PROFESSIONAL
SHAREPOINT® 2010 ADMINISTRATION

PROFESSIONAL

SharePoint® 2010 Administration

PROFESSIONAL

SharePoint® 2010 Administration

Todd Klindt
Shane Young
Steve Caravajal

WILEY

Wiley Publishing, Inc.

Professional SharePoint® 2010 Administration

Published by
Wiley Publishing, Inc.
10475 Crosspoint Boulevard
Indianapolis, IN 46256
www.wiley.com

ISBN: 978-0-470-53333-8
ISBN: 978-0-470-91245-4 (ebk)
ISBN: 978-0-470-91237-9 (ebk)
ISBN: 978-0-470-91236-2 (ebk)

Manufactured in the United States of America

10 9 8 7 6 5 4 3 2 1

For general information on our other products and services please contact our Customer Care Department within the United States at (877) 762-2974, outside the United States at (317) 572-3993 or fax (317) 572-4002.

Wiley also publishes its books in a variety of electronic formats. Some content that appears in print may not be available in electronic books.

Library of Congress Control Number: 2010926844

I'd like to dedicate this book to my wife, Jill. Without her support, strength, and tolerance for how crazy book writing makes me, this would have never been possible. Not only did she put up with the hours I spent writing this book, and taking care of our daughter, she was pregnant the whole time, giving birth a couple of days before I submitted my last content. Simply amazing. When our children grow up well adjusted and normal it will be because of her. Thanks Babe, love you so much.

—Todd

This book is dedicated to Baby Grant. Hi buddy. You are nine months old as I write these words. I hope one day you will knock the dust off this book and read this, but since there is no cow that goes moo or ghost that says boo it might be a few years from now. When you do, realize you can be or do anything you want in life. It just takes hard work and dedication. Your mother and I love you.

—Shane

To Rosemary; my wife, companion, and friend.

—Steve

ABOUT THE AUTHORS

 TODD KLINDT has been a professional computer nerd for 15 years, and was an amateur computer nerd before that. After finding out in college that his desire for food and shelter and his abilities at programming were not compatible, he decided to try being an administrator instead. He got his MCSE in 1997 and spent a lot of time taming Windows Server, Exchange Server, and the unlucky SQL Server here and there. In 2002 he was tasked with setting up a web page for his IT department. He couldn't program, and he couldn't design with HTML to save his life. He found SharePoint Team Services on an Office XP CD and decided to give it a shot. Turns out SharePoint was just what the doctor ordered. As each version of SharePoint was released, Todd became more and more enamored with it. In 2005 Todd was awarded Microsoft's MVP award for Windows SharePoint Services. Since then he has written for a couple of SharePoint books, a couple of magazine articles, and had the pleasure of speaking in more places than he can believe. To pay the bills he's a SharePoint consultant and trainer with SharePoint911. He can be found on Twitter dispensing invaluable SharePoint and relationship advice as @ToddKlindt. For the web 1.0 folks he also has a blog at http://www.toddklindt.com/blog. Todd lives in Ames, Iowa with his lovely wife Jill, their two daughters Lily and Penny, and their two feline masters, Carlos and Louise.

 SHANE YOUNG has over 14 years experience architecting and administering large-scale server farms using Microsoft enterprise technologies. For the past six years, he has been working exclusively with SharePoint Products and Technologies as a consultant, author, and trainer. He has architected SharePoint solutions for clients ranging from 20 to 50,000 users. Shane has been awarded the SharePoint Server MVP designation for five consecutive years. He is also a renowned speaker at national and international Microsoft conferences. He is the author of several of the leading SharePoint 2007 and 2010 SharePoint Training courses, several Microsoft whitepapers, numerous books, and various SharePoint 2010 videos. You can contact Shane on Facebook, LinkedIn, Twitter@ShanesCows, via email at shane@sharepoint911.com, his blog at http://msmvps.com/shane or through his company's website at http://www.SharePoint911.com. Shane lives in Cincinnati, Ohio with his wife Nicola, his son Grant, and their two dogs.

 STEVE CARAVAJAL is a Principal Architect with the Microsoft Corporation. Steve has 23+ years experience in technology and product development, consulting, and training. At Microsoft, Steve's focus includes architecting enterprise solutions that include SharePoint, Office, and custom .NET applications. He has been architecting, deploying and customizing SharePoint solutions for over 10 years. He holds a Bachelor of Science degree in Chemistry and Mathematics, a Doctoral degree in Chemistry and Computer science, and he is an Adjunct Professor at a couple of local universities. Steve has several patents and published articles, speaks at conferences and has written two previous books: *SharePoint 2007 and Office Development Expert Solutions*, and *Inside SharePoint 2007 Administration*. He has also written and managed the development of numerous enterprise software applications in C++, Java and .NET.

ABOUT THE TECHNICAL EDITORS

JENNIFER MASON has dedicated the last seven years to working with SharePoint. She started out as an intern focused on SharePoint and eventually began working as a full-time SharePoint consultant. She is currently working as a Senior SharePoint Consultant with the team at SharePoint911. Her focus has been on strategy, project planning, project management, governance, and best practices for implementing business solutions using SharePoint Technologies. She has worked with a range of companies at different points in the lifecycles of their SharePoint implementation. She is passionate about SharePoint, and loves using the out of the box features to bring immediate ROI to the organization. Jennifer is involved in the SharePoint community and is one of the founding members of the Columbus Ohio SharePoint Users Group. You can learn more about Jennifer by viewing her blog at `http://www.sharepoint911.com/blogs/jennifer/default.aspx`.

JEFF DEVERTER has been working with SharePoint since 2003, which was early in the "v2" product line. He has been involved in several disciplines within SharePoint, including System Planning and Architecture, Governance and Taxonomy, end user development, Security Planning and Implementation, and Training.

Jeff is currently the architect of Rackspace Hosting's SharePoint offering. Before joining Rackspace, Jeff worked with Fortune 100 Financial Services companies including World Savings (Golden West Financial) and USAA (United Services Automobile Association), where he worked as an Enterprise Architect over Collaboration and Enterprise Search.

CREDITS

ACQUISITIONS EDITOR
Paul Reese

PROJECT EDITOR
Sara Shlaer

TECHNICAL EDITORS
Jennifer Mason
Jeff DeVerter

CONTRIBUTING AUTHORS
Bill Baer
Darrin Bishop
Chris Caravajal
Randy Drisgill
Ryan Keller
Jennifer Mason
Larry Riemann
Laura Rogers
John Ross

PRODUCTION EDITOR
Eric Charbonneau

COPY EDITOR
Luann Rouff

EDITORIAL DIRECTOR
Robyn B. Siesky

EDITORIAL MANAGER
Mary Beth Wakefield

ASSOCIATE DIRECTOR OF MARKETING
David Mayhew

PRODUCTION MANAGER
Tim Tate

VICE PRESIDENT AND EXECUTIVE GROUP PUBLISHER
Richard Swadley

VICE PRESIDENT AND EXECUTIVE PUBLISHER
Barry Pruett

ASSOCIATE PUBLISHER
Jim Minatel

PROJECT COORDINATOR, COVER
Lynsey Stanford

COMPOSITOR
Craig Johnson, Happenstance Type-O-Rama

PROOFREADERS
Nancy Bell and Beth Prouty

INDEXER
Johnna VanHoose Dinse

COVER DESIGNER
Michael E. Trent

COVER IMAGE
© Loic Bernard/istockphoto

ACKNOWLEDGMENTS

THANKS AGAIN NICOLA. You should get some kind of Wife of the Year award as you deal with me writing these darn books or working around the clock to meet some insane deadline. I never understood how you did it and now you also manage to take care of our new son Grant as well. Just crazy if you ask me. I love both of you more than you can imagine.

I wasn't going to call out the dogs, Tyson and Pugsley, but since they are staring at me right now I feel I have to. Thanks boys! You have kept my feet warm all of the long nights it took to get this book out the door.

A big shout out goes to my friends at Microsoft. There are far too many to name but all of you have been part of my 2010 learning curve and I couldn't have written this book without each of you being along for my journey. I look forward to working with all of you for years to come.

To my fellow authors Todd and Steve: When do we write the next one? HA. Every time we finish one of these things you promise me never again. I will say it now: You guys are liars. So let's get to work. Next one we will blame on Steve.

I want everyone who reads this to know I think Jennifer Mason is one of the most amazing people I have ever met. She was the primary tech editor on this book and also a contributing author. How she managed to make heads or tails of all the details of SharePoint 2010 we threw at her I will never know. Of course, I still haven't figured out how she ate donkey meat either, so I guess I will live unknowing. If she ever runs for president be sure to vote for her. Thanks Jen.

To all of the contributors along the way: I owe you a debt of gratitude. Your additions, ideas, reviews, etc. are a huge part of this book and I am guessing it is impossible for me to express my thanks, so I will not even try. You guys were amazing. Jeff, you get a little extra thank you for getting those tech edits done overnight during the final push. You must have had a time machine or something; I couldn't have done it.

Normally I would also thank all of the employees of SharePoint911 for their help, but each of them ended up pitching in to get this book out the door so they got thanked in the previous paragraph. Cannot give them too much praise, it might go to their heads.

To the entire team at Wiley: Thanks for letting me be part of another successful book project.

Last but not least is Sara. You should be nominated for sainthood after seeing this book through. The frantic pace at the end, translating our chapters from rubbish into English, and being patient with our childlike attention spans are your three miracles. Where do I sign you up? Thanks Sara.

I love you little Sparky!

—Shane

WHAT CAN I SAY THAT SHANE ALREADY HASN'T? There was a large cast of people who came together to make possible the book you're holding in your hand, or the e-book that's on your screen. While Steve, Shane, and I are the pretty faces of the book, the other folks are the show ponies. None of this could have been possible without them.

First I want thanks some friends who helped write chapters. Darrin Bishop was the brains behind the PowerShell chapter. He's not that bad, for a developer. I also want to send a shout out to Bill Baer for helping with the chapter on high availability. Bill knows more about keeping SharePoint running than I know period. I can only imagine his hat is the secret to his powers.

My fellow SharePoint911ers deserve a round of applause as well. They helped tremendously, picking up the slack when we needed help. Thanks everyone.

Once the chapters were written, the tech editors, Jen and Jeff, had to try to sort out the mess that was sent to them, which was no small feat. Thanks for keeping us honest.

At some point I probably should acknowledge those other jokers whose names follow mine on the cover, Shane and Steve. I can't believe after having written one book together already we convinced ourselves to do it again. If I'm going to write a book, I want it to be with those yahoos. They're great to bounce ideas off of, and when my motivation is low, one of them is always ready and willing to mock me until I get back into action. Thanks guys. Couldn't have done it without you. You ready to start our next one yet?

And finally, Sara. Every word Shane wrote about Sara is true. If I get to vote for sainthood, Saint Sara will be a reality. Thanks for your guidance, Sara.

—Todd

WELL, I GUESS WE (TODD, SHANE AND I) didn't learn our lesson, and we wrote another book together. Working with these guys is like herding cats, excepts cats are easier. Having said that, I would do it again, but this time I would ask Todd and Shane to actually write something. It's been great guys; let's do it again.

Besides these two jokers, our technical editors, Jen and Jeff, deserve a lot of credit for keeping us honest. And a very special thanks to Sara, our editor; she is the person that brought it all together. Suffice it to say that without her this book wouldn't have happened. Putting up with Shane and Todd is extremely difficult, and Sara handled it well. Needless to say that we were behind schedule most of the time but Sara always provided the encouragement and kick in the pants when we needed it, and in a way that wasn't as painful as it might have been. So Sara, thank you so much for all your help.

Finally, how can I possibly thank enough the most important person in my life, my wife Rosemary. She always stands beside me, even when I overextend myself and end up being really grumpy. Being together for 33 years seems like only yesterday; I hope she will put up with me for at least 33 more.

—Steve

CONTENTS

FOREWORD

THE PAST THREE YEARS HAVE BEEN AN AMAZING JOURNEY for us here in the SharePoint group at Microsoft, and it's been a humbling experience to have been part of the team that delivered SharePoint 2010 into the hands of customers and partners across the globe.

I've worked on the team since before the release of SharePoint Server 2007. I've been deeply involved with our attempts to learn how customers deploy and use the software, and been active in the efforts we make to get feedback from customers and partners on what really works, and most importantly, where we can improve.

I really believe that since the 2007 release we've listened and learned and made significant changes and investment across the platform to release a product that has been shaped by you, the people on the front line deploying, configuring, and managing SharePoint on a daily basis—and this release has your fingerprints all over it.

So why should you buy this book?

Well, the deployment and admin landscape of SharePoint 2010 has changed in several ways, from governance to service architecture to security, and anyone tasked with installing and managing SharePoint 2010 should have a great reference book on a shelf within reaching distance of their desk to get the most out of this new release.

Shane, Todd, and Steve cover these changes and updates in an easy-to-read style, but in the depth you'll want to get your job done with confidence. They cover everything from architecture and planning, governance, how to use Windows PowerShell with SharePoint, security, taxonomy, Enterprise Content Management, and the list goes on. It's 800+ pages packed full of SharePoint 2010 IT professional guidance and advice that I'm sure will become a well-thumbed trusted advisor.

I've known Shane, Todd, and Steve for as long as I've worked in the SharePoint team. Shane and Todd are MVPs (Microsoft Most Valuable Professionals), and all three have been deeply involved in pre-release programs for SharePoint 2010 for at least 18 months prior to its release, so they certainly have the credentials to put their names on the front of this book.

Reading this book will give you the advice and guidance to plan, deploy, and manage SharePoint 2010, whether you're a seasoned SharePoint Server 2007 admin or fresh out of school with SharePoint 2010. I know that I've learned a few things myself by reading it, and I'm sure you'll learn a lot as well.

—RICHARD RILEY
Group Product Manager, SharePoint
Redmond, WA
May 2010

INTRODUCTION

IT SEEMS JUST YESTERDAY we were all feverishly hitting F5 on MSDN or TechNet, hoping, praying for those SharePoint 2007 downloads to appear. Fast-forward three years and now we have SharePoint 2010. SharePoint 2007 seems so quaint and antiquated compared to the shininess of SharePoint 2010. We have been using SharePoint since it was a wee lad in 2001 and our fascination with it has continued to grow with each version. In this book we packed in every SharePoint 2010 administration nugget we could. Most were learned after taking and retaking many classes at the school of hard knocks. It's our hope that we can share some of these lessons with other like-minded SharePoint 2010 administrators.

WHO THIS BOOK IS FOR

Are you a SharePoint administrator who wants to know more about SharePoint 2010? Are you a SharePoint power user who wants to know how to translate your SharePoint 2007 prowess to SharePoint 2010? Are you trying to pretty up SharePoint so that it doesn't look like SharePoint? Are you a SharePoint developer who has a devil of a time communicating with those blasted administrators? Then this is your book. This book was written mainly by SharePoint administrators, but we brought in experts in other areas to round it out. We brought in developers to help explain Features and Solutions with more definition. We brought in branding experts to explain how branding has changed in SharePoint 2010 and demonstrate all the marvelous things you can do. We brought in end user experts to cover all the different ways to leverage the Office clients with SharePoint 2010. They even covered workflows for us, at no extra charge. While this book was written with the SharePoint 2010 administrator in mind, it covers a variety of topics that are of interest to people in all areas of SharePoint.

WHAT THIS BOOK COVERS

From start to finish, this book is all SharePoint 2010. While no book can cover everything, we gave it the old college try. The focus is mainly on administrative topics. We cover some SharePoint 2010 theory to get the foundation built. We show you the new SharePoint 2010 user interface so that you can get around without too much fumbling. Then we cover the behind-the-scene changes in architecture to get you ready for the next part, installation. We walk you through the installation and upgrade next and show you all the options you have.

After you're comfortable with installation and noodling around in the interface, we start exploring different chunks of functionality that SharePoint 2010 has to offer. All the fan favorites are here: Search, claims, the taxonomy service, Business Connectivity Services, Enterprise Content Management, and even social computing. It's all in here.

Having the functionality isn't enough; we also cover how to administer the server, both with Central Administration and our new best friend, Windows PowerShell. A functional website is nice, but having a good looking, functional website is even better. Our branding chapter can make that dream a reality.

We've tried to make sure this book is well rounded. To that end, we covered some non-traditional administrator topics, like how to build workflows, use SharePoint Designer, and how the Office clients and SharePoint 2010 interact. These lean more toward power user topics, but the questions still come to the administrators and it's up to us to make it all work.

We even reached across the aisle and enlisted the help of a developer to get the scoop on how Features and Solutions have been improved in SharePoint 2010. Normally we wouldn't associate ourselves with developers, but for the sake of making this book complete we did it, and we don't regret it.

HOW THIS BOOK IS STRUCTURED

We organized this book so that it could be read front to back, like a romantic novel. Don't read the last chapter first — you'll ruin the ending. The first three chapters are SharePoint 2010 theory, outlining changes and explaining new terminology. Then we cover installation in excruciating detail. After you have SharePoint 2010 installed, the rest of the book covers discrete areas of functionality in each chapter. While you could stay up all night reading it cover to cover, you can also use it as a reference book. Did the boss just see Business Intelligence in bold print in a trade rag and decide your SharePoint 2010 installation needs it? No worries; read Chapter 20 and get up to speed on it.

WHAT YOU NEED TO USE THIS BOOK

Having a SharePoint 2010 installation to noodle around with while reading this book will definitely come in handy. This will enable you to follow along with the examples in the book, and maybe you'll provide helpful feedback for a subsequent edition.

If you don't have a SharePoint installation yet, you can follow the directions in Chapter 4 and install one. Microsoft has a trial license available for SharePoint Server, so all you'll need is a willing Windows 2008 server and some time.

Having some knowledge of SharePoint 2007 will help too, but it's not necessary. Where we can, we compare the SharePoint 2010 experience with the SharePoint 2007 one. If you've used SharePoint 2007, you'll find those comparisons helpful.

 This book was written against a Release Candidate build of SharePoint 2010. While our SharePoint 2010 prowess is above reproach, our ability to predict the future is not so hot. We've done everything we could to make sure that what you read here matches the final product for SharePoint 2010. In cases where things are different, we blame sunspots, or maybe volcanoes.

CONVENTIONS

To help you get the most from the text and keep track of what's happening, we've used a number of conventions throughout the book.

➤ We *highlight* new terms and important words when we introduce them.

➤ We show keyboard strokes like this: Ctrl+A.

➤ We show filenames, URLs, and code within the text like so: persistence.properties.

➤ We present code in monofont type:

```
This is the style for code examples.
```

SOURCE CODE

While you can likely type most of the Windows PowerShell cmdlets used in this book more quickly than you could download, copy, and paste them into your shell, we have made the longer scripts available for download at http://www.wrox.com. When at the site, simply locate the book's title (use the Search box or one of the title lists) and click the Download Code link on the book's detail page to obtain the source code for the book. Code that is included on the website is highlighted by the following icon:

**Available for
download on
Wrox.com**

 Because many books have similar titles, you may find it easiest to search by ISBN; this book's ISBN is 978-0-470-53333-8.

Once you download the code, just decompress it with your favorite compression tool. Alternately, you can go to the main Wrox code download page at http://www.wrox.com/dynamic/books/download.aspx to see the code available for this book and all other Wrox books.

ERRATA

We make every effort to ensure that there are no errors in the text or in the code. However, no one is perfect, and mistakes do occur. If you find an error in one of our books, like a spelling mistake or a faulty piece of code, we would be very grateful for your feedback. By sending in errata, you may save another reader hours of frustration, and at the same time you will be helping us provide even higher quality information.

To find the errata page for this book, go to http://www.wrox.com and locate the title using the Search box or one of the title lists. Then, on the book details page, click the Book Errata link. On this page, you can view all errata that has been submitted for this book and posted by Wrox editors. A complete book list, including links to each book's errata, is also available at www.wrox.com/misc-pages/booklist.shtml.

If you don't spot "your" error on the Book Errata page, go to www.wrox.com/contact/techsupport.shtml and complete the form there to send us the error you have found. We'll check the information and, if appropriate, post a message to the book's errata page and fix the problem in subsequent editions of the book.

P2P.WROX.COM

For author and peer discussion, join the P2P forums at p2p.wrox.com. The forums are a Web-based system for you to post messages relating to Wrox books and related technologies, and to interact with other readers and technology users. The forums offer a subscription feature to e-mail you topics of interest of your choosing when new posts are made to the forums. Wrox authors, editors, other industry experts, and your fellow readers are present on these forums.

At http://p2p.wrox.com, you will find a number of different forums that will help you, not only as you read this book, but also as you develop your own applications. To join the forums, just follow these steps:

1. Go to p2p.wrox.com and click the Register link.

2. Read the terms of use and click Agree.

3. Complete the required information to join, as well as any optional information you wish to provide, and click Submit.

4. You will receive an e-mail with information describing how to verify your account and complete the joining process.

 You can read messages in the forums without joining P2P, but in order to post your own messages, you must join.

Once you join, you can post new messages and respond to messages other users post. You can read messages at any time on the Web. If you would like to have new messages from a particular forum e-mailed to you, click the Subscribe to this Forum icon by the forum name in the forum listing.

For more information about how to use the Wrox P2P, be sure to read the P2P FAQs for answers to questions about how the forum software works, as well as many common questions specific to P2P and Wrox books. To read the FAQs, click the FAQ link on any P2P page.

1

What's New in SharePoint 2010

WHAT'S IN THIS CHAPTER?

➤ New installation and upgrade features

➤ Changes to Central Administration

➤ The impact of the Ribbon

It's been said before, but these are exciting times. We don't yet have the flying cars we were promised years ago, but we have SharePoint 2010. Seems like a fair trade. When flying cars do come around, I'm sure they'll be complicated to use at first. SharePoint 2010 is the same; it's a little complicated under the hood. Consider this book your mechanic's guide. The next several hundred pages will cover the deep technical details that SharePoint administrators will need to get SharePoint 2010 up and running and purring like a kitten.

This chapter serves as a jumping-off point. It covers some of the bigger changes that SharePoint 2010 has to offer. It's a teaser to really get you excited about SharePoint 2010, from the administrator's point of view. Once your appetite is whetted, you can read up on these topics in more detail in later chapters, which provide the nitty-gritty details of SharePoint 2010's functionality. There's a lot to get excited about, so we'd better dig in.

INSTALLATION

Of course, before you can see any of the great new things that SharePoint 2010 can do, you have to install it. This section covers what's new in the SharePoint 2010 installation process.

System Requirements

Before you can install SharePoint 2010, make sure you meet all of the system requirements. The minimum requirements for installing SharePoint 2010 are a 64-bit operating system running either Windows Server 2008 with SP2 or later or Window Server 2008 R2. The OS will need at least .NET 3.5 with SP1 installed as well. On the database back end, SharePoint 2010 requires SQL Server 2005 with SP2 or later or SQL Server 2008. SQL must be 64-bit also.

There is no 32-bit version of SharePoint 2010, not even for demonstration environments. It's all 64-bit now. Fortunately, any hardware on which you would install SharePoint 2010 these days is 64-bit capable. The 32-bit environment is comfortable, like an old pair of shoes, but now is a great time to move to 64-bit if you haven't already. In addition to being necessary to run SharePoint 2010, it also brings a lot of benefits like better CPU utilization and support for RAM over 4GB. Once you start using SharePoint 2010, you'll see why that last point is very important. 4GB is the bare minimum of RAM necessary to make SharePoint 2010 bearable to use, and 6GB is a better starting point.

Installation Options

After the hardware and software is squared away it's time to start installing some SharePoint bits. The installer has gotten a facelift and boasts a number of improvements. The process is kicked off with the friendly splash screen shown in Figure 1-1.

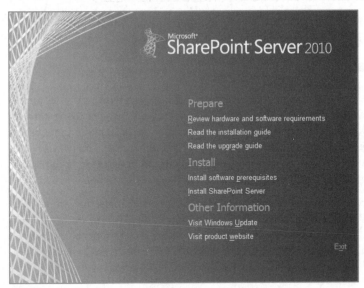

FIGURE 1-1

Along with installing the SharePoint 2010 software, the splash screen has links to other activities. The first group of links is documentation to help prepare for the install. This includes guidance on hardware requirements as well as install and upgrade guides. You might be tempted to skip them, since you already have this book. However, these links are dynamic, so they will always have the latest information. We're flattered you bought the book, but you should read those guides anyway.

The second section of links installs both the SharePoint 2010 bits themselves and any software prerequisites your system needs. The prerequisite installer is a really great tool and a welcome addition to the install process. It will not only download the current version of any software SharePoint 2010 relies on, but also install and correctly configure IIS and other components on your server. It supports both an unattended mode and installing the prerequisites for a local location, removing the need to get them from the Internet.

The second link in this section starts the setup for SharePoint 2010. The install process itself isn't very different from the SharePoint 2007 install process we all know and love. It supports the standard guided GUI install as well as the same scripted install options that SharePoint 2007 did. You can script the installation of the bits by passing the setup process a `Config.xml` file with all your settings. You can then script the configuration of SharePoint 2010 with PowerShell.

While installing SharePoint 2010 is very similar to installing SharePoint 2007, there are a couple of new twists. First, the install requires a *farm passphrase*. Just like it sounds, this passphrase is needed to add or remove a server from a farm. This passphrase is then used as the basis for encryption between farm members. SharePoint 2007 used the install account for some of this functionality, but problems arose if the user who installed SharePoint wasn't available later. The passphrase addresses that issue.

In addition, the installer now checks for a couple of Group Policy Objects (GPOs) before it installs. For example, there is a GPO that can be used to block SharePoint installations. This enables a company to control the proliferation of SharePoint farms in its environment. The installer checks this GPO to verify that it's OK to install. If it is, then the install checks for the presence of another GPO that assigns SharePoint servers to a specific Organization Unit (OU). This enables a common set of settings for all of your SharePoint 2010 servers, and makes it easy for administrators to keep track of all the SharePoint farms in their environment. Chapter 4 covers installation in greater depth.

Upgrade and Patching Options

Not everyone will be new to SharePoint. Many people have poured a lot of sweat and blood into SharePoint 2007 farms. These farms are the backbones of their organizations. In order for SharePoint 2010 to make it into these organizations, the upgrade path will have to be clear and without a lot of roadblocks. Fortunately, Microsoft also invested a lot into the upgrade experience. They're understandably proud of SharePoint 2010 and have gone to great lengths to ensure that everyone can install it.

The first glimpse we had of the SharePoint 2010 experience showed up in SP2 for SharePoint 2007. SP2 included a new STSADM operation, `preupgradecheck`. This operation interrogated your SharePoint 2007 databases and alerted you to any potential roadblocks on your upgrade to SharePoint 2010. It reports on the following key components of your farm:

➤ Servers and amount of content

➤ Search configuration

➤ Features

➤ Solutions

➤ Site definitions

➤ Alternate access mappings

➤ Language packs

It will also alert you to the following potential issues:

- ➤ Large lists
- ➤ Orphaned data
- ➤ Views and content types that use CAML
- ➤ Databases with modified schemas

The results of the upgrade check are saved to an XML file and an easy to read .HTM file. The check is read-only, and it can be run multiple times as you clean up issues it discovers.

Not to be outdone, SharePoint 2010 offers the same functionality, at least at the content database level. The PowerShell cmdlet `Test-SPContentDatabase` will interrogate both SharePoint 2007 and SharePoint 2010 content databases and determine whether they can be upgraded and added to a SharePoint 2010 farm. Like its older brother `preupgradecheck`, `Test-SPContentDatabase` does not make any changes to your databases, so you can run it without fear on your production environments.

Upgrade Methods

There are two upgrade methods for upgrading from SharePoint 2007 to SharePoint 2010: in-place and database attach. The in-place upgrade is just what it sounds like; it upgrades your SharePoint 2007 to SharePoint 2010 on your existing hardware. With the second option, you can attach back-ups of SharePoint 2007 content databases to a SharePoint 2010 web application and they will be upgraded automatically.

It may seem like the upgrade options are limited, but the true power lies in the details. Many downtime mitigation techniques are available that enable use of either of the two upgrade methods with limited downtime for end users.

The first downtime mitigation feature, support for read-only content databases, made its premiere in SharePoint 2007 SP2. This feature allows read-only copies of SharePoint 2007 content databases to be rendered while the actual databases are being upgraded. SharePoint will recognize that the database is read-only and will remove all UI elements that allow users to add or edit content. SharePoint 2010 also supports upgrading multiple databases simultaneously. This reduces upgrade time as long as the hardware, mainly the SQL servers, can handle the I/O needed to do the upgrades.

If that isn't enough to keep the users happy, there is a second option. SharePoint 2010 supports redirecting traffic to an existing SharePoint 2007 farm during upgrade. This enables users to continue to use the same URL, but they are given a client-side 302 redirect until the content is available on SharePoint 2010.

Another feature that will make users happy is Visual Upgrade. Visual Upgrade allows sites upgraded to SharePoint 2010 to use the SharePoint 2007 master page and CSS. By default, upgraded sites will maintain the familiar SharePoint 2007 look and feel. A site administrator can view the site with the SharePoint 2010 interface before finalizing its upgrade. This enables time both for training and for fixing any pages that will not upgrade gracefully.

As if that weren't enough, the logging experience is also better. Each individual upgrade event generates its own log file, which makes it easy to keep track of what happened. There is also an error-only log. This greatly reduces the amount of work it takes to determine what went wrong, in the unlikely event of an upgrade failure.

Patching

You can't talk about upgrading without also considering patching, which is like a mini upgrade. Not to be outdone by the improvements to the upgrade process, the patching process has gotten some love in SharePoint 2010 as well. To give the SharePoint administrator some flexibility in applying patches, the patches can be laid down during business hours, but the corresponding database upgrades can be put off until a time when the downtime is less obtrusive. SharePoint 2010 is also more tolerant of rolling out patches to the members of a farm. While you won't want to leave your SharePoint out of sync for days on end, things will run better in the long run if you leave them that way for a few hours to apply the patches.

 Regarding upgrades, Microsoft documentation sometimes uses the shorthand V2V for "Version to Version." In that vein, patching is similarly referred to as B2B, or "Build to Build."

How will you know if your SharePoint servers need patching, or your databases updating? Another new addition to SharePoint 2010, Health Rules, will alert you to these situations. Finally, the patching team has taken steps to reduce the number of reboots needed when patches are installed. If at all possible, processes will be stopped to allow files to be updated. While we are unlikely to reach a point when SharePoint doesn't need to be patched, at least the process isn't very painful. To find out more about upgrading and patching SharePoint 2010, turn to Chapter 5 where it is covered in stunning detail.

CENTRAL ADMINISTRATION

All these administrative improvements to SharePoint 2010 would be worthless if you couldn't find the knobs and levers needed to make them work. Therefore, a lot of attention was also given to Central Administration. Much like the improvements made to the IIS 7 Manager, Central Administration is now more flat and wide, instead of deep. As you can see in Figure 1-2, instead of having two tabs across the top like it did in SharePoint 2007, Central Administration now has links to the most common tasks on the front page, and eight links on the left if you need to find tasks that aren't exposed on the front page. This provides two immediate benefits; it makes things easier to find and it results in fewer mouse clicks to accomplish tasks.

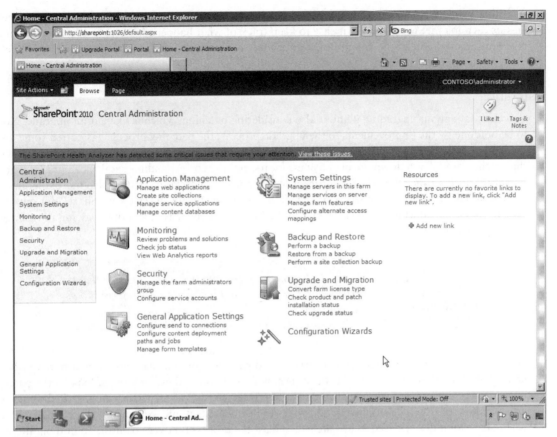

FIGURE 1-2

To make this design workable, Central Administration has also embraced the Office Ribbon. Once you drill down to the object you want to work on, the Ribbon shows up on the top of the page with all the options for that object. Figure 1-3 shows the Ribbon in action.

This enables SharePoint to pack more administrative punch into each page in Central Administration. As mentioned earlier, this makes links easier to find and requires fewer clicks to find the tasks you want to accomplish. Another benefit is that you spend less time clicking from page to page to accomplish tasks.

On the front page of Central Administration is a heading for each of the eight main areas of administration, mirroring the areas in the left navigation pane. Under each of these headings are some of the common links inside each one. For instance, under the Backup and Restore heading is a link to perform a site collection backup (refer to Figure 1-2). If the task you're looking for isn't on the front page, click the heading, either on the front page or on the left navigation pane, to see all of the options. Clicking Backup and Restore takes you to a page that shows all of the backup and recovery options provided with SharePoint 2010 out of the box. The other sections behave the same way. The front page of Central Administration provides the general topics, while the full complement of specific options are available when you click the heading link.

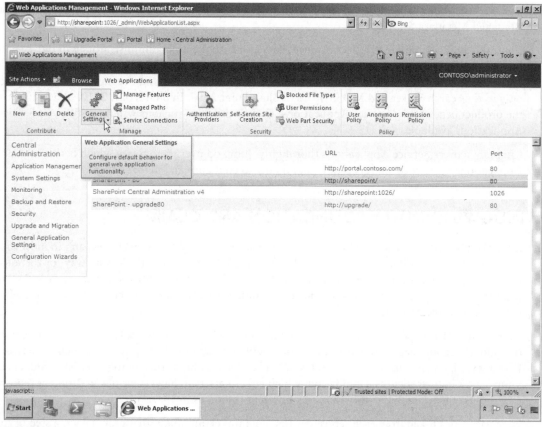

FIGURE 1-3

SERVICE APPLICATIONS

Another exciting addition to SharePoint is Service Applications. If you have used MOSS 2007, then you may be familiar with its Shared Service Provider (SSP) architecture. The SSP was a central service that shared common resources with one or many web applications. This enabled SharePoint to do one crawl, for instance, but provide the search functionality to all the web applications in the farm without duplicating effort. The SharePoint 2007 SSP was an all-or-nothing affair. Your web app could only be associated with a single SSP, consuming all SSP services; and it was difficult, if not impossible, to delegate authority over different parts of the SSP.

Service Applications represent the evolution of the SSP. The SSP model had some pretty common pain points, which the change to Service Applications addresses. In SharePoint 2010, all the Service Applications are separate. Examples of Service Applications include Search, Profile Import, Business Data Catalog and Managed Metadata. This means they can be turned on and off as needed, enabling you to pick and choose only the ones you are actually using. This saves resources and reduces the attack vector. Service Applications can also be given their own permissions. This enables you to give one user the capability to manage Search without that user being able to do anything with the Managed Metadata Service.

Central Administration is security trimmed, so Service Application administrators will only see the Service Applications to which they have access. As an added bonus, Service Applications are available in all versions of the product. Windows SharePoint Services 3.0 did not have SSPs. They were only in the Search Server and MOSS SKUs of SharePoint 2007. In SharePoint 2010, all versions of the product benefit from Service Applications, though different versions will have different Service Applications available.

Chapter 7 covers Service Applications thoroughly. Jump on over there to see which Service Applications come with SharePoint 2010 and how to configure and manage them.

WINDOWS IDENTITY FOUNDATION AND CLAIMS

It's a complicated world we live in. We all have to access many different websites, and in most cases each one requires a different username and password. What's worse is there is no way for them to know about each other and keep your information synchronized. If only there was a way to use one identity over many resources, or a way for many authentication sources to be used in one SharePoint farm. Good news; now there is.

SharePoint 2010 supports claims-based authentication, which is a powerful and flexible authentication model. Claims-based authentication works with a variety of identity systems, such as Active Directory, LDAP directories, and even LiveID. The glue that holds this all together is a product set known as Windows Identity Foundation, which enables users to have identities in different repositories and use them simultaneously to access different resources in SharePoint.

Each user gets a token from each repository that contains claims about that user. This is a step beyond just proving identity, or authentication, as we're accustomed to with SharePoint 2007. A user's token can also contain claims about the user. Think of it as user metadata. This might be the user's manager, birthday, location, and so on. One of the advantages of using claims is its support for federation. That means if the appropriate trusts are put into place, companies can trust each other's authentication providers and use their own credentials to log into another's SharePoint farm.

Sound complicated? Well, it is. Fortunately, we devote an entire chapter, Chapter 9, to explaining claims-based authentication and how to use it with SharePoint 2010.

HEALTH AND MONITORING

Installing SharePoint 2010 or upgrading your current SharePoint 2007 farm to SharePoint 2010 is only half the battle. Keeping it running is the tough part. SharePoint 2010 includes a lot of functionality, which means a lot of moving parts. Like any good machine, someone has to keep an eye on all these parts to ensure that they're working; and when they're not working, be able to figure out why. SharePoint 2010 introduces several ways for administrators to keep an eye on how SharePoint is running, as well as ways for SharePoint to proactively keep an eye on itself, and in some cases fix itself if something is wrong.

Health and Monitoring has been given so much focus in SharePoint 2010 that it has its own heading in Central Administration. The left navigation pane in Central Administration has a Monitoring link that exposes all the new options available (see Figure 1-4).

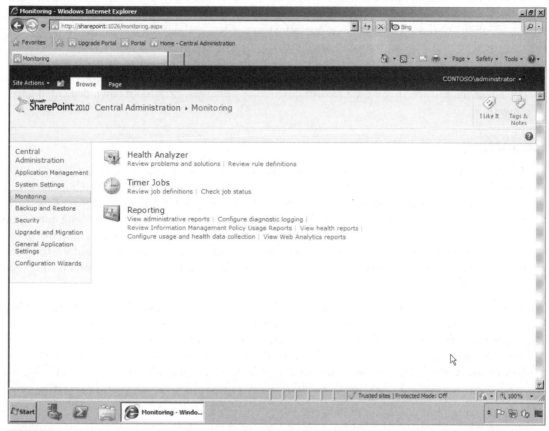

FIGURE 1-4

Health Analyzer

The first option under the Monitoring heading is the Health Analyzer. This amazing piece of software is one way that SharePoint monitors itself. Out of the box, SharePoint Server comes with 52 definitions of behaviors that it knows can go wrong with a SharePoint server, like the C drive running out of space. Each of these 52 situations is written into a rule, and periodically SharePoint reviews these rules to determine whether SharePoint is in trouble. If any rules are triggered, an administrator can be alerted, and in some cases, such as heavily fragmented database indexes, SharePoint can just take care of the problem itself. Click the "Review problems and solutions" link to see what problems SharePoint has found with itself if you haven't been alerted. The rule set is extensible, so new rules may appear in service packs or patches, and independent software vendors are able to write rules as well.

Timer Jobs

The capability for monitoring Timer Jobs was weak in SharePoint 2007 but it has also been substantially upgraded in SharePoint 2010, and you now have more granular control over the Timer Jobs. By clicking a definition, you can alter its schedule or disable it completely. You also now have the capability to run a Timer Job as a one-off when needed, without interrupting or changing the existing schedule. This is invaluable when it comes to troubleshooting. A new Timer Job Status page gives you real-time status information about running Timer Jobs. This page lets you see at a quick glance which Timer Jobs will be running next, which Timer Jobs are currently running, and the Timer Job history. If you want to drill down to any of areas, each has its own dedicated page as well.

Reporting

The final tab in the Monitoring section is Reporting. From this tab you can look back and see what SharePoint has been up to. A variety of reports are available here; there's something for everybody. It's your one-stop shop for SharePoint reporting. The first link is for Administrative reports. For example, a folder for Search reports enables you to see search metrics such as how long queries take, how long crawls take, and so on. This enables you to see potential problems with your environment before your end users start complaining about them. Another great aspect of the administrative reports is that they are extensible. They are stored in a document library, so you can upload reports of your own.

Another piece on the reporting page is the configuration for SharePoint's diagnostic logging. Here you can set diagnostic levels and the location and number of log files that are created. You can also enable a new feature called Event Flood Protection, which keeps your log files from being flooded with rapidly occurring errors, instead dropping them after a few instances and then periodically writing events to the log to let you know the error is still occurring. This option makes the log files much easier to read and saves space as well.

Another set of reports you can use to keep an eye on your farm are the health reports. These reports surface the slowest pages in a web app, or on a server. Again, this enables you to be proactive by finding the problem pages in your farm before your end users get around to letting you know about them. Speaking of end users, those same health reports can tell you who your most active users are as well. If you want the full array of usage reports for your web app, those are there too, under Web Analytics Reports. These reports show you daily hits, referrers, and other metrics about your web app. These are similar to the usage reports at the site collection level in SharePoint 2007.

This is just the tip of the monitoring iceberg. If you want to read about SharePoint 2010 monitoring in stunning Technicolor, turn to Chapter 15.

MANAGING SHAREPOINT 2010 WITH WINDOWS POWERSHELL

As we've shown already, SharePoint 2010 has a tremendous number of administrative additions, including both new functionality and improvements on ways to do old things. One example of the latter is the transition to Windows PowerShell as the command-line administrative environment. We had it pretty good with STSADM in SharePoint 2007, but Windows PowerShell takes it up to a whole new level. Our old friend STSADM is still included with the product, but it's deprecated. It's time to say your good-byes and get friendly with its replacement. Windows PowerShell not only enables you to do everything that STSADM did, but it provides a much better environment for scripting and looping through objects. No longer are administrators limited to the operations included with STSADM. No longer are you at the mercy of developers to write code to access the SharePoint object model. Windows PowerShell allows mere administrators to get access to SharePoint objects, if you choose, and to do things that were never possible before. For instance, if you want to see the last time the security was changed on a site collection, you can use a Windows PowerShell script like this:

```
PS C:\> $site = Get-spsite http://portal.contoso.com
PS C:\> $site.LastSecurityModifiedDate

Sunday, December 20, 2009 3:26:15 AM
```

In SharePoint 2007 you had to write code to get that information. That example might not be very exciting, but once you read Chapter 10 and see what Windows PowerShell can do with SharePoint 2010, you'll be a believer.

MANAGED ACCOUNTS

One of the dichotomies faced by SharePoint 2007 administrators was service accounts and passwords. On the one hand, administrators wanted to increase security by having multiple service accounts, and regularly changing those accounts' passwords. On the other hand, the process to change service account passwords was complicated and very prone to error, which could cause downtime. What was a SharePoint 2007 admin to do?

Those days are over. In SharePoint 2010 that pain has all been removed by the magic of *managed accounts*. Much like managed paths, managed accounts are accounts those for which we've told SharePoint, "These are all yours, you take care of them." Once we give SharePoint that flexibility, it can change the passwords as needed, and keep itself updated as it does so. It will even respect any GPO-based password restrictions and change account passwords accordingly. You still have the option to manage an account manually if you need to change the password and log in as a specific user. This is all managed in Central Administration or through Windows PowerShell.

Does this all sound too good to be true? Well, it's not. You can find out more about it in Chapter 8.

RECOVERING FROM DISASTER

We don't mean to alarm anybody, but there are barbarians at the gate. Every day there are forces trying to take down your much beloved SharePoint farms. These forces could be in the form of malicious users, bad software, brown-outs, floods, locusts, or even failing hard drives. Any of these can take down your SharePoint farm or result in lost data. Trust me, your end users aren't very understanding of either situation.

Fortunately, SharePoint 2010 comes with some great disaster recovery options out of the box. These options range from content recovery options like the two-stage recycle bin, to disaster recovery options like database mirroring and farm-level backups. Backup and recovery is an important enough concept that it has been given its own heading in Central Administration.

To address most common backup needs, the backup options have been divided into two levels, Farm and Granular, which is at the site collection or site level. Figure 1-5 shows all the different options.

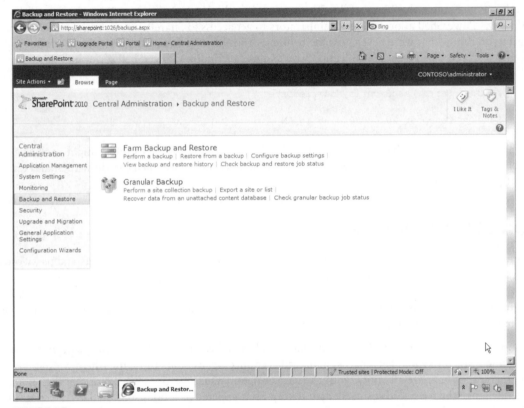

FIGURE 1-5

Chapter 12 is dedicated to backups and disaster recovery techniques. Hopefully you'll never need to use any of them, but like a Boy Scout, you should always Be Prepared.

THE NEW AND IMPROVED USER EXPERIENCE

Figure 1-2 gave you a glimpse of the SharePoint 2010 user interface. You saw that Central Administration has the Ribbon that was first introduced in the Office 2007 clients. The Ribbon (also referred to as the "fluent UI") not only made it into Central Administration, it also exists on all SharePoint content sites as well. All the advantages the Ribbon provides in Central Administration also exist in the content web apps. Even web pages have the Ribbon to make editing them easier. Figure 1-6 shows a wiki home page with the Ribbon.

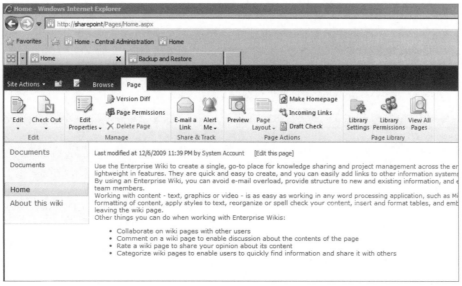

FIGURE 1-6

The Ribbon offers access to the most common tasks for the object selected. In Figure 1-6 that object is a page, so all the tasks associated with pages are available in the Ribbon. The page can be edited or checked out, and the permissions can be altered. The Ribbon is just part of what gives SharePoint 2010 a better *user experience*, also called the *UX*. The UX offers other improvements too, such as inline editing, more consistent theming and branding, and improved multilingual support. Some of these changes are significant, and will result in some growing pains for users. Chapter 2 covers all the improvements to the UX, as well as techniques to make the transition easy for your users.

SUMMARY

SharePoint 2010 brings a lot to the table for SharePoint administrators. This chapter provides some of the highlights of the product, and gives you a taste of what the subsequent chapters cover. This book contains all the SharePoint 2010 information administrators need to know. The product is big, so get comfortable; there's a lot of exciting material still to come.

2

The New and Improved User Experience

WHAT'S IN THIS CHAPTER?

➤ Browser support in SharePoint 2010

➤ Updated user interface features

➤ Using sites, lists, libraries, and and views

➤ Working with pages in SharePoint

➤ Using the Multilingual User Interface

You may find yourself wondering what a chapter on the SharePoint user experience is doing in an administration book. Well, the answer to that is twofold. First, it is important for administrators to know at least a little about what SharePoint 2010 can do from a user's standpoint and how it differs from its predecessor, SharePoint 2007, in terms of functionality. It's one thing to know how to deploy, configure, and maintain SharePoint from the backend, but it's another to actually understand what the program can do, what end users will be experiencing, and how it can help your organization. Often, administrators are the ones who will get questions from end users regarding functionality or how to accomplish certain tasks. Having an understanding of the interface will allow administrators to help users more quickly. In addition, some settings can only be enabled at a site level. Understanding Central Administration is only half of the picture. Turning on the option to allow incoming e-mail for document libraries, for example, is done in Central Administration, but what about when a user needs help actually configuring a document library to receive e-mail? Knowing the structure and setup of the user side of SharePoint is just as important as knowing the administration side.

This brings us to our second point. While much of the new functionality SharePoint 2010 brings to the table is for users, a lot of this information applies to administrators as well. The Ribbon interface, for instance, is used extensively throughout SharePoint 2010, in both

Central Administration and in regular SharePoint sites. Understanding how it works is crucial for administrators to do their jobs, as well as being able to help users with issues they may experience.

SharePoint 2010 offers a great new interface for accomplishing tasks. The core functionality of SharePoint still remains and in many area has been vastly improved upon. Lists, libraries, and page editing are all still around, as they have been in previous versions, but what makes SharePoint 2010 such a departure from what we've all come to know and love is *how* users will interact with these items. This chapter helps you get cozy with the ins and outs of the new user experience, or UX, in SharePoint 2010.

SharePoint 2010 is a large, complex product. Although this chapter is designed to give you a fairly thorough overview of using the SharePoint 2010 interface, it would be impossible to cover every aspect of it in detail in a single chapter. Therefore, this chapter covers some of the most commonly used areas in SharePoint 2010.

BROWSER SUPPORT

As you probably already know, SharePoint 2010 sites are accessed through a web browser. With SharePoint 2010, Microsoft has put effort into making it more standards-compliant, meaning it will render and behave more similarly between different browsers than in past versions. There are different levels of browser support, however, so you shouldn't expect that all features in SharePoint 2010 will work in exactly the same way when accessing the site with different browsers.

There are two main levels of browser support Microsoft has identified to work with SharePoint 2010: Supported, and Supported with known limitations.

A supported browser is a browser that is known to be 100% compatible with all features and functions in SharePoint 2010. Fully supported browsers include Internet Explorer 7 32-bit and Internet Explorer 8 32-bit. These browsers support all ActiveX controls used in SharePoint 2010 to provide the best and richest editing experience.

Supported browsers with known limitations are browsers that can access and use most of the SharePoint 2010 functionality, but there are some components that either will not work or that require a workaround to achieve the same functionality as a fully supported browser, since they may not support all the ActiveX controls used in SharePoint 2010. These browsers also have documentation readily available that lists the known limitations and workarounds. Some of these browsers include 64-bit versions of Internet Explorer 7 and 8, Firefox 3.6 and higher (on Windows), and Safari 4.04 on Mac OS X 10.6.

 Internet Explorer 6 is officially an unsupported browser to use with SharePoint 2010. Due to the advanced authoring components used in SharePoint 2010, more modern and standards-based browsers should be used instead.

It's important to mention that these browsers can all be used to browse a SharePoint 2010 site with no impact on functionality. These limitations generally come into play when you are actually working with SharePoint 2010.

For more information on browser support, see `http://technet.microsoft.com/en-us/library/cc263526(office.14).aspx`.

CHANGES TO THE SHAREPOINT 2010 USER INTERFACE

Figure 2-1 shows a screenshot of a typical out of the box SharePoint 2010 site. If you are familiar with SharePoint 2007, you'll notice that while many of the familiar items still exist on the page, a few of them have been shuffled around a bit, and they're accompanied by a few new items as well.

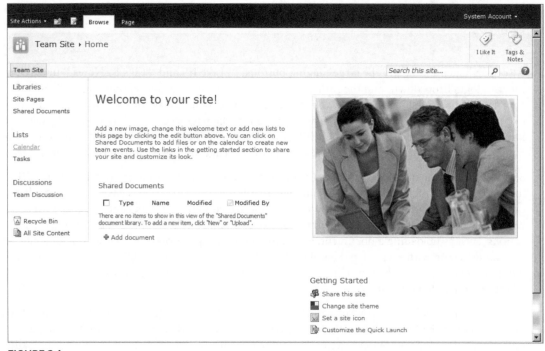

FIGURE 2-1

Notice that the Site Actions menu has been moved from the right side of the page to the left. The All Site Content link has also been repositioned from the top of the left navigation menu to the bottom. A few other changes to the interface include the new site navigator icon — the folder and arrow icon — next to the Site Actions menu, which provides a tree structure of the current page's location in relation to the rest of the site, providing a quick way to navigate back through the site after going a few levels deep.

In SharePoint sites, such as an Enterprise Wiki site or Team site, the site name in the title area of the site also can serve as the root of the breadcrumb trail. Some additional, contextual, functionality has also been built into the breadcrumb trail. For example, when working with a list, the last entry of the breadcrumb trail displays the list view name and also serves as a drop-down to select a different view (see Figure 2-2).

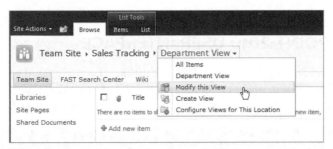

FIGURE 2-2

Also worth mentioning are the large tagging buttons, "I Like It" and "Tags & Notes," underneath the user login drop-down, and the rating stars that appear on some SharePoint pages. These are covered in more detail in Chapter 17, but basically they serve as a way for users to tag certain pages to be available to them quickly, as well as a way to rate the page's content. Higher-rated pages will have more relevance in search results, while lower-rated pages can serve as a good indicator to site owners that they may want to revisit the content on the page and revise it to meet the users' needs.

Several other UI enhancements have been made to the experience of working with SharePoint 2010 — in particular, the addition of pop-up windows. In SharePoint 2007, it was easy to get lost when performing certain tasks, as every click led to a new screen with new links and options. Often, it wasn't always apparent where SharePoint had taken you during the course of performing certain actions, such as uploading a document, especially with multiple browser windows opening and screens switching with every step. SharePoint 2010 addresses this problem by introducing pop-up windows that open over the top of a page but never fully cover the page, so you still have a sense of where you are in SharePoint.

These pop-ups aren't new browser windows that open, but rather just new SharePoint windows opening within the browser, letting a user perform an action, then closing, with the changes reflected on the page without ever actually leaving the current screen. A good example is uploading a document into a document library, as shown in Figure 2-3. Instead of leaving the document library itself, a small pop-up window opens when the Upload button is clicked in the Ribbon, and the entire upload process can be carried out in the pop-up. The pop-up then closes and the document appears in the library without the user ever having left the page. This approach keeps SharePoint fairly "flat," as opposed to "deep," much like the new approach to Central Administration, which you'll learn about in Chapter 6. There is less drill-down through SharePoint to get to the item you want.

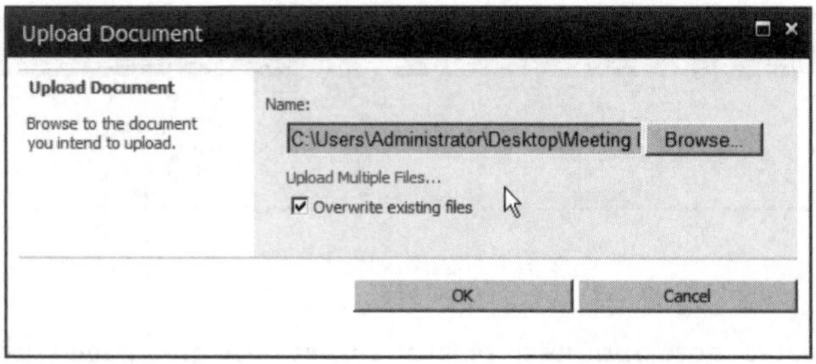

FIGURE 2-3

The Ribbon

Perhaps one of the most obvious and important changes to the SharePoint UX is the addition of the Fluent UI, or the Ribbon, as it's more commonly known. The Ribbon interface is now an integral part of the SharePoint 2010 experience for both administrators and users alike. It works very much like the Ribbon in the Microsoft Office 2007 and 2010 suite of clients. Also like the Office clients, the options available in the SharePoint 2010 Ribbon change depending on the task being performed, such as editing a page, working with an image, or working with a list. Tasks and functions are built into a visual, contextual menu. We will examine more specific details of the Ribbon and how it can be used in various areas of the site later in this chapter.

The Ribbon is divided into several tabs and categories, with different functions available depending on where in a site a user is working. You may also notice that the icons and text in the Ribbon change size, expanding when more screen real estate is available, very much like the Office clients. If the browser window is fairly small, smaller icons are used, some icons are grouped together in a drop-down menu, and very little text is displayed. With larger browser windows, more text is displayed with the Ribbon buttons, and many icons are much larger. This functionality helps manage the available real estate available in the Ribbon without reducing its functionality.

Love it or hate it, there's no getting around using the Ribbon. There is no option to turn it off, and nearly every aspect of SharePoint uses the Ribbon to perform tasks in some way or other, from basic to complex. Administrators and users will likely find that the SharePoint 2010 Ribbon makes completing most tasks easier than in previous versions. Figures 2-4 and 2-5 show examples of the Ribbon.

FIGURE 2-4

FIGURE 2-5

The main purpose of the Ribbon is to enable more options to be available at once on a page without adding additional clutter to the site. Using this approach, users should find that in most cases, fewer clicks are required to perform a simple task. Additionally, users who are familiar with using the Office 2007 clients will feel right at home in SharePoint 2010, as they share a similar interface. Working with SharePoint 2010 will feel more like working with programs users already know, helping them to become more productive.

Using the Ribbon doesn't take much effort — generally, it is exposed when it is needed, collapsed when it's not, security trimmed from view if you don't have permission to use its functionality (for example, editing a page), and some options are grayed out if they can't be utilized at the moment. As mentioned earlier, the Ribbon interface is contextual, meaning that the set of available options varies according to the page or location in a site. Users get a different set of Ribbon options for working in a list than they do when working on a page. As you will learn in Chapter 6, Central Administration even features its own Ribbon menus, such as on the Service Application page.

CREATING A SITE

The site creation process in SharePoint 2010 takes one of two forms: the "classic" way that we've all become familiar with from SharePoint 2007, and the new, fancy Silverlight-driven way. If Silverlight is installed for the client browser accessing the SharePoint site, the user will be presented with the fancy new site creation process. If not, or if the user is accessing the SharePoint site with a browser with known limitations when working with SharePoint 2010, the classic site creation process used in SharePoint 2007 will be presented. To begin the site creation process, click the Site Actions menu, and then click New Site.

Figure 2-6 shows the new Silverlight-powered site creation window. The new Silverlight site creation approach was designed to streamline and expedite the site and list creation process, since both now use the same interface. By dividing site types into categories, which can be filtered by clicking the category name on the left, it's easy for users to find the type of site they want to create.

Users can select a category, choose a site type from the icons displayed, and then assign a name and URL to the site on the right workpane. Clicking the More Options button lets you enter a description for the site, set up unique permissions, and choose whether the site navigation will use the same items as the parent site or use its own unique permissions.

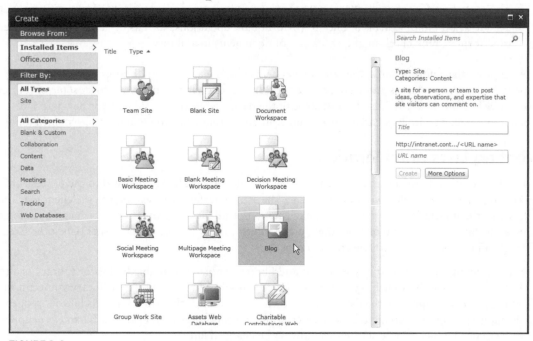

FIGURE 2-6

LISTS AND LIBRARIES IN SHAREPOINT 2010

Lists and libraries are still at the core of the SharePoint platform and where much of the power in SharePoint lies. In SharePoint terms, a *list* is a collection of data stored in rows and columns, similar to a spreadsheet. A *library* is a specialized type of list that enables the storage of files, such as documents, images, and even web pages, in addition to the data that can be collected in the list. The functionality of lists and libraries continues to improve with each version of SharePoint, and this version is no exception. In fact, performance in SharePoint 2010 has increased to the point where lists and libraries are capable of storing up to 50 million items. In addition to this vastly increased capacity are a few other notable changes to working with lists and libraries:

➤ The Ribbon — As mentioned earlier, the Ribbon is used just about everywhere in SharePoint 2010, lists and libraries included. The Ribbon provides a user-friendly interface for working with lists and libraries by offering up front a host of frequently used list options that were previously buried in menus or several layers deep in settings screens. Creating a column or view is now only a single click away.

➤ Inline editing — A new way of working with lists in SharePoint 2010 is the capability to edit each item in the list directly on the page without opening the datasheet view or the individual item.

➤ Tabular Views — This allows individual checkboxes to appear beside list items, enabling users to select multiple items at once to perform bulk operations, such as deleting list items or performing bulk check-in and check-out of documents in a library.

Along with these new features, the same components that make lists and libraries in SharePoint so powerful, such as columns and views, also return. In the following sections, we cover some of the new features in more detail. We also look at some of the returning features, and how the new interface makes interacting with lists and libraries a little different from what you might be accustomed to.

Creating Lists and Libraries

In SharePoint 2010, the process of creating lists and libraries is almost identical to the process of creating a new site, as the two processes share the same interface now (as long as the client machine has Silverlight installed). To get started, navigate to the All Site Content page, which can be accessed from the Site Actions menu or from the Quick Launch menu on most types of sites. Click the Create button in the toolbar to start the creation process.

You can immediately filter the types of list and library templates available by List or Library or further refine the search by clicking a category. Once you select the type of list or library you want to create, you can simply give the list a name and create it, or click the More Options button to open the additional options: giving the list a description and choosing whether the list's name will appear in the Quick Launch. These settings can always be changed later.

The various list templates available are actually nothing more than lists with pre-configured columns and views. You'll learn about creating your own views later in this chapter, in the "Creating Views" section. In addition, these list templates are also based on content types, which are actually collections of columns stored at the root site level and then pulled down and copied into the newly created list. You can find more details about content types in Chapter 16.

Of course, if none of the list templates provided meet your needs, then you can easily build a custom list instead. A custom list provides only one column called Title, which all lists contain. From there, you can build out your list with columns and views.

Working with Lists

Once you have created your list, it's time to start working with it. Overall, the major functions of working with a list aren't that much different than in SharePoint 2007, but you now have more avenues for list management. The Ribbon is displayed as soon as the list is created, providing you with options for nearly every task you will need to accomplish when working with a list. In addition, the list's name appears in the Quick Launch by default (unless you set this option to No during the list creation process), and you also have a link to add a new item directly on the page.

Adding content is as simple as clicking a link on the page. Clicking the Add New Item link will open a pop-up, enabling you to quickly enter a new item into the list. When you are finished adding your item, click OK and the page will refresh, with your new item showing.

If you need to collect more information for each item in the list, you can create new columns simply by clicking the Create Column button in the Ribbon under the List tab. Filling out the Create Column screen (shown in Figure 2-7) and clicking OK will add a new column to the list.

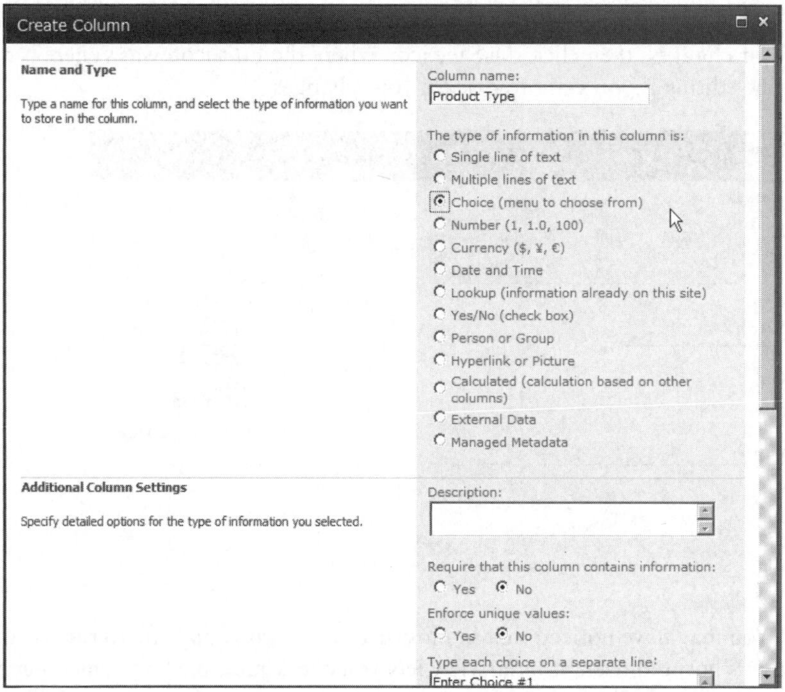

FIGURE 2-7

Datasheet View

A good way to quickly work with large quantities of data in a list, or to add data to the list quickly, is to utilize the Datasheet view. The Datasheet view opens the list in a view that very closely resembles the Excel interface, allowing you to quickly move between the cells of information and update or change them, or add new items to the list. Items added in the Datasheet view still must meet the parameters set in the Create Column screen, such as whether a cell is required. In addition, some information cannot be edited in the Datasheet view. Another thing to keep in mind is that only the current view of the list will open in the Datasheet view. This view can be a little intimidating to some users, and it can be easy to do real damage to a carefully constructed list

Inline Editing

Microsoft offers some improvements to the list editing experience with SharePoint 2010. First up is *inline editing.* As we stated earlier in this chapter, inline editing enables you to edit individual lines in a list without having to open the Edit Item window or switch to the Datasheet view. Inline editing is done directly on the list page. It is actually a component of the view displaying the list, and isn't on by default. Enabling inline editing is a simple process. To enable it for your current view, click the Modify View button in the Ribbon, scroll down to the section called Inline Editing, expand this section, and then check the box to Allow Inline Editing. Click OK to save the change to the view, and you've just enabled inline editing. (Views are covered in more depth later in this chapter.) To use inline editing, click the small Edit icon that now appears to the left of each line in the list as you hover the mouse cursor over it (see Figure 2-8). The fields in each column for the line item will become editable. Make your changes, then click the Save icon where the Edit icon was. There is also a Cancel icon to close inline editing if you want to discard your changes.

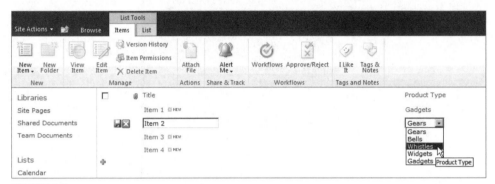

FIGURE 2-8

Tabular Views

Next up is Tabular view. You may have noticed that in most lists a checkbox appears to the left of each line item as the mouse is hovered over. Tabular view lets you check multiple line items, thereby enabling actions to be performed in bulk on the selected items. Most commands are unavailable when multiple items are checked, as many item-related commands in a list can only be performed individually; however, multiple items can be deleted at the same time using the Tabular view feature. Additional options become available when working with Tabular view in libraries, which is covered in the "Using the Ribbon with Lists" section later in this chapter.

Another feature that has been carried over from SharePoint 2007 but implemented more subtly in this version is the list item drop-down menu. Hovering over an item in the list will highlight the entire line in a border, and display a drop-down menu next to the text in the Title column. Clicking the drop-down will bring up a few options, all but one of which are available on the Ribbon. The only item that doesn't have a corresponding Ribbon button is Compliance Details. Selecting this will open a window that displays any compliance information that may be associated with the list item.

Compliance Details is a new option in SharePoint 2010 that lists the associated information and settings applied to a document. This is part of the new Records Management features included with SharePoint 2010, and is a way for users and administrators to easily see what retention policies and settings (if any) have been applied to the document.

Aside from the lists we've already described, several other types of list templates are also available for use on a SharePoint site. Here are a few notable list types in SharePoint 2010:

➤ Discussion Board — A list used as a full-fledged discussion board

➤ Links — A simple list of links to other web pages or documents

➤ Tasks — Can be used by a team or an individual to track progress of a project

➤ Project Tasks — Similar to the Tasks list, but provides a Gantt chart, which can be opened in Microsoft Project for additional tracking capabilities

➤ External List — Enables you to browse data from an external list within the SharePoint interface

➤ Survey — Use to create a survey to collect information from others in the organization

Using the Ribbon with Lists

As you work with your list, you'll notice that the Ribbon's items and tabs change when working with the various list components. When a new list is created, the Ribbon displays two tabs by default, List and Items.

The List tab contains items relevant to working with the list as a whole; columns and views are created from this menu, views can be changed, users can set up alerts for the list, and the list settings page can even be accessed from here, which opens up a page with more options for working with the list. Other options include viewing the list as an RSS feed if this functionality has been enabled for the site and list, exporting the list into an Excel spreadsheet, syncing to SharePoint Workspace, as well as other options for opening the list in SharePoint Designer and InfoPath to further customize it.

The Items tab contains buttons and options for working with individual list items. From this tab you can add new items, edit existing items, delete items, and manage item-level permissions. There are also options for using workflows in the list, as well as the capability to attach a file to a list item. You can use the tagging and "I like it" features from the Item tab as well.

Although all the buttons are visible at any given time, some buttons are not available, or enabled, in some scenarios. This is part of the contextual nature of the Ribbon — when an item can't be used, it is grayed out. When an action is performed that allows the Ribbon item to be used, it will again become available to click.

For example, when the Item tab is initially selected, the only button available on the Ribbon is New Item. Everything else is grayed out. Hovering over the Ribbon will present the user with a description of the item but also provide a message saying that the control is unavailable. However, checking the box next to an item or clicking on an item's line in the list (without clicking the item's Title link) will make more of the Item tab's buttons available. When using Tabular view, you may also notice that just about every option in the Ribbon becomes unavailable if more than one item is selected. The only options available are New Item and Delete. The capability to delete multiple items at once is in itself a handy feature.

As you work with the various types of lists, you'll notice that the Ribbon displays different options. For instance, working with a Calendar view of a list, as shown in Figure 2-9, provides different options in the Ribbon than working with a standard view of a list.

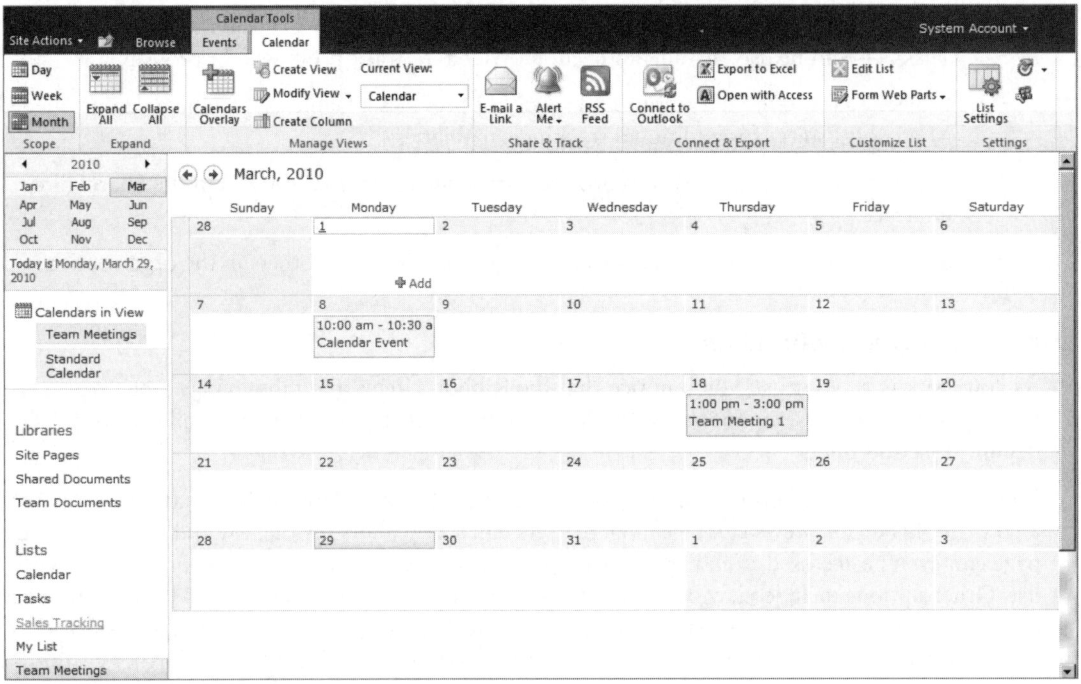

FIGURE 2-9

Working with Libraries

Working with libraries in SharePoint 2010 is very similar to working with lists. As you'll recall, libraries are nothing more than specialized lists designed for storing items. Instead of creating list items, the idea behind a library is that documents, images, and other files can be uploaded or created directly in the library. Generally, the same ideas that can be applied to lists in SharePoint also apply to libraries.

Libraries can be set up to create a specific file type when the New Document button is clicked in the Ribbon. For example, if the library is set up with a Word document as the default document type, then clicking the New Document button will create a new Word document in the library and then open the Word client to begin working with the document. Conversely, clicking the Upload button in the Ribbon or the link to Add New Document will open a pop-up window that enables you to upload a document from the client computer. The upload process is more streamlined in this version of SharePoint because it utilizes the pop-up window, eliminating the need to open multiple screens to upload and fill out metadata. The entire process is handled directly in the pop-up window; you don't need to leave the library.

Single file upload isn't the only upload option that has gotten a facelift. The multiple file upload has also been improved, adding drag and drop functionality to SharePoint libraries. To upload multiple files, you can either click the Upload button's drop-down and select Multiple File Upload, or click the Upload button and select the link on the upload pop-up to Upload Multiple Files. Then simply drag your files into the space indicated and click OK. Once the files are uploaded, click Done. If the drag and drop functionality isn't convenient, you can also browse for the files using a standard file-browsing Windows interface. Figure 2-10 shows the Upload Multiple Documents pop-up window.

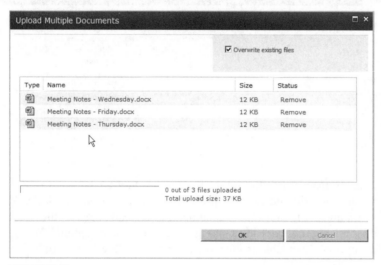

FIGURE 2-10

 The multiple file upload interface is available when the Microsoft Office clients are installed on the computer accessing the SharePoint site. The drag-and-drop functionality is available when using the Office 2010 suite of clients. In fact, the improved multiple file upload interface will also work with SharePoint 2007 when using Office 2010 on your computer.

Several types of libraries are available, such as a document library (which is the most commonly used type) and a picture library. The picture library is notable in that it doesn't actually use the Ribbon interface, but instead continues to use the menu-driven interface from SharePoint 2007.

Using the Ribbon with Libraries

The Ribbon used in libraries utilizes many of the same buttons as the Ribbon that appears when working with a list. There are some key differences, however. The major difference between the List and Library Ribbon is in the Connect & Export group. The List commands in this group enable you to use the list to work with other programs such as Excel, Visio, Outlook, and Project. There are fewer commands in the Library tab's Connect & Export group. You can still connect the document library to external clients, but there is also an icon to open the document library as a regular Windows Explorer window, as shown in Figure 2-11. This can be extremely handy when importing a large number of items into a SharePoint document library. Keep in mind, however, that when you are uploading multiple documents, either through Explorer view or through the multiple file upload interface, no metadata can be assigned to the files until after they are already uploaded.

FIGURE 2-11

The Documents tab is quite different from a list's Items tab. The options here enable you to check in and check out documents for editing, edit and view the properties of a document, check the version history of a document, set unique permissions for a document, download copies of files in the library to your computer, and set up and use workflows, along with several other options. You'll also notice that the New Folder option is available as long as the option to allow folders to be created is enabled.

The Check In and Check Out options enable you to check out a document (or multiple documents) to yourself to prevent others from editing the document while you work on it. This helps keep documents in sync as people work on them and prevents users from overwriting one another's work.

The Edit Document button in the Open & Check Out group will open the selected document in the associated client application. (Not all document types can be opened from SharePoint and saved back into SharePoint. In some instances, a document may need to be opened, saved to the local machine, and re-uploaded into SharePoint as a new version.)

In the Manage section of the Ribbon, the View Properties button and Edit Properties button enable you to view and edit the selected item, respectively. The View Properties button may cause some initial confusion, as it actually refers to the action of viewing the properties of the selected document and not looking at properties of the current view. Also in the Manage section is the capability to set unique permissions on a document, and the option to delete a document.

When using Tabular view, most of the Ribbon items disappear, leaving only a couple of options available for working with the selected documents, such as Check Out (or Check In if the selected documents are checked out) and Delete. This new functionality makes working with many documents at once much easier than in previous versions.

Columns = Metadata

Columns can still be created in a SharePoint list and/or library, just as in previous versions; and because you can create columns in your list, you can associate metadata with each list item. Basically, *metadata* is data about data. When uploading a document to a library, certain information is automatically collected about the document, such as who uploaded it, when it was created, and when it was last modified. This information about the document is the document's metadata. The same holds true when creating new items in a list.

Additional custom metadata can be added to a list or library in the form of columns. *Columns* refer to the extra type of information being collected about an item in a list or library. Creating a column enables you to collect and store additional information in the list about each item. To create a column, simply click the Create Column button in the Ribbon under the List tab (or Library tab if working with a library). The Create new column screen can also be accessed from the List or Library Settings screen.

You can create many different types of columns in order to collect metadata for items in a list or library. Table 2-1 outlines the various types of columns available in SharePoint 2010.

TABLE 2-1 SharePoint 2010 Column Types

COLUMN TYPE	DESCRIPTION
Single Line of Text	Allows users to enter a custom value for the column, up to 255 characters.
Multiple Lines of Text	Allows users to enter multiple lines for a custom value for the column. Additional options allow for rich text editing.
Choice (menu to choose from)	Allows users to select pre-determined options from a drop-down menu, radio buttons, or checkboxes, which allow for multiple selections.
Number	Allows only numbers to be entered. Options include configuring decimal places, maximum and minimum allowed values, and whether the number should show as a percentage.
Currency	Similar to the number column. Displays the number entered as the selected type of currency.
Date and Time	Allows users to enter a date and optionally a time using a date picker. Date and time columns can be useful when creating Calendar views or used as filtering options.
Lookup	This column can be used to look up values from another list or library in the same site. Not all types of columns can be used with the lookup column.
Yes/No (check box)	A simple checkbox that can be used to indicate that a condition is true or not based on whether the box is checked. When filtering with a yes/no column, the value of the check is either a 1 (for yes, or checked) or 0 (for no, not checked).

continues

TABLE 2–1: SharePoint 2010 Column Types *(continued)*

COLUMN TYPE	DESCRIPTION
Person or Group	This column is essentially a "people picker" column that enables users and groups from the site to be looked up.
Hyperlink or Picture	Allows users to enter a URL to a site (internal or external) or an image in the site, depending on whether the option is selected to format the URL as a link or a picture.
Calculated	This column uses values from other columns in the same list in an equation to produce a value. The equations used in calculated columns are very similar to the types of equations used in Excel.
External Data	A new column for SharePoint 2010 that allows external content types to be browsed and used as metadata in a list. External content types must be enabled by an administrator before this column is available.
Managed Metadata	Also new to SharePoint 2010, this allows values from a managed metadata term store to be browsed and selected. (See Chapter 16 for more about managed metadata.)

When creating a new column, it's important to look at the Additional Column Settings section below the column type selector. This section varies according to the type of column that's chosen, allowing various settings to be applied to further refine the type of data being collected. In addition, each column type can be configured to require that users enter something into the column, ensuring that the type of information that needs to be collected by an organization is being collected. Once the column is created, it can be populated with the corresponding type of data. Tagging list items with all this metadata can come in handy when working with filtering and creating views of the data, which is covered in more depth later in the chapter. Additionally, metadata can be searched, making it easy to find information in lists and libraries in this way.

 This section has been referring to columns, but when you are adding a new item to a list or editing the properties of a document, you will notice that what you create as a column actually displays as a field to collect the information. In fact, they are one and the same. When viewing the entire list, the fields containing the information you entered are displayed in a column, but when working with an individual item, the information collected in the column is simply displayed as a field for usability purposes.

Working with Folders

Inevitably, one of the first questions many users ask when they begin working with SharePoint lists and libraries for the first time is, "Can't I just put my stuff in a folder in SharePoint?" The answer is yes, but with some caveats. Users love folders. They're familiar with the concept, their entire computer has documents and images all filed away in specific folders throughout the hard drive, and they probably have dozens more folders hanging out on a file share on a server somewhere too. However, folders have inherent drawbacks, such as ending up with duplicate files and multiple versions of the same file scattered throughout a department on several users' machines, as well as on a file share. Keeping track of a single document becomes a task in itself (although SharePoint can help mitigate this mess). Unfortunately, users have been trained over the years to organize things in folders, so as an administrator, you need to understand that it's only natural for users to ask about organizing their documents within folders when moving to SharePoint. It's your job to help them understand why they ought to use metadata instead to organize their content.

While your natural reaction might be to "encourage" them either by osmosis or by using a ruler over the knuckles, you can probably do better than that. Try to explain to users how metadata helps them get better search results and how tagged content, coupled with custom views, gives them more flexibility. When they bury content in folders it is hard to get a view of all the content at once; for example, maybe you want to see all of the expense reports. With metadata it is easy to create a view that shows all expense reports.

This isn't to say that folders don't have their place in SharePoint 2010. They can come in handy in many situations. In fact, just about every type of list and library supports using folders. Some of these lists enable the use of folders by default (such as a document library), while others need the option enabled before folders can be created (such as a custom list). Folders can also be useful when you need to work with permissions on a set of documents or items in a library. Although individual items can be assigned unique permissions, it can quickly become a nightmare managing permissions on dozens of documents in the same library. Instead of managing the permissions on each document individually, documents that require the same permissions can be grouped together in a folder, which can have its own set of permissions. This makes permission management much easier. To enable or disable the use of folders in a list or library, click the List/Library Settings button in the Ribbon, under the Library tab. Click the Advanced Settings link, and select Yes or No to make the "New Folder" command available (see Figure 2-12).

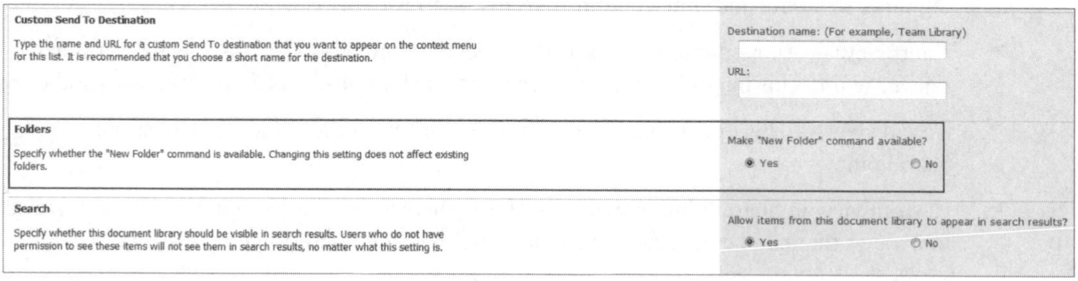

FIGURE 2-12

In addition, using folders can help scale a document library or list. Say, for example, that you have a particularly large document library, and your organization is using the large list throttling feature to only allow views of 2,000 items at a time. You could create several folders and divide the documents up between the folders, skirting around the 2,000-item per view limit imposed on the site without having to create custom views. In most cases, however, creating views based on metadata still offers more flexibility in terms of browsing through the content. For more information on large list throttling see Chapter 3.

Creating Views

SharePoint 2010 still offers the option to create different views of lists and libraries. *Views* are simply a way to reorganize and structure the data stored in a SharePoint list or library in meaningful ways. Multiple views can be created on a list or library, and can be used to group, sort, and filter the data. Sorting and filtering data is possible because of the list's metadata. For example, you could create a view that shows all documents that were last modified by a particular user. Similarly, you could create a view that groups all items in a list that meet the same criteria based on information entered into a column.

Types of Views

You can create several types of views for any given list:

➤   Standard view — This is the most commonly used type of view. It presents the data in the list in the standard row and column format. You choose which columns you would like to display, the order in which they should appear, how they display, and how many items show at once, among other options. You can also group and filter data based on information in each column.

➤   Datasheet view — This is similar to the Standard view, but it opens the list in the Datasheet by default. Like the Standard view, you can choose which columns are displayed and in which order. You don't have quite as many options for formatting the view as with a Standard view, however.

➤   Calendar view — This view displays the items in the list in a calendar format. Not all lists can utilize the Calendar view, however. Calendar views must be based on some kind of starting time, so a date and time column is necessary to use this view.

➤   Gantt view — Along the same lines as the Calendar view, this view also requires a starting time to work. This builds the list into a chart to track events or progress over a period of time.

➤   Access view — This opens the Access client to work with the values in the list outside of SharePoint.

➤   Custom view in SharePoint Designer — This opens SharePoint Designer 2010 to create custom views that can be modified and styled, such as with conditional formatting.

➤   Standard view, with Expanded Recurring Events — This option appears when creating new views based on the Calendar list template and is basically a Standard view that shows all occurrences of a recurring event.

When creating a view, it is important to consider how you want the data displayed. Probably the most commonly used view type is the Standard view, as it offers many options for configuring the view, such as grouping and filtering the data, as well as a few formatting options for how the data will be displayed. You can see the various view options on the dialog shown in Figure 2-13.

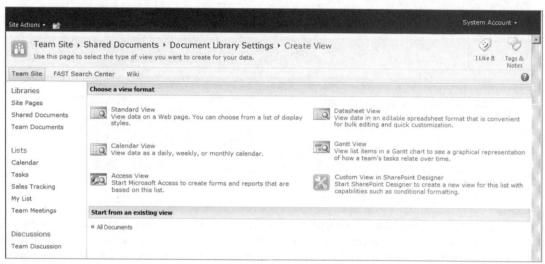

FIGURE 2-13

Creating a Standard View

To begin creating a view in a list or library, click the Create View button in the List or Library tab in the Ribbon. This will open the view selection screen. The rest of this section covers the creation of a Standard view. When creating a Standard view, you begin by giving the view a name and specifying whether this new view will be the default view that opens when the list or library is open. A word of caution here: For performance reasons, it is generally best to limit the number of items displayed by the default view of a list to a relatively small number if possible. Otherwise, the server may take a performance hit while rendering all the items in the list every time the list is opened.

In the next section on the page you have the option to make this new view public (any user can select the view) or private (it appears only for your use). Next, you will see a list of all the available columns in the list. Select the ones you'd like to display in your view by checking the boxes next to them, and choose the order in which to display them by changing the numbers to the right of the column names. Column order is set from left to right, with number 1 being the first column on the left (see Figure 2-14).

Scrolling down the page, the next section enables you to sort the items in the list by a column, and allows for a second level of sorting by another column. For example, suppose you have a list of employees and you have set up two columns, one for Department and another for Personnel. You could sort the view first by the Department column, and then do a second sort on the Personnel column. The list would display all the departments alphabetically, and all the employees of each department alphabetically as well.

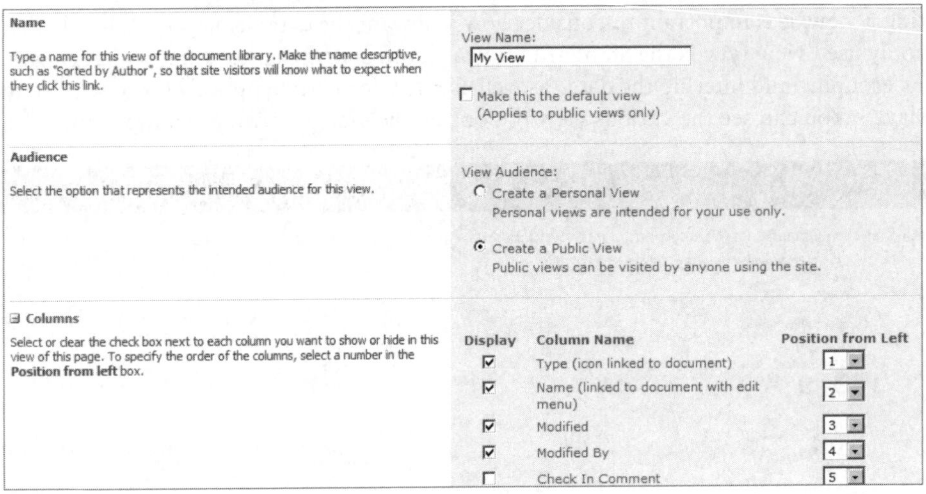

FIGURE 2-14

The next section of the view creation screen enables you to filter the data in the view, showing only a subset of the list's information. By default, the view is not filtered. You can set up the view to filter out items based on criteria set in the drop-down menus and fields in this section. To do so, select which column will be used as the filter, and then choose the type of comparison to use from the drop-down menu. Options include "is equal to," "is not equal to," "is greater than or equal to," "contains," and several others.

Finally, in the field below the comparison drop-down, type in the value that should be compared. Basically, you are having SharePoint compare the selected column to the value you have entered, and if it finds items in the list that meet that criterion, it will display only those items. You can even create more than one filtering criterion as well, using an And/Or operator, by selecting either the And or the Or radio buttons, and then filling in the criteria for the second level of filtering. Up to ten columns can be used to filter the data in a list. Filtering can be a very powerful way to view only a subset of the data in the list.

The next several sections in the view creation screen are all collapsed, so if you want to set any of the options you need to click the section name to expand it. Here is a rundown of all these collapsed sections and how they affect the view:

➤ Inline Editing — You can check the box to allow inline editing on the view. Off by default.

➤ Tabular View — This allows multiple item selection in the list. On by default.

➤ Group By — This option allows the list items to be sorted into groups.

➤ Totals — This will keep a running total of the number of items in a column or perform other calculations, such as the sum of all numbers in a numeric column. Set on a per-column basis. Off by default.

➤ Styles — Use this option to choose a different style in which to present the list. Most styles result in simple cosmetic differences. Some, such as the Preview Pane and Boxed styles, present the list in a different format. The Preview Pane style shows a preview of the list item when it is hovered over. The Boxed styles present each list item in a separate box. Some styles work better for displaying different types of data than others, so try a few out to see what style works best for your list.

➤ Folders — If you are using folders in the library or list, you can choose whether to show the folders or just show all items in the list or library at once.

➤ Item Limit — This value sets the number of items that are displayed at once. If your list has more items than are set to display, you can page through the list to view the remaining items (30 is the default value).

The last section on the create view page is new to SharePoint 2010, and that is the capability to adjust some settings for this view when viewing it on a mobile device. You can choose to make the view the default view that displays when the list is opened on a mobile device, as well as choose whether or not the view should even be available for viewing on mobile devices. You can set the number of items to display at once for the mobile view when a page with the list on it is open with a mobile device. The idea is similar to the number of items set in the Item Limit section.

Once you have all your settings the way you'd like them, click OK to create your view. The list will display with your newly created view. The view is associated with the list, so whenever the list is open, you can change the list's view to the custom view you created. You can do this in two ways. When opening a list, the last item in the breadcrumb trail displays the current view's name. Clicking on the drop-down arrow next to this name will show a list of all views associated with the list (along with options for creating a new view or modifying the view that is currently displaying, and options for configuring the available views for the list). The second way to change the view is to click the List or Library tab in the Ribbon and select the view from the Current View drop-down menu, as shown in Figure 2-15.

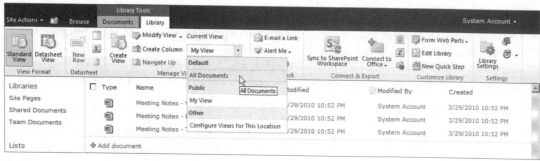

FIGURE 2-15

Modifying a View

Custom views and even the preconfigured views provided out of the box can be modified simply by selecting the view you'd like to work with and clicking the Modify View button on the List or Library tab in the Ribbon. This opens the same screen as clicking the Create View button does, enabling you to change any settings you need.

The Modify View button also has a drop-down menu associated with it. Clicking the drop-down provides the additional option to modify the view using SharePoint Designer 2010, which offers additional options for changing the view, such as turning on conditional formatting for the list. For example, a company may use a SharePoint list to keep track of inventory. Modifying this list in SharePoint Designer could enable them to set conditional formatting on the list to highlight a line item when its inventory falls below a set value. See Chapters 22 and 23 for more information on using SharePoint Designer.

Creating Other View Types

As mentioned earlier, you can create several other types of views for a list. The process is relatively similar to setting up a Standard view, with some differences that will be pointed out in the following sections.

 Note that below the available view formats is the option to create a new view using an existing view as a starting point. This can be useful if you are creating several similar views with only a few minor differences, such as showing or hiding a column or two. Instead of having to set all your options for each version of the view, you can select an existing view from the list, which copies the view's settings, and then create a new view from it.

Datasheet View

Creating a Datasheet view is identical to the process of creating a Standard view, but with fewer options. You still select which columns to display and in which order, set any sorting or filtering properties, whether you want each column totaled, how folders should be displayed, and how many items should be shown at once. Once these few options are set, you have a Datasheet view.

Calendar View

Creating a Calendar view uses the same familiar interface but requires you to provide a few different settings. Calendar views are based on date and time columns, so your list must have a date and time column on which to base the calendar. Just about any list can have a Calendar view created, provided it has a date and time column. For example, suppose you have built a custom list of events for your organization, and you'd like to display it in a Calendar view. You have a column for when the event starts, and another column for when the event ends. In the Time Interval section, choose what date and time column will be used for displaying when events start (the Begin drop-down) and when they end (the End drop-down), as shown in Figure 2-16.

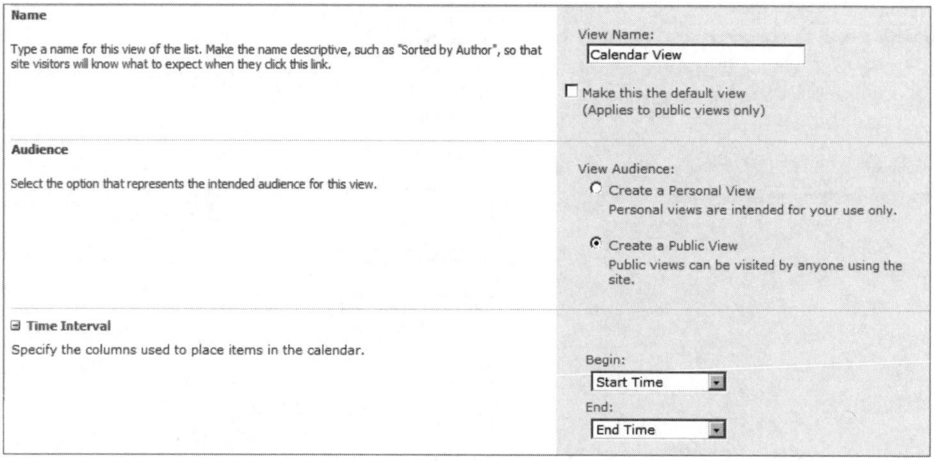

FIGURE 2-16

The next section enables you to specify which columns should be displayed as information in the calendar's various views. Calendar views can be displayed as a week, a month, or a day. In the Month View Title drop-down, select the column you'd like to display as the item's title in the month view. Similarly, choose which column information should display for the week view and day view. Generally, you'll want to use the same title for each. Week view and day view also offer the option of specifying a column to use as a subtitle, as the views offer more room for text than a month view. For instance, you could use a column that has location information or a quick description of the event as the subtitle of the event.

Next, you can choose whether the default value of the calendar should open to a month view, a week view, or a day view. You can change the view when using the calendar; this simply defines how the calendar is displayed when it is initially opened.

The final two sections are identical to creating a standard view. You can filter events from the list so only certain events show up. For example, you could set a filter that shows events for only a certain department or group. This way, all the events are maintained in a single location, but each group can have a view that shows only the events relevant to them.

Another nice addition to SharePoint 2010 calendars are calendar overlays. Now you can have more than one calendar's items displaying in a single calendar view. These items can be from an Outlook calendar stored in Outlook Web Access (OWA) or Exchange, or they can be other SharePoint calendars.

When working in a list's calendar view, click the Calendar tab in the Ribbon, and then click Calendars Overlay. Click the New Calendar link to add in a calendar either from OWA or SharePoint. Choose whether the calendar is a SharePoint calendar or Exchange calendar and fill in the information below as appropriate. Figure 2-17 shows the options for adding a SharePoint calendar as an overlay. Click OK to save the overlay information. You can toggle the overlay on and off by clicking the Calendars Overlay button and checking or clearing the checkbox next to each overlay's name. Up to ten overlays can be added per calendar view.

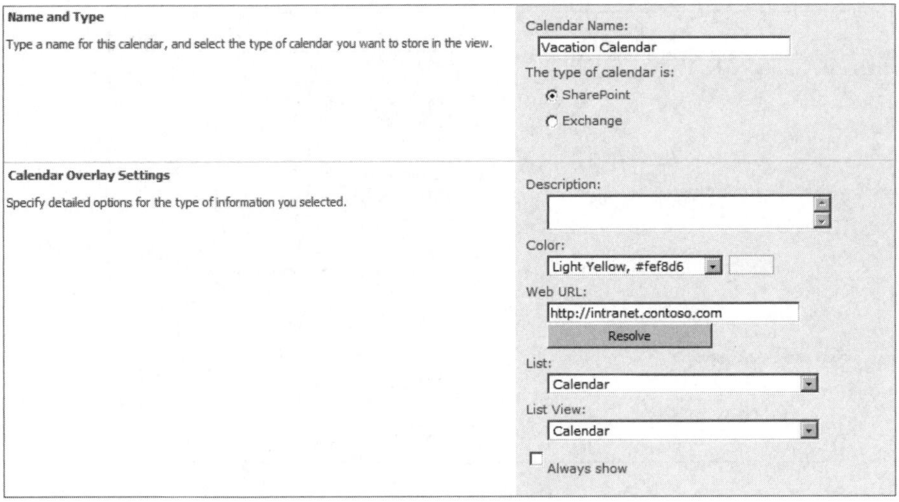

Name and Type		Calendar Name:
Type a name for this calendar, and select the type of calendar you want to store in the view.		Vacation Calendar

The type of calendar is:

○ SharePoint
○ Exchange

Calendar Overlay Settings

Specify detailed options for the type of information you selected.

Description:

Color:
Light Yellow, #fef8d6

Web URL:
http://intranet.contoso.com

Resolve

List:
Calendar

List View:
Calendar

☐ Always show

FIGURE 2-17

Gantt View

A Gantt view is a good way to display a set of information over a period of time. It's similar to a calendar in that it displays events and tasks by date, but displays them in a chart with bars representing the length of time the task or event will take place. Creating a Gantt view is like a hybrid of creating a Calendar view and a Standard view. You still select which columns to display and in which order, and like a Calendar view you still select columns to represent the start and end dates for each item. You have additional options too, such as selecting a column to represent the task's percentage of completion.

The rest of the Gantt view creation process is almost identical to the process for creating a Standard view. Once you create this view it will also be available for selection from the View drop-down.

Access View and Custom View in SharePoint Designer

The final two options on the create view screen, Access View and Custom View in SharePoint Designer, are available only if these programs are installed on the client machine accessing the site. As you may have guessed, each of these view types is made outside of SharePoint in the application you choose. An Access view will open Access and allow you to work with a list, while selecting a Custom view in SharePoint Designer will open SharePoint Designer, allowing you to add additional view formatting, such as conditional formatting, to the list.

Creating views in these two programs is out of the scope of this chapter, but you can refer to Chapter 18 for information on integrating SharePoint with the Office clients, and Chapter 22 to learn about SharePoint Designer 2010.

List View Web Parts

When a list or library is created in SharePoint, a corresponding Web Part is automatically created and made available for use throughout the site on a page. You'll learn more about using Web Parts in the following section, but for now you should be aware that any library and list created can also be used on just about any page in a site. Users may find it useful to have a Web Part that lists newly uploaded documents or recent announcements directly on the company's intranet home page.

List view Web Parts are also particularly useful in that they are directly tied to the list from which they are created. This also gives users the flexibility to update information on a web page without having to actually edit the content of the page itself — the List view Web Part is all maintained in the list itself. Another benefit of being able to use a List view Web Part is that it offers all the flexibility of being able to display any views created for the list, as well as have its own views created specifically for it. For example, you could create a list of events whose default view is a Calendar view when the list is open, and at the same time you can have the same list displayed on a web page, but in a Standard view format.

Yet another use for these List view Web Parts is the capability to display more than one instance of the same list on a page, with each instance displaying a different view. Or, you can even display many lists on a page, making it easy to compare information between lists. Perhaps you have a document library with specific views created that display only certain documents at a time. You can have two Web Parts of the document library on a web page, and set each Web Part to a unique view, so each shows different documents. When any documents that meet the criteria in the views are added to or removed from the library, the Web Parts on the web page will automatically reflect the changes.

WORKING WITH SHAREPOINT PAGES

Now that you know quite a bit about how lists and libraries work in SharePoint, this section describes how the new SharePoint 2010 interface has changed and improved the page-editing experience.

When browsing a SharePoint page, you are actually seeing the compilation of many different components all quickly rendered by the server and served to the browser. The two main components of a SharePoint page are the master page and the page layout. In very basic terms, the *master page* is the container for the overall site layout. It holds the basic structure of the site, such as the location of the navigation, search, and the Ribbon. It also houses the *page layout*, which is generally the main body of the page and contains the page's content. Refer to Chapter 23 for more detailed information on master pages and page layouts. When you are editing a SharePoint page in the browser, you are actually working with the page layout to add content to the site.

The page-editing experience in SharePoint 2010 is a little different from that found in previous versions. Again, the Ribbon plays a major part in editing a page — in fact, it's probably used even more extensively when editing a page than when working with lists and libraries.

Fortunately, the Ribbon has been very tightly integrated with the page-editing experience, to the point that many users will likely find that adding content to a SharePoint page is not much different from working in Microsoft Word. Just like the Office clients, the Ribbon is also contextual when working with various items. Different options appear in the Ribbon when working with a picture than when working with a List view Web Part, for instance. Before you can even begin working extensively with the Ribbon, however, you need to first begin to edit the page.

When browsing a page normally, the Ribbon is very discreet. Only the Browse and Page tabs are visible; the Ribbon menu itself is collapsed. By default, the Browse tab is selected. Next to these tabs is the Edit Page icon, which looks like a pencil on a piece of paper (see Figure 2-18). Clicking this icon is only one of several ways to begin the editing process. You can also edit the page by clicking the Site Actions button and then selecting Edit page, or click the Page tab in the Ribbon and click Edit Page. Note that only users with permission to edit pages will be presented with these options.

FIGURE 2-18

Exploring Edit Mode

Using the Ribbon to edit pages in SharePoint is actually a lot like using it in lists and libraries. Each tab is divided up into groups, and each group consists of several different options represented by icons (with the exception of the Browse tab, which doesn't have a menu, but instead simply lets you browse the current page). As you work with various components of a page, additional tab options appear in the Ribbon, and other buttons become active when certain actions are performed on the page.

When a page is opened in Edit mode, you'll notice a few changes. First, you'll notice that the Ribbon has grown a bit. Under the Editing Tools heading, two new tabs now appear in the Ribbon — Format Text and Insert — under the heading "Editing Tools. The Format Text tab provides you with a menu very similar to Word's Home tab, with options for formatting the text on the page. You can change the font, the font size and style, its justification, create numbered and bulleted lists, and even change the font color. There is even a Spell Check button, and advanced users can edit the HTML markup directly to achieve exactly the formatting they want. Editing a SharePoint page also provides the capability to copy, cut, and paste content to and from the page, and even features Undo functionality. This tab drives home the point that editing a SharePoint page is more like working in a Word document than creating a web page. You also have options such as Save and Check Out, which are covered in more detail later. Figure 2-19 shows the additional options that become available in the Ribbon when the page is in Edit mode.

FIGURE 2-19

The Insert tab allows you to do what you would expect it to — that is, insert content on the page. You can insert a table, a picture, or multimedia in the form of video and audio; create links to other websites; upload and create a link to a file on the fly; and insert any reusable content stored in the Reusable Content list, various Web Parts, an existing list, and a new list created on the fly (see Figure 2-20). The Insert tab provides a host of options to add content, making it extremely easy to spruce up a web page without much effort. You'll be taking a more detailed look at these options in a bit.

FIGURE 2-20

When a page is in Edit mode, you will notice that switching back to the Page tab allows a few additional options to become available.

As you edit pages in SharePoint, you can save your changes to the server so others can see them. During the editing process, you can click the Save button in the Ribbon (either on the Format Text tab or the Page tab) to simply save your changes and stop editing. You also can click the drop-down arrow underneath the Save button for additional options, such as the capability to save content and continue editing, or to stop editing altogether. With the latter option, you are prompted to save your changes or discard your changes.

One final point to note about Edit mode is that the page is divided into blocks, called zones. In these zones you can place content such as text or Web Parts. How content is placed depends on the type of page you are working with, but generally just about any type of content can be added to a SharePoint page.

Adding Content to Pages

SharePoint 2010 utilizes several different page options, which are available on different site types. A team site, for example, features what are called *Text Layouts*. You have several different text layouts from which to choose, and their function is to reorganize the zones on the page to allow for more design options when formatting content. Using these text zones, you can add Web Parts and text directly. Other zones will allow only Web Parts to be inserted.

Other types of SharePoint sites utilize *Page Layouts* instead of Text Layouts. Sites that utilize the Publishing infrastructure of SharePoint, or that have the Publishing Feature enabled, will use Page Layouts. Page Layouts provide some flexibility over Text Layouts in that they can be edited in SharePoint Designer, and users with appropriate permissions can create and upload custom Page Layouts to meet their needs.

Direct Page Edits

Many Text Layouts and Page Layouts allow for direct page editing. As the name implies, direct page editing is the capability to edit directly on a page. This function was available in SharePoint 2007 with page content controls, but in SharePoint 2010, editing text and content on a page is now even easier. Indeed, adding and editing text on a SharePoint page is as easy as clicking on the page and starting to type. We keep emphasizing that editing SharePoint pages is similar to working with a Word document, and with the improved direct page editing, it truly is.

When working with text on a page, the Ribbon switches to the Format Text tab. As you work with the text on the page, you can use SharePoint's Live Preview mode to preview most formatting changes before committing to them. To use Live Preview, highlight the text you'd like to change and hover the mouse cursor over, for example, a new font size in the size drop-down in the Ribbon, as shown in Figure 2-21. The highlighted text will temporarily change to the new size, letting you see if you like the change. You can also use Live Preview to experiment with different fonts, as well as styles and markup styles.

FIGURE 2-21

The Ribbon features more than just items for working with text on a page. Additional tasks that can be performed with a Ribbon include cutting, copying, and pasting text to and from a SharePoint page just as you would any other application. Undo and Redo buttons also help with the editing experience, as well as the capability to edit the HTML that makes up the page. In the Markup group in the Ribbon, you can choose to edit the HTML Source, or convert any existing HTML on the page into XHTML, which helps increase the page's browser compatibility. SharePoint 2010 features a robust spell check as well.

Dealing with Save Conflicts

When more than one person is working on a web page at the same time, they may run into a save conflict. A save conflict occurs when user A and user B are making changes to the same web page, and user A saves the page while user B continues working. With SharePoint 2010, when you try to save the page, a window opens with several options:

➤ Continue Editing — You can continue editing, but you will need to manually merge any changes you make later.

➤ Merge Changes — A second window opens with the most current version of the page so you can merge changes or additional text from your version of the page with the saved version.

➤ Discard Your Changes — This option deletes any changes you've made to the page in favor of the version that's been saved before yours.

➤ Overwrite the Page — This option discards the version saved by another user and replaces it with your version.

In most cases, you will probably want to choose Merge Changes, to at least look at the changes made by the other user. You can always close the newly opened window and save the changes again, choosing Overwrite the Page to discard the other user's changes.

Checking Pages In and Out

The problem of save conflicts can be mitigated by using the check-out tools built into SharePoint. In the Ribbon, you can click the Check Out button to check the page out to yourself. Checking out a page is essentially the same idea as checking out a document from a library. Basically, the page is exclusively yours to edit and change while you have it checked out.

 One note of caution here: If you have started editing a page before you check it out, your changes will be deleted, so check out a page before you begin editing it. If you have changed a page and need to check it out, save your changes first and then check the page out.

You can check in and out from the Ribbon, just as you can check out documents or items in a library or list. Click the Check Out button to check the current page out to yourself, preventing other users from being able to edit the page as you work on it. The Check Out button becomes the Check In button, and also provides you with a few additional options in the drop-down menu below the button. If you accidentally checked the page out, you can always discard the check out (which also discards any changes made to the page) by clicking the Check In drop-down menu and selecting Discard Check Out.

When a user with edit rights browses to a page that is currently checked out, a message is displayed at the top of the page indicating that the page is currently checked out, and to which user it is checked out. In addition, note that saving a page does not check the page in. If a page is checked out, then it remains checked out until it is checked in. You can, however, check a page in to save the page.

Overriding Check Outs

Administrators and users with the Override Check Out permission can override another user's checked out page. The Override Check Out permission is built into the Design permission level. If you browse to a page that is checked out to another user, the Check Out/In button is replaced with an Override Check Out button. If you have sufficient rights, then you can click the button to change the check out to yourself, which will discard the other user's changes and allow you to begin editing. Be aware, though, that there is no prompt to warn you that you will be discarding another user's changes when overriding a check out from the Ribbon.

Users with override permission can also check in the page from the Pages library for another user. This is done by clicking the drop-down menu for a page in the Pages library and selecting the Check In option, or clicking the Check In button in the Ribbon. Checking in a page for another user is less destructive than overriding the check out, as it will save the changes to the page, and then check it in. Checking in a document for another user can only be done from the Pages library and not from the page itself. This method also lets you know that you are checking in a document for another user, and tells you how long the page has been checked out.

Publishing

When using a site with Publishing features enabled, you will have an additional tab in the Ribbon for publishing content. You will still be able to save a page's content as you are working on it; but *publishing*, in SharePoint terms, means that the final version of the page is hidden from anyone without proper rights until the Publish button is clicked. Publishing a SharePoint page is the same concept as publishing a book. The book is available only to the author and editors during the creation process; until it is published, the public doesn't have access to it. The same concept applies to SharePoint — the page author and other individuals with proper rights are the only ones who can see the page as it's being worked on, but other general users of the site can't see the contents of the page until it has been published.

When the Publish button is clicked, SharePoint will check the page for any draft items and spelling errors before committing the changes, as well as give you a text field to type comments about what has changed in this published version of the page. You can exit out of the checking pop-up to check the spelling from the Format Text tab, or click the link in the status bar that opened to see a report of all spelling errors and draft items on the page that will be published (see Figure 2-22).

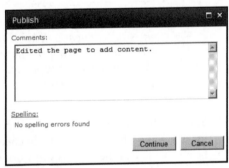

FIGURE 2-22

If you are working on a previously published page, users will see the last published version of the page before you began editing it. SharePoint serves up the last published version of the page until a new version is published to take its place. Because SharePoint 2010 still supports versioning, it is possible to roll back to a previously published version of a page, as long as versioning is turned on for the library containing the SharePoint pages.

If a user with rights to edit a page browses to a page that's being edited, a message is displayed indicating that the page is published and that it's also checked out and being edited by another user. The user editing the page also has a notice under the Ribbon saying that the page is currently checked out and editable.

Working with Web Parts

Web Parts are specialized components that perform certain tasks. You can think of SharePoint Web Parts as building blocks for adding additional content and information to your web page.

It's one thing to add text to a page. It's another to add additional content in the form of video and audio, lists, RSS feeds, and data compiled from throughout a SharePoint site. An exhaustive treatment of how they are used is beyond the scope of this chapter. This section provides a high-level overview of the process of adding Web Parts to the page and the general experience of working with them.

Adding a Web Part

From the Insert tab, you can easily add images, tables, links, Web Parts, and lists. Adding Web Parts to a SharePoint 2010 page is different than in previous versions. When you click the Web Part button on the Insert tab, a Web Part picker opens at the top of the page, just below the Ribbon, as shown in Figure 2-23. At the left is a filter tree for the list of Web Parts, organized by category. The middle pane displays the available Web Parts for the selected category, and the right pane contains information about the selected Web Part. After selecting a Web Part, you can choose the zone it should be dropped into using the Add Web Part to: dropdown (that is, if multiple zones are available). Click the Add button to insert the Web Part onto the page where the blinking cursor was left in a rich text field, or into a specific zone selected in the drop-down at the bottom of the right panel.

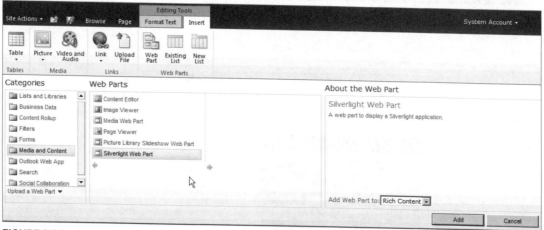

FIGURE 2-23

Not all available Web Parts are displayed on the Ribbon. To see the full list of web parts that are available on the site, click the Web Part button.

You can also upload a file directly from the Insert tab into a SharePoint library and create a link to the document on the page, all without leaving Edit mode. The new Reusable Content Web Part can be used for elements that are frequently reused when creating pages, such as a copyright line, a byline, or a quote. You can view all the reusable content configured on the site and open the list in which it's contained to add new content for use later.

Another novel addition to the Ribbon is the capability to create a new list on the fly directly from the Ribbon using the New List button. A pop-up window will open, from which you can choose your list template and give the list a name. The newly created list will appear on the page.

Using the Ribbon to Work with Web Parts

When a Web Part is selected on the page, a new contextual tab opens in the Ribbon. Depending on the Web Part selected, various options are available. For instance, inserting the new Media Web Part (from the Media and Content category) will open both the Options tab under the Web Part Tools header and another Options tab under the Media header (see Figure 2-24). The Media Web Part lets you add a Silverlight media player to the page to play audio and video clips. As you might guess, the Options tab under the Web Part Tools header contains options for working with the Web Part in general (such as opening its properties or deleting it), whereas the Media heading's Options tab pertains specifically to the selected Web Part. Not all Web Parts have a dedicated tab in the Ribbon, but they all will open the Web Part Tools Options tab.

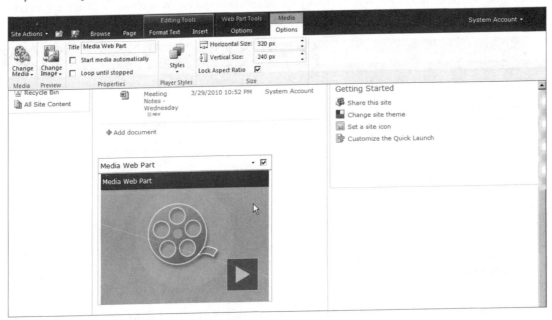

FIGURE 2-24

Many users familiar with older versions of SharePoint will also recognize the tool pane for working with Web Parts. Clicking the Web Part Properties button in the Ribbon will open the familiar tool pane along the right side of the screen, which contains options for working with the selected Web Part. You can change the Web Part's title and description and chrome state (whether its title and border display), as well as other options specific to that Web Part.

Overall, working with Web Parts in SharePoint 2010 isn't very different from past versions. Some Web Parts will have additional options in the tool pane depending on the type of Web Part. Figure 2-25 shows the tool pane for the Shared Documents library Web Part. The Content Query Web Part, for example, enables you to aggregate content from your site based on its content types. It has many different options for configuring the query used to gather its content, something that other Web Parts do not need and therefore do not feature. This tool pane can also be accessed from the Web Part's drop-down menu, which appears to the far right of the Web Part's title. Click the drop-down arrow and select Edit Web Part to open the tool pane.

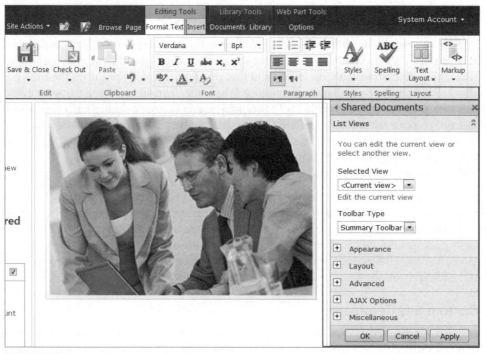

FIGURE 2-25

A new option found on the tool pane for some Web Parts that wasn't found in previous versions of SharePoint is the AJAX Options section. Expanding this enables you to use the Asynchronous Updates option for certain lists. For example, you may have asynchronous updates turned on if a Web Part is taking a particularly long time to load. Allowing asynchronous updates enables the rest of the page to load without waiting for the Web Part. It can finish loading after the rest of the page has been displayed, which makes for a better user experience. A few other options are also available for using asynchronous syncing, such as whether to allow manual and automatic refreshing of the Web Part, and defining the interval between each refresh.

When working with List view Web Parts on a page, a section opens in the Ribbon called List Tools. These list tools are, in fact, the very same Ribbon tabs that appear when working with a list directly. In other words, you can perform any action in a list through its List view Web Part that you would if you had the list open on the screen.

As you can see, the interface for editing pages and working with Web Parts has been significantly overhauled for SharePoint 2010, providing an intuitive way to work with various components of the page at once, usually without having to even leave the page in order to add images, media, text, and other Web Parts. These changes provide a much more pleasant experience for users and administrators alike, increasing productivity dramatically. Because many user-centric experiences have been revamped to more closely mimic the Office client interface that users are already familiar with, they should have an easier time adapting to the changes.

USING SITE TEMPLATES IN SHAREPOINT 2010

Suppose you are setting up several team sites in order for various groups to be able to work on projects together. It's been decided that each one of the sites will contain several custom lists and document libraries, all with custom columns set up, and that certain items will appear on the site's home page, so that any new project site that is created looks the same. Instead of having to create every single project site from scratch, and build every list, library, and custom columns each time a new site is requested, you can create one version of the site that can be made into a *template* and reused any time a new site needs to be created. You can save just the site's structure as a template, or you have the option to save any content built into the site as well, such as Web Parts added to a page, pictures and documents in a library, and items in a list.

The process is essentially the same as the site template creation process in SharePoint 2007. Sites can be created, configured, and saved as reusable templates; and you can use the browser interface or SharePoint Designer to make changes to a site. However, one difference is that SharePoint 2010 automatically packages up site templates as solution files with .wsp extensions. A WSP file is actually nothing more than a CAB file. You can even browse the contents of a WSP file by appending .cab to the end of the filename on the desktop and opening it with Windows Explorer.

Creating Custom Site Templates

In technical terms, a SharePoint custom site template is based on an existing site, which was created from a SharePoint site definition. Basically, a site definition is SharePoint's blueprint for creating the various types of sites that are available. In other words, when a site is created in SharePoint, the site is created following the instructions laid out in the site definition file. The site definition specifies which features are activated on the site, which libraries and lists are initially available, and other components of the site.

When you build a site to be used as a site template, you are adding to the set of functionality that makes up an out-of-the-box site. You can also remove functionality by deactivating features you aren't going to use. You are never actually touching the site definition file, but rather modifying a site that was created based on it. The differences between the original, out-of-the-box site and the changes you have made is essentially what defines your custom template.

 One thing to be aware of is that any changes made to site definition files may render site templates and existing sites based on that site definition useless. It's generally frowned upon to modify a site definition file in the first place, but doing so after sites have been provisioned can cause havoc in your SharePoint environment.

Saving a Template

After you have built out your site, click the Site Actions menu and select Site Settings. Under the Site Actions header, click Save as Template. After filling in the File name field, you can fill in the Template name field (see Figure 2-26). The filename is how the solution file is displayed, and the template name appears as a template selection during the site creation process. Give the template a description so users creating sites from the template will know what it should be used for. Optionally, you can choose to include content in the template, which will include all content from libraries and lists.

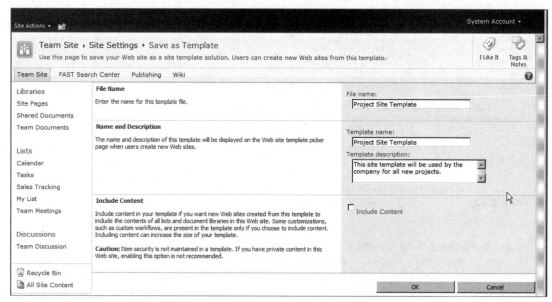

FIGURE 2-26

 Security is not maintained in templates, so any content you save in the template will become available to anyone who creates a site based on that template.

Click OK to save the template. Not all sites can be saved as templates, however. For instance, if a site has the SharePoint Server Publishing feature enabled at the site or subsite level, then the option to save the site as a template is not enabled.

When you saved a template in SharePoint 2007, it was saved in a Template Gallery. Because SharePoint 2010 saves site templates as solution files, site templates are now stored in the Solution gallery in the top-level site collection. You can access the Solution Gallery from the Site Settings screen by clicking Solutions, under the Galleries Header on the Site Settings screen. Because the template is stored as a solution, it can be activated and deactivated as needed from the Solutions Gallery. Site template solutions are automatically activated after they are created. If you need to deactivate a solution, simply put a check in the box next to the solution name and click the Deactivate button in the

Ribbon. This will open a confirmation pop-up, warning that you will lose the capability of the solution if it is deactivated, as shown in Figure 2-27.

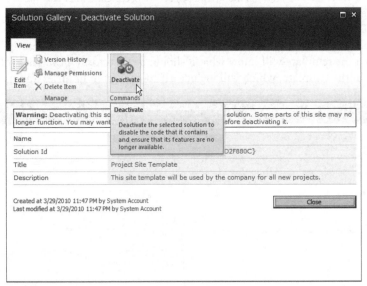

FIGURE 2-27

You can activate a feature using the same method, but clicking the Activate button instead of Deactivate. You will receive a warning on the Activate pop-up window warning that you should only activate solutions you trust. If you're working with site templates you created yourself you know they are safe to use. Go ahead and click the Activate button again in the pop-up's Ribbon to turn on the template. Its status will be listed as Active in the Solution gallery. Now the template is available to use in all subsites in that site collection. From within the Solution Gallery, you can download a copy of the template file to upload into other SharePoint 2010 site collections or even farms.

Creating a Site from a Site Template

Creating a site from a custom site template is identical to the normal site creation process. Any custom site templates that have been activated in the Solution Gallery will show up in the Blank & Custom category on the left. Select your custom site template from the available templates, give the site a name and URL, and you can begin creating sites from the template. Just as in SharePoint 2007, you can also customize which site templates are available during the creation process when building out a site based on the Publishing template. This is done from the Site Settings page. Under the Look and Feel header, click on Page Layouts and Site Templates.

On this page, you can choose whether to allow any site template or only specify a select few. On a subsite, you can specify whether the subsite should inherit its available site templates from its parent site, or whether it should use a unique set of templates. The available page layouts section below the site template selection area also uses the same interface for selecting which page layouts should be available.

List Templates

Lists and libraries can also be saved as templates in exactly the same manner as site templates. From the List Settings page, click the Save as Template link to begin the save process. Just like saving a site template, you can give the template file a filename, a display name, and a description. You can also choose to include the list content, but lists do not retain security settings, so consider that before making any sensitive information available as a template to everyone.

The only difference between the site template and the list template is that list templates are stored in the List Template Gallery instead of the Solution Gallery. They are, however, solution files that can be reused. When creating a list from a custom list template, look for your custom templates in the Blank & Custom category on the left side of the Create window.

MULTILINGUAL USER INTERFACE

Many multinational companies with offices spread across the globe may need to deploy SharePoint 2010 in the local language of each branch. Fortunately, SharePoint 2010 offers an easy way for administrators to install language packs for various languages on the server farm, enabling the creation of new sites in a local language, and the interface of existing sites to be translated into the languages installed on the server.

Installation and Configuration of SharePoint 2010 Language Packs

Installing language packs is a fairly straightforward process. Both SharePoint Foundation 2010 and SharePoint Server 2010 have language packs available to install. SharePoint Foundation 2010 only needs the SharePoint Foundation language packs, but if you are running the full license of SharePoint Server 2010, you need to install both the SharePoint Foundation and the SharePoint Server language packs. Language packs for SharePoint 2010 can be downloaded from the Microsoft Download Center at http://www.microsoft.com/downloads.

When downloading the language packs, you should create a unique folder for each, or at least provide a unique name, as the names of the SharePoint Foundation language packs all share the same filename, meaning it's possible that downloading one language pack can overwrite files of another. Every front-end web server will need a language pack installed for every language you want to use.

To begin the installation, first launch the SharePoint Foundation language pack for the selected language. When you launch the language pack's installation file, you'll be presented with a license agreement. The installation interface is written in the language of the language pack you are installing, which may look confusing at first. However, the installation process uses a standard Windows interface. Check the box below the user agreement and click the Next button (keeping in mind that "Next" is written in the language pack's local language). The language pack will install. Figure 2-28 shows the installation of a French language pack.

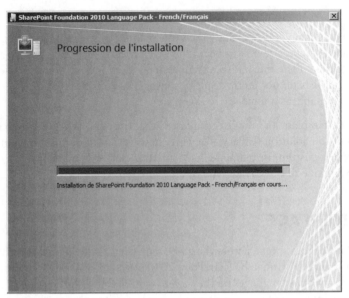

FIGURE 2-28

When the installation finishes, you are prompted to run the SharePoint Products and Technologies Configuration Wizard. If you are only running SharePoint 2010 Foundation, you can click the Finish button to launch the wizard. However, if you need to install a SharePoint Server 2010 Language Pack, you do not need to run the configuration wizard until after the other language pack has been installed. In addition, if you are installing multiple language packs, you do not need to run the configuration wizard after each language pack installation, only after all the language packs have been installed. This can help mitigate downtime when installing language packs in a production environment.

If you are running SharePoint Server 2010, install the SharePoint Server 2010 Language Pack. The installation process is identical to the Foundation language pack installation. After you have finished installing the last language pack, you can leave the box checked to automatically launch the configuration wizard, or you can manually start the configuration wizard by clicking Start ➪ All Programs ➪ Microsoft SharePoint 2010 Products ➪ SharePoint 2010 Products Configuration Wizard. For more information about using the configuration wizard, see Chapter 3.

After the configuration wizard is complete, you will have successfully installed and configured a language pack to use the Multilingual User Interface.

Using the Multilingual User Interface

Once your language packs have been installed, you can take advantage of the Multilingual User Interface (MUI). Before you can change the display language of an existing site, the newly installed language needs to be enabled. This is done on a per-site basis. From the Site Settings page, select Site Administration ⇨ Language Settings. On this page, you will see the default language of the site and any alternate languages that have been installed. Check the box next to the languages you wish to make available on the site collection. Below the Alternate language section, you are presented with the option to overwrite existing translations, as shown in Figure 2-29.

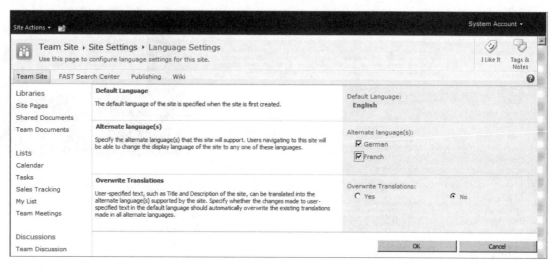

FIGURE 2-29

By default, some SharePoint content is translated into other languages when chosen. For example, some default SharePoint column headings are automatically translated into a selected language, such as the Title column that appears in virtually all SharePoint lists by default. When this option is set to No, you can make changes to the default SharePoint column headers in the default language without affecting any translations made to the column header. If you set the setting to Yes and change the name of the column in the default language, your change will overwrite any translations that may already be in place and display the default language even if an alternate language is selected.

Interface Translation

Once you turn on alternate languages, you can change the language of the SharePoint interface. Click your name in the upper right corner of the screen, hover over Display Language, and choose which language you'd like the site translated into. The Ribbon, Site Actions Menu, Site Settings menu, and other SharePoint components will be translated into the selected language, as shown in Figure 2-30. SharePoint will not translate any custom content on the page into the language chosen. Another thing you will notice is that the navigation may be displayed by its URL instead of by its name, or it may not be translated. SharePoint does not translate the site titles automatically.

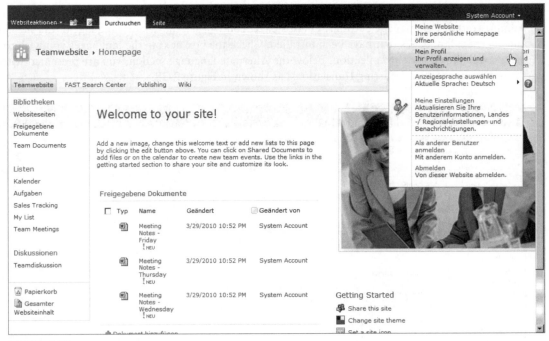

FIGURE 2-30

Navigation Translation

You can set up custom-translated navigation using the MUI. It doesn't matter if SharePoint has created your navigation automatically based on your site structure or you have created the entire site's navigation manually — either way, you can create multilingual navigation. One thing to keep in mind with multilingual navigation is that the translation is not done automatically for you. Setting up navigation translation is done manually. Although this can be a time-consuming process, it will likely produce a more accurate translation than a machine translation would.

Until the navigation translation is set up, when you switch display languages, your navigation items will be displayed in the site's default display language until additional languages have been enabled for a site. Consider the following scenario: A portal site's default language is English, and a subsite is created that has German set as the default language. The English portal will only display the title given to the German site in its navigation until English is enabled as an alternate language on the German site. Then, an alternate site name translation could be provided in English for the German site, and the English translation would then appear in the English site's navigation.

To create translations for the languages in the navigation, you have a couple of options, depending on how the navigation is set up. If SharePoint has built the navigation automatically by displaying the current site's children sites, navigate to a subsite. Because SharePoint is pulling the navigation information from the subsites, you need to make the changes at that subsite level. Open the Site Settings page and click the Title, Description, and Icon link. Then, change the language. In the Title field, type your translated title. You aren't overwriting the default language title here, but simply creating an alternate title to display when the new language is selected. You can also enter a translated description if you wish. Click the OK button to save the changes. Now, when you return to the parent site and change the language, your navigation will also change to show the translated site title (see Figure 2-31).

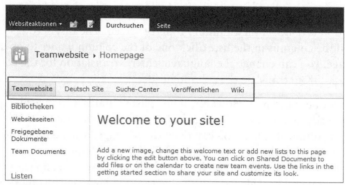

FIGURE 2-31

If you have links in your navigation that were created manually, you can use a similar process. Instead of heading to a site to make the changes, you can enter translations for navigation links and headers from the Modify Navigation page, which can be accessed from the Site Actions menu. Once you open this page, you can change languages. Select the navigation link you would like to change, and click the Modify link in the navigation toolbox (it will be translated, so it's good to be familiar with the link's location in the default language). You can replace the default text with your translated text, and then click OK to save your alternate navigation text. Changing the display language also changes your manually created links to the alternate language.

These techniques work for both the top navigation links and Quick Launch links. Many items in the Quick Launch, such as the headings for the different list type categories, the Recycle Bin link, and the View All Site Content link, are automatically translated into the selected language. Any custom lists that show on the Quick Launch menu are not automatically translated, but you can easily change this using the methods just described. You will also learn how to translate list titles in the next section.

List Translation

Lists can also have some translation applied to the title, description, and column headers. Translation can't be done on individual list items, however. Column titles that are pre-built into a list are automatically translated into the selected language. Custom columns are not automatically translated. You can, however, manually translate the column titles and descriptions for custom columns. The process for translating list names, descriptions, and column headers is fairly similar to the process of translating navigation.

The easiest way to translate a list title is to open the list in its default language and open the List Settings screen. Then, click the "Title, description and navigation link." On this screen, switch to the desired language and type your translated title and description, and click OK. You can repeat this process for as many languages as needed. You may notice that, depending on the navigation settings for your site, the name of the list didn't change in the Quick Launch menu. If this is the case, you can adjust the translation manually as outlined in the previous section.

Changing a column header translation is done on the Column Property screen. The List Settings page contains a section that lists all the columns in the list. Click one of the column names to open its properties. On the properties page, you can change the language, enter a translation for the column name and description, and click OK to translate the column header.

Generally, individual list items cannot be translated. However, if your list contains a Managed Metadata column type, you can take advantage of the Managed Metadata's ability to store translated labels for each term. In Central Administration, you can open the Managed Metadata Service Application(s) that serve content to the rest of the site. (See Chapter 7 for more about the service application architecture, and Chapter 16 to learn about the Managed Metadata service application.) In each term group, you can open a term and provide a default value for each language installed on the server. For instance, if you have the term "elephant," you can also add the translated Spanish term "elefante" and the German term "Elefant." SharePoint will realize that both of these translated terms are synonymous with the English term "elephant."

Multilingual Site Creation

In addition to being able to change the language of the interface and navigation, you can also set a site's default language during the site creation process. Any new site can be built with any of the installed languages as its default language, not just the default language of the SharePoint installation. For example, the default language of the root site may be English, but suppose a company has a French-speaking branch. Their portal homepage can be built to have a default language of French, so its interface and the menus are all written in French. A Spanish-speaking branch's portal home page can be created with Spanish as the default language. Not only will the interface display in the chosen default language, any text automatically generated by SharePoint (such as the Welcome message that displays when a Team site is created) will also display in the chosen default language. Figure 2-32 shows a subsite created with German set as the default language. All menus will display in this language as well. Regardless of the default language, you can still have SharePoint translate its interface by selecting a new language.

Creating a site with the MUI is the same as creating a site normally. The only difference is that you have the capability to select the default language from the Select Language drop-down in the Create pop-up during the site creation process. The rest of the process is identical. Keep in mind, though, that new sites are not automatically configured to allow language translation. You need to enable other languages to be displayed from the Site Actions menu before you can translate your newly created site into another language from its default.

FIGURE 2-32

Exporting and Importing Translations

A nice feature of the SharePoint 2010 MUI is the capability to export and import translation resource files. These resource files are XML files that contain references to items that can be translated. By translating the values in this file, an administrator can quickly provide translations of many components of the site in a relatively short amount of time without having to open every site, navigation item, list, and column.

On the Site Settings screen for a site, in the Site Administration section, there is a link to Export translations. On the Export Translations screen, you can choose which language(s) to export into files. The next section of the screen, Export Text, enables you to choose whether to export all items that can be translated or just the items that have not been translated yet. The translation resource files can be edited in just about any program that can open an XML file (even Notepad). This section doesn't get into the details of editing this XML file, but generally speaking, anything toward the bottom section of the file in a <value> node can be translated. Replace the text in the <value> nodes with the translated text. When the changes have been made to the file, you can save it and import the translations into the site.

Importing the file into the site is also done from the Site Settings screen. Under the Site Administration heading, click Import Translations. You can browse the computer for the translation resource file and select the language to which the translations should be applied. Click the Import button, and you have added additional translation to the site, without having to open every page and manually add translations.

SUMMARY

We hope that this chapter has given you some good insight into what has changed in the SharePoint 2010 user experience. Using SharePoint is now more like using the Office client programs than in any previous version, which should make editing and working with SharePoint pages a less daunting task for users. The addition of the Ribbon to the SharePoint interface has made working with nearly every aspect of SharePoint 2010 a different experience from what many users may be used to, but it has put more options for working with pages, lists, and libraries right in front of the user. Creating columns and views in lists is all done with the help of the Ribbon. Editing pages also relies on the Ribbon now in order to make changes to text and add Web Parts to the page.

The Live Preview mode now built into SharePoint gives users a good way to check how changes look before committing to them. Custom site templates provide administrators with a quick way to create new sites with preconfigured settings, which can be transferred to other SharePoint sites because site templates are built as solution files now. Finally, the Multilingual User Interface of SharePoint 2010 has been updated, enabling you to provide alternate translations for many items that appear in the SharePoint interface. Site navigation, site titles and descriptions, column headers in lists, and list names and descriptions can all have alternate translations based on the available language packs. You can even create sites with different default languages.

As you can see, there is a lot going on in SharePoint 2010!

3

Architecture and Capacity Planning

WHAT'S IN THIS CHAPTER?

- ➤ SharePoint products and licenses

- ➤ Critical non-SharePoint servers

- ➤ Hardware specifications

- ➤ Tools for controlling your deployment

SharePoint 2010 has greatly expanded its functionality from previous versions. New features include the following:

- ➤ Office web applications, where you can display and edit Office documents in the browser

- ➤ The Fluent UI, aka the Ribbon

- ➤ An enhanced social experience, including tagging and notes

- ➤ More flexibility regarding how web applications consume services through service applications

- ➤ A full-scale business intelligence offering through tools such as Performance Point Services, Reporting Services, and Excel Services

Those and about a million (not an exact number) other new features in SharePoint 2010 are reasons why people are so excited about the product. Of course, all of that new functionality means that users will deploy SharePoint for more tasks than ever before — and that increased traffic leads to more demands from a hardware perspective. As a result, administrators can antici-pate a strong increase in the number and size of servers in their farms. In short, it is expected that the same user from SharePoint 2007 will come to a SharePoint 2010 farm with more requests per second (RPS).

To help you scale, the Shared Services Provider (SSP) from 2007 has gone the way of the Dodo bird. In its place, Microsoft has introduced a new services architecture that is infinitely more configurable, which also means it is infinitely more complicated.

This chapter begins with a primer on the different versions of SharePoint 2010 you can expect to see, including a brief overview of SharePoint in the cloud. Then, because a SharePoint DVD isn't good for much more than a coaster until you have the supporting servers on which to install it, you will learn all of the software requirements you are expected to bring to the table.

Armed with the necessary software knowledge, the discussion will turn to hardware, including the amount of metal you will need, ways you might consider scaling up versus out, and where virtualization might come into play. Finally, the chapter describes some of the clever new tools available that will help you keep SharePoint in check in your environment.

While this might not be as exciting as a blockbuster Hollywood movie, it will turn you into what every good summer blockbuster needs: a superhero. Therefore, read carefully and make sure you picked up your cape from the dry cleaners.

WHAT'S IN A NAME?

As it turns out, in the Microsoft world there is quite a bit to a name. If you have any past SharePoint experience, you probably know the names of the previous products, Windows SharePoint Service 3.0 (WSS) and Microsoft Office SharePoint Server 2007 (MOSS). And given the success of these two products, it is pretty reasonable to assume their names would continue. This time around, the names are SharePoint Foundation and SharePoint Server 2010.

The key change here to note is the removal of Windows and Office from the product names. This speaks volumes about the success of SharePoint. The product is now considered to stand on its own and is no longer part of the Windows or Office groups. Being decoupled from these two groups will open the door for SharePoint to be more agile going forward and will be nothing but good news for everyone in the SharePoint fan club.

SharePoint Foundation

SharePoint Foundation will continue the legacy that WSS has established over the years and should keep that friendly price point that makes it so attractive. The name SharePoint Foundation is a perfect match for what the program brings to the table. As an administrator, it is easy to think of the product only in terms of the features you readily see in the browser — things like creating team sites and collaborating on content within lists and libraries, or features such as blogs, wikis, RSS feeds, alerts, and easy browser-based customizations.

Yet underneath all of that great functionality is where some of the true power of SharePoint is hidden. Here, the foundation provides developers with a great platform to build from. Out of the box, it handles storage, web presentation, authorization, user management, and has an interface into the Windows Workflow Foundation — and because all of this functionality is easily accessible through the object model, APIs, and web services, it can greatly accelerate a developer's job. Rather than build all of those infrastructure pieces for every web-based product, developers can leverage SharePoint Foundation and concentrate on just building the solution.

SharePoint Server 2010

SharePoint Server 2010 is considered the premium product. It offers additional collaboration capabilities and extends the scenarios beyond Foundation. Through its tools, it enables better aggregation and displaying of content, which makes building things such as portals much simpler. It also introduces additional web content management tools that enable developers to use Server as a platform for building Internet-facing websites.

This is all done by extending the capabilities introduced by SharePoint Foundation. Any time you install SharePoint Server, the Foundation product is installed automatically as well. Keep this in mind as you manage your environments, making sure you keep current on both Foundation and Server issues, as you really have both products. When you are doing tasks like applying service packs or adding third-party applications, this knowledge might just change how you go about things.

Standard and Enterprise

As in the past, SharePoint Server 2010 is available primarily in two flavors, either Standard or Enterprise. Standard introduces core functionality like social, search, and advanced web and enterprise content management. Enterprise focuses primarily on adding functionality through new service applications, introducing business intelligence, line of business integration, reporting, and some Office client services such as Visio.

This is all provided through a *client access license* (CAL) model. You only need to run one setup program, which puts all of the binaries on the server; and based on the license key you enter, either the Standard features will be available or both the Standard and Enterprise features. You are required to have an appropriate CAL for each user accessing SharePoint Server 2010.

 SharePoint licensing is a notorious black hole and cannot be covered completely in this book, as each scenario is unique and should be treated as such. The information provided here is guidance to help you understand the concepts in order to make more informed decisions and to understand the platform as a whole, but it should not be considered the final word on licensing. Please consult your license reseller or Microsoft Licensing for specifics before making any purchase.

For Internet Sites

Because of the tremendous popularity of SharePoint on the intranet, a new trend has been for companies to also host their Internet site on SharePoint. From a business perspective this can greatly reduce the cost through the reuse of a familiar tool. By not having two separate platforms to create "websites," it is no longer necessary to maintain two separate yet similar skill sets. This also reduces licensing and hardware costs because some systems, such as development environments, can be used for both internal and external projects. This is usually not possible if you have two separate products in place. For most companies, reducing training, licensing, development, and administrative costs sounds like just the answer bean counters are looking for.

While MOSS had an Internet license, it was an all-or-nothing model. It included all of the MOSS Enterprise features, which typically meant a hefty price tag. However, many companies only wanted the core web content management (WCM) functionality, not those extra features and their associated cost. Microsoft heard these pleas loudly and clearly, and addressed the issue in SharePoint Server 2010.

There is now a SharePoint Server 2010 for Internet Sites Standard license as well as an Enterprise license. You will often hear this license referred to by its acronym, FIS, regardless of what version they truly mean. The goal of introducing the Standard license is to offer smaller sites the capability to deploy on Server for their web presence. It is then throttled to permit only a set amount of traffic, and will not have the Enterprise features available. However, it should be just what the doctor ordered when it comes to getting a simple WWW site up and off the ground.

One very important thing to understand about FIS is where it is applicable. Remember that everyone who will access the SharePoint Server site needs a CAL. When building an intranet portal, it is easy to count how many employees you have and to purchase a CAL for each one of them; but when you stand up http://www.company.com and make it available to the world, now how many CALs do you need? There are roughly 1.8 billion people on the Internet, and potentially every one of them can come to your website. That's a lot of CALs to buy. Luckily, this is where FIS comes into play. It allows unlimited non-employee access to your SharePoint Server. The reason why non-employee is emphasized is because this license does not cover any of your employees and there has been a lot of confusion over the license in the past. The proper FIS license can help you control the cost of your SharePoint Server deployment, but great care should be taken to use it properly.

Search Server 2010

For most users, one of the major downsides of SharePoint Foundation is its lack of a powerful search feature. Foundation can provide search results of the SharePoint content from within a given site collection, but that is all. It cannot pull search results from multiple site collections, and cannot add external content sources such as file shares or Exchange public folders.

In addition, many users have become very reliant on the use of a search engine in their daily lives. Bing and Google are typical first stops for most users as they explore the Internet for everything from buying a new car to figuring out why their in-laws give them a headache. For most of these users, it is only logical that they should be able to discover information at work in the same manner. SharePoint Server 2010 can provide this full-scale enterprise search presence, but not everyone can afford to deploy it. Other users look to some type of appliance to index and search the intranet, but these devices can be difficult to administer and even more cost prohibitive. Enter Search Server 2010 Express and Search Server 2010.

Search Server 2010 Express (SSX) is a free product from Microsoft that essentially takes SharePoint Foundation and adds to it the intranet searching capabilities. You gain the capability to add content sources such as file shares, other SharePoint sites, websites, and Exchange public folders. You also get the Search Center template and all of the associated Web Parts. To avoid stealing all of the thunder from Chapter 14, this simple feature list will have to suffice for now; but if any of that interests you, consider deploying SSX instead of Foundation, or if you have Foundation already deployed, you can simply upgrade Foundation to SSX.

The only real shortcoming of SSX is that it cannot be configured to be high availability. While Search Server 2010 can be configured to avoid any single point of failure, including the Search components, SSX does not offer that capability. It can only be deployed to one server in the farm; there is no infrastructure for deploying it on multiple servers to create redundancy. If you need a high-availability solution, you need to move up to full Search Server. The only downside to the full version is that it is a for-purchase product.

Fast Search Server 2010

In early 2008, Microsoft purchased Fast Search and Transfer. Fast was considered the "best in breed" high-end search tool set. In the 2010 product line, it has been incorporated as an addition to the SharePoint Server platform, adding lots of new functionality, including the following examples:

- ➤ Visual search and best bets

- ➤ Extreme scale, with a billion documents possible

- ➤ Enhanced multiple language capabilities

- ➤ Better handling of unstructured data through metadata extraction

- ➤ Better handling of structured data such as numbers, dates, etc.

Adding all of this to SharePoint's already very powerful search engine is a huge win. There will be two different licenses for this feature: Fast Search Server 2010 for SharePoint will be used along with the Server Enterprise CAL in intranet deployments, whereas Fast Search Server 2010 for Internet Sites will be used in conjunction with FIS for public websites.

These two Fast products have been completely integrated into the SharePoint platform, providing an easy to use management interface and Windows PowerShell cmdlets. From a development perspective, they are also plugged into the object model (OM) the same way normal SharePoint Server Search is. Therefore, users don't have to learn anything new in order to get results returned. Instead, they make the same calls to the Search OM, and Fast returns information in place of the normal search engine.

There is a third license worth mentioning even though it is outside the scope of this book — Fast Search Server 2010 for Internet Business. This license will not be used in conjunction with SharePoint, but instead for custom public websites. For example BestBuy.com uses Fast to help consumers find all those gadgets and gizmos they love to buy. Unlike SharePoint, which is usable as is, this product is more a set of tools that need to be assembled to provide an amazing search experience.

SharePoint Online

Another push for SharePoint from Microsoft will be SharePoint in the cloud, hosted by Microsoft. If you are looking to deploy SharePoint using this model, then you can probably stop reading the book at the end of this section because in SharePoint Online, the entire server infrastructure is hosted and maintained for you. This model removes the administrative overhead of SharePoint and lets the business focus just on using the power that is SharePoint. (While this might be great for the business, it does eliminate the need for a SharePoint administrator, so many of us will consider this license option the enemy.)

There are actually two models to consider with SharePoint Online: shared and dedicated. The shared model provides you with a slice of a shared farm and enables you to use SharePoint out of the box. Server-deployed code and customizations are not permitted. The dedicated model enables you to run your own farm, and you are allowed to make approved customizations to the server. Any change must be packaged in a solution package and validated by Microsoft before being deployed to the server. All licenses are bought per user.

This offering has also been expanded from previous versions to add some new licensing options. One of these is the concept of the "deskless worker." These are users you can add at a lower price point, and they have mostly read-only access to SharePoint. There are also models available that can support hosting a partner collaboration site and public-facing Internet sites.

 This chapter covers SharePoint Online because it is an additional available SKU in this product cycle, but you have other notable options if you are looking at a hosted scenario. Companies such as RackSpace.com and Fpweb.net offer hosted SharePoint environments that you may find a little more flexible than SharePoint Online. Of course, hosting internally is still the best option, but it is good to know your enemies.

OTHER SERVERS

So you signed up to be a SharePoint administrator? Well, congratulations, you are also now responsible for a whole host of software. Since SharePoint isn't an operating system (yet!), you need to have the right operating system in place in order to deploy SharePoint. Additionally, SharePoint stores 99% of the content and configuration in a database, so SQL Server has to enter the conversation sooner, rather than later. Also, most deployments want to take advantage of SharePoint's ability to send notification e-mails, and some even take advantage of its ability to receive e-mails. Even though you may not directly be responsible for these products, they will affect your livelihood. Users don't call to complain that SQL Server isn't working; they call to complain that they cannot access SharePoint. It is your job to determine that it is because SQL Server is not responding. This section covers the ins and outs of these various pieces of this puzzle.

Windows Server

SharePoint is available only as 64-bit software, so by extension it can only be installed on servers with 64 bits or more. And don't bother looking, there is no 32-bit "test" version hiding out there.

The authors have looked under every rock on the Internet and inside Microsoft; and like unicorns, it doesn't exist.

For production deployments, you will be installing on either Windows Server 2008 SP2 and later or Windows Server 2008 R2 and later. The following editions of Windows Server are supported:

➤ Standard

➤ Enterprise

➤ Datacenter

Noticeably absent to some is the Server Core installation of Windows. Unfortunately, it does not allow all of the necessary components that are required for SharePoint to operate to be installed, so SharePoint will not install on Core. Also, the Web Edition is not supported, which is probably a good thing — thanks to its limited memory capacity, it would not perform very well.

Required Additional Software

After you have Windows installed, the server needs to be included as a member of an Active Directory (AD) domain. SharePoint does not support local machine accounts for any type of farm deployment, and the configuration wizard will error out if you try to use a local account.

Most administrators realize that something like IIS needs to be installed on the Windows Server in order for SharePoint to render web pages. They are often tempted to install this manually, which is safe to do but probably a waste of their time. The server also has roughly a dozen other prerequisite software packages that need to be installed, including the Web Server (IIS) Role. Thankfully, there is a SharePoint Products and Technologies Preparation Tool that will install and configure all of these for you when the time comes. That tool, and all of its intricate details, is covered in the next chapter.

BUT I ALREADY DID "X" TO MY SERVER!

If you already installed IIS, PowerShell, or one of the other prerequisites, don't worry; all is not lost. The prerequisite installer tool will check up on you. If you did successfully install and configure one of the requirements, the tool will skip it and move on to the next one. In the case of IIS, if you enabled the role but didn't configure it the way SharePoint needed, the prerequisite installer will just make the necessary changes. So keep that chin up; all is good.

Another common mistake to avoid is adding the server to a domain, or even promoting it to a domain controller (typically only done on a test virtual machine) after adding programs to the server. Programs such as IIS and SQL Server don't always take too well to these changes. Make any computer name changes (which adding to a domain does) as soon after installing Windows as possible. Then you can safely continue with getting it ready for SharePoint.

Windows Vista and 7

In order to appease your friend the developer, Microsoft has introduced the capability to install SharePoint using a standalone install, for development purposes, on certain versions of Windows Vista *x*64 and Windows 7 *x*64. These editions are as follows:

➤ Windows Vista SP1 and later.

  ➤ Business edition

  ➤ Enterprise edition

  ➤ Ultimate edition

➤ Windows 7 RTM and later.

  ➤ Professional edition

  ➤ Enterprise edition

  ➤ Ultimate edition

➤ The N and KN editions of the preceding software will also work.

It is absolutely not supported to use a Windows Vista or 7 installation for a production farm. They should only be used for developers who wish to do SharePoint development locally on their own machine. If development is done in these environments, then it is highly recommended that developers have a test environment to validate their solution before deploying to production. These types of deployments are a little more tedious in the initial configuration and are discussed more in the next chapter.

SQL Server

Get used to it: SQL Server just became your best friend. Because everything inside of SharePoint, including all of your content, lives inside a SQL Server database, as SQL goes so does your farm. For example, do you know what the most common performance bottle neck is in SharePoint? SQL Server. Therefore, in order for you to be good at your job, at a minimum you need to understand what is going on in SQL Server. Ideally, you will start sucking up to your resident database administrator (DBA) to ensure that your SharePoint databases are well cared for.

As with the Windows Server requirement, SharePoint also requires SQL Server to be 64-bit. 32-bit SQL Server is not supported. The 64-bit editions of SQL Server that are supported are SQL Server 2005, SQL Server 2008, and SQL Server 2008 R2. SQL Server 2005 requires Service Pack 3 plus cumulative update package 3 for SQL Server 2005 Service Pack 3 (KB967909). SQL Server 2008 requires Service Pack 1 plus cumulative update package 2 for SQL Server 2008 with Service Pack 1 (KB970315). SQL Server 2008 R2 will be supported at its RTM build or later.

E-mail Servers

SharePoint comes with a handy piece of functionality that enables it to send e-mails. This is often used to notify users that they have been granted access to a particular site. Users can also subscribe to an alert whereby they are notified when items are modified on a particular list or library. And with a little extra work, SharePoint workflows can be configured to e-mail users as necessary.

In order for SharePoint to send these e-mails, it needs to be configured with an outbound e-mail server. The SMTP server you point SharePoint at needs to allow anonymous relay from SharePoint. Unfortunately, SharePoint cannot be configured to provide authentication information when sending e-mails. In most environments, anonymous relay is not permitted, because for years evil spammers have used anonymous relays to avoid detection as they flood you with offers for low-cost medicines and opportunities to invest in dubious banks. In this case, you can ask the e-mail administrator to add the IP addresses of all SharePoint servers to the list of servers that are allowed to anonymously relay mail. If this is not acceptable, then your second option is to install the SMTP service on one of your SharePoint servers and then configure it as necessary. You will need to ensure that it can correctly send outbound e-mail and that it allows all anonymous relay from all the SharePoint servers in the farm.

Another requirement for outgoing e-mail is that port 25, the default SMTP port, is not blocked between your servers. Such a blockage can happen at the firewall level or at the local server level. Some antivirus vendors configure their software to block port 25 outbound on all machines. This will stop SharePoint from sending e-mail, so be on the lookout.

Incoming E-mail

A lesser-known feature of SharePoint is its ability to receive incoming e-mail and then route that e-mail to the appropriate list or library based on the To: address. This enables scenarios such as having salespeople in the field e-mail in their expense report to a special e-mail address. That e-mail would be routed to the SharePoint server and then the attachment could be extracted and uploaded to the appropriate document library. From there, whatever business process needs to take place could be invoked. A simpler scenario might be setting up an e-mail address for a discussion forum. Then, any time you send an e-mail to that address, the e-mail becomes a discussion item in the list. Once in SharePoint, it is easily indexed so it can be discovered later; and because it is now a normal list item, the discussion can continue.

Configuring this functionality requires the help of the e-mail administrator, and it is worth noting that it does not require the use of Exchange. This is a multi-step, complex process that touches several pieces, but the core steps are as follows:

1. Install and configure one of your SharePoint servers to run the SMTP service. This server will then need to be set up to accept e-mail for the domain you define for SharePoint. Typically, it would be something like @sharepoint.company.com.

2. Configure your corporate e-mail server to route mail for the @sharepoint.company.com domain. The idea is that when your corporate e-mail server receives that e-mail, it just passes it over to the SharePoint server.

3. Go to SharePoint Central Administration and enable incoming e-mail. You will need to tell SharePoint that it is looking for e-mails in the @sharepoint.company.com domain.

4. Now someone with the manage list permission level can go into his or her list and associate an e-mail address with the list — for example, doclib1@sharepoint.company.com.

5. This associated e-mail address would now need to be configured as a valid contact on the e-mail server.

With this configured, e-mails will be sent to doclib1@sharepoint.company.com. Your corporate e-mail server will relay that mail to the SMTP service running on the SharePoint server. The SMTP service will then take that e-mail and put it in a maildrop folder. The SharePoint timer service checks that folder once a minute by default, looking for e-mail. When it finds an e-mail, it routes it to the appropriate list or library based on the address.

While that is a simple scenario, many configuration options are available. You can, for example, configure Exchange Server and Active Directory to allow users to create their own e-mail addresses. This is done through the creation of an additional Organization Unit in your domain. This is a more complex scenario, but it eliminates the administrative burden of having to set up e-mail contacts each time a new list or library requires mail functionality.

You can find detailed configuration information, with multiple scenarios and troubleshooting steps, on TechNet (http://technet.microsoft.com/en-us/library/cc262947(office.14).aspx).

Text Message (SMS) Service Settings

That is right — SharePoint has become so cool that it can even send text messages. And since SharePoint still isn't old enough to drive, you don't even have to worry about it texting and driving. Once the service is configured, users can choose to have alerts sent to e-mail or text message or to both.

The service is pretty straightforward to set up from within Central Administration and can be scoped at either the farm or the web application level. You will need to provide the URL of an SMS sending service. If you don't have one handy, you can click the link on the Mobile Account Settings page in Central Administration to find one based on your preferred wireless provider. Just watch out for this functionality: It can easily become a runaway cost.

HARDWARE REQUIREMENTS

Build it and they will come. Underpower it and they will complain. (No user has ever complained that SharePoint is too fast.) Of course, with budgets being very tight, you will feel the pressure to keep hardware costs as low as possible. This tension between functionality and cost creates a fine line to walk.

Perhaps the easiest way to start thinking about hardware is to do a comparison of the minimum recommended requirements from MOSS 2007 and the minimums for SharePoint Server 2010 (see Table 3-1).

TABLE 3-1 MOSS 2007 versus Server 2010 Recommended Minimum Hardware Requirements

	MOSS 2007	SERVER 2010
Processor	2 core / 3 GHz	4 core / 2.5 GHz
RAM	2GB	8GB

Note that part of this discrepancy is that Microsoft has done a better job of setting the minimum bar this time. Despite these recommendations, it is not practical today to run a MOSS 2007 server with less than 4GB of RAM. Even taking that into account, it is safe to assume that SharePoint 2010 will require at least twice as much hardware as an existing SharePoint 2007 farm. This is assuming properly sized 2007 hardware today. Experience has shown that SharePoint farms tend to range from vastly undersized desktop-class machines running thousands of users, slowly, to super-computer-class machines that on their best day use 20 percent of their resources to serve 100 users. So if you are going to make hardware assumptions at least in part based on your 2007 environment, make sure you understand how that hardware is utilized today. The next few pages describe the different server types and how the hardware considerations vary for each.

Web Servers

Often referred to as web front-end (WFE) servers, these are the machines ultimately responsible for the rendering of the SharePoint pages. They typically do not have a high CPU load because they attempt to cache as much content as possible to avoid doing the same work over and over. To do caching properly, the server does consume quite a bit of RAM, so be sure to dedicate a substantial portion of your spending on this server to RAM.

A key consideration when determining how much memory you might need is the number of application pools you plan to have. In a nutshell, *application pools* are the various IIS processes that listen for incoming web traffic and then handle it accordingly. In Task Manager, you will see each application pool as `w3wp.exe`. For example, when you create a new SharePoint web application and choose a new application pool, you get a new instance of this process running. Now when you access SharePoint, this process is actually receiving your request and coordinating with SharePoint to render your page. When SharePoint is caching content in memory, it is being stored in RAM associated with this process.

Part of this consideration, though, is that every application pool has a certain amount of overhead associated with it, the process, and the memory it needs to do its job. Therefore, for each new application pool you create, your RAM requirements will increase, so plan accordingly.

This role requires very little local storage and does not need to be optimized in any way. The only storage this machine is doing is the SharePoint root, all of the local ULS and IIS logs, and possibly some disk-based BLOB caching. In other words, don't get carried away here and create a 10GB C: drive. SharePoint occasionally needs to have extra space for temporary files, maybe to unpack a solution or to deploy a service pack, so an 80GB or 100GB C: drive is reasonable for your WFE.

 SharePoint root *refers to a folder structure:* `C:\program files\common files\` `Microsoft shared\web server extensions\14`. *In SharePoint v3, the* `\12` *folder was called the* 12 *Hive, so you may hear some people refer to the SharePoint root as the "14 Hive." If you do, try not to make fun of them.*

Application Servers

Application server is the generic name for servers that are responsible for providing resources for the various service applications. The tricky part of sizing these boxes is that each service application has a different usage profile, so the requirements will vary depending on what is running on the box and how heavily that functionality is being used. In addition, when building out an application tier, you should consider scaling out versus scaling up. In other words, is it better to have one large application server with a lot of resources but a single point of failure, or several smaller boxes running the same services that provide fault tolerance but require more administration? The following sections describe some of the key types of application servers and their individual considerations.

Query Server

A query server is the server responsible for responding to user search requests. When a user opens a SharePoint page, types into the search box, and presses Search, that request is routed by the WFE to the query server. The query server processes the request and then forwards the information back to the WFE for security trimming and rendering of the results.

This server uses CPU and memory to process the request and will try to cache as much of the index as possible within RAM. This role is also unique in that it requires local storage on the machine. The query file is kept on local disks and processed on the server. In environments with large indexes (one million plus items) and high search demand, it is best to optimize the storage of this file for fast retrieval. Conversely, in smaller environments it is not unusual to see the WFE and query server on the same machine.

The Search architecture for SharePoint 2010 is completely new compared to 2007 and is covered in full detail in Chapter 14.

Index Server

You will hear the index server also referred to as the *crawl server*. Unlike its predecessors, this version is stateless, which means it does not store any information locally. Therefore, your index server does not have any extra disk storage requirements. Typically, indexing of content is a processor-intensive task, so consider additional CPU capacity if you are in an environment with intensive indexing requirements. This tier is also covered extensively in Chapter 14.

Excel Services

Excel services and the other service applications that are focused on Office client tasks and compatibility features are generally more CPU heavy. This is because they typically do not have any storage and are only being used to offload processing from the clients to the server. These features generally require the business units to work with their data differently. They are often not in high demand, especially during early phases of a SharePoint rollout. Therefore, don't overscale for this functionality until you confirm that the business adoption will increase demand.

Usage and Health Data Collection

The Usage and Health Data Collection service application might be the most data-intensive piece of SharePoint. It enables the collection of all the diagnostic and usage data from your entire SharePoint farm into one database. This database can then be used for reporting, and is even flexible enough to accommodate custom reporting. Early results have shown that in large environments, this feature creates a very large SQL load, especially on the storage side. Therefore, in order to fully utilize it, you may want to consider putting it onto its own SQL server. Check out Chapter 15 for full details, but make sure that the amount of usage of this functionality factors into your farm planning.

SQL Servers

It turns out there are entire multi-book series on this one topic and even if you have read all of them you still wouldn't have a definitive answer about sizing your SQL Server. Therefore, as you approach sizing this particular box or boxes, don't be afraid to ask for help. Also, keep in mind that over the years, the main bottleneck in most SharePoint farms is SQL Server performance.

The key thing to remember is that all of the standard SQL Server hardware best practices are important. SQL Server loves memory and will utilize every bit it can get its hands on, so you should plan accordingly. Eight GB of memory should be the absolute minimum you consider, and 16GB or even 32GB might be appropriate in a heavily used environment. CPUs require the same consideration; a quad-core processor might get you started, but boxes with multiple quad-core processors are more common.

Even if you buy enough CPU and RAM, you still are not out of the woods. Disk configuration has as much, if not more, to do with performance. You will need to plan for the number of spindles your SQL Server has access to and how they will be configured; and to do this properly, you need to consider the amount and shape of data you plan to store in SharePoint. You should be following the SQL best practices specifying that the data (*.mdf) and log (*.ldf) files are on different disks, and that the log files are optimized for write. When you are considering which databases to optimize first, the order is as follows:

1. Tempdb (a SQL System database)
2. Search databases
3. Content databases

While tempdb should clearly always be the first database optimized, your needs for the Search databases and content databases may vary based on your specific scenario. For example, if you have created a content database for collaboration that is excessively large (greater than 100GB), then in order to minimize locking issues you may need to move that database to optimized disks instead of the typical content database that will perform adequately on a basic RAID 5 volume. The key here is to make sure either you understand all of your SQL disk requirements before you purchase the box or you have access to a flexible solution, such as a SAN, for storing your databases.

 Check out the TechNet SQL Server TechCenter at http://technet.microsoft .com/en-us/sqlserver/default.aspx *for guidance on planning and sizing a SQL Server deployment.*

Finally, when it comes to SQL Server, SharePoint doesn't really care how you set it up. As long as SQL Server is running a supported version and can serve databases back to SharePoint, it doesn't matter whether SQL Server is dedicated to SharePoint or is shared with other applications in the company. Nor does SharePoint care whether SQL Server is clustered or doing database mirroring or even transparent encryption. SharePoint will simply call to a SQL Server instance for a database, and if it gets data back it is happy.

Mixing and Matching Servers

Now that you have an understanding of the different types of servers, you need to consider how those will be deployed onto physical hardware. As you combine them, you need to consider the hardware profile of each, and what the server will need to support the aggregate load.

One Server

This is a configuration you will typically see only for demonstration and evaluation purposes. In the example shown in Figure 3-1, all SharePoint server roles and SQL Server will be configured to run on one machine.

Two Servers

A two-server configuration is generally considered the minimum point of entry for a small SharePoint deployment. In this scenario (see Figure 3-2), all of the SharePoint services will run on one server, and SQL Server will run on a separate server.

SharePoint Server 2010
WFE Server
Application Server
SQL Server

FIGURE 3-1

SharePoint Server 2010
WFE Server
Application Server

SQL Server

FIGURE 3-2

Three Servers

By adding a second server with SharePoint installed, you create the possibility to reach a high-availability solution (see Figure 3-3). By putting some type of network load-balancing (NLB) device in front of SharePoint, you can ensure that the WFE services are fault tolerant. Make sure your NLB device is configured for persistent sessions. This is a SharePoint requirement and covered in more detail later in the chapter. Then, by configuring the service applications to run on both machines, you can avoid one server crashing and causing you to have a bad day.

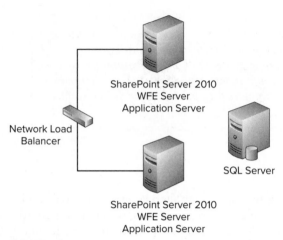

FIGURE 3-3

Four or More Servers

This is where you start making choices. Figure 3-4 shows a scenario in which the environment has been optimized for performance and availability for the WFE and query roles, but the downside is that the application tier does not provide high availability. This is generally not a good idea, so you may want to skip straight to introducing a fifth server to the farm in order to bring high availability to the other service applications. You will not need another NLB device because service applications handle their own load balancing.

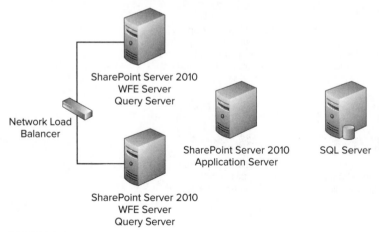

FIGURE 3-4

At this point, you probably get the idea that you can scale out any of the various service applications as necessary to meet your needs, which leads to our next topic: server groups.

The Search service application architecture is the most complex and demanding of all the service applications. For many administrators, the majority of their farm architecture will be based on meeting the demand of this feature. Please see Chapter 14, which explains all of the components of the Search architecture in full detail, including additional farm topologies for optimizing the Search service application.

Server Groups

A *server group* refers to the logical concept of grouping similar SharePoint service applications together on the same physical hardware. This enables you to add servers, which means additional capacity, for each tier as demand increases. This also segregates the performance impact of the various service applications. Figure 3-5 shows an example.

Web Group

Search Group running Index and Query

Business Intelligence Group running Excel Services and Performance Point Services

Other Service Application Group running all other service applications and Central Administration

SQL Server Group hosting Search databases only

SQL Server Group hosting Content databases only

SQL Server Group hosting all other SharePoint databases

FIGURE 3-5

This example isolates the web, search, business intelligence (BI), and all of the other service applications. Now, if business adoption of the BI increases beyond the current capacity, it will not affect the performance or stability of the rest of the farm. It is also simple to purchase another server, install SharePoint onto the box, and then add it to the farm. Once it is a member, you would then add it to the BI group by configuring it to only run the Excel and Performance Point services. Note that you will not see the term "server group" in Central Administration anywhere; it is only a logical concept.

Notice also in Figure 3-5 that SQL Server has been exploded out into various logical groupings. The performance characteristics and demands of different databases can vary greatly, and in large environments it can be very helpful to configure and manage each one separately.

Other Hardware Notes

Now that you have gotten the hang of all this hardware, the following sections describe a few more considerations to think through before you move on.

The Network

Network connectivity between the servers in your farm is hugely important. At a minimum, all servers in the farm should be connected through gigabit connections. The hard requirement here is that each server should be connected by a gigabit connection with less than one millisecond of latency. This precludes most companies from having a SharePoint farm with servers in multiple, geographically dispersed data centers.

For many companies, the sheer volume of network traffic generated between the members of the farm is overwhelming. In order to better control this traffic, they move all of the inter-farm traffic to a dedicated virtual local area network (VLAN). This is like the server groups discussed earlier. By grouping all of this traffic, it is easier to monitor and administer in the case of any issues. A dedicated VLAN is not a requirement for SharePoint, but in a large farm it is often recommended.

Network Load Balancers

In order to achieve high availability of the SharePoint web applications, it is necessary to introduce a tool to do network load balancing. This can be either a hardware-based tool, such as an F5 device, or an external software solution, such as ISA or TMG Server, or even something as simple as the built-in Windows Network Load Balancing (NLB) feature.

Hardware-based solutions are generally best, as they offer the most configuration options and usually the best performance, but they are also typically very expensive. The software-based solutions such as TMG provide a happy middle ground, especially if you are already using them in your environment. They include just enough options and monitoring to make the cut. Although using the Windows NLB is free because Windows provides it out of the box, it is a very rudimentary feature. It cannot do tasks like validate whether the server is serving valid pages, and instead only confirms that the server responds to ping traffic. For mission-critical scenarios this is not an ideal solution.

Regardless of which option you choose, you must configure NLB properly. You are required to set the NLB to a persistent or sticky session or single affinity, meaning when a user opens a browser and navigates to SharePoint their entire session must be against one WFE. SharePoint caches too many requests and does not share that cache across WFEs, so if users are constantly moving from server to server, it is possible for them to have erratic results.

Server Drives

When you configure SharePoint, it is generally a good idea to get everything possible off of the C: drive. For example, navigate to Central Administration and change the diagnostic logs to be hosted on the E: drive instead of the C: drive. Remember that this is a farm-wide setting, so all servers in your farm now must have an E: drive or they will get errors and stop logging. This is inconvenient but not the end of the world. The end of the world happens if you try to add a server to this farm now that doesn't have an E: drive. You will get file I/O errors running the configuration wizard and it can take a long time to figure out the cause. That is why it is recommended that all of the SharePoint servers in your farm have standard drive letters. A simple design choice like that can greatly reduce your headaches going forward.

Virtualization

Now that you have learned about hardware considerations, the question that logically follows is, "Which servers can I virtualize?" After looking at some of those server groups, it is very easy to see some opportunities.

Typically, when it comes to virtualization, it is recommended that you start at top of the farm and work your way down. Web front ends have almost no disk requirements and generally are consuming RAM and some CPU. They virtualize very well. How well application servers virtualize depends on what service applications they are hosting. For example, if you have a server group that is only hosting things like Office Web Apps and the Managed Metadata service, they would virtualize easily — again, because they have almost no disk requirements.

Your query and index servers can be virtualized but the benefit will depend on your performance expectations. Crawling 10 or 20 thousand items once a day is a pretty light load, and will virtualize without issue. However, trying to crawl 100 *million* items virtualizing and getting the performance you need would be extremely difficult.

The moral of the story when it comes to virtualizing SharePoint servers is that you should first understand how hard that server is working and where its first bottlenecks occur. If you can safely virtualize without reducing performance, then do so. Also, if you are building test and development environments where performance is not a critical factor, then virtualization is the way to go.

Should you virtualize SQL Server? That question generates almost as much passionate debate as Mac versus PC. Virtualizing SQL Server and achieving acceptable performance is possible; unfortunately, your average virtualization administrator, in partnership with your average SQL Server database administrator, cannot do it well. It is too complex a configuration for someone to stumble through. As a SharePoint administrator, you already know that SQL Server is going to be the factor holding your farm's performance down; do you really want to gamble with virtualization, which is likely to further decrease that performance?

TERMINOLOGY

One of the biggest challenges for SharePoint administrators new and old is the vocabulary. SharePoint is littered with words, such as "site," that have about a dozen different meanings (no one is ever really sure what a site actually is, and many consider it suitable that *site* is a four-letter word). To this end,

Figure 3-6 is here to save the day. Once you can speak to the entire hierarchy from top to bottom your job is complete, you have practically conquered SharePoint — so study hard.

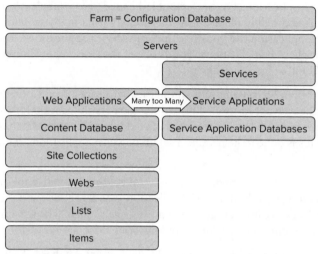

FIGURE 3-6

Starting from the top you see Farm = Configuration Database. This means that each SharePoint *server* can belong to only one farm. A farm can be a single server (refer to Figure 3-1) or something as complex as what is shown earlier in Figure 3-4. A farm refers to all of the servers that are using the same configuration database. When you run the configuration wizard, you choose to connect to an existing configuration database (join a farm) or create a new configuration database (create a farm). All servers in a farm, therefore, share everything, including the fact that there is only a single Central Administration site that controls all servers in the farm.

Below this, in the column on the right, you come to Services. These are the actual services on the server that run to provide functionality to the Service Applications. For example, the Excel Service Application you create in Central Administration from Manage Service Applications is a Service Application Connection point. That Service Application Connection point is the proxy to the instances of the Excel Service that is running on the server(s) in the farm. Don't worry if that isn't completely clear; Chapter 7 is dedicated to the inner workings of service applications.

Finally, at the bottom of the right-hand column you have Service Application Databases. Some service applications require database(s) to store information in order to work, while others do not. This is just one of the many reasons why using SharePoint 2010 means you will be getting to know SQL Server.

Web Applications, at the top of the left column, are the actual SharePoint websites you visit. Because they appear in IIS, you will hear people refer to them as sites, websites, IIS sites, and other creative things. However, it is very important that you refer to them as *web applications* or *web apps* for short, as everything in the SharePoint management interface and all of the documentation always refers to them as web applications. Examples are http://portal.company.com, http://www.company.com, https://extranet.company.com, or http://team.

Between Web Applications and Service Applications you see a double-headed arrow labeled Many to Many. This is your reminder that this is the only place on the hierarchy with a many-to-many relationship — in other words, one web application can consume multiple service applications, and service applications can also service multiple web applications. This is one of those seemingly infinite configuration options that make SharePoint so fun to architect.

Every time you create a new web application, SharePoint will automatically create a new Content Database for you and associate it with the web application. This will be the default location for storing content from the web application. It is possible for you to also create additional content databases to associate with the web application. This is done to help scale. Two unique web applications cannot share a content database.

That brings you to the most important concept in SharePoint: the Site Collection. Site collections are the unit of scale in SharePoint. The easiest way to think of a site collection is as a bag, because they are really just a boundary or container. They are not actually content users can touch. The reason why this "bag" is so important is because it determines a lot about how your information is stored.

Site collections are a storage boundary and are stored in one and only one content database. They cannot span multiple databases. When you create a site collection it is created in a database and that is where it will stay unless you manually move it. If, for example, you want to limit all of your content databases to 40GB because that is the largest size you are comfortable with, then you need to ensure that no site collection is larger than 40GB. Similarly, if you have multiple site collections (and everyone does), then you would need to apply quotas to those site collections to ensure that the sum of the site collections doesn't exceed your 40GB database limit. For instance, if you had 10 site collections, then you would want to set your quotas to 4GB per site collection.

Site collections are the only objects in SharePoint to which you can apply a storage quota. If you want to limit a user to storing only 10GB of content in a particular document library, there is no way to do that. You would have to set that entire site collection to a 10GB limit. If you have two document libraries and you want to give each one 10GB of storage, then you have to ensure that each document library is in its own site collection.

Even if you have no intention of holding users to limits, quotas are generally recommended for all site collections, as they serve as a checkpoint and keep you from having runaway site collections. If a user calls and says that he is getting warnings or errors because he has met his quota, it is a simple process for you to increase his quota, and it gives you a chance to ask, "So what are you doing with SharePoint that you need so much storage space?" It would be good to know if he is just backing up his MP3 collection to SharePoint.

Site collections also serve as an administrative boundary. Site collection administrators are a special group of users who have complete power over the site collection without necessarily having any access to other site collections. There is an entire menu on the Site Settings page of configuration options that only a site collection admin can make (see Chapter 8). If you have two groups, such as

HR and Accounting for example, in the same site collection and one of them comes to you because they need to administer one of these special settings, you will have to do some rearranging. If you make Nicola from Accounting a site collection administrator, then she can fully administer the account site as needed but she also has full control over the entire site collection, including the HR web. You need to instead move the Accounting web to its own site collection and then make Nicola an administrator there.

Site collections are also boundaries for out-of-the-box functionality such as navigation and the various galleries. This can be a drawback of many site collections. Out of the box, it is impossible to enforce consistent, self-maintaining navigation across site collections. The galleries such as the themes, Web Parts, lists, and solutions are all scoped at the site collection level. For example, if you need a list template to be available to multiple site collections, then you have to manually deploy it to each.

Site collections also serve as security boundaries. The All People list and the various SharePoint groups are all scoped at the site collection level and are not accessible for reuse outside of the site collection.

 Developers and Windows PowerShell refer to a site collection as an SPSite. *So when you hear that word, equate it to site collection.*

Inside of site collections you have one or more *webs*. A web is the object that is referred to throughout the user interface as a site. It can also be called a subsite or a subweb. Again, because the term *site* can be very confusing, whenever possible refer to these as webs. This is the first object users can actually touch. You can apply security to it, and it contains all of the user content. Each web has its own *lists* (libraries are just a special type of list) and all of those lists store *items*, which refers to the actual content, such as documents and contacts.

As you look at the hierarchy from Web Applications to Items, remember that it is a one-to-many relationship going down but a one-to-one relationship going up. That is, an item can belong to only one list, a list can belong to only one web, a web is part of only a single site collection, a site collection lives in only one content database, and a content database can be associated with only one web application.

Still a little fuzzy? Try this metaphor to understand how these pieces work together: Web applications are the landfill. Content databases are giant dumpsters. A site collection is a big, black 50-gallon garbage bag. And webs, lists, and items are pieces of trash. Your users spend all week creating garbage, continuously stuffing it in the garbage bags, with each piece of trash existing in only one garbage bag at a time. Each garbage bag can hold only 50 gallons of trash (quotas) before it is full, after which the user has to either ask for a new garbage bag or get a bigger garbage bag. That full garbage bag is placed in a dumpster, and it is not possible to put a garbage bag in more than one dumpster without destroying it. Dumpsters are serviced only by one landfill but that landfill can handle thousands of dumpsters without issue. How was that? Clear as mud?

CONTROLLING DEPLOYMENTS

SharePoint 2010 ships with more than a handful of tools that will help you to keep it under control — from tools that block and/or discover rogue deployments to built-in throttling capabilities that will help to prevent lost data and oversized lists from destroying your farm.

Blocking Rogue Deployments

SharePoint, especially Foundation, is sneaking into more and more enterprises. Business units who don't want to go through the proper channels have been caught standing up their own SharePoint servers in alarming numbers. That wouldn't be so horrible, but these rogue servers often house business-critical data but have no backups and no redundancy. IT generally doesn't find out about them until it is too late and someone has already lost critical data. To help prevent this SharePoint 2010 has implemented a new registry key:

```
HKLM\Software\policies\microsoft\SharePoint\14.0\blocksharepointinstall
```

If you set the dword `blocksharepointinstall` equal to 1, the installation of SharePoint is blocked. The key challenge is getting this registry key added to all of the machines in your farm in time, as it is not there by default. It will not affect servers that already have SharePoint installed. Also, you need to keep this key a secret between you and this page. If a user knows to look for it they can remove it from the registry and then install SharePoint anyway. If you are considering using this key it is probably easiest to create a group policy object that adds it to all the machines in your domain.

Registering SharePoint Servers in Active Directory

Rogue SharePoint servers have become an issue in many large enterprises, but sometimes blocking them as described in the previous section is considered too drastic. Wouldn't it be great if you could keep track of every server in your Active Directory that someone installed SharePoint on, so you could find the culprits and smack them on the hand with a ruler? With a little AD work you can. When a SharePoint farm first comes online it will attempt to register itself through an Active Directory Service Connection Point, also referred to as an AD Marker. The challenge is this container is not in AD by default; you must create and configure it before SharePoint is deployed. If you do it after the fact, existing farms will not be registered.

To configure this you must be a domain administrator and have access to a domain controller. Then you will need to follow the steps documented here: `http://blogs.msdn.com/opal/archive/2010/04/18/` `track-sharepoint-2010-installations-by-service-connection-point-ad-marker.aspx`.

HTTP Throttling

A potential challenge SharePoint administrators have faced in the past and are certain to see again is lack of resources and the odd behaviors it produces. One scenario is an overworked WFE server. As a WFE is processing requests, it might reach a point where it is not immediately responding to a request due to a lack of resources. It will then begin to queue requests, but it has a limited capacity for storing requests also. If the queue fills up, then it will just start indiscriminately dropping requests until it catches up. While this is not a big deal for a typical GET request, what if you are a user who has just spent an hour taking a survey or filling out an application? If that PUT request is dropped, your hour was spent in vain and you will have no option but to start over.

To avoid this issue, Microsoft has introduced HTTP Throttling to protect a server during peak load. By default, this feature monitors the available memory in megabytes and the ASP.NET requests in queue. As it monitors these counters, it generates a health score for the server on a scale from 0 to 9, with 0 being the best. The monitor checks every five seconds by default. If the score is 9 for three consecutive tests, then the server will enter a throttled state. In this throttled state, SharePoint will return a 503 server busy message to all GET requests, including the crawler if you happen to be indexing. In addition, all timer jobs will be paused, which enables the server to concentrate on finishing existing requests and hopefully makes room for anyone doing a PUT request, like that user who just spent an hour filling out a form. The monitoring continues every five seconds, and throttling is disabled after one occurrence of a score below 9.

This feature can be configured using Central Administration, to be enabled or disabled per web application. Using Windows PowerShell, you can go a step further and view and edit the thresholds using the following cmdlets:

```
Get-SPWebApplicationHttpThrottlingMonitor
```

```
Set-SPWebApplicationHttpThrottlingMonitor
```

 You can introduce your own counters, but that requires object model code, a topic outside the scope of this book.

The health score is exposed to all HTTP requests. If you use a tool like Fiddler (www.fiddler2.com) that enables you to inspect your web traffic, you will see in the header under Miscellaneous the value X-SharePointHealthScore. The place this truly comes into play is with the Office clients.

The Office 2010 client programs are aware of the score and can use it to adjust their behavior. For example, if you are using the PowerPoint Broadcast feature (covered in Chapter 18), it knows to watch the health score and to adjust the frequency of its updates based on the score.

Large List Throttling

SharePoint 2010 will support lists up to 50 million items; so much for that horrible rumor that SharePoint only supports up to 2,000 items in a list. That rumor is a case of people not getting their facts straight. Previous versions of SharePoint did have a recommendation to not exceed more than 2,000 items in a list *view* because of the performance strain it caused your farm. Think about what happened behind the scenes when a user tried to view 3,000 items in a list. First, the SQL Server had to generate a query to return all 3,000 items at once. Next, that information had to be sent to the WFE server and added to the page. Finally, the user had to download the page with its 3,000 items and wait on Internet Explorer to render all of that content. It could literally take minutes to return the page. Sadly, there was nothing to stop users from doing this or even to monitor that activity until now. SharePoint 2010 vastly improves this scenario.

With SharePoint 2010, we have controls that we can configure to prevent these types of activities. Figure 3-7 shows the Resource Throttling screen in Central Administration. You can access this screen by navigating to Application Management ⇨ Manage web applications. Then select your web application, click the drop-down for General Settings, and select Resource Throttling. All default settings are shown.

The List View Threshold, which is set to 5000 by default, represents the maximum number of items a standard user can return in a view. As users approach the limit, they will see the screen shown in Figure 3-8, which tells them how many items they have and where the throttling limit is set.

The following relevant settings are available:

➤ **Object Model Override** — This setting specifies whether a developer can override the throttling through the object model code to allow their code to run.

➤ **List View Threshold for Auditors and Administrators** — This setting is used to grant special power users a larger threshold. You can set a user up as an auditor through the Manage web applications screen. You first add a Permission Policy and enable the Site Collection Auditor permission policy level. Then, using User Policy, also on the Manage web applications Ribbon, select the new permission level you created.

➤ **List View Lookup Threshold** — This setting is used to control the number of lookups that can be specified.

➤ Daily Time Window for Large Queries — This setting is also referred to as "happy hour." It allows you to set a time of day when throttling is disabled and views are unrestricted.

➤ **List Unique Permissions Threshold** — This setting limits the number of unique permissions a given list can have. This is a good idea, as you can run into performance problems if a list has too many unique permissions coupled with too many items. Security trimming is a great but expensive feature at times.

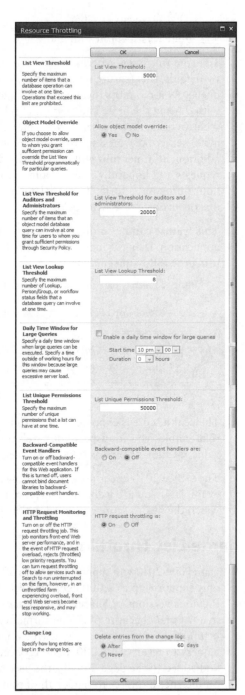

FIGURE 3-7

The remaining settings are not part of the list throttling feature.

When users exceed this limit, they will see a warning message in the browser stating "Displaying only the newest results below. To view all results, narrow your query by adding a filter." This will show the last 1,000 modified items.

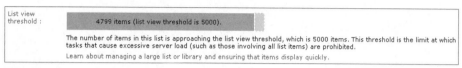

List view
threshold :

4799 items (list view threshold is 5000).

The number of items in this list is approaching the list view threshold, which is 5000 items. This threshold is the limit at which tasks that cause excessive server load (such as those involving all list items) are prohibited.

Learn about managing a large list or library and ensuring that items display quickly.

FIGURE 3-8

SUMMARY

In this chapter you reviewed the plethora of SharePoint 2010 SKUs that are available and how each one may be applicable to your situation, except for that cloud business. With that knowledge, key considerations of the other infrastructure pieces in the farm were discussed. Don't ever overlook these boxes, as they are the key to your success. Remember: No one calls to say your Windows box isn't working; they only call to complain SharePoint is broken.

In the section on terminology, you learned a bit about SharePoint's vocabulary, including how evil the word "site" is and why you should avoid it like the plague. Finally, you were introduced to SharePoint's out-of-the-box tools, which can help you manage its sometimes overwhelming collaboration and content management features.

Installing and Configuring SharePoint 2010

WHAT'S IN THIS CHAPTER?

➤ Running prerequisiteinstaller.exe and setup.exe

➤ Avoiding standalone installation

➤ Running the Config Wizard

➤ Running the Central Administration Wizard

➤ Handling post-setup configuration

➤ Installing SharePoint 2010

Please read this chapter! It has become commonplace for IT professionals and consultants to just "wing" the installation and configuration of software, figuring if there are any issues along the way a quick trip to Bing will get them squared away. While this may be true, it is hardly considered best practice.

This chapter walks you through all of the steps necessary to get your users a SharePoint site they can access. Starting with installing the software and then working through running the two configuration wizards, you will be on your way. Once you are done with the wizards, you will make some additional changes to Central Administration. With all of the knobs turned and the buttons pressed, you will then create a web application and site collection. At that point you are ready to turn over SharePoint to the users. Then there is nothing to do except cross your fingers and hope for the very best. Or if you are the proactive type you can check out Chapter 15 where monitoring is covered.

audits—essentially, walking through the install and configuration steps performed to build out a server farm and discovering and correcting the errors found with the initial installation. Can you hazard a guess as to how many of those farms were configured 100% correctly? The answer is zero. While it is true that some of them only had minor issues, the vast majority of them had major issues. How were these servers deployed? By the "Next, Next, Bing it" method. It just doesn't work.

So read this chapter before attempting to install and configure your server. That way, if it is ever audited, you can get the highly coveted "Your server is perfect!" feedback.

THE PREREQUISITES INSTALLER

SharePoint installation has followed the lead of a lot of the other Microsoft server software, and now includes its own tool, the Products Preparation Tool, to install all of those pesky little programs that are required to make your farm run. Figure 4-1 shows the list of these programs.

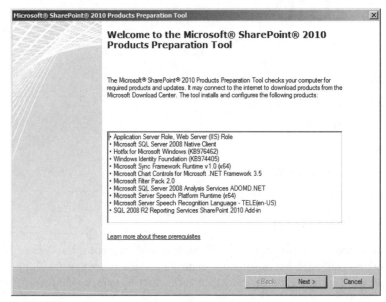

FIGURE 4-1

By default, when you run the tool it first configures IIS for you with the necessary settings. Then it checks for each of the listed programs and if they are not installed, or if the wrong version is found, the tool will access the Microsoft Download Center and download and install them for you automatically. Depending on changes made to your server and other updates you may have previously installed, you may have to reboot at this point. SharePoint will prompt you if this is necessary. Also, if a reboot is required to continue running the prerequisite installer you will be prompted to click Finish to perform the reboot. Then when you log back into the server the prereq installer will automatically pick up where it left off.

For some administrators, the process of having the tool automatically access the Internet to download all of these files is either not possible or not preferable. If you find yourself in this situation, you can manually download the files from the Internet. The easiest way to ensure that you are getting the correct files is to use the link from Figure 4-1 labeled "Learn more about these prerequisites." Clicking the link takes you to a TechNet page that contains links to all of the installers. With these installers in hand you have two options. The first option is to install each program individually to get everything your server needs; this would be ideal in one-off situations. The other option is to take advantage of the command-line switches available to the prerequisite installer by running the following command:

```
PrerequisiteInstaller.exe /?
```

Figure 4-2 shows the available installer command-line options.

FIGURE 4-2

Armed with this information, it is now possible for you to create a command line that installs all of the prerequisites for you from the locations to which you downloaded them. As you can tell, this is a pretty long command line and would not be much fun to write, so it's probably not something you would want to do for a one-time install. Conversely, if you are trying to streamline the process and make it repeatable across servers, this might just be the ticket.

WHERE IS PREREQUISITEINSTALLER.EXE?

Looking for PrerequisiteInstaller.exe? If you have a CD/DVD with SharePoint 2010 on it from Microsoft there is a good chance on the root of that disc you will find the EXE in question. But, if you are like most people, you just have an OfficeServer.exe or SharePoint.exe you downloaded from Microsoft.com. In this case you cannot access the individual files by default. To access the files you will need to extract out the contents of the EXE you downloaded first. To do this, open a command prompt, navigate to where you downloaded OfficeServer.exe, and then run the following command:

```
OfficeServer.exe /extract:c:\install
```

This will extract all of the SharePoint files and you can then find the preparation tool at `c:\install\PrerequisiteInstaller.exe`.

When the prerequisite installer finishes, you should be greeted with an Installation Complete message. If any part of the process failed, you will see an error message and a link to the log file. It is a fairly concise, easy to read log file, so if you are getting errors don't be afraid to crack it open. In most cases it will make it clear what installation or upgrade failed and why.

Two common issues seen with the prerequisite installation to this point are not having connectivity to the Internet from your SharePoint server and having PowerShell 1.0 already installed. The Internet issue is pretty obvious, along with the work-arounds noted above for manually downloading them; but the PowerShell issue requires a bit more explanation. If you are running on Windows Server 2008, there is a decent chance that you have already activated the Windows PowerShell feature. Some products will even activate this automatically when they are installed; SQL Server is an example of an application that installs PowerShell when it is installed. This feature uses Windows PowerShell 1.0 but SharePoint requires Windows PowerShell 2.0. When the prerequisite installer runs, it sees that Windows PowerShell 2.0 is not installed so it tries to download and install it. However, because Windows PowerShell 1.0 is already installed, the 2.0 version fails to install, causing the prerequisite installer to fail. At this point, you need to access Windows Server Manager, deactivate the Windows PowerShell feature, and then run prerequisiteinstaller.exe again.

RUNNING SETUP.EXE

Now that the prerequisites are out of the way, running setup.exe is the next logical step. Fortunately, setup does a little checking of its own before it does too much. It will check your system and confirm that you have indeed installed all of the prerequisites and that no reboots are needed prior to running setup. Fortunately you have read the previous section and you have gotten all of the necessary supporting programs installed.

The need to reboot is a by-product of all the updates that were installed by the prerequisite installer. Unfortunately, that tool is sometimes too lazy to tell you to reboot, so setup has to step in and deliver the bad news. Take advantage of the time to go get a drink. If it is the middle of the day the vending machine would be a good place to look for one, but if it is the middle of the night the executive refrigerator/bar might be calling your name.

If setup should fail for any reason, the best place to look for details is the logs at `c:\program files\ common files\Microsoft shared\web server extensions\14\logs`. Sometimes setup will give you a handy link, but often you need to find it on your own. Now you know where to look.

Choosing Your Installation Type

After you get through the checks and licensing, you will find yourself facing a crucial decision. Your choice on the screen shown in Figure 4-3 can make or break you; it is here that you must decide between a Standalone install or a Server Farm install.

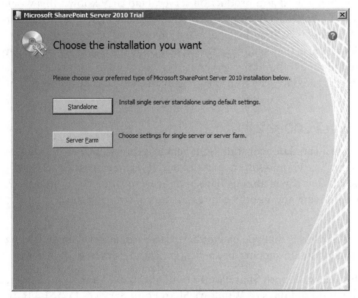

FIGURE 4-3

The real question is do you want a SharePoint environment you can be proud of and show off to your dog or do you want something that will make your four-legged friend laugh at you?

Standalone Install

You may have heard standalone installs referred to as basic installs or single-click installs. They have been around since the early days of SharePoint and are not going away any time soon. They are meant, with good intentions, for the casual evaluation of SharePoint, the idea being that you click "Standalone install" and a few minutes later, with no effort on your part, there is a running SharePoint farm for you to evaluate. The install process will take care of all the details for you. These include installing a new instance of SQL Server 2008 Express, configuring SharePoint to store all databases on that instance, configuring all of the necessary service applications, and creating a web application and, finally, a site collection. You are ready to dive headfirst into evaluating SharePoint. Not so fast.... .

There are a lot of things you should take time to consider before jumping headfirst into this type of install. The remainder of the section reviews some of the common questions/issues you need to consider before choosing your installation type. Once you read through the rest this section, it should be clear why Standalone or Basic installs are not recommended. Remember, should you choose to proceed, you have been warned!

SharePoint, the Proof of Concept That Lasts Forever

It is very common for an organization to quickly stand SharePoint up for "a simple proof of concept (POC)." The goal of the POC, to try it for one project and see how well it meets the business needs. Experience has shown that during the POC a lot of permanent, business-critical information ends up stored within SharePoint. This leaves many unsuspecting administrators stuck supporting a server that they built as a POC that is now being used as a production server. Had they known this would happen, they would have never built the POC using temporary methods, knowing it was unsupportable. The best advice? Even if the business is calling this an evaluation or POC or some other silly word and even if they double pinky promise they will have no expectations of this server being permanent, do not believe them. Take the time to build the server as if it will be used for production data. Experience has shown that this is the only way to protect against the POC that becomes the production environment.

Do You Want SQL Server Express 2008?

That is right, folks. When you choose a standalone install, SQL Server Express 2008 is installed and configured for you free of charge. SharePoint will then use that SQL Server instance for storing all of your SharePoint databases. What if you already have SQL Server installed on the server? It doesn't matter; SharePoint will still create and use the Express instance, ignoring the previously installed SQL Server.

The biggest drawback to SQL Server Express is that you cannot have databases larger than 4GB in size. It's unlikely that you would buy this big book to support an application with less than 4GB of data.

SQL Server Express is provided for use with both SharePoint Foundation and SharePoint Server, unlike in the past. Way back in the good old days of Windows SharePoint Services (WSS) 3.0, if you did a Basic install it was configured to use the Windows Internal Database (WID) engine, which did not have size limits. Because SharePoint Foundation is not part of Windows, like WSS was, it cannot use WID. If you are upgrading from WSS 3.0, this change does have some ramifications, as discussed in Chapter 5.

SQL Express 2008 does not include any GUI based managed tools, such as SQL Server Management Studio, which is the GUI tool for managing SQL Server. You can use the command-line tool `osql.exe` to manage SQL Express. Or, a much better idea is to download the free tool Microsoft SQL Server 2008 Management Studio Express, available from `http://www.microsoft.com/downloads/details .aspx?familyid=08E52AC2-1D62-45F6-9A4A-4B76A8564A2B&displaylang=en`. This will give you the GUI tools you are used to, and a fighting chance to manage your SQL databases.

It is possible to upgrade the instance of SQL Express to a real version of SQL Server. Check out `http://msdn.microsoft.com/en-us/library/ms143393.aspx` for an article on how to upgrade SQL Server, as that topic is outside the scope of this book. Keep in mind, however, that this won't negate the other pitfalls of a standalone install, including the fact that SharePoint will always know you chose standalone, which prevents you from adding additional servers to your installation and may limit your upgrade options down the road.

What Kind of Permissions Do You Want?

It is very easy to ignore what is happening behind the scenes when you do a standalone install. After all, isn't that the point? If you were paying attention to the process you would have noticed you were never prompted for a username or password. Instead of prompting you for the accounts you want to configure SharePoint to run with, it will use the Network Service and Local System accounts. SharePoint uses these accounts to configure the authentication for services, database connections, and application pools. These two special accounts are used for everything in place of real credentials. For example, your SharePoint Timer service, which is the lifeblood of SharePoint, is configured to use Network Service.

While these accounts are great to get you going and to keep you from fretting about creating service accounts, they are at the mercy of the system. Whenever a new Windows or .NET hotfix comes out, you have to proceed with extreme caution and confirm that they haven't reset some permission, thereby disabling SharePoint from running error free. It has happened with previous versions and it will most likely happen again. Your SharePoint accounts are so important that Chapter 8 spends a great many words discussing how and when to use them and what permissions they need. A basic install just bypasses all of that—not an ideal situation.

Forever Is a Long Time

When you choose a standalone install you are committing to it forever. That's because SharePoint always knows you originally did a standalone install. This will constrain a lot of your options going forward. For example, you will lose the capability to add additional SharePoint servers later when you want to scale out your system. Chapter 3, which discusses the farm architecture and capacity, explains how simple it is to add capacity after the fact by just plugging in a new server to the farm. With a standalone install you cannot add additional servers. If adding another server is an absolute must, then you must back up your data, format the server and start over from scratch. That doesn't seem like much fun.

Your upgrade options may also be limited. Basic installs of 2003 were not able to use all of the 2007 upgrade options. Fortunately, 2007 basic installs aren't limited in this way when upgrading to 2010, but who knows what the story will be moving from 2010 to the next version? That is another risk of this install method.

Patching

Windows Update will only consider installing a SharePoint patch for you if you have done a standalone install. Patching SharePoint servers is a critical task that needs to be undertaken with thought and planning. The idea that Windows Update might decide to install one at 3:00 a.m. on Tuesday is a little scary.

The patching mechanisms in SharePoint 2010 have been drastically updated and are actually pretty cool. Wouldn't you prefer to be at the helm playing with those new options, rather than be at the mercy of Windows Update? Check out Chapter 5 for all of the patching excitement.

Standalone Installation for Developers

There may be one small case where a Standalone install is a decent option. For SharePoint 2010, both Foundation and Server, Microsoft allows the installation of SharePoint on Windows 7 and Vista SP1 or SP2. (It does require a 64-bit operating system.) The idea is that developers can install SharePoint locally, avoiding the need to have a server to do their work. If you choose to go with this model, then a basic install is the only choice. It is also highly recommended that developers have access to SharePoint running on Windows Server to test their code, and that the development environment matches the configuration of production as closely as possible. For more details and a step-by-step guide to installing on a Windows client machine, check out `http://msdn.microsoft.com/en-us/library/ee554869(office.14).aspx`.

The Standalone Installation Process

If this list has not convinced you to avoid a standalone install, or if you need to do one for a specific reason, such as to create a single-server development environment installation on Windows 7 or Windows Vista, the process is simple.

When you click Standalone from the splash screen, the install begins immediately. The process will install all of the bits necessary for SharePoint. Once completed, it will then automatically run the Configuration Wizard for you. No input is required. If everything goes correctly, the next time you are prompted is from an Internet Explorer window. Here you choose what template you would like to use for the root site collection. The install automatically creates a web application at `http://<YourServerName>`. At the Choose your template screen, you can also upload a custom template to the gallery and use that template, which is a nice touch.

Hopefully, you have read this section and will heed its warnings. Standalone installs are very simple to get up and running, but they lock you into a limited set of options and present a lot of potential nightmares going forward. If you do find yourself running a standalone install, the best advice is to back up the databases and format the C: drive.

Server Farm Install

You finished reading the previous section and you get it—don't do a standalone install—so you click Server Farm like a good SharePoint administrator and what is your reward? Take a gander at Figure 4-4 to see.

Eek! The default setting is Stand-alone. How is Stand-alone different from the Standalone install we just feverishly avoided? Other than their spellings, not a gosh darn thing. That's right; Microsoft wants you to do a standalone install so badly they make you avoid it twice. Luckily, you are smart enough to know better, so select Complete before clicking Install Now.

A complete install will install all of the SharePoint bits on your server but will do nothing to configure them. Once the install is done, you run the configuration wizards to configure things as necessary. The key advantage of this approach is that you have complete control of all the service accounts you use, and what features are activated. In addition, you are free to reconfigure the server at a later time because all of the functionality is already installed. This flexibility may not seem important on day one, but as you work with SharePoint and need to scale in new business requirements, you will grow to appreciate it.

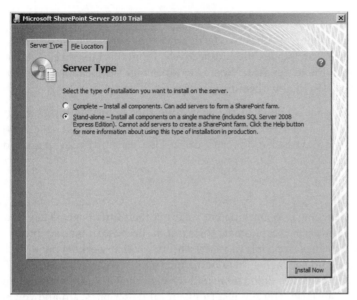

FIGURE 4-4

WEB FRONT END ONLY INSTALL

SharePoint Server 2007 had a third (advanced) install option called Web Front End (WFE). This option provided you with the flexibility of adding the server to a farm and using accounts as you wanted, but it lacked some of the components. The server only had the capability to act as a web front end, serving up SharePoint pages. You would sometimes see these servers used in large environments or for public-facing SharePoint sites. The benefit was that they had a smaller attack vector because there were fewer bits on the server to be exploited.

The major drawback was you couldn't use a WFE-only server as a query or index server. You lost all deployment flexibility because you couldn't move the server roles around. For example, if you wanted to rearrange your hardware before upgrading to this version, reallocating WFEs wouldn't be possible. In order to go from a WFE-only install to a complete, you have to uninstall and reinstall, something to keep in mind when choosing between the two.

WFE-only was so infrequently used that Microsoft has removed it from the GUI installer completely in SharePoint 2010. If you are part of that small minority who still needs that functionality, it is available through a scripted install.

Choose a File Location

The File Location tab on the dialog in Figure 4-4 has two fields where you can specify locations for the SharePoint Server files and the search index files, respectively. From this tab you can change either from their default C: location without any issue. You can also change the locations later, so don't agonize over the settings if you don't know them now.

Notice there no setting for changing what is known as the SharePoint root or the "14 hive," the files located at `c:\program files\common files\Microsoft Shared\web server extensions\14`. This is intentional; those files should always be left on the C: drive. They generally take up around 1GB of space at maximum.

Scripted Install

For some administrators all of that clicking does nothing but wear out their little finger. They find themselves for one reason or another wanting to automate their install. Because of this, scripted installs have grown in popularity over the last couple of years. The idea is that working out all of your configurations ahead of time and packaging them into a nice script can greatly accelerate your recovery plans. This is because, instead of doing an install through the GUI and then reading through documentation to rebuild your farm, you can just run your initial scripts again and you are ready to start restoring data.

The first step is modifying a `config.xml` file with your settings. SharePoint has several files with default settings that you can use as a jumping-off point. If you are doing your install from the downloaded EXE file, then you have to work a little bit to get to them. First, extract the files from the EXE by running the following command:

```
Officeserver.exe /extract:C:\install
```

 If you aren't familiar with how this works refer back to the sidebar "Where Is PrerequisiteInstaller.exe?" from earlier in this chapter.

After extracting all the files to `c:\install`, look in `c:\install\files`, where you will see several folders. Each of those folders contains a different `config.xml` file. If you open one of the files with your favorite XML editor, such as Notepad, you will see that the file is pretty self-explanatory. The contents of `c:\install\files\setup\config.xml` are as follows:

```
<Configuration>
    <Package Id="sts">
        <Setting Id="LAUNCHEDFROMSETUPSTS" Value="Yes"/>
    </Package>

    <Package Id="spswfe">
        <Setting Id="SETUPCALLED" Value="1"/>
    </Package>

    <Logging Type="verbose" Path="%temp%" Template="SharePoint Server
```

```
Setup(*).log"/>

        <Setting Id="SERVERROLE" Value="SINGLESERVER"/>
        <Setting Id="USINGUIINSTALLMODE" Value="1"/>
        <Setting Id="SETUPTYPE" Value="CLEAN_INSTALL"/>
        <Setting Id="SETUP_REBOOT" Value="Never"/>
</Configuration>
```

This is the configuration file that SharePoint uses for defaults when you run the normal GUI setup by running `setup.exe`. Let's look at a couple of quick changes you can make.

Look at the line that reads:

```
<!--<PIDKEY Value="Enter Product Key Here" />-->
```

If you remove the `<!--` from the beginning, and the `-->` from the end, you can add your product key and get a line like this:

```
<PIDKEY Value="11111-22222-33333-44444-55555" />
```

This might be a good idea if you are putting the files on a file share to be reused often. I also recommend changing `SERVERROLE` to `APPLICATION` in the next line so that the default is no longer Stand-Alone:

```
<Setting Id="SERVERROLE" Value="APPLICATION"/>
```

Those are little novelty tricks to save you some typing and clicking. The real power comes from customizing `c:\install\files\setupsilent\config.xml`. Modify this file with your desired `SEVERROLE` and `PIDKEY` and then pass a reference to the file. Now the install magic just happens. Use a line like the following at the command prompt:

```
C:\install\setup.exe /config c:\install\files\setupsilent\config.xml
```

If all of your settings are acceptable, the install will just run for you. It may take a couple of attempts to get everything right, but once you do you are on the road to a scripted install.

 One gotcha to watch out for is that the `config.xml` *file is case sensitive.*

While there is no SharePoint 2010 reference available yet, the settings are very close to, if not exactly the same as, those used with SharePoint 2007. You can find that reference at `http://technet .microsoft.com/en-us/library/cc261668.aspx`.

USING THE SHAREPOINT 2010 WIZARDS

SharePoint 2010 provides two wizards to help you get a new SharePoint farm up and running: the SharePoint Products and Technologies Configuration Wizard (Config Wizard) and the Initial Farm Configuration Wizard (Central Administration Wizard). The Config Wizard is used to create a new SharePoint farm or add your server to an existing farm. The Central Admin Wizard is used to help you provision service applications.

Configuration Wizard

After the install finishes you are brought to the configuration wizard (which could be called the *grey wizard*—more on that later). This tool is responsible for helping you create or join a SharePoint farm and then configuring all of the necessary databases and files for that farm to work.

Connecting to a Server Farm

A SharePoint server farm is one or many SharePoint servers that share the same configuration database, as explained in Chapter 2. The first important decision you need to make when running the configuration wizard is whether you want to "Connect to an existing server farm" or "Create a new server farm." More simply put, do you want to attach to an existing configuration database or create a new configuration database?

If you choose to connect to an existing server farm, you are prompted to enter the SQL Server that hosts the database, after which you click Retrieve Database Names, and then you select the configuration database, as shown in Figure 4-5. After that you will need to enter the farm passphrase (covered a little later in this chapter) to join the farm. You will also have the opportunity to specify this server as the host for SharePoint Central Administration if you wish.

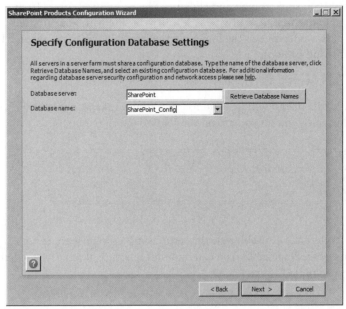

FIGURE 4-5

With this information, the wizard can then run. It will configure the files and registry on your server with the proper settings and permissions, and add your server to the SharePoint farm and register it with the appropriate databases. By default, this server will also host the web application role, so all web applications, except for Central Administration, will be created and available on this server.

> **WHAT ABOUT DUPLICATE DATABASE NAMES?**
>
> You shouldn't encounter any database name conflicts. If you are using the same SQL Server to host multiple SharePoint farms, then you should have multiple instances of SQL Server configured. Avoid having two SharePoint farms using the same SQL instance; managing those databases can quickly become a nightmare, and security is very touchy.

Creating a New Farm

If you choose to create a new farm, the options are slightly different but similar. You will be taken to a screen to specify the Database Server and Name. It is recommended to use the default database name of SharePoint_Config. You will also need to enter the username and password for your server farm account.

Establishing the Farm Account

It is very important to assign the correct settings for the server farm account. This account needs to be part of the domain, but it only needs to be a regular user and not a domain admin. As part of the configuration wizard, SharePoint will elevate this account's access as necessary. It will be given the SQL Roles of dbcreator and securityadmin. The account will also be added to the following local security groups:

➤ IIS_IUSRS

➤ Performance Log Users

➤ Performance Monitor Users

➤ WSS_ADMIN_WPG

➤ WSS_RESTRICTED_WPG

➤ WSS_WPG

The account is also given the following Local Security Policy - User Rights Assignments:

➤ Adjust memory quotas for a process

➤ Logon as a service

➤ Replace a process level token

The account will be used for the following Windows Services:

➤ Windows SharePoint Services Timer V4

➤ Windows SharePoint Services User Code Host V4

Finally, the account is used for the application pool for SharePoint Central Administration, the Topology Web Service, and the Security Token Service. With all of that it is very clear that this account should be considered carefully.

The Farm Passphrase

In the next dialog of the Config Wizard, SharePoint prompts for the farm passphrase. The passphrase is used to secure farm communications and will have to be provided by any additional servers joining the farm. You should choose a reasonably strong passphrase and document it in a safe place. Recovering a lost passphrase is very difficult if not impossible. Changing the passphrase is possible after the farm is online using the Windows PowerShell cmdlet `Set-SPPassPhrase`.

Central Administration Settings

In the next screen, the Central Administration settings enable you to configure a port number and authentication method for your Central Admin web application. It is recommended that you use a port number that is easy to remember for remote administration.

For authentication methods, the default is NTLM, which should be used unless you need the Central Administration web application to use Kerberos authentication; typically this is not necessary. Each web application has its own authentication settings, so using NTLM for Central Administration does not preclude you from using Kerberos on a different SharePoint web application.

Advanced Settings—SharePoint Foundation Only

The last screen of the Config Wizard enables you to confirm the settings you have chosen before committing to them. If you are doing anything other than a SharePoint Foundation install, you will see an Advanced Settings button that is grayed out. If you are doing a SharePoint Foundation install, this button is enabled. If you click the button, you are taken to the Enable Active Directory Account Creation Mode screen shown in Figure 4-6.

Active Directory Account Creation Mode (ADACM) is an interesting but mostly unused feature of SharePoint. It allows your SharePoint farm to be set up to automatically create Active Directory users when you add them to SharePoint. These new accounts are created in the organizational unit (OU) specified on the screen. You can even have SharePoint e-mail a notification to users when their account is created, along with the password. This is a truly automated scenario that works very well in hosted environments.

Of course, there is a down side. You cannot use existing Active Directory accounts to access SharePoint, only accounts created through this mode. So if you are deploying SharePoint in ADACM, you cannot use your existing AD account to access SharePoint. Users hate having one username and password; can you imagine telling them they need a second username and password to access SharePoint? Now you can see why this mode is not used very often. And remember, it is only available in Foundation, not Server.

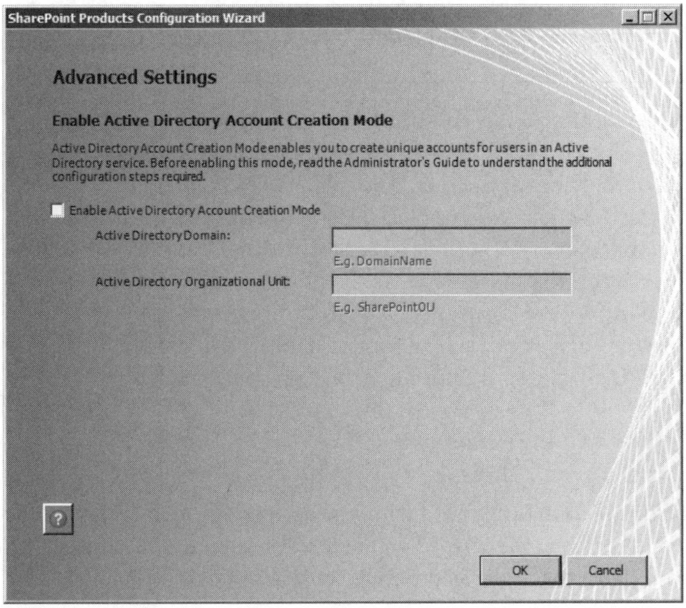

FIGURE 4-6

Other Uses for the Configuration Wizard

After configuration, it is typical to forget about this powerful tool, but that would be a mistake. While its main focus in life is running after setup.exe to get things squared away, it comes into play throughout the life of the server. It can be used to change the server that hosts the Central Administration site, commit patches and upgrades to the farm, and cleanly remove a server from the farm before being decommissioned.

Error Handling for the Configuration Wizard

If the Config Wizard encounters any errors it will fail and give you the basics of the error along with a link to the log file. In the log file, which is located in 14\logs, you will be able to trace through the full details of the error. The most common error seen at this point is related to connecting to the SQL Server, due to either network issues or security settings on the SQL Server.

Central Administration Wizard

SharePoint thought having the grey wizard was so cool that for 2010 it now has added a *white wizard*. After running the grey wizard (also known as the SharePoint Products and Technologies Configuration Wizard), Central Administration opens up the white wizard (also known as the Initial Farm Configuration Wizard). On the first page of this white wizard, you can either have SharePoint automatically provision service applications for you using default settings or choose to configure everything manually. Service applications are covered in great detail in Chapter 7.

> **WHAT DO THE WHITE WIZARD AND GREY WIZARD HAVE TO DO WITH ANYTHING?**
>
> In the grand scheme of things… nothing. SharePoint 2010 is packed full of wizards with very similar names that do similar tasks. So in order for the authors to keep track of them they have taken to referring to them by color. The SharePoint 2010 Products and Technologies Wizard, which is also called the configuration wizard by some, uses grey as the primary color for all of the screens while the Initial Farm Configuration Wizard is run on pages that have white as the primary color. So the names grey wizard and white wizard were born. Also, if you are fan of the Lord of the Rings books or movies you may also recall a very similar naming situation. At the end of the day what you call the wizards are not important; keeping track of which one does what is.

If you choose to have SharePoint help you configure your farm, you are taken to a screen where you can select an existing managed account or have the wizard create one for you, and then select which of the service applications you wish to have the wizard configure for you.

The wizard will also create a web application at `http://servername` and will prompt you for what template to use for the site collection. The account you are logged in with will be made the site collection administrator. If you are like most users, you probably won't use this site collection so you can safely click Skip.

Managed Accounts

New to SharePoint 2010 is the concept of *managed accounts*. With a managed account, you register a domain account with SharePoint, which stores the account and its password for reuse. Then, any time you specify an account in SharePoint—whether it is for application pools, database connections, or services—you have to select one of your managed accounts. The major upside of this is that now you have one interface for managing password changes for all of your managed accounts, unlike previous versions where password changes were a complete nightmare. Also, if you choose, you can have SharePoint handle the management of this account's password altogether.

For example; if you have a domain policy that passwords must be changed every 60 days, either you can configure SharePoint to notify you by e-mail so you can come into SharePoint and change the password manually or you can set SharePoint to automatically change the password in Active Directory. That way, you don't need to remember who knows the service account passwords because only the SharePoint farm does. If you need to manually change the password for any reason, you can change it from within SharePoint using PowerShell. Working with managed accounts is covered in greater detail in Chapter 6.

Error Handling for the Central Administration Wizard

The Central Administration wizard also has some built-in error handling. If an individual service application fails, Central Administration will provide you with an error message listing the service app that failed, details of the failure, and a correlation ID along with a Next button. It will continue with the other service applications that remain to be configured. You can also look in the ULS log in `14\logs` for more details. In Chapter 15, you will learn about correlation IDs and how they make your life about a million times easier.

CENTRAL ADMINISTRATION POST-SETUP CONFIGURATION

Although Chapter 6 covers SharePoint administration and how to poke around Central Admin, a couple of topics need to be covered here to get your farm off the ground successfully. This section provides insight into recommended configuration changes you should make before you let the users in and they make a mess.

Outgoing E-Mail

If you are familiar with SharePoint 2.0 or 3.0 outgoing e-mail settings, then this page should look very familiar, as it hasn't changed in years. You will need to specify the outbound SMTP server along with the From and Reply To e-mail addresses.

The outbound SMTP server can be any e-mail server that allows anonymous relay from the SharePoint server. Because anonymous relay is typically frowned upon, you may need to have your e-mail server administrator enable anonymous relay for the IP address(es) of your SharePoint server(s).

Secure Store Service

The Secure Store Service is a service application that acts as a credential manager. For example, when you set up the PerformancePoint Services application's unattended service account, the information is stored in the Secure Store Service database. While you are configuring these other service applications, it isn't always apparent they are having issues because the Secure Store Service isn't configured, so it is best to configure the service as part of the initial farm configuration.

Thankfully, there is very little to do with this configuration. Simply open the service application and generate a new key. When you generate the key you will need to specify a passphrase for the hash. Be certain to record this passphrase in a safe place. Once the key is generated, your work is done. Pretty simple, but it should save you some confusion later.

Configuring a Search Schedule

Another good idea is to configure a generic search schedule as part of your initial configuration. This way, while your users are "just testing," they don't get frustrated because the search feature doesn't work. All of Chapter 14 is dedicated to search, and there is a lot of great stuff to learn in order to search correctly; but skipping ahead for now and just enabling an incremental crawl, even just once a day, will go a long way toward avoiding angry phone calls later. This crawl will populate the index with information so when your users use the search box to find items they can get results. Keep in mind that it is easy to overwhelm your server with a too aggressive schedule, so set it to every few hours at most or every day at best until you have learned more about search and understand your data.

Monitoring Drive Space

While you are wrapping up your server configuration it is a good time to think about drive space. By default, everything is going to be on the C: drive of your server. This may be okay if you have a 500GB C: drive, but insufficient space can pose a major problem. Some items you should consider are as follows:

➤   IIS logs

➤   Web application directories (`C:\inetpub\*`)

➤   SharePoint ULS logs

➤   SharePoint usage data collection

➤   SharePoint search index

Consider whether it makes since to move some of these files to another drive.

Other Thinking Points

There are a few more things for you to consider. What is your backup strategy? Asking yourself when the server goes down or after an executive needs his or her vacation pictures restored is too late. Once the server is installed and you give users access, you are responsible for their data no matter what your agreement with them might have been, so you better be backing up that data before you let them in. Chapter 12 has plenty on the topic so enjoy the read.

Congratulations! The day you became a SharePoint administrator you also became a SQL administrator. Even if you have great DBAs watching over those SQL Servers, 99 percent of your data is stored there so their problems are your problems. You need to be very vocal in communicating with the DBAs about what they can and cannot do with your databases. And do you know where your performance bottlenecks are most likely to occur? That's right—on the SQL Server.

Chapter 3 discussed the new HTTP throttling feature and how it enables the server to protect data being written to the server during heavy load periods. If you are doing a VM install of SharePoint on underperforming hardware, consider disabling HTTP throttling. It can cause you some headaches on your slow VM while trying to protect you.

STEP-BY-STEP INSTALL

You have learned a lot over the previous several pages about the various installation and configuration options you face while building a SharePoint farm, and the reasoning behind a lot of the recommendations that were made. This section now brings it all together with clear, step-by-step install instructions that will enable you to go from a simple Windows and SQL Server install to a running SharePoint farm.

The Environment

This walk-through uses two servers. One server will be the Active Directory domain controller, with SQL Server 2008 running on it. The second server will be configured only with a pre-RTM SharePoint Server 2010 Enterprise installation. Both machines are actually virtual machine guests.

ServerDC

The first server, named ServerDC, is running Windows Server 2008 R2 (64-bit) with all current Windows Updates installed. It has been preconfigured as an Active Directory domain controller for the Contoso domain. SQL Server 2008 has been installed and has had Service Pack 1 and Cumulative Update Package 2 (KB970315) applied.

ServerSP

The second server, named ServerSP, is also running Windows Server 2008 R2 (64-bit) with all current Windows Updates installed. It is a member of the Contoso domain.

Accounts

Three accounts have been created for this scenario. In most production scenarios you will have additional accounts. The accounts are Contoso\SP_Admin, Contoso\SP_Farm, and Contoso\SP_ServiceApp. Each account has been configured only as a domain user. Additionally, SP_Admin has been given the following additional rights:

➤ Added as a local administrator on ServerSP only

➤ From SQL Management Studio running on ServerDC, the account has had a SQL login created with the roles of dbcreator, public, and securityadmin, as shown in Figure 4-7.

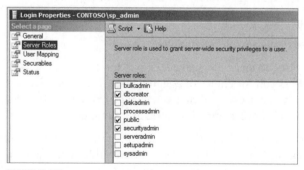

FIGURE 4-7

The Install

Enough messing around and getting things in order. Time to jump in and get this thing installed.

1. Log in to ServerSP as Contoso\SP_admin.

2. Download `OfficeServer.exe` to your server desktop.

3. Open a command prompt and change directory to your desktop by running the following command:

```
CD Desktop
```

4. Run the following command to extract the contents of `OfficeServer.exe`, as shown in Figure 4-8:

```
OfficeServer.exe /extract:c:\install\SharePoint2010
```

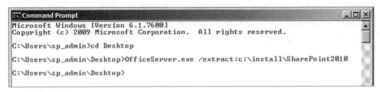

FIGURE 4-8

5. Click OK at the "Files extracted successfully." message.

6. Close the command prompt window and use Windows Explorer to navigate to `c:\install\SharePoint2010`.

7. Double-click on `PrerequisiteInstaller.exe`.

8. Click Next at the Welcome screen. Read and accept the license terms and click Next.

9. At the Installation Complete screen, click Finish. If you have any errors, click on the log and review the errors. Correct those errors and re-run the prerequisiteinstaller.exe.

10. From the `c:\install\SharePoint2010` folder, double-click `setup.exe`.

11. Enter your product key and click Continue.

12. Read and accept the license terms and click Continue.

13. STOP! This is a very easy place to make a mistake by going too fast. The "Choose the installation you want" screen offers you the choice of a Stand-alone install or a Server Farm. As described earlier in this chapter, it is essential that you change from the default Standalone option to Server Farm before clicking. Figure 4-9 serves as a reminder.

14. STOP! Another easy mistake to be made. In the next screen, Stand-alone is again the default, but for goodness' sake, click the button for Complete. After double-checking that you clicked Complete, you can click Install Now. The installation will run.

15. When the install completes, the Run Configuration Wizard screen will appear. Leave the check box selected and click Close.

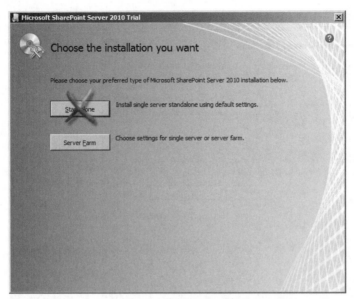

FIGURE 4-9

 If you are planning on installing the Office Web Applications (OWA), which are covered in Chapter 19, you need to deselect the check box to prevent the Configuration Wizard from running. You then need to run the OWASetup.exe and walk through that install as detailed in Chapter 19.

16. The Welcome Screen will display; click Next.

17. A warning will appear that IIS and SharePoint administrative and timer services will be stopped. Click Yes.

18. The Connect to a server farm screen will open. Select Create a new server farm and click Next.

19. At the Specify Configuration Database Settings screen, input your information as applicable. Figure 4-10 shows the settings used based on server names and accounts in the example scenario. After confirming your selections, click Next.

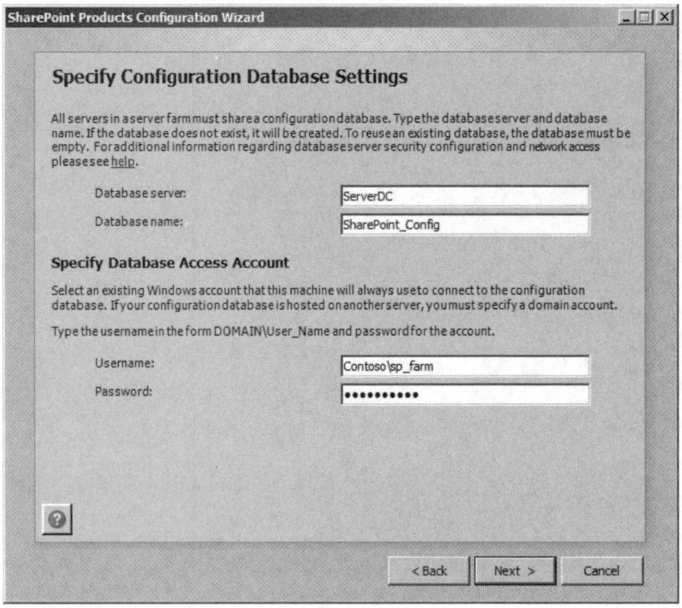

FIGURE 4-10

20. At the Specify Farm Security Settings screen, enter and confirm your passphrase. Be sure to document your passphrase for future reference.

21. At the Configure SharePoint Central Administration Web Application screen, it is recommended that you specify a port number. In the example, 5555 is used because it is easy to remember.

22. Keep the authentication provider for Central Admin at the default of NTLM and click Next to continue.

23. From the Completing the SharePoint Products Configuration Wizard screen, confirm your settings and click Next. This will start the configuration process, which takes a few minutes.

24. At the Configuration Successful screen, click Finish.

25. SharePoint Central Administration opens automatically. Depending on the configuration of your browser you may be prompted to log in. You should also confirm that the site is an Internet Explorer Trusted site or a Local intranet zone. If prompted, you can choose to participate in the Customer Experience Improvement program or not and then click OK, as shown in Figure 4-11.

26. Central Admin now takes you to a page asking "How do you want to configure your SharePoint farm?" Click Start the Wizard.

27. Enter the username and password of a new managed account. For this example, use `Contoso\SP_ServiceApp`. Remember to add the `domain\` in front of your username as shown in Figure 4-12.

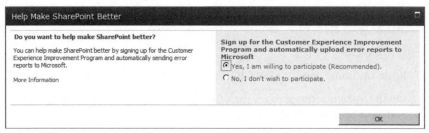

FIGURE 4-11

FIGURE 4-12

28. By default, all of the service applications will be selected except for the Lotus Notes Connector. Make any necessary changes and then click Next.

29. After a few minutes you will be brought to a page to create a site collection in the web application SharePoint automatically created for you. Enter a Title and Description and then select a template to use. Figure 4-13 shows an example.

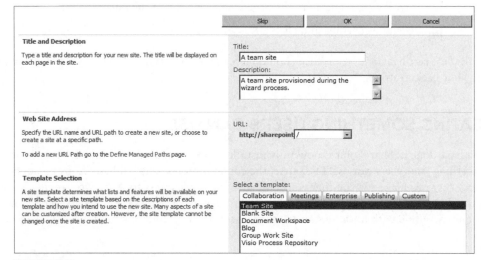

FIGURE 4-13

30. When the wizard completes, SharePoint will return a page with a list of the service applications that were created. Click Finish.

31. Configure Outgoing e-mail:

 a. From the home page of Central Admin, click System Settings.

 b. On the System Settings page, click Configure outgoing e-mail settings from the E-mail and Text Messages (SMS) section.

 c. Specify the Outbound SMTP server and the From and Reply to addresses, and then click OK.

32. Configure the Secure State Service:

 a. From the left-hand navigation pane, click Application Management.

 b. Click Manage service applications from the Service Applications section.

 c. Scroll down the page and click Secure Store Service.

 d. From the ribbon, click Generate New Key.

 e. Enter and confirm a passphrase and click OK.

 f. When finished, you should see the message "There are no Secure Store Target Applications in this Secure Store Service Application." This is normal.

33. Set a simple search crawl schedule:

 a. From the Central Admin home page, select Manage service applications.

 b. Click the Search Service Application.

 c. From the left-hand navigation pane, click Content Sources.

 d. Hover over Local SharePoint sites and click the drop-down arrow.

 e. Select Edit.

 f. Scroll to the bottom of the page and click Create schedule.

 g. Define a schedule and click OK.

With these settings done, your farm should be ready to rock and roll. Now would be a great time to put your backup strategy in place.

CREATING SOMETHING USERS CAN USE

You have done it. SharePoint is now fully installed and configured—all that is left is creating something your users can use. Of course, the configuration wizard did create a web application at `http://servername` for you that you could give the users access to, but if you are like some geeks you prefer server names like BigScaryMonsterFromSpace or Server128323-City-State-Country-Company. While both of those names are great for IT, they kind of stink for Betty in accounting.

So instead, create a web application like `http://portal.company.com` or `http://DepartmentName` to get users started. Remember that whatever host header you choose you will need to create a DNS record that points that host header at your SharePoint server. For the following example we use `portal.contoso.com`. A DNS host (A) record was created to resolve `portal.contoso.com` to the IP address of ServerSP.

One side track before you create your web application. You should use a new unique account for the application pool. For the example use `Contoso\SP_PortalApp`. This account needs to be a domain user. You also need to register this as a managed account before creating the web application.

The following sections walk you through the main steps: creating a managed account, a web application, and a site collection, and adding users.

Creating a New Managed Account

Follow these steps to create a new managed account:

1. From the home page of Central Admin, click Security.

2. Click Configure managed accounts from the General Security section.

3. Click the Register Managed Account link.

4. Enter the username and password. For this example use Contoso\SP_PortalApp for the username.

5. Leave the other default settings and click OK.

Creating a Web Application

Follow these steps to create a web application:

1. From Central Admin, select Application Management.

2. Click Manage web applications from the Web Applications section.

3. From the Ribbon, click the New icon.

4. For Authentication, accept the default of Classic Mode Authentication. (For more information on the differences between Classic Mode and Claims Based, check out Chapter 9.)

5. In the IIS Web Site section, select Create a new IIS web site. (Remember that in SharePoint terminology this is called a web application.)

6. For the port enter 80.

7. For Host Header enter **portal.contoso.com**.

8. Confirm your web application settings to match those shown in Figure 4-14 and then scroll down the page.

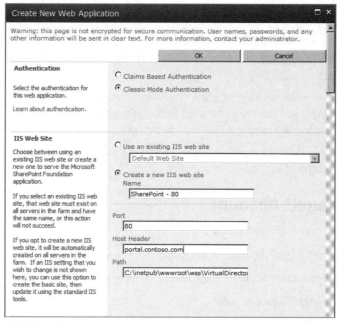

FIGURE 4-14

9. For the fields Authentication provider, Allow Anonymous, Use Secure Sockets Layer (SSL), and Public URL, accept the defaults.

10. In the Application Pool section, select the Configurable drop-down and change it to your new managed account. For this example, select Contoso\SP_PortalApp.

11. Change the Database Name from WSS_Content_*<big GUID string>* to WSS_Content_ *yourhostheader*. For this example, the database name used was WSS_Content_Portal, as shown in Figure 4-15.

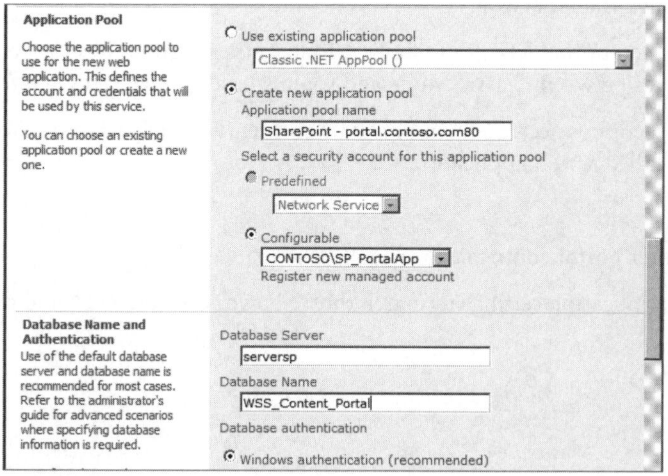

FIGURE 4-15

12. Scroll down the page and select Yes for the Enable Customer Experience Improvement Program. (This is optional but it is a good idea.)

13. Keep all other defaults and click OK.

14. Once the process is complete, click OK at the Application Created window.

Creating a Site Collection

Follow these instructions to create a site collection:

1. Click Application Management from the left-hand side of the page.

2. Click Create site collections from the Site Collections section.

3. Change the web application to your new web application by clicking the drop-down next to http://Servername and selecting Change web application.

4. From the pop-up window, click your web application. For this example, it is SharePoint - portal.contoso.com80.

5. Enter a Title and Description.

6. The URL will be at the default of http://webapplication/. For this example, it is http://portal .contoso.com/, as shown in Figure 4-16.

7. Scroll down the page and choose a template. This will be the template used for the root web in the site collection. You may also elect to choose <select template later…> from the Custom tab. This allows site collection administrators to choose their own template.

8. Enter a Primary and Secondary Site Collection Administrator.

9. Choose No Quota.

10. Click OK. You will get a page with Top-Level Site Successfully Created message. Click OK.

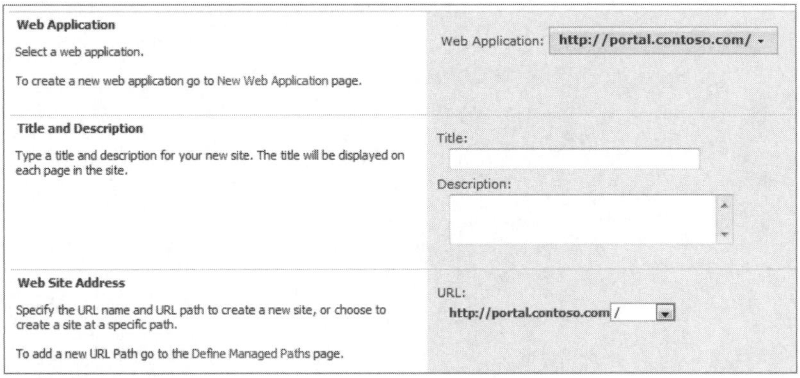

FIGURE 4-16

Add Users

The last step is to quickly grant access to the necessary users. For example, if you want everyone to try out SharePoint, you can set up Domain Users to have contributor access.

1. Navigate to your new site collection. For the example, that's http://portal.contoso.com.

2. Log in as the site collection administrator.

3. There will be a slight delay the first time the site is accessed. Once the page opens, click Site Actions ⇨ Site Settings.

4. Click Site permissions from the Users and Permissions section.

5. Click the Grant Permissions button from the Ribbon.

6. Enter domain users and select the members group from the drop-down.

7. Click OK. SharePoint is now ready for use.

SUMMARY

As you have seen from this chapter, while the install is not overly complicated, there are some opportunities for mistakes, but also many chances to make your life easier going forward. Take the time to proactively consider the installation process, and never fall for the line that "The server doesn't matter, it is just a POC." With the knowledge you gained from this chapter, you should be on your way to a great experience with SharePoint 2010. Finally, if you only take one idea from this chapter, remember that standalone installs are the devil.

5
Upgrading from SharePoint 2007 to SharePoint 2010

WHAT'S IN THIS CHAPTER?

➤ Supported upgrade methods

➤ Considerations for upgrading your farm and content

➤ Patching your SharePoint 2010 farm

SharePoint 2007 has been good to us. For many of us, SharePoint 2007 was where SharePoint started getting taken seriously. No more getting sand kicked in its face when it was at the beach; SharePoint was a force to be reckoned with. Because of that, it almost seems disrespectful to talk about abandoning it for its newer, flashier sibling SharePoint 2010. Take heart, SharePoint 2007 understands. We sat down and had a long talk with it. "Dear SharePoint 2007, it's not you, it's me…"

You have a lot of good options for moving your SharePoint 2007 content and farm to SharePoint 2010. In this chapter, we cover those options in detail, as well as discuss some ways to make the upgrade less painful for you, and your end users. At no extra charge, we also talk about upgrade's cousin, patching, and how that has improved in SharePoint 2010. There is a lot to cover, so let's dig in.

UPGRADE CONSIDERATIONS

While this chapter is chock full of great upgrade information, most of you are here for the "how." A lot of planning goes into upgrading, and there are a lot of gotchas to look out for, which are no fun. Of course, what you want is the nitty gritty about how to actually upgrade your SharePoint 2007 farms to SharePoint 2010. Don't worry, we'll get to all that later, but first we need to lay down some upgrade ground rules. After covering the basics, we will dig in with more details about each of the topics.

What Can You Upgrade?

Before we can talk about how to upgrade, you need to be clear about what you can actually upgrade. The only supported platform you can upgrade to SharePoint 2010 is SharePoint 2007 — and not just any old SharePoint 2007, it has to be at least service pack 2 (build 12.0.0.6421 to its friends) or later. (If you try to pull the wool over SharePoint 2010's eyes and attempt to upgrade an older version, it will stop you, call you bad names, and leave you feeling ashamed.) This is true for both upgrade options: in-place and database attach.

Speaking of those upgrade options, let's talk about those a little. An *in-place upgrade* takes place when you install SharePoint 2010 on your existing SharePoint 2007 machines. It functions nearly the same as the in-place upgrade from SharePoint 2003 to SharePoint 2007 did, only without all the failures and swearing. An in-place upgrade runs on your existing SharePoint 2007 hardware and maintains all your URLs. This is a good fit if you want to upgrade a small environment and use the same machines and URLs. The ins and outs of in-place upgrades are discussed later in the chapter in great detail.

Your other upgrade method is a *database attach*. With this method, you take databases from a SharePoint 2007 farm (service pack 2 or later, of course) and you attach them to a fully functional SharePoint 2010 farm. When a database is attached, SharePoint 2010 will upgrade it and render its content. You are allowed to attach content databases, Microsoft Project databases, and SharePoint profile databases to a SharePoint 2010 farm. This method requires SharePoint 2010 be a new installation on new hardware.

Both of these methods require some planning and testing to be successful. The most useful tool you can use to discover any upgrade issues you have in SharePoint 2007, and determine how much trouble they will be to upgrade, is SharePoint 2007. In service pack 2, Microsoft introduced a new STSADM operation, *preupgradecheck*, that scours your SharePoint 2007 farm looking for problems. While running preupgradecheck is not required when doing either type of upgrade, it is recommended. It will do a thorough inventory of your SharePoint 2007 farm and report any problems it finds. Not only can these problems impede your upgrade, it may be beneficial to your existing SharePoint 2007 farm to fix them sooner rather than later. Even if your farm does not have any issues, the report that preupgradecheck creates is a good point-in-time snapshot of your farm that is very easy to create. Figure 5-1 shows how to run the preupgradecheck from a command line, and what the output looks like.

This report indicates that the user has an unsupported version of SQL Server, so an in-place upgrade is not possible. The last line of the report directs the user to view an HTM file. This file is where you can get in-depth information about your farm. Figure 5-2 shows the first page of this report.

FIGURE 5-1

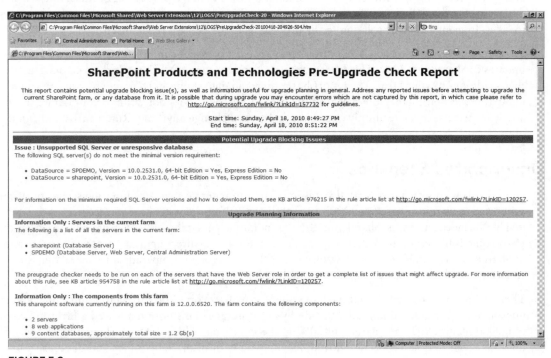

FIGURE 5-2

Here you can find more information about the upgrade blocking error found. Note the bottom of the report, which shows some of the components in the farm. This is one of the reasons this report is handy, even before you begin your upgrade. Here is a partial list of the problems preupgradecheck looks for:

➤ Farm is at service pack 2 or later

➤ Supported operating systems (Windows Server 2008 SP2 64-bit or Windows Server 2008 R2)

➤ Database schemas have not been modified

➤ Configuration database does not have any site orphans

➤ Content database does not have any data orphans

➤ Farm is not still in a gradual upgrade from SharePoint 2003

➤ Databases are read only

➤ Invalid entries in `web.config`

➤ Custom site definitions

➤ Large lists

➤ Views and content types that use CAML

Knowing what problems there are is great, but it can be a bit overwhelming if you run preupgradecheck and your screen fills up with red errors. Fortunately, the HTML report is full of links, and when it finds a problem it will direct you to a web page that describes the problem further, and offers ways to fix it. In many cases the solution to the problem is in the HTML report itself.

Preupgradecheck uses an XML definition file, so the list of issues can be updated with cumulative updates to SharePoint 2007. Third-party vendors can also supply XML to clear up errors caused by their additions to your farm. The report has a time and date stamp in its name, so you can run it as many times as you'd like. Note that running preupgradecheck does not write to your databases in any way. Because it is a read-only operation, it does not change anything. Run it early, and run it often.

Unsupported Scenarios

Now that you know what you can do, it is important to reiterate some unsupported scenarios. It's not supported to upgrade SharePoint 2007 to SharePoint 2010 if it doesn't have service pack 2 or later on it. That includes databases. SharePoint 2010 cannot attach a database that is from a farm earlier than SharePoint 2007 service pack 2. That also means there are no direct upgrades from previous versions of SharePoint, either. If you have a SharePoint 2003 farm, you must upgrade it to SharePoint 2007 service pack 2 before you can upgrade to SharePoint 2010.

There is one upgrade option that we had going from SharePoint 2003 to SharePoint 2007 that is missing now: the gradual upgrade, or side-by-side upgrade. This option allowed a farm to be running SharePoint 2003 and SharePoint 2007 at the same time. This allowed a slower, more controlled upgrade. That option has been removed, leaving you with in-place upgrades and database attach options.

Upgrade Best Practices

Before you get too far down the upgrade road, we should take a short detour to the backup and restore rest stop. Chapter 12 covers backups in SharePoint 2010, but if you're doing an upgrade, you will need good backups of your SharePoint 2007 environment as well. Nothing makes a grown man scream like a little girl as bad as realizing they don't have any backups — or even worse, realizing the backups you have cannot be restored. Any upgrades you do should be tested thoroughly in a test environment. Creating that test environment and populating it with data is a great way to test your SharePoint 2007 backups. Not only will this give you a great test environment that approximates your production environment, it also ensures that you have backups that will actually restore.

Now that we've covered the dos and the don'ts of upgrading, let's take a closer, more intimate, look at the upgrade methods and how to use them.

IN-PLACE UPGRADE

The most obvious path to upgrading SharePoint 2007 to SharePoint 2010 is an in-place upgrade. This method is the simplest, and boils down to clicking Next ⇨ Next ⇨ Finished. Tada! Congratulations, you have SharePoint 2010. Well, maybe it's not quite that easy, but that's the gist of it. When you do an in-place upgrade, you're installing SharePoint 2010 on the same hardware as your existing SharePoint 2007 farm, and for the most part everything stays the same. For example, URLs are the same for your users, settings are retained, custom code is still installed, customizations are still there, and application pools run as the same accounts. If you were to envision your "dream" SharePoint upgrade, this would be it.

Before you set this book down and try to do an in-place upgrade of your current SharePoint 2007 farm, however, there are also some cons. It's not all roses and kittens. Your current hardware and software must support SharePoint 2010 before you can do an in-place upgrade. That means all of your SharePoint 2007 servers have to be 64-bit Windows Server 2008 or Windows Server 2008 R2. Your SQL Server must also support SharePoint 2010 for your in-place upgrade to work. These software requirements are laid out in stunning detail in Chapter 3.

Another con to consider is downtime. While you are doing the in-place upgrade, your entire farm will be offline for the duration of the upgrade process. If you have multiple machines in your SharePoint 2007 farm, you need to successfully upgrade them all before any of your content is accessible. If the upgrade is not successful, your content will likely not be accessible until the upgrade finishes, depending on where it failed. In addition, when the in-place upgrade runs, it works serially on one machine. If you have multiple web applications and multiple content databases, they will be upgraded one at a time, even if you have multiple machines in your farm. This means that you cannot take advantage of all your hardware during upgrade and the rest of your machines in your farm are just standing around with their hands in their pockets. All of this leads to increased downtime.

Planning Your In-Place Upgrade

Because of the downtime issues, in-place upgrades are better suited for small environments. In larger environments, the downtime needed to do an in-place upgrade may be too long. In-place upgrades may also not be suited for environments with significant custom code or other customizations. That sounds contradictory. One of the benefits of an in-place upgrade is that the customizations in SharePoint 2007 are maintained. However, in order for your upgrade to be successful, your custom code must run in both SharePoint 2007 and SharePoint 2010. Steps have been taken by Microsoft to increase the possibility of this working, but it is not 100 percent reliable.

While the underlying DLL structure has changed dramatically between SharePoint 2007 and SharePoint 2010, Microsoft has put stubs into the DLLs to forward SharePoint 2007 style calls to the new SharePoint 2010 DLLs. This enables most SharePoint 2007 era code to run on a farm upgraded to SharePoint 2010. Of course, the code should be upgraded to use the correct SharePoint 2010 DLLs, but this helps get your environment up and running more quickly, as all of your custom code does not need to be reworked for SharePoint 2010 before you can upgrade.

The Feature framework has also been enhanced to ease your transition to SharePoint 2010 (see Chapter 13 for details on Features). It recognizes new settings in the `feature.xml` file that enable it to run different code for SharePoint 2007 or SharePoint 2010. Since SharePoint 2007 doesn't understand these entries, it happily ignores them. This enables you to update your Features while you're still running SharePoint 2007 so that when you upgrade to SharePoint 2010, your Feature is ready to go.

SharePoint 2010 looks for an `UpgradeActions` section in the `feature.xml` file. In this section, you can define versions of your feature, and how to handle upgrading from version to version. When you trigger a Feature upgrade in your farm, SharePoint 2010 checks the `feature.xml` file to determine the steps necessary to upgrade your Feature, at the four scopes: farm, web application, site collection, and site. While this is more of a topic for our developer friends, it's good to have a cursory knowledge of it for planning purposes.

Table 5-1 provides a list of common customizations in SharePoint 2007 and recommendations on how to deal with them when upgrading to SharePoint 2010.

TABLE 5-1: Common SharePoint 2007 Customizations

CUSTOMIZATION	GOOD CHOICE	BETTER CHOICE
Custom Web Parts	Probably work out of the box with SharePoint 2010	Test on sample server, plan to rewrite for SharePoint 2010
Custom event handlers	Probably work out of the box with SharePoint 2010	Test on sample server, plan to rewrite for SharePoint 2010
Third-party add-ins	Contact vender for information on SharePoint 2010 support	Contact vender for information on SharePoint 2010 support
Custom Site template	Create a site with the Custom Site template before upgrade	Recreate in SharePoint 2010, preferably as a Solution package and Feature
Custom site definition	Create UDF file for upgrade	Migrate to an out-of-the-box site template and deploy customizations as a Solution package and Feature

CUSTOMIZATION	GOOD CHOICE	BETTER CHOICE
Customized (unghosted) pages	Reset to site definition	Reset to site definition, and reapply customizations
Custom code or pages in /_layouts	Probably work out of the box with SharePoint 2010	Test on sample server, plan to rewrite for SharePoint 2010

If your SharePoint 2007 servers meet muster, and if your SQL Servers are compliant with SharePoint 2010, what will your in-place upgrade get you? As mentioned earlier, the appeal of an in-place upgrade is that your environment doesn't change. All of your users' bookmarks will continue to work. All of your web applications and site collections are there. If you were running Officer Server or Search Server, then a new SharePoint 2010 search environment will be created with all of your old settings, and you'll be able to use your SharePoint 2007 index file and property store until you can run your first full crawl.

Finally, any customizations you've made to your environment in terms of custom master pages, custom themes, and CSS will all be available in your upgraded farm via Visual Upgrade mode. Visual Upgrade is covered later in this chapter, but at a high level it enables SharePoint 2010 to render pages with the SharePoint 2007 master pages and styling. If an in-place upgrade will work in your environment, it does offer a very attractive option.

Performing the In-Place Upgrade

Executing an in-place upgrade is fairly painless after you have tested your environment and verified that it can be upgraded. You start it just like you would a regular install. First, run the prerequisite installer to get all the software prerequisites installed. Then start the SharePoint 2010 install.

1.   On the first screen of the setup, instead of asking if you want to do a Standalone or Server Farm install, you will see a screen like the one in Figure 5-3, indicating that a previous version of SharePoint has been detected and that if you continue it will be upgraded.

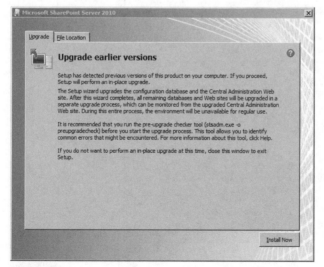

FIGURE 5-3

Click Install Now to continue the upgrade process.

2. Next, if you're upgrading MOSS to SharePoint Server, you'll need to enter your license key. Your SharePoint 2010 license key must match your SharePoint 2007 key. For instance, if your SharePoint 2007 farm is running a trial key, you will need to enter a trial key for SharePoint 2010. If your licenses don't match, you'll get an error like the one in Figure 5-4.

After you enter a license key that satisfies the installer, it starts installing the SharePoint 2010 bits. Figure 5-5 shows the installation progress bar.

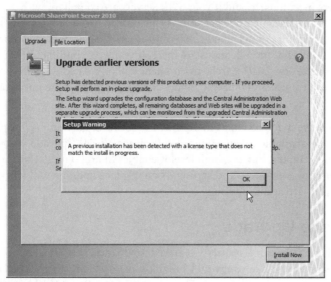

FIGURE 5-4

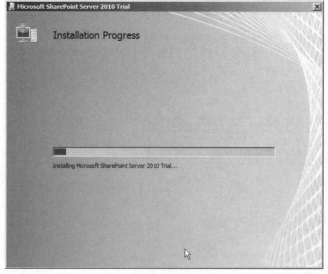

FIGURE 5-5

3. Just like a non-upgrade install, the first stage only lays down the SharePoint bits. After that part is finished, the SharePoint Products and Technologies Wizard, or PS Config for us lovers of brevity, will be started automatically to do the actual upgrade. Figure 5-6 shows the welcome screen when PS Config starts after the install.

FIGURE 5-6

For better or for worse, there isn't much to configure with in-place upgrades. The one important decision to make is whether upgraded content should be rendered as it was in SharePoint 2007 or with the new SharePoint 2010 interface. Figure 5-7 shows the dialog of options and explanations. The facility SharePoint 2010 uses to render content with the SharePoint 2007 interface is called Visual Upgrade. It is covered in more detail later in this chapter, as it pertains to both in-place upgrades and database attach upgrades. The default option is to preserve the SharePoint 2007 look and feel. You'll learn more about it later, but for most in-place upgrades, preserving the SharePoint 2007 look and feel is the best option. After you've selected which interface the content should use, SharePoint gets to the business of upgrading your content.

The steps it takes are in a very deliberate order. The most important objects are upgraded first, to give SharePoint a more solid footing should the upgrade fail and need to be restarted. The first step is to upgrade your configuration database. Once that is successfully done, the installer moves on to the Central Administration web application and upgrades it, including its content database. It then moves on to upgrading any settings that are specific to the server on which it's running. For instance, when you're running the upgrade on the server that is running search, the search components are upgraded at this stage.

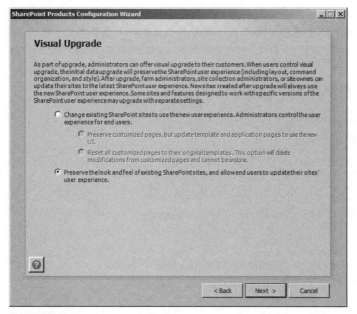

FIGURE 5-7

Once all that is done, SharePoint continues diligently down the road of upgrading your farm. The next stop on its trek is your web applications. Now that all the important groundwork is upgraded, it can move on to the fun stuff. The installer starts walking through the web applications in your farm. For each web application, it walks through and upgrades your site collections one at a time. If for some reason a site collection cannot be upgraded — for example, because it's based on a custom site definition that hasn't been dealt with — the installer will skip that site collection and move on to the rest. If that should happen, you can fix the issue and use the Windows PowerShell cmdlet `Upgrade-SPContentDatabase` to upgrade any objects in the content database that were not upgraded the first time around. This is just one way the in-place upgrade has improved since its last incarnation for upgrading SharePoint 2003 to SharePoint 2007. In the next section, you'll learn about the improvements in more detail.

Once all of your site collections are upgraded, or SharePoint has at least given it the old college try, the upgrade process finishes. If you have multiple servers in your farm, it's now time to run the installer and PS Config on the rest of your servers. Because the back end is fully upgraded at this point, the other members should upgrade quickly and smoothly.

If your current SharePoint 2007 farm is WSS, the preceding upgrade steps probably looked complete. If you are using MOSS, you probably wondered where your Shared Service Providers (SSPs) fit in. Because SSPs are gone in SharePoint 2010, their upgrade process is a little more involved. SSPs had two main components: databases and services. Each is upgraded a bit differently. After Central Admin has been upgraded but before your web applications are upgraded, the installer looks at its upgrade roadmap to see if there are any exit ramps for SSPs. If there are, the installer takes a quick detour over there and upgrades the SSPs and wires everything up for them. For each SSP that exists, the install cracks it open and creates the corresponding service applications. For each SSP in your SharePoint 2007 farm, your upgraded SharePoint 2010 farm will have the following service applications:

➤ Search Administration Web Service

➤ Search Service

➤ Application Registry

➤ Business Data Connectivity

➤ Excel Calculation Services

➤ State Service App

➤ Taxonomy

➤ User Profile

A picture is worth 1,000 words, so Figure 5-8 shows a MOSS Enterprise farm upgraded to SharePoint 2010. It is a list of the service applications that were created from the very cleverly named SSPs, SharedServices1 and SharedServices2.

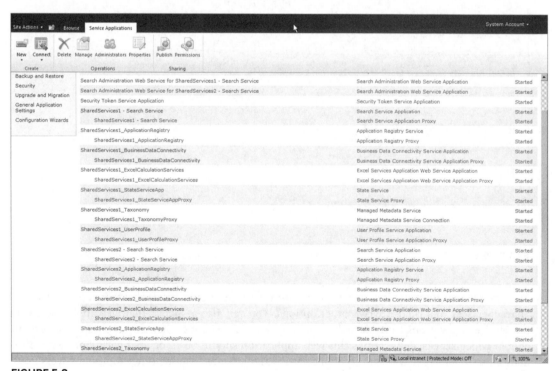

FIGURE 5-8

You can see how the SSP was broken up and how each old SSP was reborn as eight service applications. When the installer moves to the next step, where it upgrades the web applications, it will wire each web application up with the service applications that match the SSP it was using in SharePoint 2007. After the upgrade is finished, you can associate web applications to service applications from whichever legacy SSP you would like. You can also delete unnecessary service applications that were created during the upgrade process. For instance, you may not need two search service applications in SharePoint 2010. You can associate all of your web applications with one and delete the other. Figure 5-9 shows the service application associations for a web application associated with SharedService1 in SharePoint 2007.

FIGURE 5-9

You can see that the default associations are for the service applications that were created from SharedService1, but there are two other options. You can also associate that web application with the service applications from SharedService2, or you could choose the custom option and pick and choose which service applications this web application should be associated with. For more information, see Chapter 7, which is all about service applications. Among other topics, it covers how you can create your own service application proxy groups and edit the existing ones. These are valuable when you have done an upgrade with multiple SSPs and you want to clean up your service applications.

That covers how the SSP services are upgraded from SharePoint 2007 to SharePoint 2010, but we still have the matter of those pesky SSP databases to attend to. The good news is that these are straightforward, because not much upgrades. One of the problems with SharePoint 2007 was that most of the SSP content was stored in one database. With service applications in SharePoint 2010, that is no longer the case, so there is no direct upgrade path for the SSP database. The notable exception to that is the Search property storage database, which SharePoint 2010 can upgrade for its Search to use. This also means you can do searches in SharePoint 2010 before the Search service application has crawled your content. For farms with a lot of content, this is very convenient. Figure 5-10 shows the databases for the Search service application that was created from SharedService1.

Search Application Topology

Category	Server Name	Status
Admin		
Administration Component	SPDEMO	Online
Crawl - SPDEMO\SharedServices1 - Search Service_GathererDB_4859cbddaa744a9fbba2a2506cf0c096		
Crawl Component 0	SPDEMO	Online
Databases		
Administration Database : SharedServices1 - Search Service_AdminDB_de6083da84d24b47868a9270d8da9bba	SPDEMO	
Crawl Database : SharedServices1 - Search Service_GathererDB_4859cbddaa744a9fbba2a2506cf0c096	SPDEMO	
Property Database : SharedServices1_Search_DB	SPDEMO	
Index Partition - 0 - SPDEMO\SharedServices1_Search_DB		
Query Component 0	SPDEMO	Online

FIGURE 5-10

In the list of databases, you can see that one of them differs from the others. The administration database and the crawl database have GUIDs at the end of their names and include "Search Service." The property database is different, though: Its name is ShareServices1_Search_DB. The first two databases were created by the installer when it upgraded the SSP. The property store database is the SharePoint 2007 search database, so it has its old name. Chapter 14 covers Search inside and out, and explains the role each of these databases plays.

To manage SSPs in SharePoint 2007, each SSP had its own Admin site. Because service applications are managed in Central Administration now, these SSP Admin sites are unnecessary. The installer does not upgrade them because there is no corresponding SSP Admin site to upgrade them to. If you browse to one of your SharePoint 2007 SSP Admin sites after you upgrade to SharePoint 2010, you will be greeted by the friendly page shown in Figure 5-11.

Once you have made the BDC changes that the page suggests, it is safe to delete the legacy SSP Admin site. If it was on its own web application, then you can delete that as well.

FIGURE 5-11

In-Place Upgrade Improvements

If you have made it this far reading about in-place upgrades, one of two things is probably true: Either you never tried an in-place upgrade from SharePoint 2003 to SharePoint 2007 or you did and you are so shocked that someone is actually suggesting an in-place upgrade to SharePoint 2010 that you just had to read the rest so that you could mock it appropriately. Rest assured, the authors of this book did battle with in-place upgrades to SharePoint 2007 and there are very few marks in the "win" column. It was a pretty tough course, and for the most part it was one to be avoided. In most cases, users did gradual upgrades instead. As you learned earlier, that is no longer an option in SharePoint 2010. It's time to go back to the drawing board and give in-place upgrade another look.

The list of problems with the SharePoint 2007 in-place upgrade is long and well known. Fortunately, Microsoft took that list of problems, scratched out "Why SharePoint 2007 in-place upgrade is for the birds" at the top, and replaced it with "Things to do correctly in SharePoint 2010 in-place upgrade." There were two main issues with SharePoint 2007 in-place upgrades. One, it didn't take much to make it fail. Any number of timeouts could affect it on the SharePoint side or the SQL Server side. In addition, SQL servers ran out of drive space. One time, an office window was left open and a cool breeze crashed an in-place upgrade. It was very fragile; your environment had to be just right for the in-place upgrade to succeed. The other issue made the first one worse. If for any reason your upgrade failed (and there were many reasons it could), there was no way to salvage the upgrade. You couldn't free up drive space on your server, or close that office window and pick up where you left off. Although that made the decision about what to do next very easy, the bad news is that the answer was to recover everything from backups and start all over — not a very appealing option.

The in-place upgrade in SharePoint 2010 addresses both of those issues, in spades. To address the issue of failures, Microsoft has removed most of the timeouts that caused failures upgrading to SharePoint 2007. Long operations will no longer cause an upgrade to fail. Can we get an "Amen!"?

Other common failure points have also been addressed, and no longer cause upgrades to fail. Leave all your office windows open; SharePoint doesn't care.

Of course, that was only part of the problem; the other part was what to do after a failure. To address that, Microsoft has made the upgrade process restartable. If something does prevent your upgrade from completing successfully, it can be continued after you address the problem. Figure 5-12 shows an upgrade failing because the SQL Server does not meet SharePoint 2010's minimum requirements.

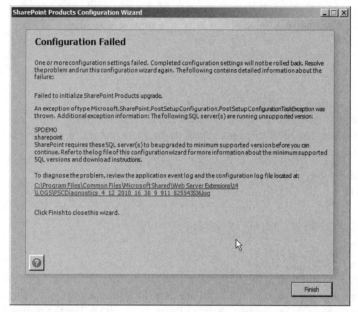

FIGURE 5-12

This error appeared after the SharePoint 2010 bits were installed and the configuration wizard had started to run (after everything was configured as shown earlier in Figure 5-7). After all that, the installer tries to start upgrading the configuration database but errors out because SQL Server doesn't support it. If this error had happened during an upgrade to SharePoint 2007, it would have been followed immediately by the thump of a head hitting a desk, followed by whimpering and later, loud sobbing. In this case, however, the fix was easy. First, the SQL Server instance was upgraded to a suitable version. Then the configuration wizard was run again. It just picked up where it left off, happily upgrading to SharePoint 2010 like nothing ever happened.

Because the failure occurred before the configuration wizard was able to complete, rerunning it was the obvious way to restart the upgrade process. If the upgrade fails after the configuration wizard finishes, or the configuration wizard finishes with errors, you can use the Windows PowerShell cmdlet `Upgrade-SPContentDatabase` to restart the upgrade on a content database. While you should certainly do everything you can to ensure a successful upgrade if something goes wrong, rest assured you have options to salvage all your work without resorting to backup tapes or begging deities for help.

Note also in Figure 5-12 a link to a log file to help you troubleshoot the error. The upgrade walks through every step the configuration wizard went through as it upgraded your farm, right up to the point it failed. To make troubleshooting easy, a new upgrade log is created for each upgrade session. This keeps the upgrade log files from becoming any more cumbersome than necessary. In addition, when an upgrade fails, a special upgrade log is created, with `-error` appended to it. This error log contains only things that went wrong during that specific upgrade session, enabling you to zero in on the information you need to find the problem. If for some reason the upgrade process is unable to write out the upgrade log (due to a drive being full or a permissions issue), then the upgrade won't start. This prevents any upgrading from happening without it being properly logged.

DATABASE ATTACH

The second method for upgrading content to SharePoint 2010 is the database attach method. In this method you already have a SharePoint 2010 farm installed and configured. To upgrade your content, you attach a SharePoint 2007 (service pack 2 or later) content database, which SharePoint 2010 will upgrade. Sounds easy, doesn't it?

The database attach method requires that you have separate hardware for your SharePoint 2010 farm; you cannot use your SharePoint 2007 hardware unless you remove SharePoint 2007 from all of the machines and install SharePoint 2010 on them. The database attach method also usually results in different URLs for your web applications, as the corresponding SharePoint 2007 farm is typically online at the same time.

The main advantage of the database attach method is control. When you do an in-place upgrade, you don't have much control. You cannot control the order in which the web applications or site collections are upgraded, and you can only upgrade one database at a time, which can be a waste of resources if your SharePoint boxes and SQL Server box can handle more. With the database attach method, you can attach multiple databases at the same time and upgrade them in tandem. The limiting factor is disk I/O on the SQL Server box. Before doing this in production, test your SQL Server box by testing database attach upgrading. Start by doing two databases at once and time the upgrade. Then redo the upgrades and add a third database. Once your SQL Server is saturated, you'll notice that your upgrade times will dramatically increase. Also keep an eye on the disk queue length on the SQL Server. That will let you know how well the disk subsystem is keeping up.

Because you are starting the database upgrades manually with this method, you also have control over the order in which databases are upgraded. With an in-place upgrade, you can't control which web applications are upgraded first, and they're all offline until the upgrade is finished. Conversely, using the database attach method, SharePoint 2010 is already online and rendering content. You have control over which databases you attach, and their content is available as soon as the database is attached. (Our recommendation is to always upgrade the content database that contains your resume first. You can never be too careful.)

There are some considerations when doing database attach upgrades. Because you are attaching content databases only, none of your customizations will be included. Any customizations will have to be manually moved to your new farm. For instance, if the sites stored in the content database require any third-party software to function, that software will have to be installed on the new SharePoint 2010 farm to which the database is attached.

The database attach method also means more work for the administrator and may require access to the SQL Servers if the backups are being moved from one SQL Server to another. You may also need to factor in time and network bandwidth if you have to shuffle databases around.

Another benefit of the database attach method is that it enables you to combine the content databases from multiple farms and consolidate your environment. You may have had multiple SharePoint 2007 farms for a variety of reasons: scale, isolation, hardware, and so on. SharePoint 2010 fixes a lot of those issues, so it might make sense to combine those separate SharePoint 2007 farms into one massive SharePoint 2010 farm. You can use the database attach method to do this before you upgrade all of your SharePoint 2007 farms to SharePoint 2010. Create the additional web applications on your SharePoint 2010 farm and attach the content databases to the appropriate web application.

If you can live with those considerations, then maybe a database attach upgrade will work for your environment. You can use either STSADM or Windows PowerShell to attach content databases to SharePoint 2010. This chapter focuses on Windows PowerShell.

 For plenty of information on Windows PowerShell, see Chapter 10.

The Windows PowerShell cmdlet you will use to attach to attach the database is `Mount-SPContentDatabase`. In your perusal of Windows PowerShell cmdlets, you may stumble across the `Upgrade-SPContentDatabase` cmdlet, but that cmdlet is not necessary when doing a database attach unless part of the database attach upgrade fails. The `Upgrade-SPContentDatabase` cmdlet retries or resumes a failed upgrade. To prevent that, you should check your content database for potential problems. There's a Windows PowerShell cmdlet for that, too: `Test-SPContentDatabase`. While it's not necessary to test a content database before you mount it, it is a good idea. When you run `Test-SPContentDatabase` you need to provide it with a database name and the URL of the web application to which you want to attach it. You need to supply the web application because solutions and features can be scoped at the web application level. A site collection in an attached database may work fine with one web application but not work at all with another. Figure 5-13 shows running `Test-SPContentDatbase` against a SharePoint 2007 database.

Note that you run `Test-SPContentDatabase` against a database that is in SQL but has not yet been attached to SharePoint. It's easy to fall into the trap of assuming that SharePoint can only deal with databases that it knows about. That's not the case here. As shown in Figure 5-13, `Test-SPContentDatabase` has found a couple of problems with the database. A couple of Web Parts that it references do not exist in the `http://upgrade` web application. Notice, though, that neither issue is enough to block the upgrade, as the `UpgradeBlocking` property for both errors is `False`. Both of those errors are something that we can live with and fix later if the need arises. We will use the `Mount-SPContentDatabase` cmdlet to add it to our farm, which will upgrade it automatically if it is from SharePoint 2007. Figure 5-14 shows the command to use to attach your SharePoint 2007 database to your SharePoint 2010 farm. Note the percentage, indicating the progress of the upgrade process. You can also watch the upgrade progress in Central Administration. Click

Upgrade and Migration in the left navigation pane and check Upgrade Status in the Upgrade and Migration page.

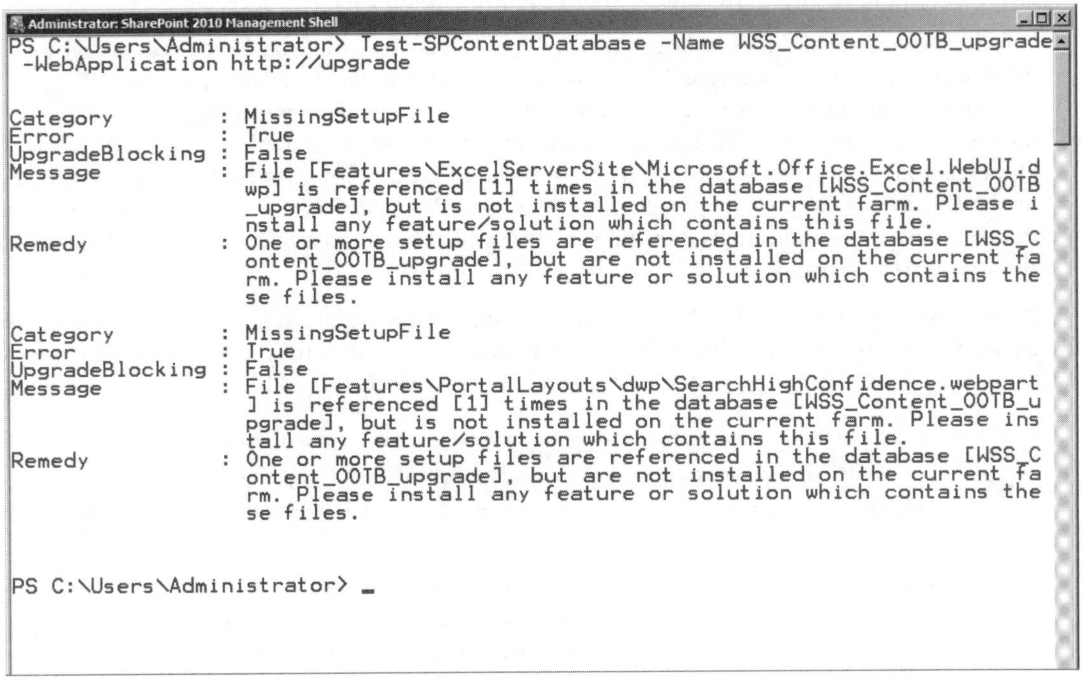

```
Administrator: SharePoint 2010 Management Shell                                    _ □ ×
PS C:\Users\Administrator> Test-SPContentDatabase -Name WSS_Content_OOTB_upgrade
 -WebApplication http://upgrade

Category         : MissingSetupFile
Error            : True
UpgradeBlocking  : False
Message          : File [Features\ExcelServerSite\Microsoft.Office.Excel.WebUI.d
                   wp] is referenced [1] times in the database [WSS_Content_OOTB
                   _upgrade], but is not installed on the current farm. Please i
                   nstall any feature/solution which contains this file.
Remedy           : One or more setup files are referenced in the database [WSS_C
                   ontent_OOTB_upgrade], but are not installed on the current fa
                   rm. Please install any feature or solution which contains the
                   se files.

Category         : MissingSetupFile
Error            : True
UpgradeBlocking  : False
Message          : File [Features\PortalLayouts\dwp\SearchHighConfidence.webpart
                   ] is referenced [1] times in the database [WSS_Content_OOTB_u
                   pgrade], but is not installed on the current farm. Please ins
                   tall any feature/solution which contains this file.
Remedy           : One or more setup files are referenced in the database [WSS_C
                   ontent_OOTB_upgrade], but are not installed on the current fa
                   rm. Please install any feature or solution which contains the
                   se files.


PS C:\Users\Administrator> _
```

FIGURE 5-13

```
Administrator: SharePoint 2010 Management Shell                                    _ □ ×
PS C:\Users\Administrator> Mount-SPContentDatabase -Name WSS_Content_OOTB_upgrad
e -WebApplication http://upgrade
29.06%_
```

FIGURE 5-14

We mentioned earlier that this can also be done with STSADM. STSADM is old and kind of dusty, and we don't recommend using it; but if you lose a dare and need to attach a SharePoint 2007 database to a SharePoint 2010 farm with STSADM, you can use the command STSADM -o addcontentdb to do it. If you wanted to use STSADM to replace the Windows PowerShell command in Figure 5-14, you would use this:

```
Stsadm -o addcontentdb -url http://upgrade -databasename WSS_Content_OOTB_upgrade
```

Figure 5-15 shows the finished product. Even though Test-SPContentDatabase indicated that errors would occur with the upgrade, SharePoint 2010 upgraded it anyway, enabling you to browse the site collection in that content database.

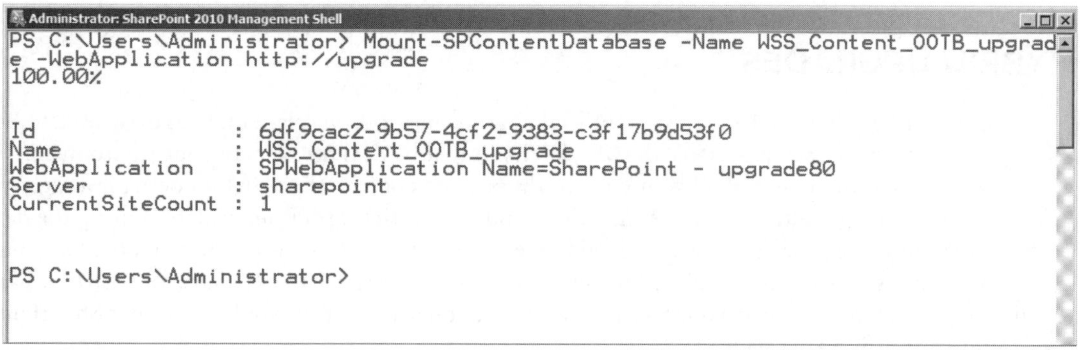

```
Administrator: SharePoint 2010 Management Shell                                    _ □ ×
PS C:\Users\Administrator> Mount-SPContentDatabase -Name WSS_Content_00TB_upgrad
e -WebApplication http://upgrade
100.00%


Id                  : 6df9cac2-9b57-4cf2-9383-c3f17b9d53f0
Name                : WSS_Content_00TB_upgrade
WebApplication      : SPWebApplication Name=SharePoint - upgrade80
Server              : sharepoint
CurrentSiteCount    : 1


PS C:\Users\Administrator>
```

FIGURE 5-15

You can use the Get-SPSite cmdlet, as shown in Figure 5-16, to see what site collections you have just added to your farm with your upgraded database.

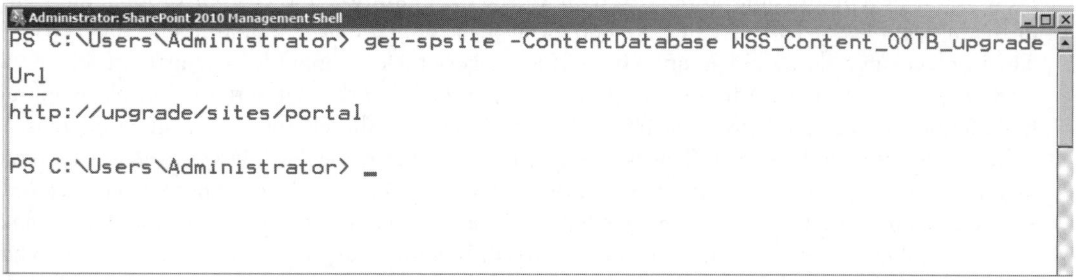

```
Administrator: SharePoint 2010 Management Shell                                    _ □ ×
PS C:\Users\Administrator> get-spsite -ContentDatabase WSS_Content_00TB_upgrade

Url
---
http://upgrade/sites/portal

PS C:\Users\Administrator> _
```

FIGURE 5-16

As mentioned before, one of the big benefits of the database attach method is that you can attach multiple databases at one time. To do this, open multiple SharePoint Management Shell windows and run the Mount-SPContentDatabase command in them.

When you use Mount-SPContentDatabase to upgrade databases, you will notice that the content looks like it did in SharePoint 2007. This is by design. It demonstrates Visual Upgrade, functionality that Microsoft created to ease the transition to SharePoint 2010. It is covered in more detail later in this chapter. If you want your content rendered with the SharePoint 2010 interface, add the -UpdateUserExperience parameter to your Mount-SPContentDatabase command.

This section has spent a lot of time covering attaching content databases because we think that is what the majority of people will do, but content databases are not the only SharePoint 2007 databases that can be attached to SharePoint 2010. Project Server 2007 databases can also be attached to a SharePoint 2010 farm that is running Project Server 2010. Project Server 2007 did not support customizations, so attaching those databases is pretty straightforward.

A SharePoint 2007 SSP can also be attached to a SharePoint 2010 farm. Not all of it can be used by SharePoint 2010 because of the change in architecture, but SharePoint 2010 can take a SharePoint 2007 SSP database and use it as a Profile Services database.

HYBRID UPGRADES

In this chapter we have covered the two official upgrade methods: in-place and database attach. Both work well, but they each have some drawbacks that might be deal breakers in your environment. The in-place upgrade maintains all of your customizations and configuration, but it doesn't leverage your hardware by doing multiple databases at a time, and your entire farm is unavailable during the duration of the upgrade. The database attach addresses those issues but requires you to redo all of your customizations and settings, and will likely require extra hardware to get SharePoint 2010 up and running on before you move your SharePoint 2007 databases over. It would seem that SharePoint administrators just can't win … .

What if we told you that you can have your cake and eat it too? Using a combination of the in-place upgrade and the database attach, you can get the best of both worlds. To use the hybrid method, simply detach all of the content web application content databases from your SharePoint 2007 farm. Don't get carried away and detach your central admin content database — leave that one attached. Now you have a SharePoint 2007 farm with all the configuration and customizations, but none of the big databases. The next step is to do an in-place upgrade of that SharePoint 2007 farm. The in-place upgrade should go quickly, as there is very little to upgrade. The infrastructure will be upgraded and Central Administration will be upgraded, but that's it. After the in-place upgrade has completed successfully, you finish it up by attaching your SharePoint 2007 content databases to your new SharePoint 2010 farm. This is where you get to leverage the flexibility of the database attach method. You can attach the databases in the order in which you want the content to come back online. In addition, because the farm was upgraded in-place, it is accessible. As soon as the database is attached and upgraded, the content can be browsed. If your hardware can support it, you also have the option to attach multiple databases. In other words, the hybrid method has all the benefits of the in-place upgrade with the flexibility of the database attach method. Looks like this book just paid for itself.

As if that were not enough, the hybrid method offers yet another option. If you have another SharePoint 2010 farm already standing, it could upgrade your SharePoint 2007 databases while the in-place upgrade is running. Content databases are portable, so while your production farm is doing the in-place upgrade, or even while it is attaching your content databases, you could have another SharePoint 2010 farm upgrading your databases in tandem. When they are upgraded in the test SharePoint 2010 farm, simply detach them and reattach them to your production farm. Because they have already been upgraded, the hard work is finished and they will be online in a matter of seconds. The hybrid approach has great potential; I think it's going to go places.

DATABASE ATTACH WITH AAM REDIRECT

If your SharePoint 2007 farm has a lot of content and a lot of customizations, none of the options talked about already may work for you. An in-place won't work because it will take too long. A database attach won't work because it would be too much work and too costly to rebuild all of your customizations and get extra hardware. Even the hybrid won't work because of the amount of time it will take to upgrade all of your databases. What's a large SharePoint 2007 farm to do?

There is one final tool in the SharePoint 2010 upgrade toolbox, the database attach with Alternate Access Mapping (AAM) redirect upgrade method. Like it sounds, this is basically the database attach method, but with a twist. You start the same way, with a SharePoint 2010 installation in tandem with your SharePoint 2007 farm. You end the same way, by detaching your SharePoint 2007 content databases and attaching them to your SharePoint 2010 farm. There's an extra step in the middle, though, and that's where all the magic occurs. For our example, our SharePoint 2007 farm has a web application at `http://portal.contoso.com`, where all of our content resides. We give that web application a second AAM for `http://oldportal.contoso.com`. When we create our SharePoint 2010 farm, we also give it a web application at `http://portal.contoso.com`. However, when we create that web application, we don't do it in Central Administration, we do it with STSADM and add an extra parameter, `redirectionurl`. It would look like this:

```
stsadm -o addzoneurl -url http://portal.contoso.com -zonemappedurl
http://portal.contoso.com -urlzone default -redirectionurl
http://oldportal.contoso.com
```

That's the magic. Now, when SharePoint 2010 gets a request for a page on a site collection that it can't find on the `http://portal.contoso.com` web application, it sends the browser an HTTP 302 redirect to the same site collection but at `http://oldportal.contoso.com`. This sends requests to the SharePoint 2007 farm where the content exists. Then when you move a SharePoint 2007 content database to SharePoint 2010, SharePoint 2010 no longer redirects the site collections in that content database to SharePoint 2007. This enables you to upgrade your SharePoint 2007 farm over the course of days or weeks, as your content is always online in either SharePoint 2007 or SharePoint 2010. Once all of your SharePoint 2007 content databases have been attached to your shiny new SharePoint 2010 farm, you can retire your SharePoint 2007 farm.

The redirect works well for web browsers, as they understand HTTP 302 redirects. Office applications, however, aren't quite so understanding. It's unlikely that users will have shortcuts directly to a document, but it is possible. Also keep in mind that this is scoped at the site collection level. When a request comes in to a SharePoint 2010 web application with a redirection URL, SharePoint 2010 checks its list of site collections for that web application to see if there is a match. If there is, SharePoint 2010 attempts to render the content. If not, SharePoint 2010 sends the browser the HTTP 302 redirect. If SharePoint 2010 has the site collection but not the specific web or page in the request, the user will get a much less friendly HTTP 404 error.

OTHER UPGRADE OPTIONS

So far, this chapter has covered how to get your SharePoint 2007 content into SharePoint 2010. There are a couple of other techniques that can be used in conjunction with your upgrade to make things smoother for your end users. In the remainder of the chapter, we cover how to use Visual Upgrade to slowly introduce SharePoint 2010 to your users. We also cover some techniques you can use to minimize the downtime your users experience while you are upgrading.

Visual Upgrade

To help ease the upgrade to SharePoint 2010, Microsoft added a new feature, Visual Upgrade. Visual Upgrade enables the rendering of content using the SharePoint 2007 master pages and CSS files in SharePoint 2010. This enables you to separate the binary upgrade to SharePoint 2010 from the interface. You can upgrade your back end to SharePoint 2010 without having all of your SharePoint 2007 customizations ready for SharePoint 2010. While your content is in SharePoint 2010 it will look like SharePoint 2007 and it will be able to take advantage of your SharePoint 2007 master pages and CSS. This is important, as SharePoint 2007 master pages and CSS files will not upgrade to SharePoint 2010. They aren't upgraded if you do an in-place upgrade, and they aren't upgraded if you do a database attach. The interfaces of the two versions of SharePoint are different enough that the elements of the master pages and CSS don't map easily. Instead of doing the upgrade poorly, SharePoint doesn't do it at all.

When doing any of the upgrade methods described earlier, the default is always to render the content in the SharePoint 2007 style. This demonstrates one of the philosophies Microsoft followed when designing the upgrade experience, "Do no harm." If you don't understand what Visual Upgrade is and you choose the default options, your content will upgrade and render the way that it always has. No harm has been done. After the upgrade is finished, you can choose the SharePoint 2010 interface when you're ready for it. Earlier, in the discussion of in-place upgrades, you saw in Figure 5-7 where you are offered the choice. The default value is to preserve the look and feel of SharePoint 2007. When upgrading with a database attach, the site collections will maintain the SharePoint 2007 interface unless you specify an interface upgrade with the -UpdateUserExperience parameter. No matter how you get content into SharePoint 2010, you need to deliberately choose the new interface.

Since SharePoint has done everything in its power to keep you from having the SharePoint 2010 interface, how do you get it? You have a few choices. The easiest way is with your browser, in the site itself. Figure 5-17 shows a portal site that was upgraded. It has the SharePoint 2007 interface. In the Site Actions drop-down menu is a new entry, Visual Upgrade. This will be available to site collection administrators.

If you click this option, you'll be taken to the Title, Description and Icon page in Site Settings. At the bottom of the page are the Visual Upgrade settings, as shown in Figure 5-18.

There are three options. The first, Use the previous user interface, is the SharePoint 2007 UI. The second option, Preview the updated user interface, uses the SharePoint 2010 interface, but it leaves the Visual Upgrade option in Site Actions in case you want to switch back. It's for site collection administrators with commitment issues. The final option, Update the user interface, uses the SharePoint 2010 interface and removes the Visual Upgrade setting from Site Actions. This is the option to use if you are sure you will no longer need the SharePoint 2007 interface. You can switch back afterward using Windows PowerShell if necessary.

Figure 5-19 shows the same site in SharePoint 2010 Preview mode. The Visual Upgrade option is still present in the Site Actions menu so you can switch back to SharePoint 2007 UI, or commit to the SharePoint 2010 UI.

FIGURE 5-17

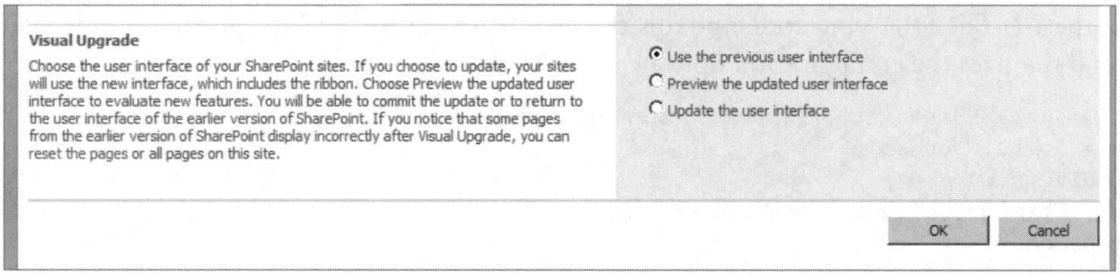

FIGURE 5-18

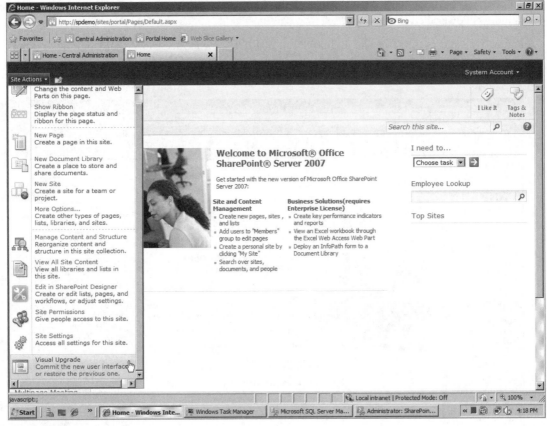

FIGURE 5-19

Once you choose Update the user interface from the Visual Upgrade page, that option is removed from Site Actions. Again, this is scoped at the web level, so that setting must be changed for each web that is upgraded.

Changing the Visual Upgrade setting for all the webs could be cumbersome if there are a lot of them. Fortunately, you can use Windows PowerShell to do this more efficiently. Each web has two settings that need to be changed: which version of the UI to use, and whether the Visual Upgrade setting is enabled in the UI. The following code updates the web from Figure 5-17 to the SharePoint 2010 interface and removes the configuration option:

Available for download on Wrox.com

```
$site = Get-SPSite http://spdemo/sites/portal
$web = $site.RootWeb
$web.UIVersion = 4
$web.UIVersionConfigurationEnabled = $false
$web.Update()
```

Code file Chapter05_code.txt

That works well for one or two webs, but it could be slow going for a few hundred webs. One of the benefits of Windows PowerShell is its ability to loop through objects. The following code will loop through all of the site collections in a content database, then loop through all of the webs in those site collections, and set them all to the SharePoint 2010 interface and turn off the Visual Upgrade setting:

```
$db = Get-SPContentDatabase WSS_Content_OOTB_upgrade
$db.Sites | Get-SPWeb -limit all | ForEach-Object {$_.UIversion = 4;
$_.UIVersionConfigurationEnabled = $false; $_.update()}
```

If you want a quick report showing which interface each web in a site collection is using, you can use the following code:

```
$site = Get-SPSite http://spdemo/sites/portal
$site | Get-SPWeb -limit all | sort-object uiversion -desc | select url, uiversion
```

The output should look something like Figure 5-20.

FIGURE 5-20

This makes it easy to discover which webs need to be upgraded. It could be expanded to run across the entire farm if a larger report were needed. Be sure to test out Visual Upgrade when planning your farm upgrade; it provides tremendous flexibility and eases the upgrade for the end users.

Mitigating Downtime with Read-Only Databases

No one likes downtime, and SharePoint users are no different. Sadly, there is no such thing as a "no downtime upgrade." However, using some of the techniques in this chapter, you can control and minimize the downtime you have to experience.

Earlier in this chapter we covered the database attach with AAM redirect upgrade option. This is a great way to control downtime, as you have both farms (SharePoint 2007 and SharePoint 2010) online at the same time. When we discussed the hybrid method, we mentioned another downtime mitigation technique: upgrading your databases on multiple farms at the same time, and then attaching them quickly to your production SharePoint 2010 farm. These both work well, but your SharePoint 2007 content has to be offline during the duration of the upgrade. You don't want users changing content in SharePoint 2007 while you're upgrading the database.

We have one more trick up our sleeves to help minimize downtime. Behold, the read-only database! Beginning with service pack 2 for SharePoint 2007, SharePoint can now gracefully handle a content database being set to read-only in SQL Server. If the database is read-only, SharePoint will render its content, but not allow any changes. If you couple that with the other techniques, you shorten the amount of time SharePoint 2007 content is unavailable while upgrades are happening. In the database attach with AAM redirect method, you would set the content database to read-only and copy it over to SharePoint 2010 to be upgraded. Once it's upgraded in SharePoint 2010, simply detach it in SharePoint 2007.

This technique could even be used with an in-place upgrade. In that case, you would need to stand up a temporary SharePoint 2007 farm to host the read-only content while the production farm is being upgraded. It's a little extra work, but if your environment needs uptime it's worth considering.

PATCHING SHAREPOINT 2010

It seems almost anticlimactic to cover patching after covering all the great improvements that have been made to upgrade, but since we promised it in the Introduction it only seems fair to follow through.

Patching SharePoint 2007 wasn't a bad experience, as long as your farm was exactly one server and didn't have much content. As soon as you added that second machine, or started getting a few GBs of content, things got scary in a hurry. *Patching*, at its most basic level is simply an in-place upgrade. The upgrading that was covered earlier in the chapter is referred to as a *version-to-version* or a *v2v* upgrade, since we are upgrading from the SharePoint 2007 version to the SharePoint 2010 version. Patching is referred to as a *build-to-build* or *b2b* upgrade, as it is only upgrading to a newer build of the same version. Under the covers though, they're very similar. Not identical twins, but maybe fraternal twins.

We've already covered the shortcomings of the 2007 in-place upgrade, and two of those were of particular concern when patching. The patching process ran serially and could take a long time with large content databases. There was no way around that. Second, if the patch failed there was no way to resume. It was time to dust off those backup tapes and order some pizza. Both of those problems and a whole lot more get addressed in the SharePoint 2010 patching story.

One of the most liberating improvements in patching with SharePoint 2010 is that the binaries on your farm can be at a newer version than the databases those binaries are using, if both builds are in the same compatibility range. The compatibility ranges should be between service packs, meaning that any database that is SharePoint 2010 SP1 or higher should be able to be rendered by binaries that are at the same build or later, but before SP2. This gives you the freedom to upgrade your binaries without immediately upgrading your databases at the same time. Walking through all your databases and upgrading them is the most time intensive part of patching, so being able to postpone that is a huge advantage. You'll be able patch the binaries running on your servers quickly and take advantage of any fixes or security updates without having to incur the downtime penalty of upgrading your databases too. You can postpone the lengthy database upgrade part to a more convenient time, like over the weekend. Also, since the binary upgrade isn't coupled to the database upgrade, you can do the database upgrades in waves instead of all at once. This is especially handy if you have user bases in different time zones. While you shouldn't plan on leaving your farm in this condition for weeks or months, you can safely do it for a few days.

If you do decide to upgrade your content databases, you can do it manually with Windows PowerShell using the `Upgrade-SPContentDatabase` cmdlet. Provide `Upgrade-SPContentDatabase` with the name of the content database you want upgraded and it's off. Like `Mount-SPContentDatabase`, you can run multiple copies of this at once to make the upgrades go more quickly if your hardware can handle it. When you get around to finalizing your patch installation with the configuration wizard, any content databases that are not already upgraded will get upgraded, along with any service application databases that need to be upgraded.

Not only can your databases be out of sync with the binaries installed on your server, but the servers themselves can be at different build levels as well. This is truly an advanced move, however, and should only be used when necessary by trained professionals. If you do choose to patch your servers individually it's recommended that you do tiers of them at a time. For example, if you have several servers running the Search component, try to keep their patch level in sync. If you have multiple web front ends (WFEs), keep them in sync. If you want to improve uptime by patching your WFEs in waves, then make sure all the WFEs that are accepting end user traffic are at the same patch level. This means you can't stagger them in and out of your load balancer as you patch. For instance, if you have four WFEs you can pull two of them out and patch them while two stay in. Before you add the two patched WFEs back into rotation, pull out the two unpatched WFEs. That way all the WFEs serving pages to end users are at the same patch level at all times. It won't be the end of the world if they're mismatched, dogs and cats won't be living together or anything, but it will likely result in an inconsistent or confusing experience for the end users. That will mean angry phone calls to you, and none of us wants that.

After all the servers in your farm have a patch installed, you need to run the configuration wizard on them all to finalize it. If you try to be sneaky and run the configuration wizard before all of the servers in your farm are at the same patch level, you'll get a very stern talking to from it while it glowers at you over its glasses. It will tell you which servers are out of sync and wait patiently for you to get your act together and install the patch on them before it proceeds. As with SharePoint 2007, you do have to run the configuration wizard on each and every server in your farm. Unlike SharePoint 2007, the steps are very fluid. It doesn't matter in what order you run it on the servers and there is no coordination needed. In SharePoint 2007, the configuration wizard would stop at various stages while it was running, and advise you to go to other servers in your farm and complete steps. In SharePoint 2010, the configuration wizard handles that all itself by writing entries in the Config DB file as different machines complete different tasks. After the configuration wizard is running on all of your servers, you can feel free to go out and have a nice dinner, followed by a very fattening dessert. The configuration wizard will finish the farm upgrade all on its own and start serving out pages without any human intervention. It will upgrade any content databases you have not already upgraded with `Upgrade-SPContentDatabase` and it will upgrade any other databases that need to be upgraded. When you get back from dinner, click OK a couple of times and your farm is officially patched.

SUMMARY

The road from SharePoint 2007 to SharePoint 2010 is not a complicated one. There are several paths you can take, depending on what's best for your environment. If you have customizations you want to keep, you can do an in-place upgrade. If you want more control over your upgrade, the database attach method might be appropriate for you. If you have complex needs, or the desire to flex your SharePoint muscle, you can choose one of the advanced methods. Once you figure out which method you're going to use, you have other options to help guide your SharePoint 2007 farm easily toward SharePoint 2010 without upsetting your users too much. Upgrading to SharePoint 2010 will be an adventure, for sure, but it will be a good one, and well worth it.

Using the New Central Administration

WHAT'S IN THIS CHAPTER?

➤ Using the Farm Configuration Wizard

➤ Setting up Managed Accounts

➤ Finding your way around the new and improved interface

➤ Using the Ribbon in Central Administration

➤ Backing up and restoring your site with Central Administration

Now that you've laid down the SharePoint bits and finished running through the SharePoint Configuration Wizard, you get your first taste of using SharePoint 2010 when Central Administration launches.

This chapter mainly serves as a general overview of Central Administration. Many topics require more than just a few pages to adequately cover; in fact, some topics actually have entire chapters dedicated to them. In this chapter we'll hit the major highlights of Central Administration, and point you to different areas in this book that cover certain topics in more detail.

A QUICK OVERVIEW OF THE NEW CENTRAL ADMINISTRATION INTERFACE

If you could navigate Central Administration in SharePoint 2007 with your eyes closed, you might be in for a bit of a shock when you first look at Central Administration in SharePoint 2010. One of the first things you will notice about the new Central Administration is that it looks nothing like the Central Administration in SharePoint 2007 that we came to know and love. In SharePoint 2010, all tasks and links are divided into one of eight categories. You can see these categories on the home page of Central Administration, both in the Quick Launch and in the body, as shown in Figure 6-1. Underneath each category header are several links, which enable you to access some of the more frequently used pages in each category, right from the home page. Clicking the headings of each category will take you to that category's page, which features additional subcategories and links related to the category. Although this new layout is vastly different from SharePoint 2007's Central Administration, it may also seem somewhat familiar to you: the new categorical approach is visually and structurally similar to the look and feel of the Control Panel in Windows Vista and Windows 7.

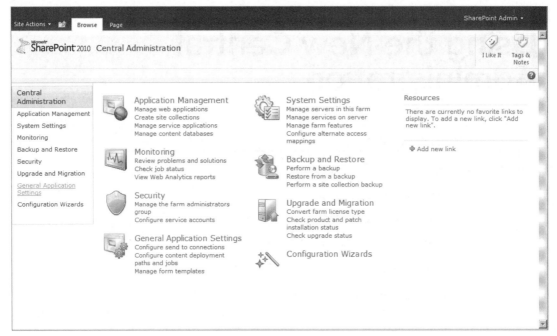

FIGURE 6-1

As you click through some of the links in the various pages, you will encounter several pages that look nearly identical to their SharePoint 2007 counterparts. In many instances, how you configure certain settings hasn't changed a bit, only the way they are accessed.

Aside from the reorganized settings, Central Administration also makes use of another major change to the SharePoint platform: the Ribbon. The Ribbon interface (also known as the Fluent UI) was introduced with the Office 2007 suite of clients. In the Office clients, the Ribbon was used to make more tasks available to the user at one time, while logically grouping them together. In SharePoint 2010, this same idea is carried over. The Ribbon interface is designed to make accessing settings and performing tasks easier for both administrators and users.

 Using the Ribbon interface from a user perspective is covered in Chapter 2.

The Ribbon isn't used in Central Administration as extensively as it is in the normal user interface, but understanding how it works will make your life easier. This chapter covers some of the basics of the Ribbon as it pertains to Central Administration.

As you start using Central Administration, you'll notice that its structure is much "flatter" than SharePoint 2007. By using the categorical approach to organizing the content in Central Administration, tasks and settings can usually be accessed in fewer clicks than it used to take in SharePoint 2007. Because the links are divided among eight categories, many administrators will likely discover that finding links is much quicker, as there is less guesswork as to where a link would logically be located.

FIRST THINGS FIRST

You just finished up the install and are greeted by Central Administration. This section gives you an overview of the steps taken the first time you access Central Administration post install. (If the install has already been done and you are just accessing the server for the first time you can skip this section and jump forward a page or two to the "Managed Accounts" section.)

Central Administration fires up for the first time immediately after the SharePoint Configuration Wizard finishes its tasks. A pop-up window opens first, and you'll be asked if you'd like to participate in the Customer Experience Improvement Program (CEIP) to make SharePoint better. Make your selection and click OK to close the pop-up. Central Administration offers to help you through the initial setup process right off the bat by asking if you'd like to run through the Farm Configuration Wizard (see Figure 6-2). You can choose to run through the wizard now or run it later if you wish. Generally, you'll probably want to run through the wizard, as it enables you to provision a default set of service applications and create a web application to start exploring SharePoint 2010. It's pretty short — only a couple of options and questions and you'll be ready to go. Of course, you can also configure the farm manually and skip the wizard altogether if you wish. The wizard simply provides a one-stop-shop for getting up and running with SharePoint 2010. Chapter 7 covers the manual process for provisioning service applications.

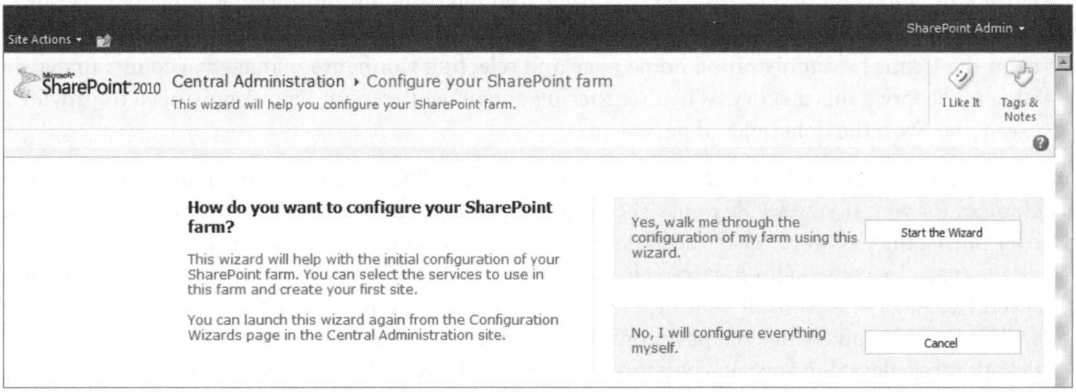

FIGURE 6-2

If you accidentally close the Central Administration window, or are accessing the server for the first time and are looking for the site, you can easily open it from the Start menu. Simply click Start ➪ All Programs ➪ Microsoft SharePoint Products ➪ SharePoint 2010 Central Administration.

The Farm Configuration Wizard

If you decide to walk through the Farm Configuration Wizard, select the option to Walk me through the settings using this configuration wizard … and click Next. If you chose to skip the Farm Configuration Wizard, you can always run it later from the Central Administration home page.

The first screen in the Farm Configuration Wizard lets you choose or create a *managed account* (see the following section) that will be used as the service account. This service account will run the service applications that you select to have the wizard create. You can set up additional instances of the service applications with any account you choose later as well.

Below the Service Account section, you'll see that you can choose which service applications will be provisioned by the wizard for the farm. Note that nearly all the services are checked for you. If you know you aren't going to be using certain services, you can deselect them. It's easy to create new service applications later and add them to the default set, so don't get too hung up on choosing the right set of services out of the gate.

Managed Accounts

Managed accounts are a brand new concept in SharePoint 2010. They are designed to give administrators more control over the domain accounts that are used to run the various components of SharePoint. When an account is registered with SharePoint, administrators can maintain the account from within SharePoint, without worrying about how a change, such as a password change, will affect the SharePoint farm.

When a domain account is registered with SharePoint as a managed account, it can be used to run various components of the farm, such as application pools or service applications. The account used to install SharePoint is automatically registered as a managed account. When you run the Farm Configuration Wizard for the first time, you have the option to register as many service accounts as you will need. You can also add more accounts later by clicking the Security category from the Central Administration home page and selecting Configure managed accounts under the General Security subcategory. When registering a managed account, you simply need to provide the username (with the domain) and password.

Next, you can configure whether you'd like to have SharePoint automatically handle the password changes for you. If you decide to use the automatic password change option, SharePoint will take over setting the password for the account in Active Directory for as long as the account is registered as a managed account. This is extremely useful because it completely removes the burden of managing several account passwords. If your organization also enforces a password change policy, SharePoint will detect this and change the password a set number of days before the expiry of the policy. The default is two days, but you can configure the number of days beforehand that SharePoint will change the password. You can also have SharePoint notify a user or group of users via e-mail before the password is changed by checking the option to start notifying by e-mail. Below this checkbox is the scheduler for setting when and how often the password will be changed. You can have the password changed automatically every week, specifying the days and times during which the change can occur; or you can have the password change monthly, choosing a day and time range during which the password can be changed, or choosing a specific day and time, such as the fourth Tuesday at 3:00 a.m. All of the preceding options are shown in Figure 6-3.

Account Registration

Service accounts are used by various farm components to operate. The account password can be set to automatically change on a schedule and before any scheduled Active Directory enforced password change event.

Enter the service account credentials.

Service account credentials
User name

```
ntoso\sp_PortalAppPool
```

Password

```
••••••••••••
```

Automatic Password Change

Automatic password change enables SharePoint to automatically generate new strong passwords on a schedule you set. Select the Enable automatic password change checkbox to allow SharePoint to manage the password for the selected account.

If an account policy based expiry date is detected for the account, and the expiry will occur before the scheduled date and time, the password will be changed on a configured number of days before the expiry date at the regularly scheduled time.

Choose to enable e-mail notifications in order to have the system generate warning notifications about upcoming password change events.

Specify a time and schedule for the system to automatically change the password.

☑ Enable automatic password change
  If password expiry policy is detected, change password
  [2] days before expiry policy is enforced
☑ Start notifying by e-mail
  [5] days before password change
○ Weekly   ⦿ By date: starting every month between
⦿ Monthly   [2 AM ▼] [00 ▼] on the [7th ▼]
  and no later than
  [3 AM ▼] [00 ▼] on the [7th ▼]
○ By day: starting every month
  [12 AM ▼] [00 ▼] on the [first ▼] [Sunday ▼]

FIGURE 6-3

You don't have to allow SharePoint to change the passwords automatically; you can still easily manage password changes from within Central Administration now, knowing that changing the password on a managed account will go smoothly. (In SharePoint 2007, administrators often ran into issues when changing passwords on accounts SharePoint relied on, but this is no longer a problem.) From the Managed Accounts page, you can click the Edit button next to the account whose password you'd like to set. From this screen, you can change the password by checking the box next to Change password now, and either have SharePoint automatically generate a strong password, use a new password, or use an existing password.

Accounts can also be removed from SharePoint as long as they are not associated with any farm services (see Chapter 7 for more on service applications). In that case, you can click the X in the Remove column of the Managed Account list. If SharePoint has been managing the password for this account, you will not know what it is, but fortunately you have the option to change the password as you disassociate the account from SharePoint. You can check the box to change the password on the Remove Managed Account screen, and specify a new password for the account.

An additional consideration: If someone goes into AD directly and changes the password for the account without telling SharePoint, your managed accounts will not work. SharePoint needs to know the account's password to use it. If you need to change the password it is best to use the preceding option of changing the password from SharePoint and not using an AD tool.

CENTRAL ADMINISTRATION CATEGORIES

From the Central Administration home page, you'll notice that some of the most commonly used actions are immediately available under the heading for each category. For instance, you can start creating site collections in a single click from the home page with the link Create site collections under the Application Management header. Similarly, you can quickly start a backup by clicking the Perform a backup link under the Backup and Restore header. The rest of the actions found in each category can be accessed by clicking the category's header or its corresponding link in the Quick Launch. Another nice feature added to this new Central Administration site is the use of tooltips when hovering over a link. Throughout Central Administration, hovering the mouse over a link will give you a brief description of what that link opens.

The following sections describe the various categories and what you can do with each.

Application Management

The Application Management category is likely the area of Central Administration you will use the most. As you might guess from its name, Application Management is the location from which you manage your web applications and service applications and related items, such as site collections and databases. This category includes a good portion of the links that were found in the Application Management tab of SharePoint 2007's Central Administration. In SharePoint 2010, the Application Management category is further divided into several subcategories, each pertaining to a specific area.

Web Applications

In the Web Applications section (see Figure 6-4), you can access a list of all the web applications available in the farm, as well as configure alternate access mappings. Clicking the Manage web applications link will open a list of all of the web applications you have running in the farm.

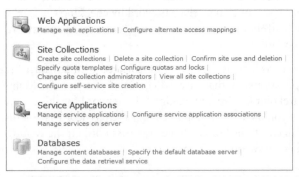

FIGURE 6-4

You'll notice that initially you can't do a whole lot with the Ribbon, as nearly every button is grayed out with the exception of the New button. Once you select a web application on the page, the Ribbon lights up and gives you many other options that can be used for changing the settings for the selected web application. You'll also notice that many options that were available from the Application Management tab in SharePoint 2007 now live on the Ribbon, reducing link clutter on the page (see Figure 6-5).

FIGURE 6-5

Managing the Web Applications enables you to make widespread changes to your sites. Because Web Applications are one of the highest levels of SharePoint containment, any settings you make from the Manage Web Applications screen will affect any site collections contained in the selected Web Application.

A few notable Ribbon items that you may end up using include the Extend button, which enables you to extend the selected Web Application to a different IIS website than the one on which it is currently hosted. You can use this in conjunction with Alternate Access Mappings to allow the same content to be accessed from more than one URL.

The Delete button enables you to remove the Web Application from SharePoint. You also have the option to remove the IIS website and the content database as well if you wish.

The General Settings button, as you might guess, enables you to set some of the basic settings for the Web Application. Here is where you can enable RSS feeds for all the site collections in the Web Application, as well as set the maximum upload size for files. The General Settings button also has a drop-down from which you can set other options. Some of these are covered in subsequent chapters, so we won't cover the rest of the options in great detail.

 Some of these options can be accessed from other areas of Central Administration, too. While exploring Central Administration, you will find that several options can be found in more than one place.

Let's head back to the Application Management page. Alternate Access Mappings (AAMs), under the Web Applications subheader Configure alternate access mappings, provide a way to access the same SharePoint content from different URLs. This can be useful if external users in an organization will access the SharePoint site using a different URL than the internal users. If you are familiar with setting up AAMs in SharePoint 2007, there's nothing new this time around. The interface is exactly the same. SharePoint enables you to configure up to five different zones, or entry points, as alternative URLs that point to the same Web Application.

AAMs also need to be configured if the SharePoint site is behind a reverse proxy server (such as Microsoft Forefront Threat Management Gateway 2010). In this scenario, the URL that end-users type to access the site may not be the actual URL of the SharePoint site, but rather a URL that the reverse-proxy server hands off to SharePoint. An alternate access mapping allows SharePoint to receive the request and return the correct content.

Site Collections

In this subcategory, all your site collection needs are met. Most of these items, which were found on the Application Management tab in SharePoint 2007, now have their own featured page, enabling you to more easily find what you need. You can create and delete site collections from the various Web Applications in the farm, set quota templates and apply quotas to individual site collections, change the administrators of the site collections, and set up self-service site creation for users. For the most part, working with site collections in Central Administration is exactly the same as it was in SharePoint 2007. In most cases, you choose the web application and site collection you'd like to work with, and then configure the settings available on the screen.

The process of creating a site collection in SharePoint 2010 is identical to that in SharePoint 2007. You still choose the web application that will contain the site collection, give it a name, pick the template, and assign an administrator and quota (if desired). Configuring and applying quotas is also the same, as is the capability to set up confirmation e-mails and notification for site usage and deletion. One addition to the site creation process is the ability to create a site collection without specifying a site template. This is done by selecting the Custom tab on the site template selector and choosing <Select template later...>. The first time the new site collection is accessed by a site collection administrator, the template selector will be displayed. Using this new feature means that a SharePoint administrator can set up a site collection for a group of users, but let the site collection's administrator make the call on which template is most appropriate for his or her needs.

Service Applications

Service applications are a new concept to SharePoint 2010. In a nutshell, service applications are the replacement for the Shared Services Provider (SSP) used in MOSS 2007. Unlike the SSP, which housed all available services, such as search, people services, Excel Calculations, and other services shared between web applications in the farm, in SharePoint 2010, service applications are individual components that can be individually associated with web applications. This approach offers much more flexibility than the SSP model from SharePoint 2007. Because not all services need to be running on any given web application, this can save on overhead. You will learn much more about service applications in Chapter 7, so this section serves more as a quick introduction to working with service applications in Central Administration.

When you click the Manage service applications link, you are presented with a list of all the available service applications that were configured during the initial farm configuration. This management page also utilizes the Ribbon for efficient management of the service applications. You can create additional instances of service applications using the New button. You can select which type of service application you'd like to create, and a pop-up window opens, enabling you to create a new service application. Figure 6-6 shows a list of service applications, with the Managed Metadata Service highlighted.

When working with service applications, you'll probably use the Manage and Properties buttons most often. The Properties button enables you to adjust general settings for the service application (such as its name), while the Manage button opens the management options for the selected service application. This is where you'll actually work with the service application. For example, selecting the Search Service Application and clicking Manage in the Ribbon opens the Search Administration page.

Service applications aren't contained in a completely separate web application like the SSP was. Instead, they're all individual components that can be accessed directly from Central Administration.

Each service application has a slightly different interface, but you'll find that it's a rather seamless transition from working in Central Administration to managing a service application.

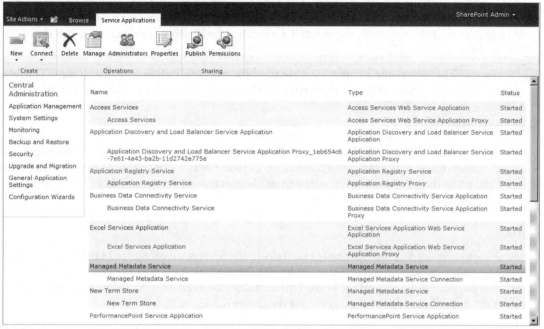

FIGURE 6-6

Databases

Also finding a home in the Application Management category is the subcategory Databases. Using these links enable you to specify the default database server, as well as manage the content databases in the farm. The interface on the Manage content databases screen is nearly the same as in SharePoint 2007, with the addition of a couple of extra columns that provide some additional information. In addition, the column headers are now more descriptive, specifically indicating that they are referring to site collections.

Just as in SharePoint 2007, clicking the database name will enable you to configure properties of the database, but this time around you get more information and options to set. You can specify a failover database server on this screen, set the search server, and adjust the database capacity for the number of site collections permitted in the selected Web Application. By default, you can create 15,000 site collections, and a warning event is triggered when the number of site collections reaches 9,000. You can adjust these values to meet your needs. You may want to revisit Chapter 3 for more information on architecture and capacity planning.

From this screen, you can also check the database schema versions by clicking on the database name. This is helpful to determine the patch level of the SharePoint farm. In SharePoint 2010, you can actually install patches to SharePoint without upgrading the databases at the same time. This enables you to mitigate downtime during patch installations. Although you can run SharePoint and the databases at different patch levels, you will want to synchronize them as soon as it's feasible by running the SharePoint 2010 Products Configuration Wizard.

New to SharePoint 2010 is the capability to assign a specific server to be responsible for the timer jobs that run against a particular content database. While this likely wouldn't be a common setting, if you do need to take advantage of it, the interface for setting that is also on this page. You can read more about this in Chapter 15.

Finally, you can remove the content database from the web application from this screen. This won't delete the database from SQL; it simply removes the association with the web application.

System Settings

Administrators familiar with SharePoint 2007 will recognize many of the pages in this category. As stated earlier, many of the screens in SharePoint 2010 are nearly identical to SharePoint 2007, but how you get to them has changed. System Settings houses many of the pages that can be used to make farmwide settings.

Servers

As shown in Figure 6-7, there are only two links in the Servers subcategory: Manage servers in this farm and Manage services on server. Clicking the former link will open a page that lists all the servers that are part of the SharePoint farm. This includes all servers with SharePoint actually installed on them, but not the SQL servers where the databases reside.

To remove a server from the SharePoint farm, click the Remove Server link in the row of the server's name. This page is largely informational. Clicking on the server name will open the Services on Server page (which is actually the equivalent of clicking the Manage services on server link from the System Settings category page and selecting the desired server).

FIGURE 6-7

On the Services on Server page, you'll see all the services currently running on the selected server. These services are configured based on the type of role the server plays in the farm. Next to the service name is the service's status. This is either stopped or started, and next to that is the related action that can be performed (i.e., stopped services can be started and vice versa). You'll notice that some of the service names are hyperlinks and some are not. Clicking the hyperlinked names opens a page where you can make additional configurations before or after the service has been started.

E-mail and Text Messages (SMS)

This subcategory has three links. Configure outgoing e-mail settings enables you to specify a server in your network set up with SMTP to send messages from the SharePoint farm. There isn't much to configure here; simply enter the server, the From: address, and the Reply to: address, and you've just enabled outgoing e-mail from the SharePoint farm.

Setting up incoming e-mail is only a little more involved. To use incoming e-mail, the SMTP feature needs to be enabled on the server. If it's not enabled, you'll receive a notice dialog box when you access the Configure incoming e-mail settings page. Once again, the settings page for incoming e-mail is identical to SharePoint 2007. First, decide whether you are going to enable incoming e-mail for your farm. Then, decide whether you want to let the server handle all the dirty work (with Automatic mode) or whether you want to configure the SMTP drop folder yourself (with Advanced mode).

Next, you can specify if you want to enable Directory Management Service, which is basically a fancy way of saying that the e-mail can be tied in with your Active Directory and Exchange systems if you so desire. You can also set the e-mail display address and the e-mail drop folder as well, if you are working in Advanced mode. If you chose Automatic mode, you have the option to either specify safe e-mail servers or simply allow e-mail from all e-mail servers. Once incoming e-mail is configured, a SharePoint timer job will check the e-mail drop folder that the SMTP service uses to drop off messages, and route them to the appropriate list or library.

Finally, you can enable SharePoint to send out text message alerts via an SMS service. If your organization subscribes to a text message service, you should have a username and password for your account. Simply specify the URL of the service, enter the username and password you have been provided with, and you have set up a mobile account to send alerts to any user who has chosen to be alerted with a text message when an item in SharePoint changes that meets the alert criteria. If you aren't subscribed to an SMS service, Microsoft has made the process easy by providing a link directly on the Mobile Account Settings page that displays a list of compatible services.

Farm Management

The last stop in the System Settings category is the Farm Management subcategory. This section contains links to various widespread settings that affect the entire farm.

 Notice that you have another link to configuring AAMs here. Because we've already covered AAMs, we'll skip right over that link.

You can manage features scoped to the farm level from this subcategory by clicking the Manage farm features link (you'll learn more about Features in Chapter 13). Essentially, features are bits of functionality that can be turned on or off in a subsite, a site collection, a web application, or the entire farm. This list happens to include all out-of-the-box features scoped to the farm level. If you know you won't be using a particular feature in your organization, you can deactivate it to remove its functionality. Generally, however, you will probably want to leave most of these features activated, as they affect every server and web application in your farm.

The Manage farm solutions link is the SharePoint 2010 equivalent of the Solution management link from SharePoint 2007. Also known as the Solution Store, this is where any installed solution packages that have been added to the farm are stored. From here, you can deploy or retract solutions using a GUI interface. If you prefer using STSADM or PowerShell, you can also deploy and retract solutions from a command prompt.

Any user-submitted solutions can be managed with the Manage user solutions link. This screen offers administrators the option to block any solutions they wish. To block a solution from running in the farm, simply browse for the solution file and optionally provide a message informing users that their request is being blocked. You can also set how SharePoint handles multi-server scenarios and solutions. You can allow solutions to run only on the server on which the request was made, or on other servers running the User Code Service.

The Configure privacy options link is simply a page where you can specify whether you would like to send information to Microsoft regarding the SharePoint farm. You can opt in or out of the Customer Experience Improvement Program, as well as decide if you'd like to automatically send any errors related to Microsoft. Finally, you can choose whether you'd like to display help from the locally installed help files or whether you'd like to use the online help from Microsoft.

Lastly, administrators can use the Configure cross firewall access zone link to enable SharePoint to send externally accessible URLs in alerts. This is useful if the site is being set up with SSL. Choose the web application, and then choose the zone that will be used as the cross firewall access zone from the drop-down list.

Monitoring

Monitoring in SharePoint 2010 has been improved, offering more insight into the state of your farm. The Monitoring category contains three subsections: Health Analyzer, Timer Jobs, and Reporting (see Figure 6-8). This section is meant only as a primer and the real meat on these topics is presented in Chapter 15.

FIGURE 6-8

Health Analyzer

SharePoint 2010 introduces a new feature called the Health Analyzer (sometimes called the Best Practices Analyzer). This rule-based tool periodically scans the farm, checking various components and settings of SharePoint and comparing them to a rule bank.

If any settings are found that don't match the rule, the Health Analyzer will display a prominent notice on the home page of Central Administration, as shown in Figure 6-9. This alerts administrators to potential issues they should be aware of: A yellow bar indicates that the Health Analyzer has found items that may need attention, while a red bar indicates more serious issues.

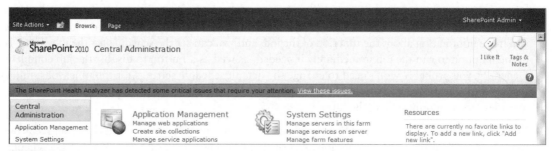

FIGURE 6-9

 This section covers the Health Analyzer only briefly. To learn more about this and other monitoring capabilities, see Chapter 15.

In the Health Analyzer subcategory, you can take a look at any issues that have been detected during the various scans performed on the farm. If you have received a notice about any issues on the home page of Central Administration, you can also click the link within the notice to access this same page. On the Review problems and solutions page, you can scan through the various reports, which are divided by category. Out of the box, the Health Analyzer uses more than 50 rules, spread out among four different categories. Also indicated is which server is causing the error, and even which service is triggering the Health Analyzer. Clicking the name of an issue will open a pop-up window with more detailed information about the rule. Some rules even provide an option to allow SharePoint to automatically correct the problem. If you have already corrected the issue that SharePoint is complaining about, you can use the Reanalyze Now button in the pop-up's Ribbon to rescan the farm for that rule ahead of its scheduled scan.

But what about the rules themselves? The second link in the Health Analyzer subcategory, Review rule definitions, is for actually seeing what rules the Health Analyzer is using to compare the farm settings. You can manually launch a scan with any rule by clicking the rule name and choosing Scan Now from the Ribbon in the pop-up window that opens. This screen also lets you adjust the settings and schedule of the rules. You can even disable rules you find to be incessantly irritating by setting their schedule to OnDemandOnly. This way, SharePoint won't automatically scan the farm with that rule. For instance, you may have set up a single-server test farm, and every week a warning message appears informing you that databases exist on servers running SharePoint Foundation. In this case, such behavior is expected and required, so you could open the rule, click Edit Item in the Ribbon, change the schedule drop-down to OnDemandOnly, and then save the rule.

Timer Jobs

Timer jobs are somewhat similar to the Health Analyzer in that they run periodically, but their function is to keep the farm up and running, not to scan for issues. Each of these small scheduled jobs has a particular task to accomplish according to a schedule, which you can look at by clicking the Review job definitions option under the Timer Jobs subcategory. From this screen, you get view the schedule for each job, as well as the web application(s) some jobs are associated with. Clicking on a job's title gives you more information about the function of the job, and you can set the schedule for the job. There is even an option to run the job immediately if needed, as well as a button to disable the job completely. Generally, you probably won't need to change the default schedule settings for the timer jobs, unless you need to adjust them for troubleshooting purposes. Note that you can't change what each timer job does; you can only set its schedule.

You can also check the status and history of timer jobs with the Check job status link. Scroll through the page to look at the various timer jobs and their states. The report displays jobs that are scheduled, jobs that are currently running, and jobs that have run. If something in the farm seems to be hung up, checking this page can indicate whether the problem is being caused by a timer job.

Reporting

In the Reporting subcategory, you can check out a variety of different reports that SharePoint automatically compiles. Clicking the View administrative reports opens a library that houses performance reports. For example, you can look at several search-related charts to see how the search function is performing.

Clicking the Configure diagnostic logging link enables you to customize the logging for SharePoint events to the Windows Event Log and trace logs. You can drill down through the various categories of events and change the settings for a specific component by checking the box next to its name, then setting the drop-downs below the category list. Any category that has been modified will appear in bold text. This can help you troubleshoot if you know you are only logging errors, or you can turn on verbose logging to get more information about what a particular component is doing. Remember, however, that enabling verbose logging on services can create larger log files, so you may want to temporarily change the logging type, and then reset the logging levels to their defaults.

Below the Event Throttling section on the Diagnostic Logging page, you can toggle Event Log Flood Protection (EVFP). EVFP is designed to keep your logs from becoming cluttered with hundreds or thousands of the same events repeating every couple of seconds if a server component begins to have issues. If SharePoint detects that the same event has been logged five times in two minutes or less, EVFP kicks in and stops logging that event for another two minutes. This can help manage the size of the log files significantly.

Speaking of log files, below the EVFP toggle is a section where you can set the location of the SharePoint trace logs. Because the trace logs can eventually grow rather large, it's recommended that you set up a location on a drive other than C: for the log files. You can set the number of days that log files should be kept, and even set the amount of disk space they should be allowed to consume, which helps you keep logs under control if you don't move them from the C: drive.

Also in the Reporting subcategory is a link for viewing health reports. These reports can give administrators a good snapshot of who is using the farm and how pages in the farm are performing. Select the Slowest Pages report from the Quick Launch menu on the left to see which pages in the farm suffer from the slowest performance. This can be helpful for finding any performance issues with pages or Web Parts in the site.

In addition to viewing the health reports, you can also configure the usage and health reports by clicking the Configure usage and health data collection link. This screen enables you to configure whether or not SharePoint should collect site usage information and health information. Ideally, you want to ensure you're collecting this information to better understand how the site is being utilized, what pages are most popular, and who is using the site. You can also configure what types of events are logged. By default, all types of events are logged, but you may want to consider logging only specific events you really care about. Like the trace logs, you can specify where the log files should be kept, and how much disk space they should be allowed to take up. An important note about both trace logs and usage logs is that if you choose to change the log file location, you must select a location that exists on every SharePoint server in the farm. For example, if you decide that the logs should reside on `F:\SharePointLogs`, then every server in the farm needs to have an `F:\SharePointLogs` folder so that the log files are written to the same location on each server. The usage and health monitoring configuration page also lets you choose whether to log health data collection or not; and it provides links to modify the health logging schedule and the log collection schedule, which are simply timer jobs.

Last in the Monitoring category is the Web Analytics Report. This informative page shows you the running total for the number of page views for each of the web applications in the farm, the total number of unique visitors per day, and the number of search queries performed. Clicking a web application's name opens a more detailed view of the usage for that web application. You can also modify the date range by clicking the Change Settings link in the blue Date Range bar and selecting one of the preset date ranges, or setting your own custom date range from the More drop-down in the Ribbon.

Backup and Restore

Chapter 12 is dedicated to SharePoint backup and recovery, so this section will serve more as a general overview of using Central Administration as a backup and recovery tool. Figure 6-10 shows the backup and restore tasks that you can perform through the Central Administration interface (see Figure 6-10).

FIGURE 6-10

A new and welcome addition to SharePoint 2010 is the capability to perform more granular backup and recovery. Instead of only being able to back up content databases or the entire farm, as you were limited to in the SharePoint 2007 Central Administration backup, you can now back up site collections, subsites, and even lists from this interface. Previously, restoring any content smaller than a content database from a backup generally meant having to set up a separate recovery farm, restore the content database, then export the content from the recovery farm using STSADM.EXE and import it back into the production farm. Now, this can all be done from the Central Administration interface. In addition, SharePoint databases and database snapshots that aren't even attached to the farm can be used to browse and recover content from within Central Administration.

The Backup and Restore category is divided into two subcategories: Farm Backup and Restore, and Granular Backup. The Farm Backup and Restore subcategory enables you to perform high-level backups of the entire farm or individual Web Applications, as well as recover from these backups. Conversely, the Granular Backup subcategory is where you perform your backups and exports of site collections, webs, and lists.

If the backup and restore functionality in Central Administration has you frothing at the mouth, wait until you read Chapter 12, which is all about backups and high availability. It'll drive you wild.

Security

The Security category, shown in Figure 6-11, is all about ... well, security! From this page, you can manage user security to the farm and set web application user policies, configure the farm's managed accounts, block file types, and set up information rights management.

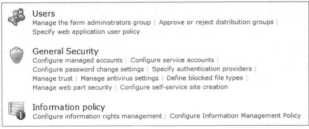

FIGURE 6-11

Users

Let's start with the Users subcategory. Your SharePoint farm always needs at least one administrator. The account used to run the SharePoint 2010 Products Configuration Wizard is automatically added to the farm administrators group, as is the local server administrator. If you need to add specific users in your organization to the farm administrators group, you can do so here. One thing to consider, however, is that anyone in this group essentially has rights to anything and everything contained in the farm. That's important to keep in mind when determining who should get what permissions. Consider whether a user could accomplish the tasks he or she needs with fewer permissions, such as to a Web Application or a site collection. It's generally considered best practice to not go wild and give a large number of people farm administrator access if you can avoid it.

The Approve or reject distribution groups link opens a list from which you can manage the distribution groups used for incoming e-mail. This can be useful if your users have created so many distribution groups within e-mail-enabled document libraries that the number has become unwieldy. This is actually nothing more than a SharePoint list, which makes it easy to manage.

The Specify web application user policy link opens the Policy for Web Application page, which enables you to add users and groups to the Web Applications in the farm. Select a web application and you can manage the users already associated with it, or add users. This can be used as an alternative to giving users full Farm Administrator access if they need access to multiple web applications. You can choose one of four permission policies for users and groups for the web applications: full control, full read, deny write, and deny all. Keep in mind that these policies affect the entire web application, so any setting made for a user or group here applies to all site collections contained in that web application. Notice that the account used to run search crawling is automatically given full read permissions to the site.

You also have the option to make an account operate as a system account, whereby any changes made to SharePoint will register as being made with the name System Account, rather than the user who actually made the change. It's worthwhile to note that this is the only place in SharePoint where you can deny someone access in SharePoint.

General Security

Moving on to the General Security subcategory, you'll find items pertaining to the overall security and accounts used in the farm. The first two links, Configure managed accounts and Configure service accounts, sound fairly similar, but their function is different. The Configure managed accounts link is where you can register domain accounts with SharePoint so that SharePoint is responsible for them (as described earlier in the section "Managed Accounts"), whereas the Configure service accounts link opens a page from which you can manage existing account associations with the various services on the farm.

You can have the passwords of managed accounts registered with SharePoint automatically changed to comply with the organization's policies, and a few settings related to changing passwords can be found in the link Configure password change settings. Despite the name, this page doesn't actually allow you to set the passwords for your accounts; it simply allows you to configure notifications and set a timer for the password change. You can configure how many days prior to the change the notification will be sent out (the default is 10 days), and how many days prior to the change the e-mail should be sent out. In the last section on the Password Management Settings page, you can adjust the amount of time SharePoint waits to change the password after notifying the services that new passwords are about to be applied. This time window is necessary for the services to finish up any running tasks before their managed accounts receive a new password. The default is 45 seconds. You can also adjust how many times SharePoint should attempt to change a password before failing.

Next up is the link Specify authentication providers. Here you can see a list of the various authentication zones and provider names. Clicking on the zone name will enable you to edit the authentication for that zone. Several common configuration options are available here, including the capability to enable or disable client integration for the Office clients, and enabling or disabling anonymous access for the site. Like many settings in Central Administration, these are also configured per web application. Additional settings that can be made include the authentication type and IIS authentication method, and whether or not users should be required to have Use Remote Interfaces Permission.

In the General Security subcategory, you can also manage inter-farm trusts and the associated root certificates. This page employs light use of the Ribbon, allowing you to create new trusts or edit existing trusts. Clicking an existing trust name will open the options Edit and Delete in the Ribbon. Creating a new trust involves giving the trust a name and pointing SharePoint to the root authority certificate. All trusts require a *root authority certificate*. If you are setting up a trust to provide trust to another farm, you need to provide SharePoint with a *token issuer certificate*. Once you have configured your trust, you can return to them later to edit the settings if desired.

You can manage how an antivirus program interacts with SharePoint by clicking the Manage antivirus settings link. You can set how the antivirus scanner will treat documents that are uploaded and downloaded, and whether or not it should attempt to clean any infected documents it discovers. You can also adjust the length of time the scanner runs before it times out, as well as the number of threads used for scanning. Depending on your server performance when running scans, you may want to adjust these numbers.

Another important security practice SharePoint employs is to limit the types of files that can be uploaded. You can find the list of blocked files by clicking the Define blocked file types link. SharePoint 2007 also had a blocked file list, and it's largely the same in SharePoint 2010. Out of the box, SharePoint 2010 blocks nearly 100 file types, but you can add your own to the list by entering the extension of the file type. This is configured per web application, so if you have more than one web application you can have a different set of files blocked for each.

The last major link in the General Security subcategory is Manage web part security. This page enables you to configure how users are allowed to interact with aspects of Web Parts. As in previous SharePoint versions, Web Parts are still one of the building blocks for providing information on a SharePoint page; and also like previous versions, many of those Web Parts can be connected to provide and consume data from one another, allowing for dynamic presentation of content. You can choose to disable the Web Part connections option (its default is enabled), and specify whether or not they are allowed to access the Online Web Part Gallery, which contains Web Parts developed by Microsoft and potentially other third-party vendors. If you choose to allow users to access the Online Web Part Gallery, you may need to modify the `web.config` file to allow the server access to outside galleries. Finally, on this page you can allow your users to edit scriptable Web Parts; and you can restore the default settings if necessary. Again, these settings can be changed per web application.

The General Security subcategory also provides another link to configuring self-site creation, which can be accessed from a number of other areas in Central Administration as well.

Information Policy

The Information Policy subcategory lets you configure information rights management (IRM) for the farm by clicking the Configure information rights management link. By default, IRM is turned off, but you have the option to use the default server running Windows Rights Management Services listed in Active directory, or specify your own server running RMS. Once IRM has been enabled, you can set the IRM policies for the farm by clicking Configure Information Rights Management Policy. Out of the box, SharePoint 2010 comes with four preconfigured policies: Labels, Barcodes,

Auditing, and Retention. Clicking the policy name enables you to edit the settings for that policy, such as whether or not the policy should be decommissioned or remain active. Decommissioning a policy doesn't remove it from any document libraries and lists that currently use it, but it will prevent new libraries and lists from being able to consume it.

Upgrade and Migration

As shown in Figure 6-12, the Upgrade and Migration category only has one subcategory, Upgrade and Patch Management. This subcategory contains only a handful of links.

Upgrade and Patch Management
Convert farm license type | Enable Enterprise Features |
Enable Features on Existing Sites | Check product and patch installation status |
Review database status | Check upgrade status

FIGURE 6-12

This is where you will find links to convert your SharePoint license type (for example, from a trial version to a licensed version), as well as select which feature set to use if you've recently activated an enterprise license. To activate a license, simply click Convert farm license type and type or paste your license in the field and click OK. Once you've done that, you can head over to the Enable Enterprise Features link to switch the set of features from the standard set to the Enterprise set. Once you turn on Enterprise features, you can't undo it.

If you've been running SharePoint 2010 for a while and have created several sites, and you then upgrade your license type, the newly available Enterprise features may not be activated in your existing sites. You can use the Enable Features on Existing Sites link to push down the newly activated set of features to any sites that were created before the license conversion. Any sites made after the license conversion will already have the new feature sets.

The Check product and patch installation status option provides a report of all the various components and products on the server, including their current patch level. This can be useful in determining what version of a particular product you're running. This is a nice centralized place to find version information, especially if you are running a larger farm with many services running on the various servers. You can show all the products installed on the farm, or view the list filtered by individual servers.

Selecting View database status provides another report of all the various databases connected to the farm, and what type of database they are (content database, metadata service database, configuration database, etc.).

Finally, if you are upgrading from SharePoint 2007 to SharePoint 2010 using the database attach method (which you learned about in Chapter 5), the Check upgrade status link will become a good friend of yours. Once you add a SharePoint 2007 database to the farm, you will see any active and previous upgrade sessions (see Figure 6-13). The page refreshes periodically during the upgrade process, keeping you informed of the status, and reports any errors encountered during the upgrade. Refer back to Chapter 5 for more information on using this page during the upgrade process.

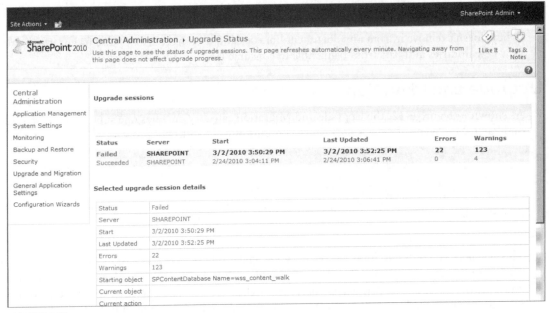

FIGURE 6-13

General Application Settings

The General Application Settings category, shown in Figure 6-14, is one of the larger categories found in Central Administration. There's a lot that you can do here to change how users will interact with SharePoint 2010. In this category, you'll find options for controlling how client-side applications interact with SharePoint 2010, such as InfoPath and SharePoint Designer, as well as settings in SharePoint that apply to Web Applications. In addition, because Central Administration's interface is pluggable, it is possible for additional links and sections to display here when using products that integrate with SharePoint. For instance, a Reporting Services section is added if the SQL server is running Reporting Services in SharePoint integration mode.

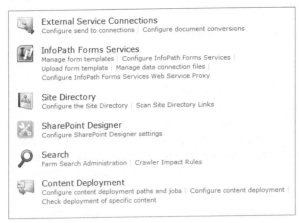

FIGURE 6-14

External Service Connections

Starting in the External Service Connections subcategory, you'll find a couple of links that can be used to send and convert documents in the SharePoint farm. The Configure send to connections link enables you to configure custom send to locations for the selected web application. This makes use of the Content Organizer feature available in SharePoint 2010. In a site collection, this feature can be enabled and configured to allow management of documents submitted to a drop-off folder. Using the Configure Send To Connections page in Central Administration, you can take this a step further and enable documents to be submitted across multiple site collections, a boundary that many organizations found themselves up against in SharePoint 2007.

Configuring send to locations requires that the Content Organizer site collection feature is enabled on the site collection that will receive the documents. Once the feature is activated, you will have additional options on the Site Settings page under the Site Administration headers: Content Organizer Settings and Content Organizer Rules. You can use these pages to customize the settings for the drop-off folder and how the documents will be routed in the site collection.

At the very bottom of the Content Organizer Settings page is a URL for a web service. Copy this URL; and then back in Central Administration, paste the URL in the Send to URL field on the Configure Send to Connections page. You can give the new connection a name, decide what action will be taken, and give the send to an explanation of what will happen. Once configured, your new send to destination will be available in the Send to menu in the Documents tab of the Ribbon.

SharePoint 2010 also allows for document conversions using pre-installed and third-party software. Settings for managing document conversions can be found in the Configure document conversions link under the External Service Connections subcategory. In order for document conversions to be enabled, two services must be started first (by default, they are disabled). To enable them, open the System Settings category and click Manage services on server. Look for the two services Document Conversions Launcher Service and Document Conversions Load Balancer Service. Next to each, click the link to start the services. You can configure additional options by clicking the service names, such as specifying the communication scheme for the services to utilize (http or https), the port number the services will use to communicate, and which server in a multi-server farm will act as the conversion load balancer. Once these services have been started, you can continue the configuration of document conversions under the General Application Settings category. SharePoint 2010 comes with four converters preinstalled, and third-party applications may add additional converters.

InfoPath Forms Services

This subcategory contains all the links you need to start utilizing the tight integration between InfoPath 2010 and SharePoint 2010. Use the Manage form templates link to keep track of all the available InfoPath forms that are enabled on the server. You can filter the list using the List View filters in the Quick Launch menu, and you can upload your own custom templates. You can further manage the templates by clicking the drop-down arrow around each template name: You can activate, deactivate, quiesce, and delete the templates (keeping in mind that templates tied to existing workflows or deployed using a feature can't be removed or modified). If you upload a custom InfoPath template, you can also deploy it to site collections using the drop-down menu.

To quiesce *a template means that no new connections will be allowed to use the template, and any existing connections will be gradually timed out in an effort to minimize data loss.*

The Configure InfoPath Forms Services link opens a page of general settings related to the InfoPath Forms Service. Most of these options are fairly self-explanatory. You can use this page to set additional options that can enable additional features in InfoPath forms, such as allowing forms to use embedded SQL authentication when connecting to external data sources; to configure thresholds for user sessions when using InfoPath forms; and even to set the time-out settings and maximum amount of data transfer allowed for sessions.

The Upload form template link opens the same page that can be accessed from the Manage Form Templates page. Simply browse for a form and verify its compatibility with the Verify button. Below that, you have the option to choose how existing forms are upgraded. You can choose to upgrade existing forms while preserving active connections to the older version of the template, or you can choose to upgrade the forms immediately and close any existing connections. When you have made your selections, click the Upload button to upload your form template into the template gallery. Similar to the template gallery is the data connection library, accessed with the Manage data connection files link. You can upload InfoPath data connection files to Central Administration to manage them centrally if you wish.

Finally, clicking the Configure InfoPath Forms Service Web Service Proxy link gives you the option to enable a proxy to be used for connections between web services and the InfoPath Forms service application. You can read more about service application proxies in Chapter 7.

Site Directory

The Site Directory subcategory contains just a couple of options. In SharePoint 2007 you had the option to create a *master site directory* that would automatically list all site collections in a single location. This could be very useful if your organization has a large number of site collections throughout the farm, as having a centralized list of all the available site collections could be a time saver. This idea is carried over to SharePoint 2010. While each site collection can have its own site directory, you can also create a site that will become the master site directory. Click the link Configure the Site Directory in the Site Directory subcategory and simply enter the URL of the site directory site collection in the field. You can specify whether all sites should be added to the site directory, and whether or not they are required to be categorized.

Clicking the Scan Site Directory Links option under the Site Directory subcategory enables you to specify a scan on a view of the site directory list to check for broken links. Each view in SharePoint 2010 has a unique URL, which can be copied and pasted into the field for scanning. Your site directory may have views that display only sites in a particular category, and you may want to only scan a particular view instead of scanning the entire site directory.

SharePoint Designer

When Microsoft began offering SharePoint Designer 2007 as a free download, many administrators immediately began having visions of the SharePoint Apocalypse: users wreaking havoc on a finely tuned SharePoint deployment, unghosting pages left and right, and deploying custom designs. There were a few ways to address how SharePoint Designer 2007 could interact with SharePoint and keep it under control, but in many cases administrators simply kept SharePoint Designer under wraps in hopes that their general user base wouldn't discover it.

SharePoint Designer 2010 is also available as a free download from Microsoft, but now it offers more options for restricting its use, which can be set on a more granular level. Individual site collections can have the use of SharePoint Designer restricted as needed. The use of SharePoint Designer can be set per Web Application, which will affect all site collections in that Web Application. As shown in Figure 6-15, all the options for using SharePoint Designer are checked by default in Central Administration, but not at the site collection level, which provides flexibility regarding who can do what with it.

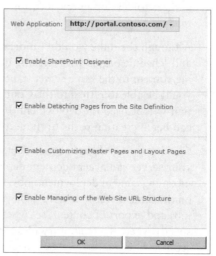

FIGURE 6-15

For example, in Central Administration you can completely disable the use of SharePoint Designer for all site collections in a Web Application if you wish, or you can select which set of permissions administrators will be allowed. Keep in mind that deselecting an option in Central Administration for SharePoint Designer will make that option unavailable in all site collections within the selected Web Application.

Search

Under the Search subcategory you'll find a link to the Farm-Wide Search Administration page and a link to the Crawler Impact Rules page. Both of these links can also be found in the Management page for the Search Service Application. Briefly, the Farm-Wide Search Administration link will open a page that gives you a general overview of the Search topology in the farm. You can see any proxy servers set up for Search, how long the timeout is set to, and whether or not Search should ignore SSL warnings. You can configure all of these options by clicking the respective values set to each property. Below that is a list of all search-related service applications. Clicking the name of the service application will open the management screen for that service application, while clicking the Modify Topology link enables you to view and modify the topology of Search in the farm. You can also add new search databases or modify the properties of existing databases.

Clicking the Crawler Impact Rules link enables you to control how the crawler affects performance. For example, you can choose whether you want a specific number of simultaneous requests to be made by the crawler, or if you'd rather have only one document requested at a time with a specified pause between requests. This is all handled on a per-site basis, so different sites can have different rules.

You can read all about Search and its various settings in more detail in Chapter 14.

Content Deployment

We've nearly made it to the end of our tour of the General Application Settings category. Last up we have the subcategory of Content Deployment. Content deployment is the production of content in one site collection that will then be ported to another site collection. Often, in public-facing websites, authors will create content in an authoring or staging environment, and the content deployment schedule will port that content to the production destination. These can be as elaborate as separate farms or as simple as separate site collections in different Web Applications. This enables authors to develop in one location without worrying about accidentally publishing content that isn't ready yet.

Although the links wouldn't indicate it by the order they're in, creating a content deployment path and schedule begins with clicking the Configure content deployment link if you're going to be deploying content to the same server. Once you have actually configured content deployment for the server, you'll be able to return to the Configure content deployment paths and jobs link to set up the paths that will be used for deployment. If you have a second environment that will receive the content, you can begin creating paths to the second environment right away.

Clicking the Configure content deployment link opens the Content Deployment Settings screen. Before your server can accept content deployments, you'll need to enable it. Choose the option to Accept incoming content deployment jobs, which allows you to set up Web Applications and site collections on the same server to receive deployments. Next, you choose which server will handle the deployment jobs and export of content, set whether you'd like to use SSL encryption to deploy the content, and specify where the temporary files for incoming content should be stored. By default, the location is set to `C:\ProgramData\ContentDeployment`, but you can set your own location. It would be advisable to move this location off the C: drive, especially if you know you will be relying heavily on content deployment in your organization. Lastly, you can configure how many records should be kept for each deployment job that runs. The default is 20. When you are finished, click OK to save your configuration.

Once you've configured the content deployment for the server, you can start creating deployment jobs. Click the Configure content deployment paths and jobs link to see a list of the deployment jobs you have set up (obviously the list will be empty the first time you click it). Create a new deployment job by clicking the New Path link. You need to specify a name, and optionally a description, for the path you want to create for deploying content from one location to another. Next, choose the source Web Application and source site collection. Once that is specified, you provide the URL of the Central Administration site on the destination server (or, if the destination is on the same server, the URL of Central Administration you're already working in). If you configured content deployment to utilize SSL, you need to ensure that the Central Administration URL begins with `https://`. If you don't use SSL, then you will receive a warning message as you type the URL, letting you know that the traffic won't be encrypted.

Below that, enter the username and password of an account that has access to the destination Central Administration. Click the Connect button to verify that the connection works. Choose the destination Web Application and site collection from the respective drop-downs. By default, the option to deploy user names is checked, which will associate the username of the original author with the deployed content. To finish creating your path, choose what security information you want to send with the deployment and click OK. You've successfully created a path through which you can deploy content.

Once you have configured content deployment and set up a path, you can now set up a job schedule. From the Manage Content Deployment Paths and Jobs page, click the New Job link to associate a deployment job with a particular path. Give the new job a name and description. Next, choose which path you will be associating the job with from the drop-down. If your version of SQL Server supports SQL snapshots, SharePoint can utilize them to speed up the deployment process significantly. By default, SQL snapshots are not used. Next, choose whether an entire site collection or individual webs (subsites) within the site collection will be deployed with the job. To select individual subsites, click the Select Sites button and from the tree that opens, you can select individual sites or entire branches of the site tree by clicking the name and selecting either the site or the branch to be deployed. Click OK to close the pop-up.

Next up you can create the deployment schedule. You can run the job as a one-time only deployment or you can create a repeating schedule. Deployments can run once a month, once a week, once a day, once an hour, or every so many minutes. Choose your option and set the desired time schedule for the deployment. Under the schedule, you can optionally choose to send e-mail notifications to people when the deployments run. Clicking OK will create the job. Paths can have multiple jobs associated with them, which can be useful if different areas of the destination site need to be updated on different schedules, or if a one-time job needs to be run before the next scheduled job. If you create a new job for a path, you will have one extra option in the job creation screen, enabling you to deploy only new content to the destination or all content regardless of whether it is new or not.

From the Manage Content Deployment Paths and Jobs link, you can manage your paths and jobs by clicking the drop-down around them. You can even test jobs to ensure that they will run and to spot any potential issues before actually running a job, and view the history of previously run jobs (see Figure 6-16). The Status column also creates hyperlinks to view more details about the current status of the job in question.

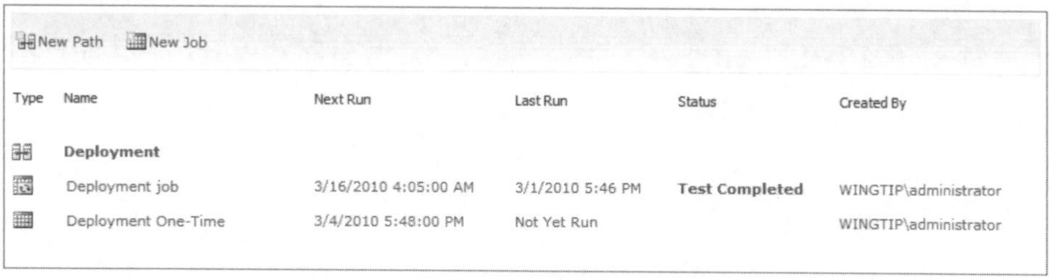

Type	Name	Next Run	Last Run	Status	Created By
	Deployment				
	Deployment job	3/16/2010 4:05:00 AM	3/1/2010 5:46 PM	**Test Completed**	WINGTIP\administrator
	Deployment One-Time	3/4/2010 5:48:00 PM	Not Yet Run		WINGTIP\administrator

New Path   New Job

FIGURE 6-16

Finally, the last link on the General Application Settings category is Content Deployment Object Status. This page provides a report on the content deployment jobs that have run. You can check specific content by entering a URL into the field and clicking the Check Status button. This will return a report of the source and destination object details. You can use this page to check for warnings and errors if the content doesn't seem to have deployed properly.

Configuration Wizards

The final category we'll cover in Central Administration is the Configuration Wizards category. There isn't a lot to explain here; this category contains a link to run the Farm Configuration Wizard (see Figure 6-17).

FIGURE 6-17

If you skipped that step during the initial configuration of SharePoint, you can run it from here. SharePoint 2010's wizard framework is fully pluggable as well, so it's conceivable that this list could be expanded in the future, either by Microsoft or by third-party vendors. For example, a third-party tool might include a wizard to walk you through the setup, and a link to it could be stored here.

SUMMARY

Whew, we made it! We've covered nearly every aspect of SharePoint 2010's Central Administration. What a ride! There is definitely a lot to take in, but the more you work with Central Administration the more you will find that it makes your life as an administrator easier. You'll find more detailed information about many of these topics we've covered here later in the book. This chapter was basically a start-to-finish tutorial demonstrating where you can find the various settings in the newly designed interface. Hopefully, you now have a better idea of where to look when searching for an elusive setting.

7

Understanding the Service Application Architecture

WHAT'S IN THIS CHAPTER?

➤ What happened to Shared Services Providers?

➤ Service application basics

➤ Administering service applications

➤ Multi-tenancy in SharePoint 2010

Put your thinking cap on. This chapter is going to plunge you headfirst into the depths of SharePoint service applications. On the surface, they are pretty straightforward — heck, you can just run a wizard to get started — but truly unlocking their power takes a bit more effort. Service applications are the way SharePoint 2010 provides most of its services. Think of something like Search or Excel Services. These are offered as individual services that can be consumed in a variety of ways. Out with the rigid Shared Services Providers and in with the flexible service applications.

Groups, connections, proxies, services, delegated administrators — what is all of that stuff? As with most things technical, terminology is critical; and unfortunately, once you learn the key SharePoint terms, you will find that half of them have a doppelganger in Windows PowerShell. Ugh.

However, once you have a grip on the terminology and the plumbing, it's time for the fun part. After looking at the fundamentals in Central Administration and then strolling through some of the key cmdlets, you'll be ready to get your hands dirty.

Then once you think you have things under control, you learn a new trick. Some of the service applications can be configured to be multi-tenant, meaning that a specific instance of the service application can be set up in a way that makes each site collection think it is using a dedicated service, when in reality they are sharing.

Get excited. You may think this chapter will be boring, but it's a non-stop thrill ride through one of the most important pieces of SharePoint.

FAREWELL TO THE SHARED SERVICES PROVIDER

If you are familiar with MOSS 2007, then you know all about those lovely things called Shared Service Providers (SSPs). They enabled services to be packaged and provided in MOSS. An SSP consisted of Search, Profiles, Audiences, and My Sites; and if you were cool enough to have the Enterprise CAL, then they also brought Excel Services and the Business Data Catalog (BDC) to the party. You would then associate one or more SharePoint web applications with the SSP to consume these services. The web application had to get all of its services from one SSP, which caused scaling nightmares for many administrators.

For example, suppose you currently host your intranet at `http://intranet` and it is associated with the Enterprise SSP. Then Human Resources comes to you and says they need to have their own, isolated copy of the BDC to protect their data. First you would have to create for them a unique web application, `http://hrweb`. Then you would have to create an HR-only SSP and associate their web application with the new SSP. Then you could set up the BDC. The only problem is that when you create the new SSP, you also get a new instance of all of those

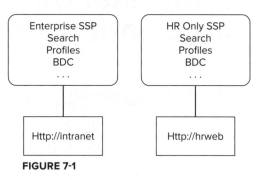

FIGURE 7-1

other services, like Search, as shown in Figure 7-1. If HR would like to be able to search, then you have to configure Search for this SSP because they could not associate their web app with the corporate SSP and its Search index. You can see how this could quickly become a black hole of redundant services and duplicate data.

In SharePoint 2010 this is no longer the case. Instead, all of those individual services can stand on their own as service applications. Table 7-1 shows the list of the service applications available and some information about them.

TABLE 7-1 Service Applications

SHAREPOINT FOUNDATION SERVICE APPLICATIONS		
	Has Database	**Cross-Farm Capable**
Business Data Connectivity	Yes	Yes
Usage and Health Data Collection	Yes	No
Web Analytics	No	Yes
Microsoft SharePoint Foundation Subscription Settings Service	Yes	No

SHAREPOINT SERVER 2010 STANDARD SERVICE APPLICATIONS		
	Has Database	**Cross-Farm Capable**
Managed Metadata Service	Yes	Yes
Search	Yes	Yes
Secure Store Service	Yes	Yes
State Service	Yes	No
User Profile Service	Yes	No
SHAREPOINT SERVER 2010 ENTERPRISE SERVICE APPLICATIONS		
	Has Database	**Cross-Farm Capable**
Access Service	No	No
Excel Service	No	No
Visio Graphic Service	No	No
Word Automation Services	No	No
PerformancePoint Service	No	No

Note that service applications are part of all the SharePoint 2010 editions, including Foundation. This is great news for administrators and should help reduce some of the previous inconsistencies in administering SharePoint.

The best way to think about service applications is take the old SSP and explode it out so that each piece stands alone. So instead of buying a combo meal, now you can get the burger, fries, and drink separately — and if for some reason you want two drinks and no fries, that's fine too. Everything is ala carte. To put that in SharePoint terms, we can return to the example described earlier.

Currently, your company uses http://intranet for all SharePoint sites. For security reasons, the Human Resources group wants to have its own BDC, so you begin by creating a web application for them, http://hrweb. Then you provision a new BDC service application named HR only BDC. Now you can associate http://hrweb with that service application and all of the other service applications, as shown in Figure 7-2.

As you can see, now HR has access to all of the same service applications as before, including the Enterprise BDC, and they have their own BDC. The other Intranet users are unaffected in terms of access; they are merely excluded from the HR only BDC, thus giving HR its desired isolation.

What was such a huge nightmare in the previous version of SharePoint is now a piece of cake in SharePoint 2010. Even better, the service application architecture is infinitely configurable. Of course, as you already know, infinitely configurable also means it can be infinitely complex. Fear not; this chapter will help you work through those infinite loops.

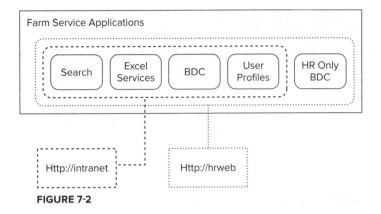

FIGURE 7-2

SERVICE APPLICATION FUNDAMENTALS

Before you can begin to work with service applications it is important to get a handle on all of the pieces involved and how they interrelate. There are a series of connections and associations to get from your web application to search results and the better you understand the pieces the easier it is to wire it all together.

The Connection Structure

In order to provide service applications that are flexible and scalable, the services are actually offered through a series of connections and associations (see Figure 7-3).

SharePoint web applications are associated with service application *groups*, which are made up of one or more service application *connections*. Each service application connection connects the service application to the service application group. A given service application consumes one or more service application *services*. Finally, some of those service applications have databases for storage, while others do not. You already know what web applications are, so the following sections will help you make sense of these interrelated elements.

Service Application Groups

The *group* is the piece you associate with your web applications. When you created your first web application back in Chapter 4, it was set to use the default

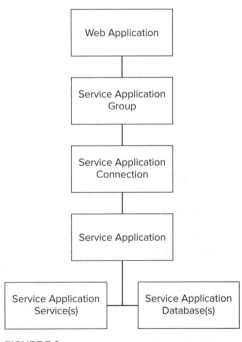

FIGURE 7-3

service application group, as shown in Figure 7-4. Notice that when the default is selected, all of the checkboxes are grayed out. You cannot edit the default group from this screen.

FIGURE 7-4

The default group is automatically provisioned for you. If you used the initial Farm Configuration Wizard, then all of the service applications are part of this group. When you manually create a service application, you can choose to include it in the default group or not by using the checkbox shown in Figure 7-5 (more on that later in the chapter).

FIGURE 7-5

This group enables you to associate a web application with a bunch of service applications. If the default group doesn't meet your needs, you can you can use the [custom] option. This enables you to specify which service applications you want to use for the web application. Keep in mind that although [custom] appears in the group drop-down menu, you cannot reuse this "group." When you create a web application and specify [custom], you choose the service applications available to that web application. If you then create a second web application and select [custom], you will not see the service applications you chose for the first web application. This is a unique instance of [custom]. It is not reusable.

Proxy groups or *application proxy groups* are other terms you may hear for service application groups. This is how they are referred to in the SharePoint 2010 Management Shell and in the object model (OM).

 To create a group you can reuse, you need to use the SharePoint 2010 Management Shell and run the `New-SPServiceApplicationProxyGroup` *cmdlet. You will learn more about this cmdlet in the section "Service Application Administration" later in the chapter.*

Service Application Connection

The *service application connection* is actually what most people are thinking about when they create the service application from Central Administration. This connection connects the web service that runs for the service application and accepts requests from the web application to the service application group. In other words, the web application is associated with a service application group that says, "Here are all the service applications you can use." That way, when the web application wants profile information, for example, it knows what User Profile web services to call. If you look in IIS, you will see a website named SharePoint Web Services. If you drill through this list, you can find these service application connections and their web services. If you configured your farm with the Farm Configuration Wizard, then they will be named and listed as a 32 character GUID and not a logical name.

Like the service application group, the service application connection is known by a few other names. *Proxy* and *application proxy* are sometimes used, especially when dealing with the SharePoint 2010 Management Shell and the OM. Avoid the temptation to use these terms, as the word "proxy" is one of those overused IT words, used in about a bazillion places. Just don't do it.

Service Application

The *service application* is your main purpose in this somewhat complicated connection matrix. Service applications provide the services you need once you have access to them. When you create a new service application, you automatically get the accompanying service application connection point and the database(s), covered next.

Service Application Database(s)

As mentioned earlier, not all service applications have a storage requirement. For example, Excel Services does not store data; it only facilitates the display of data stored somewhere else, so it doesn't need a database. Conversely, Search has intensive storage needs, so it actually has multiple databases. The Managed Metadata service only needs one database to do its job.

When a service application needs a database, you will be prompted to provide a name when manually creating the service application. Each database is unique to an individual service application. For example, if you create an Enterprise BDC service application and an HR Only BDC service application, you will have two unique databases. A single database and service can be used to host data that needs to be kept logically separate, but additional planning and PowerShell cmdlets are required. More on that later.

Service Application Service(s)

Last, but certainly not least, are the *service application services*. You can find these hanging out in Central Administration on the Application Management page. Under Service Applications, click Manage services on server. The link is also on the System Settings page.

The services are the true workhorses in the stack. When you make a request to Excel Services, for example, you go through the connections listed above and finally get to the service application. It facilitates your request but all the actual processing and work is done by the Excel Calculation Services running on one or more servers in your farm.

These services are one of the key ways you scale service applications. If, due to heavy usage, you find that you need more performance from Excel Services, then you could start the Excel Calculation Services on another server in your farm. That way, when you make requests of the Excel service application, it will distribute the request between both of the servers running the services. You can continue to add servers running the service until you achieve your performance target.

You will find that each service application can handle this load balancing of the services in its own way. Excel services has a setting to control the load balancing. Managed Metadata just does the load balancing on its own. And Search... well, you'll find several pages in Chapter 14 to explain how Search balances the load.

Tying It Up with an Example

Take a look at Figure 7-6, which provides a schematic diagram of the concepts just described.

Looking first at the left side of the diagram, the company has a SharePoint web application, http://intranet (1a), that is associated with the default (2a) service application group. The default service application group has three service applications in it: Enterprise BDC (4a), Enterprise Managed Metadata (4b), and Enterprise Excel Services (4c). These are connected to the default service application group by the three service application connections (3a, 3b, 3c). These connections are not something that administrators can actually touch; they are created when the service application is created and they enable the web applications to talk to the associated service applications. The Enterprise BDC stores its content in its database (5a) and uses the Business Data Connectivity Service (6a) running on the server. You can also see that the Enterprise Managed Metadata service application has a database (5b) and a service (6b). Finally, Enterprise Excel Services does not have a database but is using the Excel calculation service (6c).

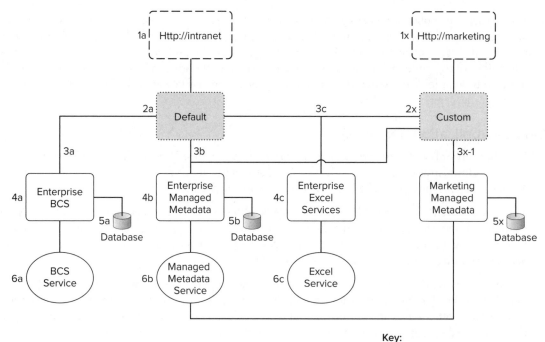

Key:
1. Web Application
2. Service Application Group
3. Service Application Connection
4. Service Application
5. Service Application Database(s)
6. Service Application Service(s)

FIGURE 7-6

That was pretty straightforward, so now take a look at a slightly more complicated scenario by looking at the right side of the figure. The company has a second web application at `http://marketing` (1x). They are using the [custom] (2x) service application group. Now for the twist. There are once again three service application connections. The connection (3b) to the Enterprise Managed Metadata (4b) and the connection (3c) to the Enterprise Excel Services (4c) are reused, demonstrating that a service application can be connected to multiple service application groups. Enterprise Managed Metadata continues to use the same database (5b) and service (6b) as before, because it is the same service application. The same is true for Enterprise Excel Services and its service (6c).

And the final twist: Marketing has a unique service application, Marketing Managed Metadata (4x) that is connected (3x) to the [custom] group. This service application has a unique database (5x) for its storage but it uses the same Managed Metadata Service (6b) as the Enterprise Managed Metadata service application did.

That's it, folks. If you grasp these relationships, you know everything you need to know about service applications. Ok, maybe not everything, but you are off to a solid start. Dig in and keep reading.

Connecting across Farms

Once you understand the service applications and all of their connections in your farm, the next logical step is to add more connections. Some of the service applications are capable of being published and then consumed across different SharePoint farms. Even more impressive is the fact that all of the service applications except the User Profile service application don't even require the two SharePoint farms to be in trusted Active Directory domains.

Before you can publish or consume the service applications between two farms, you have to establish a farm *trust*. This is done by using the SharePoint 2010 Management Shell to create and register certificates between the two farms. This is covered in greater detail in the section "Service Application Administration" later in the chapter.

After the farm trust is configured, you can go to the publishing farm and select the service application you want to publish. Once it is published, you will get a URL for accessing the published service.

From the consuming farm, you simply connect to the published service by providing the URL. Then the connected service application can be added to a service application group, and will provide services just as if the service application had been part of the farm. Figure 7-7 shows an example of four farms at work.

Farm 1 introduces a new concept, an *enterprise services farm*. This is something typically seen only in large companies. The idea is that a farm is created and maintained exclusively to provide services to other SharePoint farms throughout the organization. This way, the services farm can be optimized for hosting services and can be maintained in the same manner. For example, a Search index might contain several million items, requiring several days to do a full crawl, and hours to do an incremental crawl. In order to do this efficiently, you need to optimize your hardware for Search. If you have three SharePoint farms and each maintains its own Search service application, it would be very expensive to do a lot of repetitive crawling of content. Instead, a much better solution would be to maintain the index in one farm and just consume the service from the other farms.

Farm 2 is a simple farm for publishing content, maybe hosting just informational websites or similar content. In this farm, the demand for service applications is low, and all of the service applications it does require are provided by the enterprise farm. Therefore, this farm actually has no local service applications and is just optimized for displaying SharePoint content.

Farm 3 is a collaboration farm and is a busy place. This farm has demands for all types of service applications — some are consumed from farm 1, and others are hosted locally. The locally hosted service applications are those that are not capable of being published across farms, so they must reside in the farm where they are needed. Note that the Managed Metadata service application from farm 4 is being consumed. Other than that, there is nothing special about this scenario other than the flexibility of consuming service applications from multiple farms.

Farm 4 is very similar to the collaboration farm in nature. It is hosting its own web applications and is consuming local and remote service applications. Additionally, it has published the Managed Metadata service application for consumption by farm 3. Although all three farms are using the default group in this example, this isn't a requirement. You very well could have configured the [custom] group in any of the farms to consume the cross-farm service applications.

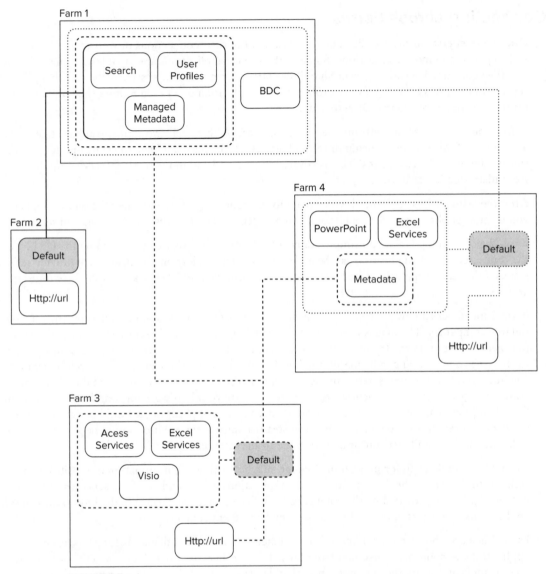

FIGURE 7-7

Service Applications As a Framework

You have probably noticed by now that all of the service applications act slightly different. This is because service applications are really a bunch of individual services built to plug into a framework.

The great thing about this framework is that anyone can plug into it. It is hoped that as third-party vendors and developers start writing code for SharePoint 2010, they will take advantage of the framework and use it to add their functionality. That way, instead of needing to create a custom third-party application to administer their added SharePoint functionality, they will just plug right into Central Administration. If they need a service to run, they can just add it to services on the server, giving administrators a consistent experience.

There are already two instances of this today. The Microsoft Office Web Applications and Project Server 2010 are not strictly parts of SharePoint 2010. But when they were developed, their respective groups at Microsoft chose to add their functionality through the service application framework. That way, when you need to administer either tool, you can simply select Central Administration ⇨ Manage service applications. For example, after you install the Office Web Applications you will see both a service application and a service on the server named Word Viewing Service, along with a few others. From an administrator's perspective, there is no difference between these service applications and one provided out of the box with SharePoint 2010.

SERVICE APPLICATION ADMINISTRATION

Now that you have a working knowledge of the fundamentals, it is time to put that knowledge to work. In this section, you will learn how to operate all the knobs and switches that enable you, as a SharePoint administrator, to do your job.

Creating a New Instance of a Service Application

In Chapter 4, you took advantage of the Farm Configuration Wizard to create several default service applications. That was a great way to quickly get up and running with SharePoint 2010.But now you are ready for prime time, and HR is screaming for its own instance of the Managed Metadata service application. They would like to name it HR Only Metadata. The following steps describe how you would create it for them:

FIGURE 7-8

1. Open Central Administration.

2. In the Application Management section of the home page, click the link to Manage service applications.

3. Here you can see all of the service applications currently available in your farm. In the Ribbon, click the New button and select Managed Metadata Service, as shown in Figure 7-8.

4. For Name, enter HR Only Metadata.

5. Confirm you have the correct Database Server listed.

WHAT IF EVERYONE WANTS THEIR OWN MANAGED METADATA SERVICE?

If there are other divisions in the company that feel they need to have their own Managed Metadata service, there is an additional way to solve this. By using what Microsoft terms a partitioned service application, data and processing can be kept separate despite being in a single process and database. This is discussed in greater detail later in this chapter.

If you want to host this database, or any other database, on a different SQL Server, you merely need to ensure that permissions are set up. Once that is done, you can just enter the new server's name. Typically, the permissions you need are found in your farm administrator account. This is the account you specified when you ran the SharePoint Products and Technologies Configuration Wizard (the gray one) when the farm was first configured. The SQL rights this account needs include dbcreator and securityadmin on the existing or new SQL Server that you are trying to use. Also, the SQL Server will need to meet the minimum SharePoint requirements for SQL.

6. Most of the time you will choose Use existing application pool for Application Pool. Then, in the drop-down menu, select SharePoint Web Services Default, as shown in Figure 7-9.

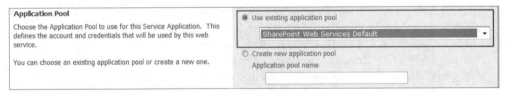

FIGURE 7-9

For optimal performance, the current best practice is to keep all of your service applications in one application pool. This may change as the product evolves, but it makes the most sense for now. Application pools consume a great deal of resources, and performance testing has shown that you will get the best results if all of your service applications are in one application pool.

7. At the bottom of the window you will see some stuff about Content Type hub and Report syndication errors. Leave these two fields alone for now (and check out Chapter 16 for more information on their use).

8. The last checkbox, Add this service application to the farm's default list, is checked by default. Leave it as is. Later in the chapter you will learn how to change this setting after the fact if necessary.

9. Leave all other settings at their default and click OK. After the service application is created, you will be returned to the Manage service applications page.

Using the Ribbon to Manage Service Applications

Service applications are built and then bolted into SharePoint through the framework. Part of that framework allows developers to utilize the Ribbon to manage their service applications. But because there is no hard set of rules about what they do with the buttons on the Ribbon, you will see a variety of behaviors. In this section you will learn the primary uses of the various Ribbon commands.

When looking at the various management screens and options you will see that some service applications use all of the buttons on the Ribbon, while others use almost none. This flexibility is the power at work. As an administrator you will just have to apply the knowledge learned here to each service application and figure out exactly how it works.

The Manage and Properties Buttons

Now that you have your HR Only Metadata service application, you need to be able to administer it. The first thing to take a look at is the properties. You do this by clicking once to the right of the service application. This will highlight the service application, enabling the available options on the Ribbon, as shown in Figure 7-10. (If you are taken to the Manage service application screen after clicking, then you accidently clicked the name of the service application. Press the Back button in your browser and try again.)

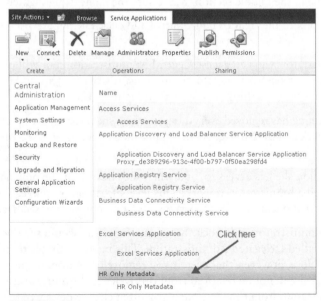

FIGURE 7-10

Now click the Properties button on the Ribbon. That pops up a window showing the same settings you specified when you created the service application. Most of the service applications allow you to access this screen. Here, you can check information (such as what database name you used) or adjust settings if you change your mind about something (such as the application pool). After you are done looking around, click Cancel to return to the Manage service application screen.

Now click the Manage button on the Ribbon. This will take you to the page for managing the actual service application. In the case of HR Only Metadata, you are now taken to the screen for defining terms and all of those other fun things you can do with managed metadata. All of the service applications that have something to manage have their own manage interface. This is just another piece of the framework.

In short, use Properties to look at or change settings you configured when creating a service application. Use Manage to access the service application and do whatever it is your service application was meant to do.

Setting Up a Delegated Administrator

Now that you have found this awesome manage screen for managing the managed metadata terms, wouldn't it be great if you could give someone in HR access to add all of the terms? Well, you are in luck. You can add someone from Human Resources as a delegated administrator quite easily:

1. Ensure that you are still at the Manage service applications screen in Central Administration.

2. Click to the right of HR Only Metadata.

3. Click Administrators from the Ribbon.

4. Enter the name of the HR user and click Add (for example, Contoso\JenniferH).

5. You will now see the user's name in the middle section. Make sure the name is highlighted.

6. In the bottom section, click the box to the right of Full Control and click OK. Figure 7-11 shows an example.

Now the HR user is a delegated administrator who can access Central Administration, but will only see those service applications to which they have been granted permissions. If Contoso\JenniferH logs into Central Administration, she will see something very similar to Figure 7-12.

That's a lot of white space. Security trimming has removed everything to which she doesn't have access, which is pretty much everything. If she clicks on the Manage service applications link, she will see what is shown in Figure 7-13.

She can see only the one service application she has access to, and when she clicks on it she only has the option of Manage. This is a delegated administrator at work. This level of trimming enables you to delegate the management of specific components without worrying about compromising security.

If you were to log back in as the real administrator and check the permissions, you would see the user has been added to a special group called Delegated Administrators. This makes it simple to find everyone who has been granted access. Note, however, that even if you remove users from managing all of the service applications, they still will not be removed from this Delegated Administrators group. Therefore, be sure to do a little cleanup from time to time if you often change delegated administrators.

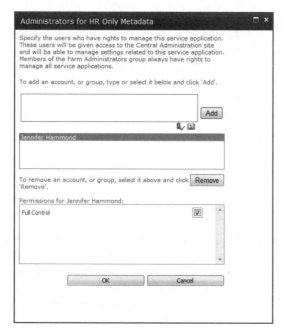

FIGURE 7-11

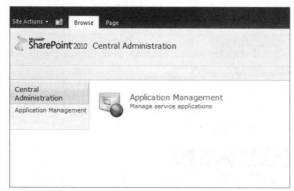

FIGURE 7-12

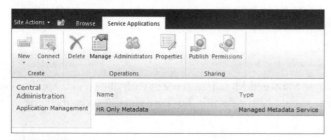

FIGURE 7-13

Managing Service Application Groups

After all that very exciting information about how great these groups are, it is time you learned how to use and consume them. After a brief walk through the GUI tools, we'll take a look at some of the hardcore things you can do with the SharePoint 2010 Management Shell.

Using Your Mouse to Manage Groups

Put that fancy mouse you have on your desk to work and follow these steps:

1. Open Central Administration.

2. Click Application Management.

3. In the Service Application section, click Configure service application associations.

From this screen you will see a list of all of your service applications and the Application Proxy Group with which each one is associated. This is where all that terminology you studied comes in handy. You already know that "application proxy group" means service application group, and that "application proxies" really means service application connections, right? The nice thing about this screen is you can now click on one of the proxy groups to change its connections if necessary. For example, if you wanted to remove HR Only Metadata from the default group, this is how you would do it:

1. Click on the proxy group Default.

2. Deselect HR Only Metadata.

3. Scroll down the page and click OK.

Now all of the web applications that are associated with the default service application group will no longer have access to the HR Only Metadata group.

When you first got to the Configure Service Application Associations screen, you may have noticed that because you have multiple Managed Metadata service applications in your farm, one appears as [default] and the other(s) as [set as default], as shown in Figure 7-14.

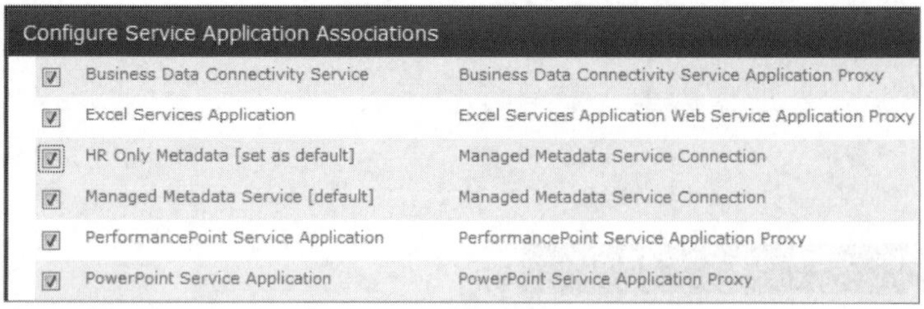

Configure Service Application Associations	
☑ Business Data Connectivity Service	Business Data Connectivity Service Application Proxy
☑ Excel Services Application	Excel Services Application Web Service Application Proxy
☑ HR Only Metadata [set as default]	Managed Metadata Service Connection
☑ Managed Metadata Service [default]	Managed Metadata Service Connection
☑ PerformancePoint Service Application	PerformancePoint Service Application Proxy
☑ PowerPoint Service Application	PowerPoint Service Application Proxy

FIGURE 7-14

This is because you can associate multiple Managed Metadata services with one service application group, so you need to specify which one should be the default. Both are equally accessible; one of them just needs to be presented to the user first. You will see the set as default option with other service applications as applicable.

This interface for manipulating the service application connections in a service application group is the same whether you are modifying the default, [custom], or even a custom group created with the SharePoint 2010 Management Shell.

Using the Keyboard to Manage Groups with Windows PowerShell

As with just about everything related to SharePoint 2010 administration, anything you can do in a GUI you can do better with Windows PowerShell cmdlets in the SharePoint 2010 Management Shell. Chapter 10 has all of the awesome details about working with Windows PowerShell for administrative tasks. This section covers some of the key cmdlets you can use for service applications, and skips right over all of the details about using the SharePoint 2010 Management Shell. If you are new to Windows PowerShell, you might find it easier to put this section on hold until you have had a chance to dig into Chapter 10.

Depending on which components you have installed, there are approximately 105 different components related to service applications. Because it would be impossible to cover all of these without doubling this book's page count, we will instead take a look at a few of the more important ones. To discover most of the cmdlets, run the following command from the shell:

```
Get-Command *serviceapplication*
```

Have fun with the list that is returned. You will notice that each service application, such as Excel Services, has its own cmdlets, which you can use to provision a new service application without the need to use Central Administration.

Creating a New Service Application Group

After spending all that time learning about service application groups, you were no doubt dismayed to learn that you cannot create reusable groups in Central Administration. As you might guess, you can create your own group.

The cmdlet you need is `New-SPServiceApplicationProxyGroup`, and you just need to provide the `-name` property. The command is as follows:

```
New-SPServiceApplicationProxyGroup -name YourCustomGroup
```

Now you have a group called YourCustomGroup. The group is empty, of course, so now you can add a connection to it. To do this, you first need to get the Id of the connection you want to add. To achieve that, run the following cmdlet:

```
Get-SPServiceApplicationProxy
```

This will give you the DisplayName, TypeName, and Id, which is a GUID. The Id is the important part. See Figure 7-15 for example output. Keep in mind that your GUIDs will be different — or at least they should be; if they are not, you have bigger problems than this book can solve.

```
PS C:\Users\shane> Get-SPServiceApplicationProxy

DisplayName          TypeName            Id

Business Data Con... Business Data Con... 8b5a6d82-553a-4c52-8e5c-443af28100a6
Word Viewing Service Word Viewing Serv... 7ef2a5c5-e5e1-4228-8c21-668919c3e046
Word Automation S... Word Automation S... 693451b1-0fad-4130-b458-7287f4500903
State Service        State Service Proxy ad34b1e8-e531-4b21-b106-8b17d424944f
Access Services      Access Services W... 9bc562cc-84ad-4d18-98d9-8c27e472271e
Application Regis... Application Regis... 93efe2f7-141f-4e8f-ac81-18f824a8ea2b
HR Only Metadata     Managed Metadata ... f2e1ecab-8ceb-4007-9c12-c418e1349071
Managed Metadata ... Managed Metadata ... 01e0a24c-1527-4eab-a473-ee059b2c73c2
PerformancePoint ... PerformancePoint ... 2c7989f3-6208-4692-b7ea-cd3e9c8b0723
Secure Store Service Secure Store Serv... 161b62b8-1669-495f-9d10-d18b0b522e46
Test Secure Store    Secure Store Serv... abfe3190-0c36-4df7-b6a4-7c86db54a0c7
Search Service Ap... Search Service Ap... 0838df6c-0078-4b1f-93ac-35568a62685c
Web Analytics Ser... Web Analytics Ser... 6147528d-4a7b-4c6e-bccf-6fdb353df0ae
Application Disco... Application Disco... f03c67a2-2fc9-405e-b568-63da816c4659
PowerPoint Servic... PowerPoint Servic... 9ff16103-0fb1-4b1a-a3c1-1ff1ff55ca31
User Profile Serv... User Profile Serv... fd64203f-a0fd-43cc-b77d-07dc15419814
Visio Graphics Se... Visio Graphics Se... c053594d-626f-4362-ba88-69352387c34e
Excel Services Ap... Excel Services Ap... cd7a24a9-17a9-4f34-b6c4-ec605568e18e
Usage and Health ... Usage and Health ... cc2b2e15-61a5-4449-ba2f-a1454508a474
```

FIGURE 7-15

To add the Access Services connection to the group, you would run the following command:

```
Add-SPServiceApplicationProxyGroupMember YourCustomGroup -member
    9bc562cc-84ad-4d18-98d9-8c27e472271e
```

Remember that you need to enter the GUID for your service application.

If you are thinking that was a very long way to go to add a service application connection, you're right.

An Easier Way to Add Connections

Let's cheat. Now that you have the new group, you can go back to the GUI and do a little click, click, click to add the other connections to it. Navigate back to Central Administration ➪ Application Management ➪ Configure service application associations. Confused? When you get to that page, you will not see YourCustomGroup. You will not be able to see it on this page until you associate it with a web application. To change a web application's service application group association, follow these steps:

1. From the Application Management page, select Manage web applications.

2. Select the service application for which you want to change associations.

3. From the Ribbon, click Service Connections.

4. From the drop-down, select YourCustomGroup.

5. Scroll down the page and click OK.

Now go back to Configure service application associations. You should see YourCustomGroup. Click YourCustomGroup. A simple web interface will appear for selecting the service application connections you want to include in the group.

Publishing a Service Application Across Farms

Time for some more fun with Windows PowerShell cmdlets. Publishing a service application and consuming it isn't too terribly difficult and can mostly be done through the UI. The tricky part is setting up the farm trusts and getting the Application Discovery and Load Balancer Service Application secured properly. Once you knock out those two pieces the rest is a breeze.

Setting Up the Farm Trust

Follow these steps to set up the farm trust:

1. On the publishing server, create a folder at c:\PubCerts.

2. From the publishing server, open the SharePoint 2010 Management Shell. To get the certificate, type the following line and press Enter:

    ```
    $rootCert = Get-SPCertificateAuthority | Select RootCertificate
    ```

3. To export the certificate, type the following line and press Enter:

    ```
    $rootCert.Export("Cert") | Set-Content C:\PubCerts\PublishingRoot.cer
        -Encoding byte
    ```

4. Copy the c:\PubCerts folder from the publishing server to the consuming server.

5. On the consuming server, create a folder at c:\ConsumerCerts.

6. From the publishing server, open the SharePoint 2010 Management Shell.

7. To get the certificate, type the following line and press Enter:

    ```
    $rootCert = Get-SPCertificateAuthority | Select RootCertificate
    ```

8. To export the certificate, type the following line and press Enter:

    ```
    $rootCert.Export("Cert") | Set-Content C:\ConsumerCerts\ConsumingRoot.cer
        -Encoding byte
    ```

9. To get the STS certificate, type the following line and press Enter:

    ```
    $stsCert =
        (Get-SPSecurityTokenServiceConfig).LocalLoginProvider.SigningCertificate
    ```

10. To export the STS certificate, type the following line and press Enter:

    ```
    $stsCert.Export("Cert") | Set-Content "C:\ConsumerCerts\ConsumingSTS.cer"
        -Encoding byte
    ```

11. Copy the c:\ConsumerCerts folder to the publishing server.

12. Still on the consuming server, to load the publishing server's certificate, type the following line and press Enter:

    ```
    $trustCert = Get-PfxCertificate "C:\PubCerts\PublishingRoot.cer"
    ```

13. To set up the trust using the certificate, type the following line and press Enter:

    ```
    New-SPTrustedRootAuthority PublishingFarm -Certificate $trustCert
    ```

14. Return to the shell on the publishing server.

15. To load the consuming server's certificate, type the following line and press Enter:

```
$trustCert = Get-PfxCertificate "c:\ConsumerCerts\ConsumingRoot.cer"
```

16. To set up the trust using the certificate, type the following line and press Enter:

```
New-SPTrustedRootAuthority Collaboration -Certificate $trustCert
```

17. To load the consuming server's STS certificate, type the following line and press Enter:

```
$stsCert = Get-PfxCertificate "c:\ConsumerCerts\ConsumingSTS.cer"
```

18. To add the STS certificate to the trust, type the following line and press Enter:

```
New-SPTrustedServiceTokenIssuer Collaboration -Certificate $stsCert
```

19. Return to the shell on the consuming server.

20. Type the following line and press Enter:

```
Get-SPFarm | Select Id
```

21. Record that number for use later.

22. Return to the Shell on the publishing server.

23. To get the security object for the topology service application, type the following line and press Enter:

```
$security = Get-SPTopologyServiceApplication | Get-SPServiceApplication
    Security
```

24. To get the farm's claim provider object, type the following line and press Enter:

```
$claimProvider = (Get-SPClaimProvider System).ClaimProvider
```

25. To set up the new claim principal for the consuming farm, type the following line and press Enter:

```
$principal = New-SPClaimsPrincipal -ClaimType
    "http://schemas.microsoft.com/sharepoint/2009/08/claims/farmid"
    -ClaimProvider $claimProvider
    -ClaimValue <Type the ID from Step 21, don't include the <>>
```

26. To give that principal permissions in your publishing farm to the topology service application, type the following line and press Enter:

```
Grant-SPObjectSecurity -Identity $security -Principal $principal
    -Rights "Full Control"
```

27. To set the access just given, type the following line and press Enter:

```
Get-SPTopologyServiceApplication | Set-SPServiceApplicationSecurity
    -ObjectSecurity $security
```

That does it. You now have completed the process of establishing a trust between the two farms so that the publishing server can serve up service applications to the consuming farm. If you want to look at the trusts or possibly remove one, you can do that through the GUI by navigating to Central Administration ⇨ Security ⇨ Manage trust.

Publishing a Service Application

For this part, you could dive back into PowerShell, or you could use the GUI in Central Administration. Let's be "efficient" (aka lazy) and use the GUI. For this example, we will publish a managed metadata service application:

1. On the publishing server, open Central Administration.

2. Navigate to Application Management ⇨ Manage service applications.

3. Click to the right of the service application you want to make available.

4. In the Ribbon, click Publish.

5. On the Publish Service Application page, check the box for Publish this Service Application to other farms.

6. For the Publish URL, copy all of the string that begins with "urn:" and ends with ".svc." For example, it will be similar to the following:

```
urn:schemas-microsoft-com:sharepoint:service:ac40e8f87daa43d9bec93f9fa99360c7
        #authority=urn:uuid:de389296913c4f00b7970f50ea298fd4&authority
        =https://server:32844/Topology/topology.svc
```

7. Scroll down the page and click OK.

8. Click to the right of the service application.

9. From the Ribbon, click Permissions.

10. Enter the Farm Id of the consuming farm. You found this using step 21 in the previous section, "Setting Up theFarm Trust."

11. Click Add.

12. Highlight the Remote Farm: <Your Farm Id>.

13. For permissions, check the box to assign the permissions you wish to give to the remote farm. The permissions available will vary based on the service application being published.

14. Open Central Administration on the consuming farm.

15. Navigate to Application Management ⇨ Manage service applications.

16. From the Ribbon, click Connect.

17. Enter the URL for the service application you want to access from step 6 in this section.

18. Click OK.

19. Click the service application name so that it is highlighted in yellow.

20. You can choose whether or not to include this service application in the default service application group. When you are done, click OK.

21. Now you can accept the default connection name or enter your own. When you are finished, click OK.

22. At the success screen, click OK.

You can now work with the service application just as if it were part of your farm. The first time you work through this process, take your time; it is very easy to make a small mistake that causes yourself hours of troubleshooting.

MULTI-TENANCY IN SHAREPOINT 2010

No conversation about service applications would be complete without digging into the multi-tenant capabilities that have been built into SharePoint 2010. Under normal circumstance, the multi-tenant discussion usually pertains to hosted environments where a SharePoint farm is providing services to any number of different companies. But as you will see in this section, the concepts of multi-tenancy apply very directly to the enterprise as well.

Segmentation of Data and Processing

In SharePoint 2007, the walls of security and the isolation of data and services fell along the lines of Web Application to Site Collections to webs (if you need a refresher check out the "Terminology" section Chapter 3). New to SharePoint 2010 is the capability to create a new layer of segregation of data and services between the Application layer and the associated site collections. This segmentation is possible through the use of *site subscriptions*. Site subscriptions enable you to group together site collections that are part of the same web application. Site subscriptions are a logical group of site collections that can share settings (in the Subscription Settings database), features, and service data. Site Subscriptions are identified with a subscription ID. The subscription ID is used to map services, features, and sites to tenants, and to partition service data by tenant. Note the following characteristics of site subscriptions:

➤ A site can be a member of only one site subscription at a time. This prevents any conflicts with licensing schemas.

➤ There is no Central Administration interface for managing site subscriptions. Management must be handled through PowerShell, including creating, managing, and removing sites from a site subscription.

➤ Sites can only join a site group in the same web application as that specific site subscription. Sites can't join site groups associated with other Web Applications.

➤ Site subscriptions can span multiple content databases.

Once you have a site subscription with associated site collections, they can now consume data from service applications. While this concept is not necessarily new, what is new is that some of these service applications can be provisioned such that their functions and data are kept separate from other tenants who may be consuming that service application. SharePoint 2010 refers to this type of service application as a *partitioned service application*. For instance, if Enterprise Search were provisioned as a partitioned service application and associated with two site subscriptions, then search results from customer A would never be returned to customer B.

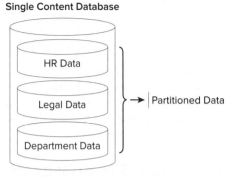

Single Content Database

HR Data

Legal Data

Department Data

Partitioned Data

FIGURE 7-16

It should also be pointed out that no changes or additions are made to the number of databases required to support this capability. SharePoint merely segments the content within the single database (see Figure 7-16).

Although nonpartitioned service applications can be created with Central Administration or PowerShell, the latter is required to provision a partitioned service application. When creating a partitioned service application in PowerShell, the addition of the –Partitioned switch is all that is required.

Some service applications do not lend themselves to being partitioned, such as those that do not store user-specific data. Table 7-2 shows which service applications within SharePoint 2010 can be partitioned.

TABLE 7-2 SharePoint 2010 Service Application Partitioning

CAN BE PARTITIONED	CANNOT BE PARTITIONED
People	Excel Calculates Services
Managed Metadata	Access Services
Business Data Connectivity	Visio Service
SharePoint Search	Word Service
Secure Storage Service	Word Viewing
Web Analytics	PowerPoint
Usage and Health Data Connection	State Service
Project\Subscription Settings	InfoPath
	Fast Search

Another set of capabilities that was previously managed at the web application layer was Features. When a Feature was installed and activated at a Web Application layer, it was automatically available for activation at the Site Collection level. In SharePoint 2010 you can now group Features together into what are called *Feature sets*. Feature sets are logical groupings of Features that are then made available for activation to a site subscription by an administrator of that site subscription.

SharePoint 2010 is smart enough to prevent the use of Web Parts that are part of a service application that is not partitioned to a specific site in a site subscription. For instance, if the farm is built with SharePoint Server Enterprise but the site subscription does not have Enterprise Search available, then SharePoint will not make the Search template (and Web Parts) available for use by the end users.

Once a site subscription is created and sites are associated with it, the sites are managed through a new site template called a Tenant Administration site. (It's called this because a hosted customer (or department) is referred to as a "tenant." The Tenant Administration site gives the administrator full administrative rights over the site collections, including permissions to create new sites if self-service site creation is enabled.

Creating a Site Subscription

When you are ready to start working with SharePoint in the Hosted mode, keep in mind that nearly all of your system administration will be done through PowerShell, as these new features are not built into the SharePoint Central Administration console. This is true for creating site subscriptions, feature sets, and partitioned service applications, and provisioning Tenant Administration sites. The PowerShell cmdlet to create a new site subscription is:

```
New-SPSiteSubscription
```

When building your site subscriptions, using variables for your commands will enable them to be reused and/or nested within other cmdlets. For example, to create and view a new site subscription, use the following:

```
$SiteSub = New-SPSiteSubscription
```

Once you have the subscription, you need to get the site collection(s) you want to add to the subscription into a variable. To add a *single* site collection to a variable use the following command:

```
$TargetSite = get-spsite http://portal.contoso.com/sites/marketing
```

To add *all* site collections within a web application to a variable, use this command:

```
$TargetSite = Get-SPWebApplication http://portal.contoso.com | Get-SPSite
```

Now that you have your site collection(s) in a variable, use the following command to add their subscription:

```
$TargetSite | foreach-Object{set-SPSite -Identity $_ -SiteSubscription $SiteSub}
```

To view all the site collections that are now part of the site subscription you would just type the name of the variable:

```
(Get-spsitesubscription $SiteSub).sites
```

From here you could create the Tenant Administration site using the PowerShell cmdlet `new-spsite`, making sure to identify the site template as `tenantadmin#0`:

```
New-spsite -url http://portal.contoso.com/sites/tasite -template "tenantadmin#0"
      -owneralias domain\username -sitesubscription $SiteSub
```

As previously mentioned, site collections aren't the only SharePoint artifacts that can be grouped; Features can be grouped into Feature sets.

Another benefit to site subscriptions is that usage analysis data and logging data is also segmented, like the user data. This enables the IT pro to troubleshoot and debug based on a specific site subscription. In addition, segmenting the usage data enables a hosting company or enterprise that's using a charge-back model for IT services to charge according to usage based on data, processes, or number of users.

Multi-Tenant Use Cases

You should now have a basic understanding of the use of multi-tenancy in the traditional hosted services scenario. To summarize:

A hosting company decides that they would like to be able to sell SharePoint services to their customers. All of the customers will be different individuals or companies that want to ensure that their information is kept separate from the other sites that are hosted on the common infrastructure. Windows SharePoint Services (WSS) 3.0 included mechanisms to keep a customer's content separate from other customer's data, but what was lacking was the ability to separate processing and data from additional services like Enterprise Search.

These customers would need to be provisioned using an STSADM command and be given site collections that would be held in shared web applications. The hosting company was also bound to using WSS because of the common Shared Service Provider found in MOSS. One of the challenges that the SSP created in this specific scenario was with Enterprise Search. Enterprise Search was designed to index all content associated with that SSP. The query service would then provide results to users when requested. The challenge specific to this scenario is that there was the very real possibility of exposing customer A's data to customer B via Enterprise Search as there we lacked the capability to segment the data based on site collection. Adding SSPs was not an option as there is a limit on the number of SSPs that can be provisioned in a single farm.

SharePoint 2010 fixes this through Service Application Partitioning. Partitioning creates very real boundaries between information and processing based on site subscriptions, making it impossible to expose customer A's data to customer B. As previously mentioned, provisioning must be done when the service application and proxy are created. Now let's apply the concept of partitioning to the enterprise.

Partitioning in the Enterprise

Just as it would in a hosted scenario, a large enterprise needs to handle data and services in ways similar to the Hosted world. Consider, for instance, managed metadata. There are terms within the organization that need to be controlled by one central group and consumed by the entire organization. There are also terms that ought to be defined and managed by individual corporate divisions or departments. The same holds true for Enterprise Search. A partitioned Enterprise Search service application would enable content from the General Council department to remain wholly separate from content from other divisions, as depicted in Figure 7-17.

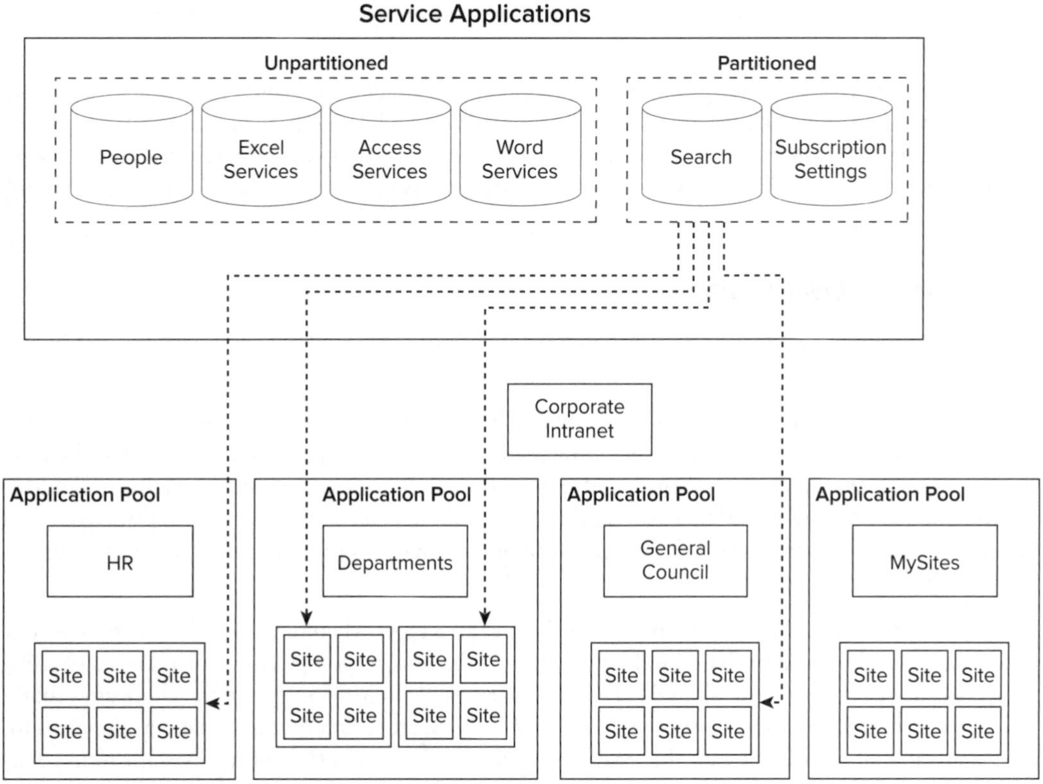

Service Applications

FIGURE 7-17

The ability to segment this data and to create Feature sets gives both the multi-tenant hoster as well as the enterprise customer an opportunity to offer different tiers of services to their customers. The hosting company can provision a single farm and provide SharePoint Foundation, SharePoint Server Standard, and SharePoint Server Enterprise products. To take things one step further, they could also layer on additional third-party tools to enhance their product offering and more easily manage the provisioning and billing of those services.

From the enterprise customer's point of view, they can now provide multiple versions of SharePoint to their users on a single farm. For instance, only half of a company's 10,000 employees may need SharePoint Foundation capabilities. The remaining user community may need SharePoint Server Enterprise features. Individual SharePoint farms can now have multiple licensing schemas associated with them in a way that is easier to manage and control. In this case, only 5,000 users would need SharePoint Server Enterprise licenses, while the remaining users would use SharePoint Foundation licensing — and all of this would be perfectly acceptable to Microsoft.

The additional capabilities provided by the service application architecture, as well as the partitioning features available in SharePoint 2010, provide additional scalability previously not available in SharePoint. For instance, as Enterprise Search grows in content size and usage, it can now be segregated into its own SharePoint farm created for the purpose of providing Search services to the content farm(s). These types of farms, known as service application farms, provide services and data to other SharePoint farms; they are not directly consumed by users (see Figure 7-18).

Multi-Farm Hosting

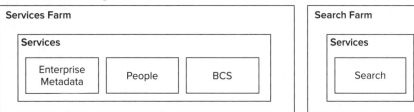

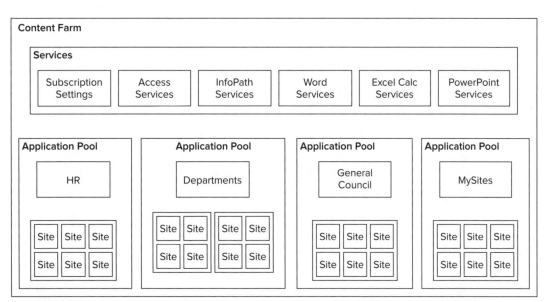

FIGURE 7-18

SUMMARY

The new service application framework in SharePoint 2010 provides a vast improvement over the shared service provider model offered previously. This new paradigm for sharing resources and managing services is scalable, flexible, and robust. As a SharePoint administrator who needs to make your farm sing, it is relatively easy to scale from a small, simple farm all the way up to multi-server farms with just a few simple clicks of the mouse or taps of the keyboard. And when you start to feel like even all of that flexibility isn't enough, you can also incorporate the use of multi-tenancy.

Now that you are familiar with all of the options for connecting your web applications to service applications, even from remote farms, you can rest easy. Although SharePoint can be configured in a seemingly infinite number of ways, this chapter has described how you can harness and manage its impressive capabilities. You have Central Administration for the easy tasks, and a large set of Windows PowerShell cmdlets for when you need to take things to the next level or just show off how cool you really are.

8

Securing and Managing Site Content

WHAT'S IN THIS CHAPTER?

➤   The administration hierarchy

➤   Security terminology

➤   User permissions

➤   Permission levels

➤   Security groups

➤   Granting users access

As the capabilities and use of SharePoint technologies continue to increase, so does the amount of content stored in SharePoint sites. To maintain and manage this content, you need an effective security structure in place to ensure that this content is only accessed by users with the proper permissions. To assist administrators with this gargantuan task, configuration options exist to grant users access with both broad and fine-grained settings. Additionally, you can configure this access at several hierarchical levels, making it easy to secure content throughout an environment. The security structure built at the onset of a SharePoint deployment plays a major role in the overall success or failure of the solution and is not to be taken lightly. In this chapter you get an in-depth look at the security configuration options available with SharePoint 2010 and how they can be used to lock down your environment.

REVIEWING THE TERMINOLOGY

Before diving into how site security can be set up, it is vital to understand the vocabulary that represents the various components of user access. These terms are often dependent upon each other so it is easy to get subjects confused. Be sure to have a firm grasp of these concepts before moving on to the next sections:

➤ **Permissions** — These are single units of access that represent specific tasks that can be performed at the list, site, or personalization level. Permission levels are made up of sets of permissions. SharePoint ships with a list of permissions. This list cannot be edited or added to, and permissions cannot be deleted.

 Although you can't delete a permission, you can control the permissions that are available for a site collection. For example, if you have a site collection that is storing archived content and you want to eliminate the possibility of users deleting list and library items, you can remove the permission to "Delete Items." This type of configuration can be made from Central Administration.

➤ **Permission levels** — Permission levels are pre-defined sets of permissions that are used to grant users access to content in SharePoint. The level of access that users with the assigned permission have is based on the permissions that make up the permission level. Several permission levels are created by default. These permission levels vary according to the type of template you use to create your site collections and sites. Each permission level is covered in detail later in this chapter, in the section "Permission Levels."

➤ **Users** — The smallest value to which access can be granted. This value corresponds to an account in Active Directory or another host application for user accounts.

➤ **Groups** — A group is a set of users who will have identical access needs. Users in the same group typically have the same role within an organization. Using groups, rather than granting permissions to individual users, makes it easier to manage user access.

➤ **Securable objects** — Securable objects are levels within SharePoint 2010 that can be "locked down," or secured, by setting specific user access. Sites, lists, libraries, and items are all securable objects. User access at each of these levels can be customized so that only the appropriate or approved users have access to the content.

➤ **Inheritance** — Inheritance is used to describe how user access is created by default within SharePoint. Whenever a securable object is created, it is created with the same user access as its parent. For new sites that you create, you specify whether you want the site to "inherit" permissions or whether the site should have customized permissions. When user access is inherited, any changes made to the parent securable object(s) will update the child securable object(s). When permissions aren't inherited, no updates are made to the access users and groups have within the securable object(s). If you choose to customize your user access and not inherit from the parent site, it is paramount that you document any changes to your security structure so that your team is aware of which sites will not be automatically updated.

This does not mean that membership to groups will not be updated; it means that the access that users or groups have will not be updated. Group membership can be edited in any site within the site collection, but these changes will affect the group for the entire site collection.

➤ **Site groups** — These are specific groups that are created for you by default when a new site is created. The types of groups that are created vary according to the site template used to create the site. The "Security Groups" section goes into more detail regarding the different types of groups and how they can be used within SharePoint 2010.

ADMINISTRATION HIERARCHY IN SHAREPOINT 2010

User access can be set at several hierarchical levels in a SharePoint 2010 environment. This helps break up the task and responsibility of security administration. At the higher levels, IT members will most likely be responsible for managing security for the server farm down through the services, features, and site collection administrator levels. This gives your IT department control over the servers and provisioning and managing site collections. Once site collections and sites have been created, along with the corresponding lists, libraries, pages, etc., the responsibility of securing content should be redirected to the users that "own" the specified content. This takes a large burden off of your IT department, and allows them to focus on maintaining the SharePoint environment as a whole, rather than managing every little piece. At the site collection level is the site collection administrator. This is typically a manager or department head that oversees all the users and content within a given site collection. Moving down the chain, individual users or power users can be delegated control of child sites, lists, and libraries. Note that if you intend on having non-IT staff manage security at the lower levels, an extensive amount of training is recommended, as well as an effective backup/restore plan. Having such high access allows those users to perform a wide variety of tasks, some of which can be fatal for environments. In the next few sections, each hierarchical level is covered in more detail.

Server or Server Farm Administrators

The server farm access level includes two groups:

➤ **Local Administrators** — Members of this group are also members of the Farm Administrators group. In addition to all the administrative tasks they can perform as farm administrators, local administrators can perform additional activities, even tasks unrelated to the SharePoint environment, on servers in the farm — including installing patches and service packs, administering IIS, starting/stopping services, SQL maintenance, reviewing Event Viewer logs, etc. Like farm administrators, these users do not have access to SharePoint sites by default. To manage users in this group, you must do so from the server itself.

➤ **Farm Administrators** — Members of this group have administrator access to all servers in the server farm. With this access they can perform any administrative task within the Central Administration site. Users in this group can also use PowerShell cmdlets for various administrative activities and assign users administrative roles for service applications. By default, this group does not have access to SharePoint sites, but it is possible for them to give themselves access through a web application policy.

To manage server farm administrators, follow these steps:

1. From Central Administration, select Site Settings ⇨ People and Groups.

2. Click Manage the farm administrators group. Here you can add and remove users from this group.

3. To add a user, click the New drop-down menu and select Add Users, as shown in Figure 8-1.

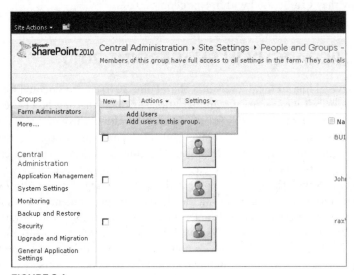

FIGURE 8-1

4. To remove a user, click the checkbox next to his or her name and then click Actions ⇨ Remove Users from Group, as shown in Figure 8-2.

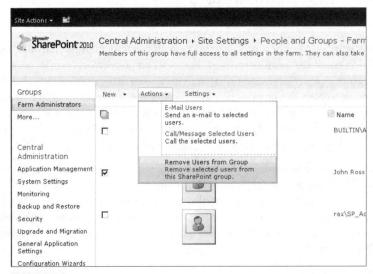

FIGURE 8-2

Although farm and local administrators do not have access to SharePoint sites by default, they can access and configure anything in Central Administration. With this access, they can grant themselves permissions by adding themselves to the Site Collection Administrators group for a site collection or by creating a web application policy that will grant them access to any site collection within that particular web application.

Service Application Administrators

Service application management is delegated to two groups. For more details check out Chapter 7.

➤ **Service Administrators** — Delegated by members in the Farm Administrators group, these users can manage settings for a specific service application within the server farm. These users cannot access any other service application unless they are given access by a farm administrator. Members of this group cannot create new service applications or perform any farm-level operations. To manage the Service Administrators, go to Central Administration ➪ Manage Service Applications (under the Application Management header). Highlight a service and in the Ribbon, under the Service Applications tab, click on Administrators.

➤ **Feature Administrators** — Delegated by farm or service administrators, members of this group are associated with a specific feature within a service application. Users can manage the subset of service application settings related to this feature, but only for this feature. Most service applications do not have this flexibility. An example of one that does have this capability is the User Profile service application. Here you can drill down and give users very specific permissions such as the ability to only manage audiences or profiles. To manage the Feature Administrators, go to Central Administration ➪ Manage Service Applications (under the Application Management header). Highlight a service and in the Ribbon, under the Service Applications tab, click on Permissions. If the service is available in the Permissions for user section you will see multiple permissions you can assign.

Site Collection Administrators

Members of the Site Collection Administrators group have Full Control permission level settings for all sites within the site collection. This access cannot be overridden for this site collection except through a web application policy, and this access is available to all content, whether the users are given explicit permissions or not. In addition to the administrative capabilities, the Primary and Secondary Site Collection Administrators receive additional notifications for quotas and user access requests. The Primary and Secondary Site Collection Administrators are specified when the site collection is created.

To manage users in a Site Collection Administrators group you have two options. For the first option:

1. Open Central Administration.

2. Click Application Management.

3. Under Site Collections, click Change site collection administrators. On the Site Collection Administrators page that appears (see Figure 8-3), you must select a site collection, and then you can add users as Primary or Secondary site collection administrators. Only one user can be added as a Primary site collection administrator; likewise for the Secondary site collection administrator. User groups cannot be entered for either of these sections.

FIGURE 8-3

The other option for managing the Site Collection Administrators group is from the site collection itself:

1. From the top-level site in your site collection, click Site Actions ⇨ Site Permissions.

2. In the Permission Tools tab, click Site Collection Administrators to display the screen shown in Figure 8-4.

3. Here you can add and remove users from this group, similarly to the method shown earlier for farm administrators.

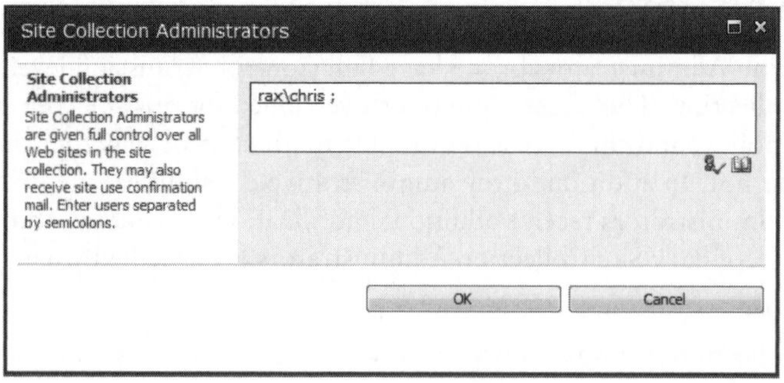

FIGURE 8-4

As a rule, the Site Collection Administrators group can never be empty. If you try to remove all the users, you will receive an error. If you find a way to do it programmatically, very bad things happen.

Site Administration

Users in the Site Owners group have been added to the Owners group and have Full Control to content on this site. Unlike site collection administrators, this access can be overridden by customizing permissions settings on a child site or lower level. By default, if you specify this at site creation, a [*site name*] Owners group is created. This group's members will have full control to the site.

Administration Beneath the Site Level

Management of content below the site level does not always require group membership:

➤ **Document library or list** — There is no specific group that manages content at this level, but permissions can be configured. This is useful when you want only a small portion of your content, on one site, to have restricted access.

➤ **Individual items** — Similar to the previous level, there is no set group that administers individual items at this level, but permissions can be configured. Providing granular control over user access is a powerful feature in SharePoint 2010.

UNDERSTANDING PERMISSIONS

When SharePoint is installed, a set of permissions is created. This set can be viewed by opening Central Administration and clicking on Application Management ➪ Manage Web Applications. From there, highlight a web application and click on User Permission (in the Ribbon, under the Web Applications tab). Not only can you view the available permissions, you can select the permissions that will be available for the web application and its site collections.

It is these permissions that enable administrators to configure user access at a granular level and, by doing so, secure content at various levels within SharePoint sites. Each permission level is one of three types of permissions: List, Site, or Personal. As previously mentioned, these permissions are combined to create *permission levels*. This method is the recommended approach for configuring SharePoint security. Figure 8-5 shows a partial list of the available options; for a more comprehensive look at permissions, see Table 8-1. This table provides the list of all permission levels, including what type of permission it is. It also displays the default permission levels that have each of these permissions out of the box.

TABLE 8-1: User Permissions

PERMISSION	DESCRIPTION	TYPE	PERMISSION LEVEL
Manage Lists	Create and delete lists, add or remove columns in a list, and add or remove public views of a list.	List	Full Control, Design, Manage Hierarchy
Override Check Out	Discard or check in a document that is checked out to another user.	List	Full Control, Design, Approve, Manage Hierarchy
Add Items	Add items to lists, and add documents to document libraries.	List	Full Control, Design, Contribute, Approve, Manage Hierarchy
Edit Items	Edit items in lists, edit documents in document libraries, and customize Web Part pages in document libraries.	List	Full Control, Design, Contribute, Approve, Manage Hierarchy
Delete Items	Delete items from a list, and documents from a document library.	List	Full Control, Design, Contribute, Approve, Manage Hierarchy
View Items	View items in lists, and documents in document libraries.	List	Full Control, Design, Contribute, Read, Approve, Manage Hierarchy, Restricted Read
Approve Items	Approve a minor version of a list item or document.	List	Full Control, Design, Approve
Open Items	View the source of documents with server-side file handlers.	List	Full Control, Design, Contribute, Read, Approve, Manage Hierarchy, Restricted Read
View Versions	View past versions of a list item or document.	List	Full Control, Design, Contribute, Read, Approve, Manage Hierarchy
Delete Versions	Delete past versions of a list item or document.	List	Full Control, Design, Contribute, Approve, Manage Hierarchy
Create Alerts	Create alerts	List	Full Control, Design, Contribute, Read, Approve, Manage Hierarchy

PERMISSION	DESCRIPTION	TYPE	PERMISSION LEVEL
View Application Pages	View forms, views, and application pages; enumerate lists.	List	Full Control, Design, Contribute, Read, Approve, Manage Hierarchy
Manage Permissions	Create and change permission levels on the website and assign permissions to users and groups.	Site	Full Control, Manage Hierarchy
View Web Analytics Data	View reports on website usage.	Site	Full Control, Manage Hierarchy
Create Subsites	Create subsites such as Team sites, Meeting Workspace sites, and Document Workspace sites.	Site	Full Control, Manage Hierarchy
Manage Web Site	Grant the ability to perform all administrative tasks for the website, as well as manage content.	Site	Full Control, Manage Hierarchy
Add and Customize Pages	Add, change, or delete HTML pages or Web Part pages, and edit the website using a Microsoft SharePoint Foundation compatible editor.	Site	Full Control, Design, Manage Hierarchy
Apply Themes and Borders	Apply a theme or borders to the entire website.	Site	Full Control, Design
Apply Style Sheets	Apply a style sheet (.css file) to the website.	Site	Full Control, Design
Create Groups	Create a group of users that can be used anywhere within the site collection.	Site	Full Control
Browse Directories	Enumerate files and folders in a website using SharePoint Designer and WebDAV interfaces.	Site	Full Control, Design, Contribute, Approve, Manage Hierarchy
Use Self-Service Site Creation	Create a website using Self-Service Site Creation.	Site	Read, Contribute, Design, Full Control

continues

TABLE 8-1 *(continued)*

PERMISSION	DESCRIPTION	TYPE	PERMISSION LEVEL
View Pages	View pages in a website.	Site	Full Control, Design, Contribute, Read, Approve, Manage Hierarchy, Restricted Read
Enumerate Permissions	Enumerate permissions on the website, list, folder, document, or list item.	Site	Full Control, Manage Hierarchy
Browse User Information	View information about users of the website.	Site	Full Control, Design, Contribute, Read, Limited Access, Approve, Manage Hierarchy
Manage Alerts	Manage alerts for all users of the website.	Site	Full Control, Manage Hierarchy
Use Remote Interfaces	Use SOAP, Web DAV, the Client Object Model, or SharePoint Designer interfaces to access the website.	Site	Full Control, Design, Contribute, Read, Approve, Manage Hierarchy
Use Client Integration Features	Use features that launch client applications. Without this permission, users must work on documents locally and upload their changes.	Site	Full Control, Design, Contribute, Read, Limited Access, Approve, Manage Hierarchy
Open	Allow users to open a website, list, or folder in order to access items inside that container.	Site	Full Control, Design, Contribute, Read, Limited Access, Approve, Manage Hierarchy, Restricted Read
Edit Personal User Information	Allow a user to change his own user information, such as adding a picture.	Site	Full Control, Design, Contribute, Approve, Manage Hierarchy
Manage Personal Views	Create, change, and delete personal views of lists.	Personal Permissions	Full Control, Design, Contribute, Approve, Manage Hierarchy
Add/Remove Personal Views	Add or remove personal Web Parts on a Web Part page.	Personal Permissions	Full Control, Design, Contribute, Approve, Manage Hierarchy
Update Personal Web Parts	Update Web Parts to display personalized information.	Personal Permissions	Full Control, Design, Contribute, Approve, Manage Hierarchy

PERMISSION LEVELS

Permission levels are the sets of permissions that administrators use to grant users access to site content. Depending upon the access a user or group of users require, an administrator can use the out-of-the-box permission levels or create one that will fulfill the user access requirements.

Unlike permissions, permission levels are manageable from the site where they are being used. From the Site Permissions page, you can access the current permission levels available for your site. It is here you can create your own permission levels, delete existing permission levels, and modify existing permission levels.

There are a few "best practices" when it comes to managing permission levels:

➤ *It is not a good idea to modify a default permission level. If a default permission level is not configured the way you like, you can create a new permission level.*

➤ *When you create a new permission level, you are often only changing one or more permissions assigned to a default permission level. To ensure that you keep all the desired permissions, make a copy of the default permission level and then edit the permissions for the copied permission level.*

➤ *It is not recommended to delete a default permission level. If you don't think you need it, there is no harm in keeping it. If you need it down the road, you won't have to create it from scratch and risk not configuring it the same way it was originally.*

By default, a set of permission levels is available when a new site is created. This set of permissions will depend upon the site template that was used to create the site. For team sites there are six default permission levels:

➤ **Full Control** — Users and groups with this permission level will have access to everything on the site and can perform any site administrative tasks. This shouldn't be confused with site collection administrators. Users and groups with Full Control permissions cannot perform site collection administrative tasks.

➤ **Design** — Can view, add, update, delete, approve, and customize. A step up from Contribute, this permission also allows users to customize the site and its pages. Additionally, this group can approve items that are in containers with Content Approval enabled. For the most part, users and groups with this permission level can do anything on the securable object except for administrative tasks.

➤ **Contribute** — Can view, add, update, and delete list items and documents. This is the standard permission level used to grant users access to content and containers when they need to add, edit, and delete content.

➤ **Read** — Can view pages and list items and download documents. This is the standard permission level for users and groups you want to access content, but not have the permissions to add, edit, or delete content.

➤ **Limited Access** — Can view specific lists, document libraries, list items, folders, or documents when given permissions. This permission level cannot be assigned. Instead, it is the result of customizing permissions for a securable object. In essence, when you see this permission level for a user or group, the users have access to a securable object in the current container, but not to all the securable objects in the container.

➤ **View Only** — Can view pages, list items, and documents. Document types with server-side file handlers can be viewed in the browser but not downloaded. The key concept here is that users and groups with this permission level can't download copies of documents with server-side file handlers.

Figure 8-5 shows the permission levels for team sites.

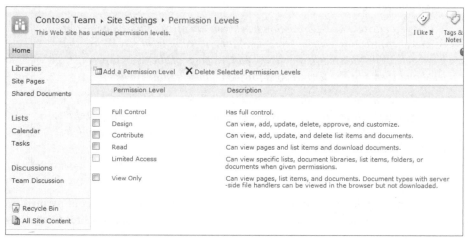

FIGURE 8-5

To see all of the default permission levels, you have to create a site based on a Publishing site template. Only the Publishing site template deploys the total set of permission levels. These include the permission levels available with the team site as well as those in the following list:

➤ **Restricted Read** — View pages and documents. For Publishing sites only. This permission level is similar to the Read permission level, but it only has four of the eleven Read permission level permissions. Key distinctions are that users with this permission level will not be able to create alerts, browse user information, or use client integration.

➤ **View Only** — View pages, list items, and documents. If the document has a server-side file handler available, users can only view the document by using that file handler. Again, this permission level is based on the Read permission, but it doesn't have all the same permissions. A few key distinctions are that users with this permission level will not be able to open list and document library items, browse user information, or use client integration.

➤ **Approve** — Edit and approve pages, list items, and documents. For Publishing sites only. This permission level is designed to work with the Publishing Approval workflow template. Users and groups with this permission level will be able to edit and approve items submitted, and leverage the Publishing Approval workflow. They will also be able to approve items in lists and document libraries that have Content Approval enabled.

➤ **Manage Hierarchy** — Create sites; edit pages, list items, and documents. For Publishing sites only. Similar to the Design permission, this permission level allows users to edit the design and components that make up the site. This permission level does not include all the permissions that users with the Design permission level have. A key difference is that users with the Manage Hierarchy permission level cannot approve items leveraging the Publishing Approval workflow or Content Approval features.

Figure 8-6 shows the default Publishing permission levels when using the Publishing template.

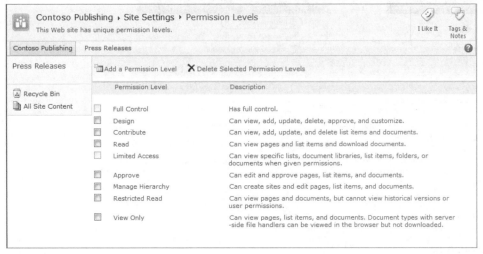

FIGURE 8-6

An important thing to remember when working with these permission levels is that, for the most part, moving down the hierarchy of permission levels, levels will contain all the permissions of the permission levels that precede them. Therefore, Full Control contains all the permissions of all the permission levels combined. The Contribute permission will have all the permissions of Read, Restricted Read, View Only, and Limited Access.

Creating a New Permission Level Based on an Existing Permission Level

Depending on your environment, you might find that the default permission levels aren't adequate for the user access needs of your organization. One of the most common issues is that the Contribute permission level allows users to have Delete Items permission. To remedy this problem, you can create a new Contribute Without Delete permission level and base this new permission level on the default Contribute permission level. Rather than build a new permission from scratch, you can start with the Contribute permissions and then deselect the Delete Items permission and you will be good to go. The following procedure will walk you through this process:

1. Navigate to your top-level site.

2. Click on Site Actions and select Site Permissions (or Site Actions and select Site Settings for the Publishing site options). Under Users and Permissions, click on Site Permissions.

3. In the Ribbon, click on Permission Levels (see Figure 8-7).

FIGURE 8-7

4. Select the permission level that you want to use as a reference for your new permission level. For this example, the Contribute permission level will be selected.

5. Scroll down to the bottom of the page and click Copy Permission Level (see Figure 8-8).

6. You will be prompted to give the copied permission level a name, a description, and the desired permissions. Since all that is needed is to remove the Delete Items permission, simply scroll down to that permission and deselect it.

7. Scroll down to the bottom of the page and click Create. This will create your new permission level. Note that the permissions list in Figure 8-9 now includes Contribute Without Delete.

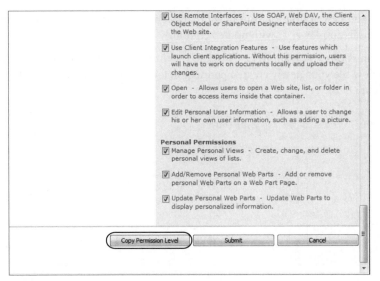

FIGURE 8-8

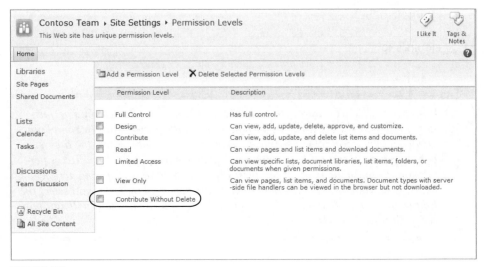

FIGURE 8-9

Creating a Permission Level from Scratch

If the default permission levels don't provide a good starting point for a permission level your environment requires, you have the option to create a permission level from scratch. You start with a blank slate and select the desired permissions that will be needed.

1. Follow steps 1-3 in the preceding set of instructions to navigate to the Permissions Level page.

2. Click Add a Permission Level.

3. Enter a name and description for your new permission level. For this example, the name will be Custom Permission Level 1, with no description.

4. Select the permissions you want to be associated with the permission level and click Create. You should now see your newly created permission level in the Permission Levels page, as shown in Figure 8-10.

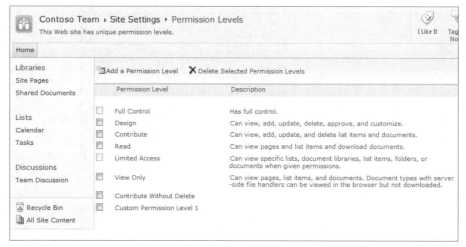

FIGURE 8-10

 In step 4 of this procedure, you may notice that when you click on a permission, others are automatically selected. Some of the permissions in SharePoint are dependent upon others — selecting one automatically selects the others. For example, several other permissions are dependent on the View Items permission. Because many other permissions are related to performing actions on items, it is prudent to first be able to view the item. Therefore, if you select the Edit Items or Delete Items permissions, for example, SharePoint will automatically select the View Items permission.

Editing an Existing Permission Level

As previously mentioned, sometimes the permissions that exist on your sites are not exactly what you are looking for. Fortunately, you can edit these permission levels by selecting and deselecting the individual permissions that make up the permission level.

 Following Microsoft "Best Practices," editing default permission levels is not advised. Instead, edit custom permission levels.

The following procedure will walk you through editing a permission level that exists on a site based on the Team site template:

1. Follow the steps in the earlier instructions to navigate to the Permissions Level page.

2. Click the permission level you want to edit. If you select the Full Control or Limited Access permission levels, you will notice that all of the permissions are grayed out. You will not be able to edit these permission levels. If you select a permission level other than these two, you can deselect current permissions and/or add permissions.

3. When finished, click Submit. This will save the changes you have made. Note that this change will affect this entire site collection.

Deleting a Permission Level

In the event that you no longer wish a permission level to be available, you can remove it from the Permission Levels page:

1. Follow the steps in the earlier instructions to navigate to the Permissions Level page.

2. Select the permission level you want to delete. For this example, the Custom Permission Level 1 will be deleted. Select this permission level and click Delete Selected Permission Levels. As the option states, you can delete more than one permission level at a time if you so choose.

3. Once you click Delete Selected Permission Levels, a pop-up window will appear asking you to confirm the deletion of the selected permission level (see Figure 8-11). Click OK.

4. The selected permission level will be deleted and will no longer be available from the Permission Levels page.

FIGURE 8-11

 When you delete a permission level it will no longer be available. When the permission level is removed, any users or groups that are leveraging this permission level for access will be removed from the Site Permissions page. In order for these users or groups to have access again, you must grant them one of the available permission levels.

SECURITY GROUPS

So far this chapter has covered the individual permissions that make up permission levels and how these permission levels are used to grant users and groups access to SharePoint content. Now it is time to discuss the users and groups that will be assigned the previously stated permission levels.

SharePoint Security Groups

SharePoint security groups are groups of users that are created from within the browser and can be used within a given site collection. By default, SharePoint creates security groups (site groups) when a new site collection is created. The groups that are created vary according to the template that is used. The following are the site groups that may be created:

➤ **Site Collection Administrators** — This group is created for all site collection templates. It has Full Control permissions and can do anything on this site collection. These permissions cannot be overridden. When a new site collection is created, the creator has to specify a value for the primary site collection administrator, and he/she will have the option to enter a user for the secondary site collection administrator. These specified users are added to the Site Collection Administrators group and will be able to perform the administrative tasks associated with the site collection. These options are available from the Site Settings menu on the top-level site collection (see Figure 8-12). These users will also be the only users who can view the members of the Site Collection Administrators group. The Site Collection Administrators group is also accessible from the Site Permissions page of the top-level site, as shown in Figure 8-13.

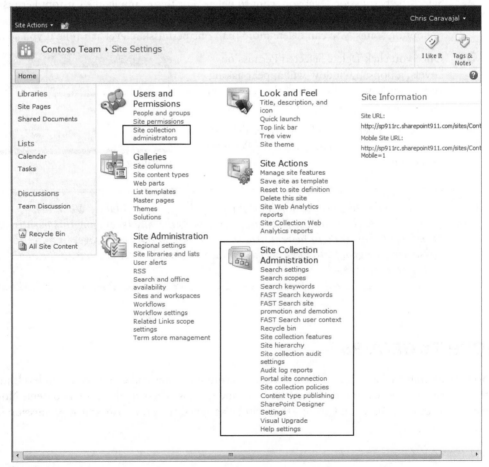

FIGURE 8-12

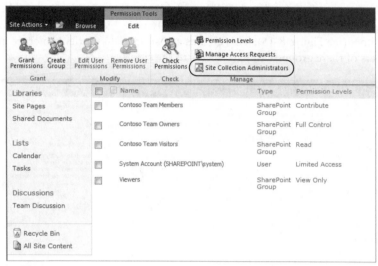

FIGURE 8-13

➤ **[Site collection name] Owners** — This group is created for all site collection templates; by default, members of this group will have Full Control.

➤ **[Site collection name] Members** — This group is created for all site collection templates; by default, members of this group will have Contribute access.

➤ **[Site collection name] Visitors** — This group is created for all site collection templates; by default, members of this group will have Read access.

➤ **Viewers** — This group has View Only access, and is created for Collaboration and Meeting site templates.

➤ **Approvers** — This group has Approval access, and is created for Enterprise site templates and Publishing site templates.

➤ **Designers** — This group has Design access, and is created for Enterprise site templates and Publishing site templates.

➤ **Hierarchy Managers** — This group has Manage Hierarchy access, and is created for Enterprise site templates and Publishing site templates.

➤ **Restricted Readers** — This group has Restricted Read access, and is created for Enterprise site templates and Publishing site templates.

Configuring Permissions During Site Creation

When you create a new site, within an existing site collection, you select your template and then you enter a name, URL, and description for your site. To configure permissions during site creation, from the Create screen click the More Options button. The Permissions options will appear, as shown in Figure 8-14. The default value is to Use same permissions as parent site — that is, inherit permissions from the parent site. This means that access to the new site is the same as that used on the parent one. No new groups will be created.

If you select Use unique permissions (as shown in Figure 8-14) and click Create, you will be prompted to configure three new user access groups: [*New site name*] Owners, [*New site name*] Members, and [*New site name*] Visitors (see Figure 8-15). This creates a customized security structure and only users who are members of these groups will have access to the site.

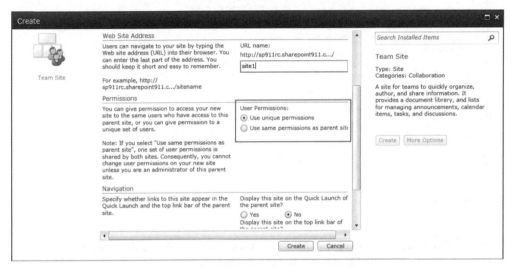

FIGURE 8-14

FIGURE 8-15

The available default permissions will vary with the version of SharePoint 2010 you are running. SharePoint Foundation 2010 does not have all the same permissions that SharePoint Server 2010 has.

Adding a SharePoint Security Group

In addition to site groups and groups that are created when a new site is created using unique permissions, you can create your own SharePoint security groups, assuming you have sufficient permissions. This group will be usable within the entire site collection, not just within the site in which it was created. When you assign a permission level to the group, that access applies to the current securable object and all child securable objects.

This is an area where people are easily confused. When you create a SharePoint group, you can specify the group's permission level or you can leave it blank. If you leave it blank, you can always configure the group's access to another securable object. If you configure the group's access, the access will only be for that securable object and any securable objects that inherit permissions from the parent. Once the SharePoint security group is created, you can navigate to any securable object's permission settings page and add access for the group.

To add a SharePoint security group, follow these steps:

1. Navigate to the People and Groups page in any site within your site collection by clicking Site Actions ⇨ Site Settings.

2. Under the Users and Permission header, click People and Groups. By default, the page will display the first SharePoint group that is listed in the Current Navigation under Groups. To see all groups within the site collection, click on the link for Groups (see Figure 8-16) to open the All Groups page.

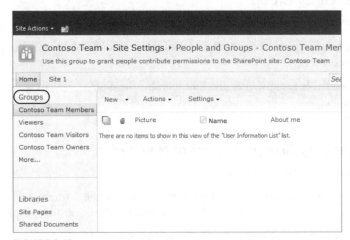

FIGURE 8-16

3. Click the New drop-down menu and select New Group, as shown in Figure 8-17.

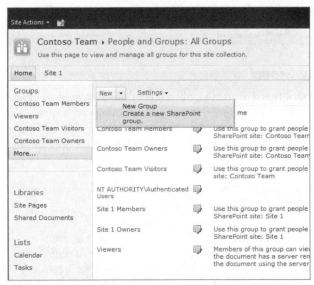

FIGURE 8-17

4. Enter a name and description for the new group. For this example the name will be New Group 1, with no description. Specify the Group Owner (only one user can be the group owner). Typically, the only people who can view the membership of the group are the members of that group. Additionally, only the Group Owner can edit the membership of the group. For obvious reasons, it is not a good idea to give several users this capability. You can also configure if and how you want to receive membership requests.

5. Click Create. Your group will now be created.

Deleting a SharePoint Security Group

Deleting a SharePoint security group is simple:

1. Navigate to the All Groups page (see steps 1 and 2 of the preceding "Adding a SharePoint Security Group" procedure).

2. When viewing the available groups, click the Edit icon for the desired security group.

3. Scroll down and click Delete.

Managing SharePoint Security Groups in Current Navigation

To manage SharePoint security groups, follow these steps:

1. Navigate to the People and Groups page (follow steps 1 and 2 of the "Adding a SharePoint Security Group" procedure). This procedure describes how to edit the groups displayed here.

2. Select Settings ⇨ Edit Group Quick Launch, as shown in Figure 8-18.

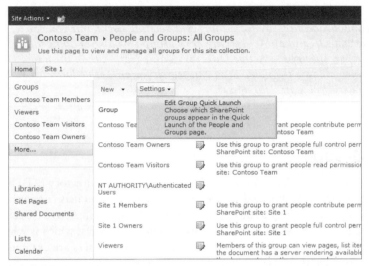

FIGURE 8-18

3. Enter or remove one or more security groups from the displayed groups.

Adding Users to SharePoint Security Groups

To add users to SharePoint security groups, follow these steps:

1. Navigate to the All Groups page (follow steps 1 and 2 of the "Adding a SharePoint Security Group" procedure).

2. Select a group by clicking on the name of the group.

3. Click the New drop-down menu and select Add Users.

4. Enter the user's name and validate.

5. Select whether or not you want to have an e-mail sent to the user informing them of their new access.

6. Click OK.

Deleting Users from SharePoint Security Groups

To delete users from SharePoint security groups, follow these steps:

1. Navigate to the All Groups page (follow steps 1 and 2 of the "Adding a SharePoint Security Group" procedure).

2. Select a group by clicking on the name of the group.

3. Select the users you want to remove.

4. Click Remove Users From Group.

The two preceding procedures are for adding and deleting users, but you can follow the same steps to add an Active Directory group to a SharePoint group. In the people picker, specify the Active Directory group, rather than the name of a user, and then validate the name. You can search for an Active Directory group the same way you search for a user.

Active Directory Groups

In addition to using SharePoint security groups, you can also use Active Directory (AD) groups. For security, you must use AD e-mail-enabled security groups. Distribution lists cannot be used. In order for an object to be used in security it must have a Security ID (SID) in Active Directory. User accounts have SIDs, so they can be used. Distribution lists do not have SIDs, which is why they cannot be used as security objects in SharePoint. AD groups and individual users are granted permissions in similar fashion. As such, their use is covered later in this chapter.

SharePoint Security Groups versus Active Directory Groups

Because you can use either SharePoint security groups or Active Directory groups, let's discuss the benefits and downsides to using either option. In most cases, it really depends on the environment and the governance policy in place.

In most environments, the AD structure is much older than the SharePoint implementation and already setup. If your SharePoint security structure needs match those of the current AD setup, then it will be much easier to deploy AD groups, rather than recreate the same structure and add users to SharePoint security groups. If this is not the case, and your SharePoint site structure has completely different user access configuration needs, this is a picture-perfect example of when to choose SharePoint security groups over AD groups.

Another thing to consider is the user who will be managing the security structure and user access. With AD, it is almost always an information technology specialist, who may or may not have SharePoint access. With SharePoint, the site collection administrator or site owner may be an IT professional, but there is a good chance that it will be a manager or power user, who will not have AD access. Most organizations avoid turning control of IT application security over to a non-IT professional. In situations where the site collection administrator and/or site owners are non-IT members, a combined approach is common. One significant drawback to AD groups is discoverability. There is no way in SharePoint to see the members of an AD group, making it difficult or impossible to know who has access to something if AD groups are used.

Special Groups and Authentication Options

There might not always be a user or group that exactly fits the bill when you want to add permissions at a large level. If you need to provide access to a large group of people that is dynamic, you may need to employ some special tactics to open your content to everyone that needs access.

➤ **All Authenticated Users** — One AD group that can be very useful is the NT AUTHORITY\ Authenticated Users group. This group represents any and all users who authenticate to your

AD domain. The advantage to using this group is that for environments that will be accessible by all your domain users, this guarantees access for all your users and is easy to manage. The downside is that this group represents all your users, granting them all access. Imagine if this group were given access to secure content. As such, this option should be used with caution. This also includes trusted domains, not just the domain your SharePoint servers are in. If you are using a trusted domain for extranet users, for instance, they will all also have access to any content secured with NT AUTHORITY\Authenticated Users.

NT AUTHORITY\Authenticated Users is an Active Directory group. Use of this group requires Windows Integrated Security.

➤ **Anonymous Access** — This authentication method allows any user(s) to access your SharePoint sites. Primarily seen with Internet sites, this option is useful when the users who will be accessing your content do not have corresponding user accounts in your domain. Anonymous Access can only be enabled at the web application level. Once enabled, it can be available for all site collections and sites within the web application. Since this is configurable at the site level, it is up to the site collection and site administrators whether they want this enabled in their environments. Similar to using the NT AUTHORITY\Authenticate Users group, this option should be used with caution. Anonymous access can be configured from the Site Permissions page, as shown in Figures 8-19 and 8-20.

Anonymous Access can only be configured at the site level once it is enabled in Central Administration in the authentication settings.

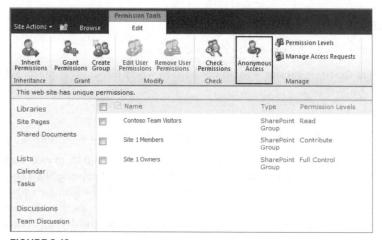

FIGURE 8-19

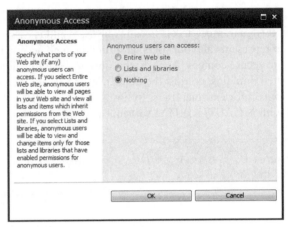

FIGURE 8-20

GRANTING PERMISSIONS

Giving users access can be achieved in three ways: You can grant access to SharePoint security groups, to AD groups, or directly to users. Fortunately, the same procedure is used for each option. As previously stated, you must grant access to the specific securable object. For many environments, users will have different access for the various sites in the SharePoint environment.

For the following procedures, you will follow the first two steps to start:

1. Navigate to the securable object. In this example, the securable object will be a site.

2. Select Site Actions ➪ Site Permissions.

Granting Access to a Top-Level Site

To grant access to a top-level site, continue with the following steps:

1. Because this is at the top-level site, you do not have to worry about inheritance. Select Site Actions ➪ Site Permissions.

2. Click Grant Access.

3. Enter the user name(s), AD group name, or SharePoint group name and validate.

4. When granting permissions, you can add the desired user or AD group to an existing SharePoint group or you can give permission directly. The drop-down menu of existing SharePoint groups also shows the corresponding permission level for each group. Adding a new entry to this group gives that user the listed permission level. If you select Grant users permission directly, the permission levels options will be displayed and you can select the desired access (see Figure 8-21).

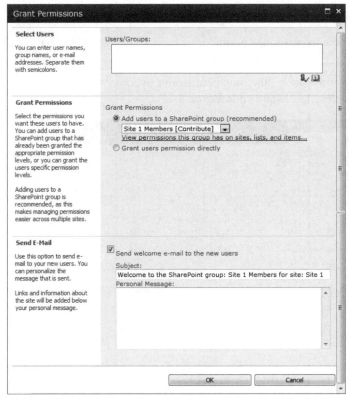

FIGURE 8-21

 You cannot add a SharePoint group to another SharePoint group. This is known as "nesting" and it is not compatible with SharePoint 2010. If you try to nest groups, SharePoint will give you an error. Therefore, if you plan to grant access by adding to a SharePoint group, your entry must be a user or AD group.

5. Select whether to e-mail the user(s) a notification.

6. Click OK.

 When you first configure security for your site collection, although it may seem more convenient to give individual users direct access, it is not recommended. It might be manageable with a couple dozen users, but imagine doing this for several hundreds or thousands of users. It would be an administrative nightmare.

Breaking Inheritance and Granting User Access

Follow the instructions below to customize permissions for a securable object that is inheriting permissions from its parent:

1. You can confirm that the site is inheriting permissions by looking at the status bar running horizontally across the page, as shown in Figure 8-22.

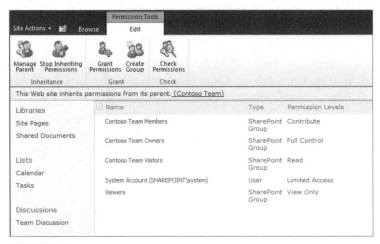

FIGURE 8-22

2. To be able to grant new permissions, you must select Stop Inheriting Permissions, indicated in Figure 8-23. A pop-up will appear asking you to confirm the request. Click OK. The status bar changes to inform you that the site is using unique permissions, as shown in Figure 8-24.

3. Select Grant Permissions. You can now customize permissions.

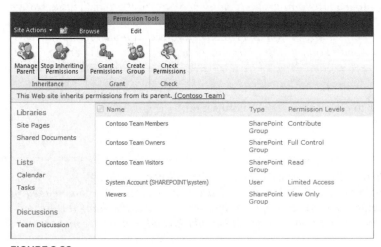

FIGURE 8-23

FIGURE 8-24

 Once a site is using unique permissions, you always have the option to inherit permissions from the parent. Simply click the Inherit Permissions link in the Ribbon. This is a nice way to reset permissions if you ever need to troubleshoot unique permissions errors.

Editing User Access

Once a user, AD group, or SharePoint group has been given access, you can edit this access from the Ribbon on the Site Permissions page (or permissions page for the corresponding securable object). To edit or remove the permissions, select the user, AD group, or SharePoint group and click Edit User Permissions or Delete User Permissions, respectively.

Managing Access Requests

If a user does not have access to your sites and tries to access them, he or she will get an Access Denied error. If the Allow requests for access setting is enabled, the error message will include the option to contact the administrator and request permission to the site. As the administrator for your sites and/ or site collection, you can configure this option from the Site Permissions page. In the Ribbon you will see a link titled Manage Access Requests. You have two configuration options: enable or disable the feature; if enabled, enter an e-mail address to receive requests. Figure 8-25 shows the screen with the feature enabled.

FIGURE 8-25

WEB APPLICATION POLICY

The access options discussed in this chapter so far are related to the granular capabilities of SharePoint, and they enable administrators to give users access to content and various securable objects. At the other end of the spectrum is the option to create a *web application policy*. This is a broad configuration that will grant (or deny) a user or group access to an entire web application. This can be handy if auditors are coming in, or if the legal department needs to search for content based on keywords. Web application policies are the only place in SharePoint where a user or group can be denied access to an object. You can use them to verify that an entire group cannot access a specific web application. For instance, if you have many domains in your environment, you can prevent members from a specific domain from accessing a web application, despite any attempts from site collection administrators to give them access. The nice part about this option is that this policy cannot be overridden by security settings in the sites themselves.

To set up a web application policy you must be a farm administrator and make the configuration in Central Administration. Follow these steps to create a web application policy:

1. Open Central Administration.

2. Click Security. Under Users, click Specify web application policy. Here you can add, edit, or delete selected policies. Click Add Users.

3. Select the web application and zone for the policy. Click Next.

4. Enter the user(s) and select the permissions. By default, there are four permissions levels to choose from: Full Control, Full Read, Deny Write, and Deny All.

   If none of the default levels will suffice, you can create your own permission policy. From the Central Administration homepage, click Manage Web Applications. Select a web application and click the Permission Policy link in the Ribbon.

5. In the Choose System Settings section, be very careful. Here you can specify the entered account to operate as the System account. This is rarely selected. Do not select this option for regular users. The only time this is okay is when you have a new service account that needs complete access — Farm Administrators, Email Service account, Email Crawl account, Application Pool accounts, overall administrative account (i.e. any administrative user account).

6. Click Finish.

SUMMARY

Configuring security and user access can be a daunting task and heavy responsibility. Be sure to have a firm grasp of the concepts in this chapter and have a clearly defined security plan before opening content to users. The following points reiterate the most important pieces of information from this chapter:

➤ Access can be granted at a granular level, with users given access to a specific piece of content in SharePoint, or a web application policy can be used to grant users access to an entire web application and its sites.

➤ Permissions are divided among permission levels, and permission levels are used to grant users access.

➤ An administrator can restrict the set of available permissions for a web application through the Central Administration site, but this requires being a member of the Farm Administrators group.

➤ SharePoint groups are available throughout an entire site collection. Membership can be managed at any level with the appropriate permissions, but access must be granted to the specific securable object.

➤ Inheritance restricts permission management. To customize permissions on a securable object, you have to stop inheritance. Inheritance can always be reset.

➤ For the sake of easy manageability, inheritance should be leveraged wherever possible.

➤ Be sure to document securable objects using unique permissions.

➤ As a general rule, the default permission levels and site groups should not be edited or deleted. If another option is needed, create it.

➤ When configuring user access, it is better to be restrictive when granting permissions. Only grant users access to content they need.

➤ Use the site groups (Owners, Members, and Visitors) as much as possible.

➤ Limit the number of users in the Site Collection Administration and Owners groups.

Adhering to these policies will help keep your server farm content secure.

Claims-Based Authentication

➤ Using claims-based identity

➤ SharePoint authentication options

➤ Creating claims-based web applications

SharePoint Server 2010 utilizes a new authentication model called *claims-based authentication* (CBA). CBA is based on the concept of *identity* and utilizes open source standards and protocols so that it works with any corporate identity system, not just Active Directory and not just Windows-based systems. Identity is represented by a security token. This token is presented to any application to which the individual is attempting to gain access. The individual's token, and therefore his or her identity, is verified by some system. This is normally some directory service that contains username and password information, but the beauty of CBA is that it is not limited to just username and password information.

CBA provides a trust-based system between applications and a centralized provider that issues the token. The application trusts the individual because they trust the provider. Therefore, in addition to providing a single sign-on environment, this alleviates the need for each application to authenticate the user, enabling the application to focus on what permissions to assign, and how the application interacts with, the user. This chapter is an introduction to CBA, and it will provide you with the knowledge necessary to begin using CBA for SharePoint websites.

CLAIMS-BASED IDENTITY

User identity is a fundamental requirement for application security, both user authentication and user authorization. Knowing who is requesting access to websites and access to object information is critical to providing a secure environment. The challenge is deciding which identity technology is the right one for a specific application, and then which one is the best across the enterprise so that you can accommodate the needs of all the applications. The solution to this can become very complicated. You need to satisfy two key requirements:

➤ How users will gain access to the enterprise's applications, regardless of their location.

➤ How different types of user information will be retrieved by the applications so that the applications can accomplish their required functions.

User Access Challenge

Will the application be accessed by employees from within the organization, from outside the organization, from the public Internet? One technology may not be enough and the organization may have to support multiple technologies. For example, you could use Windows Integrated security for internal users and Forms-Based Authentication (FBA) for users outside the organization; but we all know the complexity this introduces in terms of providing a single authentication mechanism and the need for storing different user information in multiple locations. In addition, neither Windows Integrated security nor FBA provide much information about the user, with the latter providing username and password information only. And what about providing access to partner or vendor employees? For that you need to implement *identity federation*, so that the users won't need a separate login. Finally, keep in mind that the application requiring login may exist in the cloud, as this scenario is rapidly gaining popularity; or you could have a hybrid scenario, with applications both on the premises and in the cloud.

User Information Storage Challenge

How will information about users be stored and retrieved? The application can query the user for some information, and look up other information. This may not sound like a big issue, but consider the number of different applications in an organization, and that each may need to store and retrieve information that is specific to its functionality. Even when your organization requires simple identity capability, such as all users across the enterprise authenticating using Active Directory, this type of login provides very little information about the user.

Solution

After this brief review of two key challenges, you are probably thinking that the solution is simple. Why not create a single identity approach for all scenarios that provides each application with the specific information it needs? If so, you guessed correctly. Claims-based identity satisfies these requirements.

Claims-based identity provides a common way for applications to acquire identity information from users, irrespective of whether they are inside the organization, in other organizations, or on the Internet. Identity information is stored in a *security token*, often simply called a *token*. A token contains one or more *claims* about the user. Think of a claim as metadata about the user that stays with them throughout their enterprise journey. For example, this could include username, manager's name, address, e-mail address, group memberships, etc.

Implementing claims-based identity generally requires using and understanding a set of core technologies: Windows Identity Foundation (WIF), Active Directory Federated Services 2.0 (ADFS), and

CardSpace 2.0. WIF is part of the SharePoint 2010 prerequisites, and it is automatically installed when you run the prerequisite installer as discussed in Chapter 4. The claims-based technologies are summarized in Table 9-1. Don't worry if the table contains unfamiliar terms, as they are further defined in subsequent sections of this chapter.

TABLE 9-1 Claims-Based Identity Technology for the Windows Platform

TECHNOLOGY	DESCRIPTION
Windows Identity Foundation	WIF, which was formerly called the "Geneva Framework," is a set of application programming interfaces (APIs) that can be used by developers to build claims-aware and federation-capable applications. WIF provides a framework to claims-enable your applications and to create custom security token services. This enables enterprises to use a single identity model so that applications can communicate and interoperate using industry standard protocols.
ADFS 2.0	ADFS 2.0, formerly called "Geneva Server," provides both identity federation and single-sign-on (SSO) solutions. ADFS 2.0 is a security token service (STS), responsible for issuing security tokens. It uses Active Directory as its identity store; and Lightweight Directory Access Protocol (LDAP), SQL, or a custom store as an attribute store. ADFS 2.0 supports both active (WS-Trust) and passive (WS-Federation and SAML 2.0) scenarios.
Windows CardSpace 2.0	Windows CardSpace, formerly code-named "InfoCard," is an identity selector technology that can replace usernames and passwords that you use to register with and log on to websites and online services. CardSpace stores users' digital identities, and represents the identity information in visual Information Cards. This enables users to share information with sites, review the identity of a site, and manage their digital information.

Claims-based authentication is user authentication that utilizes claims-based identity, and it opens the door to great possibilities in SharePoint Server 2010. Users can have identities in different directory stores and use them simultaneously to access different resources in SharePoint.

Using Claims Identity for Authentication

SharePoint 2010 supports claims-based authentication, which is a powerful and flexible authentication model. Claims-based authentication (CBA) in SharePoint 2010 works with a variety of identity systems, such as Active Directory, LDAP directories, and even LiveID. CBA uses several different technology components to authenticate users and enable them to present their digital identity to an application. Key components include tokens, claims, identity providers, and the Security Token Service (STS). The following steps describe the general authentication process, such as a user attempting to access a web application using a web browser:

1.   A web browser will request a token from an STS on the behalf of the user. This request is made using WS-Trust, a standard protocol for web service communication. The request typically includes the name of the user whom the token will represent and an identifier that describes the application the user wishes to access.

2. The STS performs an information look-up and verification. User information is stored in a database like SQL Server or a directory store like Active Directory or an LDAP directory. Once the information is verified and the user is authenticated, the STS issues a token, which is returned to the requestor. The STS's authority to issue tokens has been granted by some identity provider, which is also called an *issuer*. The issuer stands behind the validity of the claims contained in the token. SharePoint 2010 includes its own STS, and the identity provider would be represented by the organization.

3. The browser sends the token to the desired web application, which receives the token and the required claims. The application uses the claims information because it trusts the identity provider, referred to as a *relying party*. Once the application verifies the token signature, confirming it originated from a trusted STS, the claims are accepted and the information is used for authorization. A key benefit is that the application can focus on authorization because it no longer needs to authenticate the user. An application can specify exactly what claims it needs and which identity providers it trusts. An administrator must configure the STS to issue the right claims.

SharePoint 2010 includes an STS and WIF to claims-enable web applications, and therefore SharePoint websites can be configured to utilize CBA. To broaden SharePoint's identity capability, you could install ADFS 2.0. ADFS provides much broader support for CBA, including the capability to federate to other organizations outside the hosting organization. ADFS 2.0 is an improvement over its predecessor, ADFS 1.0, because it implements an STS that generates SAML tokens in response to WS-Trust requests. In addition, ADFS 2.0 supports both web browsers and other clients, such as Office desktop clients and those built using Windows Communication Foundation (WCF). ADFS 1.0 only supported web browsers. The ADFS 2.0 STS can be used entirely inside an organization, exposed on the Internet, or both. However, ADFS 2.0 is not required to use claims-based identity; CBA can be implemented using an STS from any vendor, or even a custom-built STS. Table 9-2 summarizes the components and open source protocols used in CBA.

TABLE 9-2 Claims-Based Authentication Components and Open Source Protocols

COMPONENT	DESCRIPTION
Token	A token contains claims about a user and a digital signature. The service that issues the token digitally signs the token in order to verify the issuer and guard against unauthorized claim changes.
Claim	A claim is any piece of information that describes a characteristic about the user.
Security Token Service (STS)	An STS creates and issues tokens. STS is a web service that issues tokens as defined by the WS-Trust security standard.
Secure Store Service	SSS is a claims-aware service that has been discussed in several previous chapters. It is responsible for decrypting the token issued by the STS to access the application ID, and retrieving credentials from the secure store database. The credentials are then used to authorize access to resources.

COMPONENT	DESCRIPTION
WS-Trust	This is an open source standard that defines the concept of an STS, and the issuing, renewing, and validating of security tokens.
Identity Provider	The organization that backs the STS and ensures that the claims are authentic
Relying Party	An application that accepts and uses a token is referred to as a relying party. The user has been authenticated by a trusted provider, and the application is relying on the information contained in the claims.
SAML	The Security Assertion Markup Language is an open source XML standard for communicating and exchanging identity information, authentication, and authorization data between different organizations. SAML provides Internet single sign-on (SSO) for organizations that want to securely connect to Internet applications that exist both inside and outside the safety of an organization's firewall.

SHAREPOINT AUTHENTICATION OPTIONS

SharePoint Server 2010 supports CBA as well as classic mode authentication (CMA). CMA was how users were authenticated in SharePoint Server 2007. In SharePoint Server 2010, you can choose between claims-based authentication and classic mode authentication when you create a web application. SharePoint 2010 is represented by three logical layers or tiers: the front-end web server tier (WFE), the application server tier, and the back-end database tier. Each tier may require authentication using an authentication provider, which supports specific authentication methods.

There are several factors to consider when choosing an authentication method. One factor is whether or not you will be using FBA. If you plan to use FBA, you will need to utilize CBA. This is a change from SharePoint 2007. You may also be considering SAML token-based authentication; if so, you will need to use CBA. If neither FBA or SAML are being planned, and identity federation is also not under consideration, then using classic mode authentication may be the preferred method.

Classic Mode

Classic mode authentication refers to the Integrated Windows authentication model supported in SharePoint Server 2007. CMA does not utilize any of the claims infrastructure, and therefore none of the claims features are available. Classic mode supports all the Windows authentication methods that were available in SharePoint 2007. Similar to the restriction in SharePoint 2007, SharePoint 2010 web applications that use classic mode are limited to one form of authentication for each zone. These different Windows authentication methods include the following:

➤ Anonymous

➤ Basic

- ➤ Digest
- ➤ Certificate
- ➤ NTLM
- ➤ Kerberos

Claims-Based

SharePoint Server 2010 CBA enables authentication using Windows Integrated security and non-Windows systems. A key concept with CBA in SharePoint 2010 is that authentication is based on an identity provider. Applications trust this provider because they are configured to utilize the provider. The beauty of the system is that any provider that meets specific Internet security standards can be used. These standards include WS-Security, WS-SecurityPolicy, WS-Trust and WS-Federation. Therefore companies have the flexibility to choose their provider, and as long as it's compliant with these standards it will be supported by SharePoint. CBA supports three different authentication providers out of the box:

- ➤ **Windows Authentication** — This includes all the same authentication methods that CMA supports, as listed above.

- ➤ **Forms-Based Authentication (FBA)** — These methods include LDAP, database or custom membership, and role providers. Note that FBA is only available when you use claims-based authentication.

- ➤ **SAML Token-Based Authentication** — These include ADFS 2.0, Windows Live ID, and third-party providers.

CREATING CLAIMS-BASED WEB APPLICATIONS

The following instructions walk you through the process of creating a claims-enabled web application. You will also configure the application to allow anonymous access. Finally, you will add FBA to the application so that you have a dual authentication configuration.

Configuring CBA with Windows Authentication

Begin by configuring CBA with Windows Authentication:

1. Create a new web application using CBA. The process for creating a new web application was discussed in detail in Chapter 4, so it isn't repeated here. Only the changes specific to enabling CBA are discussed. You must first enable CBA in the Authentication section of the Create New Web Application web page in Central Administration. The default is classic mode, so you will need to select claims mode. Notice that the Claims-Based Authentication option has been selected, as shown in Figure 9-1.

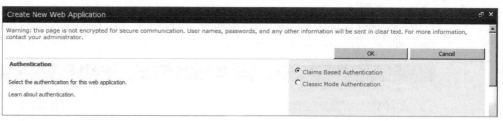

FIGURE 9-1

2. Scroll down to the Claims Authentication Types section and review the options. This section and the Sign In Page URL section are shown in Figure 9-2. Keep the default settings, which are Windows Authentication enabled and NTLM. Note that you can enable the web application to use a single URL for both Windows Authentication and Forms-Based Authentication by enabling the checkbox for both methods. This is only possible with CBA. Without CBA, you would have to create two different zones.

3. CBA may require users to log in; therefore, they may need to be redirected to a web page to enter their credentials. Do not change the default settings, which should be to use the Default Sign In Page option. Note the option to enter the URL of a custom sign in page, as shown in Figure 9-2.

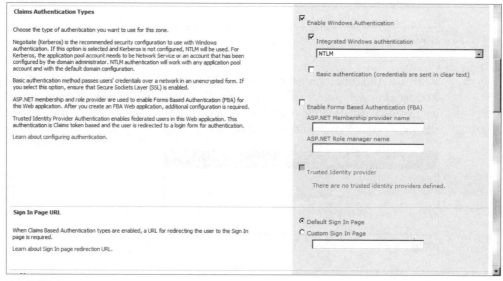

FIGURE 9-2

4. Ensure that all the other settings are configured according to your specific interests. When finished, click OK. Once the web application has been created, the Application Created web page will be displayed, as shown in Figure 9-3.

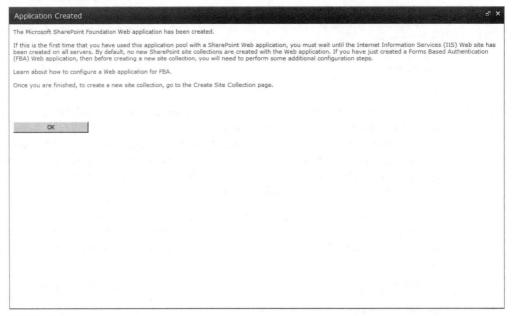

FIGURE 9-3

5. Verify the Authentication settings for the web application by browsing to the Web Applications Management web page, clicking your specific claims-enabled web application, and then clicking the Authentication Providers button in the Ribbon. The Authentication Providers dialog, shown in Figure 9-4, should be displayed.

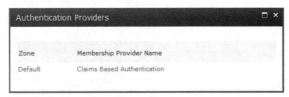

FIGURE 9-4

6. Create a new site collection within this new web application using your own preferences. You will be directed to the Top-Level Site Successfully Created web page once the process is complete. Browse to your new site collection's top-level site. This completes the process. You may need to create a new DNS entry if you used host headers for your web application, and you may need to issue the following command, `ipconfig /flushdns`, after creating the DNS entry.

Configuring Anonymous Access

You can configure your CBA web application to allow anonymous access using the following steps. These steps are similar to those used for SharePoint 2007:

1. Under Application Management in Central Administration, select Manage web applications.

2. Select the specific web application to be enabled and click the Authentication Providers button on the Ribbon.

3. Click the Default link in the Authentication Providers dialog. This should display the Edit Authentication dialog, shown in Figure 9-5.

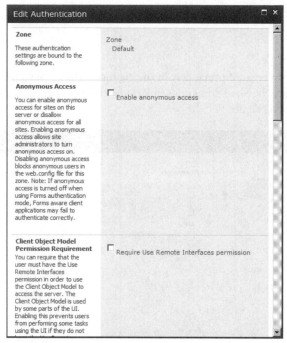

FIGURE 9-5

4. Enable anonymous access by clicking inside the Enable anonymous access checkbox in the Anonymous Access section. Click the Save button. Close the Authentication Providers dialog.

5. Return to the Web Applications Management page. With your web application selected, click the Anonymous Policy button in the Ribbon. This will take you to the Anonymous Access Restrictions dialog, shown in Figure 9-6. In the Zones drop-down box, select (All Zones); and in the Permissions section, select None - No Policy. These should be the default conditions.

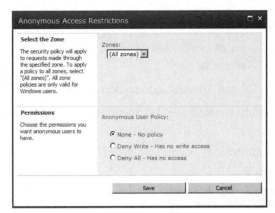

FIGURE 9-6

6. Browse to the site collection you created previously in the claims-enabled web application. From the Site Settings page, click the Site Permissions link in the Users and Permissions section. The Permissions page is shown in Figure 9-7.

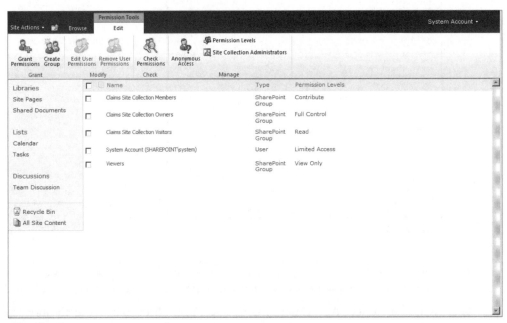

FIGURE 9-7

7. Click the Anonymous Access button in the Ribbon to display the Anonymous Access dialog, shown in Figure 9-8.

8. Select the Entire Web site option or the Lists and Libraries option, depending on what you wish to provide access to. For this exercise, select Entire Web site. When finished, click OK.

You should see Anonymous Users added to the list of users and groups on the Permissions page, as shown in Figure 9-9. This completes the configuration.

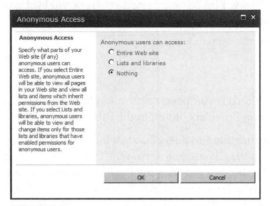

FIGURE 9-8

FIGURE 9-9

Converting to CBA from CMA

You can convert a web application that has been configured to use CMA to use CBA, but only by using PowerShell. Once you convert the web application to use CBA, you cannot return to CMA. The following PowerShell commands will complete this conversion:

```
$ConvertApp = get-spwebapplication "http://<web application name>"
$ConvertApp.useclaimsauthentication = "True"
$ConvertApp.Update()
```

Configuring Forms-Based Authentication

Using the following instructions, you will enable FBA for your existing claims-enabled website so that both Windows Integrated and FBA are being used.

Enable FBA

Follow these steps to enable FBA:

1. Navigate to the Web Applications Management page, select your claims-enabled web application and click on the Authentication Providers button in the Ribbon.

2. Click the Default link in the Authentication Providers dialog window. Scroll down in Edit Authentication dialog until you reach the Claims Authentication Types section. Enable FBA and add names for the ASP.NET membership provider and the role manager. You can choose your own names or use SQLMembershipProvider and SQLRoleManager. Click Save when you are done and close the Authentication Providers dialog. Remember the names that you have chosen because you will need to refer to them in the `web.config` file. Also, keep in mind that these names are case sensitive.

Install and Configure the SQL Server Database

The next step is to create and configure a SQL Server database that will be used for FBA:

1. Open Windows Explorer and navigate to `C:\Windows\Microsoft .Net\Framework64\ v2.0.50727`. Locate the `aspnet_regsql.exe` application and execute it. This will open the ASP.NET SQL Server Setup wizard, shown in Figure 9-10. Click the Next button.

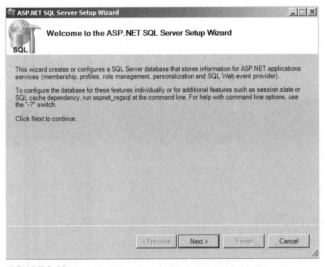

FIGURE 9-10

2. On the Select a Setup Option dialog, shown in Figure 9-11, select the Configure SQL Server for application services option. This should be the default option. Then click the Next button.

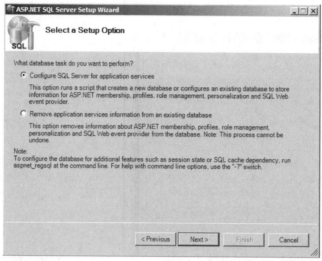

FIGURE 9-11

3. In the Select the Server and Database dialog, shown in Figure 9-12, enter the name of the SQL Server. This box should be automatically populated; if not, then enter the proper value for your installation. Use Windows Authentication and accept the default name for the database, which will be aspnetdb. Click Next.

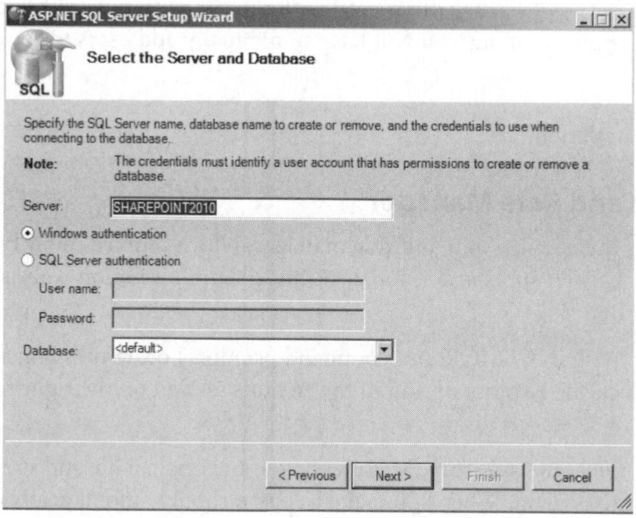

FIGURE 9-12

4. Verify that your settings are correct on the Confirm Your Settings page and click the Next button. Once the database has been created, you should receive confirmation, as shown in Figure 9-13. Click the Finish button.

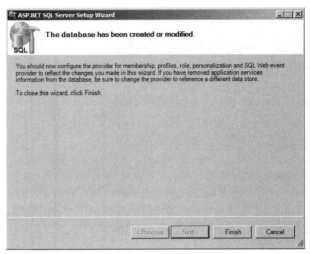

FIGURE 9-13

5. Open SQL Server Management Studio and confirm that the aspnetdb database has been created.

6. Now you can populate the SQL Server database with user information using an application on CodePlex called MembershipSeeder (`http://cks.codeplex.com/releases/view/7450#DownloadId=19598`). You can proceed with the configuration without using the MembershipSeeder application but you will have to manually add users to the aspnetdb tables.

This completes the database installation.

Configure the Membership and Role Manager

The next set of steps configures the membership and role manager, which requires modifying three different `web.config` files: for the web application, for the Central Administration website, and for the STS:

1. Open IIS Manager by typing **INETMGR** at a command prompt. Locate the claims-enabled website and select it. Click the Explore option in the Actions section on the right-hand side of the page.

2. Locate the `web.config` file in the directory. Make a copy of the original file and store the copy in the same location as the original. When you make a copy it should automatically assign it a different name compared to the original.

> *You should never modify any original SharePoint files without first making a copy. If for whatever reason you make a mistake or things don't work correctly, you can always go back to the original configuration using the copy.*

3. Open the original `web.config` file in a text editor of your choice and locate the `</SharePoint>` element. It should appear immediately before the `<system.web>` element.

4. Add the following XML to the `web.config` file between the `</SharePoint>` and `<system.web>` elements. This information enables the connectivity to the SQL Server database aspnetdb.

> *The code in these instructions is available for download on this book's website at Wrox.com.*

Available for download on Wrox.com

```
<connectionStrings>
<add name="SQLConnectionString" connectionString="data source=SQL;
Integrated Security=SSPI;Initial Catalog=aspnetdb" />
</connectionStrings>
```

Code file Chapter09_code.txt

5. The next step is to add the membership provider and the role manager configuration information. Locate the `<membership defaultProvider="i">` element and add the following information to the `<providers>` element:

```
<add connectionStringName="SQLConnectionString" passwordAttemptWindow="5"
 enablePasswordRetrieval="false" enablePasswordReset="false"
 requiresQuestionAndAnswer="true" applicationName="/"
 requiresUniqueEmail="true" passwordFormat="Hashed" description="Stores
 and retrieves membership data from SQL Server"
 name="SQLMembershipProvider"
 type="System.Web.Security.SqlMembershipProvider, System.Web,
 Version=2.0.3600.0, Culture=neutral, PublicKeyToken=b03f5f7f11d50a3a" />
```

6. Locate the `<roleManager defaultProvider="c" enabled="true" cacheRolesInCookie="false">` element, insert the following text into the `<providers>` element, and then save and close the `web.config` file:

```
<add connectionStringName="SQLConnectionString" applicationName="/"
 description="Stores and retrieves roles from SQL Server"
 name="SQLRoleManager" type="System.Web.Security.SqlRoleProvider,
 System.Web, Version=2.0.3600.0, Culture=neutral,
 PublicKeyToken=b03f5f7f11d50a3a" />
```

7. To modify the `web.config` file of the Central Administration web application, add the connection string information to the `web.config` file for the Central Administration web site just like you did in steps 1–4:

```
<connectionStrings>
<add name="SQLConnectionString" connectionString="data source=SQL;
Integrated Security=SSPI;Initial Catalog=aspnetdb" />
</connectionStrings>
```

8. Locate the `<system.web>` element and add the following information:

```
<roleManager defaultProvider="AspNetWindowsTokenRoleProvider" enabled="true"
 cacheRolesInCookie="false">
<providers>
<add connectionStringName="SQLConnectionString" applicationName="/"
 description="Stores and retrieves roles from SQL Server"
 name="SQLRoleManager" type="System.Web.Security.SqlRoleProvider,
 System.Web, Version=2.0.3600.0, Culture=neutral,
 PublicKeyToken=b03f5f7f11d50a3a" />
</providers>
</roleManager>
```

9. Insert the following code immediately after the `<roleManager>` code entered earlier in step 8, and then save and close the `web.config` file:

```
<membership defaultProvider="SQLMembershipProvider">
<providers>
<add connectionStringName="SQLConnectionString" passwordAttemptWindow="5"
 enablePasswordRetrieval="false" enablePasswordReset="false"
requiresQuestionAndAnswer="true" applicationName="/"
 requiresUniqueEmail="true" passwordFormat="Hashed" description="Stores
 and retrieves membership data from SQL Server"
 name="SQLMembershipProvider"
 type="System.Web.Security.SqlMembershipProvider, System.Web,
 Version=2.0.3600.0, Culture=neutral, PublicKeyToken=b03f5f7f11d50a3a" />
</providers>
</membership>
```

10. The final `web.config` file to be modified is the STS `web.config` file. Expand the SharePoint Web Services website in IIS Manager and select the SecurityTokenServiceApplication site.

11. Locate the `web.config` file and make a copy as you did previously.

12. Insert the following code into the `web.config` file before the `</configuration>` element, and then save and close the `web.config` file:

```
<connectionStrings>
<add name="SQLConnectionString" connectionString="data source=SQL;
Integrated Security=SSPI;Initial Catalog=aspnetdb" />
</connectionStrings>

<system.web>
<roleManager defaultProvider="c" enabled="true" cacheRolesInCookie="false">
<providers>
```

```
<add name="c" type="Microsoft.SharePoint.Administration.Claims.SPClaimsAuth
 RoleProvider,
 Microsoft.SharePoint, Version=14.0.0.0, Culture=neutral,
 PublicKeyToken=71e9bce111e9429c" />
<add connectionStringName="SQLConnectionString" applicationName="/"
 description="Stores and retrieves roles from SQL Server"
 name="SQLRoleManager" type="System.Web.Security.SqlRoleProvider,
 System.Web, Version=2.0.3600.0, Culture=neutral,
 PublicKeyToken=b03f5f7f11d50a3a" />
</providers>
</roleManager>
<membership defaultProvider="i">
<providers>
<add name="i" type="Microsoft.SharePoint.Administration.Claims
.SPClaimsAuthMembershipProvider, Microsoft.SharePoint,
Version=14.0.0.0, Culture=neutral, PublicKeyToken=71e9bce111e9429c" />
<add connectionStringName="SQLConnectionString" passwordAttemptWindow="5"
 enablePasswordRetrieval="false" enablePasswordReset="false"
 requiresQuestionAndAnswer="true" applicationName="/"
 requiresUniqueEmail="true" passwordFormat="Hashed" description="Stores
 and retrieves membership data from SQL Server"
 name="SQLMembershipProvider"
 type="System.Web.Security.SqlMembershipProvider,
System.Web, Version=2.0.3600.0, Culture=neutral,
 PublicKeyToken=b03f5f7f11d50a3a" />
</providers>
</membership>
</system.web>
```

13. The final steps in the process involve assigning permissions for users in the SQL Server data-base. First, navigate to the Manage Web Applications page in Central Administration.

14. Select your claims-enabled web application and click the User Policy button in the Ribbon. You should see the Policy for Web Application dialog, shown in Figure 9-14.

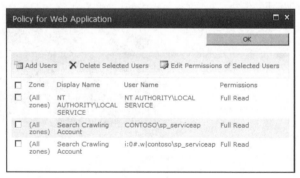

FIGURE 9-14

15. Click the Add Users link, which will reveal the Add Users dialog. Choose the Default zone in the Zones drop-down menu, and then click the Next button.

16. On the Add Users dialog, add the administrator account and assign Full Control, as shown in Figure 9-15. Click Finish, and then click OK to close the Policy for Web Application dialog.

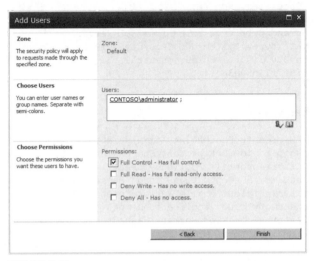

FIGURE 9-15

17. It's time to test the application. Navigate to your top-level site in your claims-enabled web application. An example is shown in Figure 9-16.

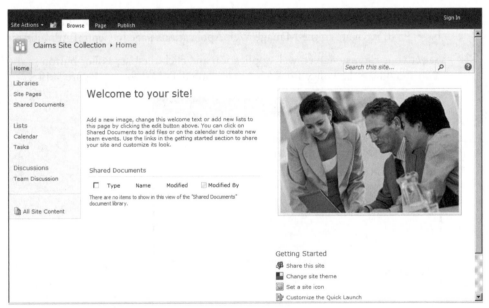

FIGURE 9-16

18. If you enabled anonymous access, you should see the Sign In link at the top, upper-right side of the page. Click the Sign In link to display the Sign In dialog, shown in Figure 9-17.

FIGURE 9-17

19. You need to choose which authentication method to use, as the website has two different methods configured. Choose Windows Authentication to sign in to the application.

20. Finally, log out of the application so that you can sign in again using FBA. The MembershipSeeder tool was used to add a user to the database for testing purposes. If you populated the aspnetdb with user information, then you can proceed to test the login.

21. Click the Sign In link and choose the Forms Authentication option to log in. You should be prompted with the Sign In dialog shown in Figure 9-18.

FIGURE 9-18

22. Enter the username and password for the user and click the Sign In button. You should be directed to your top-level site once authenticated.

At this point, you have successfully configured a web application with two different methods of authentication. For those SharePoint 2007 websites that were FBA-enabled, you will have to convert them to using CBA using the steps outlined in the exercise after you upgrade them to SharePoint 2010.

SUMMARY

Claims-based authentication is a new and powerful addition to SharePoint. It provides the capability to unify the authentication process and deliver single sign-on across applications in the enterprise, as well as between organizations and in the cloud. Because it is based on open standards and protocols, it is not Microsoft-centric. As a SharePoint administrator, you will discover that CBA provides capabilities that previously did not exist.

10

Administering SharePoint 2010 with Windows PowerShell

WHAT'S IN THIS CHAPTER?

➤ Basic Windows PowerShell usage

➤ How to use common SharePoint 2010 cmdlets

➤ The SharePoint object model

PowerShell is now the command-line tool for administering SharePoint 2010. In previous versions of SharePoint, administrators worked with STSADM.exe. Starting with SharePoint 2007, we began seeing some integration with PowerShell and SharePoint. With no commands provided we managed to create our own PowerShell commands and scripts for SharePoint 2007. To do so some of us had to get our hands dirty and either put on our developer hat or beg, borrow, and steal from friends on the Internet. Ultimately, we ended up with some PowerShell scripts for SharePoint 2007 even if we really didn't understand how they worked under the covers. With the 2010 version of SharePoint, the use of PowerShell for administration is different, much different.

Now we have commands and a management shell that installs with SharePoint 2010 — and when we say commands, we mean a lot of commands, well over 500. STSADM only boasted around 185 commands. More important, these 500 plus commands can be chained together and scripted, enabling you to create practically an infinite number of scripts and commands.

In this chapter we will get you up to speed on PowerShell in general, and then show you how to harness the power of this beast to benefit your SharePoint 2010 farm.

INTRODUCTION TO WINDOWS POWERSHELL

There is no requirement that you must use PowerShell to administer SharePoint 2010. Basically every administrative function is exposed through the SharePoint user interface. Many administrative tasks are easily done via Central Administration or Site Settings. While it is conceivable that a SharePoint 2010 administrator could avoid using PowerShell, what fun would that be? PowerShell really starts to shine when you want to perform repeatable processes or multiple tasks.

For example, you can create site collections using Central Administration — one site collection at a time. But with a little knowledge of PowerShell and the SharePoint commands you can create a comma-separated list of many site collection URLs and supporting information, and then use PowerShell's `Import-CSV` cmdlet with the `New-SPSite` cmdlet to create them with a single click of the Enter key.

> *If you are worried that STSADM is no longer available, rest assured that STSADM is still around, for now. The writing is on the wall, however; PowerShell is now the command-line tool for SharePoint administrators. Microsoft says STSADM is deprecated, which is a fancy way of saying it will be removed in a future version. Start saying goodbye to STSADM.*

MICROSOFT SHAREPOINT 2010 MANAGEMENT SHELL AND OTHER HOSTS

PowerShell is included in Microsoft Windows Server 2008 and is activated as a feature. However, it is version 1.1, and SharePoint 2010 requires version 2. Because PowerShell version 2 is a prerequisite for SharePoint 2010, the prerequisite installer will try to install it. You'll get an error if the PowerShell version 1.1 feature is activated. Simply deactivate it and run the prerequisite installer to get the correct version of PowerShell installed. Windows Server 2008 R2 comes with PowerShell version 2 already installed and enabled. You may get an error when the prerequisite installer runs, but you can ignore it. The correct version of PowerShell is installed and patiently waiting for SharePoint to come out and play.

Microsoft SharePoint 2010 Management Shell

The Microsoft SharePoint 2010 Management Shell is displayed in Figure 10-1. This is the default, out-of-the-box SharePoint command-line interface. Not much to look at. As a matter of fact, it looks a lot like the command console you used to run STSADM commands in SharePoint 2007. It is, however, a cleverly disguised PowerShell console, with the PowerShell commands registered and ready for use. Open the SharePoint 2010 Management Shell and PowerShell at the same time. If you squint, you might see that they look pretty similar. The only obvious difference is that the

SharePoint Management Shell has a black background, while the standard PowerShell background is blue. They may look similar, but only the Management Shell will run the SharePoint commands without further configuration.

 You can run STSADM commands inside of PowerShell. Add the path to STSADM to the system's path variable and call all the STSADM commands you like.

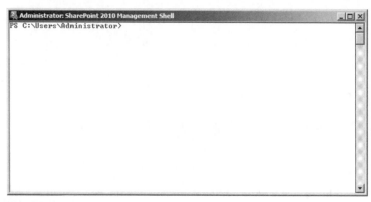

FIGURE 10-1

Run a very basic SharePoint command in both consoles — for example, Get-SPSite. The Management Shell will happily return a list of site collections, whereas the PowerShell console won't have a clue what you want it to do.

In other words, the big secret is that the SharePoint 2010 Management Shell is just the PowerShell .exe with a command-line parameter that points to a PSC1 file or a console file. The PSC1 file tells the PowerShell host to register the SharePoint commands. One other minor difference is that it also has a title bar that says SharePoint 2010 Management Shell, but otherwise the Management Shell is all PowerShell.

Using Other Windows PowerShell Hosts

While the Management Shell is the only host that is configured to run SharePoint commands, it is not the only host that an administrator can use. Administrators can choose to work with other PowerShell hosts. Two common hosts are available with Windows Server 2008 and Windows Server 2008 R2: Windows PowerShell and Windows PowerShell Integrated Scripting Environment, more commonly known as ISE. ISE is displayed in Figure 10-2. Administrators can also use many of the third-party PowerShell hosts available free or for purchase. Many of these boast a rich graphical user interface. The rest of this chapter sticks to the Management Shell because it is the lowest common denominator, but we realize that many of you will want to know how to configure these other hosts to use the SharePoint 2010 PowerShell commands, so we cover that here.

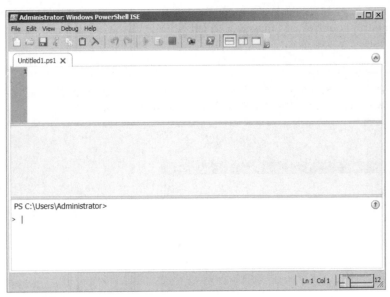

FIGURE 10-2

Adding commands is similar for all hosts. We will be adding commands to the PowerShell ISE host. ISE provides a multi-line editor with breakpoints and other help for scripting. You might need to consult the documentation for other third-party hosts.

ISE is installed with Windows Server 2008 and Windows Server 2008 R2 but it is not activated. To activate ISE, use the Add Feature screen of the Server Manager. Figure 10-3 shows the Server Manager's Add Feature screen with the ISE feature checked.

To register the SharePoint PowerShell commands with ISE you must be working locally on a SharePoint 2010 server. The SharePoint 2010 PowerShell commands do not remote.

 SharePoint 2010 commands must be run on a SharePoint 2010 server. The commands cannot be run from a client. PowerShell 2 does provide a remoting scenario whereby commands can be executed from a client to run on the server. This is a PowerShell function and not specific to SharePoint 2010. To learn more about configuring Windows PowerShell remoting with SharePoint 2010, read this blog post: `http://blogs.msdn.com/opal/archive/2010/03/07/sharepoint-2010-with-windows-powershell-remoting-step-by-step.aspx`.

Use the `Add-PSSnapin` PowerShell command to register the SharePoint PowerShell commands:

```
Add-PSSnapIn Microsoft.SharePoint.PowerShell
```

`Add-PSSnapIn` is a PowerShell command that will register commands. The Microsoft.SharePoint .PowerShell snap-in contains the registration information for the SharePoint commands.

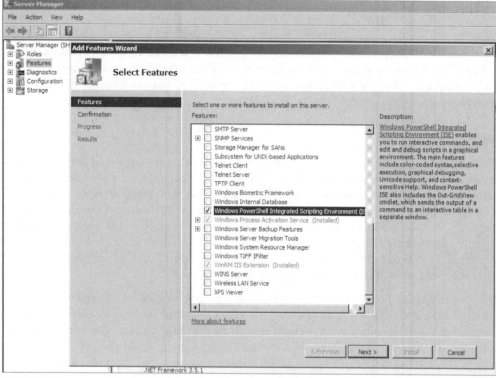

FIGURE 10-3

This will get you started. To verify that the SharePoint 2010 commands are available in ISE, simply run a SharePoint command such as Get-SPSite. ISE should respond with a list of site collections on the farm. Note one tiny issue: You are required to add the Microsoft.SharePoint.PowerShell snap-in every time you start the host. To avoid this, you can run the command to add the snap-in to your profile, which will run each time you start a host.

You can locate your profile by typing **$Profile** into the command line, which will return the path to your profile. $Profile is a variable containing the current user's profile location. The profile location may be different for each host. The ISE profile is different from the PowerShell profile, so commands for the ISE user's profile will not interfere with other PowerShell hosts. If the profile exists already, you can use the following command to open your profile:

```
Notepad $Profile
```

If the profile exists, Notepad will open it. If the profile does not exist but the directory exists, Notepad will prompt you to create a new file. Add the Add-PSSnapin command with the Microsoft.SharePoint .PowerShell value into your ISE profile and save it. You will need to restart ISE to read in the profile changes. When you need a command, variable, or function to persist between sessions, you can use the profile.

COMMANDS

PowerShell is powered by commands. Commands get things done. There are four basic types of commands: cmdlets, functions, scripts, and native commands. It is not necessarily important to know the differences among these command types to work with PowerShell and SharePoint, but it doesn't hurt either. If you are just starting out with PowerShell, you can find a wealth of general information at `http://microsoft.com/PowerShell`.

Cmdlets

Cmdlets (pronounced command-lets) are compiled commands that are registered with PowerShell. They have a very specific naming convention: All cmdlets are named with a verb-noun combination. The verb portion of the name should be one of the PowerShell accepted verbs. PowerShell defines a list of these verbs and what they mean at `http://msdn.microsoft.com/en-us/library/ms714428(VS.85).aspx`. Because the verbs are "standardized," you can usually guess the verb portion of the cmdlet. An example of a cmdlet is `New-SPWebApplication`, which has a corresponding `Remove-SPWebApplication`. You might have expected to use the verb "delete" to delete a `SPWebApplication`, but delete is not one of the standardized verbs, so it cannot be used.

Cmdlets are installed and registered. As you might have already guessed, the SharePoint commands that we will be using are cmdlets. You saw that SharePoint installed the cmdlets on the server, and the Management Shell registered them with the host using the PSC1 file; and you now know how to manually register them in the ISE. You can also create custom cmdlets, but that is a topic beyond the scope of this book. You can learn more about writing your own cmdlets in this MSDN article: `http://msdn.microsoft.com/en-us/library/dd878294(VS.85).aspx`.

Functions

Functions can contain one or more commands to accomplish a task, and can accept parameters that allow the creation of custom reusable code. They are defined in PowerShell by typing the function into the host. PowerShell then compiles the function and verifies the syntax. Functions can be reused for the lifetime of the host session. If you close the host, then you lose the function; and it will need to be entered again when you start another session with the host. You can enter functions into your profile so they will be available whenever you start a session.

 There's nothing worse than working on an award-winning function, only to lose it when you shut down the host. Consider yourself warned and save your function in your profile or at least to a text file so you can copy it later.

Functions have their place and are great for containing code that you will want to call from various other scripts or commands, but with a single chapter for administering SharePoint using PowerShell, we have no space to cover them in depth here.

Scripts

Scripts are a combination of commands, functions, and practically anything PowerShell. Because SharePoint 2007 did not have cmdlets, PowerShell scripts were very important. Now that we have more than enough cmdlets with SharePoint 2010, they are not as important for daily work. Scripts are useful for common reusable code, but SharePoint administration often results in the use of "one-liners." There is no big secret behind scripts; create a script in your favorite text editor or ISE and save it to the file system with a .PS1 file extension. Later you can run the script by typing in the filename.

Scripts, in contrast to functions or PowerShell snap-ins, survive the host shutdown and can easily be recalled. Another great benefit of the script is that once a script is created and tested, it can be saved to a script library and reused. By default, the hosts do not run unsigned scripts. Hosts will warn if you attempt to run a script that has not been signed. You can modify the security setting using the cmdlet Set-ExecutionPolicy. Because so much can be accomplished using the SharePoint cmdlets, we will not be doing much with scripts in this chapter. Scripts are only necessary if you want to chain together a complicated series of cmdlets, or walk through complicated loops.

 For security reasons, the PowerShell application is not associated with .PS1 files. The default application associated with .PS1 files is Notepad, so double-clicking a .PS1 file will open the file in Notepad. This effectively stops the user from double-clicking a malicious script and running it. If you change the file association, which is not recommended, you run the risk of inadvertently running a malicious script.

Native Commands

Native commands are commands that run outside of the host process. We have already used a native command, Notepad. If you are still hooked on STSADM.exe, you can use STSADM as a native command in the host. But with all the PowerShell goodness and the SharePoint commands, why would you?

BASIC POWERSHELL

Entire books have been written on PowerShell, so it is not possible to cover the basics in a single chapter. But we won't just you throw you to the wolves with PowerShell. Here we cover a few key things to help the newer "PowerShellers" out there (or is it "SharePointShellers"?). Many of the SharePoint PowerShell commands can be used as a one-liner or "standalone," so a true understanding of PowerShell is not always required. That said, understanding a few PowerShell concepts in conjunction with the SharePoint commands can help you along the way.

Listing the SharePoint Commands

PowerShell provides the Get-Command cmdlet to retrieve a list of available commands. The Get-Command parameter will retrieve all commands that are known to the host. Get-Command, like many commands, accepts optional parameters. Since we are interested in only the SharePoint 2010 commands, we can limit the commands displayed to just the SharePoint 2010 commands by using the optional -Module parameter. To list only SharePoint commands, execute the following command:

```
Get-Command -Module Microsoft.SharePoint.PowerShell
```

Figure 10-4 displays the output of the Get-Command cmdlet using the -Module parameter.

FIGURE 10-4

Did you catch all that? At last count there were over 500 PowerShell cmdlets included with SharePoint 2010. This might still be a few more commands than you want to list. The list can be pared down some if you use the optional -noun or -verb parameter for Get-Command. For example, if you were wondering what commands work with a Web application, use the following command:

```
Get-Command -Module Microsoft.SharePoint.PowerShell -noun SPWebApplication
```

If you need to know which command to use for backups, use the following command:

```
Get-Command -Module Microsoft.SharePoint.PowerShell -verb Backup
```

Figure 10-5 shows how you can control the output of Get-Command with the -noun and -verb parameters.

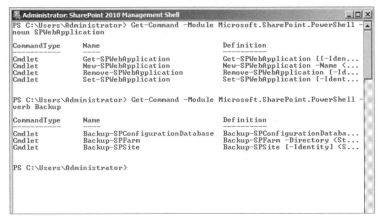

FIGURE 10-5

PowerShell Help

As shown in the preceding section, `Get-Command` will help you determine which command you should use to accomplish a task. `Get-Help` will help you understand the *usage* of a command. The `Get-Help` command is a standard PowerShell cmdlet. To get help for a particular command, simply call `Get-Help`, passing in the name of the command for which you want help. For example, if you wanted to see help about `New-SPWebApplication`, you would use the following:

```
Get-Help New-SPWebApplication
```

Figure 10-6 shows the help returned for `New-SPWebApplication`. It provides you with numerous details about the command, including parameters, examples, and usage. `Get-Help` accepts the optional parameters of `-detailed` and `-examples`. Examples of your options are shown at the bottom of Figure 10-6 under the Remarks heading. To learn more about `Get-Help`, simply use `Get-Help Get-Help` — a little redundant but it works.

PowerShell Variables

We can't ignore the topic of variables, which gets us frighteningly close to developer work. In a basic sense, variables hold information. Typically, variables don't come into play until you start doing more of the common one-liner commands. All PowerShell variables start with the `$` character and can hold any type of object.

 Certain objects in SharePoint such as `SPWeb`, `SPSite`, *and* `SPSiteAdministration`, *must be properly disposed of. One-liner SharePoint commands will dispose of all objects correctly. Storing these SharePoint objects in variables can lead to performance issues and memory leaks if the variable is not handled correctly. This section on variables specifically avoids using these SharePoint objects until the dispose subject can be addressed later in the chapter.*

FIGURE 10-6

In Figure 10-7, the variable $webApps is set to the output of Get-SPWebApplications. $webApps now contains all of the Web application (SPWebApplication) objects. You use the count property to determine how many Web applications are contained in the variable. You can display the Web applications by simply typing the variable name.

FIGURE 10-7

 Wondering which commands were used to get the output displayed in the screen-shots of the Management Shell? Just take a look at the top of the figures to see the commands following the Administrator prompt.

THE FORMERLY DREADED "OBJECTS"

We thought we would add a few words about our friends, the objects. As administrators, we have been able to stay blissfully ignorant of these pesky little devils. Until now. In previous versions of SharePoint we had STSADM. STSADM was good to us. When we needed to interact with it, we gave it strings like `http://portal.company.com`, `WSS_ContentDB`, or `domain\username`. And when STSADM replied back to us, it reciprocated with easy to understand strings. Strings are just text, so they're easy to use. We managed SharePoint with strings and we liked it. Then this fancy PowerShell comes along with its snap-ins and its cmdlets and its objects. What exactly is an object? It's complicated, but it helps to think of an object like a car. Like an object, a car has properties. Properties are information about the object, things like color, numberoftires, make, model, smellslikefeet, and so on. If we're given the object car, instead of the word "car" we can use those properties to make decisions. If we get a group of car objects, we can decide to only view the blue ones by checking the `car.color` property. That's one place where strings let us down. When we got a list of site collections from STSADM we got text. If we wanted information that wasn't in the text, we had no way to get more information, and if the information we needed was hidden somewhere in that string, we had to do complicated text manipulation to get it out. Objects make sorting this out easier.

Like our objects, cars also have methods. Methods are actions you can do with your object. In our car example a method might be start, accelerate, slowdown, rolldownwindows, driveoffcliff, and so on. Objects are the same way. We have methods associated with different object types. Those methods are one way we interact with the objects. The `SPSite` object has a `dispose` method, which flushes it out of RAM. It also has a `delete` method, which is one way to delete an `SPSite` object. See, objects aren't scary at all. Okay, maybe a little.

Hopefully after this little chat we've all become fans of objects and we appreciate them for the functionality they provide, and no longer hold their complexity against them.

It's important to note that the `Get-SPWebApplication` cmdlet does not include your Central Admin web application by default. You have to include the parameter `-IncludeCentralAdministration` for Central Administration to be included. Also, if you have only a single content web application the `.count` does not return 1, like you would expect. It returned nothing, nada, zilch.

Variables enable you to hold onto objects and data for later use in your commands and scripts. Obviously, variables do not survive a host shutdown, but you can create and set a variable in your profile. This book generally avoids using variables because so much can be done to administer SharePoint 2010 without them, which also avoids any disposal issues.

PowerShell Pipeline

The PowerShell *pipeline* is how you chain commands together. Why chain together commands? Cmdlets are usually good at one specific task such as listing SPSite objects (think site collections). You can chain together many commands to do a more specific or targeted task. The Get-SPSite command will return all site collections in the farm. The Get-SPWeb command will return a specific web object. If you needed to retrieve all SPWeb objects, you could chain the Get-SPSite command to the Get-SPWeb command using the PowerShell pipeline. To get all the SPWeb objects on the farm (excluding any within the Central Administration Web applications), use the following command, as shown in Figure 10-8:

```
Get-SPSite –Limit ALL | Get-SPWeb –Limit ALL
```

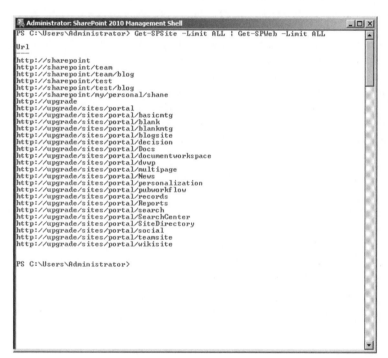

FIGURE 10-8

We cannot leave this discussion of the pipeline without at least mentioning .NET objects. The pipeline passes .NET objects between commands. The word "objects" might scare you a little, but you have been working with objects for some time now — with VBScript, CScript, and WMI, to name a few. Objects simply contain information and methods to act on the information or the environment. While you might shy away from objects, the fact that PowerShell uses .NET objects makes life a lot easier. For example, you can use a function such as Get-SPSite to return SPSite objects and send them to a command that will alter the objects. For a lot of what you do, objects will be sitting in the background.

Controlling Output

Now that you know a little about the pipeline and its use of objects, we need to take a look at how to control the output of these objects. The pipeline uses objects, but all we really work with in the Management Shell is text. No problem; PowerShell is a smart application. When an object hits the end of a pipeline, it must be captured, set to void, or formatted for the screen as text. We have already looked at using variables, so you should be familiar with the concept of capturing. *Void* is a fancy developer term for *nothing, get lost, I don't want you.* We won't worry much about void. Formatting, however, is something to worry about, because if you don't take care of formatting, PowerShell will.

In many cases it is not a big deal that we let PowerShell format our objects for display. When an object makes it to the end of the pipeline, the default formatters take effect. Many SharePoint objects have a default format, which is usually a table format with a few key properties. Let's take a look at the default formatting for the SPFarm object using the Get-SPFarm command.

In Figure 10-9 it appears that there are only two properties associated with the SPFarm object: Name and Status. While those are key properties, they are not the only properties associated with the SPFarm object. The default format for the SPFarm object displays only the Name and Status properties.

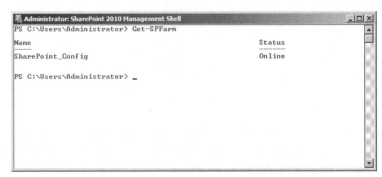

FIGURE 10-9

So how do you get to look at more properties? When you control the output, you get to decide how you want the objects formatted. You control the format using the format commands, the most common of which are Format-List and Format-Table. There are a few others, but this section looks at only these two common formatting commands.

Format-List will display object properties in list format. Each object gets one or more rows to display a property and a value. When you see text fly across the screen during some of your outputs, you can probably assume that you are looking at objects formatted in list style. At this point, we'll go ahead and send our SPFarm object to the Format-List command. Figure 10-10 displays the SPFarm object's properties in List view. The Format-List command also accepts an optional Properties parameter, which enables you to provide a comma-separated list of property names to be displayed.

FIGURE 10-10

`Format-Table` will display an object's properties in tabular fashion. Each object gets a single row and one or more columns depending on what properties should be displayed. The default format for most objects is table style, so simply piping the objects to the `Format-Table` might not get you much further. What will help is the optional `Property` parameter, which accepts a comma-separated list of properties to display. You could choose to display all `SPFarm` properties using the following command:

```
Get-SPFarm | Format-Table *
```

If you do that, however, you will get a result that is practically unreadable because you attempted to put too many columns in such a small amount of space. The `Format-List` command is better for showing a large number of properties. For example, instead of displaying all properties, you can display only the `DisplayName`, `Status`, and `BuildVersion` properties. Figure 10-11 shows the result of using the following command:

```
Get-SPFarm |Format-Table -Property DisplayName, Status, BuildVersion
```

Due to space limitations, this chapter doesn't cover many other formatting commands and even output commands to pipe content to files, including CSV. To learn more, use these two help commands:

```
Get-Help Format
Get-Help Out
```

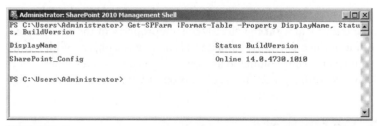

FIGURE 10-11

 To clear the screen, use CLS, *which is an alias for Clear-Host.*

USING SHAREPOINT COMMANDS

With more than 500 individual SharePoint 2010commands, one chapter cannot possibly cover them all. This section will get you started working with some of the more common SharePoint commands for PowerShell.

Working with the Farm

The Farm is the top-most SharePoint administrator object, containing key properties and collections associated with the SharePoint farm. The term "farm" can be confusing, especially in a single-sever environment. A *farm* is one or more servers that share the same configuration database. The association of farm and configuration database is carried through as the farm's name is the configuration database name.

In SharePoint 2007, we used the Farm object quite often when we scripted commands to get to all the collections and properties. With the many SharePoint 2010 commands, you can now access many of these properties using a more specific command. The farm still contains many key properties and methods that can be used for administration. For example, you can determine the farm's status, display name, and version.

You can access the farm using the Get-SPFarm command (refer back to Figure 10-9). The output of this command is nothing special. The default formatting for the SPFarm object is to display the Status and DisplayName. However, you learned earlier how to control formatting of the objects, so feel free to modify the output of the SPFarm object.

To access a specific property on the SPFarm object, use dot notation (.). You could also do this using a variable, but this has its own complications, which are covered at the end of this chapter when we cover object disposal. For example, to access the BuildVersion property of the SPFarm object, use the following command:

```
(Get-SPFarm).BuildVersion
```

The parentheses tell the command that you want the BuildVersion property of the *result* of the Get-SPFarm command. The result of the Get-SPFarm command is an SPFarm object. Without the parentheses, PowerShell would interpret your command as "get the BuildVersion property of the Get-SPFarm command," which does not have a BuildVersion property. Figure 10-12 shows the result.

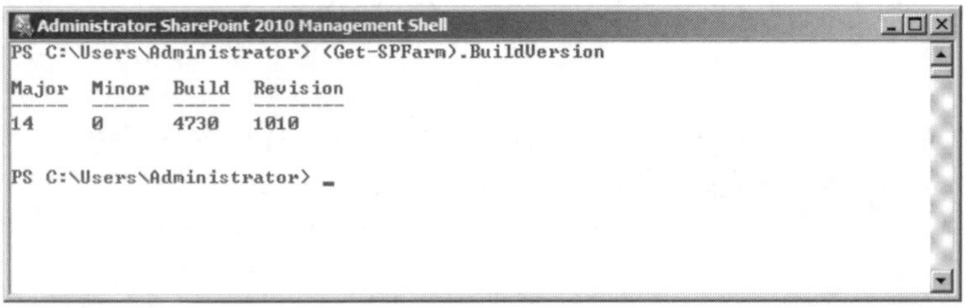

FIGURE 10-12

There are quite a few methods for the SPFarm object, but we won't cover any of these because SharePoint includes specific commands for many of these methods, such as backup and restore. There's no point spending time learning how to work with the object model when you can simply call a command.

Besides viewing and accessing properties of the farm, you can also back up and restore the farm using PowerShell and SharePoint commands. The backup command is Backup-SPFarm; and the restore command is Restore-SPFarm. The purpose of these cmdlets is obvious thanks to the nice verb-noun naming convention.

The backup command requires a Backup method and Directory parameter. If you don't include these parameters, the command will prompt for them. The BackupMethod can be Full or Differential. The directory is the location where you want the files to be placed. Just supply the path, not the file-name, for the Directory parameter. There are also optional parameters for the Backup-SPFarm command. Use Get-Help Backup-SPFarm to see these optional parameters. One particularly interesting parameter is the ShowTree parameter. Figure 10-13 displays the Backup-SPFarm command and its output.

Backing up would be useless if we could not restore the data. Restore-SPFarm requires the Restore method and a directory where the backup should be located. The Restore method can be either overwrite or new. Overwrite will overwrite the original location, whereas new will create a new database. Figure 10-14 shows the help for Restore-SPFarm.

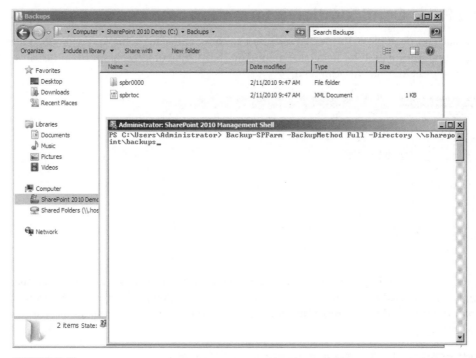

FIGURE 10-13

FIGURE 10-14

Retrieving Farm Configuration Information

We need to touch on the topic of the Get-SPFarmConfig command. This command will return farm-level configuration information for items that are not on the SPFarm object. Figure 10-15 displays the output of the Get-SPFarmConfig command.

```
Administrator: SharePoint 2010 Management Shell                              _□×
PS C:\Users\Administrator> Get-SPFarmConfig


WorkflowBatchSize                    : 100
WorkflowPostponeThreshold            : 15
WorkflowEventDeliveryTimeout         : 5
DataFormWebPartAutoRefreshEnabled    : True
ASPScriptOptimizationEnabled         : True


PS C:\Users\Administrator> _
```

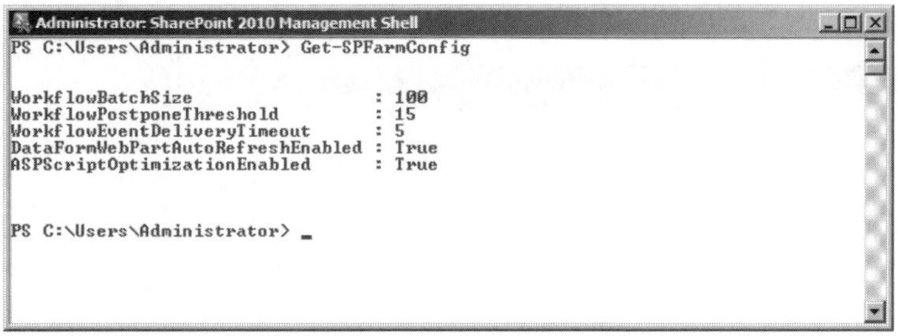

FIGURE 10-15

You can use the corresponding Set-SPFarmConfig to modify the values. It is a little bit more than a single command. You need to get the FarmConfig into a variable, change the value of the property, and then pipe the modified FarmConfig variable to the Set-SPFarmConfig command. Figure 10-16 shows the output.

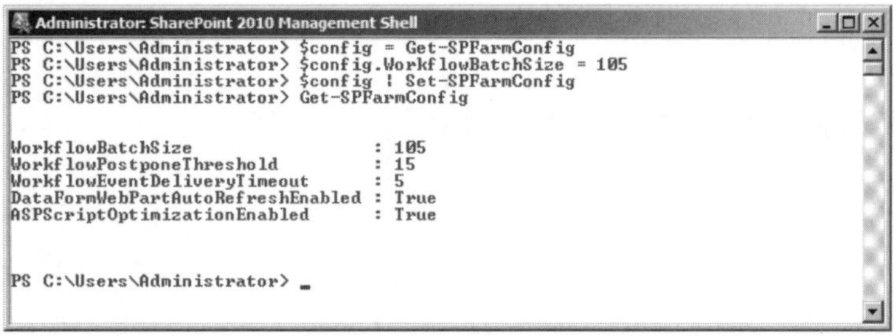

```
Administrator: SharePoint 2010 Management Shell                              _□×
PS C:\Users\Administrator> $config = Get-SPFarmConfig
PS C:\Users\Administrator> $config.WorkflowBatchSize = 105
PS C:\Users\Administrator> $config ! Set-SPFarmConfig
PS C:\Users\Administrator> Get-SPFarmConfig


WorkflowBatchSize                    : 105
WorkflowPostponeThreshold            : 15
WorkflowEventDeliveryTimeout         : 5
DataFormWebPartAutoRefreshEnabled    : True
ASPScriptOptimizationEnabled         : True


PS C:\Users\Administrator> _
```

FIGURE 10-16

The commands in Figure 10-16 modify the farm's WorkFlowBatchSize property. This property determines how many workflows can be processed at one time by the farm. The default value for this is 100. The lines above change this setting to 105 and writes the value back to the farm.

Working with Web Applications

Every SharePoint site collection is associated with a single Web application. The SPWebApplication object represents a Web application. The Web application contains many properties that an administrator might want to look at, such as those associated with the Recycle Bin, Official File, List throttling, and status. Using the SharePoint commands, you can list all Web applications including the Central Administration Web application, create new Web applications, remove Web applications, and modify Web application properties.

First, let's see all the Web applications on the farm. The Get-SPWebApplication command will display all the Web applications on the farm except for the Central Administration Web application. That is probably a good thing, as you probably don't want to treat the Central Administration Web application the same way we treat your content Web applications. To get all Web applications on a farm, including the Central Administration Web application, use the Get-SPWebApplication command with the IncludeCentralAdministration switch parameter, as shown in Figure 10-17.

FIGURE 10-17

Getting all the Web applications might not be exactly what you need. Sometimes you need a single Web application. To retrieve a single Web application, you use the Identity parameter. This parameter is smart enough to accept a name, Url, or Id of the Web application. You rarely see the –Identity parameter actually named. Normally, you can omit the name of the parameter, and name only the Url or Id, as shown in Figure 10-18.

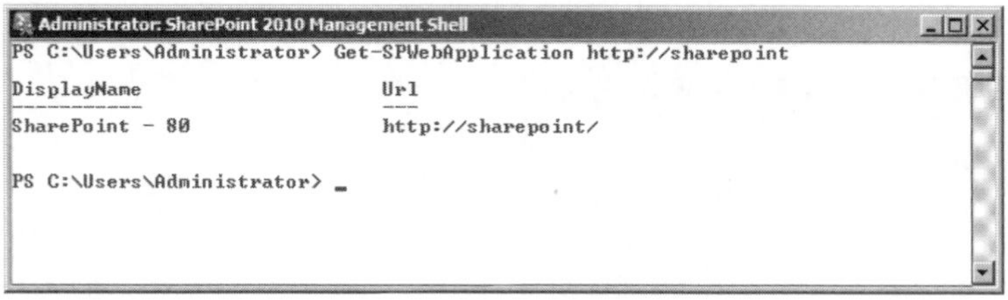

FIGURE 10-18

The SPWebApplication has a lot of properties and methods. To see the properties of this specific Web application, you can pipe it to Format-List as shown in Figure 10-19.

As Figure 10-19 demonstrates, the web application object has a lot of properties. To be honest, all the SharePoint objects have a lot of properties. How are we supposed to discover all these properties and keep track of them? Fortunately we have a command for that. Get-Member will return the members of the object passed into it via the pipeline. To determine what properties and methods are available on the SPWebApplication object, use the following command (the output is shown in Figure 10-20):

```
Get-SPWebApplication http://sharepoint | Get-Member
```

FIGURE 10-19

FIGURE 10-20

If piping the output through `Format-List` gives you more information than one screen can handle, you can additionally pipe it through the `More` command:

```
Get-SPWebApplication http://sharepoint | Get-Member | More
```

This will give you one page of output at a time. Press the spacebar to see the next screen. You can also scroll one line at a time by pressing the Enter key.

To access a specific property on the `SPWebApplication` object, use the dot notation described earlier. To access the Id of the http://sharepoint Web application, use the following command:

```
(Get-SPWebApplication http://sharepoint).Id
```

While it is nice to be able to access the Web applications, you might just want to create or remove a Web application. It's clear why you might want to remove a Web application, but why would you want to create a new one using PowerShell? Creating a new Web application is a great way to repeatedly build out your demo environments. The `New-SPWebApplication` cmdlet, shown below and in Figure 10-21, creates a new Web application, which contains many parameters — some required and some optional. The following simple example demonstrates how to create a new Web application. To see all the parameters, use `Get-Help New-SPWebApplication`.

```
New-SPWebApplication -Name "Portal" -Port 80 -HostHeader portal.contoso.com -Url
http://portal.contoso.com -ApplicationPool DemoAppPool -ApplicationPoolAccount (Get
-SPManagedAccount contoso\SP_serviceapps)
```

FIGURE 10-21

 When trying the code in Figure 10-21 you may get an error telling you that you need "machine privileges." This happens if your SharePoint 2010 Management Shell was not started with the Run as Administrator option. Without elevated permissions SharePoint can't always access what it needs. If you get any errors like this, make sure your management shell window has "Administrator:" at the beginning of the title bar.

You can use the `Get-SPWebApplication` command to verify that the Web application was created, but astute readers will notice that the newly created `SPWebApplication` object was formatted for the screen already. You could capture the `SPWebApplication` in a variable or pass the object onto another command via the pipeline. If you do capture the object in a variable, make sure you read the section "Disposing of SharePoint Variables" at the end of this chapter. Notice that we are calling the `Get-SPManagedAccount` command to retrieve an `SPManagedAccount` object, which is required for the AppPool account. You can see what managed accounts you have by using the `Get-SPManagedAccount` command with no parameter, as shown in Figure 10-22.

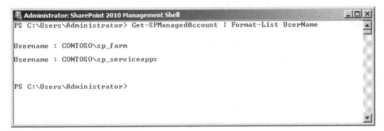

FIGURE 10-22

Now that you know how to create a web application using the SharePoint commands, it would be useful to learn how to remove an `SPWeb` application. It probably comes as no surprise that to remove a web application, you use the `Remove-SPWebApplication` command. This command requires you to select a specific web application, which prevents the deletion of multiple applications at once. Figure 10-23 shows how to remove the web application you just created.

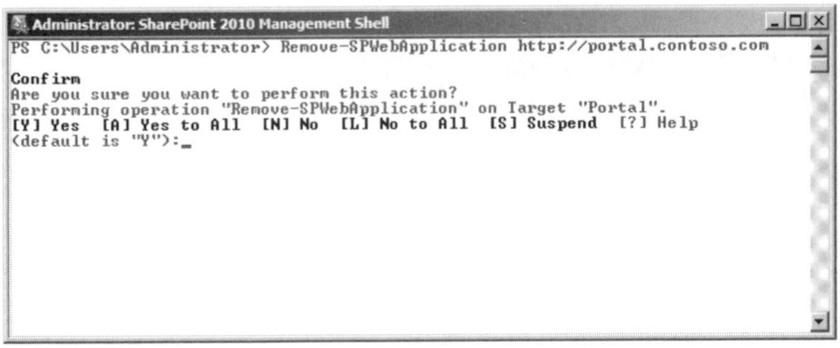

FIGURE 10-23

Notice how PowerShell is smart enough to prompt you before it destroys your precious information. Yes, there is a way to "override" this helpful prompt, but we will leave that as an exercise for readers who want to learn enough about PowerShell to change this setting and take responsibility for the consequences. We don't need any midnight phone calls when you accidentally delete your web application.

Working with Site Collections

The site collection level is where life gets interesting, for a number of reasons. First, since the 2003 version of SharePoint there has been a disconnect between the way the site collections are referred to in the Administration UI and object model. Next, the objects that you will be working with in this section require the proper disposal; otherwise your application might just start to hiccup, or worse.

Let's start by clarifying that a site collection is represented in the SharePoint object model as an SPSite. That should be enough clarification for the purposes of this section. We have looked at site collections in various chapters of this book already. The site collection belongs to one and only one Web application. The site collection is generally defined as a boundary for items such as content types and permissions. Like other objects in SharePoint 2010, you can list, create, modify, and remove a site collection or SPSite using the SharePoint PowerShell commands. You can also back up and restore a site collection using PowerShell.

 The SPSiteAdministration *commands* Get-SPSiteAdministration *and* Set-SPSiteAdministration *allow administrators who do not have access to the site collection to manage certain elements of it. Use of the SPSite-based commands assumes some amount of access to the site collection.*

Let's start by listing all site collections on the farm. There are two common methods to do this. If you do not need to list the Central Administration site collection (see the section "Working with Web Applications"), you can use the Get-SPSite command as described earlier in this chapter. As usual, the default formatting for the SPSite object provides only a few items for display. Figure 10-24 shows the Get-SPSite command in action.

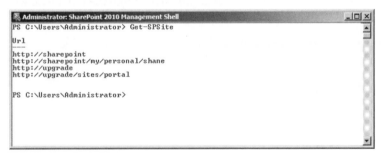

FIGURE 10-24

The Get-SPSite command, as well as other Get commands in SharePoint 2010, will return only 20 items before providing a warning that the list was limited. These commands limit the number of objects returned for performance reasons. You will greatly appreciate the limit functionality of the Get commands the first time someone tries to return hundreds of sites and webs. The Get-SPSite command has an optional Limit parameter that can be set to a number or to All if you wish to return all items. You will see how to use the Limit parameter in the following section.

If you want to include site collections associated with Central Administration, you need to start with the Get-SPWebApplication command with the IncludeCentralAdministration parameter. You then need to pipe the results to the Get-SPSite command, as shown in Figure 10-25.

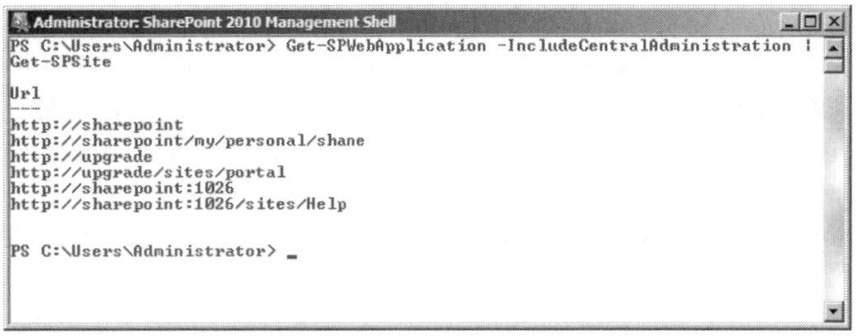

FIGURE 10-25

Of course, sometimes you need to get a single site collection or possibly a smaller subset of site collections. Using SharePoint 2010, along with some basic PowerShell commands, you have several ways to do just that.

To get a specific site collection, you can use the `Identity` parameter. Like the `Identity` parameter used with the `Get-SPWebApplication` command, you can provide the command with a few different values; and like the `Get-SPWebApplication` command, the actual word `Identity` is generally not seen. In this case, the `Identity` parameter can use wildcards as well as regular expressions (when used in conjunction with the `RegEx` switch parameter). To get a single site collection, simply pass in the `Url` as a parameter to the `Get-SPSite` command, which is piped to the `Format-List` command as demonstrated in Figure 10-26. Feel free to throw an asterisk into the mix to see what you get back.

FIGURE 10-26

The `Get-SPSite` command also has an optional `Filter` parameter that will perform server-site filtering of site collections, which provides a faster way to limit the SPSites returned. The `Filter` parameter will limit the results of the `Get-SPSite` command using a *script block*. A script block is simply a block of script enclosed by brackets. The `Filter` parameter can be used to filter on `Owner`, `Secondary Owner`, and `LockState`. Figure 10-27 shows the use of the `Filter` parameter and the script block. The `$_` represents the current object in the pipeline.

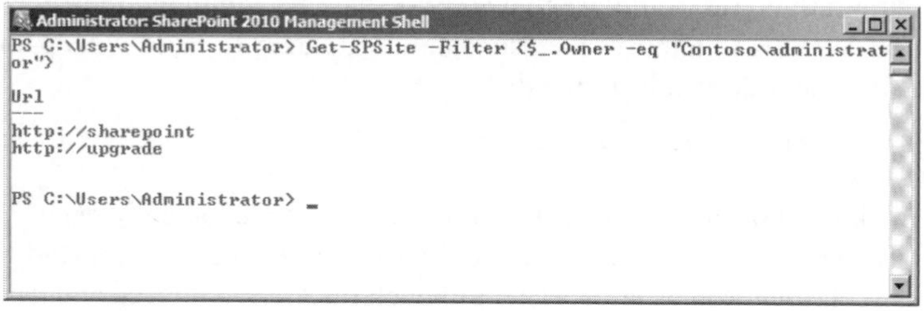

```
Administrator: SharePoint 2010 Management Shell
PS C:\Users\Administrator> Get-SPSite -Filter {$_.Owner -eq "Contoso\administrat
or"}

Url
---
http://sharepoint
http://upgrade

PS C:\Users\Administrator> _
```

FIGURE 10-27

Don't forget about using the pipeline to filter your site collections. The `Filter` parameter will only filter on `Owner`, `Secondary Owner`, or `LockState`. What happens if you need to select on other properties? If you can't seem to get from here to there using any of the preceding methods, you can always reach for the `Where-Object` command. The `Where-Object` command is a PowerShell command that uses a script block to filter objects. You commonly use the `$_` reference to the current pipeline object to check a property and decide whether to keep the object or ignore it. Use `Get-Help Where-Object` to learn more about the `Where-Object` command. The following example reaches out a little further and retrieves only those site collections that have a single `SPWeb` object, which is the root web:

```
Get-SPSite -Limit All |Where-Object {$_.allwebs.Count -eq 1}
```

Before removing any site collections, let's look at the backup and restore options. It's a good practice to back up the site in case you realize you really needed it after removing it.

By now you should be able to guess that the command to back up a site is `Backup-SPSite`. The site collection backup requires that you identify the site to back up and the path, including the filename, to save the backup image. This command by itself will back up only a single site collection. For example, to back up the site.Contoso.com/teams/IT site collection, you would use the following command:

```
Backup-SPSite http://site.contoso.com/teams/IT -path c:\backups\contoso\it\it.bak
```

While that's handy, it doesn't scale very well. Part of the "power" of PowerShell is its ability to loop through objects. Earlier in this chapter you saw how easy it is to get a list of all of your site collections. You also know how to back one up. Therefore, you may be thinking that you should be able to combine those two tasks in order to back up all of your site collections. If so, your instincts are correct. PowerShell provides exactly that capability. Behold, the "back up all of your site collections in a single script" script:

```
Get-SPWebApplication | Get-SPSite | ForEach-Object{$FilePath = "c:\backups\" +
  $_.Url.Replace("http://","").Replace("/","-") + ".bak" ; Backup-SPSite -Identity
  $_.Url -Path $FilePath}
```

There's a lot going on there, but when it's broken down it's easy to understand. The first two cmdlets get the list of web applications and site collections in the farm. The next part walks through the list of site collections and for each one creates a variable named `$FilePath` that consists of `C:\backups\` plus the name of the site collection, with the protocol (`http://`) removed and any slashes in the URL replaced with dashes. Finally, you use your old friend `Backup-SPSite` to back up the current site collection to the location you just built with `$FilePath`. So simple, yet so powerful.

You've probably already figured out that you would use the `Restore-SPSite` command to restore the backup. The `Restore-SPSite` command requires the usual standard `Identity` and `Path` parameter. To restore the `it.bak` file, use the following command:

```
Restore-SPSite http://site.contoso.com/teams/IT -path c:\backups\contoso\it\it.bak
```

Now that you have a backup and know how to restore the site collection, it is time to finally remove the site collection. To do that, you use the `Remove-SPSite` command. Like other destructive commands, you will be prompted for each site collection you want to delete. Although the `Remove-SPSite` will remove only one site collection, you are free to pass the `SPSite` object into the `Remove-SPSite` command using the PowerShell pipeline. You can now appreciate the fact that PowerShell prompts you to allow the deletion of each and every site collection.

Now is also a good time to talk about PowerShell's `WhatIf` parameter. Well-behaved cmdlets that are potentially destructive in nature support the optional `WhatIf` switch parameter, and the `Remove-SPSite` cmdlet is indeed one of those cmdlets. If you add the `WhatIf` switch parameter to the `Remove-SPSite` command, the command will not actually remove the site but instead indicate what will happen if you remove the `WhatIf` parameter. Nice touch, isn't it? It might not make sense if you are working with a single site but imagine if you ran this command:

```
$WebApps = Get-SPWebApplication -IncludeCentralAdministration
```

Now you have a variable that contains all Web applications. Suppose you later decide to remove all site collections. That is easy enough: `$WebApps | Get-SPSite | Remove-SPSite`. That is fine until you realize, too late, that you just deleted the Central Administration site collection. With the `WhatIf` parameter, you are forewarned about the pain you are about to inflict on yourself. Figure 10-28 shows you how a smart administrator can leave work on time.

Consider using the `WhatIf` parameter whenever you use a command that might destroy your data. It will help avert those frantic late-night restores and a fair amount of swearing.

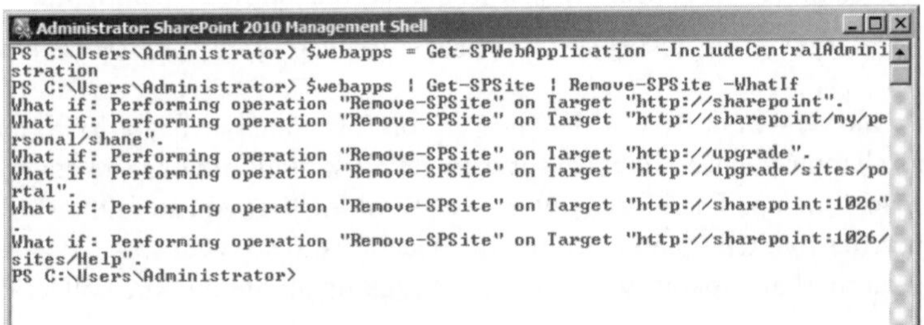

FIGURE 10-28

Working with Webs

Site collections contain webs or SPWebs if you are speaking about SharePoint PowerShell commands. Like the other main objects in the SharePoint hierarchy, you can list, add, modify, and remove webs. Administrators tend to spend a lot of time working with webs because they are so numerous and this is where end users actually do their work. The SPWeb object contains many items that end users work with, such as lists and libraries. Now is probably a good time to let you know that there are no commands to access objects below the SPWeb object. This means that there are no commands for lists, libraries, or files, to name a few objects below the SPWeb object. However, that does not mean you cannot access them via PowerShell — just that you will not find cmdlets specific to these objects. You are free to access these objects via the object model.

Listing all the webs of the farm is slightly different from listing SPWebApplications or SPSites. The Get-SPWeb cmdlet requires at least one parameter. It will not list all SPWebs on the farm if you omit the parameters. On the plus side, you are allowed wildcards, regular expressions (with the use of the −RegEx switch parameter), and filters (with a script block), similar to Get-SPSite. The Identity parameter will also accept a relative path if the Site parameter is used.

Let's look at a few ways to list SPWebs starting with a single web. To access a single SPWeb object, use the Identity parameter, passing in the Url as demonstrated in Figure 10-29.

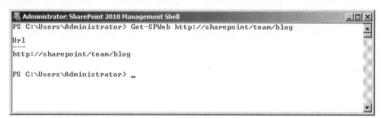

```
Administrator: SharePoint 2010 Management Shell
PS C:\Users\Administrator> Get-SPWeb http://sharepoint/team/blog

Url
---
http://sharepoint/team/blog

PS C:\Users\Administrator> _
```

FIGURE 10-29

Now use the Filter parameter to filter your SPWebs on the server side, which performs better than returning all SPWebs for further filtering. The Filter parameter can be used with the Template and Title properties of the SPWeb. Remember to use a script block with a Filter parameter. The following command returns a list of SPWebs that are based on the Blank Team site:

```
Get-SPSite | Get-SPWeb -Filter {$_.Template -eq "STS#1"}
```

The next example returns all the SPWebs in the farm, including any Central Administration webs, sorted by Url and displaying only the Title and Url:

```
Get-SPWebApplication -IncludeCentralAdministration | Get-SPSite |Get-SPWeb |
Sort-Object Url | Format-Table Title, Url
```

Figure 10-30 displays the results of the attempt to display all of the SPWebs on the farm. As discussed earlier, the cmdlet will limit the number of objects returned to 20 for performance reasons. If the number of objects is greater than 20, a warning will be displayed. To display all of the SPWebs, you need to add the Limit property set to All for both Get-SPSite and Get-SPWeb:

```
Get-SPWebApplication -IncludeCentralAdministration | Get-SPSite -Limit All |
Get-SPWeb -Limit All|Sort-Object Url|Format-List Title, Url
```

```
Administrator: SharePoint 2010 Management Shell                              _|□|×|
PS C:\Users\Administrator> Get-SPWebApplication -IncludeCentralAdministration |
Get-SPSite |Get-SPWeb |Sort-Object Url | Format-Table Title, Url
WARNING: More results were found in Get-SPWeb but were not returned.  Use
'-Limit ALL' to return all possible results.

Title                                    Url
-----                                    ---
Portal                                   http://sharepoint
CONTOSO\shane                            http://sharepoint/my/personal/shane
Team                                     http://sharepoint/team
Company Blog                             http://sharepoint/team/blog
Test                                     http://sharepoint/test
                                         http://sharepoint/test/blog
Upgrade                                  http://upgrade
OOTB Portal                              http://upgrade/sites/portal
Basic Meeting Workspace                  http://upgrade/sites/portal/basicmtg
Blank Site                               http://upgrade/sites/portal/blank
Blank Meeting Workspace                  http://upgrade/sites/portal/blankmtg
Blog                                     http://upgrade/sites/portal/blogsite
Decision Meeting Workspace               http://upgrade/sites/portal/decision
Document Center                          http://upgrade/sites/portal/Docs
Document Workspace                       http://upgrade/sites/portal/document...
DWWP                                     http://upgrade/sites/portal/dwwp
Multipage Meeting Workspace              http://upgrade/sites/portal/multipage
News Site                                http://upgrade/sites/portal/News
Personalization Site                     http://upgrade/sites/portal/personal...
Publishing Site with Workflow            http://upgrade/sites/portal/pubworkflow


PS C:\Users\Administrator> _
```

FIGURE 10-30

Creating a new web is similar to creating new site collections. You use the `New-SPWeb` command and a host of parameters to define the new SPWeb. One of these parameters, `Url` is required; but the rest are optional, such as `Name` and `Template`. The following command creates a new SPWeb based on the Team Site template:

```
New-SPSWeb -Url http://site.contoso.com/teams/IT/SP2010,
-Template "STS#1" -Name "SP 2010 Implementation"
```

Once the web has been created, the SPWeb object is returned and displayed on the screen.

You cannot back up or restore an individual web; that is reserved for the site collection and farm. What you can do is export and import a web. Because we just created a new web, let's go ahead and export it. To export the web, use the `Export-SPWeb` command, passing in the `Identity` and `Path` parameters. The `Path` parameter indicates where the exported web file will be placed, and it must include both a filename and the path. Use the `Export-SPWeb` command to export your new web:

```
Export-SPWeb http://corpNet.contoso.com/ops -Path c:\ExportWeb\opsExport.cmp
```

You can import the web into an existing or new web. The `Import-Web` command requires the identity of the web to import to and the path to the exported web file. The command to import your exported site to a new web is as follows:

```
Import-SPWeb http://corpNet.contoso.com/DemoImport -Path c:\ExportWeb\opsExport.cmp
```

Finally, you can remove your web by using the `Remove-SPWeb` command. This command is similar to the `Remove-SPSite` command. It removes one web at a time, prompting users for confirmation along the way. You can pipe an unlimited number of SPWebs into the remove command. Don't forget the earlier discussion of the `WhatIf` parameter. As shown in Figure 10-31, use the `WhatIf` parameter to see what would happen if you ran this command:

```
Get-SPSite |Get-SPWeb -Limit All |Remove-SPWeb -WhatIf
```

FIGURE 10-31

As you can see, the pipeline is very powerful. Be careful when you pipe objects into destructive commands. The WhatIf parameter and PowerShell's confirm message will help to keep you out of trouble — that is, if you pay attention!

Working with Objects below the Web Level

As mentioned earlier, SharePoint PowerShell commands generally work from the SPWeb object and above. That means you will not find commands such as Get-SPList or New-SPLibrary in the out-of-the-box commands. That does not mean that there is no way to access these and other items not exposed by the included commands. It means that we need to start thinking more like developers and attack the object model. This is exactly how we worked with SharePoint 2007 and PowerShell when we had no SharePoint cmdlets. We had to walk uphill both ways to and from school, and we liked it! This section does not delve too far into this subject, but it looks at how you can use PowerShell to list a web's lists and libraries, and add and then remove a SharePoint list. That will provide you with the foundation to move outside the commands supplied by SharePoint 2010.

Lists and libraries are children object of the SPWeb object we just looked at. The SPWeb object contains a single property, Lists, which is a collection of all its lists and libraries. To retrieve all the lists and libraries of a specific web, you can use the following command, as shown in Figure 10-32, within the Management Shell or a host with the SharePoint commands registered:

```
(Get-SPWeb http://sharepoint/team/blog).Lists
```

FIGURE 10-32

It is likely that there is a lot of text flying across your screen now as all the properties of all the lists and libraries are displayed. Unlike the previous SharePoint objects you have worked with, the SPList list object that is returned from the preceding command does not have a defined default format; therefore, PowerShell does its best formatting by dumping all the properties.

 Control+C will exit the current processing and return you to your prompt.

None of us can read that fast. Fortunately, you can control how each list is formatted and slow down some of that flying text. Run the same command, but this time send the lists and libraries out to Format-Table, which is another PowerShell formatting command, as shown in Figure 10-33.

```
(Get-SPWeb http://sharepoint/team/blog).lists | Sort-Object Title | Format-Table
    Title, Id, ItemCount, hasUniqueRoleAssignments, EnabledAttachments, EnableThrottling
```

```
Administrator: SharePoint 2010 Management Shell                          _ □ X
PS C:\Users\Administrator> (Get-SPWeb http://sharepoint/team/blog).lists | Sort-
Object Title | Format-Table Title, Id, ItemCount, hasUniqueRoleAssignments, Enab
ledAttachments, EnableThrottling

Title          ID              ItemCount HasUniqueRol EnabledAttac EnableThrott
                                         eAssignments hments           ling
-----          --              --------- ------------ ------------ ------------
Categories     6ca950a9-7...           3        False                      True
Comments       3f7c81ec-1...           0        False                      True
Links          791f1fb8-3...           1        False                      True
Master Pag...  60b39b0c-8...           3        False                      True
Photos         c5cefb1d-7...           0        False                      True
Posts          f8b99154-d...           1        False                      True


PS C:\Users\Administrator>
```

FIGURE 10-33

 Many of the lower-level objects such as SPList *and* SPListItem *will not save their changes to the content database until the* Update *method is called on the object.*

Now that you know how to retrieve all the lists and libraries contained within a SharePoint web, the following example demonstrates how to get just one specific list. The Lists property on the SPWeb object returns a collection of lists, like many of the properties associated with SharePoint objects. You can retrieve any list by using the index, Id, or title. For example, to get the third item in the lists collection, use the following:

```
(Get-SPWeb http://sharepoint/team/blog).lists[2] | Format-Table Title, Id,
ItemCount, hasUniqueRoleAssignments, EnabledAttachments, EnableThrottling
```

In the preceding example, the value 2 is used, rather than 3, because developers like to start counting at 0. Therefore, the first item in the collection is number 0, and the third item is 2.

As mentioned previously, you can also get a list by using the Id or list title. Simply replace the number 2 with the Id or Title. Go ahead and try:

```
(Get-SPWeb http://sharepoint/team/blog).lists["Links"] | Format-Table Title, Id,
ItemCount, hasUniqueRoleAssignments, EnabledAttachments, EnableThrottling
```

At this point, you know how to get down to the list level and enumerate all of your lists and libraries. Want to create a new list? Well, that one is a little tricky. First, you need to decide what type of list you will create. To keep it simple, the next example creates a Links list. The Links list template has an Id of 103, which is information you can find by looking in the SharePoint documentation. You can also get this information by running the following command:

```
(Get-SPWeb http://sharepoint/team/blog).ListTemplates | Where-Object {$_.Name -eq
"Links"}
```

To create the Links list, you need to call the Add method of the List collection you have already been working with. The Add method requires three parameters for this example: Title, Description, and `ListTemplateId`. Armed with all of this information, add that list using the following command:

```
(Get-SPWeb http://sharepoint/team/blog).Lists.Add("Demo Links List", "This is the
    description", 103)
```

Figure 10-34 shows the new, improved list of lists — now with even more Links lists.

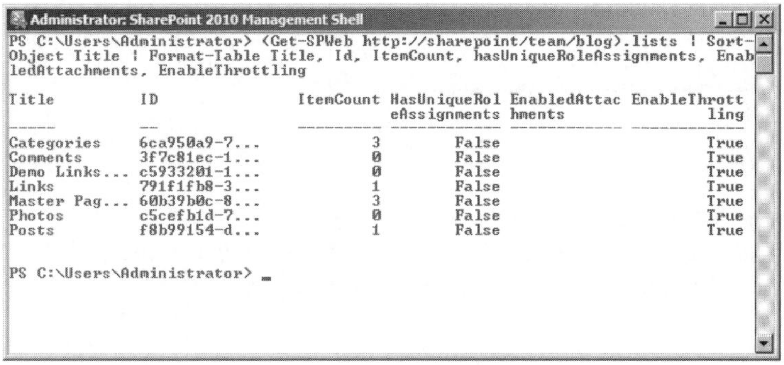

FIGURE 10-34

Finally, to close out this section you will delete your list. Yes, delete and not remove. The `Delete` method is a method of the `SPListCollection` object (the `Lists` property), and not a command in PowerShell, which is why you can use it. The `Delete` method of the List collection requires the list Id, so we are going to use a variable this time to grab the list Id in one line and use it in the `Delete` on the next line. Following are the two lines needed to delete the list you just created, and Figure 10-35 shows what it looks like.

```
$listId = (Get-SPWeb http://sharepoint/team/blog).lists["Demo Links List"].Id
(Get-SPWeb http://sharepoint/team/blog).lists.Delete($listId)
```

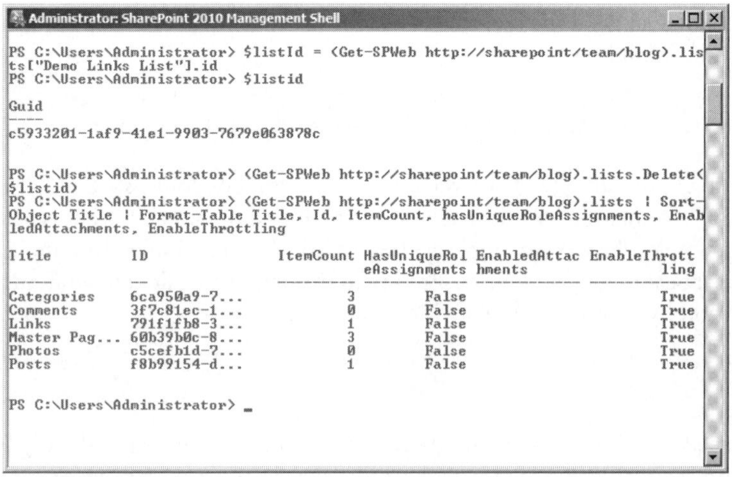

FIGURE 10-35

Again, you can verify that you did indeed remove the list by using the earlier command to list all your lists.

We can't close out this section without at least pointing you new admin developers to the key documentation that will help you with these more interesting creations: the SharePoint 2010 SDK, or Software Development Kit. Don't let the name scare you. It is actually a compiled help file or a set of web pages that provides documentation on the various objects in SharePoint. The SharePoint 2010 SDK is currently located at `http://msdn.microsoft.com/en-us/library/ee557253(office.14).aspx`. (Note that it might move later, as it contains "Office.14" in the URL. To find it after it is moved, simply search for "SharePoint 2010 SDK."

Disposing of SharePoint Variables

No chapter on working with SharePoint and PowerShell would be complete without discussing a topic that just might keep your farm up and running: disposing of your SharePoint objects. It is no myth that certain SharePoint objects need to be disposed of properly or you might see memory leaks on your beloved farm.

Although a few variables slipped into the examples, this chapter specifically avoided scenarios that required their use. It instead focused on single-line commands, which includes commands that are chained using the pipeline, because single-line commands will properly handle the disposal of SharePoint objects. The more you stick to one-liners, the less chance you have to forget how to properly clean up after yourself.

The disposal issue becomes a problem as soon as you start to capture certain SharePoint objects such as `SPSite`, `SPSiteAdministration`, and `SPWeb`, and hold on to them. They cannot be disposed of at the end of the pipeline because you are still using the object.

Luckily, there are two commands to help you work with situations in which you might run into disposal issues: `Start-SPAssignment` and `Stop-SPAssignment`. The `SPAssignment` commands help you to both track objects and then dispose of them when they are no longer needed.

This section covers two different ways of using these commands. The first command is the simple assignment method that uses the `Global` switch parameter. Basically, before you start to use objects that might need to be disposed of, you call `Start-SPAssignment` using the `Global` switch parameter. This will start the tracking of all resources being used, which quite frankly can be a lot. Once you are done working with your variables and objects, you need to call `Stop-SPAssignment` with the same `Global` switch parameter. At this point, all the objects that were tracked will be released and properly disposed of. Once you call `Stop-SPAssignment` you should not use the resources for that block of commands, as they may not work properly as they are disposed of.

Figure 10-36 demonstrates the use of `Start` and `Stop-SPAssignment` with the `Global` switch parameter.

While using the simple assignment method is simple, it does have some drawbacks. Any trackable SharePoint object between the `Start` and `Stop-SPAssignment` will be managed by the commands. This means that if you run many one-liners that do not necessarily need to be tracked, they will get tracked anyway and that is more memory that is waiting to be released.

If you know when you need to track a SharePoint object, you can manually assign your resources to be tracked. This enables you to be selective regarding the objects that are assigned for tracking and disposal. You can do this with the same `Start` and `Stop-SPAssignment` commands. With this technique, you create a new `SPAssignmentCollection` using `Start-SPAssignment` — for example, `$spAssign = Start-SPAssignment`.

```
Administrator: SharePoint 2010 Management Shell                              _□×
PS C:\Users\Administrator> Start-SPAssignment -Global
PS C:\Users\Administrator> $Webs = (Get-SPSite)[0] | Get-SPWeb
PS C:\Users\Administrator> $webs | Format-Table Title, URL

Title                            Url
-----                            ---
Portal                           http://sharepoint
Team                             http://sharepoint/team
Company Blog                     http://sharepoint/team/blog
Test                             http://sharepoint/test
                                 http://sharepoint/test/blog


PS C:\Users\Administrator> Stop-SPAssignment -Global
PS C:\Users\Administrator> _
```

FIGURE 10-36

When you need to track objects, you can use the `$SPAssign` in the pipeline. For example, you can assign all webs from a particular site collection for tracking and disposal:

```
$Webs = $SPAssign | Get-SPSite http://sharepoint | get-SPWeb
```

You can also throw in a few one-liners as we have been doing up until now. These do not need to be tracked because they will be disposed of properly. Since these objects will not be assigned to the `SPAssignmentCollection` object, they will be disposed of at the end of their lifetime and will not hold onto extra memory. Once you are done with your block of commands, you can clean up using the `Stop-SPAssignment` command, passing in the `$SPAssign` variable. Like the simple assignment, once you call `Stop-SPAssignment` you should not use the variables that were assigned to the `SPAssignmentCollection`. Figure 10-37 demonstrates the assignment of a collection of web objects and their proper disposal with the call to `Stop-SPAssignment`.

```
Administrator: SharePoint 2010 Management Shell                              _□×
PS C:\Users\Administrator> $SPAssign = Start-SPAssignment
PS C:\Users\Administrator> $Webs = $SPAssign | Get-SPSite http://sharepoint | Ge
t-SPWeb
PS C:\Users\Administrator> (Get-SPWeb http://sharepoint).Lists | Format-Table Ti
tle, ItemCount

Title                                        ItemCount
-----                                        ---------
Cache Profiles                                       4
Content and Structure Reports                        7
Content type publishing error log                    0
Converted Forms                                      0
Customized Reports                                   0
Documents                                            0
Form Templates                                       0
Forms                                                0
Images                                               0
List Template Gallery                                0
Long Running Operation Status                        0
Master Page Gallery                                 54
Notification List                                    0
Pages                                                2
Quick Deploy Items                                   0
Relationships List                                   1
Reusable Content                                     3
Site Collection Documents                            0
Site Collection Images                               0
Solution Gallery                                     0
Style Library                                       41
Suggested Content Browser Locations                  0
TaxonomyHiddenList                                   0
Theme Gallery                                       20
User Information List                               16
Variation Labels                                     0
Web Part Gallery                                    67
wfpub                                               28
Workflow Tasks                                       0


PS C:\Users\Administrator> Stop-SPAssignment $SPAssign
PS C:\Users\Administrator> _
```

FIGURE 10-37

Note in Figure 10-37 that you do not assign the SPWeb object you used to display the SPList objects. This SPWeb object is in a one-liner and will be disposed of correctly without the need for any tracking.

SUMMARY

This PowerShell thing just might catch on. As demonstrated in this chapter, it adds a dimension of power to SharePoint administration that just wasn't available to administrators in SharePoint 2007. This chapter has taken you from being a PowerShell newbie to using advanced techniques on your SharePoint farm, such as looping and object disposal. While we don't recommend talking to developers if it can be avoided, using PowerShell levels the playing field some. You'll be able to tell amusing anecdotes about SPSites and SPWebs and they'll laugh along. Oh, and you'll be able to better administer your SharePoint 2010 farm too.

11

Managing Navigation and Understanding Governance

WHAT'S IN THIS CHAPTER?

➤ SharePoint navigation on the Team site, the Portal site, and the Publishing site

➤ Navigating the Workspace

➤ Developing governance policies and procedures

This chapter begins by walking you through the various types of navigation and the SharePoint navigation features. We show you how to configure navigation so your users can easily access the tools and content they need.

In exploring navigation, it will become clear that an organization can benefit by implementing some type of strategy to ensure consistency. Users find it disconcerting when similar sites have different layouts or behavior; they find it easier to navigate if common menus or features are standard across the SharePoint environment. Navigation is one area of SharePoint where a commitment to strong governance can help ensure consistency.

The second part of the chapter shows you how to develop governance policies and procedures that ensure that your SharePoint environment is able to consistently provide a robust, stable working environment for your users. Good governance requires input from across the organization — management, designers, developers, and end users as well as SharePoint administrators. We explain the process by which governance is created and maintained, and give some examples of areas such as navigation where governance policies are useful.

NAVIGATION

SharePoint has several different types of navigation that can be configured within a site collection. In the first half of this chapter we review the different types of navigation available and discuss the different ways they can be used and configured within your environment. As you read this chapter, note that we are covering only what is available for configuring navigation out of the box. If further customizations are needed, custom approaches to navigation can be used. This chapter will give you the baseline you need to determine what is available out of the box, and then help you identify how to use the tools presented to build a consistent navigation for your users.

Before getting started, first consider the effect of navigation within your SharePoint environment. Navigation provides the users with the tools they need to successfully locate the different areas within your environment. This can be as simple as navigating to the Human Resources department to look for a form or to the IT department to submit a help desk request. When users access your site, they must use the navigation provided to them to access the specific content they are looking for. Users expect to access the site and *easily* move throughout it locating the content relevant to their specific tasks. Moreover, as with most WEB based resources, they expect to do this with very little training or effort. This also means that regardless of your site's content or design, if users cannot easily find things they will not be satisfied with the overall site.

As the SharePoint administrator, you are continuously presented with various solutions, ideas, and projects that are being developed within SharePoint. As you review and work with teams that are developing these solutions, the information in this chapter will help you understand your options and how they can be combined to ensure a consistent approach throughout your environment.

Understanding the Different Types of Navigation

Several types of navigation are available within SharePoint. Some are available in all cases, and others are available only when certain features, such as the SharePoint Server Publishing Infrastructure, have been enabled. This section provides a brief overview of the different elements available. The remainder of this section covers each area in additional detail. Following are the main navigation tools:

> **Bread crumbs** — These are links that provide users with information about their location within the site, relative to the rest of the site structure. From these bread crumbs, users can easily navigate to a different part of the site. These links are dynamically generated as the site is built.

> **Portal site connection** — This link, configured in the site collection administration settings, is displayed as the top-most link in the bread crumbs for the site. It enables you to always point users back to a common location, regardless of the site collection.

> **Tree View** — This setting enables you to display the hierarchy of the site in place of the Quick Launch. It provides users with a very structured view of the site.

➤ **Metadata navigation** — This feature enables you to navigate through lists and libraries based on the configuration of the managed metadata.

➤ **Team site navigation** — This provides the tools needed to navigate through team sites or sites for which publishing has not been activated. This includes the Quick Launch and top link bar tools.

➤ **Publishing site navigation** — This provides all the tools needed to configure navigation throughout publishing sites and includes the Global Navigation and the Current Navigation configurations.

➤ **Workspace navigation** — Workspace navigation is used specifically within meeting workspaces and provides additional functionality that enables navigation between meeting pages.

➤ **Navigation Web Parts** — These provide additional navigation that can be added to the various pages within the site. These Web Parts are available to all publishing sites.

Navigation is configured per site collection and the preceding list identifies the different ways navigation is provided out of the box with SharePoint. The options available to you will vary according to the different features you have activated within your site collections.

Bread Crumbs

Bread crumbs provide a "trail" that enables users to easily navigate back to the top of the site as they work within it. They are available within both Publishing and Team site collections and are dynamically created as the site content is created. The bread crumbs are displayed in the top-left corner of the site, next to the Site Actions command. A user has the ability to navigate to any point in the bread crumb with a single click. The bread crumbs are displayed only when the icon is selected and they show the hierarchy of the site based on the user's current location. Figure 11-1 shows the bread crumb for a team site collection. Within the site collection is a project site that contains several document libraries. The bread crumbs indicate that the user is currently located within the Shared Documents Library in the Project site that is part of the Team site collection.

Bread crumbs are included in all site templates. As you build sites based on the Publishing Portal template, you will notice that the appearance of the bread crumb is different from other site templates. This is because the template is referencing a different master page. Figure 11-2 is an example of the bread crumb for the Publishing Portal template.

FIGURE 11-1

FIGURE 11-2

Current Location Navigation

Another type of bread crumb navigation available for users is the current location navigation that is available for various locations within the site. A specific example is within a list or a library. This navigation displays where the user is located within the site and it can be used to navigate to a location above the current location or to additional views available for the list or the library. Figure 11-3 shows an example of this type of navigation within a document library. The view drop-down contains the different options available for the current view, as well as links to return to the Shared Document Libraries default view or the Project site home page.

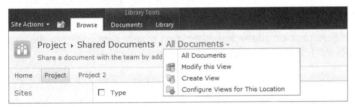

FIGURE 11-3

Portal Site Connection

A portal site connection is a configuration setting that enables you to configure a single link as the topmost link in the bread crumbs. This link is configured once per site collection and is displayed for all sites. It can represent any valid URL. When configuring the link, you are required to enter the address as well as a friendly name, which will be displayed within the bread crumbs. Figure 11-4 shows an example of a site collection that has configured the portal site connection to be the Company Intranet site.

FIGURE 11-4

The capability to connect a site collection to a different site collection is a great tool to bring consistency to your environment. As you know from Chapter 3, it is important to plan for multiple site collections so that your data can be stored in multiple databases. When your design requires the use of multiple site collections, the portal site connection functionality enables you to provide users with a shared link to a single location. This provides a seamless navigation experience, and enables administrators to divide content as needed across site collections without compromising the navigation experience for users.

Tree View

Tree View navigation provides a way to show a complete hierarchical view of the site from within the site pages. When activated, the Tree View (shown in Figure 11-5) is displayed on the left side of the site.

The Tree View is available in most site collections, and it can be combined with other page navigation elements, such as the Quick Launch or Current Navigation. The settings to control the Tree View are located in the Look and Feel options in the Site Settings page.

Team Site Navigation

This section covers the navigation options available in team sites. We are defining a team site as any site collection or site that does not have the SharePoint Server Publishing Infrastructure site collection feature activated, referred to as the publishing feature in the context of this chapter. You can determine whether the site collection is using the publishing feature by reviewing the features enabled for that site collection. This information can be accessed on the Site Settings page under the Site Collection Administration group.

Two navigation options are available within team sites: the Quick Launch and the top link bar. The Quick Launch provides a way for you to create on-page links that are persistent throughout the entire site, and the top link bar enables you to provide persistent tabs across the top of each page. Each of these options is described in more detail below.

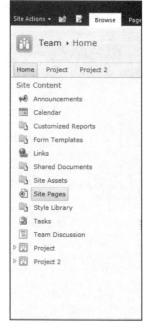

FIGURE 11-5

Keep in mind that the features available to your site collections and sites are based on licensing within the farm. Out of the box, if you create a site collection using the Team Site template, a site will be created that is using only team site features. To take advantage of the publishing navigation features, you could easily activate the publishing feature for the site collection. Once the publishing feature has been activated, the links within site actions that pertain to navigation will represent the publishing elements, which are described in detail in the next section.

Quick Launch

When a new site is created using the Team Site template, the Quick Launch is enabled by default. It contains links to the libraries, lists, and discussions within the site. The Quick Launch headings are links to a page displaying all the content of that specific type within the site, and the items under each heading are direct links to the specific content. Figure 11-6 shows an example of the default Quick Launch configuration for the Team Site template. You will also sometimes hear it referred to as the Quick Launch bar, left-hand navigation, and current navigation.

The Quick Launch can be configured dynamically as content is created or built manually through the addition of links and headings. The options for dynamically adding content to the Quick Launch are provided for you when new lists, libraries, or sites are created. As you create new content, an option will be available that enables you to select items to be added to the Quick Launch. Selecting yes for this option will add the item to the Quick Launch under the appropriate heading.

FIGURE 11-6

All links added to the Quick Launch, either manually or dynamically, are security trimmed. Links that are manually added to the Quick Launch that are items outside of the site collection are not security trimmed. *Security trimmed* refers to the process of only showing the links or items to users who have access to them. Figure 11-7 shows the default options for creating a new document library and adding it to the Quick Launch. Once you create a new list or library, you can modify its visibility on the Quick Launch through the Title, description and navigation configuration page found in the settings for the library or list.

FIGURE 11-7

You can manually configure the Quick Launch through the Quick Launch option under Look and Feel in Site Settings. From this screen you can create new headings and navigation links, and you can reorder existing links. When creating new headers you have to provide a URL and the header title. When creating new links you have to provide the URL, the link title, and the associated header. Each link must be associated with a header. To edit an existing link, simply click the edit icon displayed next to the item. Figure 11-8 shows the configuration screen for the Quick Launch.

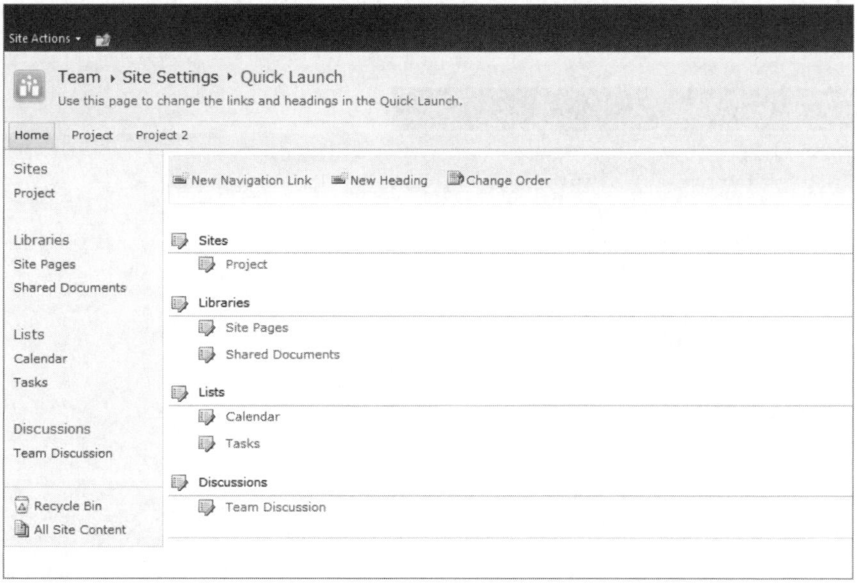

FIGURE 11-8

The Quick Launch is configured per site and there is no way to inherit the Quick Launch from a parent site. If inheritance is a requirement, then the publishing feature (available only with SharePoint Server) should be used. The Quick Launch can also be disabled for the site. The setting to disable the Quick Launch is provided in the Tree View settings located in the Look and Feel group on the Site Settings page.

Top Link Bar

The top link bar is used to provide tabbed navigation throughout the site collection. When new sites are created, they can use the same top link bar as their parent site, or use one specific to their site collection. Like the Quick Launch, the top link bar can be controlled either dynamically or manually. Any links added dynamically are security trimmed, whereas any links added manually are available to all users. You can configure the top link bar when a new site is created. On the options page that is displayed when you create a new site, select More Options. On the screen that appears, you will see the following available settings for the top link bar:

➤ **Display this site on the Quick Launch of the parent site** — This option adds the site link to the Sites header on the parent site Quick Launch Bar. If no heading for Sites exists, it will be created for you when you select this option.

➤ **Display this site on the top link bar of the parent site** — This option adds a link to the parent site's top link bar.

➤ **Use the top link bar from the parent site** — This option causes the site you are creating to inherit the top link bar from the parent site.

To change the link to a site once it has been created, you must access the top link bar options under Look and Feel in the Site Settings page and make manual modifications. From this configuration screen, shown in Figure 11-9, you can create new links, and reorder and modify existing links.

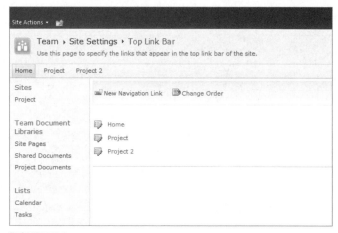

FIGURE 11-9

If the site you are working with has been configured to inherit the top link bar from its parent site, when you access the configuration screen you will see an option to Stop Inheriting Links (see Figure 11-10). Likewise, if the site is not set to inherit from its parent, when you access the configuration screen you will see an option to Use Links from Parent (shown in Figure 11-11).

FIGURE 11-10

FIGURE 11-11

Publishing Site Navigation

Navigation options within a site that has the publishing features enabled provide additional functionality over sites for which these features have not been enabled. This added functionality includes items such as multi-level navigation links and the capability to inherit the current navigation from the parent site. This section covers these differences and describes the various configuration options available.

 Once you activate publishing for a site collection, every template within that site collection will use the publishing navigation controls. This means that if you create a team site as a subsite to a publishing site, that team site will use the publishing navigation, not the team site navigation described earlier.

The first big difference in the publishing sites is the replacement of the top link bar and Quick Launch with the Global Navigation menu. Once publishing has been enabled for the site collection, the Navigation link is displayed in the Look and Feel section of the Site Settings page. This Navigation link provides the configuration settings for both the global and current navigation settings.

 When working with publishing sites, keep in mind that it is likely that they are using a custom master page. Within the master page, it is possible to hide controls or move their locations. This commonly occurs with the navigation elements. If the site you are working with does not display the navigation you are expecting based on the information provided in this chapter, the master page has probably been customized.

Global Navigation

The Global Navigation settings allow you to select the navigation inheritance, as well as limit the total number of dynamic elements displayed. The options for display include sites and pages. If you select to show sites and pages, any sites or pages created will be displayed on the Global Navigation bar. From this option you can also configure the navigation inheritance. You can select to use the same navigation elements as the parent site or create your own navigation. Figure 11-12 shows the global configuration of a site that is opting to show pages and sites. In this case, HR Department is a site and Vacation-Policy is a page.

FIGURE 11-12

Current Navigation

The Current Navigation settings allow you to determine what content is displayed on the left pane of the site. These settings can be thought of as a replacement for the Quick Launch. In fact, when you create new content you can still select to add it to the Quick Launch — it will be added as a link under the corresponding heading category. For example, a document library that is created with the option of being added to the Quick Launch will be displayed as a link to the Libraries heading.

From this screen you can also configure what level of content to display. Your options include the following settings:

➤ Displaying the same current navigation as the parent site.

➤ Display the current site, the navigation items below the current site, and the current site's siblings.

➤ Display only the navigation items below the current site.

The options just listed enable you to configure your current navigation in a variety of ways. Figure 11-13 shows an example of a site that is displaying the current items, items below that, and the sibling site's items.

Keep in mind that if none of the options listed so far for either the Global Navigation or the Current Navigation provide what you are looking for, you can always customize the links for your specific needs. The options for customizing are covered in the section "Navigation Editing and Sorting."

Sorting

From this setting you can configure to sort your content automatically or manually. If you select to sort your content manually, options for arranging the content are provided in the following section. If you select to automatically sort your content, you will be required to select a field and a sort order from the options provided.

FIGURE 11-13

Navigation Editing and Sorting

From the Navigation Editing and Sorting option, shown in Figure 11-14, you can create custom headers, or link or modify existing headers and links. To modify an existing item, select the item and use the toolbar to make your changes. You can modify the link, change the title, or move the link to a new location. Links can be moved between different headers, but a link cannot become a header and a header cannot become a link.

FIGURE 11-14

Show and Hide Ribbon

The last option you have in the publishing navigation configuration is to use the Show/Hide Ribbon option instead of automatically showing the Ribbon. This feature is only available within publishing sites. When selected, the Ribbon will not automatically display on pages; instead users access the Ribbon through the Site Actions menu. From this menu item, shown in Figure 11-15, they can select to show or hide the Ribbon.

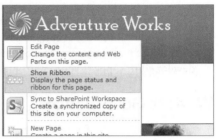

FIGURE 11-15

Workspace Navigation

The final piece of navigation to look at is the Workspace templates. These templates are used to store meeting information and come in several different varieties, such as social, decision making, and multi-page. By default, these sites use the concept of pages to manage their content. This page is a little different from the type of page in a publishing site. They are used to store additional content within the meeting. They are also used to provide navigation in place of the Quick Launch or Current Navigation. This means that the settings you configure for the Quick Launch or Current Navigation will not be displayed on the meeting site. The only way to add navigation to these templates is through the creation and management of pages. The options to create and manage the pages are available within the Pages tool pane, shown in Figure 11-16. To access this tool pane, select Manage Pages from the Site Actions menu.

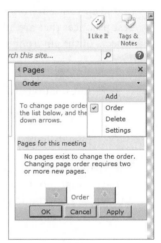

FIGURE 11-16

Next Steps

At this point in the chapter, you are likely trying to assimilate all this information and figure out which method is best to implement a navigation strategy. Who knew there could be so many options! On the one hand, you could let everyone fend for themselves and have each site develop its own methods of managing navigation. On the other hand, you could develop some guidelines and enforce that each site use the same navigation strategy.

This is just one of many examples in which SharePoint governance should be implemented. If each site used a different navigation strategy, then how would users know how to navigate? And if the system administrator is responsible for building the navigation strategy, how will that person know what the business needs? In this situation, the best-case scenario would be the business units working together with the system administrators. The system administrators know what is possible and the business units know what is needed. Working together they can develop an approach that is manageable and meets the needs of the organization. This process of working together to define strategies is the development of SharePoint governance. The remainder of this chapter covers governance and reviews different approaches to implementing it. By the end of the chapter, you will see that navigation is just one of many areas that require governance!

SHAREPOINT GOVERNANCE

This section provides a high-level overview of SharePoint governance. We first define governance and then work through some different approaches to building your team. Finally, we will review each of the major areas within SharePoint and describe the different types of policies that should be developed to support your environment.

What Is Governance?

Governance, in the SharePoint context of this chapter, is the set of policies and procedures developed to ensure that your SharePoint environment is able to consistently provide a robust, stable working environment for your users. These policies and procedures are the guiding principles that keep your environment configured for the best possible support. They are usually based on best practices that are adjusted to fit your organization's needs. Governance covers many different aspects of the environment, including the following:

- ➤ Infrastructure
- ➤ Information architecture
- ➤ Development and customization
- ➤ Support and availability

The following sections cover each of these areas and provide insight on the different questions and scenarios that should be considered as you develop your governance policies. We will also look into different ways to build your governance team, and even ways to help promote the need for governance within your environment.

Getting Started with Governance

One of the hardest parts of SharePoint governance is simply getting started! If you are in an organization like most, governance comes in one of two flavors — the lifeline to keeping things going or the thing that should have been done to avoid issues. In some places governance doesn't tend to be high on the list of priorities until something major happens that causes everyone to say, "Wow, if we had just done X, all of this could have been avoided!"

When handled correctly, governance will be the driving force of your implementation. When ignored, your implementation will be at risk on several fronts. The most common elements to suffer when governance is ignored are funding, usability, and supportability. For example, consider the situation in which many different projects are developed at once by different groups, all using SharePoint. If none of the teams building the solutions are working together using common standards, you are likely to get several drastically different solutions. This may seem fine at first; different problems require different solutions, right?

It's fine until an end user encounters a completely different look and feel for each similar site they have to access. Consider the Quick Launch — what if its location differs on every site users access? Imagine the confusion and frustration that could cause, and then imagine all the extra help desk support you would need to answer all the questions it would be flooded with! Conversely, imagine what the situation would have been like if, when new departments wanted to use SharePoint, clear guidelines were in place that outlined the purpose of the environment and the things that could and should be done to the site.

At the same time, you don't want to have to be the gatekeeper for every action, especially those that don't really matter to you and your responsibility to keep the farm running and happy. How do you find the balance? You build a team and implement governance policies! The remainder of this chapter is dedicated to providing you with the information needed to begin building and developing governance policies within your SharePoint implementation.

 While it's easy to find existing best practices and standards for governance policies, keep in mind that they need to be integrated into your specific, unique environment. Because governance policies consist of guidelines to ensure that your environment remains stable and supportable, it is critical that your team reviews the best practices and adapts them as appropriate.

Governance Team

Because SharePoint can be used for many different purposes within the organization, the team that supports the environment should be representative of the entire company. By working together, this cross-functional team will be able to develop specific policies and guidelines that represent the needs and requirements of the entire organization. The following list describes some of the key players that you should include in your governance planning:

➤ **SharePoint Owner** — This role should be filled by the person responsible for the SharePoint budget. By including them in the governance planning, you ensure that they hear firsthand the needs of the organization and how SharePoint can be implemented to solve those needs.

➤ **SharePoint Farm Administrator** — This should be the person responsible for keeping the farm up and running and happy. It is essential that this person be a key player in developing the governance policies. After all, administrators cannot successfully fulfill their job responsibilities unless they have a say in what can and cannot be done within the environment.

➤ **SharePoint Solution Architect** — This role should be filled by the person who is usually responsible for configuring the information architecture. This should be someone who understands both the technology and the business, and then merges the needs with the product to deliver the overall layout for the organization.

➤ **SharePoint Designer** — This is the person responsible for the "look and feel" of the site. Usually, this is someone who is part of the marketing or communications department, and who directs the way the organization brands its SharePoint environment.

➤ **SharePoint Developer** — This is the person responsible for developing custom solutions that will be deployed to the environment.

➤ **SharePoint End Users** — This is the person or group that represents the end users. This is a key role to include in your planning. You can build the best, most advanced system in the world, but if users are confused they won't use it or appreciate all the hard work that went into creating it. In larger organizations, this should be a cross-departmental team that represents the larger community of users.

At this point, you are likely thinking, "Who wants to put all those roles in a room and get them to work together toward one common goal? Won't it make decision making harder with multiple roles included?" The simple answer is yes — involving more people, who represent more opinions, will probably make the decision-making process take longer and will add more complexity. However, the end results will be much better than mandating decisions without input. The process of defining governance is a business activity, not technical. It will be up to the SharePoint Administrator to guide the team about what is possible then to implement the team's decisions.

Take branding as an example. As the farm's administrator, it's likely that you do not care *what* is being built, but you probably care quite a bit about *how* it is built. It is irrelevant to you what colors and fonts are chosen. What does matter to you is what is being done to the farm in order to deliver the branding solution. Are custom master pages being built? If so, are they being deployed to the farm via Features and Solutions or are they being manually deployed to each site collection? Typically, the SharePoint designer doesn't really understand the environment and *how* things need to be done; the designer just knows *what* needs to be done — the fonts, colors, and layouts that will convey the company's brand.

Or imagine if your business users were responsible for configuring the governance policies around the search feature. Clearly, this wouldn't work; they don't have the tools and skill sets needed to make decisions like that, or info about the best time to run indexing to avoid slowing down other processes. While their input is critical to ensure that search will ultimately meet the business needs, the final decision on implementation should be left to the team that is responsible for managing the server.

Defining Policies and Procedures

A governance policy can take many forms. It can be a long, detailed process that identifies everything that needs to be done for the configuration and management of SharePoint. It can also be a simple statement that identifies what is being done to manage specific areas within the environment. As stated earlier, the purpose of governance is to help you manage your SharePoint environment. That may mean you need to develop detailed corporate policies, or it may mean you just need to work through the list of recommended areas and make notes. Before creating any policy, the most important thing to do is to think through all of the business areas that will be affected and carefully plan how they will be incorporated into your environment.

Another thing to keep in mind is that governance policies should be considered "living" policies. In other words, they are not created once and never changed. They are created once and then maintained by a group of individuals, updating as necessary so that they can continually support the organization. Just as organizations change over time, so must your governance policies if they are to retain their value.

SAMPLE SHAREPOINT GOVERNANCE POLICIES

To help you get started, here are two different sample governance policies.

Client Configurations

In order to best support the SharePoint environment, support needs to be limited to specific client configurations. While every effort will be made to support multiple environments, [*company name*] will need to put limitations around the standard environments that are used to access SharePoint. The following list identifies the different supported environments and configurations:

- ➤ Windows Vista, Windows 7
- ➤ Office 2007, Office 2010
- ➤ IE 7, IE 8

In addition to the supported environments, the following environments will be tested and any issues identified and communicated to users:

- ➤ Mac OS
- ➤ Office 2003
- ➤ Mozilla Firefox
- ➤ Windows XP

[*Company name*] will make every effort to provide solutions for multiple environments, but under certain circumstances it will be necessary to use the supported configurations to take full advantage of the features available within the portal.

Site Quota Templates

Site quotas will be used to manage the team collaboration sites. Three different quota levels will be created. By default, each site will start at the level 1 quota. When a site is approaching the quota limit, the help desk will review it and make any necessary adjustments to the existing content. If no adjustments can be made, the site will be elevated to the level 2 quota. If the team is notified that they are reaching the level 2 quota, the help desk will again review the site content. If it is determined that the site will continue to require additional storage space, then downtime will be scheduled and the site will be migrated to a dedicated database.

These are just two examples of the many governance policies that can be created to support your environment.

Infrastructure

Now that we have looked at the team and how its members work together, we can start to focus on some of the key areas for which governance policies are created. Let's start by looking at infrastructure. The following list contains some of the key things that should come to mind when you start thinking about the physical environment:

- ➤ Client machine configurations
- ➤ Server topology
- ➤ Installation and configuration policies
- ➤ DNS settings
- ➤ Site management
    - ➤ Quota templates
    - ➤ Recycle Bin settings
- ➤ Usage reporting
- ➤ SQL management
- ➤ Server monitor
- ➤ Backup and restore policies
- ➤ Anti-virus/security

For each of these areas, you should record what you are doing to configure, manage, and maintain the desired configuration. By developing a plan for each area, you will be able quickly respond when issues are identified.

Information Architecture

Information architecture (IA) defines how content will be organized within your environment. Some of the key questions addressed in IA planning include the following:

- ➤ How many web applications will be created?
- ➤ When are new site collections created and where are they created?

For example, let's look at a common scenario for a mid-size organization that is getting ready to implement SharePoint. They have purchased SharePoint because of the value it provides to the organization through the fulfillment of multiple efforts. Specifically, they are looking for SharePoint to provide the following functionality:

- ➤ Corporate intranet
- ➤ Team collaboration sites
- ➤ Department collaboration sites
- ➤ Corporate extranet
- ➤ Corporate website

SharePoint probably provides an unlimited number of combinations that could be used to configure the preceding requirements — but just because you can, doesn't mean you should. Imagine what would happen if you just started creating sites as they were requested. What if you end up mixing your collaboration and intranet sites? How would your users know where they needed to be to collaborate and share content versus where they needed to be if they wanted to consume information from the organization?

At this point in the book, you are already aware of the need to plan your environment, and you are probably well on your way to planning exactly what you should be implementing. What may not be clear, however, is what planning the IA has to do with governance. It's simple, really; by creating an IA plan and assigning an owner, you are ensuring accountability — for the proposed structure, for future requests, and for all of the "exceptions" that are generated along the way. You know it will happen: As soon as you build and implement the perfect solution, a manager with enough budget money or power comes along and wants something just slightly different from what you planned. No matter how hard you plan to include everything, there will always be an exception. In this case, you deal with the exception through governance. Because you have created a governance policy that outlines the IA for the environment, you have something to fall back on as you deal with the exception. The person on the governance team responsible for creating and defining the IA will then be responsible for making a decision about where and how to address the requested exception.

Development and Customization

Development and customization governance policies will define how and when customizations are made to your environment. The customizations include anything that is not created using out-of-the-box tools, such as Office and Internet Explorer, and includes things such as SharePoint Designer customizations, sandbox solutions, and custom Web Parts. Keep in mind that these customizations can be things created in house, as well as third-party tools that can be purchased.

The key point with this area of governance is understanding what types of customizations are being made to your environment. A simple example is the deployment of customizations. Are they being deployed manually (i.e., changes are made to each web front end individually) or are they being deployed through a solution package? As you learned in Chapter 13, the only supported method of deployment is through solution packages. This is a primary example of the type of policy that should be included within your governance plans.

Another example is the use of SharePoint Designer within your organization. As detailed in Chapter 22, SharePoint Designer is a powerful tool that can be used to make many power customizations to SharePoint sites. However, like any editing tool, training is required to use it properly. Imagine what would happen to the number of support requests if every user simply opened SharePoint Designer and starting making changes to their sites! Just think of all the potential things you would have to fix or recover. Now imagine if the use of SharePoint Designer were controlled in some fashion, and only trained and educated users were able to make changes to their site using SharePoint Designer. Sure, you would still have support issues but they would be nothing compared to the first scenario.

The final area we should cover in this section is the process for deploying content to the production environment. How will customizations be approved and processed before they are deployed to production? This area includes everything from the initial deployment to any required maintenance over time. Here are some of the questions you should be thinking through as you develop your governance policies for deployment of customizations:

➤ Who needs to approve customizations? Keep in mind that this should be determined early in the process before any development or purchasing is started.

➤ What criteria and standards must customizations meet in order to be added to the farm?

➤ What is the schedule for deploying customizations to production?

➤ What development and QA environments will be in place to support the process of testing and deploying customizations?

➤ What processes and procedures need to be put in place to ensure that customizations made today will work correctly with customizations made in the future?

By taking the time to work through each of these questions, you should be able to identify specific policies and procedures that should be included within your governance plan.

Support and Availability

Support and availability covers the users' expectations of support within the environment, and is often referred to as the service-level agreement (SLA). This SLA is basically a statement clarifying what can be expected from the farm. Your organization may already have SLAs, in which case SharePoint will just become part of those same agreements. If no SLAs exist, it is important to define them for your implementation. This should be communicated clearly, so that users are not caught off guard.

For example, users may be caught off guard in the following scenario. A group or project has a tight deadline and the team is working overtime and through the weekend to wrap it up. They are storing and collaborating all of their information within their project SharePoint site. What would happen if one of their big project deadlines was scheduled during your weekend patching window? While it is true that even with an SLA in place there is no guarantee that this scenario won't happen, having one in place at least ensures that you did all you could to avoid the situation.

Another thing to consider in this area of governance is content restoration and what users should expect. This would include the different levels of restoration, such as site or list, and the expected duration of the restoration. Documenting all of this before users create content in SharePoint will go a long way toward setting realistic expectations about what they can expect in terms of support. It should be a part of a department's expectation as they adopt SharePoint that they understand the SLAs and recovery time of the farm in the event that their content is more mission critical than the SharePoint farm. If this is the case, then the department needs to either not adopt SharePoint or work through normal management channels to modify the SLAs for SharePoint. This will often include additional hardware, third-party software, or personnel.

Selling the Need for Governance

SharePoint administrators frequently claim that they want to implement governance, but just don't have the time, resources, or support from management. It's important for those administrators to understand that something is better than nothing, and anything they can do to create governance policies will help them better support their environment. It's also essential to convey the benefits of a good governance policy to others in your organization. The following sections offer some advice on different strategies you can use to help foster the need and importance of governance within your environment.

Start Small and Grow

One of the most common mistakes in the SharePoint community is that when an implementation project starts, those responsible either go all out in developing their governance plan or they do nothing at all. We would encourage those who fall under the "nothing" end of the spectrum to consider starting small. To do this, think of the key things that you will be doing within your environment, and then think of the key policies or procedures that you could put in place to better support those initiatives. Start small, and start only with the areas that make sense for your implementation. Prioritizing is critical: determine which areas of governance will be most useful and start with those. If you are going to spend the first months of your implementation focusing on using SharePoint out of the box, put the task of defining policies for customization on the back burner. If you have limited time and resources to dedicate to governance planning, start with what is most relevant and build the remainder into the future project timeline.

Communicate the Value

If you want to convince the organization to provide the resources needed to plan for governance, management needs to see and understand the value of the governance being developed — and it is your job to help them see this! If your organization is already using some form of governance, then whenever possible you should be communicating to management how it is helping and improving the way you are able to provide service. Conversely, if you don't have any governance enforced, communicate how not having it is causing problems that could be avoided. It may take time and it may take a few big events for them to recognize the value, but eventually they should provide you with the resources you need to develop, implement, and maintain the governance polices. You should also piggy-back on any defined informational governance that your company has in place. For instance, if HR has a defined plan around information that creates an availability, recoverability, and update timeline, then tie those expectations to the data in the sites (site collection) on which the data resides.

SUMMARY

We have covered a lot of ground in this chapter! We started by looking at all of the different ways to configure navigation and then discussed the importance of setting standards or guidelines concerning its use. That led to a discussion about governance and its importance within the SharePoint implementation. We concluded by looking at the different areas of SharePoint and the role that governance plays in each of these areas. Realize also that these activities are not one-time occurrences but are in a constant state of "update" as long as you have your farm. By this time, you are ready to move forward with the implementation, but not without first creating that governance plan!

12

Configuring SharePoint 2010 for High Availability Backups

WHAT'S IN THIS CHAPTER?

➤ Methods for backing up content and configuration

➤ Restoring the information you've backed up

➤ Keeping SharePoint 2010 online in the face of adversity

It's terrifying to think about, but someday, something terrible might happen to your SharePoint 2010 servers. Some mean users might delete content that they want back, right now, of course. A hard drive may decide to take an early retirement, or a stray volcano may take out your datacenter. While we all hate to think about it, these things do happen. To fend off that diabolical Murphy, you have to put some plans into place. If you plan accordingly, you can keep your SharePoint 2010 farm safe from any bad luck that might come your way.

Attacks come in different forms and not all organizations need protection from all kinds of failures or problems. Determining which of the world's evils you want to protect your servers from is the first step. In this chapter we cover the different options you have with SharePoint 2010 out of the box and what kinds of situations they will protect you against.

DETERMINING YOUR BUSINESS REQUIREMENTS

Business continuity management can be summarized as an organization's processes and procedures to create and validate a logistical plan outlining how to recover and restore interrupted critical functions within a predetermined time following a disaster or disruption. The predetermined time by which the organization will recover and/or restore is guided by several objectives, including the following:

➤ **Service-level agreements (SLAs)** — The SLA is the cornerstone of keeping the businesses or end users happy. It is a contract, an agreement between the end users and the service provider. In this case that is whoever is in charge of the keeping the SharePoint 2010 farm up. The SLA usually defines acceptable levels of downtime, both planned and unplanned, and other metrics that are defined in the following bullets.

➤ **Operational-level agreements (OLAs)** — The OLA is similar to an SLA, but it is between support groups, not between a support group and the customer. In the SharePoint environment, the SharePoint support team as well as the SQL and Active Directory support team may have responsibilities outlined in a company's OLA.

➤ **Recovery point objectives (RPOs)** — The RPO helps define the acceptable level of data loss. When this is defined in the SLA it helps keep everyone's expectations the same. Usually the shorter the RPO, the more expensive the solution. Examples of RPOs are "Anything that existed at midnight when the backups ran" or "Never lose more than two hours' worth of data."

➤ **Recovery time objectives (RTOs)** — Your RTO is how long it will take to recover from a disaster. If the RTO is three hours, then the SharePoint 2010 farm should be back on line within three hours of the failure. It's important to note that your RTO can be longer than your RPO. For instance, an example SLA may state the RPO is one hour, and the RTO is three hours. If a failure happens at 9:59 in the morning, all data that existed at 8:59 or earlier can be restored. However, since the RTO is three hours, that data may not be available until 1:00, as that's three hours after 9:59. Sounds like a great excuse for an early lunch.

These objectives apply both within and across the boundaries of the two primary scenarios in which business continuity management applies: *high availability* and *disaster recovery.*

This chapter describes these two objectives and explains how the new capabilities offered by SharePoint 2010 can help you achieve them. Keep in mind that, as with many of the new features in SharePoint, the backup and recovery features are merely facilitating the technical implementation of a business plan. You, as the administrator of the farm, will often be the driving force in the creation or updating of this business plan, but remember that your role is to provide technical guidance as to what is capable in SharePoint 2010 and to implement what the business decides.

When planning business continuity management, you should adhere to a process that begins with analysis to clarify the various scenarios and threats, and assess their potential impact, that will guide your solution design. You should also realize that there is rarely a "one size fits all" approach to this process. Different types of data require different recovery plans. Usually it is the most stringently controlled data in your organization that ends up making the hard decisions (and often the most costly decisions) for the rest of the organization, for instance, if a second failover data center is required because the data is just too valuable to the business.

The next stage is the one everyone hates, the documentation stage. Here is where you plan, document, and prepare your solution design, identifying the most cost-effective solution that meets the main requirements from the impact analysis stage. The solution design is based primarily on the objectives or requirements to which you are required to adhere as set forth by any SLAs, RPOs, or RTOs.

The next step in the process is the implementation stage, where you carry out the results of your business continuity management planning. At this point you should be prepared to test your solution and gain organizational acceptance as the next stage. Testing and acceptance is critical in order to validate that the solution satisfies the organization's recovery requirements. Commonly, in this stage of planning you may discover that the solution fails to meet expectations, perhaps as a result of insufficient recovery requirements or inaccurate recovery requirements. Other common failures at this stage in planning result from design flaws and/or implementation errors. Testing and finally acceptance is an important stage. It's what all this work has been moving us toward. All the planning and documentation is no good if the customer won't sign off on it.

Upon successful completion of the testing and acceptance stage, you can finally begin the last stage of the business continuity management process, which is maintenance. The maintenance stage includes preparation, validation, and handoff of all corresponding documentation, testing, and verification of the solution, including testing and verification of the processes and procedures required to properly execute the solution.

Because each organization has unique requirements and objectives, there is no definitive manual or set of guidelines that can ensure you find the most effective solution. Therefore, you need a thorough understanding of not only what capabilities are provided by the service you are protecting, but also what aspects of that service are critical to your operations. Remember that this is not a one-time activity, as business rules and processes can change within an organization, and adding or removing sets of data can drastically change your company's data availability requirements.

In this chapter, at a high level, we break down the three most common areas of planning associated with SharePoint 2010: content recovery, disaster recovery, and high availability. After ensuring that your business continuity management plan includes these areas, you can take advantage of the features and capabilities of SharePoint 2010 to meet your defined objectives.

CONTENT RECOVERY

Content recovery is the most frequently leveraged aspect of data restoration with SharePoint 2010. Depending on both the scope and nature of recovery, several options are available for recovering data lost through deletion or corruption, including the following:

➤ Versioning

➤ Recycle Bin

➤ SharePoint Administration Tool

➤ Windows PowerShell

➤ Central Administration

These rich capabilities used both independently and in conjunction provide a framework for your disaster recovery processes and procedures. In addition to these new and improved capabilities, SharePoint 2010 also supports the use of SQL Server snapshots as part of its content recovery scenarios.

About SQL Server Snapshots

SQL Server snapshots are a SQL Server Enterprise and Developer Edition feature that enables you to specify a point in time from which you wish to preserve the contents of a database. Snapshots do not actually make a copy of the data, but instead create a new database that is prepared to receive content from the source database as the content is replaced, changed, or overwritten. When you restore the snapshot to the live site, those previous values are reapplied to the live database, which brings the database back to the state it was in at the point in time when the snapshot was taken.

It is important to understand that adding more SQL Server snapshots for a database slows the performance of that database. This is because each time a write operation takes place on the source database, the previous value has to be registered on each snapshot.

Content Storage Overview

Understanding how content is stored and organized in SharePoint 2010 is important for understanding the technologies used to protect it. In most scenarios, *binary large objects*, or *BLOBs*, comprise the deployment. These are the individual files commonly introduced by end users, such as PowerPoint presentations, Word documents, and so on. The binary large objects are stored in data tables within one or more content databases. In SharePoint 2010, *content databases* are the smallest unit of content representation on the file system and are hosted by individual web applications. It might not be obvious, but it is worth noting that if you have good backups of your content databases, you can always recover individual documents. You may have to jump through some hoops, but the content database contains all of the content for the site collections it contains. Take care of the databases; they may get you out of a jam some time.

The binary large objects are assigned to the specific document library or folder to which they were placed within a site hosted within a site collection, which is the principal point of initial interaction that end users have with SharePoint. A site collection is a set of sites that have the same owner and share administrative settings. It contains a top-level site and can contain one or more subsites. A site is the primary means of organizing related content in SharePoint 2010 and is host to document libraries and folders.

Document libraries are a location in a site containing files of one or more large binary objects or content types. Document libraries are designed to manage and store related documents, and to enable users to create new documents of the appropriate types. A folder is a named subdivision of the content in a document library, similar to the concept of folders in a file system. The primary purpose of folders is to organize content to match the expected functionality of the library. Figure 12-1 shows the farm hierarchy.

The Recycle Bin

The Recycle Bin, initially introduced in Windows SharePoint Services 3.0, provides self-service recovery of simple content — for example, lists and list items — to users of SharePoint 2010. The Recycle Bin is enabled by default and is configured on a per-web-application basis.

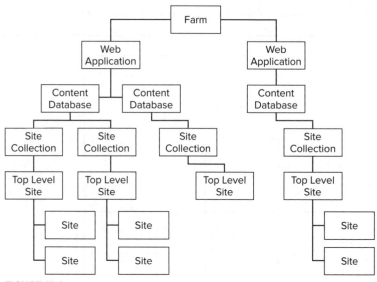

FIGURE 12-1

The Recycle Bin in SharePoint 2010 is unchanged from Windows SharePoint Services 3.0 and supports two Recycle Bin stages:

➤ **Stage 1** — The first-stage Recycle Bin is located at the site level and is available to users with Contribute, Design, or Full Control permissions. When a user deletes an item from a site, it is sent to the first-stage Recycle Bin, where it can be recovered by that user. Items located in this stage affect the overall site quota and are retained until the specified time period has been reached as configured by the administrator in SharePoint 2010 Central Administration (the default setting is 30 days).

➤ **Stage 2** — The second-stage Recycle Bin is located at the site collection level and is organized in two distinct views: the first-stage Recycle Bin just described and the second-stage Recycle Bin described here. Items deleted from the first-stage Recycle Bin are submitted to the second-stage Recycle Bin, where they can be recovered by the site collection administrator.

Items are retained in the second-stage Recycle Bin until the specified time period has been reached, similar to the first-stage Recycle Bin (the default setting is 30 days), or until the second-stage Recycle Bin has reached its allocated size limit, established by the administrator in SharePoint 2010 Central Administration, at which time the oldest items are permanently deleted. The time limit for the Recycle Bins reflects the total time after the item was initially deleted, not the time spent in either Recycle Bin stage.

When a second-stage Recycle Bin is enabled for a web application, the amount of disk space available to the second-stage Recycle Bin is defined as a percentage of the quota allotted to each individual site collection. Items stored in the second-stage Recycle Bin do not count toward the site quota; however, the size that is specified for the second-stage Recycle Bin increases the total size of the site and the content database that hosts it. If no site quota has been set, there is no limit on the size of the second-stage Recycle Bin.

Figure 12-2 provides an overview of two stages of the Recycle Bin and points of interaction.

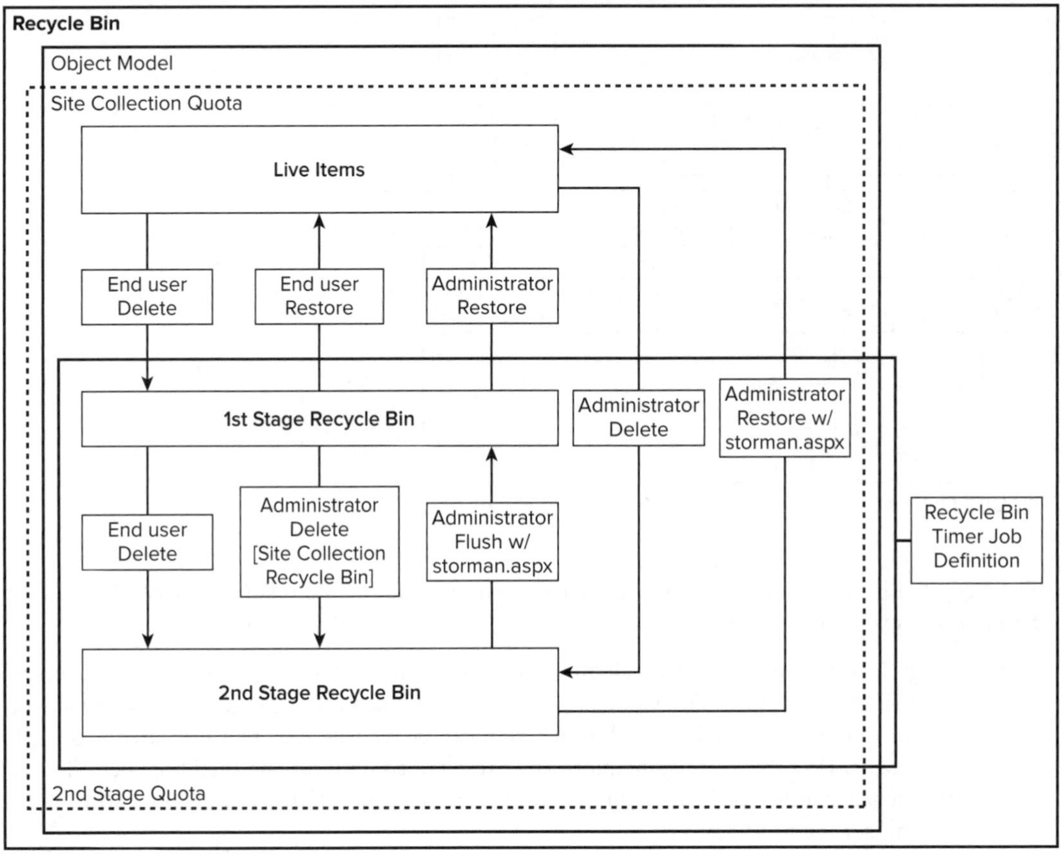

Recycle Bin

Object Model

Site Collection Quota

Live Items

End user Delete	End user Restore	Administrator Restore

1st Stage Recycle Bin

Administrator Delete

Administrator Restore w/ storman.aspx

End user Delete	Administrator Delete [Site Collection Recycle Bin]	Administrator Flush w/ storman.aspx

Recycle Bin Timer Job Definition

2nd Stage Recycle Bin

2nd Stage Quota

FIGURE 12-2

Keep in mind that the total life of a document in your SharePoint farm equals the amount of time the document is *live* in a site AND the amount of time it spends in the Recycle Bin. This time can have a significant impact on your organization's Business Records Retention Policy. Make sure that the team that manages Business Records policies for your organization is aware of and has a say in the Recycle Bin's policies.

 Each stage of the Recycle Bin can contain multiple copies of a document, even where they share the same filename and source. It is important to understand that these documents cannot be restored over an existing copy of a document or to recover previous versions or overwrite documents — that functionality is provided through versioning, discussed later in this chapter.

Configuring the Recycle Bin

The Recycle Bin is configured at the web application level by the server farm administrator. Each web application can have its own settings depending on the business processes and continuity requirements necessary to support the content hosted within that web application. To configure the Recycle Bin, use the following steps:

1. Open SharePoint 2010 Central Administration.

2. Under Application Management, click Manage web applications.

3. Click the web application whose Recycle Bin settings you want to change; you'll notice that many buttons light up on the Ribbon.

4. Click the General Settings button in the Ribbon, and then click General Settings again from the dropdown. Scroll to the bottom of the web application's general settings to find its Recycle Bin settings.

Figure 12-3 shows the Recycle Bin settings for a web application. The default retention settings have been left for the first stage, 30 days. In this example, the second stage has been turned off. This means that if a user empties the first stage, the document cannot be recovered through the Recycle Bin. Regardless of whether the second stage is turned on or not, 31 days after a document has been deleted it will no longer be able to be recovered through the Recycle Bin. Another caveat to keep in mind is that disabling the Recycle Bin entirely will immediately flush it. This means if you disable it and immediately regret doing so, there is good news and bad news. The bad news is that all of the documents that were in the Recycle Bin are gone. The good news is that your content databases have a lot of good white space in them. There's a silver lining to almost anything if you look hard enough.

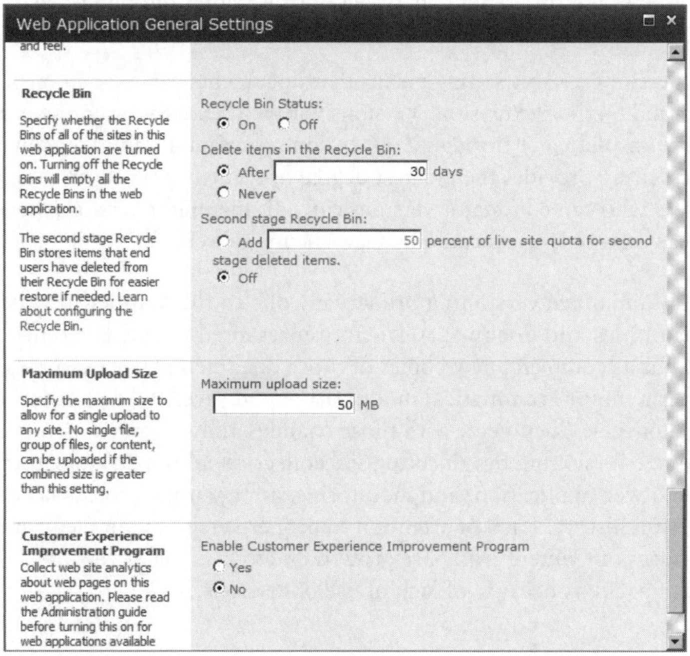

FIGURE 12-3

Keep in mind that while the first stage of the Recycle Bin counts against your site collection quota, the second stage does not. For example, if you specify a default Quota Template of 1GB per site collection on a web application, allotting a 50 percent quota for the second-stage Recycle Bin allocates 500 MB for the second-stage Recycle Bin and up to 1.5GB per site collection on the web application. This is important when sizing your content databases or trying to answer the age old question; "Why is my database so big!?" You can allocate up to 100 percent for the second-stage Recycle Bin quota.

Versioning

Versioning can be loosely compared to the Recycle Bin in that it provides self-service recovery of content for users — for example, if data loss occurs as the result of overwriting a document. Through versioning, SharePoint 2010 users can keep multiple versions of the same document in a document library; and in the event of an undesired change, such as an overwritten document or corruption, users can easily restore the previous version.

Versioning is configured by the site collection administrator on a per-site basis and is not enabled by default.

Versioning accepts the following configurations:

➤ **No Versioning** — The No versioning setting means prior versions of documents and their subsequent history, including comments, are not recoverable. No versioning is the default setting.

➤ **Create Major Versions** — This setting means that each iteration of a document becomes a full version of the document, using sequentially numbered versions (e.g., 1.0, 2.0, 3.0, etc). Users with permissions to the document library may view each updated version of a document. Note that this setting does not differentiate between draft versions and published versions.

➤ **Create Major and Minor Versions** — This setting means that documents can exist in one of two possible states, as denoted by their extension: Versions with a .0 extension represent a major version, whereas versions with a .1 through .9 extension represent a minor version of a document. This versioning setting provides the greatest degree of security granularity because in most scenarios, only users who can edit major versions can edit the minor versions associated with that item, whereas read-only users can only view the major versions.

Site collection administrators should manage versioning proactively due to the manner in which versions are maintained. Versions of files and documents are not represented as the differential between two or more documents, but as complete, new copies of those documents. For example, if a user opens a document and makes a minor grammatical modification and saves the document as a new version, it becomes a completely new document, with those changes and the previous version intact. You should proactively manage versioning by educating site collection administrators, establishing quotas on site collections in a web application, and monitoring storage utilization as needed. Figure 12-4 shows an example version history. Lack of attention to proper versioning implementation is one of the more common causes of Content Database growth due to overuse of versions, as well as causing restores of files from backups because of lack of use of versions.

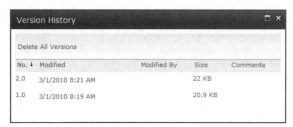

FIGURE 12-4

Enabling and Configuring Versioning

To enable and configure versioning for libraries, follow these steps:

1. Select the library for which you want to enable versioning.

2. From the Ribbon, select ⇨ Library Tools ⇨ Library ⇨ Library Settings (see Figure 12-5).

FIGURE 12-5

3. On the Document Library Settings page, in the General Settings section, click Versioning settings.

4. If you want to require content approval for your document library, click Yes in the Content Approval section. If you enable Content Approval, the Draft Item Security section will light up, giving you control over how items are handled before they are approved.

5. The Document Version History section, shown in Figure 12-6, allows you to configure how version are handled. Your options are to disable versions completely, create only major versions, or allow major and minor versions, which are known as drafts. If you enable versions, you can also limit the number of major and minor versions that are allowed. This is an important step for keeping your database sizes under control.

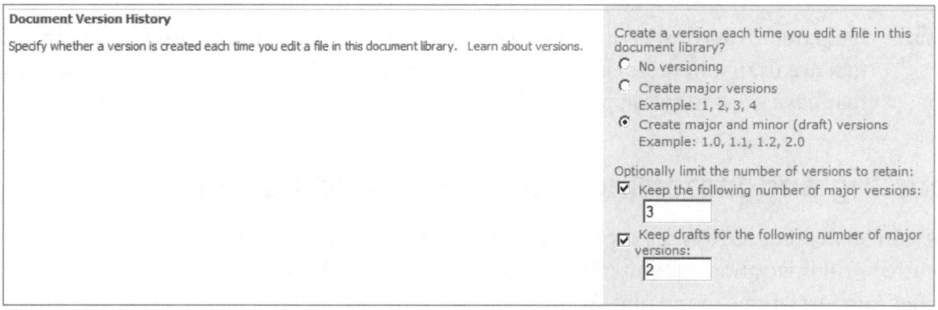

Document Version History	Create a version each time you edit a file in this document library?

Specify whether a version is created each time you edit a file in this document library. Learn about versions.	○ No versioning
	○ Create major versions
	   Example: 1, 2, 3, 4
	⊙ Create major and minor (draft) versions
	   Example: 1.0, 1.1, 1.2, 2.0
	
	Optionally limit the number of versions to retain:
	☑ Keep the following number of major versions:
	   [3]
	☑ Keep drafts for the following number of major versions:
	   [2]

FIGURE 12-6

6. If you chose to enable Content Approval in step 4, you can configure the Draft Item Security next. This allows you to control who can see draft items. In most cases, you want the bottom option. This keeps draft items from being visible to most users.

7. The last option is whether you want to force a check out before an item can be edited.

To enable and configure versioning for a list, follow these steps:

1. Select the list for which you want to enable versioning.

2. From the Ribbon, select List Tools ⇨ List ⇨ List Settings (see Figure 12-7).

FIGURE 12-7

3. On the List Settings page, click Versioning settings.

4. On the Version settings page, click Yes under Content Approval if you want to require content approval for this list. Much like with document libraries, when you enable content approval you can control the Draft Item Security at the bottom of the page.

5. In the Item Version History section, shown in Figure 12-8, you can configure whether a new version is created when a list item is edited. If that is turned on, you also get the option to control how many major versions of each item are allowed. If Content Approval is enabled you then can also control how many minor versions are kept.

FIGURE 12-8

6. If Content Approval is turned on you also have the option of limiting who can see list items that are drafts. In most cases drafts should only be visible to the author of the item and users that have the ability to approve them.

Exporting and Importing Sites, Lists, and Libraries

New in SharePoint 2010 is the capability to export lists, libraries, and sites through the SharePoint 2010 Central Administration user interface, in addition to new Windows PowerShell support and continued support of the SharePoint Administration Tool (STSADM). These new capabilities are based on PRIME (Publishing, Rollback, Import, Migration, Export), which was introduced in Windows SharePoint Services 3.0. PRIME is a feature for content migration from a source site to a destination site. The Content Migration application programming interface (API) provides a simple and flexible solution for migrating content between SharePoint sites. You can export the content related to a SharePoint Web site, along with any dependencies (e.g., security, roles, versioning, workflow, and other metadata), into a single or multiple XML-formatted files called *content migration packages*. After import to the destination site, the packaged data is extracted and interpreted. Content migration packages are portable, meaning you can also save the packages to a file server before migrating to a different server.

While the intention of the content deployment was to, well, deploy content, it can also be used as a rudimentary means of content recovery. It can be used to export lists or libraries that are of high importance (like the ones where you have your résumé, for instance) giving you a quick way to protect that data. It has another important function — getting that data back into SharePoint. Backups are great, but knowing how to get your backed up information back into production could be the difference between an "Atta boy!" and an "Outta here!" If you only need a specific list or library to be restored, you can use content deployment to shuffle content from a database restored to a different environment back to production. You could also use content deployment to move content between test and production environments.

Exporting Sites, Lists, and Libraries with Windows PowerShell

New Windows PowerShell cmdlets provide greater granularity than their SharePoint Administration Tool command-line operation equivalents. With the new Windows PowerShell `Export-SPWeb` cmdlet, you can export not only a site like you could in SharePoint 2007, but also lists and libraries, which can be restored into the same or other server farms.

To export (back up) a site, list or library with Windows PowerShell, enter the following cmdlet in the Microsoft SharePoint 2010 Management Shell:

```
Export-SPWeb -identity <Url or Guid> -path <drive:\destination>
```

The following options are available to the backup operation using Windows PowerShell:

➤ To forcibly perform the export operation, use the `Force` parameter. You can use this to overwrite an existing file.

➤ To stop the export process in the event of a warning or error, use the `HaltOnError` or `HaltOnWarning` switches.

➤ To preserve time stamps, security information, and user data, you must use the `IncludeUserSecurity` switch.

➤ To specify which type of file and list item version history should be included in the export, use the `IncludeVersions` parameter. A description of the values follows:

  ➤ Last major version for files and list items (default)

  ➤ The current version, either the last major or the last minor

  ➤ Last major and last minor versions for files and list items

  ➤ All versions for files and list items

➤ To disable file compression in the export package, use the `NoFileCompression` switch, which is recommended for better performance. Enabling compression can speed up the export process by approximately 30 percent. When content is exported it's written to the file system. When compression is enabled, that content is then compressed. You can save time by not having that final compression step run. If your export jobs are failing you may also be able to fix them by disabling the file compression. Some timeouts and other errors may be introduced by the compression process.

➤ To suppress the generation of an export log file, use the `NoLogFile` switch; otherwise, an export log is generated in the same location as the export package.

➤ To specify whether or not the backup should be executed against a snapshot, use the `UseSqlSnapshot` switch.

> *To see all of the parameters for this any or any PowerShell command, use the following syntax from the SharePoint 2010 Management Shell:*
>
> ```
> Get-help Export-SPWeb
> ```

To export a site, provide `Export-SPWeb` with the URL to the web. To export a list or library, provide `Export-SPWeb` with the URL to the specific list or library. Below are two examples. The first exports an entire site; the second only backs up a library called Docs in that web.

```
Export-SPWeb http://sharepoint.contoso.com/team -Path "team export.cmp"
Export-SPWeb http://sharepoint.contoso.com/team/Docs -Path docs.cmp
```

Exporting Sites, Lists, and Libraries with STSADM

If you are reading this book, we can probably tell a few things about you. You probably sat at the front of the class and ruined the curve for all your classmates. You're an exceptional SharePoint administrator, are better looking than your peers, and can probably dance like Fred Astaire. Either that or you are one of the authors' mothers. Regardless, if you have taken anything from this book hopefully you have picked up that Windows PowerShell should be your command line weapon of choice for SharePoint 2010. But if you have slower, less enlightened counterparts you may need to know how to do all this fancy exporting and importing with STSADM. This section covers that too.

To export (back up) a site with the SharePoint Administration Tool, open up a command prompt and change directories to the `Bin` directory of the SharePoint Root (`c:\program files\common files\microsoft shared\web server extensions\14\bin`). You can use the export operation to export lists or webs. Here is the usage.

```
STSADM -o export -url <Url> -filename <drive:\destination>
```

➤ To overwrite an existing content migration package of the same name and location, use the `-overwrite` parameter.

➤ To stop the export process in the event of a warning or error, use the `haltonfatalerror` or `haltonwarning` switches.

➤ To preserve time stamps, security information, and user data, you must use the `includeusersecurity` switch.

➤ To specify which type of file and list item version history should be included in the export, use the `versions` parameter. A description of the values follows:

  ➤ Last major version for files and list items (default)

  ➤ The current version, either the last major or the last minor

  ➤ Last major and last minor versions for files and list items

  ➤ All versions for files and list items

➤ To disable file compression in the export package, use the `nofilecompression` switch. This provides the same performance improvement with STSADM as it does with PowerShell.

➤ To suppress the generation of an export log file, use the `nologfile` switch; otherwise, an export log is generated in the same location as the export package.

➤ To specify whether or not the backup should be executed against a snapshot, use the `usesqlsnapshot` switch.

Exporting Sites and Lists with Central Administration

While PowerShell and STSADM do very impressive jobs of exporting, sometimes you just need a comfortable, mouse-friendly way to do your tasks. Get your mousing finger stretched and ready to go, because you can also export sites and lists within Central Administration.

In the next section we will discuss how to import the lists and libraries that are being exported in the following steps. Observant readers will notice there is no section on how to import lists and libraries with Central Administration. That's because there is no way to do imports in Central Administration. You'll have to use one of the command line methods covered below.

To export (back up) a site or list through Central Administration:

1. From the SharePoint 2010 Central Administration home page, select Backup and Restore.

2. On the Backup and Restore page, select Export a site or list under Granular Backup.

3. On the Site or List Export page:

   a. Select a site collection from the list of available site collections where the site or list to be exported resides.

   b. In the File location section, type the Universal Naming Convention (UNC) path of the backup folder, as shown in Figure 12-9.

c. If exporting a site, optionally select the checkbox labeled Export full security in the Export Full Security section to export the full security of the site, which includes authors, editors, time stamps, and users.

d. In the Export Versions section, optionally select whether to export all versions, only the last major version, the current version, or both the last major and minor versions.

e. Click Start Export to begin the export process.

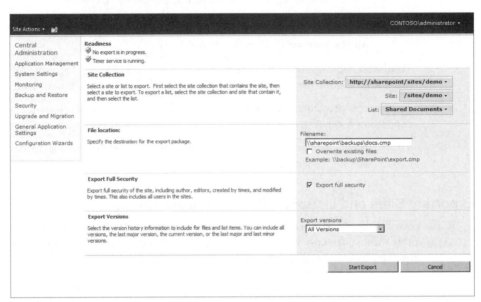

FIGURE 12-9

Workflow is not included in packages created through Central Administration, Windows PowerShell, or STSADM content deployment packages. Nor are alerts. This is because the tool we're using is focused on content deployment, so functionality that is not content is not always brought over.

Importing Sites, Lists, and Libraries with Windows PowerShell

To import (restore) a site, list, or library with Windows PowerShell, enter the following command in the Microsoft SharePoint 2010 Management Shell:

```
Import-SPWeb -identity <Url or Guid> -path <drive:\destination>
```

The following options are available to the import operation using Windows PowerShell:

➤ To stop the import process in the event of a warning or error, use the HaltOnWarning or HaltOnError switches.

➤ To preserve time stamps, security information, and user data, you must use the IncludeUserSecurity switch.

➤ To suppress the generation of an import log file, use the NoLogFile switch; otherwise, an import log is generated in the same location as the import package.

➤ To specify how to resolve situations in which a file to be imported to a site already exists in that site, including options to add a new version, overwrite the file, and delete all versions prior to insert, or to ignore the file as it exists, use the UpdateVersions switch. A description of the values follows:

➤ Add new versions to the current file (default)

➤ Overwrite the file and all of its versions (delete then insert)

➤ Ignore the file if it exists on the destination

➤ If you want to only describe the effect of the command, rather than actually perform the operation, use the WhatIf switch.

When restoring sites, lists, and libraries using the Import-SPWeb *cmdlet, all imported list or library items overwrite the previous data unless the* -UpdateVersions *parameter is passed in the operation, which requires versioning to be enabled on the destination list or library. Using* -UpdateVersions *enables you to restore the information contained in the backup without overwriting new items created in the destination list or library.*

Importing Sites, Lists, and Libraries with STSADM

If you are forced to, or if you've lost a dare, you can also use STSADM to import sites, lists, or libraries:

```
STSADM -o import -url <Url> -filename <drive:\destination>
```

The following options are available to the import operation in STSADM:

➤ To stop the import process in the event of a warning or error, use the haltonwarning or haltonerror switches.

➤ To preserve time stamps, security information, and user data, you must use the includeusersecurity switch.

➤ To specify which type of file and list item version history should be included in the import, use the updateversions parameter. A description of the values follows:

➤ Add the imported files to the current file, which is the default.

➤ Delete the current file and all its versions and replace them with the imported files.

➤ Skip the file if it exists in the destination.

➤ To disable file compression in the import package, use the `nofilecompression` switch.

➤ To suppress the generation of an import log file, use the `nologfile` switch; otherwise, an import log is generated in the same location as the import package.

➤ To suppress the output of import progress information to the display window, use the `quiet` switch. This parameter is recommended for better performance, as the buffer of the display window is small compared to writing a file.

When using the preceding import and export commands, you should confirm you are a member of the WSS_ADMIN_WPG local group on the computer where Microsoft SharePoint Server 2010 is installed to avoid errors and ensure that the operation is completed successfully.

When restoring sites and subsites, the URL specified to be restored to must have the same template applied as the backup. For example, if a site were created using the STS#0 template, the destination site must also use the STS#0 template.

Backing Up and Restoring Site Collections

Sites and site collection backup and restore in SharePoint 2010 can be accomplished through the SharePoint Administration Tool (STSADM) in addition to Windows PowerShell and Central Administration. Site and site collection backup and restore is commonly used either to recover content that has been permanently deleted from the second-stage Recycle Bin or to recover corrupted data or pages.

While creating site collection backups may seem like a compelling solution to achieve continuity, it should only be used in conjunction with an existing overall solution, and limited to use on only the most critical site collections of 15GB or smaller, as it is resource-intensive from a time, storage, and processing perspective.

Backing Up and Restoring Site Collections Using Windows PowerShell

Not only can you use Windows PowerShell for exporting and importing sites, you can also use it to back up and restore entire site collections. This section will cover that.

The cmdlet `Backup-SPSite` will make a single file backup of a site collection. In contrast to the exports we covered previously, these backups are full fidelity. They back up non-content objects like workflow and alerts. Like their content deployment counterparts, site collection backups are portable and can be shuffled around on a farm, or restored to a different farm entirely as long as the destination farm is at the same build or later than the source farm.

You can use `Get-Help` in PowerShell to get the full usage of `Get-SPSite`, but the basic usage is shown here:

```
Backup-SPSite -Identity <Site collection URL> -Path <backup file> [Force]
[-NoSiteLock] [-UseSqlSnapshot] [-Verbose]
```

➤ To overwrite a previously used backup file, use the `Force` parameter.

➤ You can use the `NoSiteLock` switch to keep the read-only lock from being set on the site collection while it is being backed up. However, using this switch allows users to change the site collection while it is being backed up, which can lead to possible data corruption during backup. Unfortunately, the time when you will discover this corruption is when you try to restore the site collection. It is not recommended to use `NoSiteLock`.

➤ If the database server is running an Enterprise Edition of Microsoft SQL Server, we recommend that you also use the `UseSqlSnapshot` switch for more consistent backups.

Some smaller server farms may optionally choose to use site collection backups as their overall business continuity management scenario. While this is not recommended to support disaster recovery due to the constraints associated with the backup of site collections, Windows PowerShell opens the door to new opportunities to develop a scripted solution that can be run on demand or scheduled as a task with Windows Task Scheduler.

An example of a solution that would iterate through and back up all site collections in a web application with Windows PowerShell could be implemented as follows:

```
Get-SPWebApplication | Get-SPSite | ForEach-Object{$FilePath = "C:\Backup\" +
$_.Url.Replace("http://","").Replace("/","-") + ".bak" ; Backup-SPSite -Identity
$_.Url -Path $FilePath}
```

Backing up your site collections isn't very useful without being able to restore them. Windows PowerShell provides a cmdlet to do just that, `Restore-SPSite`. Like you may suspect, using the `Get-Help` cmdlet will show you all of your restore options, but the basic usage is shown here:

```
Restore-SPSite -Identity <Site collection URL> -Path <Backup file>
[-DatabaseServer <Database server name>] [-DatabaseName <Content database name>]
[-HostHeader <Host header>] [-Force] [-GradualDelete] [-Verbose]
```

`Restore-SPSite` has many parameters to make your site collection restoring experience more pleasurable. You can use the `-DatabaseName` parameter to have SharePoint 2010 restore your site collection to a specific content database. If that database is not on your default SQL instance, use `-DatabaseServer` to direct SharePoint 2010 to the appropriate server. If you are restoring your site collection on top of an existing site collection, use the `-Force` parameter. If you are overwriting a site collection that is over 1GB, use the `-GradualDelete` option to reduce the likelihood of database locks as the site collection is deleted before it is overwritten.

While most site collections are URL-based, if you happen to be restoring host-named site collections, use the `-HostHeader` switch followed by the URL of the web application that is hosting your site collection.

Backing Up and Restoring Site Collections Using STSADM

There are two operations to use with STSADM to back up or restore site collections. They function very similarly to their newer Windows PowerShell counterparts.

The `backup` operation handles the backup responsibilities. `Stsadm -help backup` will give you the full usage, but here is the general usage:

```
Stsadm -o backup -url <site collection URL> -filename <filename>
```

As with `Backup-SPSite`, you have the option of using `-overwrite` to overwrite an existing backup file. You can also use `-nositelock` to prevent the site collection from being locked before it is backed up. Even `-usesqlsnapshot` is there, which you can use if you have the Enterprise SKU of SQL Server.

To restore a site collection with STSADM, enter the following command from the Microsoft SharePoint 2010 Management Shell:

```
STSADM -o restore -url <Site Collection Url> -filename <filename>
```

➤ If you are restoring a host-named site collection, use the `url` parameter to specify the URL of the host-named site collection, and use the `hostheaderwebapplicationurl` parameter to specify the URL of the web application that will hold the host-named site collection.

➤ To overwrite an existing site collection, use the `overwrite` parameter.

➤ If the site collection that you are restoring is 1GB or larger, you can use the `GradualDelete` parameter for better performance during the restore process. When this parameter is used, the site collection that is overwritten is marked as deleted, which immediately prevents any additional access to its content. The data in the marked site collection is then deleted gradually over time by a timer job, rather than all at once, which reduces the impact on server performance.

Backing Up Site Collections Using Central Administration

New in SharePoint 2010 is the capability to perform a site collection backup directly from the SharePoint 2010 Central Administration user interface. This provides administrators with a way to perform routine backup and recovery tasks without needing to log onto a server to access one of the available command-line options; however, you cannot restore site collections through SharePoint 2010 Central Administration, and you must use one of the available command-line options discussed in this chapter.

Follow these steps to perform a backup from Central Administration:

1. From the home page in Central Administration, in the Backup and Restore section, click Perform a site collection backup.

2. On the Site Collection Backup page, select the site collection from the Site Collection list.

3. Type the local path of the backup file in the Filename box.

4. Click Start Backup.

SharePoint 2010 provides a rich user interface, enabling you to view the general status of all backup jobs at the top of the Backup and Restore Job Status page in the Readiness section. You can view the status for the current backup job in the lower part of the page in the Backup section.

If you receive any errors, you can review them in the Failure Message column of the Backup and Restore Job Status page.

Verify that the user account performing this procedure is a member of the Farm Administrators group. Additionally, verify that the Windows SharePoint Services Timer V4 service has Full Control permissions on the backup folder.

Restoring Content with Unattached Content Database Data Recovery

In SharePoint 2007 restoring content from backups can be painful, and it seems like nothing ever goes right. Unless you want to overwrite your production data, you need a recovery farm to restore you database to. Then you need to extract the site or site collection from there before you can get it to your production server. Hopefully that recovery farm hasn't been used in a while, so it probably needs some Windows updates before it's happy. And if you've upgraded SharePoint on your production server with a cumulative update or service pack, your databases won't attach until you do the same to your test environment. The whole process has so many moving parts it's almost guaranteed that something will go wrong. Wouldn't it be great if you could recover content without that second farm, and without overwriting production?

Unattached Content Database Data Recovery is a feature available to the new Granular Backup capabilities in SharePoint 2010 that does just that. Unattached Content Database Data Recovery enables you to back up lists, libraries, sites, and site collections, and browse the content of a database or database snapshot attached to a SQL Server instance, but not associated with a web application. Unattached Content Database Data Recovery enables administrators to work with a content database even when a duplicate of that database is attached to its respective web application. In Office SharePoint Server 2007, these capabilities required a separate recovery server farm or web application to avoid URL conflicts that would arise if the database were attached to a production server farm.

To use Unattached Content Database Data Recovery, first attach a recent backup to either the server farm default or a separate SQL Server instance. Once the content database has been attached successfully to the SQL Server instance, refer to the following steps:

1. On the SharePoint 2010 Central Administration home page, select Backup and Restore.

2. On the Backup and Restore page, under Granular Backup select Recover data from an unattached content database.

3. On the Unattached Content Database Data Recovery page:

   a. Specify the content database server and the content database name to connect to in the Database Server and Database Name fields.

   b. Select the authentication method to be used to connect to the database, either Windows integrated (recommended) or SQL authentication.

   c. Select an operation to perform from the list of available operations: Browse content, Backup site collection, or Export site or list as shown in Figure 12-10.

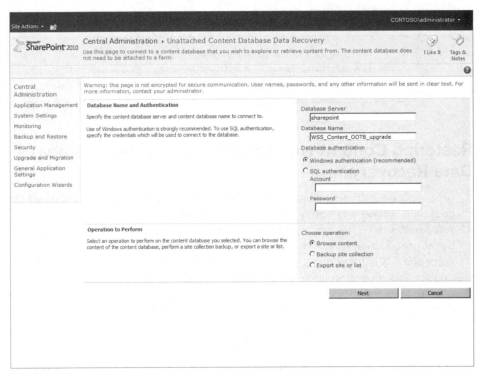

FIGURE 12-10

4. Click Next on the Unattached Content Database Data Recovery page.

5. If you elected to browse content, on the Browse content page (see Figure 12-11):

   a. Select the site collection, site, and/or list access in the Site Collection section.

   b. Select the operation to perform from the list of available operations in the Operation to Perform section: Backup site collection or Export site or list.

6. If you elected to back up a site collection, on the Site collection backup page:

   a. Select the site collection from the list of available site collections in the Site Collection section.

   b. Specify the destination and filename in the Filename field in the File location section and click Start Backup to begin the process.

FIGURE 12-11

7. If you elected to export a site or list, on the Site Or List Export page (see Figure 12-12):

    a. Select the site collection, site, or list from the list of available options in the Site Collection section.

    b. Specify the destination and filename in the Filename field in the File location section and click Start Backup to begin the process.

    c. Optionally, select the checkbox labeled Export full security in the Export Full Security section to export the full security of the site, which includes authors, editors, time stamps, and users.

    d. In the Export Versions section, optionally specify whether to export all versions, only the last major version, the current version, or both the last major and minor versions.

8. Click Start Export to begin the export process.

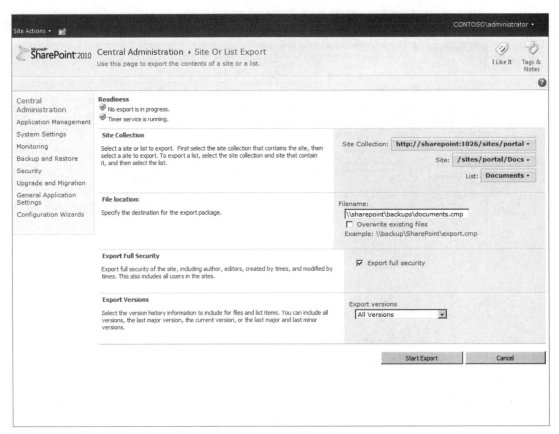

FIGURE 12-12

This section provided the basic information required to understand the methods to both successfully protect and recover content from corruption, accidental deletion, or other loss scenarios. If your organization has service-level agreements targeted specifically at content recovery scenarios, you should evaluate all of the options presented here; and through planning and practice, combine these strategies with your overall business continuity requirements, while keeping in mind that although content comprises the majority of information accessed in SharePoint, its protection alone does not provide an adequate disaster-recovery or high-availability solution. Testing is imperative to help you make an informed decision about which solution or combination of solutions should be implemented to protect your content.

DISASTER RECOVERY

Disaster recovery is the process and procedures related to preparing for recovery or continuation of technology infrastructure in the event that the primary site where that infrastructure is provided is lost due to natural disaster or some other event, making that site unavailable to continue serving users. Disaster recovery processes and procedures are commonly guided by two principles:

➤ **Recovery point objective (RPO)** — RPO is a critical value when planning a business continuity solution and is impacted by factors such as restore duration from backup and replication performance.

➤ **Recovery time objective (RTO)** — RTO is important as it dictates the total amount of time required to bring the service back online. It should be mapped to any operating-level agreements established with ancillary technologies, such as Directory Services or network infrastructure, as these services will commonly need to be available before you can offer your service to users.

It is equally important to understand that any reduction in RPO and RTO objectives will often increase the costs associated with the technologies elected to provide the business continuity management solution. This section describes several solutions available in SharePoint 2010 to facilitate a business continuity management solution.

The first step when planning the business continuity management solution is understanding what needs to be recovered in the event of a disaster, keeping in mind that in most cases content comprises a deployment (see also "Content Recovery" in this chapter). Content is the foundation for most service applications and should be prioritized in most solutions — for example, prioritizing the recovery of Search over content provides no value, as Search requires content to crawl to effectively provide value to users.

An additional consideration that applies in continuity management solutions is the protection of customizations deployed to a server farm environment. Some of these customizations can be protected adequately using the functionality provided by SharePoint 2010, but in some cases you will need to catalog, manually protect, or replicate these customizations in the destination server farm environment.

Backup and Restore for Disaster Recovery

SharePoint 2010 provides new and improved tools and capabilities to protect its content, configuration, and customizations, including extending options that were previously available only through the command line to the user interface, new features to provide greater granularity, and overall improvements in performance and resiliency. In SharePoint 2010, backup and restore capabilities are distributed across two primary areas of functionality:

➤ Farm backup and restore

➤ Granular backup

Farm backup and restore, also known as catastrophic backup and restore, provides solutions designed to enable you to backup and restore components of a server farm or the entire server farm environment, in addition to providing entry points that enable you to configure backup settings and access backup and restore history.

In addition to an entire server farm, backup enables you to protect the following components:

➤ Configuration databases

➤ Web applications, to include settings and content databases

➤ Service applications, to include settings and databases where present

➤ Services such as InfoPath Forms, State, Application Registry, and User Code Solution services

Granular Backup provides solutions designed to enable you to back up site collections, export sites and lists, recover data from unattached content databases, and access backup history.

In addition to the features provided through SharePoint 2010 Central Administration, SharePoint 2010 continues to provide backup and restore capabilities through both the SharePoint Administration Tool and new capabilities through Windows PowerShell.

> *While the SharePoint Administration Tool is still available under* `%commonprogramfiles%\Microsoft Shared\Web Server Extensions\14\` `BIN,` *we recommend that you use Windows PowerShell when performing command-line administrative tasks. The SharePoint Administration Tool has been deprecated, but it is included to support compatibility with previous product versions.*

Backing Up and Restoring Content Databases

We have already demonstrated that there are many tools in SharePoint 2010 that you can use to accomplish a task. You have the option of using Windows PowerShell, the Central Administration website, or even STSADM, if you must. Backing up content databases is no different. In this section we cover the different ways you can back up your content databases in SharePoint 2010.

Backing Up and Restoring Content Databases Using Central Administration

SharePoint 2010 provides improved backup and restore functionality out of the box, including greater granularity, improved monitoring and reporting, and greater scale and efficiency. With SharePoint 2010 backup and restore, you can back up one or more content databases in either full or differential mode.

To back up a content database using SharePoint 2010 Backup and Restore:

1. Open SharePoint 2010 Central Administration and select Perform a backup under Farm Backup and Restore.

2. On the Perform a Backup — Step 1 of 2: Select Component to Back Up page, expand the web application where the content database to be backed up is attached and select the content database you want to back up. If you want to back up multiple content databases you can only do that by backing up the entire web application. You can't back up content databases in different web applications without backing up the whole farm. Select the content databases or web applications you want to backup and click Next.

3. On the Start Backup — Step 2 of 2: Select Backup Options page, in the Backup Type section, select Full.

4. In the Backup File Location section, type the Universal Naming Convention (UNC) path of the backup folder, and then click Start Backup.

Figure 12-13 shows how the final screen will look before the backup is run.

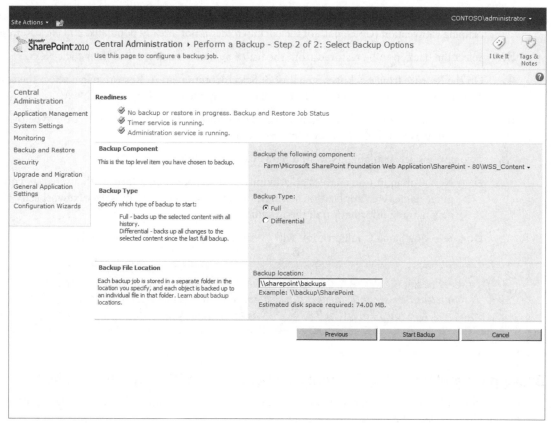

FIGURE 12-13

 To perform a differential backup instead of a full backup, simply select Differential instead of Full as the Backup Type in step 3 of these instructions. For more discussion about choosing between full and differential backups, see the "Backing Up and Restoring Content Databases Using Microsoft SQL Server" section coming up shortly.

Remember that you can view the general status of all backup jobs at the top of the Backup and Restore Job Status page in the Readiness section, and see the status for the current backup job in the lower part of the page in the Backup section.

To restore a content database using SharePoint 2010 Backup and Restore:

1. Open SharePoint 2010 Central Administration and select Farm Backup and Restore ⇨ Restore from a backup.

2. On the Restore from Backup - Step 1 of 3: Select Backup to Restore page, specify the Universal Naming Convention (UNC) path of the backup folder if not already populated and click Refresh.

3. Select the backup to be restored from the list of available backups and then click Next.

4. On the Restore from Backup - Step 2 of 3: Select Component to Restore page, select the component to be restored from the list of available components and then click Next.

5. On the Restore from Backup - Step 3 of 3: Select Restore Options page, select the type of restore to perform in the Restore Options section.

   Two options are available, New and Same Configuration:

   a. New Configuration enables an administrator to restore to a farm with a separate computer name, web application settings, or database server. If you select New, specify the new naming information in the provided fields.

   b. Selecting Same Configuration will overwrite any existing copy of the data.

In some cases, the desired content databases may not be reflected in the Central Administration user interface. If the content database is not selectable, you must use Windows PowerShell or SQL Server tools to restore it.

Backing Up and Restoring Content Databases Using Windows PowerShell

New Windows PowerShell support enables you to perform common administrative tasks, apply varying levels of backup, and restore granularity.

To back up a content database by using Windows PowerShell, enter the following command in the Microsoft SharePoint 2010 Management Shell:

```
Backup-SPFarm -Directory <Backup folder> -BackupMethod {Full | Differential}
-Item <Content database name> [-Verbose]
```

To restore a content database by using Windows PowerShell, use the following command:

```
Restore-SPFarm -Directory <Backup folder name> -RestoreMethod Overwrite -Item
<Content database name> [-BackupId <GUID>] [-Verbose]
```

For content databases that have not been previously backed up, you must use the -Full *switch.*

Backing Up and Restoring Content Databases Using Microsoft SQL Server

SQL Server provides the greatest scale and selection of backup options available to SharePoint 2010 content databases, including Full, Differential, and Incremental.

Depending on your specific recovery point and recovery time objectives, you may often be required to combine these options to provide the broadest overall coverage and facilitate rapid recovery of content. For example, many enterprises are expected to provide a 21-day, disk-based backup regimen; in this scenario, a combination of three full and 18 differential backups are implemented to meet the requirements and minimize the storage footprint.

SQL Server provides a number of options and levels of granularity for performing database backups. Full backup is the simplest form of backup with SQL Server; it provides database administrators with additional options such as the capability to perform single data file or filegroup backups. SharePoint 2010 does not support partitioning schemes, which are required to fully support multiple filegroups, so these options are not discussed here; however, while SharePoint 2010 supports multiple data files, all data files should be backed up and restored as a single unit when working with SharePoint 2010 content databases.

A full database backup provides a complete copy of the content database and provides a "point in time" snapshot to which the database can be restored; however, it does not include the time during which the backup was running. This is important to understand in order to meet specific recovery point objectives, due to the increased backup duration that occurs as the size of the database increases.

Full database backups are the easiest to use and contain all of the data in the content database. When working with a small content database of 50GB or less, the usual best practice is to rely on just full database backups. However, as noted earlier, as the size of a database increases, so does the duration of the backup; and therefore it takes more time to finish and requires more storage space. In these cases, the best practice is to supplement full backups with differential backups, in order to ensure efficiency and performance in both backup and restore.

To perform a full database backup of an individual SharePoint 2010 content database:

1. Open Microsoft SQL Server Management Studio and connect to the appropriate instance of the Microsoft SQL Server Database Engine.
2. In Object Explorer, click the server name to expand the server tree.
3. Expand Databases, and select a content database from the list of available user databases.
4. Right-click the desired content database, and select Tasks ⇨ Back Up, as shown in Figure 12-14.

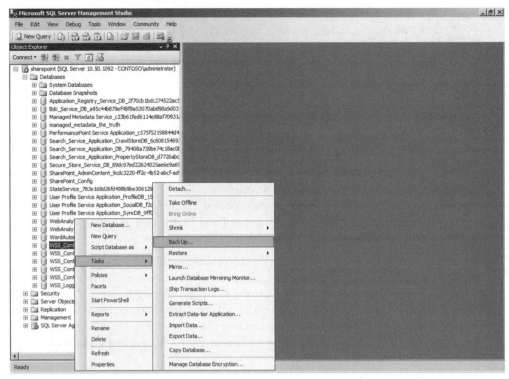

FIGURE 12-14

5. On the Back Up Database dialog, verify the database name in the Database list box.

6. In the Backup type list box, select Full from the list of available options.

7. For Backup component, click Database.

8. Either accept the default backup set name prepopulated in the Name text box or enter a different name for the backup set.

9. In large environments, provide a description of the content database in the Description text box. The description can include the database name, host web application, etc., to help database administrators easily identify the content database.

10. Choose the type of backup destination by clicking Disk. If a filename is not already populated, click Add to add one. Figure 12-15 shows the database being backed up to `C:\Backups\WSS_Content.bak`.

11. SQL Server 2008 Enterprise and later support backup compression. By default, whether a backup is compressed depends on the value of the backup-compression default server configuration option. However, regardless of the current server-level default, you can compress a backup by checking Compress backup, or you can prevent compression by checking Do not compress backup.

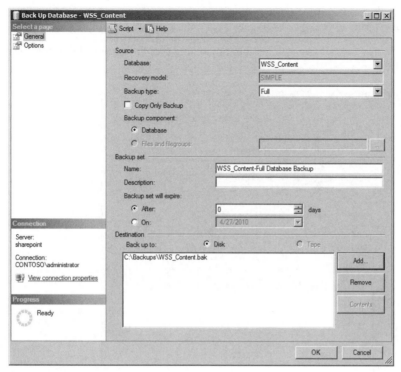

FIGURE 12-15

To restore a content database backed up through SQL Server:

1. Open Microsoft SQL Server Management Studio and connect to the appropriate instance of the Microsoft SQL Server Database Engine.

2. In Object Explorer, click the server name to expand the server tree.

3. In most disaster recovery instances you need to keep the production database online, but you need to recover an older instance to get content out. To do that you will restore the database with a different name. Right click on Databases and select Restore Database... as shown in Figure 12-16.

4. In the To database box type the name you want the restored database to have. Normally this is the database's original name with the date of the backup appended.

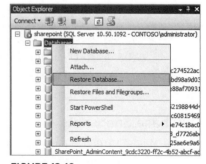

FIGURE 12-16

5. Click From device and use the ellipses to choose the database backup file you created in the preceding backup steps.

6. When the list of backup sets populates be sure to click the checkbox next to the one you want to restore, even if there is only one. Figure 12-17 shows how it should look.

7. Click OK, and if things go well you will get a happy dialog box telling you the restore completed successfully. Congratulations!

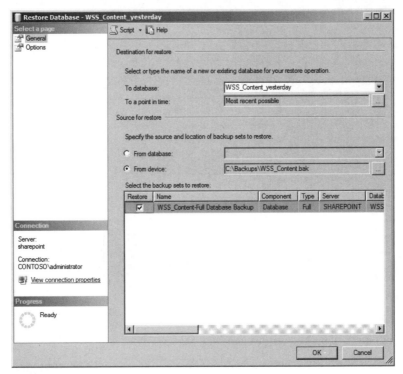

FIGURE 12-17

 If you prefer to restore over the top of an existing database you can do that too. In step 3, right-click on the database you want to restore over and select Tasks ➪ Restore ➪ Database. Then follow the same steps to restore your database.

Database Snapshots

SharePoint 2010 also introduces support for database snapshots (to learn more about snapshots, see "SQL Server Snapshots," earlier in this chapter).

Snapshots are a little tough to set up, and definitely not for the faint of heart. In this section you take a look at how to set them up, then walk through the steps. Figure 12-18 shows the before and after.

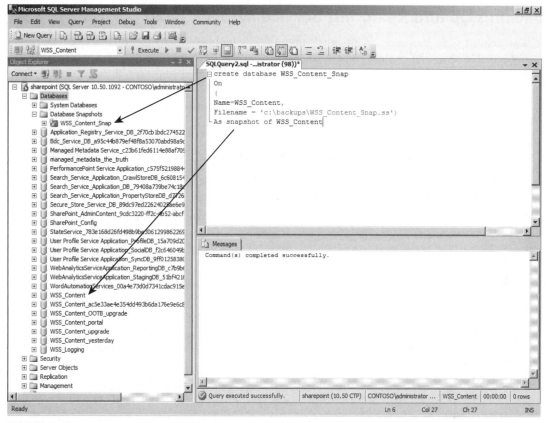

FIGURE 12-18

The query in the query window is the command that was used to create the snapshot. There is no way in the UI to do it. The first line creates the snapshot as a database named WSS_Content_Snap. The arrow points to where you will find it in the interface after it has been created. The next line, Name=WSS_Content, refers to the Logical name of the database file for the database you are making the snapshot of. In most cases it will be the same as the database name itself, as is the case here. The next line specifies the name of the file that will contain the snapshot, WSS_Content_Snap.ss. The final line specifies which database this will be a snapshot of. That's all there is to it. Once you get the query written, press the Execute button in the menu bar, sit back, and let the magic happen.

Once you have the snapshot created you can treat it like any read-only database. You can mount it in SharePoint and render out the content, or you can use it to do an unattached database restore. When you're finished with the snapshot you can delete it the same way you would a regular database.

Backing up content databases to snapshots is only available through the SQL Server management tools. When using snapshots, you should understand their limitations and requirements. For more information on this subject, see the SQL Server Books Online article at http://technet.microsoft.com/en-us/library/ms189940.aspx.

Backing Up and Restoring Service Applications

The new service application architecture not only provides new and compelling scenarios previously not possible under Office SharePoint Server 2007's SSP design, but also introduces new services, some with databases associated, that must be considered when planning your overall backup and restore strategies. Fortunately, SharePoint 2010's native backup and restore capabilities enable both backup and restore of individual service applications, with their respective content where applicable, and backup and restore of only their unique configuration settings.

Backing Up and Restoring Service Applications with Windows PowerShell

To back up a service application using Windows PowerShell, enter the following command in the Microsoft SharePoint 2010 Management Shell:

```
Backup-SPFarm -Directory <Backup folder> -BackupMethod {Full | Differential}
-Item <Service application name> [-Verbose]
```

To perform a restore, use this command:

```
Restore-SPFarm -Directory <Backup folder> -Item <Service application name>
-RecoveryMethod Overwrite [ -BackupId <GUID>] [-Verbose]
```

> *To specify which backup to use, use the* BackupId *parameter. You can view the backups for the farm by entering the following cmdlet from the SharePoint Management Shell:*
>
> ```
> Get-SPBackupHistory -Directory <Backup folder> -ShowBackup
> ```
> *If you do not specify the* BackupId, *the most recent backup will be used. You cannot restore a service application from a configuration-only backup.*

Backing Up and Restoring Service Applications with Central Administration

Follow these steps to back up a service application using Central Administration:

1. From the Central Administration home page, select Backup and Restore ➪ Perform a backup.

2. First you will choose which service application you want to back up. As with backing up content databases above, you can back up one, or all, but nothing in between. Click a service application to back up and click Next.

3. Next you can choose a full or differential backup. If you're not sure which you want, or if you haven't done a full backup yet, select full.

4. Enter a UNC path for the backup location and click Start Backup.

Of course backups are only part of the solution. Let's walk through restoring a service application from Central Adminstration.

1. From the home page in Central Administration, select Backup and Restore ➪ Restore from a backup.

2. When doing a restore, the first thing you need to do is choose which backup you want to restore from. Verify the backup location is correct, then choose the backup job that contains the service application backup you want to restore. When you have the correct one selected, click Next.

3. After Central Admin churns on your backup for a minute you'll get a page showing you which objects you can restore from this backup. Choose the server application or applications you want to restore and click Next.

4. The next page asks a very important question: do you want to restore this service application as a new service application, or overwrite the old one? If you choose to restore it as a new configuration you'll need to specify a service account password and a service name. Click Same Configuration and click OK to the warning box.

5. Click Start Restore.

Now that you've given SharePoint its marching orders it will fire off a Timer Job and start restoring your service application.

Backing Up and Restoring a Farm

A farm backup is useful when you would like to recover all elements of a server farm back to the same overall topology in addition to preserving the original farm's content and configuration. As a result, a full backup should only be considered in scenarios with extended RPO and RTO objectives due to the lengthy downtime required to effectively bring the service online on standby hardware. Most large organizations with complex topologies will elect to leverage more granular protection options that provide a warm standby solution, such as SQL Server Log Shipping, rather than implement a solution based on backup and restore.

Some of the limitations when performing a farm-level backup and restore include the following:

➤ The farm where the restore will be performed must have the same topology as the original source farm.

➤ You cannot downgrade or upgrade topologies with farm backup and restore; for example, a multi-server farm backup cannot be restored to a single-server farm, and vice versa.

➤ Farm backups cannot be restored to other product versions, such as SharePoint Server 2007.

➤ A recovery farm should not be considered to be adequate protection unless specific RTO and RPO objectives allow for such a scenario. Warm standby solutions are always preferable in disaster-recovery scenarios.

➤ In multiple-server topologies, the backup directory must be a common share that all servers in the topology can write to and read from, and all accounts in the farm should have adequate access to that common share.

Backing Up and Restoring a Farm with Windows PowerShell

To perform a farm backup using Windows PowerShell, enter the following command in the Microsoft SharePoint 2010 Management Shell:

```
Backup-SPFarm -Directory <Backup folder> -BackupMethod {Full | Differential}
[ -Verbose]
```

If an error occurs during the backup, you can view the `spbackup.log` file created in the backup directory. As a best practice, you should always use the `Verbose` switch to monitor the operation and its status.

For farms that have not been previously backed up, you must use the `-Full` switch.

To perform a farm restore, enter the following command:

```
Restore-SPFarm -Directory <Backup folder> -RestoreMethod {New | Overwrite}
[ -Verbose]
```

As with a farm backup, if an error occurs during the restore, you can view the `spbackup.log` file created in the backup directory. As a best practice, you should always use the `Verbose` switch to monitor the operation and its status.

 When using `Backup-SPFarm` *or* `Restore-SPFarm`, *you should verify that you are a member of the SharePoint_Shell_Access role on the configuration database, and a member of the WSS_ADMIN_WPG local group on the computer where SharePoint 2010 is installed.*

Backing Up and Restoring a Farm with Central Administration

Backing up your SharePoint farm in SharePoint 2010 is much the same as it was in SharePoint 2007, but in the interest of being thorough, let's go ahead and walk through the steps:

1. In Central Administration click Backup and Restore.

2. Click Perform a Backup at the top of the page.

3. On the next page click Farm under Components to back up. The entire list of options should then be selected and highlighted. Click Next.

4. Select a Full backup unless you have already done a full backup; in that case you can choose Differential. Leave the radio button next to Back up content and configuration settings checked. Type a UNC path in for the backup location and click Start Backup.

SharePoint will now kick off a timer job to back up your farm. You can view its progress on the backup job status page that shows up after the backup starts.

Backing Up and Restoring Configuration Settings

In Office SharePoint Server 2007, a limitation of the Backup/Restore feature was that farmwide configuration settings and information could not be backed up and restored to another server farm. In SharePoint 2010, you can back up and restore only the configuration settings that apply to a specific component. This capability to seamlessly back up and restore configuration settings provides robust support for scenarios such as hardware migrations, replicating settings to preproduction or development environments, or facilitating the rapid build and deployment of production environments that share common settings and topologies.

When performing a complete server farm backup in SharePoint 2010, the configuration database is included; however, it cannot be restored. There are several challenges associated with restoring the configuration database — most notably, the configuration database stores server names and topology information. Therefore, when the restore operation is taking place on a new farm, there is uncertainty about how that information should be treated. The new farm will likely have different machine names and possibly a new topology.

The new "configuration only" backup capabilities mitigate these constraints, enabling you to restore the configuration database settings that are not affected by these unique properties. The configuration only backup extracts and backs up configuration settings from any configuration database, including the current farm's configuration database, the configuration database on another farm, or a configuration database that is not associated with any farm.

Backing Up and Restoring Configuration Settings with Windows PowerShell

To back up configuration settings using Windows PowerShell, enter the following cmdlet in the Microsoft SharePoint 2010 Management Shell:

```
Backup-SPConfigurationDatabase -Directory <Backup folder> -DatabaseServer
<Database server name> -DatabaseName <Database name> -DatabaseCredentials
<PowerShell Credential Object> [-Verbose]
```

In order to successfully back up configuration with Windows PowerShell, you should be logged on with an account with the db_backupoperator fixed database role on the database server where the configuration database is stored; otherwise, you must specify the value for the DatabaseCredentials *parameter.*

To restore configuration settings with Windows PowerShell, enter the following cmdlet:

```
Restore-SPFarm -Directory <Backup folder> -RestoreMethod Overwrite
-ConfigurationOnly [-Verbose]
```

Backing Up and Restoring Configuration Settings with Central Administration

Doing a Configuration only backup in Central Administration is nearly identical to the farm backup shown earlier in this chapter. The steps are the same, but to do a configuration only backup, select Back up only configuration settings in step 4, instead of leaving the Data to back up at the default value. See Figure 12-19.

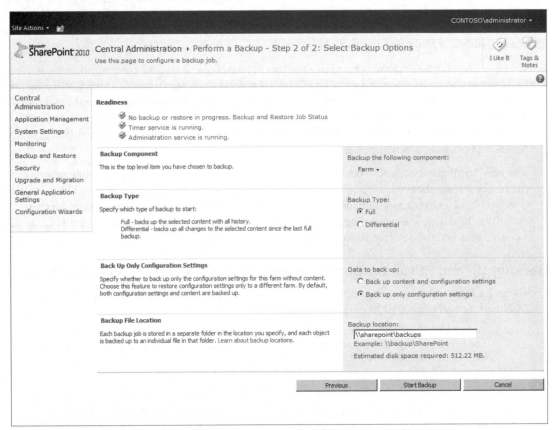

FIGURE 12-19

This backup will go very quickly: don't blink or you'll miss it.

The steps to perform a restore of configuration settings nearly mirror the earlier steps for doing a farm recovery with content. Select the Restore from a backup option in Central Administration and choose the configuration only backup you just did. You can choose to restore the entire farm configuration, or the configuration of certain components. Once you've chosen which configuration you want to restore, click Next. You're greeted with a familiar page asking if you want this restored as a new configuration or the same one. If you are restoring a farm with new computer names, web applications, or SQL servers, click New configuration, as in Figure 12-20, and click Start Restore.

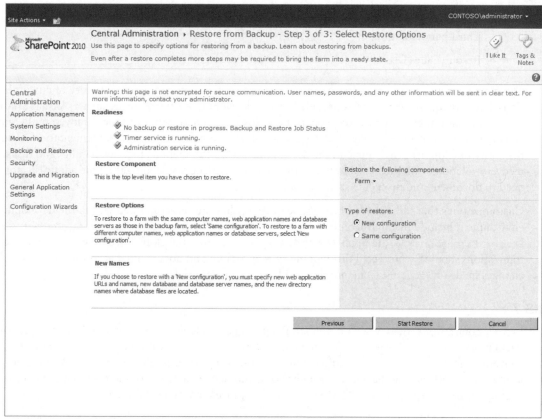

FIGURE 12-20

Customizations

Just because you have all of your content doesn't mean you have everything covered. A lot of work goes into making that pretty SharePoint page, and you have to make sure you get every last bit of supporting material. Customizations are a big part of that.

Customizations can be the most challenging piece of any recovery planning due to the dynamic nature of customizations in terms of life cycle, purpose, and location on a server. For example, with SharePoint, customizations commonly include the following:

➤ Assemblies deployed to the global assembly cache (GAC)

➤ Feature or site definition XML manifests

➤ Master pages, page layouts, and cascading style sheets (these objects are typically content database contained)

➤ Web Parts, site or list definitions, custom columns, new content types, custom fields, custom actions, etc.

➤ Coded workflow

➤ iFilters and corresponding Registry modifications

➤ Third-party solutions

➤ Resource files (.resx)

The most appropriate and seamless method of containing and managing the recovery of customizations is to leverage the capabilities provided by the development environment, such as Visual Studio Team Foundation, by which the developer or developers can maintain both the deployed build and version tree in a centrally managed system, in addition to any corresponding documentation. Using the native development environment, the development team can align its high-availability and disaster-recovery solutions with those tied to the SharePoint deployment, while mitigating the administrator's need to document and protect customizations separately.

Customizations that fall outside of the scope of those that are self-contained within the development environment include the SharePoint 14 "hive" (%COMMONPROGRAMFILES%\Microsoft Shared\Web Server Extensions\14), inetpub (%WINDIR%\Assembly), and the global assembly cache. These customizations should be protected through file system backup and documented accordingly, to include changes made to Web.Config manually outside of the object model.

IIS 7

Like customizations, there are a lot of SharePoint nuggets hidden in IIS, so it should be part of your backup plan too. The process of backing up and restoring a configuration has been made more convenient to administrators by adding command-line support through AppCmd.exe. You can use AppCmd.exe with the add backup, restore backup, and delete backup parameters to perform a full backup of the \windows\system32\inetsrv\config directory and subdirectories.

In addition to simplifying the process by which administrators can back up and restore IIS 7 configuration, IIS also includes a new feature that captures configuration history. With this new capability, IIS will automatically create history snapshots of ApplicationHost.config when a change is detected, which enables you to easily restore to a prior version. By default, IIS checks for a new version every 120 seconds and retains 10 prior versions of the file, which are stored in the %systemdrive%\inetpub\history folder. You can change any of these settings by editing the <system.applicationHost/configHistory> section in ApplicationHost.config.

 While IIS 7 enables you to perform backup and restore of configuration settings, it is not recommended to use the restore function with SharePoint 2010. These configuration settings should be used only for documentation and support-related issues when necessary, not as a recovery solution.

Warm Standby Solutions

Cold standby solutions such as backup and restore account for only a small percentage of a business continuity management plan. In addition to those solutions, you should evaluate the available technologies and capabilities of warm standby solutions that enable recovery of a SharePoint 2010 deployment with minimal disruption in the event of a disaster or major failure in the primary site. Warm standby solutions provide a second copy of the data that can be leveraged in a secondary data center if necessary.

HIGH AVAILABILITY

High availability is the implementation of a system to ensure a certain degree of operational continuity during a given measurement period, typically defined by service-level agreements (SLAs), and can encompass the entirety of a solution or just a portion thereof.

Service-level agreements are a form of contractual agreement whereby the level of service is formally defined, and they can include both performance and delivery time. For example, a guarantee of 99.9% system availability may be a facet of a service-level agreement. Service-level agreements are commonly mapped to operational-level agreements, which define internal support relationships, such as those defined between two services — for example, infrastructure and the consuming application.

SharePoint 2010 offers new high-availability scenarios that provide capabilities to mitigate downtime, promote redundancy, increase resiliency, and drive a highly scalable architecture. Among these improvements are a new service application architecture, native support for SQL Server database mirroring, and improvements to the methods by which costly operations such as large list querying and site collection deletion are handled.

Load Balancing

Load balancing can be a combination of software- and hardware-based solutions designed to distribute workload evenly across two or more computers, such as two front-end web, query, or indexing servers in a SharePoint 2010 topology. The decision to leverage a software or hardware load-balanced solution is determined by the capabilities and scale you require to meet your objectives. These can include compliance requirements, geographic needs, and overall scale and performance in addition to manageability.

SQL Server Database Mirroring

SQL Server database mirroring is becoming a popular option not only to provide a highly resilient and performance-oriented data replication solution, but also to move toward commodity storage servers and inexpensive direct-access storage (DAS). SQL Server database mirroring can serve as either a high-availability solution or a disaster-recovery solution, but it cannot be both. SQL Server database mirroring works by maintaining two copies of a single database on separate SQL Server instances.

In a database mirroring session, one database, the principal, serves the database to clients; while the other, the mirror, provides a hot or warm standby server. Whether a database is a hot standby or a warm standby is dictated by the operating mode of the mirroring session:

> ➤ **Synchronous** — In a synchronous database mirroring configuration, database mirroring provides a hot standby solution that provides rapid failover without data loss (committed transactions). This is accomplished because each transaction must be acknowledged by the

mirror before it is hardened on the principal. While this method offers the highest resiliency, there is the potential to lose inflight transactions in some scenarios.

➤ **Asynchronous** — In asynchronous configurations (i.e., sessions are not synchronized), there is the potential to incur data loss; therefore, it is considered a warm standby solution. Asynchronous database mirroring is commonly configured to support and drive disaster-recovery solutions due to its efficiencies over latent links, such as a WAN.

When implementing database mirroring with SharePoint 2010 as a high-availability solution, it must be configured synchronously in the High-safety with automatic failover operating mode, which includes a *witness server*. The witness server provides automatic failover by periodically "polling" the principal server to determine whether it is up and functioning. The mirror server initiates automatic failover only when the mirror and the witness remain connected to each other after both have been disconnected from the principal server. This configuration enables a seamless client experience if a database is compromised and unable to serve clients.

Table 12-1 provides an overview of SQL Server database mirroring availability according to SQL Server edition.

TABLE 12-1: Database Mirroring Features by SQL Server Edition

FEATURE	CORE EDITIONS		SPECIALIZED EDITIONS		
	ENTERPRISE	STANDARD	WORKGROUP	WEB	EXPRESS
Database Mirroring	Yes (full)	Yes (Single Threaded, Safety Full Only)	Witness only	Witness only	Witness

SQL Server 2008 Enterprise and Standard Editions include a number of database mirroring improvements that provide further resiliency with SharePoint 2010, including, for example, Torn Page Repair. With Torn Page Repair, a database mirroring partner will attempt to recover from corrupted pages on the mirroring database by resolving a limited set of errors, which can enable a data page to be read. If a partner is unable to read a page, it will request a copy from the other partner. If the request succeeds, then the unreadable page is replaced by the good copy, resolving the error in most cases. This illustrates only one of the many improvements in SQL Server 2008; to learn more, see also `http://msdn.microsoft.com/en-us/library/ms130214.aspx`.

Most databases in SharePoint 2010 can be configured using a standard Windows PowerShell noun and verb combination, although in some cases varying statements are required to successfully configure database mirroring. While Windows PowerShell is most frequently used to configure database mirroring, the SharePoint 2010 Central Administration user interface also provides support for configuring database mirroring — the exception being the configuration database, which must be configured through Windows PowerShell.

Note that unlike previous versions of SharePoint, SharePoint 2010 supports database mirroring without the implementation of connection aliases or middle-tier software to manage the failover. This is possible because SharePoint 2010 databases are built on the SQL Native Client (SNAC) that introduces support for the `Failover_Partner` keyword in the connection string.

Although database mirroring can be configured through SharePoint 2010, it simply enables the support for database mirroring — it does not configure mirroring at the database level, which must be completed through the SQL Server management tools or Transact-SQL prior to enabling a database with SharePoint. To learn more about database mirroring and how to configure it in SQL Server, see `http://technet.microsoft.com/en-us/library/ms189852.aspx`.

Configuring Database Mirroring for the Configuration Database

To configure database mirroring for the configuration database, enter the following command in the Microsoft SharePoint 2010 Management Shell:

```
$db = Get-SPDatabase | where {$_.Name -match "SharePoint_Config"}
$db.AddFailoverServiceInstance("mirrorservername")
$db.Update()
```

Configure Database Mirroring for Content Databases

Database mirroring for a content database can be configured with either Windows PowerShell or Central Administration.

To use Windows PowerShell, enter the following command in the Microsoft SharePoint 2010 Management Shell:

```
$db = Get-SPDatabase | where {$_.name -match "WSS_Content"}
$db.AddFailoverServiceInstance("mirrorservername")
$db.Update()
```

To configure mirroring on a content database using Central Administration, follow these steps:

1. On the SharePoint 2010 Central Administration home page, select Application Management ➪ Manage content databases.

2. On the Manage Content Databases page, select a web application from the list of available web applications, and then select a content database associated with that web application.

3. On the Manage Content Database Settings page, specify the mirror server in the Failover Database Server field.

4. Click OK.

Configure Database Mirroring for Service Application Databases

Many of the new service applications in SharePoint 2010 provide a user interface entry point to configure the failover partner when using database mirroring; however, they differ in implementation.

To configure service applications for database mirroring using Windows PowerShell, enter the following command in the Microsoft SharePoint 2010 Management Shell:

```
$db = Get-SPDatabase | where {$_.name -match "Search_PropertyStore_<GUID>"}
$db.AddFailoverServiceInstance("mirrorservername")
$db.Update()
```

Failover Clustering

While SQL Server database mirroring support has been included in SharePoint 2010, full support of failover clustering remains.

Failover clustering helps ensure that applications and services, such as SharePoint, are available when you need them. A failover cluster is a group of computers working together to increase the availability of applications and services, such as SQL Server. The clustered servers are commonly connected by physical cables and software. In the event that one of the cluster nodes fails, another node takes over; as a result, users experience a minimum of disruption in service.

The key difference between database mirroring and failover clustering is that database mirroring provides a second warm or hot standby of one or more databases, whereas failover clustering protection occurs at the server level.

To learn more about failover clustering, see `http://technet.microsoft.com/en-us/library/ff182326(WS.10).aspx`.

Read-Only Mode

SharePoint 2010 supports configuring its content databases in read-only mode. When databases are configured as read-only, SharePoint 2010 detects and seamlessly responds to the situation and disables any user interface options associated with write and edit scenarios. This enables users to continue working normally with SharePoint 2010 by allowing them to retrieve data and work with content until the environment is placed into a read/write mode. Read-only scenarios can be used in disaster-recovery solutions in the secondary environment or in a localized secondary environment during patching and upgrade. Read-only mode is configured through SQL Server management tools or Transact-SQL.

To configure a database as read-only:

1. Open SQL Server Management Studio.

2. Right-click the database to be configured as read-only, and then click Properties.

3. On the Options page, in the Other options list, navigate to the State section.

4. On the Database Read-Only entry, select True from the menu as shown in Figure 12-21 and then click OK.

Repeat the preceding steps for each database to be configured.

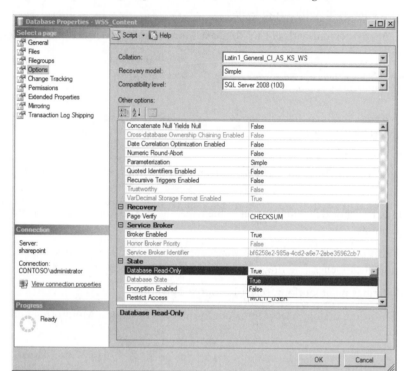

FIGURE 12-21

HTTP Request Monitoring and Throttling

SharePoint is popular, sometimes too popular for its own good. There are times when a SharePoint server can get more requests than it can handle in a timely fashion. In the dark ages, with SharePoint 2007, those requests would get dropped in a somewhat random fashion. While a user getting an error trying to get to your portal home is bad, getting that same error when hitting Submit on their vacation approval form is even worse. To help reduce the impact of an overburdened server, SharePoint 2010 introduces HTTP Request Monitoring and Throttling. Hallelujah! Vacations everywhere will be saved!

How does this all work? Every five seconds each server checks various aspects of its performance. It looks at metrics like memory available and ASP.NET requests queued, and compares them against acceptable thresholds. If the server is overworked and exceeds the defined thresholds three times in a row, the red lights start flashing and the server goes into throttled mode. Web applications that have HTTP throttling enabled get some new instructions. They will not accept any new requests. New requests will be met with a very friendly, but firm HTTP 503 error, server busy. The server will, however, accept connections from existing sessions. This should help free up server resources to let that vacation request form get submitted. No new timer jobs will be started on that server, and any running timer jobs will be paused, if they can be. The server continues to check itself every five seconds, and stays in the throttled state until all the metrics it checks fall back into acceptable ranges. All of this will be logged in the server's System log in the Event Viewer.

HTTP Request Monitoring and Throttling can be enabled through both Central Administration and Windows PowerShell on a per web application basis.

To view and change the values associated with HTTP Request Monitoring and Throttling, use these Windows PowerShell cmdlets:

```
Get-SPWebApplicationHttpThrottlingMonitor
Set-SPWebApplicationHttpThrottlingMonitor
```

You can use `Get-SPWebApplicationHttpThrottlingMonitor -identity http://www`
`.contoso.com` to return the HTTP Throttling values. To change the values, you can use
`Set-SPWebApplicationHttpThrottlingMonitor`.

To configure HTTP Request Monitoring and Throttling from Central Administration, follow these steps:

1. On the SharePoint 2010 Central Administration home page, select Application Management ➪ Manage web applications.

2. On the Manage Web Applications page, select a web application from the list of available web applications and click General Settings on the Ribbon.

3. From the General Settings menu options, select Resource Throttling.

4. On the Resource Throttling dialog, select On or Off in the HTTP Request Monitoring and Throttling section.

5. Click OK.

List Throttling

List Throttling is a new feature in SharePoint 2010 that enables administrators to proactively protect server resources from the impact of large lists and their associated views. In order to provide a consistent server response, SharePoint 2010 provides several settings that can be used to restrict queries executed against large lists. To provide the greatest amount of flexibility, these settings are configured on a per web application basis.

To configure list throttling from Central Administration, follow these steps:

1. On the SharePoint 2010 Central Administration home page, select Application Management ➪ Manage web applications.

2. On the Manage Web Applications page, select a web application from the list of available web applications and click General Settings on the Ribbon.

3. From the General Settings menu options, select Resource Throttling.

4. On the Resource Throttling dialog, specify a value for each setting you wish to configure:

    ➤ **List View Threshold** — Specifies the maximum number of items that can be retrieved in a single request. The default value is 5,000; the minimum value is 2,000.

➤ **Object Model Override** — It is possible for developers to override list throttling in the object model. In order for this to work, you must enable the Object Model Override.

➤ **List View Threshold for Auditors and Administrators** — Specifies the maximum number of items that can be retrieved in a single request through the object model for appropriately permissioned users. This value does not allow users to see more items in a list view than a standard user.

➤ **List View Lookup Threshold** — Specifies the maximum number of Lookup, Person/Group, or Workflow status fields that are returned in a single request.

➤ **Daily Time Window for Large Queries** — Specifies a date/time range and duration in which you will allow queries to run while not enforcing any configured throttling limits. Queries that have executed but not completed within the range will continue to run until complete.

➤ **List Unique Permissions Threshold** — Specifies the maximum number of unique permissions that an individual list can support.

5. Click OK.

Gradual Site Delete

Gradual Site Delete is an improvement in the manner by which site collections are deleted in SharePoint 2010, provided through the new Gradual Site Delete Timer Job Definition.

In SharePoint 2007 a seemingly innocent operation of deleting a site collection could make site collections inexplicably unavailable. When a site collection was deleted in SharePoint 2007, a SQL stored procedure was run. It was given the ID of the site collection that had been given its walking papers. The SQL stored procedure searched through all the tables in the content database that held the site collection, and deleted all rows that were associated to that ID. While this seems like a good idea, it turns out it could wreak a fair amount of havoc. A couple of tables could potentially have thousands of rows associated with a single site collection. When SQL starts deleting a large number of rows in a table it may choose to lock that table. Once it does that, all the site collections in the database will be offline until the rows are deleted and the lock is released. Users HATE that.

To help make SharePoint 2010 more resilient, this problem has been addressed. The folks at Microsoft went back to the drawing board and designed a whole new way to delete site collections in SharePoint 2010. Now when a site collection is deleted the job is broken down into smaller steps, so as to not anger SQL and elicit one of its nasty locks. First SharePoint deletes the pointer to the site collection in the configuration database, and from the Sites table in the content database. At that point it is no longer available to end users. As far as they know it is gone. Behind the scenes SharePoint has put a sticky reminder note on its monitor reminding it to delete those old rows when it gets a chance. Then, via a timer job, it deletes small groups of rows until all signs of the site collection are gone. It does this all under the cover of darkness and SQL has no idea. While this isn't technically something a SharePoint 2010 administrator can do to improve SharePoint's availability, it is worth mentioning in this section.

SUMMARY

Whew, we covered a lot of ground in this chapter. The big message is that there are many ways to look at disaster recovery and fault tolerance. The techniques you use with your environment depend on which problems you want to protect against, and what your budget is.

The first thing to consider is content recovery. We would get so much done if it weren't for those darned users. Recovering their content is one of the things we need to plan for. In this chapter we covered various methods of protecting users from themselves. These include how to use versions and recycle bins to recover data. We also discussed a variety of ways to back up content from lists, all the way to site collections.

High availability as described here crosses many boundaries and is not limited to strictly component redundancy; it not only spans technologies, but is contained and managed within the product itself, as illustrated in new resource throttling capabilities and how simple site deletion actions are managed. Like all aspects of continuity management, prior to embarking on developing a high-availability solution, you should clearly understand both your objectives and how SharePoint 2010 is intended to be used in your organization.

The cost and complexity of your high-availability solution will be largely based on your service-level agreements — a very conservative SLA may require a costly and complex solution to meet its requirements, whereas a very liberal SLA may require an inexpensive solution based primarily on warm standby solutions.

Disaster recovery is a critical component of a SharePoint deployment, and planning should begin once a topology has been identified. This planning should not only include consideration of your physical and logical topologies, but also ensure that your strategy supports all underlying RTO and RPO objectives established by your organization. The previous pages have covered some of the available technologies at a high level. While this chapter can't tell you exactly what's right for your environment, hopefully it did give an introduction to the tools you can use, and it got you thinking about what aspects of disaster recovery you need to consider.

13

Using Features and Solution Packages

WHAT'S IN THIS CHAPTER?

➤ Understanding SharePoint Features

➤ How to manage Features

➤ Working with SharePoint Solutions

➤ How to manage Solutions

➤ How to create a basic Feature and Solution Package

All SharePoint administrators should understand both Features and Solutions. While the creation of Features and Solutions is typically a development role, administrators need to understand their main components in order to manage and support them, as well as to understand a Feature or Solution's impact on the farm.

Features are a key building block of SharePoint, and much of SharePoint's own functionality is implemented using them. A *Feature* is a collection of elements that are grouped together and, though they are not required to be, usually composed of logically related elements. An element can be almost anything in SharePoint: a Web Part, a workflow, a content type definition, an event receiver, etc. Name an artifact in SharePoint and the odds are good that it can be an element in a Feature. Once Features are installed, they can be activated or subsequently deactivated so that their functionality can be enabled and disabled. As you have seen in previous chapters, the authors may have asked you to either activate a Feature or ensure that a specific Feature was already activated.

The SharePoint *Solution* infrastructure enables you to have a single deployment point for all of the servers in your farm, and to schedule deployments and updates via jobs. This in turn enables you to do more with less, because during deployments you will not need to copy files to every server in the farm, or make `web.config` changes to all servers in the farm. If a Solution has been created correctly, all of this will be handled by the Solution infrastructure. All you have to do is execute a deployment or update to the centralized solution store, and SharePoint takes care of the rest.

In addition, because you can use Solutions to schedule deployments and updates, you no longer need to pay someone to wait around until midnight for those tasks. You can simply schedule them and then confirm that they occurred later. While not everyone will feel comfortable with scheduling a deployment to be run as an automated job, those who have a test and/or staging environments are likely to use this capability because success can be verified elsewhere first.

Features and Solution Packages play a big role in deploying custom capability to SharePoint websites. This chapter discusses what Features contain, how they are activated, and how they are managed. You will also create a simple Feature so that you will have a better understanding of the process.

USING SHAREPOINT 2010 FEATURES

Features are located in the `TEMPLATE\FEATURES` subdirectory of the SharePoint root folder located at `C:\Program Files\Common Files\Microsoft Shared\Web Server Extensions\14\TEMPLATE\FEATURES`. Within the `FEATURES` directory, each Feature has its own directory; and at a minimum, that directory contains a `feature.xml` file. It is in this file where the Feature is actually defined. A Feature definition is composed of element manifests, dependencies, upgrade actions and/or properties, and is used to register functionality at a given scope within SharePoint. These directories will often have additional files and/or subdirectories that contain supporting files where the elements and other parts of the Feature are defined. For most Features, it is the elements that we care about, not so much the Feature definition itself. The elements are what define the Web Parts, workflows, menus, content type, lists, and so on that you or your users will use and interact with.

Defining Scope

Features are defined in SharePoint for a particular scope — at the farm, web application, site collection, and site level. The scope defined for a Feature determines what elements are available within it, and whether and how Feature dependencies will work for the Feature. A table showing the elements by scope can be found at `http://msdn.microsoft.com/en-us/library/ms454835(office.14).aspx`.

SHAREPOINT SCOPE NAMES

The nomenclature for scopes in SharePoint has changed over time but some of the legacy terms remain for compatibility purposes. In the online table, you will notice the current term used to describe SharePoint's scopes and another term in parentheses; for example, *Site (site collection)*. The term in parentheses is the term SharePoint uses internally to refer to the scope, and the one that it expects to see in the `scope` attribute of the Feature element in the `feature.xml` file. For example, for Features that have a Site Collection scope, you need to specify *Site* as the scope; and for Features that will have a Site scope, you need to specify a scope of *Web*. This can be a little confusing at first and is worth a review if you are having scoping issues with a Feature.

Activating and Deactivating Features

The SharePoint infrastructure allows Features to be activated and deactivated, much like using a light switch. During the activation process, SharePoint provisions elements or makes declarative elements available; and during the deactivation process, SharePoint unprovisions some of those same elements, but not all, and makes declarative elements unavailable. You can see a listing of elements and how they are provisioned/unprovisioned or made declaratively available/unavailable here `http://msdn.microsoft.com/en-us/library/ee537575(office.14).aspx`.

The difference between provisioning an element and making a declarative element available is durability. That is to say, when something is provisioned, SharePoint stores information in the configuration or content databases; and when something is declaratively made available, it is read directly from the Feature definition each time a SharePoint web application starts. As mentioned above, not all elements provisioned during activation are unprovisioned during deactivation, and content that has been created based on elements will not be removed when the Feature is deactivated either.

 The provisioning behavior described above reflects the default actions and behaviors that occur during the Feature activation/deactivation process; but using custom code, a Feature creator can change how parts of that process work.

Managing Features

SharePoint gives you the flexibility to manage things in a number of different ways, and Features are no different. You can manage Features through the user interface or via the command line, using either legacy STSADM commands or PowerShell cmdlets; and they can be installed, uninstalled, activated/deactivated, and viewed.

Managing Features via the User Interface

The user interface provides a limited amount of functionality for managing Features. It allows users with the Manage Web permission to see the visible Features for the current site or site collection. In order to manage Features scoped for the farm or web application, you must be a farm administrator.

 The Manage Web permission must be given on the root site of a site collection in order for the user to be able to manage Features at the Site Collection level.

How you get to the Feature's management page depends on the scope you want to manage.

Sites and Site Collections

To manage Site and Site Collection scoped Features, go to the Site Actions menu and choose Site Settings, as shown in Figure 13-1.

To manage Features for the site, choose Manage site features (see Figure 13-2) under the Site Actions section. To manage Features for the site collection, choose Site collection features (see Figure 13-3) under the Site Collection Administration section.

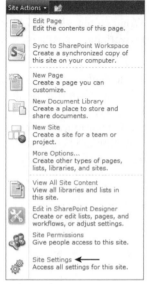

FIGURE 13-1

FIGURE 13-2

FIGURE 13-3

Farm

When managing web application and farm level Features through the user interface, you must access Central Administration. You can get to the link for managing farm Features in a couple of different ways, but the simplest way is to use the link on the Central Administration home page under the System Settings section, as shown in Figure 13-4.

Web Application

Web application Features are accessed a little differently than the other scopes because they are accessed via the Ribbon. To access web application Features, click the Manage web applications link that is available on the Central Administration home page, in the Application Management section, as shown in Figure 13-5.

FIGURE 13-4

FIGURE 13-5

Once on the Web Application Management page, you need to click one of the listed web applications in order for the options in the Ribbon to become available (see Figure 13-6).

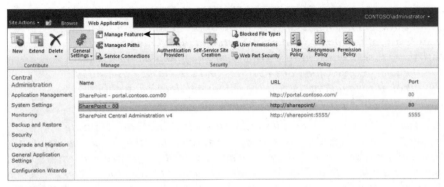

FIGURE 13-6

Table 13-1 lists the direct URLs for each page based on scope.

TABLE 13-1: Feature Management URLs

SCOPE	URL
Farm	`http://<CA-Server>/_admin/ManageFarmFeatures.aspx`
Web Application	`http://<CA-Server>/_admin/ManageWebAppFeatures.aspx`
Site Collection	`http://<Server>/<SiteCollection>/_layouts/ManageFeatures.aspx?Scope=Site`
Site	`http://<Server>/<SiteCollectionAndSite>/_layouts/ManageFeatures.aspx`

Feature Management Pages

Each of the Feature management pages allows you to activate and deactivate Features for their given scope. Keep in mind that these pages show only the visible Features for the given scope. For each Feature, the page includes an activation/deactivation button, whose status appears immediately to the right of the Feature (see Figure 13-7). A status is shown only if the Feature is active. Users can toggle the status of a Feature by using this button. The action the button will take on the Feature is determined by the current state of the Feature and the action to be taken will be labeled on the button.

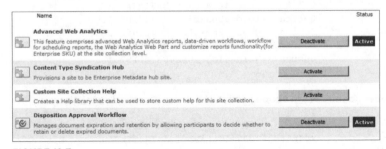

FIGURE 13-7

The user interface will not necessarily show all of the Features for a given scope because a Feature can be hidden. A Feature will be hidden when its hidden *attribute is set to* true *(this attribute can be found on the Feature element in the* feature.xml *file). For Features that are marked as hidden, your only option for managing them is the command line, using either PowerShell cmdlets or legacy STSADM commands.*

Why hide a Feature? You may not want to allow users to activate or deactivate it. For instance, you may not want users to deactivate a Feature that has an event receiver that enforces data validation when an item is added or updated in a list, or you may not want them to activate a Feature that is not intended for all sites in the farm. Another thing to keep in mind is that SharePoint shows all of the visible Features in the farm for the given scope. Therefore, if you have a lot of Features deployed on a farm, the user interface can get a bit cluttered in a hurry. For these types of environments, it is preferable to mark the Feature hidden unless it is necessary for a user to be able to control its status.

Managing Features via the Command Line

The command line provides you with all of the administrative functions needed to manage Features, such as viewing information, installing/uninstalling, and activating/deactivating. All of these functions are available from PowerShell, and all but viewing information are available using legacy STSADM commands. PowerShell cmdlets for Features include Get-SPFeature, Enable-SPFeature, Disable-SPFeature, Install-SPFeature, and Uninstall-SPFeature.

Viewing Feature Information

The PowerShell cmdlet Get-SPFeature enables you to view information about Features from the command line. Used alone, the cmdlet is pretty basic and has very limited use. It enables you to view a list of all of the Features in the entire farm or for a given scope. Executing the cmdlet Get-SPFeature by itself will yield a list of all of the Features for all scopes. The following example shows how to condition the output to view all of the Features in the farm that have a Site Collection scope level.

```
Get-SPFeature
DisplayName                        Id                                        Scope
-----------                        --                                        -----
PublishingStapling                 001f4bd7-746d-403b-aa09-a6cc43de7942      Farm
BasicWebParts                      00bfea71-1c5e-4a24-b310-ba51c3eb7a57      Site
XmlFormLibrary                     00bfea71-1e1d-4562-b56a-f05371bb0115      Web
LinksList                          00bfea71-2062-426c-90bf-714c59600103      Web
workflowProcessList                00bfea71-2d77-4a75-9fca-76516689e21a      Web
GridList                           00bfea71-3a1d-41d3-a0ee-651d11570120      Web
...


Get-SPFeature | Where-Object {$_.Scope -Eq "Site"} | Sort DisplayName
DisplayName                        Id                                        Scope
-----------                        --                                        -----
AccSrvSolutionGallery              744b5fd3-3b09-4da6-9bd1-de18315b045d      Site
```

```
AdminReportCore              b8f36433-367d-49f3-ae11-f7d76b51d251    Site
AssetLibrary                 4bcccd62-dcaf-46dc-a7d4-e38277ef33f4    Site
BaseSite                     b21b090c-c796-4b0f-ac0f-7ef1659c20ae    Site
BasicWebParts                00bfea71-1c5e-4a24-b310-ba51c3eb7a57    Site
...
```

```
Get-SPFeature -Site http://<Server>/<SiteCollectionPath> | Sort DisplayName
DisplayName                  Id                                      Scope
-----------                  --                                      -----
AccSrvSolutionGallery        744b5fd3-3b09-4da6-9bd1-de18315b045d    Site
AdminReportCore              b8f36433-367d-49f3-ae11-f7d76b51d251    Site
AssetLibrary                 4bcccd62-dcaf-46dc-a7d4-e38277ef33f4    Site
BaseSite                     b21b090c-c796-4b0f-ac0f-7ef1659c20ae    Site
BasicWebParts                00bfea71-1c5e-4a24-b310-ba51c3eb7a57    Site
...
```

Note that there is no STSADM equivalent to these PowerShell cmdlets.

Installing and Uninstalling Features

Generally, you should not install or uninstall Features outside of the Solution infrastructure, but in some cases it may be necessary. Solutions are covered in detail later in this chapter, but for now you should know that they are the preferred method for installing and uninstalling Features, rather than using the command line. To install and uninstall Features, you use the `Install-SPFeature` and `Uninstall-SPFeature` cmdlets, respectively. The following examples show how to use these to install and uninstall a Feature named HelloWorldWebPart.

Both the install and uninstall cmdlets can take a `-Force` parameter. When this parameter is specified, SharePoint will bypass some of the checks that it normally performs when the command is executed. This can be helpful when trying to troubleshoot or fix issues with a Feature.

The following PowerShell cmdlet will install the Feature:

```
Install-SPFeature HelloWorldWebPart
DisplayName                  Id                                      Scope
-----------                  --                                      -----
HelloWorldWebPart            d157638b-0fbd-4196-8683-155e24330314    Site
...
```

The STSADM equivalent is:

```
STSADM -o installfeature HelloWorldWebPart
```

The following PowerShell cmdlet will uninstall the Feature:

```
Uninstall-SPFeature HelloWorldWebPart
```

The STSADM equivalent is:

```
STSADM -o uninstallfeature HelloWorldWebPart
```

Activating and Deactivating Features

As you have seen, you can activate and deactivate a visible Feature through the user interface. Those same tasks can also be accomplished by using the PowerShell `Enable-SPFeature` and `Disable-SPFeature` cmdlets, respectively. The cmdlet names use a different nomenclature than the user interface and the legacy STSADM commands. For these cmdlets, `Enable-SPFeature` performs the activation of a Feature, and `Disable-SPFeature` performs the deactivation.

The `-URL` parameter for the enable and disable cmdlets is used to identify the web application, site collection, or site on which the cmdlet will take action.

Like the install and uninstall cmdlets, the enable and disable cmdlets support a `-Force` parameter. This parameter can also be useful when troubleshooting issues with a Feature. In the case of `Enable-SPFeature`, it allows you to issue the enable cmdlet for an already activated Feature. This can be useful if you want to update a Feature definition without first having to deactivate it.

The following PowerShell cmdlet will enable the Feature (no output is returned):

```
Enable-SPFeature HelloWorldWebPart -URL http://sharepoint
```

The STSADM equivalent is:

```
STSADM -o activatefeature HelloWorldWebPart -URL http://sharepoint
```

The following PowerShell cmdlet will disable the Feature:

```
Disable-SPFeature HelloWorldWebPart -URL http://sharepoint
```

The STSADM equivalent is:

```
STSADM -o deactivatefeature HelloWorldWebPart -URL http://sharepoint
```

 The `-Force` parameter is a useful option with Features but you should exercise caution when using it. Not all Features are built to handle being installed/ uninstalled, or activated/deactivated, repeatedly without first having the inverse command executed. For these Features, you can end up with issues that manifest themselves in many ways, such as Feature elements appearing in the system multiple times, errors being generated during the execution process that may leave things in an inconsistent state, Feature or content corruption, and so on. The possible issues with the `-Force` parameter are usually limited to complex Features but they can occur in simple ones as well, so proceed with caution.

Creating a Feature

As stated earlier, creating a Feature is generally considered a development task, but having a basic understanding of how Features are created can help you better understand how to troubleshoot issues if (when) they arise. Creating a Feature can range in complexity from very simple to extremely complicated depending on the elements and artifacts that are being used. This section focuses on creating a very basic Feature that will add a menu item to one of the menus in SharePoint and link to Wrox's website. Later in this chapter we will add this Feature to a Solution.

Creating a Feature in this manner is not considered a best practice and should not be done this way in a real-world scenario. As a best practice, Features should be packaged into Solutions and deployed with the same. The purpose of this example is to show you the mechanics of creating a Feature manually so that you can see all of the moving parts. It is recommended that you use a tool such as Visual Studio 2010 to create Features and package them in Solutions.

To begin creating the Feature, you need to create a directory in the `TEMPLATE\FEATURES` directory of the SharePoint root (`C:\Program Files\Common Files\Microsoft Shared\Web Server Extensions\14\TEMPLATE\FEATURES`). For this Feature, name the directory `MyBasicMenuItem`. This step is illustrated in Figure 13-8.

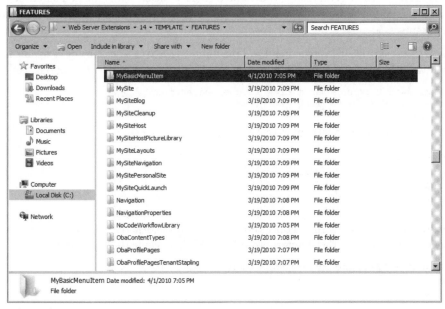

FIGURE 13-8

Inside the `MyBasicMenuItem` directory, create two files, a Feature file named `feature.xml` and an elements file named `elements.xml`. Only the Feature's filename is important; it must be named `feature.xml`. The element's filename is not important; the file can be named anything as long as it is referenced correctly from the Feature file. Once the files are created, open the Feature file in the text editor of your choice (Notepad works just fine). Inside the Feature file, add the following XML:

```
<Feature Title="My Basic Menu Button"
    Scope="Web"
    Id="6C5F196C-A287-4019-A415-C55ED1782860"
    xmlns="http://schemas.microsoft.com/sharepoint/">
    <ElementManifests>
```

```
      <ElementManifest Location="elements.xml" />
    </ElementManifests>
  </Feature>
```

Note the Scope and Id. Scope attributes, which indicate to SharePoint the level in the hierarchy at which this Feature applies; and as a result, what elements it should expect to process and handle during its activation. This Feature will be scoped at the Site level, so you specify the term "Web" (please refer to the "SharePoint Scope Names" note, earlier in the chapter, for an explanation of why these terms differ). The Id attribute is also important because it will be SharePoint's internal identifier for the Feature. This Id needs to be a unique GUID (global unique identifier). You cannot use the same Id/GUID across Features.

Note also that you specify an element manifest in the file, and that the manifest entry is pointing to a Location named elements.xml. That is the elements file you created in the directory. The path is relative to the Feature's own directory, so if you wanted to have the elements file in a subdirectory named MenuItems, you would specify MenuItems\elements.xml as the Location, but for now leave it as just elements.xml.

Next, open the elements.xml file in Notepad and add the following XML. The element in the file is a custom action that will add a menu item/hyperlink to the Site Settings menu in the Site Actions section.

```xml
<Elements xmlns="http://schemas.microsoft.com/sharepoint/">
  <CustomAction Title="Visit Wrox Web Site"
    Sequence="1"
    Location="Microsoft.SharePoint.SiteSettings"
    GroupId="SiteTasks"
    Id="MyBasicMenuItem">
    <UrlAction Url="http://www.wrox.com" />
  </CustomAction>
</Elements>
```

Your Feature is now complete. To let SharePoint know that it is there, use the Install-SPFeature cmdlet you learned about earlier in the chapter. From PowerShell, execute the following:

```
PS C:\> Install-SPFeature MyBasicMenuItem
DisplayName                    Id                               Scope
-----------                    --                               -----
mybasicmenuitem                6c5f196c-a287-4019-a415-c55ed1782860   Web
```

At this point, you might assume that now that the Feature is installed, you should see the menu item in the Site Actions menu under Site Settings, right? Nope, you still need to activate the Feature for a specific site, as this Feature is scoped at the Site (web) level. Before activating the Feature, however, take a look at the Site Actions section (see Figure 13-9) so you can compare it to what it looks like after the Feature is activated.

Now activate the Feature. You can use the Enable-SPFeature cmdlet or you can enable it through the user interface, but you should probably experiment with both:

```
PS C:\> Enable-SPFeature MyBasicMenuItem -URL http://sharepoint
```

With the Feature activated, take another look at the Site Actions section (see Figure 13-10) on the site. You can see that the menu item is now visible and ready for use.

FIGURE 13-9

FIGURE 13-10

Of course, most Features that you will see in your life as a SharePoint administrator will be far more complex than the one you just created, but this should help give you an idea of what is involved in creating, installing, and activating a Feature in SharePoint.

SOLUTIONS

Solutions are nothing more than a properly formatted .cab file that has a .wsp extension, and they are the recommended way to deploy Features and any other functionality to SharePoint. Though they differ in many ways, you can think of a .wsp file in SharePoint as being very much like an .msi file for Windows. Both contain instructions for deploying content to their respective environments.

SharePoint 2010 introduces a new type of Solution called a *Sandbox Solution* that allows Site Collection administrators to deploy and manage Solutions at the site collection level while providing the capability to throttle the amount of resources those Solutions use within the farm. They are called Sandbox Solutions because their capabilities are constrained at runtime both from a security and functional standpoint. Sandbox Solutions enable administrators to give users more freedom within their site collections, while also providing the ability for the administrator to limit users' impact on the farm.

Managing Farm Solutions

Managing Solutions is a lot like managing Features and other items in SharePoint. With Solutions, you can manage their installation and deployment through the Central Administration user interface, and even more through the command line — whether it is with PowerShell or legacy STSADM commands.

Managing Farm Solutions via the User Interface

When managing Solutions in SharePoint, you can do almost anything through the user interface. The only normal actions that you cannot perform through the user interface are adding and updating Solutions in the farm solution store. Essentially, everything else can be done through the browser. When managing a Solution through the browser, you always begin in the same place: Select Central Administration ➪ System Settings ➪ Farm Management ➪ Manage farm solutions, as shown in Figure 13-11.

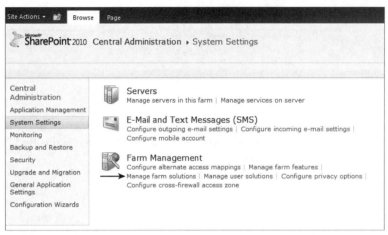

FIGURE 13-11

Deploying Solutions

To deploy a Solution using the user interface, we will start at the Solution Management page in Central Administration. The Solution Management page, shown in Figure 13-12, gives you an overview of all the Solutions in the farm, along with their deployment status and location.

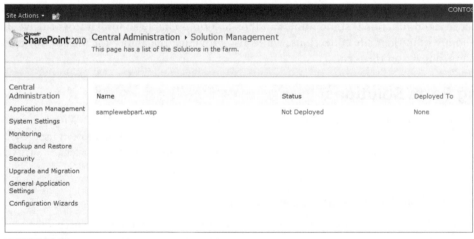

FIGURE 13-12

Here you can see that the `samplewebpart.wsp` Solution is not deployed. To deploy the Solution, click the Solution name. This will take you to the Solution Properties page, shown in Figure 13-13, which provides some basic information about the Solution, such as whether it contains web application resources, assemblies to be deployed in the global assembly cache (GAC), or a custom code access security policy, as well as previous operations and deployment status and deployment locations (if any).

FIGURE 13-13

This page also contains a link labeled Deploy Solution. Clicking this link takes you to the Deploy Solution page (see Figure 13-14). It is from this page that you take any actions needed to deploy the Solution, which include specifying when the Solution will be deployed and to where it will be deployed. By default, Solutions are set to deploy immediately and to all content web applications, or globally if no web application resources are present. Whether the Solution is set to deploy immediately or at a scheduled time, the actual deployment action is a job scheduled with the Timer Service. Given that, you can reasonably expect that the deployments will occur either close to now/immediately or near the time specified, but it will not be precise.

In addition to specifying when the Solution should be deployed, you also specify where. In cases for which no web application resources are part of the Solution, you will not have the option to specify where you would like to deploy the Solution. That's because any Solution that does not have a web application resource is considered to be a global Solution. Examples of web application resources might be SafeControl entries destined for the `web.config` file or an assembly that is headed for the web application's bin folder, to name only two. Once you specify the deployment time, and the location if applicable, all you have to do is click OK and the deployment process will be scheduled.

SafeControl entries provide the necessary registration information for custom code that allows it to be executed in the SharePoint farm. For example, these type of entries are necessary for any new Web Parts that are created.

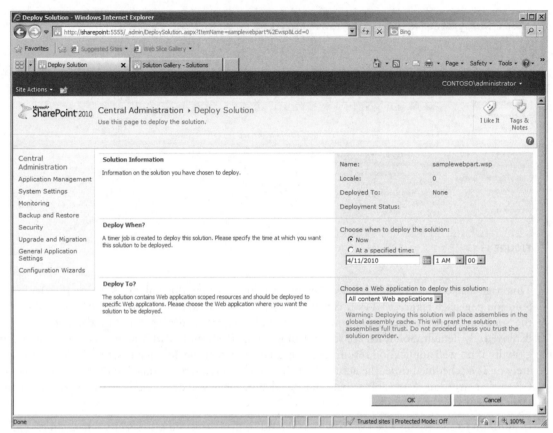

FIGURE 13-14

Retracting a Solution

To "undeploy" a Solution, simply retract it. After a Solution has been deployed, access the Solution Properties page, where you will see a Retract Solution link next to the Deploy Solution link, as shown in Figure 13-15. (Note that before the Solution was deployed, the link next to Deploy Solution was Remove Solution; this is covered in the next section.)

When you click the Retract Solution link, you are taken to the Retract Solution page, which is almost identical to the Deploy Solution page. Again, you specify when you want the action to take place and at what location. Once the information has been specified and submitted, the job will be scheduled for the retraction to occur.

Removing a Solution

You can remove a Solution only when the Solution is no longer deployed to a location. When the Solution is no longer deployed, a Remove Solution link appears next to the Deploy Solution link, where the Retract Solution link used to be (see Figure 13-16).

FIGURE 13-15

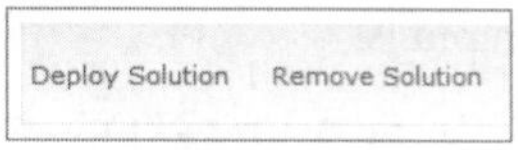

Deploy Solution | Remove Solution

FIGURE 13-16

When you click the Remove Solution link, you are prompted for confirmation; if confirmed, the Solution will be removed from the solution store. Remember that Solutions cannot be added to the solution store through the user interface, so before removing a Solution, ensure that you have or can get access to SharePoint via PowerShell if you will need to add the Solution back later.

Managing Farm Solutions via the Command Line

Like Features, the command line provides all of the administrative functions needed to manage Solutions. From the command line you can view information, add/remove/update Solutions from the solution store, and deploy/retract Solutions globally or to specific web applications.

View Solution Information

The PowerShell cmdlet `Get-SPSolution` enables you to view basic information about a Solution. Using the cmdlet without parameters, you can retrieve a list of all of the Solutions in the farm, as in the following example.

```
Get-SPSolution
Name                         SolutionId                            Deployed
----                         ----------                            --------
samplewebpart.wsp            177004f5-c0ba-4f54-80d0-e2afb78d4865 False
```

If no Solutions are in the solution store the cmdlet will return nothing.

You can retrieve a specific Solution by specifying a name, as in the following example.

```
Get-SPSolution samplewebpart.wsp
Name                         SolutionId                            Deployed
----                         ----------                            --------
samplewebpart.wsp            177004f5-c0ba-4f54-80d0-e2afb78d4865 False
```

There is no STSADM equivalent for this command.

Adding, Updating, and Removing Solutions

The capability to add and update Solutions is limited to the command line. There is no out-of-the-box functionality that will allow you do it any other way. Conversely, you can remove a Solution using either the command line or the user interface. The commands used to add, update, and remove Solutions are `Add-SPSolution`, `Update-SPSolution`, and `Remove-SPSolution`, respectively.

The following `Add-SPSolution` cmdlet is straightforward and takes a single parameter that indicates the path to the .wsp file:

```
Add-SPSolution C:\SampleWebPart.wsp
Name                         SolutionId                            Deployed
----                         ----------                            --------
samplewebpart.wsp            177004f5-c0ba-4f54-80d0-e2afb78d4865 False
```

The STSADM equivalent command is:

```
STSADM -o addsolution C:\SampleWebPart.wsp
```

Updating a Solution is a little more involved, as it can require knowledge of the Solution itself. The `Update-SPSolution` cmdlet has several parameters, some of which may be required depending on the contents of the Solution. In addition to the required attributes indicating the name of the Solution (`-Identity`) and the file path to the updated .wsp file (`-LiteralPath`), you may be required to specify one or more of the following:

➤   `-CASPolicies` — If the Solution contains a custom code access security policy

➤   `-GACDeployment` — If the Solution contains assemblies that have a target deployment location of the GAC (Global Assembly Cache)

➤   `-Time` — If you would like to schedule the update (the default is immediate)

➤   `-Force` — If you need to bypass some of the safety checks that SharePoint uses

The `Update-SPSolution` cmdlet returns no output:

```
Update-SPSolution SampleWebPart.wsp -LiteralPath C:\SampleWebPart.wsp
```

The STSADM equivalent is:

```
STSADM -o upgradesolution -name SampleWebPart.wsp -filename C:\SampleWebPart.wsp
```

Removing a Solution is straightforward. You simply call `Remove-SPSolution` with the name of the Solution. There is one catch to using the `Remove-SPSolution` cmdlet: The Solution being removed cannot be deployed globally or to a web application unless you are willing to use the `-Force` parameter (which, as you learned earlier, can leave things in an inconsistent state). The `Remove-SPSolution` cmdlet returns no output:

```
Remove-SPSolution SampleWebPart.wsp
```

The STSADM equivalent is:

```
STSADM -o deletesolution -name SampleWebPart.wsp
```

Deploying and Retracting Solutions

The commands used to deploy and retract Solutions are named using a different nomenclature; they are `Install-SPSolution` and `Uninstall-SPSolution`, respectively. The `Install-SPSolution` cmdlet has some of the same optional parameters as the `Update-SPSolution` cmdlet (`-GACDeployment`, `-CASPolicies`, `-Time`), and they serve the same purpose. The required parameters for the cmdlet are the name /identity of the Solution and the web application to which it should be deployed. The web application parameter takes one of two forms: The `-AllWebApplicaitons` parameter instructs SharePoint to deploy the Solution to all content web applications, whereas the `-WebApplication` parameter enables you to specify a specific web application for deployment. The `Install-SPSolution` cmdlet returns no output.

```
Install-SPSolution SampleWebPart.wsp -WebApplication http://sharepoint
```

The STSADM equivalent is:

```
STSADM -o deploysolution -name SampleWebPart.wsp -url http://sharepoint
```

To retract the Solution, use the following cmdlet:

```
Uninstall-SPSolution SampleWebPart.wsp -WebApplication http://sharepoint
```

The STSADM equivalent is:

```
STSADM -o retractsolution -name SampleWebPart.wsp -url http://sharepoint
```

Managing Sandbox Solutions

There are two aspects to managing Sandbox Solutions: the administrator's and the user's. An administrator will manage settings for Sandbox Solutions from Central Administration. The throttling capability can be managed from the Site Quotas and Locks page, which is accessed from the Configure quotas and locks link in the Site Collections management section (see Figure 13-17).

FIGURE 13-17

When you navigate to the page, notice the section toward the bottom, shown in Figure 13-18. Here you can set the maximum number of points that a Solution in the particular site collection can use. Points are a metric that is used to measure the resources used by a Solution. When the specified threshold is surpassed, the Solution will not function until the next day (after midnight).

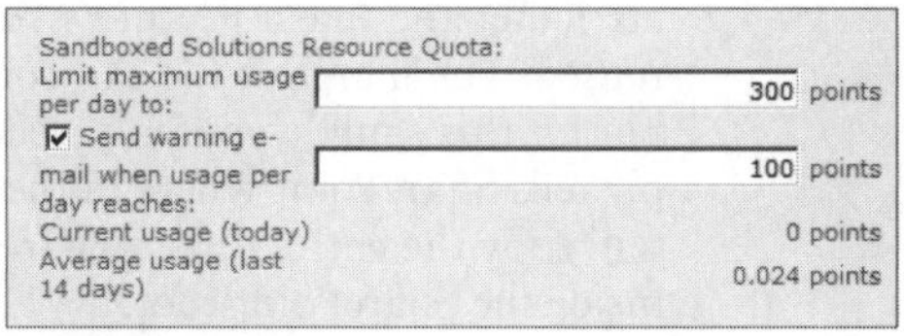

Sandboxed Solutions Resource Quota:
Limit maximum usage per day to: 300 points
☑ Send warning e-mail when usage per day reaches: 100 points
Current usage (today) 0 points
Average usage (last 14 days) 0.024 points

FIGURE 13-18

Creating Solutions

Creating a Solution in SharePoint is generally a straightforward task, but it can be a little tricky at times because you are editing text and XML files by hand (much like you did when creating a Feature). When creating a Solution by hand, you generally need to create two files: `manifest.xml` and `sharepoint.ddf`. The filename of the `.ddf` file is not important, but the filename of the manifest must be `manifest.xml`. As you have learned so far in this chapter, the manifest file is the instruction set that tells SharePoint what items are being provisioned to the file system and elsewhere when the Solution is added to the solution store, as well as what items should be provisioned when deploying to a web application.

The `.ddf` file, however, has not been covered yet. That's because this file does not concern SharePoint in any way. The `.ddf` file is merely a means to an end — and that end is the creation of the Solution files (aka the *cab* file). The `.ddf` file is an instruction file for the `MAKECAB.EXE` utility that comes with Windows;

and, no surprises here, it makes a cabinet file based on the .ddf file specified as one of the command-line parameters.

For this example, you will be packaging the Feature you created earlier in the chapter into your Solution.

1. Start by creating a directory structure to mimic your desired Solution file structure. For this Solution, the desired structure will be pretty basic. Begin by creating a directory named MySolution. The MySolution directory can be created anywhere on your system, but in this case you create it off of the c:\ drive.

2. Inside the MySolution folder, create a folder named MyBasicMenuItem (note that it is the same name that you created for your Feature). When that is complete, you should have a structure that looks like the one shown in Figure 13-19.

FIGURE 13-19

3. Now that you have the directory structure, you want to add a manifest.xml file to the MySolution directory. Place the following XML inside that file:

```
<Solution SolutionId="53C17DBB-EB22-48E2-B81D-B17EE68A9395"
          xmlns="http://schemas.microsoft.com/sharepoint/">
  <FeatureManifests>
    <FeatureManifest Location="MyBasicMenuItem\feature.xml"/>
  </FeatureManifests>
</Solution>
```

Notice that the manifest file contains a unique identifier in the form of the SolutionId attribute; and like a Feature's Id attribute, the SolutionId is a GUID and should not be reused. The manifest file can contain any of the items that are part of the Solution schema, but for this sample you only need to include a Feature manifest. The Feature manifest simply tells SharePoint where in the Solution file a Feature definition is located, and SharePoint will copy the entire directory from inside the Solution file to the TEMPLATE\FEATURES folder inside the SharePoint root.

4. Now that you have the manifest file created, you need to add the Feature files into your structure. Copy the feature.xml and elements.xml files that you created earlier in this chapter to the MyBasicMenuItem directory. Once those files are copied, your Solution structure is complete and should resemble what is shown in Figure 13-20 and Figure 13-21.

5. With the Solution structure and its contents complete, you are now ready to package the contents into a .wsp file. To do this, you need to create a .ddf file that you can reference when calling the MAKECAB.EXE utility. A .ddf file is straightforward; it basically contains a listing of the files and directories that need to be included/created in the file. You can visit the following link for more information on the MAKECAB.EXE utility: http://msdn.microsoft.com/en-us/library/bb417343.aspx# microsoftmakecabusersguide. Following are the contents of the .ddf file you will use to package your Solution. Name the file **MySolution.ddf** and place it in the MySolution folder you created at C:\MySolution.

```
manifest.xml

.Set DestinationDir=MyBasicMenuItem
MyBasicMenuItem\feature.xml
MyBasicMenuItem\elements.xml
```

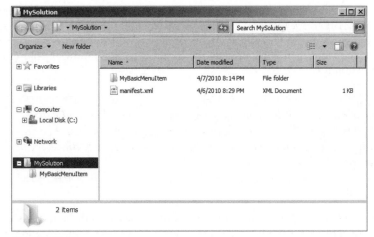

FIGURE 13-20

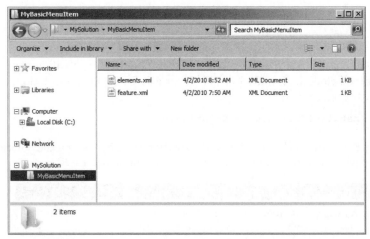

FIGURE 13-21

6. The file references are relative to the path from which the MAKECAB.EXE utility is run. Execute the MAKECAB.EXE utility from the C:\MySolution directory as follows:

```
C:\MySolution>makecab /F MySolution.ddf /D
CabinetNameTemplate=MySolution.wsp /D DiskDirectory1=wsp
Cabinet Maker - Lossless Data Compression Tool

805 bytes in 3 files
Total files:            3
Bytes before:           805
Bytes after:            376
After/Before:           46.71% compression
Time:                   0.09 seconds ( 0 hr  0 min  0.09 sec)
Throughput:             9.25 Kb/second
```

After the command completes successfully, you will have a newly created Solution file located at `C:\MySolution\wsp\MySolution.wsp`. Remember that this is just an ordinary Cabinet file, so if you want to view the contents of the file all you have to do is rename the file extension to `.cab` and then you can view the contents with Windows Explorer or your favorite compression tool.

 Before moving forward with this part of the example, ensure that the Feature from earlier in this chapter has been deactivated from any sites, uninstalled from the farm, and its directory removed from the `TEMPLATE\ FEATURES` *directory in the SharePoint root.*

7. With the Solution file created, you are ready to add the Solution to the solution store; and after that you can activate the MyBasicMenuItem Feature. To install the Solution, use the `Add-SPSolution` cmdlet you learned about earlier in the chapter:

```
PS C:\> Add-SPSolution C:\MySolution\wsp\MySolution.wsp
Name                           SolutionId                              Deployed
----                           ----------                              --------
mysolution.wsp                 4afc1350-f354-4439-b941-51377e845f2b    False
```

8. Once the Solution has been successfully added to the solution store, it will need to be installed/deployed before the Feature is available for use. To deploy the Solution, use the `Install-SPSolution` cmdlet:

```
PS C:\> Install-SPSolution MySolution.wsp
```

You can verify the status of the Solution in the solution store by visiting the Solution Management page in Central Administration, as shown in Figure 13-22.

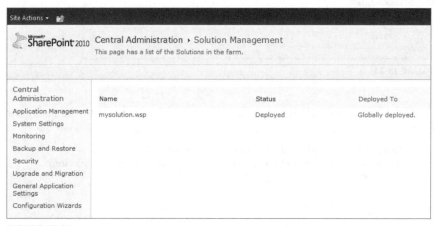

FIGURE 13-22

The only thing you have left to do after the Solution has been installed/deployed is activate the Feature for the appropriate site. You can use the same cmdlets that you used during the Feature example (`Enable-SPFeature`) or you can use the Manage Site Features user interface.

SUMMARY

As you have seen in this chapter, Features and Solutions are essential ways of adding functionality to SharePoint. While there are other ways you can add functionality to SharePoint, those methods are not recommended. Features and Solutions come with a host of useful options, tools, and commands that were designed to make your life as an administrator easier, and they should be used whenever possible.

14

Configuring and Managing Enterprise Search

WHAT'S IN THIS CHAPTER?

➤ SharePoint Foundation Search

➤ SharePoint Server and Search Server

➤ FAST Search

➤ All the bells and whistles of Search

Who doesn't need Search these days? In the early days of the Internet search engines were either unknown or considered weird things that the geeks (like the authors of this book) would use to find those cool nuggets of information on the Internet. You know the ones, like how to build your own BBS using 286s or what was the code for invincibility in Doom. Fast forward to today and now everyone and their dog uses search to explore the Internet. And it works great for finding anything and everything you can imagine. It even works just as well to find those Doom codes. Unfortunately, Internet search engines cannot reach inside your corporate network. And even if you buy one of those "Internet search devices" and put it inside your network they generally don't do a very good job of indexing (cataloging) your corporate data. That's because the online search engines are optimized for following the billions and billions of links on the Internet and determining relevancy that way. Your intranet doesn't have the same type of linking, so the results fall short.

The challenge is your users want to search, they even expect it. They don't want to dig through a file share to find their spreadsheet. Think about it; what is one of the most popular features in Outlook 2007 and 2010? The instant search capabilities of e-mail. Once again, people don't want to categorize and organize e-mail; they want to have a big pile that search can deal with. If only there was a way to effectively provide search results from the intranet.

Enter SharePoint 2010 in all of its Search glory (hear the trumpets?). For a lot of companies evaluating SharePoint, Search is one of the most compelling reasons to invest in the platform.

SharePoint Search not only does a fabulous job of indexing your SharePoint installation, but can reach out and index the rest of your enterprise. File shares, Exchange public folders, other web sites, line of business data, even Lotus Notes databases can all be added to your SharePoint index by the index servers. Servers? Yes, that's right; SharePoint 2010 has made some major architectural changes, including supporting multiple index partitions and even using multiple index servers to populate them. All of these changes extend SharePoint Server Search's upper limit to 100 million items. And if you want to go beyond that you should look at one of the new SKUs introduced, FAST Search. With FAST, having 1 billion items in the index becomes a real possibility.

A fancy new architecture and some new SKUs wasn't enough for the Search team. They have also invested quite heavily in updates to the user experience. Things like wild card searches, support for Boolean operators, and a refinement panel are all now available. You will also see a new Search-specific master page that provides more screen real estate, and AJAX support for rendering Web Parts — and extensible Web Parts this time around.

When you first begin to administer Search, it will seem very familiar as the Search administration pages that were introduced with MOSS 2007 at the infrastructure update have been retained in SharePoint 2010. But don't overlook this chapter, as there is gold in them thar hills. Several small nuggets have been added to give the administrator more control. Features like setting content priority, search of case sensitive locations, and a whole list of new reporting options will excite even the most jaded administrator. Also, watch for some changes: protocol handlers are out, BCS connectors are in, and introducing claims to the farm. This chapter will help you unlock all of the power of this favorite feature of both administrators and users.

THE DIFFERENT VERSIONS OF SEARCH

In Chapter 3 you learned that there are a lot of different SKUs for SharePoint. This chapter looks at the way Search functions in three key product sets:

➤ SharePoint Foundation Search

➤ SharePoint Server and SharePoint Search Server

➤ FAST Search Server 2010 for SharePoint and FAST Search Server 2010 for Internet Sites

 FAST Search Server 2010 for Internet Business is not covered in this book. While it shares a similar name, it is a standalone product that has nothing to do with SharePoint.

SHAREPOINT FOUNDATION SEARCH

SharePoint Foundation continues the proud heritage of Windows SharePoint Services as an environment that is easy to deploy, configure, and use. Once deployed, it gives users convenient access to the key features they need to start collaborating. Search is no exception to this. Foundation Search will index all of your SharePoint content and provide basic search results with very little effort. And once you enable the indexing, the administration and UI have no settings to configure — they just work. But don't gloss over this section; there's some important info here to help you get the most out of Foundation Search.

Setting Up Foundation Search

Foundation Search does need a little nudge from you, the SharePoint administrator, before it goes into auto-pilot mode for the next couple of years. You need to start the service and ensure that all of your content databases know to use the service you start. Follow these instructions to get things going:

1. Open Central Administration.

2. Under System Settings, click Manage services on server.

3. At the bottom of the list click Start (to the right of SharePoint Foundation Search).

4. Choose the proper service account; if you are doing a least privileged install, then you should create a new managed account for Search.

5. For Content Access Account, enter a username and password as shown in Figure 14-1. Keep in mind:

    ➤ This should be a unique, dedicated only for Search account.

    ➤ Always enter accounts in the form domain\username.

FIGURE 14-1

6. Make any changes to the Search Database screen that you need. For most options, the defaults will work well. Figure 14-2 shows an example.

7. If applicable, specify a Failover Server.

8. For Indexing Schedule, you need to choose the proper schedule for your needs. You will need to balance the need for more frequent index updates with the performance capacity of your server(s). If you are unsure, start with the default of once an hour and then adjust from there based on user feedback and system performance. Figure 14-3 shows a default schedule.

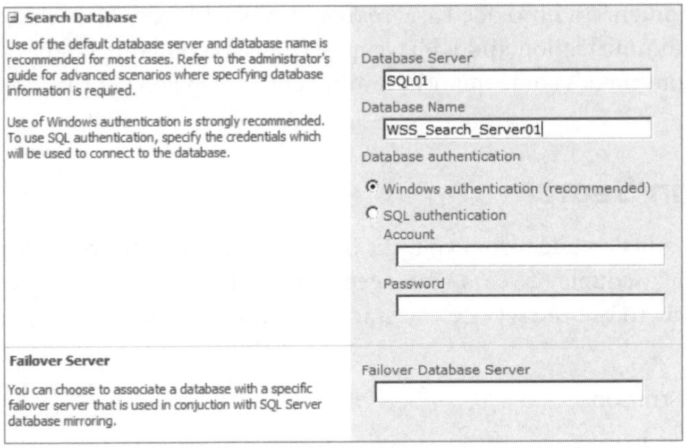

FIGURE 14-2

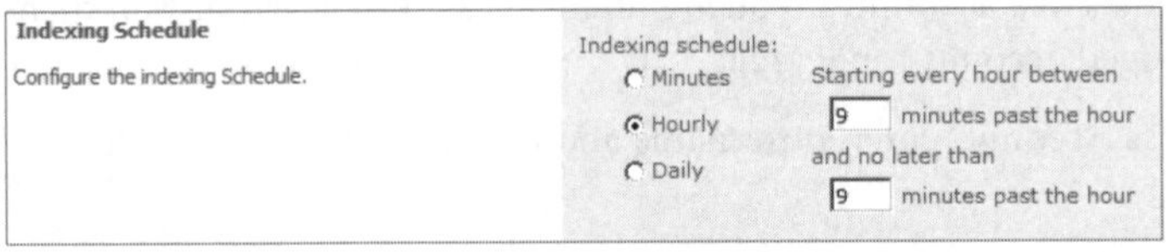

FIGURE 14-3

9. Scroll to the bottom of the page and click Start.

After a minute or two of processing you will be taken back to the Services on Server page and the status for SharePoint Foundation Search will be started. (You may see the name of the service updated to SharePoint Foundation Help Search.) Now, with Foundation Search running, you need to ensure that all of your content databases are assigned an indexer. The indexer will be the server on which you just started the Search service.

1. From Central Administration, go to Application Management.

2. Under the Databases section, click Manage content databases.

3. Click the name of your content database.

4. Scroll down the page to Search Server and select your index server from the drop-down.

5. Click OK. If you have multiple content databases you will need to repeat these steps for each of them.

With the Search Server value updated, the next time the indexer runs based on the schedule you defined earlier, the selected content database will be indexed. If, like your impatient authors, you do not want to wait, you are in luck. You can use the `stsadm.exe` command shown here to start a full crawl immediately:

```
Stsadm.exe -o spservice -action FullCrawlStart
```

With Foundation it is possible to have multiple index servers by simply start-ing the service on multiple servers. If you do this, you can then distribute the load by content database. And as long as you have your site collections spread across multiple databases, you have a solution that has distributed the load of indexing. Keep in mind, though, that this is not making your indexing high availability. If one index server goes down, then the other server will not pick up and respond to requests in its place. You would first have to set all of the content databases to be indexed by the surviving index server and then run another crawl.

Remember that you have to be in the SharePoint Root folder and then `\bin` to run the command. Or you can take the easier way and open the SharePoint 2010 Management Shell, since `stsadm.exe` is already in the path.

The message "Operation completed successfully." will return quickly. This does not mean the index is done, just that it is started. If you want to know when it is complete, you can monitor Event Viewer on the server. You will see an Event 85: "A master merge has completed for catalog Search." Now you have search results.

Search Results

Take a look at Figure 14-4 for an example of Foundation Search results.

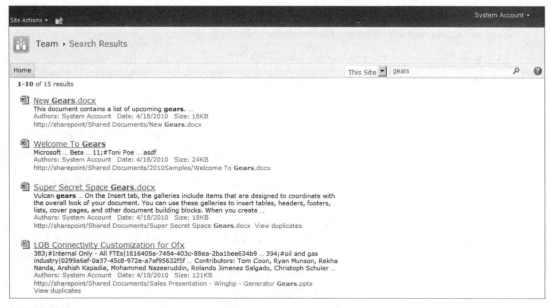

FIGURE 14-4

Here you can see the simplicity at work again. No tabs to navigate search result pages, no refinement panel to drill down based on metadata, no federated results, no advanced search options. Just good old-fashioned SharePoint content search results. To understand exactly where those results come from, Figure 14-5 shows an example hierarchy.

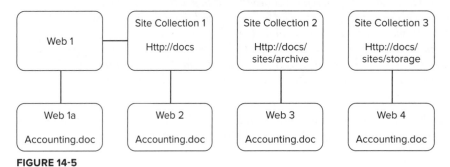

FIGURE 14-5

If you run a search for Accounting.doc from each of the locations shown in Figure 14-2, you will see the following results:

➤ **Site Collection 1** — You will get results from all four sites: Web 1 a, Web 2, Web 3, and Web 4.

➤ **Web 1** — You see the results only from Web 1 a.

➤ **Web 1 a** — You see the results only from Web 1 a.

➤ **Web 2** — You see the results only from Web 2.

➤ **Site Collection 2** — You see the results only for Web 3.

➤ **Web 3** — You see the results only from Web 3.

➤ **Site Collection 3** — You see the results only for Web 4.

➤ **Web 4** — You see the results only from Web 4.

From the root web at the root site collection, Search will return results from the entire web application. This is the only location that will return all results. Searching from any of the other locations will return results only from that spot in the site collection and down the tree, as shown when you are on Web 1 and you see results for Web 1 a but not Web 2. Web 1 and Web 2 are in the same site collection but they are in different branches.

Why does that root site collection get these magical powers? In fact, it isn't magic, just fun with query strings. Go to the root site collection and search for test. Then look at the URL `http://docs/_layouts/searchresults.aspx?k=test&u=http%3A%2F%2Fdocs`. If you break that down starting from the ?, you can see there are two parameters. The `K=test` parameter means "do a search for the keyword `test`." The & means there is another query string coming. The `u=http%3A%2F%2Fdocs` parameter translates to "return search results for URLs that start with `http://docs`." Because every web in the web application starts with `http://docs`, you got results from the whole web application.

Just for fun, what happens if you manually remove the `u=http%3A%2F%2Fdocs` *from the URL and press Enter? You get results from the entire farm. Very interesting; maybe you should add that to your secret SharePoint hacker notes.*

Remember that the search results you see, even if you are manipulating the query strings, will only be items to which you have permissions.

SECURITY TRIMMING

SharePoint will only show you search results for content you have access to, and for which SharePoint understands the security. This is called *security trimming*. For example, when you index your Windows file share, SharePoint can match your AD permissions on the share to the AD account you are logged into SharePoint with and trim your search results. But if you set up SharePoint to index an external source, maybe using a cookie or a secret anonymous back door, SharePoint doesn't understand these permissions. It will then show you all of the results for that source. If you need to have security trimming for these external repositories, you should look into developing a custom security trimmer. That is another one of those "developer" topics that is outside the scope of this book.

User Interface Features

A couple of user features are worth noting. Wildcard and Boolean searches work with Foundation and are covered in greater detail later in the chapter in the "SharePoint Server and Search Server" section. This means you can do searches like *share** or something fancy like *"Human Resources" AND policy*. This former does a search for anything that begins with *share*. The latter will search for anything that has the words *Human* and *Resources* together and has the word *policy* in it.

Foundation will automatically create *contextual scopes* for you. A contextual scope can help you narrow down your search results. It enables you to do a search of This Site or This List. To access the contextual scope for This List, navigate to the list and then do your search from the Search box at the top of the page. It will default to searching your current list. You can then click the drop-down menu to select This Site. Interestingly enough, if you look at the URL when you search This List, you will see the same `u=<your URL location>`, once again opening the door for some search results manipulation if necessary.

Site Search Administration

If you look for Search settings from the Site Settings page, you will not find much. The only search-related option is Search and offline availability. This setting allows you to control whether the current web is included in search results and how to handle any ASPX pages you may be using.

That's it; you are done with your tour of Foundation site search administration. Clearly, there are a lot of positives here; but keep reading. The next section covers SharePoint Server Search and Search Server. As you drool over those features, don't forget that the Express version of Search Server is free, and you can bolt it right on top of Foundation with ease. Wow — a free solution and a more awesome Search.

SHAREPOINT SERVER AND SEARCH SERVER

This section covers the following products:

- ➤ SharePoint Server 2010 Standard
- ➤ SharePoint Server 2010 Enterprise
- ➤ SharePoint Server 2010 for Internet Sites Standard
- ➤ SharePoint Server 2010 for Internet Sites Enterprise
- ➤ Search Server 2010 Express
- ➤ Search Server 2010

This is the money section of the chapter. Most readers probably have one of the aforementioned products or are bugging their bosses to get one. Foundation Search is great for getting started, but it lacks the level of control you may be hoping for. FAST Search is amazing, but its price tag can be a tough hurdle to overcome in smaller environments — so that leaves you here, in a very nice and comfortable place.

Search Server versus SharePoint Server

A very common question that first pops up in this conversation is "If I have SharePoint Server what do I get by adding Search Server?" The answer is simple: nothing at all. Search Server is only a subset of the functionality available in SharePoint Server and cannot be installed on an existing SharePoint Server installation.

An example of a key difference is that SharePoint Server can index Active Directory information about your users after you configure and do a profile import, which is covered in Chapter 17. While Search Server can index SharePoint sites, it does not have a mechanism for doing the profile import from Active Directory, so it is unable to index user information. We will note similar limitations on Search Server throughout the chapter; otherwise, assume Search Server can perform the covered feature.

The follow-up question is "What is the difference between Search Server and Search Server Express (SSX)?" Again the answer is simple: scale. SSX can only be deployed on one server in the farm. You cannot add more servers to make Search high availability. Search Server can be scaled in the same fashion as SharePoint Server, providing high availability for search and the capability to scale to somewhere in the ballpark of 100 million items. Yikes! Of course, that power comes at a price. Express is free, whereas regular Search Server is not.

Configuration and Scale

In Chapter 3 you took a good look at farm topologies and scale points. Noticeably absent from that chapter was a detailed discussion of Search. That wasn't author laziness; the Search team at Microsoft chose to build their own tools for configuration of their service application. To access this tool, go into Central Administration ➪ Manage service applications and click on your Search service application. At the bottom of the administration window you will see the screen shown in Figure 14-6.

FIGURE 14-6

Here you can view and modify all of the wonderful Search components. You want scale and high availability? Well, here it comes by the truckload. As indicated in the figure, there are four sections in the Search Application Topology: Admin, Crawl, Index Partition, and Databases. The first three are each addressed in the following sections. The various databases are associated with the various other components so they are discussed throughout as relevant.

Admin

In the Admin section of this screen you will find the Administration component. This is the boss of Search. It tells all of the other components and servers what to do by managing the topology. This component cannot be made redundant but that is okay; if this server is offline, then the rest of the servers will continue serving their role. No changes to the Search topology can be made while this server is offline. This server is responsible for such items as starting crawls, reassigning crawl tasks if it finds a crawler unavailable, and similar tasks.

To store all of this information, this component uses the administration database. This database has all of the search configuration information, so when you learn how to create a new crawl rule, this is where you will find it.

A final note about the Admin component: It cannot be readily moved to a different server, so it will live forever on whatever server you first provision it on. This might affect your planning if you are very particular about what is hosted on which server.

Crawl

You might think of the Crawl component as your indexer. This is the piece that will connect to your content, bring it down to the server, generate the index, and extract the necessary metadata. Notice I did not say the crawl component is your index server. This is because one crawl server can host multiple crawl components.

The big change from MOSS 2007 is that the crawler does not store a copy of your index. Instead, the crawler is stateless. It simply marks the content as crawled in the crawl database and then pushes the changes for the index off to the appropriate query server. Additionally, it will take all your search property information and push it off to the property store database.

The Crawl component keeps track of what it needs to crawl and what has been crawled in the crawl database, along with the crawl schedule and other details necessary for crawl operations. And the exciting part: You can have multiple crawlers assigned to the same crawl database. For you MOSS 2007 fans, this means no more relying on only one index server to build your index; now the sky is the limit regarding how much hardware you can throw at creating the index. Another benefit of the crawler having a dedicated database is it does not add load to the property database while crawling.

By default, if you have more than one crawl database associated with a service application, the load is spread between the databases by host name. Using host distribution rules, it's possible to specify that a certain host (think content source like `http://portal` or `\\server\share`) is specifically tied to a crawl database. And because you assign Crawl components to specific crawl databases, you can now ensure that you have your most powerful crawlers working on that database. You may even choose to have that crawl database on a dedicated SQL Server.

 If you have multiple databases and you want to find out what hosts are in what database, you can do that in the crawl log. Details about this cool capability follow later in the chapter.

Index Partition

You just learned about crawlers, and how they create an index but don't store the actual index. The storage is actually done by the Query component. The Query component is responsible for responding to search queries. When a user on a SharePoint site types "Cow" in the search box and hits Search, the web server hands that off to the Query Component server, more often than not just called the *query server*. The query server then digs through the index and property database to come up with a list of items for the search. Security trimming then takes place, and finally the web server renders those results back to the user.

If you want to add scale, you can actually divide the index into multiple partitions, or pieces (as described later in this chapter). That way, you can assign each partition to a query server. For example, if you have one million items in your index prior to partitioning, it might take one second to find your search results. If you divide that into two partitions and put each partition on its own query server, your index still has one million items in it but each query server has only 500,000 items in its partition to look through. Now your query results can be aggregated and returned to your browser in .5 seconds. That is how you scale the query servers for faster results.

An important threshold for an index partition is 10 million items, the maximum number supported in a partition. Also, remember that each time you want to introduce a new partition you need to introduce a new query server. Very little is gained, and more than likely you actually will decrease performance, if you have only one query server and you try to break your index up into two partitions with both living on the same query server. Unlike the crawl databases that are divided up by hosts, the index partitions try to maintain a very close balance. So each item is sent to an index partition based on a hash of its document id. This method provides better scale with query partitions.

Now you have two query servers but each one has half the index (its own partition). Next you need to configure redundancy. Partitions can also have mirrors. The mirror partition can be configured to respond to queries only if the primary partition is unavailable, or it can be a fully functional mirror that responds to queries. The balancing of query traffic is handled by the Search Admin component and is automatic. Typically, your index partition will be served by only one Query component, and configured with a failover mirror.

The final piece here is the property database. This database stores all of the metadata associated with the index partition(s) to which it is connected. An index partition is associated with only one partition database, but a partition database can be connected to multiple index partitions. This SQL Server database can become a bottleneck over time as it grows. If that is the case, you can either move the database to a bigger, badder SQL Server or reduce the number of partitions associated with it.

Adding a Server to the Search Topology

Consider a scenario in which the server farm is fully configured with everything, including SQL Server, running on one machine. Another server, ServerRC, has been purchased, has the same version of SharePoint Server 2010 Enterprise installed, and is added to the farm. The initial configuration wizard has been run on the new server. This started the appropriate services on this server. To add the second server to your Search topology, follow these steps:

1. Open Central Administration ⇨ Application Management ⇨ Manage service applications.

2. Find your search service application and open the Manage interface. Remember that Search topology is defined per Search service application if for some reason you have more than one.

3. Scroll down the page and click Modify (refer to Figure 14-3).

4. Click New, and from the drop-down select Crawl Component.

5. For Server, select your new server's name. For this example, it is ServerRC.

6. For Associated Crawl Database, select the Crawl Database from which you want this crawler to work.

7. If necessary, change the Temporary Location of Index. This location will only be used for creating the index updates before pushing them out, and it should remain relatively small. It will not increase in size as your index grows. Check out Figure 14-7 for an example and then click OK.

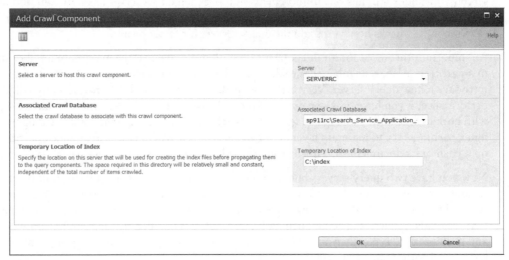

FIGURE 14-7

8. You are returned to the Manage Search Topology screen, where you will see Pending creation next to your new component. Click the Apply Topology Changes button at the bottom of the screen, unless you plan to also add the Query component in the next set of steps. If so, skip this step. A processing screen will appear and process for a few minutes. Once it is complete, you are all set.

You now have configured the two servers to share the load of the one crawl database. The next logical step is to configure your new server to also be a query server. With the second Query component, you will get a second index partition, so you will want to define a mirror for each of your two partitions:

1. Return to the Search administration screen and click the Modify Search Application Topology button.

2. Click New. From the drop-down, select Index Partition and Query Component.

3. For Server, select your new server.

4. For Associated Property Database, choose the database you want this query component to use. You haven't created any additional ones, so there should only be one item in the list.

5. Location of Index is an important consideration. This is where the physical index files will be stored on the server. Ensure that you have enough storage capacity in your chosen location. If at all possible, this should be on its own dedicated drive.

6. Leave the Set this query component as failover-only at its default setting of unchecked as illustrated in Figure 14-8.

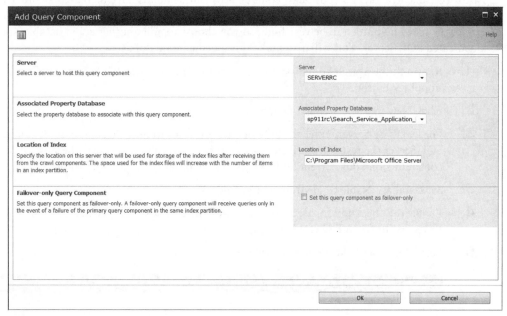

FIGURE 14-8

7. After you confirm your settings, click OK. This will automatically create Query component 2.

8. Now you have the two partitions you need to set up the mirrors. Hover over Query component 1, click the drop-down, and select Add Mirror.

9. For Server, choose the server that is currently not hosting this partition.

10. Confirm that your Index location is correct. (Remember that the C: drive is a bad place.)

11. Check the box for Set the query component as failover-only.

12. Click OK.

13. Repeat steps 8–12 for Query component 2.

14. You are returned to the Manage Search Topology screen. You will see Pending creation next to your new component. Click the Apply Topology Changes button at the bottom of the screen. A processing screen will appear and process for a few minutes. Once it is complete you are all set.

Now both servers are participating in serving Search queries and helping to crawl all of the content. You also have solid redundancy. In most environments the preceding actions will be sufficient. You have the capacity to crawl a lot of content in a reasonable amount of time and your Search components are high availability. Note that this does not include SQL Server. It is up to you to implement a high-availability solution for the databases, whether that is SQL Server clustering, taking advantage of the database mirroring support, or some third-party solution.

Scaling Up with Crawl Databases

Fast forward a little bit and your SharePoint deployment demands have increased again. You now want to add the crawling of your very large file server. Because of the size and nature of the data, you expect the crawling burden to be very high, so you choose to add another crawl database running on a dedicated SQL Server. You will also make this a dedicated database.

1. Return to the Search administration screen and click the Modify Search Application Topology button.

2. Click New and select Crawl Database.

3. For Database Server, enter the SQL Server you want to host this database. It can be the same SQL Server the rest of your farm uses, or if you're trying to add scale because of performance constraints on your current SQL Server, it may be a dedicated SQL Server.

3. Set Database Name to anything you would like.

4. Enable the checkbox for Dedicate this crawl store to hosts as specified in Host Distribution Rules, as shown in Figure 14-9.

5. Leave the other fields as is and click OK.

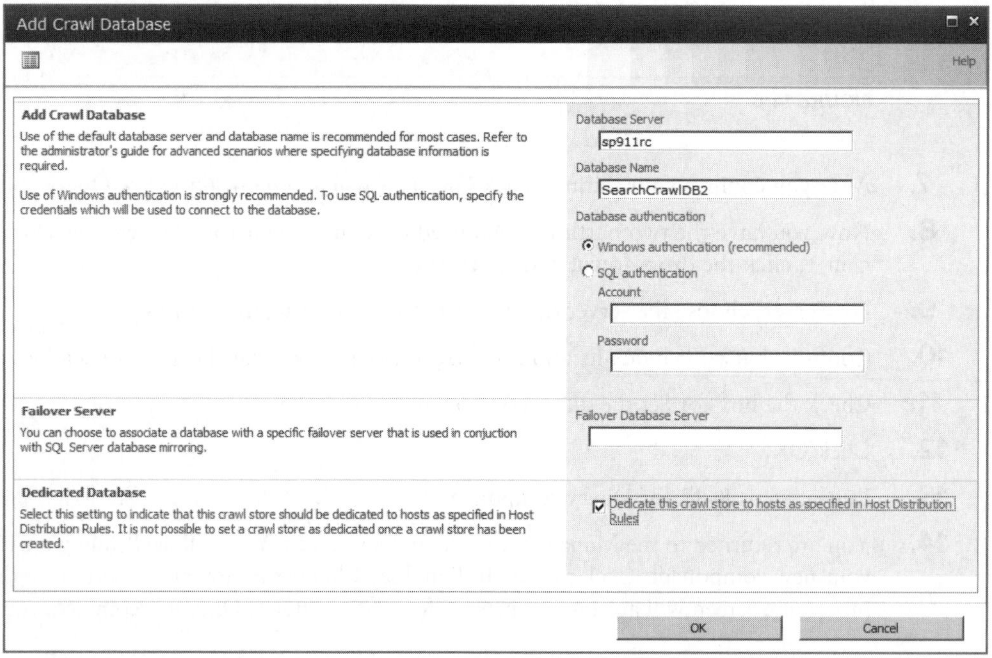

FIGURE 14-9

At the bottom of page you selected the option to Dedicate this crawl store to hosts as specified in Host Distribution Rules. This rule tells the database to not store anything that is not specifically added by a host distribution rule, which you will create in the next section. If you do not make this crawl database a dedicated database, then Search will automatically balance the load in this database with the other crawl database. Don't forget to click Apply Topology Changes once you are done making updates to your topology.

If you were to now go straight into adding a host distribution rule, you would not see your new crawl database listed. That's because you have not associated your new crawl database with a crawl component, making it useless. To fix this, you need to follow the previous steps for creating a new crawl component, but this time select the new crawl database you created. Do this on Server1 and ServerRC.

Adding a Content Source and Host Distribution Rule

In these steps you will add a file share content source and then add it to the crawl database you specified earlier:

1. Go to the Search Administration page.

2. On the left side of the page, click Content Sources.

3. Click New Content Source.

4. Specify a Name.

5. For Content Source Type, choose File Shares.

6. For Start Addresses, enter the UNC path to the share(s) you want to crawl — for example, `\\FileServer\Share`. Note that the search crawl account needs to have "read access" to the share(s) being crawled.

7. For Crawl Settings, the default is normally correct. Crawl the whole share, not just the root folder.

8. For now, leave the crawl schedule set to None. (Crawl schedules are covered later in the chapter.)

9. Content Source Priority gives you the opportunity to mark a content source as high priority. This way, if overlapping content source crawls are taking place, you can specify which should have priority.

10. Skip over Start Full Crawl. You will do that the old-fashioned way in a moment.

11. Click OK. Figure 14-10 shows a sample configuration.

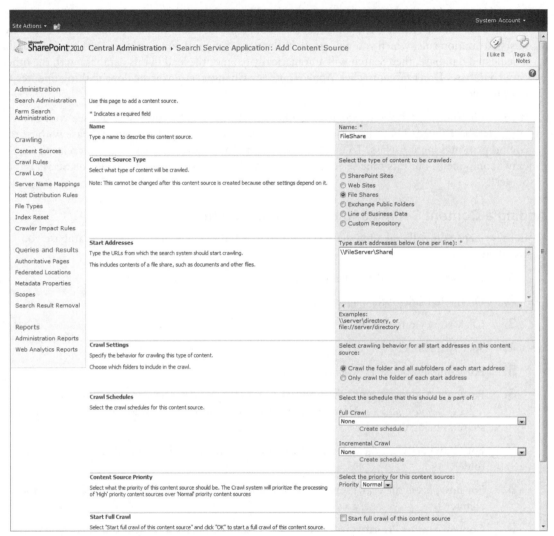

FIGURE 14-10

Creating a Host Distribution Rule

Now your file share content source is created. Before you start that full crawl, you need to set up your host distribution rule:

1. On the left side of the screen, click Host Distribution Rules.

2. Click the button for Add Distribution Rule.

3. For Hostname, enter FileServer. (Do not use slashes, just the actual host name. For example, if you had a content source of `http://portal.contoso.com`, your hostname would be `portal.contoso.com`. `FileServer` is used as the hostname here to keep up with the previous file share configured for `\\FileServer\Share`.)

4. From the Distribution Configuration, select the crawl database that you created in the earlier section.

5. Click OK.

6. Click Apply Changes. This will check to determine whether any content must be moved from one crawl database to another to comply with your new rule. If so, you are warned that this takes time and that any active/pending crawls will be paused for the duration of the move. Click the Redistribute Now button when you are ready to commit to the changes.

Starting a Crawl

With all of that done you are now ready to do a crawl of your content sources and watch them split up across the databases:

1. Click Content Sources on the left side of the screen.

2. Hover over File Share (your content source), click the drop-down, and select Start Full Crawl.

3. Click Search Administration on the top left.

4. Now you can get a nice can of Mountain Dew, and sit back and watch the crawler go.

Perfect! Now you have your entire file share in one dedicated crawl database with two dedicated crawlers. Keep in mind that your dedicated crawlers are still on the same crawl server as the other crawlers. If you needed more scale, you could introduce more servers into the farm, create new crawl components on those servers, and then assign those crawlers to this crawl database and remove the current two. Scaling up is as flexible as Silly Putty.

Matching Crawl Databases to Hosts

For the final trick when it comes to playing with crawl databases, you need to look at the crawl logs:

1. On the left side of the Search Administration page, click Crawl Log.

2. From the top menu bar, click Host Name.

   Behold! All of your crawl databases are listed, and each one shows what hosts are included in the database.

Take a gander at Figure 14-11. It doesn't reflect the preceding steps, but rather includes some interesting things to test your knowledge.

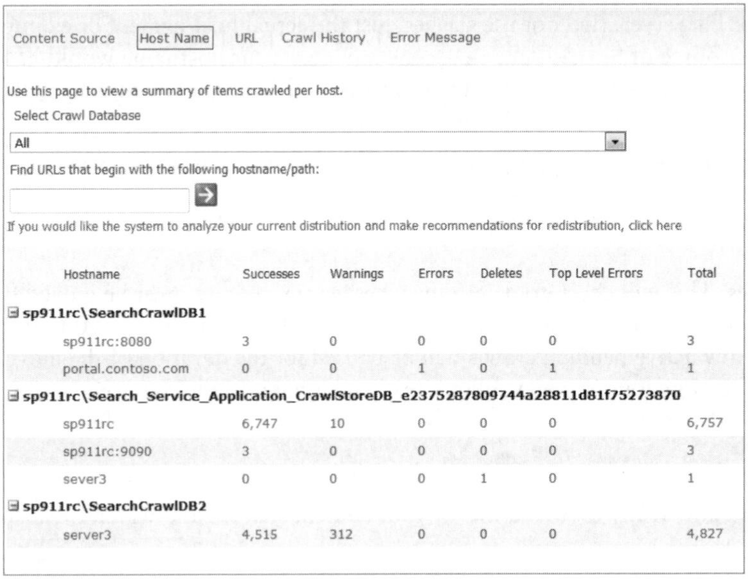

| Content Source | Host Name | URL | Crawl History | Error Message |

Use this page to view a summary of items crawled per host.

Select Crawl Database

| All | ▼ |

Find URLs that begin with the following hostname/path:

| | → |

If you would like the system to analyze your current distribution and make recommendations for redistribution, click here

Hostname	Successes	Warnings	Errors	Deletes	Top Level Errors	Total
⊟ **sp911rc\SearchCrawlDB1**						
sp911rc:8080	3	0	0	0	0	3
portal.contoso.com	0	0	1	0	1	1
⊟ **sp911rc\Search_Service_Application_CrawlStoreDB_e2375287809744a28811d81f75273870**						
sp911rc	6,747	10	0	0	0	6,757
sp911rc:9090	3	0	0	0	0	3
sever3	0	0	0	1	0	1
⊟ **sp911rc\SearchCrawlDB2**						
server3	4,515	312	0	0	0	4,827

FIGURE 14-11

There are three crawl databases. Search_Service_Application_CrawlStoreDB_ e2375287809744a28811d81f75273870 is the original crawl database that was created using the Initial Farm Configuration Wizard. The "Initial" in its name is a good reminder of its limitations. SearchCrawlDB1 and SearchCrawlDB2 were manually created using the Modify Topology button. SearchCrawlDB2 was configured to Dedicate this crawl store to hosts as specified in Host Distribution Rules.

Looking at the hosts, you can see content distribution at work. There are six content sources. Server3 has a host distribution rule to force it into SearchCrawlDB2. The remaining five were spread across the remaining two databases. Three of the content sources begin with sp911rc, but because they are separate sources, based on the port, they are divided accordingly.

At the top of the page there is also a link that says "If you would like the system to analyze your current distribution and make recommendations for redistribution, click here." Clicking that button on this server produces the report shown in Figure 14-12.

That's rather impressive. Search looked at how your hosts were currently distributed versus the amount of content in each and suggested changes to better balance the databases. Keeping perfect balance is very difficult, as each host has to reside in only one crawl database; but in an environment with many hosts, this can go a long way. At the bottom is a Redistribute Now button if you want to have the changes implemented for you. If you click this button, SharePoint will automatically configure new Host Distribution rules for you and update the crawl databases as necessary. Don't forget that all crawls are paused while this process runs.

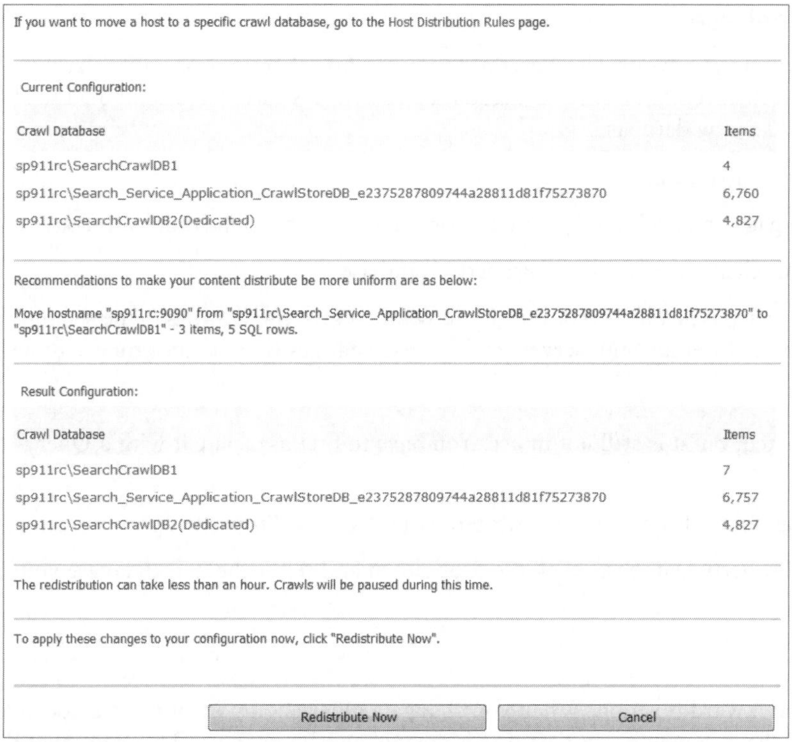

If you want to move a host to a specific crawl database, go to the Host Distribution Rules page.

Current Configuration:

Crawl Database	Items
sp911rc\SearchCrawlDB1	4
sp911rc\Search_Service_Application_CrawlStoreDB_e2375287809744a28811d81f75273870	6,760
sp911rc\SearchCrawlDB2(Dedicated)	4,827

Recommendations to make your content distribute be more uniform are as below:

Move hostname "sp911rc:9090" from "sp911rc\Search_Service_Application_CrawlStoreDB_e2375287809744a28811d81f75273870" to "sp911rc\SearchCrawlDB1" - 3 items, 5 SQL rows.

Result Configuration:

Crawl Database	Items
sp911rc\SearchCrawlDB1	7
sp911rc\Search_Service_Application_CrawlStoreDB_e2375287809744a28811d81f75273870	6,757
sp911rc\SearchCrawlDB2(Dedicated)	4,827

The redistribution can take less than an hour. Crawls will be paused during this time.

To apply these changes to your configuration now, click "Redistribute Now".

Redistribute Now	Cancel

FIGURE 14-12

Once the rules are created, you will be brought back to the Host Distribution Rules page. Here you will see a Redistribution status across the top of the page, with a percentage complete. The page will automatically refresh every 10 seconds while the distribution runs.

After everything is done you can return to the Auto Host Distribution page and let it check again. You will see something similar to Figure 14-13.

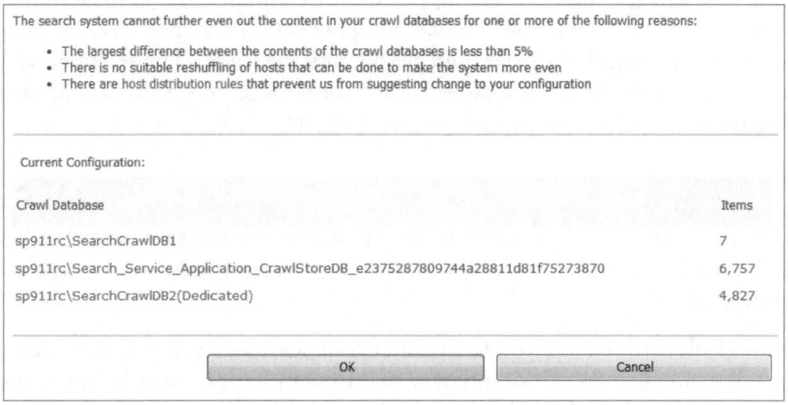

The search system cannot further even out the content in your crawl databases for one or more of the following reasons:

- The largest difference between the contents of the crawl databases is less than 5%
- There is no suitable reshuffling of hosts that can be done to make the system more even
- There are host distribution rules that prevent us from suggesting change to your configuration

Current Configuration:

Crawl Database	Items
sp911rc\SearchCrawlDB1	7
sp911rc\Search_Service_Application_CrawlStoreDB_e2375287809744a28811d81f75273870	6,757
sp911rc\SearchCrawlDB2(Dedicated)	4,827

OK	Cancel

FIGURE 14-13

Adding a Property Database

Now imagine that after looking at your query performance you find that your property database has become the bottleneck. Your overabundance of metadata and SQL disk I/O have combined to slow things down. Time to add a new database:

1. Open Search Administration.

2. Scroll down the page and click the Modify button under Search Application Topology.

3. From the toolbar, click New and select Property Database.

4. The defaults here are typically good, but if you want to give the database a new name or have it hosted on a different SQL server, make those changes now. Once you are done click OK.

Now the database is created, but it is still not in use. You have to first associate it with a Query component:

1. Click Query Component1, and from the drop-down select Edit Properties.

2. For Associated Property Database, click the drop-down and select the new database you created.

3. Click OK.

Now you are still in an awkward position. When you change a Query component to be associated with a new property database, a new index partition is created as a by-product. That's because the index partition is associated with a specific property database and cannot be changed. This means that you now need to reevaluate your index partitions. For example, the partition you just created doesn't have a mirror. You need to add a mirror to it. And the old partition is gone but the mirror of that partition is still floating out there associated with the wrong property database. Once you get everything straightened out, be sure to apply your changes.

The Search UI

After you put so much work into configuring your topology and then working through the administration interfaces, it's easy to assume you are done. Don't clock out quite yet. While the UI is a wonderful thing that will "just work," there is so much more you can get out of it with a little understanding and tweaking. Even more exciting is the fact that you can delegate this work to a site collection administrator. The following sections describe some of the ways you can tweak the UI.

The Search Box

Everyone knows how to use the Search box: You enter your search query, hit Search, and then get the results. Pretty straightforward — but as noted in the SharePoint Foundation section, you can do a handful of cool things in this box:

➤ **Wildcard searches** — Wildcards enable you to broaden your search by using symbols to represent characters. For example, you can simply type *Sh** to search for all words that begin with the letters Sh. Note that the wildcard search works only for the end of the word. You cannot search for *point only share*. Also, keep in mind that while wildcard search can help you find more good results, it is also going to return more bad results. Relevancy is greatly reduced when search for wildcards.

➤ **Boolean searches** — This searching method enables you to narrow or broaden your search using terms such as AND, OR, and NOT. It is important that you capitalize the Boolean terms properly. Also worth noting is the use of " " around phrases. For example, you could do a search such as *("Accounting Policy" or "Accounting Procedures") AND Termination*. This would return all search results that have either Accounting Policy and Termination or Accounting Procedures and Termination.

➤ **Range refinements** — You can do range refinements using the =, >, <, <=, and >= operators. The previous version of SharePoint accepted these operators to help you refine property restrictions; it just didn't do it very well. Who knew those could be used for something more than making emoticons?

➤ **Property searches** — For years we have had a property search capability but it was apparently secret. In the search box, you can type *title:"Vacation policy"* or *author:Shane* and do a search on specific properties. Any of the Managed Metadata properties can be used. They are discussed later in the chapter.

Relevancy Improvements

Every iteration of a good search engine improves the magic that drives search results, and SharePoint is no exception. Although most of the updates are closely guarded secrets, there are a couple that can be shared.

Phrase matching support has been added. For example, when you search for *sales presentation*, results with sales and presentation together will be ranked higher than results with sales and presentation in the document but not together.

Clickthroughs count. A clickthrough is the way the search page captures your activity. When you do a search and get back results, Search continues to monitor your activity by noting which links you click. For example, if you search for *policy*, and after reviewing the list of files you click on the third document, SharePoint makes a note of that. Over time, if people searching for *policy* continue to click on the third document, SharePoint will adjust that document and return it higher in the results. This is a pretty powerful feature, driving better search results as your users simply do their normal activities.

In Chapters 16 and 17 you learned about different ways of adding metadata to documents. One of the features was social tagging. Whether it is on pages, documents, or entire sites, tags are a help to Search. Search looks at these social tags and gives increased weight to tags, especially if the same content is tagged repeatedly with the same tag. Once again, Search knows your users matter and it updates its indexes to reflect their activities.

Refiners

When you do a search, notice the list of properties on the left-hand side of the page, as shown in Figure 14-14. These are called *refiners*. For example, you can click on Word under Result Type and your search results will be narrowed down to only include Word documents. You could then click on a specific author to further refine your results. This list of refiners is built from the first 50 search results, meaning it is not all inclusive if you have a large set of results. A small note if you were using FAST Search — the refinement panel is based on all the search results, not just the top 50.

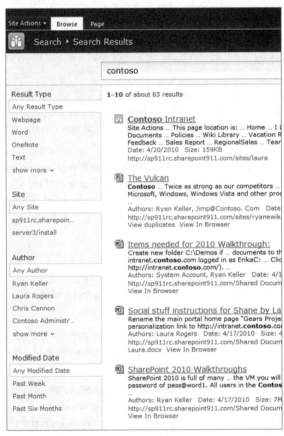

FIGURE 14-14

Search Alerts and RSS Feeds

Sometimes you might need to do the same search repeatedly. And while the search page is pretty cool and you enjoy checking it every day, repeating a search may not be the best use of your time. A better option would be to click the search alert icon (labeled 1 in Figure 14-15) to get search alerts. This way, every time the search results are updated for your query, SharePoint will send you an e-mail. You could also use the RSS Feed icon (labeled 2 in the figure) to subscribe to an RSS feed of your search results.

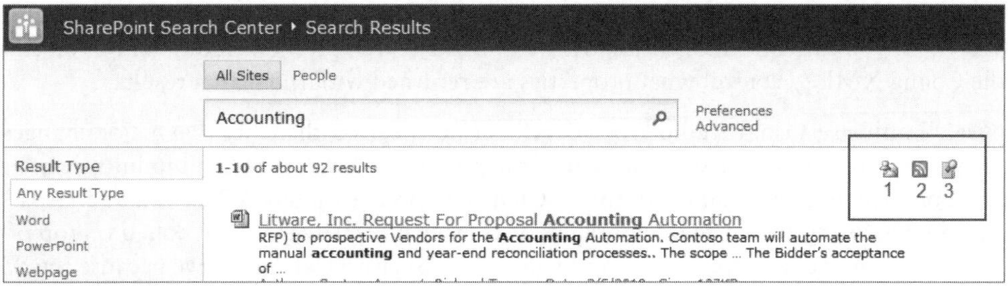

FIGURE 14-15

Windows 7 Desktop Search Add-on

If you perform your search from a Windows 7 machine you will see the Desktop Search icon (labeled 3 in Figure 14-15). Clicking this icon will add a search connector to your Windows 7 desktop Search. With this connector you can search your SharePoint site right from your Windows machine. (You will see your SharePoint site in Explorer under Favorites.)

View in Browser

If you have the Office Web Applications installed (see Chapter 19), the View in Browser link will appear, giving your users the option to quickly view the document in the browser without having to download it. Functionality previously only available with third-party hardware now just works out of the box with no effort on your part.

Query Federation

Query federation enables you to add search results from any OpenSearch-compliant search engine to your SharePoint site. These results appear in a separate Web Part on the right-hand side of the screen and are not intermixed with your SharePoint results. Also, this Web Part is asynchronous by default, which means it will load independently of the rest of the page, so you aren't waiting on it to get your SharePoint results. For example, you might set up a special search page for your research group that searches your SharePoint indexes and Bing at the same time, helping the group to discover information quicker and with one search instead of two.

This federation is also very useful in scenarios where a company is geographically dispersed and has multiple SharePoint farms. Often these companies want to have search results from all farms but don't want the hassle and expense of having SharePoint crawl across the WAN. Instead, they set each farm to crawl itself, and then use Search Federation to display results from both farms on the same page. Remember, though, these are two separate sets of results and will not be combined.

Extensible Web Parts

Extensible Web Parts sounds an awful lot like a developer topic, and for the most part it is, but as a good admin you should be familiar with some of the options.

The first option is done through the browser. By editing the page and then modifying the search results Web Parts, you can introduce custom XSLT to make search prettier. Additionally, you can modify the Config XML to control what properties are returned with the search results.

From a pure, "I only use Visual Studio type" developer perspective, there are two major changes to note. First, most of the search Web Parts are now public, so developers can tap into them and extend functionality. A great example of this is what the FAST team did. When you add FAST Search, you are just using the normal SharePoint Search Web Parts with FAST bolted on top of them. This reduces their development time and your administrative learning curve because the Web Parts have a very familiar feel to them. The second thing to note is that there are no more hidden query objects. In SharePoint 2007, the communication between the Web Parts was not accessible by developers, so if they wanted to add a Search Web Part to the page they would have to perform their own query for search results instead of taking advantage of the results being used by the out-of-the-box Web Parts.

Did You Mean...?

The "Did you mean..." feature offers suggestions based on what you have searched for. Figure 14-16 shows the user searched for *sahrepoint*, and even though there were no results, Search suggested *sharepoint*. If you click the link, the search will be re-run with *sharepoint* in place of *sahrepoint*. The downside of this functionality is that it isn't configurable.

> *Oddly, if you are trying to find this Web Part in the list, look for Search Summary.*

FIGURE 14-16

Search Suggestions

As shown in Figure 14-17, Search will offer suggestions as you type. It "learns" to offer these auto-complete suggestions over time by tracking the searches of users.

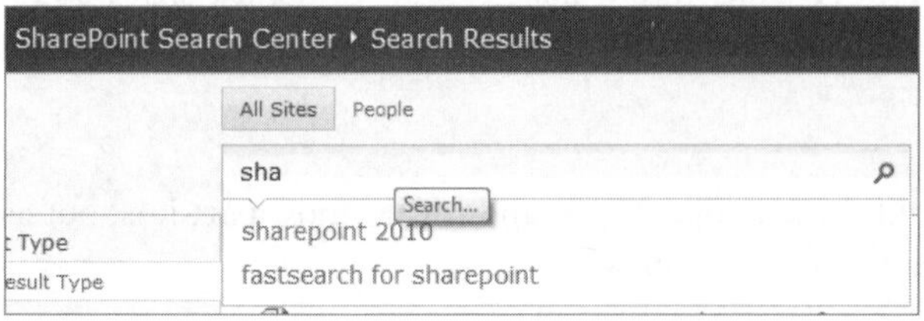

FIGURE 14-17

Search Administration

There are two places to administrate SharePoint Search. At the site collection level, site collection administrators have a set of tools and settings they can make for just their site collection. At the service application level you can also administrate settings that affect all site collections associated with the service application.

At the Site Level

When you specify someone as a site collection administrator, you give them a world of new buttons and knobs to operate. An important set of these knobs is for Search. These knobs are all located under the Site Collection Administration section on the Site Settings page.

Search Settings

The first option is Search settings. From Search settings you can specify what Search Center to use for the site collection, how the drop-down box should behave, and what search results page you would use if you did not have a Search Center defined. Interestingly enough, for most templates you do not get a Search Center by default, so even though you have SharePoint Server you are using the Foundation Search UI. Yucky. Let's look at how to fix that:

 If you are unfamiliar with the term, a Search Center is a special SharePoint web template customized for search. It is preconfigured with a search page, a search results page, and it uses a special master page. This master page maximizes the screen space for displaying search results.

1. Create a new site collection using the Team Site template at `http://yourwebapp/sites/st`.
2. Open the site collection as a site collection administrator.
3. Click Site Actions ⇨ New Site.
4. Choose Basic Search Center as the template.
5. Set the name to Search Center.
6. Set the URL to SearchCenter.
7. Click Create.

Now you have a Search Center ready to use; it just needs to be connected:

1. Click Site Actions ⇨ Site Settings.
2. Under Site Collection Administration, click Go to top level site settings.
3. Under Site Collection Administration, click Search settings.

4. For Site Collection Search Center, select Enable custom scopes (such as "All Sites") by connecting this site collection with the following Search Center:, and enter **/sites/st/SearchCenter** in the box.

5. For Site Collection Search Dropdown Mode, select Show scopes dropdown.

6. Confirm that your settings match those in Figure 14-18 and then click OK.

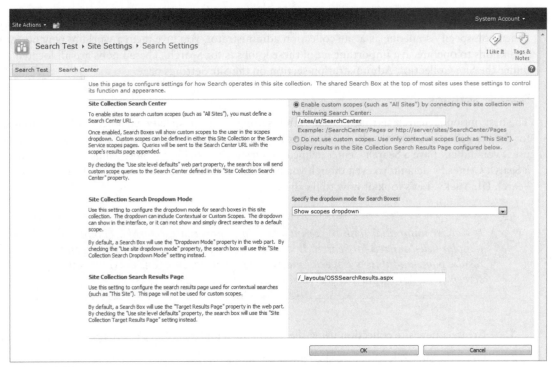

FIGURE 14-18

7. Test it out by navigating to the root of your site collection and doing a search from the box at the top of the page. If you get search results from the Search Center you just created, you are all set.

 If you try to create an Enterprise Search Center using the previous steps you will get an error message. To use this template you must first activate the site collection feature SharePoint Server Publishing Infrastructure.

Search Scopes

The next setting in the Site Collection Administration menu is for Search scopes. Scopes are covered later in the chapter in the "Queries and Results" section. This is the menu you use to determine what global search scopes you will use in your site collection or to create your own specifically for this site collection.

Search Keywords

From the Search Keywords screen you can add a keyword and then associate best bets with the keyword. This is best explained with an example. You get back from a company trip to Hawaii for the SharePoint is Awesome Conference and try to find the blank expense report. You open SharePoint and do a search for "expense report" and get about 5,000 results. Yikes. Somewhere in there is the blank report along with the HR policy covering what is acceptable for reimbursement. Good luck finding those needles in the haystack.

To avoid this, you can set up a keyword called "Expense Report." With the keyword you can add a definition like "You have three days to submit these to accounting with your manager's signature to get reimbursed." Then you can associate best bets with this keyword and definition.

A *best bet* is a link to content that is most likely to be what the searcher is looking for. So you would have best bets to the blank expense report and the policy file. Now when you search for "Expense Reports," you will see something similar to Figure 14-19. Note that keywords and best bets are defined per site collection, which might alter your planning for their use.

FIGURE 14-19

At the Service Application Level

The Search Administration page on the Search Service Application is your one-stop-shop for all things search-related. On this page, you'll find the System Status section, which provides you with a report of your search status. Below the System Status report is the Crawl History. This provides you with a report of the most recent crawls, including what was crawled, what type of crawl it was, when it started and ended, how long it took, and the number of successes or errors encountered during the crawl. Below the Crawl History is the Search Topology section, which gives you an overview of the various Search components in your farm. Figure 14-20 shows the Search Administration page.

FIGURE 14-20

Along the left side of the Search Administration page are links for setting up the different configuration options for Search in your farm. These links are divided into four categories: Administration, Crawling, Queries and Results, and Reports. The following sections briefly cover each of these links.

Administration

The Administration category contains two links. The first link, Search Administration, as you may guess, is a link to the Search Administration page. When navigating through the Search settings, this link can take you back to the home page for administering Search. The second link, Farm Search Administration, takes you to the high-level administration page for setting up components of the farm's Search.

Crawling

This is where you will be spending the bulk of your time as you configure the Search Service Application to crawl content in your farm, as well as check the status of previous crawls, set up crawl rules, manage your index, and configure the file types that should be crawled, among other options. The following list outlines the available Crawl settings.

➤ **Content Sources** — SharePoint can't crawl what it can't find. Use the Content Sources link to define what SharePoint will be crawling. Lucky for you, SharePoint was nice enough to auto-matically create a default content source for you, which includes all your existing SharePoint web applications, as shown in Figure 14-21. (Any web applications added after Crawl is con-figured are also automatically added to this default source.)

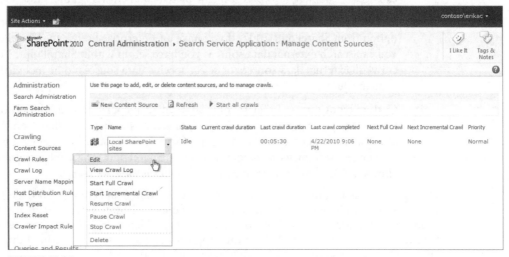

FIGURE 14-21

You can create a new content source by clicking the New Content Source link on the tool-bar. You are not limited to crawling SharePoint sites, however. SharePoint 2010 enables you to create six different types of content sources:

➤ **SharePoint sites** — You can set up a separate content source for SharePoint sites other than the default content source. This can be helpful if you need to create separate crawl schedules for different web applications.

 If you are using claims authentication on the SharePoint web application, the claim is stored. If you are using NTLM, the ACL is stored. The exception to this is when the ACL exceeds 64KB; in this case, Search will automatically convert it to a claim to avoid problems with an oversized ACL.

➤ **Web sites** — Non-SharePoint websites can be crawled and indexed by SharePoint Search, and made part of the Search index. For instance, maybe your organization uses SharePoint to host its intranet, but the public-facing Internet site is a traditional website. Because useful information is also posted on the public site, you could set up a crawl source of that website to include in SharePoint Search results.

➤ **File shares** — SharePoint Search isn't limited to crawling only websites. You can also provide a path to a shared network drive to index the files and content there. This can be helpful for organizations that have a large amount of content on a network share. If a wholesale migration of that content into SharePoint isn't practical or feasible, crawling the share can be a handy way to provide easier access to those files.

➤ **Exchange public folders** — SharePoint knows how to talk to Exchange to index public folders. In addition, Exchange 2007 and 2010 have change logs that SharePoint can access, enabling it to perform true incremental crawls against these sources.

➤ **Line of business data** — This option is similar to the Business Data content source option from SharePoint 2007. If you have an Enterprise license for SharePoint 2010, you can search external data sources you have set up within SharePoint. You can crawl all external data sources or select specific data sources to be included in the content source.

➤ **Custom repository** — In SharePoint 2010 you can connect to additional content sources by creating your own custom connectors. Protocol handlers from MOSS 2007 have been deprecated and replaced with these connectors. The best part is that the connector framework is common across SharePoint. The same technology that allows the BDC to connect to external sources is used by Search.

Once you've specified the name of your new content source and configured the options, you are essentially ready to go. You can also create a crawl schedule when you create the content source, or set it later. Any content source can be edited later by clicking its name on the Content Sources page (or by clicking the drop-down around it and selecting Edit). You can't change the content source's type once it has been set, however.

From this page, you can also start the crawls of your various content sources by clicking the drop-down menu for the content source and selecting the type of crawl you want to perform. During a crawl, you can monitor the progress from this page as well.

➤ **Types of crawls** — Setting up a crawl schedule is one thing, but your Search Service is just going to sit there twiddling its thumbs until it knows when it's supposed to do something with those content sources you created. That's where a crawl schedule comes in handy. Setting a crawl schedule tells SharePoint when and how often to crawl a content source, and what type of crawl to perform.

Two types of crawls can be scheduled — a *full crawl* or an *incremental crawl*. A full crawl is one that crawls every bit of content it can find on the web service, and keeps crawling until there is nothing left to crawl. Because full crawls cover all content in a content source, they can be fairly lengthy — especially if you have a lot of content. Conversely, an incremental crawl is generally much faster. It crawls only content that has been changed since the last crawl was performed. It does this by referencing the change log. Incremental crawls typically run much more often than full crawls.

➤ **Setting a crawl schedule** — When creating or editing a content source, you can set the crawl schedule at the bottom of the page. If no crawl schedule is set, click one of the Create schedule links. You can choose from daily, weekly, or monthly (see Figure 14-22). The specific settings vary according to the option chosen. You can get pretty granular when setting up a crawl schedule. Full and incremental crawls can be run on different schedules. A general rule of thumb is that you want to set your crawl to run during a low-usage time for the sites, such as very late at night or on a weekend, when traffic to the site is typically low, especially for a full crawl. Incremental crawls can run more frequently, and it's usually recommended to do so to keep the search results fresh. Also, it's best to avoid running crawls during backup times to prevent unnecessary server strain.

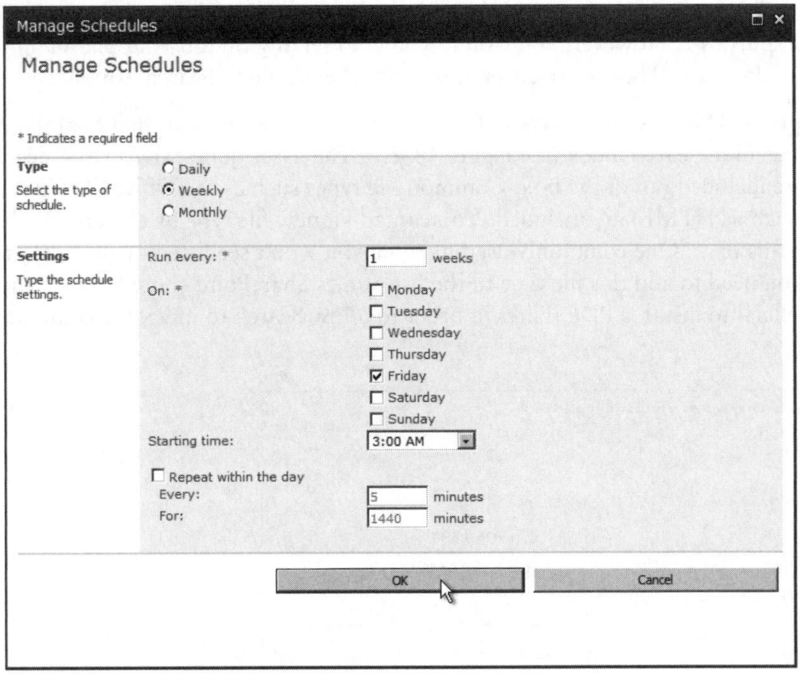

FIGURE 14-22

➤ **Crawl rules** — By default, Search is eager to go out and crawl everything it can find. That's awfully generous of it, but you may want to restrict some places. You can do this by setting a crawl rule to exclude content. (Crawl rules can also be used to include specific content in an area that has otherwise been excluded from search.) Once you tell SharePoint which URL it should exclude (or include) and set a few additional parameters, you will have a newly created crawl rule. You can even set up a crawl rule to crawl a specific set of content with an account other than the default search account. This can come in handy if you need to crawl a site using basic authentication — simply set up a crawl rule to use the basic authentication account to search the site.

➤ **Crawl log** — The crawl log is a detailed report of the crawl activity in your farm. If you notice your search results seem a little "off," you should head to the crawl log to see what's going on. SharePoint keeps track of all the items it is able to reach successfully, which content it had trouble reaching, and which areas it could not reach. You can use the links at the top of the Crawl Log page to filter and drill down into your crawl results.

➤ **Server name mappings** — Server name mappings are used when search results display a path to a file that may cause access issues, or when the actual location of a file pulled into Search shouldn't be revealed to users. For instance, you may have a shared drive mapped but do not want to display the actual path to that drive for security reasons. You could set up a mapping to change how SharePoint displays the path to that file to users performing the search.

➤ **Host distribution rules** — In farms with more than one Search database, you can use this page to set a specific host for a crawl database. You can use this for optimization or organization purposes. However, you won't be able to set any rules if your SharePoint farm has only one database. These were covered in the earlier section "Search Topology."

➤ **File types** — This lists all the types of documents (by file extension) that SharePoint is set up to include in its search index (see Figure 14-23). The list is quite extensive — nearly 50 file types are included out of the box. Common file types such as the Office file types and web file types (such as HTML) are included. You can add a new file type by clicking the New file type link on this page. One commonly used file type you won't see listed by default is the PDF file type. You need to add this file type to the list of files SharePoint should index (and it would be beneficial to install a PDF iFilter in order to allow Search to index the contents of PDF files).

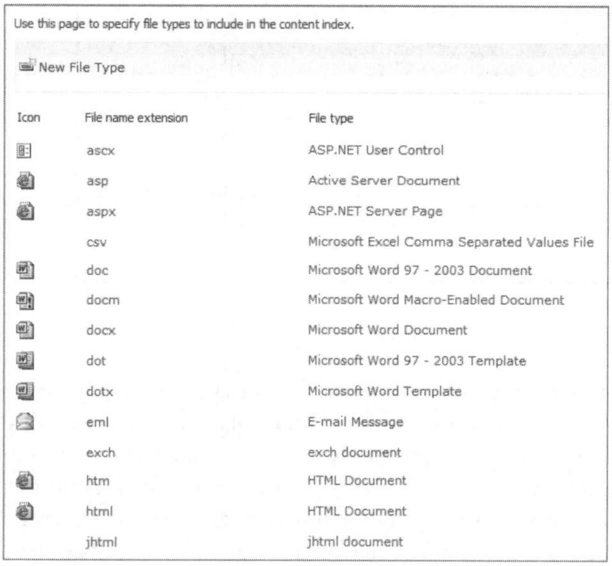

Use this page to specify file types to include in the content index.

New File Type

Icon	File name extension	File type
	ascx	ASP.NET User Control
	asp	Active Server Document
	aspx	ASP.NET Server Page
	csv	Microsoft Excel Comma Separated Values File
	doc	Microsoft Word 97 - 2003 Document
	docm	Microsoft Word Macro-Enabled Document
	docx	Microsoft Word Document
	dot	Microsoft Word 97 - 2003 Template
	dotx	Microsoft Word Template
	eml	E-mail Message
	exch	exch document
	htm	HTML Document
	html	HTML Document
	jhtml	jhtml document

FIGURE 14-23

➤ **Index reset** — Generally speaking, SharePoint Search works just the way it should. However, sometimes a change is made on the SharePoint server that prevents Search from working correctly, or it just isn't behaving the way it should. Or, maybe you're noticing more errors than successes in your crawl logs. In these cases, you may need to reset the search index, which completely deletes everything in the index, including the search property database, until a full crawl is run. Usually you would want to use this as a last resort, especially if performing a full crawl takes a massive amount of time in your environment.

This page also gives you an option to deactivate search alerts during the reset. This prevents you from flooding your users' in-boxes with search alerts (if they've signed up for them) as the site is re-indexed. You'll need to reenable the alerts once the site has been recrawled. (This is done from the Search Administration page. In the System Status section, click the Enable link next to Search alerts status.)

➤ **Crawler impact rules** — SharePoint provides administrators with a way to control the impact that Search has on the server through the use of crawler impact rules. Even on powerful hardware, the search process can heavily tax a server or even the farm, depending on how your farm is configured. Although it is best to run crawls at times when very few people are using the server, this isn't always possible. That's where crawler impact rules can come in handy. If you have a heavily used site, you can tell SharePoint to throttle itself back a little when crawling that site. Conversely, if you have an extremely large number of documents on which you want to perform a full crawl as fast as possible, you can use crawl rules to help with this too.

You have a couple of options when setting crawl impact rules. You can increase or reduce the number of simultaneous documents requested by search at a time. This can impact server performance, so pay attention to how SharePoint behaves when changing this setting. If you notice significant slowdown during a crawl, you may want to lower the number of documents requested. You also have the option to request one document at a time and specify an amount of time for SharePoint to wait before requesting the next. Although crawl times will be significantly increased, server impact is negligible.

Crawler impact rules can also be quite helpful when you are crawling content that is located outside of SharePoint. Because you are a savvy SharePoint administrator, you have configured your SharePoint indexing server with a lot of muscle. This can't necessarily be said for every server in your enterprise. Many a server has been brought to its knees when a multi-threaded indexing process is unleashed on an unsuspecting WEB server. In this case, use crawler impact rules to limit the number and frequency of the external server requests.

Queries and Results

The Queries and Results section in the Search Administration page's quick launch lets you configure settings related to how Search queries are handled and how results are displayed. You can use this area to fine-tune your users' search experience. Available settings include the following:

➤ **Authoritative pages** — Administrators can specify which pages in the site are the most authoritative, or contain the most relevant information for which users are likely to be searching. You can specify as many authoritative pages as you want, and even assign pages as the most authoritative, second-most authoritative, and third-most authoritative. Likewise, you can even specify pages that should be demoted in search results. SharePoint's search results are calculated using these pages, and the way it displays results are weighed against the pages' content and the level of authoritativeness assigned to them.

➤ **Federated locations** — A feature introduced to SharePoint 2007 with the Infrastructure Update was the capability to incorporate federated locations into SharePoint search results pages. This feature has been carried over to SharePoint 2010 and is available out of the box. Setting up federated locations enable a user's query to be performed on multiple, alternative sources along with the standard SharePoint search index. Internet search engine results can be incorporated into the results, as well as databases and search scopes defined for SharePoint. This can give users richer results and provide them with more information than they would otherwise receive.

Search connectors can be downloaded from Microsoft and imported as a new location in the federated locations. In addition, you can specify triggers for when federated search content should display in the results, and set patterns and prefixes that narrow the results to more specific options. Numerous options and configurations are available when using federated search locations, a topic beyond the scope of this section.

➤ **Metadata properties** — Nearly all content in SharePoint has some sort of metadata associated with it, which Search can use when ranking content for display on the results page. Metadata is also used when filtering search results (e.g., by document type or author). The metadata properties link in Search Administration shows the mapping properties set up for each bit of metadata. A mapped property is how SharePoint Search maps the available metadata fields to other metadata properties it knows about.

➤ **Scopes** — Scopes provide a way for users to narrow their search results before even performing a query. Generally, when a search is performed, it is done against all the content in the index. While this is useful for broad searches, sometimes users may want to search only a specific site or set of data. Scopes can be set up to narrow the field of search down to a smaller subset of the entire search index. When you set up a scope, you first give it a name, then define the rules that will apply to the scope. A specific scope can use a different results page than a standard search.

When setting up the rules, you define the type rule that will be associated with the scope. A scope can be set up to search a specific web address (or addresses), a specific property, a content source you have defined, or all content. Various configurations are associated with each rule type, and rules can be used to include or exclude content, or to return a very narrow set of results by requiring the results to match the query exactly. In addition, more than one rule can be created for a scope. For instance, you could create a scope that queries only a specific site for documents created by a specific person. Or, perhaps you want to create a scope that searches all the content available except for one specific site. In that case, you would create a rule for that scope to include all content in the site, and a second rule to exclude the specific site from the results. As you can see, scopes can be set up to be as specific as you need them to be.

Every 15 minutes, the scopes are updated to include the results specified. Therefore, when you create a new scope or modify an existing scope, you may not have results right away, until the update is run. You can force an immediate update from the Search Administration page in the System Status section. There is a Start update now link next to Scopes needing update.

➤ **Search result removal** — If you need to remove content from the search results immediately, then you have come to the right place. There are several reasons why you might want to remove content from your search results — perhaps some sensitive documents have been uploaded to a document library with incorrect permissions, or perhaps your company is starting work on a project to which only a few select people should have access. Although setting the proper permissions for sites will take care of the majority of issues that could occur with search accessing content it's not supposed to, it's possible that a user could accidentally set the wrong permissions for a site or document library, exposing the content to Search.

If this happens and you need to immediately remove the content from appearing in search results, simply enter the address of the site in the field on this page and click the Remove Now button. This will remove the specified URLs from the search results immediately, and add the addresses to the Crawl Rules to exclude that content from future crawls.

Note that while removing a document or correcting permissions issues will prevent users from accessing content, it will still show up in the search results until the next scheduled crawl. This is because the search results are returned from the index compiled from the last crawl, so real-time results are not displayed. Using the Result Removal tool is much faster than waiting for the next crawl to run or even starting a new crawl to update the index. The added benefit is that it also creates the crawl rule for you.

Reports

As an administrator, you may feel that you have a perfectly configured Search service application. Your content sources and scopes have been defined, your crawl schedules have been set, and life is good. However, your users may feel otherwise if they don't seem to be getting the results they're expecting. How would you know this? By checking out the available reports in this section, administrators can gain great insight into how Search is being used on the site, what users are searching for, and whether that content is actually being found.

➤ **Administration reports** — This is actually a link to the Administrative Report Library, which can also be accessed from the Monitoring category in Central Administration. This library has several reports available out of the box relating to Search, which can be used to track the overall performance of Search and see how long it's taking to crawl each content source, how fast it's crawling each type result, and how long it takes for queries to return results. Clicking the report name generates a graph of information that you can use to check the performance of Search. Data is compiled over time, so you can select a date range to filter the data accordingly. Refer to Chapter 6 for more information about using the administrative reports.

➤ **Web Analytics reports** — This link takes you to the real meat for finding out how users are using Search. The web analytics was enabled automatically for you if you used the Farm Configuration Wizard during the initial setup process. On this page, you can see the total number of queries performed on the site, as well as the average number of queries per day. Other reports available appear in the quick launch area, and give you a graphical representation of the number of queries over time (see Figure 14-24), as well as the Top Queries, and how often those queries were performed. You can also see what queries gave your users zero results with the No Queries Results report.

In the Ribbon on the Web Analytics Reports page, you can click the Analyze tab to refine the reports, change the dates, and even export the report to an Excel spreadsheet. These reports can be particularly useful when tracking Search trends over time. You can use these to set up best bets on the various sites to help users find the content they are looking for, or pass the reports on to site collection administrators or content owners to help them refine the content of their sites appropriately to help users find what they're after as quickly as possible.

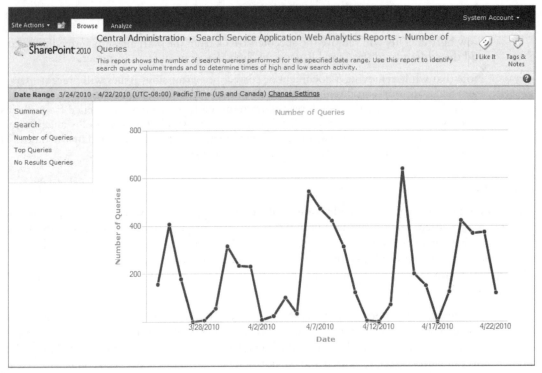

FIGURE 14-24

As you can see, there is a lot going on with the Search Administration page, and a lot of configuration options. Although all the various options can make setting up Search properly seem a little intimidating, we hope this overview has provided a strong base from which you can further explore this robust feature.

Other Search Features

A couple more Search features worth mentioning are Mobile Search and People Search:

> ➤ **Mobile Search** — SharePoint 2010 has made some great strides forward with enhanced mobile support. One such advance is the addition of Mobile Search. From the mobile browser, the user can do a search and even choose a scope. Search results are displayed with a simplified interface, as shown in Figure 14-25. No graphics, no previews or suggestions, just what they came for — search results. If you want to see how this works from the comfort of your desktop PC, you can. From your Search site, click Site Settings. On the right side of the page, click the Mobile Site URL. Now have all the fun of a mobile experience without wearing out your thumbs.

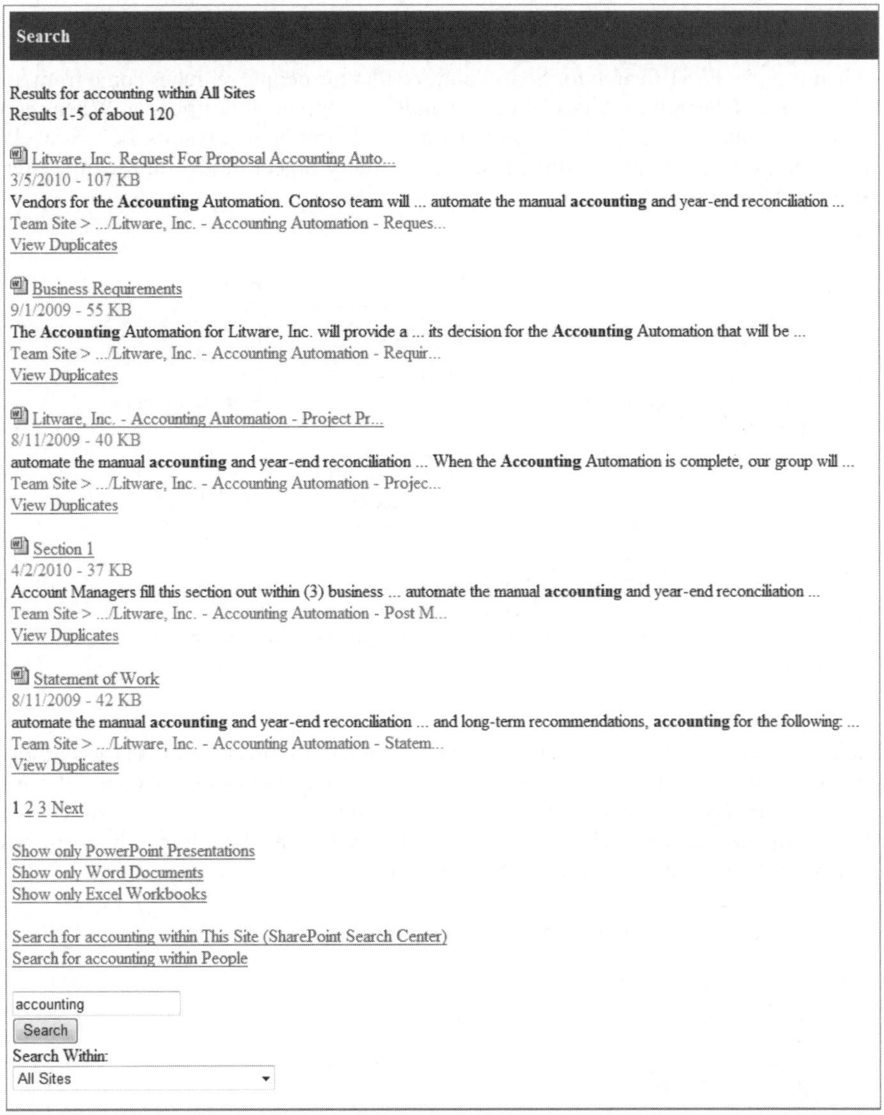

Search

Results for accounting within All Sites
Results 1-5 of about 120

📄 Litware, Inc. Request For Proposal Accounting Auto...
3/5/2010 - 107 KB
Vendors for the **Accounting** Automation. Contoso team will ... automate the manual **accounting** and year-end reconciliation ...
Team Site > .../Litware, Inc. - Accounting Automation - Reques...
View Duplicates

📄 Business Requirements
9/1/2009 - 55 KB
The **Accounting** Automation for Litware, Inc. will provide a ... its decision for the **Accounting** Automation that will be ...
Team Site > .../Litware, Inc. - Accounting Automation - Requir...
View Duplicates

📄 Litware, Inc. - Accounting Automation - Project Pr...
8/11/2009 - 40 KB
automate the manual **accounting** and year-end reconciliation ... When the **Accounting** Automation is complete, our group will ...
Team Site > .../Litware, Inc. - Accounting Automation - Projec...
View Duplicates

📄 Section 1
4/2/2010 - 37 KB
Account Managers fill this section out within (3) business ... automate the manual **accounting** and year-end reconciliation ...
Team Site > .../Litware, Inc. - Accounting Automation - Post M...
View Duplicates

📄 Statement of Work
8/11/2009 - 42 KB
automate the manual **accounting** and year-end reconciliation ... and long-term recommendations, **accounting** for the following: ...
Team Site > .../Litware, Inc. - Accounting Automation - Statem...
View Duplicates

1 2 3 Next

Show only PowerPoint Presentations
Show only Word Documents
Show only Excel Workbooks

Search for accounting within This Site (SharePoint Search Center)
Search for accounting within People

accounting
Search
Search Within:
All Sites

FIGURE 14-25

➤ **People Search** — People Search is covered in more detail in Chapter 17 but some highlights are worth mentioning here. Phonetic and nickname matching is very powerful. For example, search for the name *fillups* and you will get results for "Phillips." Similarly, if you are looking for Jeff but cannot remember if it is Geoff or Jeff, no worries: Search for *Jeff* and get both. Looking for *Bill* will get you results for William as well. This is very powerful for enhancing discoverability.

Earlier we noted some "secret" improvements were made to relevancy. That goes for People Search as well. As a matter of fact, the people relevancy is so good in SharePoint 2010 that even when you use FAST Search for SharePoint, results for people searches come from SharePoint Search. FAST Search for SharePoint only indexes content — not people. When search queries include people results, content results from FAST and People results from SharePoint search are brought together in one unified set in the query object model on the query server, as shown in Figure 14-26.

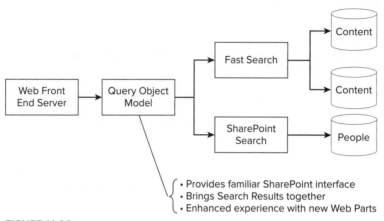

FIGURE 14-26

When it comes to People Search, one of the most popular queries is searching for one's own name. Search recognizes this type of query, returning the results in a special box, as shown in Figure 14-27. It indicates how many times people did a search that lead to you and what keywords they were searching when they found you. This insight can help you tune your My Site to make you easier to find (or harder if you are the shy type).

FIGURE 14-27

FAST SEARCH

FAST Search for SharePoint Sites and FAST Search for Internet Sites take all of the goodness described in the previous section and give it a giant shot of adrenaline. SharePoint Search can view results in the browser using the OWAs? FAST Search can preview PowerPoint presentations within the actual search results. SharePoint Search has refiners for the first 50 documents? FAST does it for all documents in the results set. SharePoint Search can handle some 100 million items in the index? FAST is looking at closer to one billion items. You get the drift. Everything to the extreme.

This section offers a brief look at some of the key FAST differentiators. Because FAST was a bit late to the game for this version of SharePoint, documentation for it is still limited. As FAST matures, expect entire books dedicated to it.

Thumbnails

One of the first things you'll notice when you do a FAST Search is the thumbnails that show up in the search results. This is useful if you are doing a search and can't remember which document you are looking for just by seeing the title. A quick thumbnail of the documents helps to determine the right one.

Scrolling Preview

Clicking on the thumbnail of a PowerPoint document opens a scrolling preview of the slides, enabling you to determine whether it has the content you might be looking for. If you consider this on a larger scale, imagine if you were looking for information in a presentation but couldn't remember exactly which slide deck had the specific file you were looking for. You could do a search and then open each slide deck one by one, which might take several minutes; or you could quickly take a look at the slides directly from the FAST Search results page, which would take only seconds to find the content you want.

Similar Results

Have you ever searched for a document, finally got to what you were looking for, and then thought to yourself that it would be great if you could find more documents just like the one you found? Results in FAST Search enable users to click a Similar Results link to view other content that is similar to a specific document. Essentially, FAST looks at the metadata for the original document and calculates which other documents are most like it.

User Context

Every organization has groups of users, and each group views content across the organization in a unique way. Salespeople generally care about different things than server administrators care about. One of the most powerful capabilities of FAST Search is the capability to target different user contexts. More simply, a user context is a group of users — you can think of it similarly to a search scope. Search administrators can define a user context based on values specified by a user's profile. You could specify a user context based on office location, specialty, interests, project experience, or even hobbies. Once the user context has been defined, you can use it for all sorts of fun things — such as best bets, visual best bets, or for promoting or demoting documents. The user context itself is just the definition of a group of users. The real power is how it can be used in combination with other features to target content at different groups.

Visual Best Bets

SharePoint has always had best bets (covered in the "SharePoint Server" section earlier in the chapter). In a nutshell, they allow an administrator to return for specific links when a user searches on a specific keyword. For example, you can configure SharePoint to specify to always show a link to the proposal template when a user does a search on the term proposal.

FAST Search takes the idea of best bets to the next level with *visual best bets*. Basically, it is exactly what it sounds like it is — a best bet with a picture. Administrators can control several aspects of the visual best bet to gain even greater control over when it shows. Not only can the keyword be used to determine when the visual best bet is displayed, it can be further controlled by specifying the start and end date, and for which user context to show the visual best bet. For example, maybe there is a project management conference scheduled and you want the visual best bet to be displayed only during the month before the conference and only to project managers who type in a specific search term (see Figure 14-28).

FIGURE 14-28

Promote/Demote Documents

FAST Search enables search administrators to specify content that should get a boost or decrease in relevancy ranking. This can be done for all users or for a specific group. For example, imagine a scenario in which different proposals were submitted for project work. Perhaps one proposal is successful and the other is not. Search administrators could provide a relevancy boost to the successful proposal and decrease the relevancy of the unsuccessful document, affecting the results when someone searches on the keyword proposal.

Promotions and demotions can be targeted at specific groups. Using the previous example, maybe it is necessary to adjust the relevancy of the proposals for only project managers — search administrators could specify the user context to target, as well as the start and end date indicating how long the promotion or demotion should apply for the content.

SUMMARY

This chapter provided you with a basic tour of the main components of Search. In addition to setting up Search and adding servers and databases, you now know how to create host distribution rules, refine searches, administer Search, and much more. Understanding these fundamental aspects of Search should enable you to continue your exploration of this large topic with confidence, and to further enhance the search experience of your users.

15

Monitoring SharePoint 2010

WHAT'S IN THIS CHAPTER?

➤ Improvements in diagnostic log management

➤ Using correlation IDs

➤ Using the logging database

If you've made it this far you've got SharePoint 2010 installed and running. You've created a web application or two and uploaded some content. You've probably configured some service applications and sent them off to do their work. SharePoint is doing its thing and life is good. You might be tempted to lean back in your chair and put your feet up, but your adventure is not finished. While SharePoint might be spinning like a top now, the day will come when there are problems. When that happens, you will need to know how to find out what's troubling SharePoint so that you can fix it. A lot of work has been put into monitoring in SharePoint 2010. So much has been added that Monitoring has been given its own tab in Central Administration. SharePoint will report errors, but you need to know where to find them. This chapter will show you how to keep an eye on SharePoint, both in proactive and reactive ways so that you can keep your SharePoint servers in tip-top shape. This will enable you to fix SharePoint when it's broken, as well as see where problem areas are before they become bad enough that your end users complain. Nobody likes that.

UNIFIED LOGGING SERVICE

We will start our journey toward SharePoint monitoring enlightenment with the Unified Logging Service (ULS). To the seasoned SharePoint administrator, the ULS logs are nothing new. They have been around for a version or two of SharePoint. SharePoint 2010 carries on that tradition but improves on it. The ULS surfaces information in three different places; trace logs, Windows Event Viewer, and a new reporting database. This chapter covers all three areas and explains how they differ.

ULS is sort of like SharePoint's tattletale. It is only a logging service; it does not act on any of the events that it sees. However, as you'll see later in this chapter, SharePoint monitoring is more than just the ULS logs and is not always passive. The ULS service's purpose in life is to provide the SharePoint administrators or operations teams with all the information they need to solve problems, or head problems off at the pass. The hope is that with all the information that ULS provides, you should be able to spend fewer resources keeping an eye on SharePoint; and in the unlikely event of a SharePoint problem, the ULS should provide you with the information you need to resolve the problem quickly.

Trace Logs

When most SharePoint administrators hear "ULS" they immediately think of the ULS logs that they have been using for years with previous versions of SharePoint. In SharePoint 2010 these are officially referred to as the trace logs. The trace logs have a similar address to their counterparts in previous versions of SharePoint. You can find them in the Logs folder of `C:\Program Files\Common Files\Microsoft Shared\Web Server Extensions\14\`. That's quite a mouthful, so Microsoft has lovingly christened that path the "SharePoint Root." You may also hear some less refined people refer to it as the "14 Hive."

Figure 15-1 shows what you can expect to see if you look for the ULS trace logs in Explorer. The filename consists of the server name, the date in four-digit year, month, and date order, followed by the time in 24-hour format. You'll also notice that the duration between log file creation is always exactly 30 minutes apart, at least while the machine is on. This is the default setting, although you can use Windows PowerShell to change this. See the sidebar for more information on using PowerShell with trace logs.

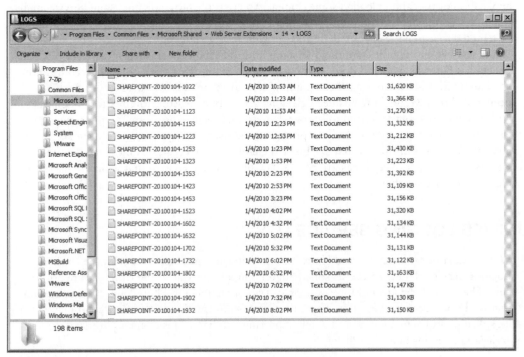

FIGURE 15-1

If you open one of the trace logs, you will see that it is packed full of great SharePoint information, probably more than you need on a daily basis. The good news is that you will probably access the trace logs only when you're researching a problem. The bad news is that even then, there still might be more information presented than what is really helpful for troubleshooting your issues. You'll see later how to control how much information is added to the trace logs.

Improvements from SharePoint 2007

If you used SharePoint 2007 at all you're probably asking yourself what's so special about trace logs in SharePoint 2010. We're glad you asked. While they are similar in intent, the trace logs received a number of really exciting improvements. Figure 15-1 hinted at the first improvement; the log files are smaller. A lot of changes have made that possible. From Figure 15-1 you can see that by default the log files themselves are compressed on the drive, using NTFS compression. Because the logs are text files and consist of a lot of repeating data, they compress very well. The files in Figure 15-1 each show a size of around 31MB, but each actually uses around 13MB on disk due to the compression. That's over 50% smaller and the only penalty is some CPU cycles. To make the files even smaller, many of the noisy events that were written to the SharePoint 2007 log have been removed.

To better manage the information written to the trace logs, the throttling interface has been given a complete overhaul. In SharePoint 2007, the information written to the trace logs could be controlled, to a point. Unfortunately, it wasn't very useful. If the diagnostic levels were increased to troubleshoot a problem, it was impossible to determine which settings had been changed. Moreover, even if you knew which levels had been changed, there was no way to determine what they had been changed from. It was a mess. In SharePoint 2010 this has all been fixed.

To get to the new Event Throttling settings, go into Central Administration and click Monitoring on the left navigation pane. Figure 15-2 shows all the Monitoring links.

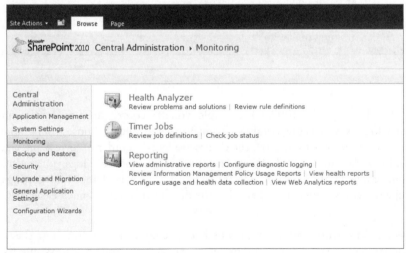

FIGURE 15-2

In the Reporting section, click "Configure diagnostic logging" to get to the Event Throttling settings, shown in Figure 15-3. Compared to SharePoint 2007, you'll notice a wider variety of categories. This makes it easier to determine which category covers the event you want to find. Expand the category to see the settings each contains. This demonstrates two improvements over SharePoint 2007. First, you have more granular ability to find the settings you're looking for. One of the diagnostic categories in SharePoint 2007 was General/Administration, which isn't particularly helpful when you're trying to find where you can increase logging. Second, the interface has checkboxes so you can alter multiple events at once.

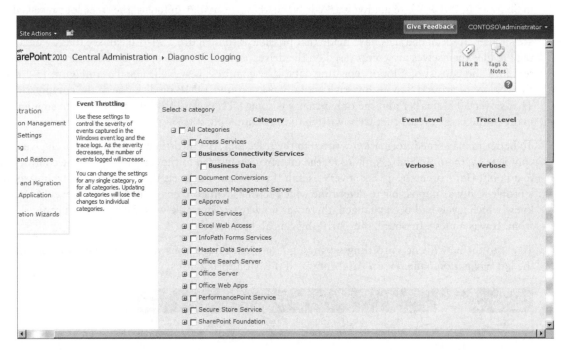

FIGURE 15-3

Some features are shared with SharePoint 2007. For example, you can control how much information is written to the trace logs as well as the Windows Event Viewer. You can choose from among several logging levels. For the Windows Event Log, the events are listed in order of fewest messages to most: None, Critical, Error, Warning, Information, and Verbose. For the trace logs you can select None, Unexpected, Monitorable, High, Medium, or Verbose. You can easily change both settings for multiple events on one screen. As you can see, altering the diagnostic levels is much easier in SharePoint 2010.

Easy alterations can be a good feature, but it can also be bad. It enables you to fine-tune the changes you need, but it can also mean changing many settings back once you've successfully fixed the issue you're investigating. Fortunately, SharePoint 2010 provides improvements in that area as well. Any time you change a diagnostic level, that category appears in bold in the interface (refer to Figure 15-3).

It's one thing to know which settings have been changed; it's another to know what to reset them to. Have no fear; SharePoint 2010 takes care of that too. One of the event levels to which you can set a category is Reset to default, as shown in Figure 15-4.

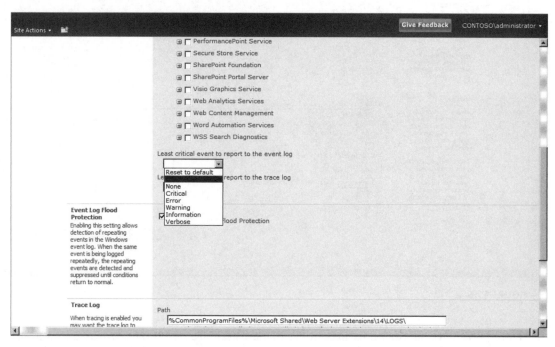

FIGURE 15-4

The combination of those two improvements makes it easy to get your diagnostic levels back to their defaults after you've cranked them up to investigate an issue.

Trace Log Settings

A few other settings are related to the trace logs. They involve the location of the trace logs and how long to keep them. As noted earlier, by default they are written to the Logs directory of the SharePoint Root. You can, and probably should, move them to a different location. That's because in most cases Windows is installed on the C: drive, and the SharePoint Root must be on the C: drive. Therefore, it's a good idea to leave the C: drive with as much free space as possible. Moving the trace logs to a different drive reduces the possibility of filling up the C: drive. Figure 15-5 shows SharePoint writing the trace logs to D:\SharePoint\Logs.

Keep in mind that this is a farm-level setting, it is not per server. Any path you put here must exist on all servers in the farm. If you try to enter a path that does not exist, SharePoint will not let you save it. This is also a concern when you add new servers to your farm; make sure they also have the trace log path available.

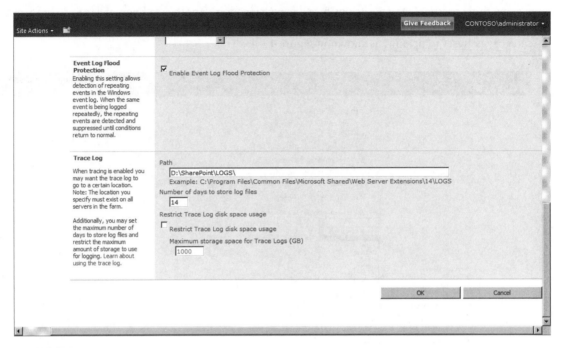

FIGURE 15-5

Figure 15-5 shows the other trace log settings that are available to you. They are used to restrict the storage space used for trace logs. You have two methods to control their growth. One option is to control how many days' worth to keep. The default value is 14 days; with this value, on day 15 the logs from the first day are deleted. The other option is to absolutely restrict the amount of drive space available to the trace logs. The default, and maximum, value is 1000GB. If you choose to restrict drive space, then both settings are used to control the logs. If the logs are small and don't hit the space restriction, then they will be pruned based on the day restriction. If the logs are very active and they reach the space restriction before the day restriction, they will be pruned.

Trace Logs Administration with Windows PowerShell

Windows PowerShell can be used for many amazing tasks. The following sections demonstrate the PowerShell cmdlets useful for working with trace logs.

Configuring Diagnostic Log Settings with Windows PowerShell

If you're the scripting type, you can use Windows PowerShell to view and configure SharePoint's diagnostic log settings. You can use the cmdlet Get-SPDiagnosticConfig to get a list of the farm configuration settings. If you want to change any of the settings, use the cmdlet Set-SPDiagnosticConfig to assign the values you want. The following command will change the number of days SharePoint keeps the trace logs to 30 days:

```
Set-SPDiagnosticConfig -DaysToKeepLogs 30
```

Changing Logs with Windows PowerShell

You also have the option to use Windows PowerShell to set and get the logging level for specific categories. Running the cmdlet `Get-SPLogLevel` with no parameters will report the logging level for all categories. If you want to change a category's level, use `Set-SPLogLevel` to alter the category's value.

PowerShell can also manipulate the trace files themselves. `New-SPLogFile` tells SharePoint to create a new trace file. This is a great diagnostic technique. If you create a new trace file before you start troubleshooting, you will know exactly which file contains the error. To take it another step, use `Merge-SPLogFile` to merge all the trace files in your farm into a single file on the local computer.

To get the entire list of trace file–related cmdlets, use the following command:

```
Get-command -noun splog*
```

Correlation IDs

There is one addition to the trace logs that does help you hone in on the information you need. SharePoint 2010 introduces correlation IDs. Correlation IDs are unique GUIDs that are assigned to each user conversation with SharePoint. They are like breadcrumbs that a SharePoint administrator can use to follow a user around and see what they were doing if there is a problem. Nothing is more frustrating when troubleshooting than when you ask a user, "What were you doing when you got the error?" and they reply, "Nothing." Correlation IDs are like flashlights guiding us through the fog of unhelpful users.

Correlation IDs will surface when SharePoint crashes in the browser. The user will still get the ever helpful "An Unexpected Error Has Occurred" message or something else equally helpful. On top of that, though, they will get a correlation ID in the form of a Globally Unique IDentifier, or GUID to its friends. GUIDs are randomly generated and in the form of "601487bc-1a65-4d4a-70dd-bf9c01e57e8b." There will a correlation ID in this form on the error page, like you see in Figure 15-6. As a SharePoint administrator, you can take this correlation ID and search through your trace logs to follow the user's conversation with SharePoint, as well as see exactly which lines in the trace logs deal with that failure. Figure 15-7 shows some of the corresponding trace log entries to the error shown in Figure 15-6. No more searching through trace logs trying to figure out which lines pertained to which errors. Now it is all mapped out for you, with a lighted path.

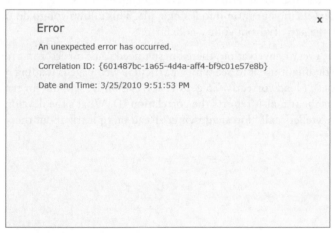

Error

An unexpected error has occurred.

Correlation ID: {601487bc-1a65-4d4a-aff4-bf9c01e57e8b}

Date and Time: 3/25/2010 9:51:53 PM

FIGURE 15-6

FIGURE 15-7

To make your troubleshooting even easier, correlations IDs are persisted across servers in your farm. So if a user initially hits SERVER1, which is running the web front end role, and that renders an Excel spreadsheet that is calculated on SERVER2, the correlation ID for the conversation will be the same on SERVER1 and SERVER2. The correlation ID is even available as a filter if you are doing SQL tracing on your SQL server. You can use the Windows PowerShell cmdlet `Merge-SPLogFile` to merge the trace logs from all the servers in your farm into a single file. This allows you to do one search for the correlation ID and get the activity from your whole farm.

Since a correlation ID is generated for every conversation, there doesn't need to be an error in order for you to follow the conversation. You might use it to see why a particular web page is loading slowly, or why a certain Web Part doesn't load correctly. To get the correlation ID without an error page you can enable the developer dashboard, as it reports the correlation ID. What's the developer dashboard, you ask? This is what storytellers call "foreshadowing." Read on to learn about the developer dashboard.

Developer Dashboard

While this book is squarely aimed at SharePoint administrators, we need to cover a new piece of functionality called the *developer dashboard*. Despite what the name may suggest, it's not just for developers. The developer dashboard is dashboard that shows how long it took for a page to load, and which components loaded with it. A picture is worth 1000 words, so Figure 15-8 probably explains it better.

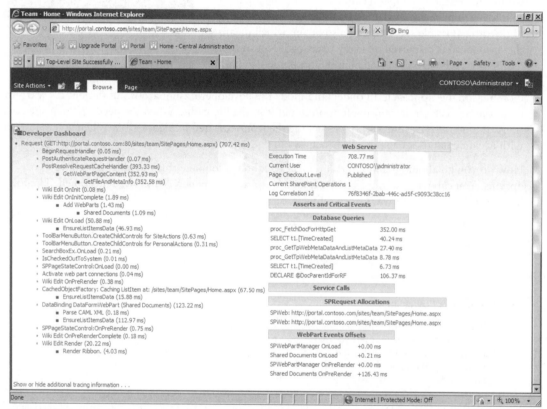

FIGURE 15-8

This dashboard is loaded at the bottom of your requested web page. As you can see, the dashboard is chock full of information about the page load. You can see how long the page took to load (708.77 ms) as well as who requested it, its correlation ID, and so on. This info is useful when the helpdesk gets those ever popular "SharePoint's slow" calls from users. Now you can quantify exactly what "slow" means as well as see what led up to the page load being slow. If Web Parts were poorly designed and did a lot of database queries, you'd see it here. If they fetched large amounts of SharePoint content, you'd see it here. If you're really curious you can click the link on the bottom left, "Show or hide additional tracing information" to get several pages worth of information about every step that was taken to render that page.

FIGURE 15-9

Now that you're sold on the developer dashboard, how do you actually use it? Like we mentioned before, it is exposed as a dashboard at the bottom of the page when it renders. The user browsing the page must be a site collection administrator to see the developer dashboard, and it must be enabled in your farm. By default it is shut off, which is one of the three possible states. It can also be on, which means the dashboard is displayed on every page load. Not only is that tedious when you're using SharePoint, but it also has a performance penalty. The third option, ondemand, is a more reasonable approach. In ondemand mode the developer dashboard is not on, but it's warming up in the on deck circle, waiting for you to put it in the big game. When the need arises, a site collection administrator can turn it on my clicking the icon indicated in Figure 15-9. When you are finished with it, you can put it back on the bench by clicking the same icon.

How do you go about enabling the developer dashboard to make this possible? You have two options. You can use sad, old STSADM, or you can use shiny new Windows PowerShell. The following code shows both ways of enabling it.

Using STSADM:

```
stsadm -o setproperty -pn developer-dashboard -pv on
stsadm -o setproperty -pn developer-dashboard -pv off
stsadm -o setproperty -pn developer-dashboard -pv ondemand
```

Using Windows PowerShell:

```
$dash = [Microsoft.SharePoint.Administration.SPWebService]::
ContentService.DeveloperDashboardSettings;
$dash.DisplayLevel = 'OnDemand';
$dash.TraceEnabled = $true;
$dash.Update()
```

Notice that at no point do you specify a URL when you're setting this. It is a farm-wide setting. Never fear though; only site collection administrators will see it, so hopefully it won't scare too many users if you have to enable it for troubleshooting.

Logging Database

Microsoft has always made it pretty clear how it feels about people touching the SharePoint databases. The answer is always a very clear and concise, "Knock that off!" They didn't support reading from or writing to SharePoint databases, period. End of story. That became a problem, however, because not all of the information administrators wanted about their farm or servers was discoverable in the interface, or with the SharePoint Object Model. This resulted in rogue administrators, in the dark of night, quietly querying their databases, hoping to never get caught.

SharePoint 2010 addresses this by introducing a logging database. This database is a repository of SharePoint events from every machine in your farm. It aggregates information from many different locations and writes them all to a single database. This database contains just about everything you could ever want to know about your farm. Even better, you can read from and write to this database if you would like, as the schema is public. Do your worst to it, Microsoft doesn't care.

Microsoft's reason for forbidding access to databases before was well intentioned. Obviously, writing to a SharePoint database potentially puts it in a state where SharePoint can no longer read it and render the content in it. We all agree this is bad. What is less obvious though is that reading from a database can have the same impact. A seemingly innocent but poorly written SQL query that only reads values could put a lock on a table, or the whole database. This lock would also mean that SharePoint could not render out the content of that database for the duration of the lock. That's also a bad thing. This logging database, however, is just a copy of information gathered from other places and is not used to satisfy end user requests, so it's safe for you to read from it or write to it. If you destroy the database completely, you can just delete it and let SharePoint re-create it. The freedom is invigorating.

Figure 15-10 shows some of the information that is copied into the logging database.

SQL Logging Database	
Feature use	Page Requests
Search Queries	Site Inventory Usage
Timer Jobs	Rating Usage
Content Import Usage	Content Export Usage
Server Farm Health Data	NT Events
SQL blocked queries	SQL high CPU/ IO queries
Site Inventory	Search Crawl
Search Query statistics	Query click-through
Users' ratings	...and more

FIGURE 15-10

Configuring the Logging Database

How do you use this magical database and leverage all this information? By default, health data collection is enabled. This builds the logging database. To view the settings, open SharePoint Central Administration and go into the now familiar Monitoring section. Under the Reporting heading, click "Configure usage and health data collection," as shown in Figure 15-11.

FIGURE 15-11

Let's start our tour of the settings at the top. The first checkbox on the page determines whether the usage data is collected and stored in the Logging database. This is turned on by default, and here is where you would disable it, should you choose to.

The next section enables you to determine which events you want reported in the log. By default, all eight events are logged. If you want to reduce the impact logging has on your servers, you can disable events for which you don't think you'll want reports. You always have the option to enable events later. You may want to do this if you need to investigate a specific issue. You can turn the logging on during your investigation, and then shut it off after the investigation is finished.

The next section determines where the usage logs will be stored. By default they are stored in the Logs directory of the SharePoint Root, along with the trace logs. The usage logs follow the same naming convention as the trace logs, but have the suffix .usage. As with the trace logs, it's a good idea to move these logs off of the C:\ drive if possible. You can also limit the amount of space the usage logs take, with 5GB being the default.

The next section, Health data collection, seems simple enough: just a checkbox and a link. The checkbox determines whether SharePoint will periodically collect health information about the members of the farm. The link takes you to a list of timer jobs that collect that information. When you click the Health Logging Schedule link, you're taken to a page that lists all of the timer jobs that collect this information. You can use this page to disable the timer jobs for any information you don't want to collect. Again, the more logging you do, the greater the impact on performance. Figure 15-12 shows the health data collection timer jobs.

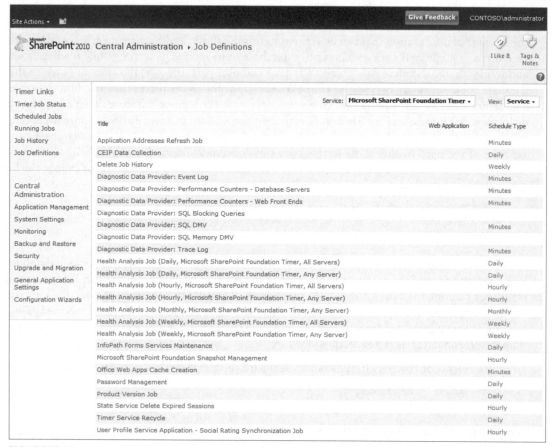

FIGURE 15-12

Clearly, SharePoint collects a vast amount of information. Not only does it monitor SharePoint-related performance, such as the User Profile Service Application Synchronization Job, it also keeps track of the health of non-SharePoint processes, like SQL. It reports SQL blocking queries and DMV (dynamic management view) data. Not only can you disable the timer jobs for information you don't want to collect, you can also decrease how often they run, to reduce the impact on your servers.

The next section of the Configure web analytics and health data collection page is the log collection schedule, which enables you to configure how frequently the logs are collected from the servers in the farm, and how frequently they are processed and written to the logging database. This lets you control the impact the log collection has on your servers. The default setting collects the logs every 30 minutes, but you can increase that to reduce the load placed on the servers.

The final section of the page displays the SQL instance and database name of the reporting database itself. The default settings use the same SQL instance as the default content database SQL instance, and use the database name WSS_Logging. Although the page recommends using the default settings, there are some pretty good reasons to change its location and settings. Considering the amount of information that can be written to this database, and how frequently that data can be written, it might make sense to move this database to its own SQL server. While reading from and writing to the database won't directly impact end user performance, the amount of usage this database could see might overwhelm your SQL server, or fill up the drives that also house your other SharePoint databases. If your organization chooses to use the logging database, keep an eye on the disk space that it uses, and the amount of activity it generates. On a test environment with about one month's worth of use by one user, the logging database grew to over 1GB. This database can get huge. If you need to alter those settings you can do so in Windows PowerShell with the Set-SPUsageApplication cmdlet. The following PowerShell code demonstrates how to change the logging database's location:

```
Set-SPUsageApplication -DatabaseServer <Database server name> -DatabaseName
<Database name> [-DatabaseUsername <User name>] [-DatabasePassword <Password>]
[-Verbose]
```

Specify the name of the SQL server or instance where you would like to host the logging database. You must also specify the database name, even if you want to use the default name, WSS_Logging. If the user running the Set-SPUsageApplication cmdlet is not the owner of the database, provide the username and password of an account that has sufficient permissions. Because this database consists of data aggregated from other locations, you can move it without losing any data. It will simply be repopulated as the collection jobs run.

To get the full list of PowerShell cmdlets that deal with the Usage service, use Get-Command as follows:

```
get-command -noun spusage*
```

Consuming the Logging Database

We've talked a lot about this logging database, what's in it, and how to configure it, but we haven't yet covered how you can enjoy its handiwork. There are many places to consume the information in the logging database. The first place is Central Administration. Under Monitoring ➪ Reporting are three reports that use information in the logging database. The first link is View administrative reports. Clicking that link takes you to a document library in Central Administration that contains a few canned administrative reports. Out of the box there are only search reports, as shown in Figure 15-13, but any type of report could be put here. Microsoft could provide these reports, or they can be created by SharePoint administrators.

The documents in this library are simply web pages, so click any of them to see the information they contain. These particular reports are very handy for determining the source of search bottlenecks.

This enables you to be proactive in scaling out your search infrastructure. You are able to see how long discrete parts of search take, and then scale out your infrastructure before end users are affected.

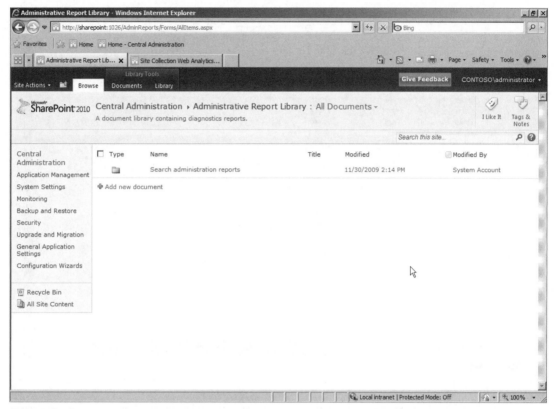

FIGURE 15-13

The next set of reports in Central Administration are the health reports. These reports enable you to isolate the slowest pages in your web app, and the most active users per web app. Like the search reports, these reports enable you to proactively diagnose issues in your farm. After viewing details about the slowest pages being rendered, you can take steps to improve their performance. Figure 15-14 shows part of the report. To view a report, click the Go button on the right.

The report shows how long each page takes to load, including minimums, maximums, and averages. This gives you a very convenient way to find your trouble pages. You can also see how many database queries the page makes. This is helpful, as database queries are expensive operations that can slow down a page render. You can drill down to a specific server or web app with this report as well, since the logging database aggregates information from all the servers in your farm. Pick the scope of the report you want and click the Go button. The reports are generated at runtime, so it might take a few seconds for it to appear. After the results appear, you can click a column heading to sort by those values.

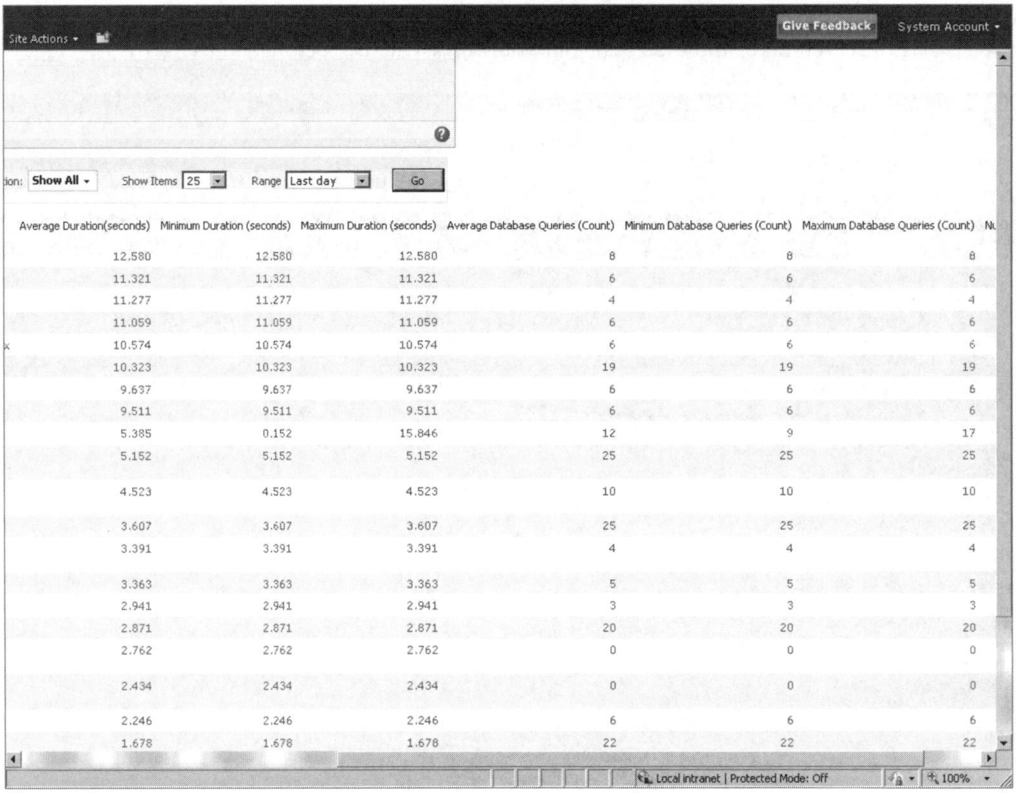

FIGURE 15-14

The third and final set of reports in Central Admin that are fed from the logging database are the Web Analytics reports. These reports provide usage information about each of your farm's web applications, excluding Central Admin. Clicking the View Web Analytics reports link takes you to a summary page listing the web apps in your farm, along with some high-level metrics like total number of page views and total number of daily unique visitors. Figure 15-15 shows the Summary page.

When you click on a web application on the Summary page you're taken to a Summary page for that web app that provides more detailed usage information. This includes additional metrics for the web app, such as referrers, total number of page views, and the trends for each, as shown in Figure 15-16.

The web app summary report also adds new links on the left. These links enable you to drill further down into each category. Each new report has a graph at the top, with more detailed information at the bottom of the screen. If you want to change the scope of a report, click Analyze in the ribbon. This shows the options you have for the report, including the date ranges included. You can choose one of the date ranges provided or, as shown in Figure 15-17, choose custom dates.

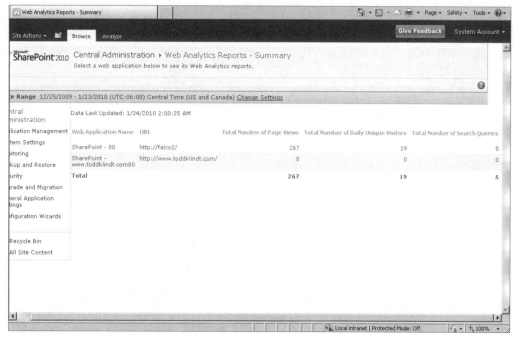

FIGURE 15-15

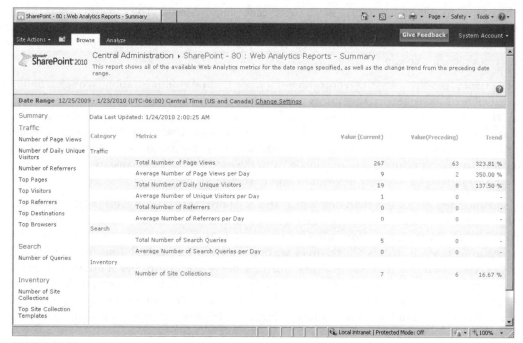

FIGURE 15-16

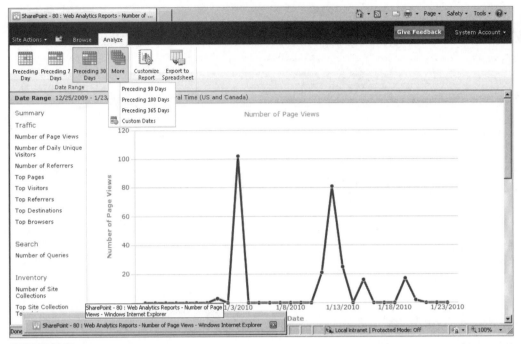

FIGURE 15-17

This gives you the flexibility to drill down to the exact date you want. You can also export the report out to a CSV file with the Export to Spreadsheet button. Because this is a CSV file, the graph is not included — only the dates and their values. These options are available for any of the reports after you choose a web app.

As mentioned, the web analytics reports do not include Central Administration. While it's unlikely that you'll need such a report, they are available to you. The Central Admin site is simply a highly specialized site collection in its own web app. Because it is a site collection, usage reports are also available for it. To view them, click Site Actions ⇨ Site Settings. Under Site Administration, click Site web analytics reports. This brings up the same usage reports you just saw at the web app level. You also have the same options in the ribbon, with the exception of being able to export to CSV. Figure 15-18 shows the browser report for Central Admin.

Because these reports are site collection web analytics reports, they are available in all site collections as well as in Central Admin. This is another way to consume the information in the logging database. You can view the usage information for any site collection or web, just open Site Actions ⇨ Site Settings to get the web analytics links. You have two similar links: Site Web Analytics reports and Site Collection Web Analytics reports. These are the same sets of reports, but at different scopes. The site collection–level reports are for the entire site collection. The Site-level reports provide the same information but at the site (also called *web*) level. You have a further option of scoping the reports at that particular site, or that site and its subsites. Figure 15-19 shows the options available at the site level.

FIGURE 15-18

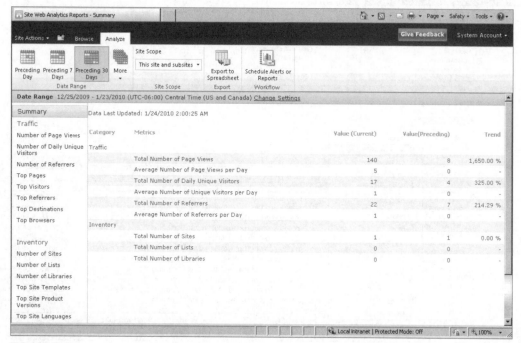

FIGURE 15-19

You may also notice another option that was not available in the Central Administration web analytics reports, the capability to use workflows to schedule alerts or reports. You can use this functionality to have specific reports sent to people at specific intervals, or when specific values are met. This is another way that you can use the logging database and the information it collects to be proactive with your SharePoint farm.

There is one final way to consume the information stored in the logging database: directly from SQL. Although it might feel like you're doing something wrong, Microsoft supports this method. There are several ways to access data in SQL Server databases, but we're going to demonstrate how to do it in SQL Server Management Studio with regular SQL queries.

SQL Server Management Studio allows you to run queries against databases. Normally, it's a very bad thing to touch any of the SharePoint databases; the logging database, mentioned earlier, is the only exception to that rule. Open Management Studio and find the WSS_Logging database. Go ahead and poke around; it's fine. You'll notice the large number of tables in the database. Each category of information has 32 tables to partition the data. It's obvious this database was designed to accommodate a lot of growth. Because of the database partitions, it's tough to do SELECT statements against them. Fortunately, the database also includes a Views feature that you can use to view the data. Expand the Views node of the database to see which views are defined. Figure 15-20 demonstrates getting the information from the Usage tables. Right-click on the view and click Select Top 1000 Rows.

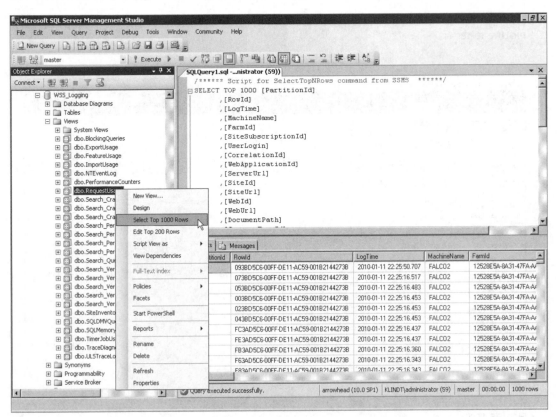

FIGURE 15-20

This shows both the query that is used and the results of that query. You can use this view and the resulting query as a template for any queries you want to design. Remember that if you do happen to do any damage to the logging database, you can simply delete it and SharePoint will re-create it.

Health Analyzer

By now you've seen there are a lot of ways for you to keep an eye on SharePoint. What if there were some magical way for SharePoint to watch over itself? What if it could use all that fancy monitoring to see when something bad was going to happen to it and just fix it itself? Welcome to the future. SharePoint 2010 introduces a feature called the Health Analyzer that does just that. The Health Analyzer utilizes Timer Jobs to run rules periodically and check on system metrics that are based on SharePoint best practices. When a rule fails, SharePoint can alert an administrator in Central Administration, or, in some cases, just fix the problem itself. To access all this magic, just select Monitoring ⇨ Health Analyzer.

Reviewing Problems

How do you know when the Health Analyzer has detected a problem? You're probably familiar with the window shown in Figure 15-21. You fire up Central Admin and there's a red bar running across the top. That's the Health Analyzer alerting you that there's a problem in the farm. To review any problems, click the View these issues link on the right.

FIGURE 15-21

When you click the link you're taken to the Review problems and solutions page. (Even if there are no problems, you can get there by clicking Monitoring ⇨ Review problems and solutions in Central Admin.) This page shows you all the problems that the Health Analyzer found in the farm. Figure 15-22 shows some problems common with a single-server farm.

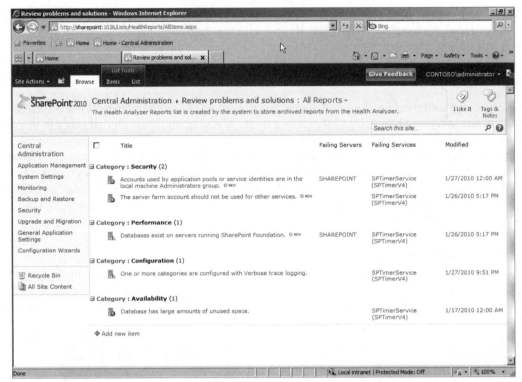

FIGURE 15-22

Clicking any of the issues will bring up the definition of the rule and offer remedies for it. Figure 15-23 shows details about the first problem.

SharePoint provides a summary of the rule. This particular error indicates that one of the app pool accounts is also a local administrator. In most situations this is a security issue, so SharePoint discourages it. SharePoint categorizes this as having a severity level of 1, and therefore an Error. It also tells you this problem is in the Security category. The next section, Explanation, describes what the problem is and to which application pools and services it pertains. The following section, Remedy, points you to the Central Admin page, where you can fix the problem, and an external link to a page with more information about this rule. This is a great addition and gives SharePoint the ability to update the information dynamically. The next two sections indicate which server is affected by the issue, and which service logged the failure. The final section provides a link to view the settings for this rule. You'll learn more about the rule definitions later in this chapter.

That's a rather in-depth property page, and it's packed with even more features. Across the top is a small ribbon that gives you some management options. Starting on the left is the Edit Item button. This lets you alter the values shown on the property page. You could use this to change the error level or category of the rule. It isn't recommended that you alter these values, but if you do you can keep track of the versions with the next button, Version History. The following button enables you to set an alert if the item changes. You have these options because these rules are simply items in a list, so you have many of the same options you have with regular list items.

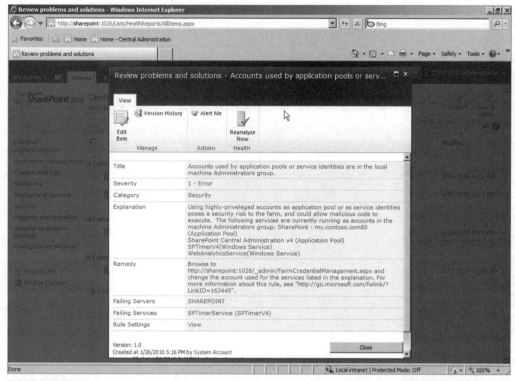

FIGURE 15-23

You may notice one more button: for each rule you have the option to Reanalyze Now. This lets you fire off any rule without waiting for its scheduled appearance, which is great for ensuring that a problem is fixed once you have addressed it. You won't have to wait for the next time the rule runs to verify that it has been taken care of.

Some problems are not only reported, but can be fixed in the property page as well. Figure 15-22 showed another problem under the Configuration category. It noted that one or more categories were configured with Verbose trace logging. This configuration issue can contribute to unnecessary disk I/O and drive space usage. The Health Analyzer alerts you when this value is set. This problem is pretty easy to fix; simply set the trace logging level back to its default. For problems like this, SharePoint offers another option, Repair Automatically. Figure 15-24 shows this functionality in action.

Clicking the Repair Automatically button allows SharePoint to fix the problem. Then click the Reanalyze Now button, click Close on the property page, and reload the problem report page. The trace logging problem should no longer be listed. This is almost bliss for the lazy SharePoint administrator.

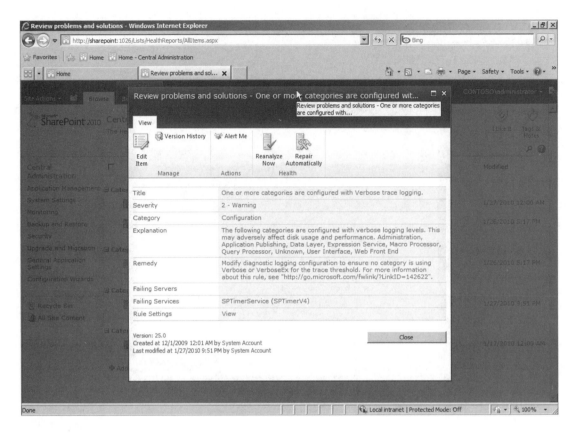

FIGURE 15-24

Rule Definitions

The real power of the Health Analyzer lies in its impressive set of rules. Out of the box, SharePoint 2010 comes with 52 rules. You can see the entire list and details about each rule by clicking Monitoring ➪ Health Analyzer ➪ Review rule definitions. You will see a screen like the one shown in Figure 15-25.

As you can see, the rules are broken down by category. Figure 15-25 shows three of the categories: Security, Performance, and Configuration. There is a fourth and final category on the second page of rules: Availability. The default view shows several pieces of information about each rule, including the Title, the Schedule of how often it runs, whether it's Enabled to run, and whether it will Repair Automatically. Wait, Repair Automatically? You read that right; some rules can be configured to automatically repair problems when they find them.

Figure 15-25 shows several rules that by default are set to repair automatically. One example is "Databases used by SharePoint have fragmented indices." Once a day, SharePoint checks the indices of its databases, and if their fragmentation exceeds a hardcoded threshold, SharePoint will automatically defrag the indices. If the indices are not heavily fragmented, it does nothing. This is a great use of Repair Automatically. It's an easy task to automate, and there's no reason it should need to be done manually by an administrator. Some rules, like "Drives are running out of free space," don't seem like quite as good candidates for SharePoint to fix by itself. You don't want it deleting all those copies of your resume, or your Grandma's secret chocolate-chip cookie recipe.

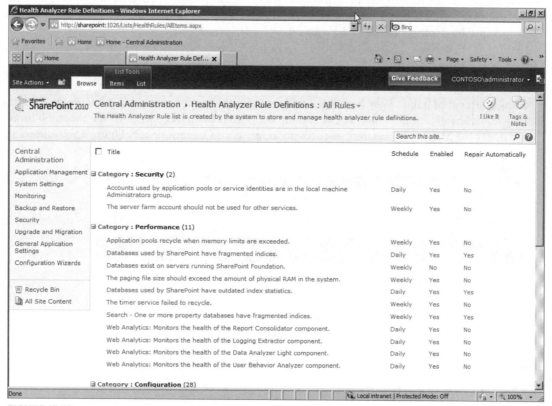

FIGURE 15-25

If you want to change the settings of any of the rules, including whether it Repairs Automatically or not, simply click the rule title, or click the rule's line and select Edit Item in the ribbon. Here you can enable or disable whether a rule will run or not. In the single-server environment shown, it would make sense to disable the rule that reported databases on the SharePoint server. It's nothing that can be fixed, so getting alerts about it does you no good. You could also choose to change how often a rule is run, but it is not a best practice to change the details of a rule other than enabling the rule and Repair Automatically.

Finally, because the rules are simply items in a list, the rules list is extensible. More rules can be added later by Microsoft or third parties.

Timer Jobs

Timer jobs are one of the great unsung heroes of SharePoint. They have been around for several versions of SharePoint, and they get better with each version. Timer jobs are the workhorses of SharePoint. Most configuration changes are pushed out to the farm members with timer jobs. Recurring tasks like Incoming E-Mail also leverage timer jobs. In SharePoint 2010, timer jobs have been given another round of improvements. A lot of the functionality covered in this chapter relies on timer jobs, so you have seen some of those improvements already. This section drills down a little deeper into how timer jobs have improved.

Timer Job Management

When you enter Central Admin it is not immediately obvious that timer jobs have gotten such a shiny new coat of paint. They have links to essentially the same two items in SharePoint 2010 that they do in SharePoint 2007: job status and job definition. In SharePoint 2010 the timer job links are under the Monitoring section, as there no longer is an Operations tab. Figure 15-26 shows their new home.

FIGURE 15-26

Let's start our tour of the new timer job features by looking at the timer job definitions. Again, this page is largely unchanged from its SharePoint 2007 counterpart. You get a list of the timer jobs, the web application they will run on, and their schedule. You can also change the jobs that are shown by filtering the list with the View drop-down in the upper right-hand corner. Figure 15-27 shows the Job Definitions screen.

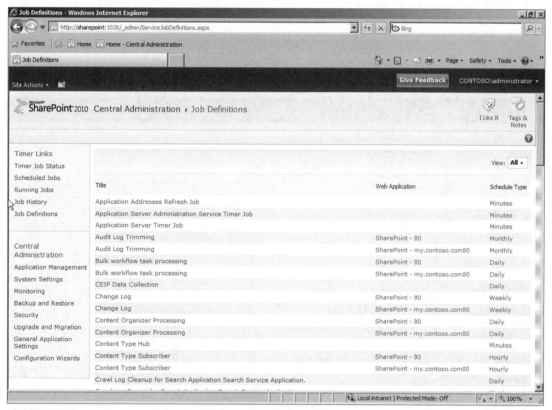

FIGURE 15-27

Again, not a huge improvement over the timer job definition management provided in SharePoint 2007. To really see what's new, click one of the timer job definitions. Hopefully you're sitting down, because otherwise the new timer definition page, shown in Figure 15-28, might knock you over.

It includes all of the same information provided in SharePoint 2007, including the general information on the job definitions screen and the buttons to disable the timer job. However, there are two new, very exciting features. First, you can change the timer job schedule in this screen. In SharePoint 2007 you need to use code to do this. This gives you a lot of flexibility to move timer jobs around if your farm load requires it. That's a great feature, but it's not the best addition.

The best addition to this page, and arguably to timer jobs in SharePoint 2010, is the button on the lower right, Run Now. You now have the capability to run almost any timer job at will. This means no more waiting for the timer job's scheduled interval to elapse before knowing if something you fixed is working. This is the same feature that enables the Health Monitoring discussed earlier in the chapter to fix issues and reanalyze problems. You are no longer bound by the chains of timer job schedules. You are free to run timer jobs whenever you want. That alone is worth the cost of admission.

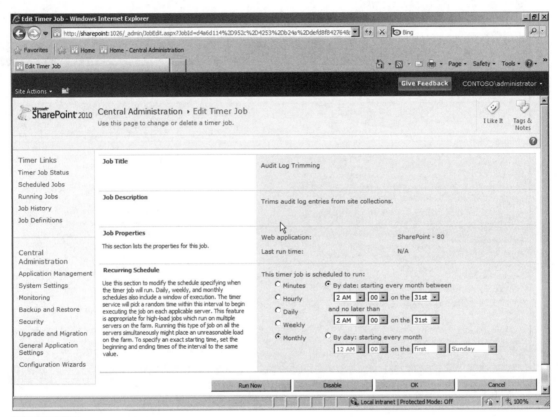

FIGURE 15-28

Timer Job Status

The other link related to timer jobs in Central Admin is Check job status. This serves the same purpose as its SharePoint 2007 counterpart. However, like the timer job definitions, it has gotten a new coat of paint. Figure 15-29 shows the new Timer Job Status page. Like the SharePoint 2007 version, it shows you the timer jobs that have completed, when they ran, and whether they were successful or not.

SharePoint 2010 takes it a step further. Notice that the Succeeded status is now a hyperlink. Simply click this link to get more information. Figure 15-30 shows the full Job History page, with a job highlighted. You can also get to this page by clicking Job History in the left navigation pane.

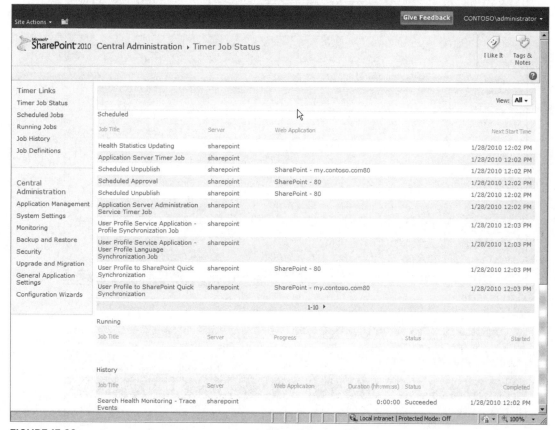

FIGURE 15-29

Figure 15-30 also shows another great addition, the capability to filter and view only the failed jobs. That helps with troubleshooting, as you can see all the failures on one page, without all those pesky successes getting in the way. To take it a step further, you can click on a failure and get information about why that particular timer job failed, as shown in Figure 15-31.

In this case, the Health Statistics timer job failed because of a timeout issue. Now you have some real information to use to get to the bottom of the problem.

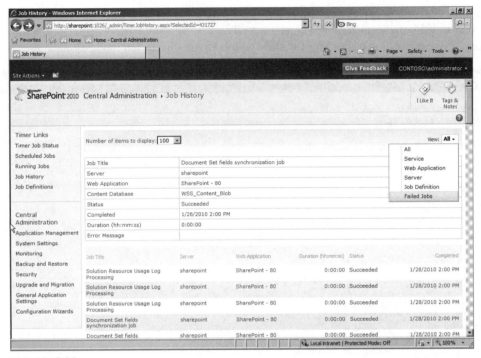

FIGURE 15-30

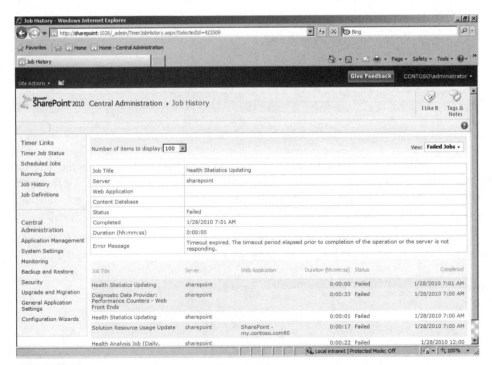

FIGURE 15-31

The Timer Job Status page serves as a dashboard. You've already seen how it shows the timer job history, but it also shows the timer jobs that are scheduled to run, as well as the timer jobs that are currently running. Refer back to Figures 15-29 and 15-30; Figure 15-29 shows all three sections with scheduled jobs on the top followed by running jobs and finally the timer job history. If you want more complete information on any of these sections you can click the appropriate link on the left under Timer Links. This gives you a page dedicated to each section. Figure 15-30 is an example of the history page. Figure 15-32 shows the running timer jobs in the Timer Job Status page. Along with showing the timer jobs that are running, you can also see the progress of each job, complete with a progress bar. If you have many jobs running at once, you can click Running Jobs in the left navigation pane to access a page dedicated to reporting the timer jobs that are currently running.

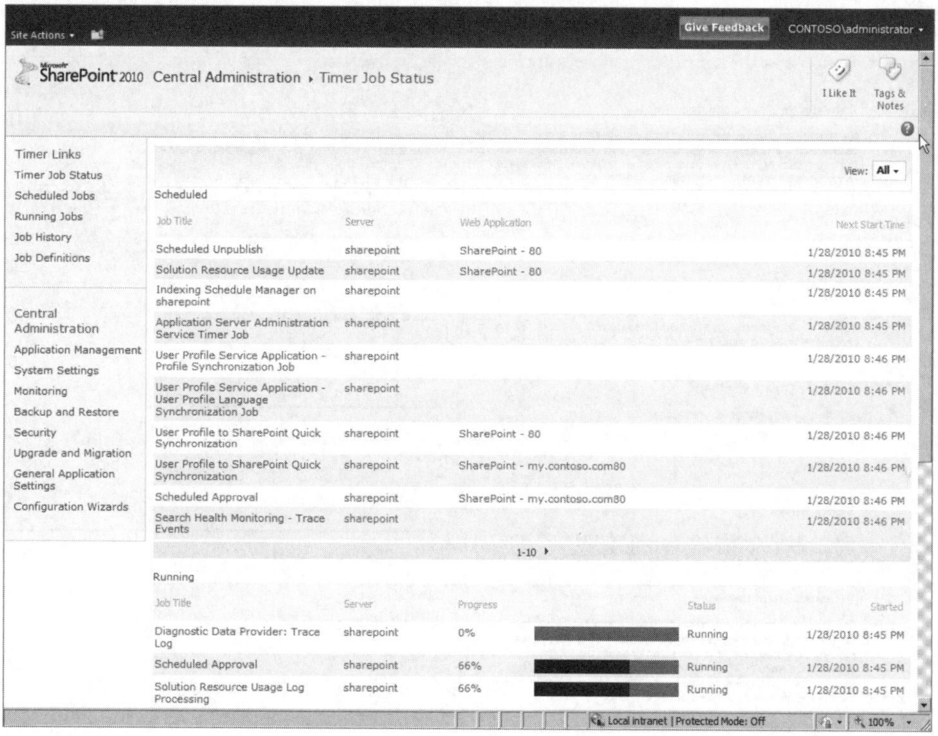

FIGURE 15-32

Here's one final timer job improvement: SharePoint 2010 introduces the capability to assign a preferred server for the timer jobs running against a specific content database. Figure 15-33 shows how it is configured in Central Admin.

This setting is set per content database, so it is set on the Manage Content Database Settings page (go to Central Administration ⇨ Application Management ⇨ Manage Content Databases). Being able to set a particular server to run the database's timer jobs serves two purposes. From a troubleshooting standpoint, you can use this to isolate failures to a single box, if you're having trouble with a specific timer job or content database. You can also use this to move the burden of timer jobs to a specific server. This server could be one that is not used to service end user requests, so having it be responsible for timer jobs will allow another scaling option.

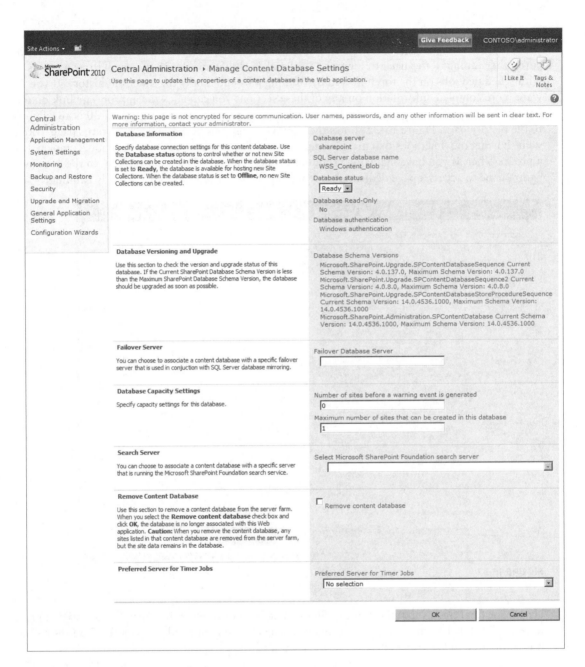

FIGURE 15-33

Again, you can take your administrative experience to the next level with Windows PowerShell. There are five cmdlets that ship with SharePoint that deal with timer jobs. To discover them use `Get-Command`:

```
PS C:\> Get-Command -noun SPTimerJob
```

You can use PowerShell to list all of your timer jobs using `Get-SPTimerJob`, and then choose to run one with `Start-SPTimerJob`.

SUMMARY

The monitoring capabilities in SharePoint got a serious shot in the arm with SharePoint 2010. The trace logs now take up less space, but somehow also hold more helpful information. The interface for configuring them has also been drastically improved. You also now have a database that is dedicated to logging and reports, and you can access it with Microsoft's blessing. The software has also become more self-sufficient. Not only can it monitor itself and let you know when there are problems, it can also fix some problems on its own. A wide variety of reports keep an eye on various aspects of the server, enabling you to proactively monitor it. Finally, even timer jobs have been improved. You can now run them at will, and you have much better diagnostic tools to watch over them. In short, the monitoring experience in SharePoint 2010 is much improved over earlier versions.

16

Managed Metadata Service Applications

WHAT'S IN THIS CHAPTER?

➤ Configuring managed metadata

➤ Metadata navigation

➤ Publishing content types

Two powerful features in SharePoint 2010 are metadata and content types. *Metadata* enables users to quickly and easily classify specific data about documents and list items within SharePoint by using list columns. *Content types* take metadata to the next level by providing a way to group a collection of metadata with a specific template. These content types can then be associated with many different lists within the site collection. Different content types can reference the same metadata (site columns), and content types can branch into several different levels.

An example of this scenario would be an organization that wants to create a *standard* document content type with three required metadata columns. By associating this content type with each of the document libraries, the organization provides a way to collect consistent data from many different locations. They could then create an additional *department* document content type that inherits from the standard document content type, thus allowing each department to add additional fields to the standard document. Using this approach enables an organization to manage the metadata and determine how it is associated with each of the different content types.

This functionality was provided within SharePoint 2007, but it was difficult for an organization to deploy and manage it on a large scale. The biggest problem arose when an organization needed to make different content types or site columns available to many different site collections as these are natively only available within the site collection in which they were created. In order to do this within the 2007 framework, solutions would have to be created to deploy the content types and site columns to each of the site collections. With the release of SharePoint 2010, the

Managed Metadata service, sometimes called the *Taxonomy* service, enables you to create and manage column types and content types in one centralized location that then serves as a "hub" for the rest of the SharePoint farm. These terms can even be consumed across different SharePoint farms. This enables you to create and manage content types at a global level.

ADVANTAGES OF THE MANAGED METADATA SERVICE

The Managed Metadata service offers a new way to look at content types and metadata. It allows you to provide a collection of metadata and content types to all sites within the SharePoint farm. This framework is managed at a farm level, where various settings such as preferred values and synonyms can be configured, yet it can still be expanded within sites that are subscribing to the service. Consistency and usability is improved at a global level, but functionality and the ability to customize remain in the hands of the users. Managed Metadata service offers some distinct advantages:

- ➤ **A global framework** — As described earlier, organizations often want to guide all of their departments to use specific columns and content types, but also provide some flexibility so that each department can extend the base schema to meet its specific needs. Through managed metadata and content type publishing, the Managed Metadata service within SharePoint 2010 provides this base schema. Site collections can consume the services and then extend them as needed to meet their specific needs.

- ➤ **Consistency in data entry** — The Managed Metadata service provides several key features that enable consistent entry of data. For instance, by configuring preferred values you can provide alternative selections to users when they are entering values. For example, if a user enters the term "car" or "vehicle," an alternate suggestion of "automobile" can be displayed for their selection. This feature provides a way to easily guide users to enter the preferred values for common words. In addition, as users are entering values for keywords, suggestions of previous keywords are displayed for selection. Because options are being presented to users, it is less likely that multiple terms for the same items will be entered.

- ➤ **Improved usability** — In addition to enabling users to quickly and easily tag data based on a global structure, many new features greatly improve usability, including type ahead, preferred values, and recently used values. These features are available both in the SharePoint UI and within the Office applications. Users will be able to learn one approach to entering data that can be used across multiple applications.

NEW MANAGED METADATA SERVICE FEATURES

In addition to the usability features mentioned in the previous section, the new Managed Metadata service includes three major new feature improvements for column types, content types, and filtering.

Column Types

Two new types of site column can be configured at a global level: Managed Metadata and Managed Keywords. Managed Metadata is a choice field that is configured to pull from levels within the global term store, and the Managed Keywords field is a text field that references a global store.

> ➤ **Managed Metadata** — Within Central Administration, you can create *term stores* that are used to populate various column types within SharePoint lists and libraries. Term stores are collections of like values. These term stores can be populated manually or through a .csv import file. The terms, or keywords, in the term store are managed at a global level, and then consumed by sites and webs within the environment.
>
> Examples of entries within a term store could include some of the following values:
>
> > ➤ Departments
> >
> > ➤ Offices
> >
> > ➤ Categories
> >
> > ➤ Project Status
>
> By adding these values at a global level, consistency across multiple sites and webs can be maintained. Instead of each site needing to maintain a column of the various departments within the organization, one centralized, managed list can be maintained. Combining this feature with the usability improvements such as type ahead and the data entry suggestion features enables users to easily and quickly enter standard organization data values.
>
> ➤ **Managed Keywords** — Managed keywords are similar to managed metadata, with the key difference being that the end user is able to enter new terms into the store — that is, terms that did not previously exist.

Content Types

Content types, mentioned earlier, are a powerful addition to any organization. They allow for standard templates, metadata, and workflows to be associated with different list items and document types. They provide a way for an organization to easily guide its users through adding content to the site, by showing them the specific metadata and workflows that should be associated with their content.

For example, at a global level the organization may want to collect the following information about each project document:

> ➤ Name
>
> ➤ Owner
>
> ➤ Keywords

Each department may want to also collect the following information:

➤ Project name

➤ Project type

➤ Assigned resources

In such a scenario, the organization would be able to take the global project document content type and expand it to capture the additional fields. Because the content type is based on the parent, Project Document, any changes to Project Document would be pushed down to the extended content type. Once the framework is in place, the rest of the organization will be able to work within that framework to meet their specific needs. As mentioned earlier, SharePoint 2010's Managed Metadata service stores these content types in a "hub," to be accessed and used across multiple site collections.

Filtering

One the key benefits of configuring and consuming the managed metadata available in the farm is the ability to take advantage of the new filtering features. These features allow for multi-level filtering within the managed metadata columns. This filtering is made available within the standard list views, as well as within the site navigation in the Quick Launch area. The remainder of this chapter provides an in-depth look at configuring, maintaining, and using these new features.

GETTING STARTED WITH THE MANAGED METADATA SERVICE

The Managed Metadata service is provided to different sites through the creation of a service application. This section describes the steps required to create and define the service application.

The Service Applications Architecture

Service applications in SharePoint 2010 provide the framework for sharing content and services across multiple web apps, sites, and webs. Service applications are new in SharePoint 2010 and replace what is currently provided by the Shared Service Provider in SharePoint 2007. For a more detailed look at what makes up a service application, refer to Chapter 7.

Configuring Managed Metadata Services

Configuring the Managed Metadata service in SharePoint 2010 is pretty straightforward. Follow these steps to create and prepare a new instance of the Managed Metadata service for use within the environment.

1. Open Central Administration and click the Application Management link. The Application Management screen has an entire section dedicated to the management of service applications, as indicated in Figure 16-1. These options enable you to create and edit new and existing service applications.

FIGURE 16-1

2. Click the link to the Manage Service Applications page. A listing of all service applications will be displayed. You can see all the services, their types, and their current status. Selecting any of these services will load the Ribbon, giving you quick access to the configuration elements of the service. Figure 16-2 highlights the Managed Metadata service and the corresponding Ribbon.

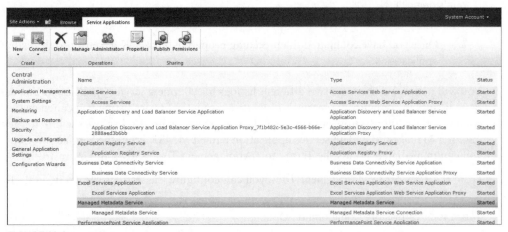

FIGURE 16-2

3. To create a new Metadata service application, select the New option from the Ribbon and select Managed Metadata service to load a new page where you can enter the service information. Table 16-1 shows the options available for configuration.

TABLE 16-1: Managed Metadata Service Application Configuration Options

OPTION	DESCRIPTION
Name	A short name used to describe the Managed Metadata service application.
Database Server	Name of the server that is hosting your SharePoint databases.
Database Name	The specific database that will be used to store the service information.
Database Authentication	The type of authentication used to access the information stored in the database. Windows Authentication is the recommended configuration for this setting.
Failover Server	The server that will be used as the failover server. For more information on using a failover server, refer to Chapter 12.
Application Pool	Defines the identity that the service will run as. This service can run using an existing application pool or a new one can be created.
Content Type Hub	The URL entered in this property will be used as the hub for all content types. This will point to a separate site collection.
Report Syndication Import Errors	Select this option if you would like this service to report synchronization errors.
Add this service application to the farm's default list.	Select this option if you want all sites to be connected to this service by default.

4. Once you have configured the preceding properties, click OK to return to the listing of service applications.

You will notice that there are two different listings for your new service application. You can select these listings to configure the service's properties. From the Service listing you can view the properties, configure the administrators, and manage the term store. Figure 16-3 shows the link to the Service listing for a Managed Metadata service application named MMS1. From the Service connection listing you can immediately access the Term Store Management Tool, shown in Figure 16-4.

From the Term Store Management Tool, you can configure the settings shown in Table 16-2.

TABLE 16-2: Term Store Configuration Options

OPTION	DESCRIPTION
Available Service Applications	Provides the capability to navigate between available Service Applications
Sample Import	Provides a sample import .csv file
Term Store Administrators	A collection of users or groups who have full control of the term store

OPTION	DESCRIPTION
Default Language	Specifies the default language
Working Languages	Specifies each of the languages available for the service application

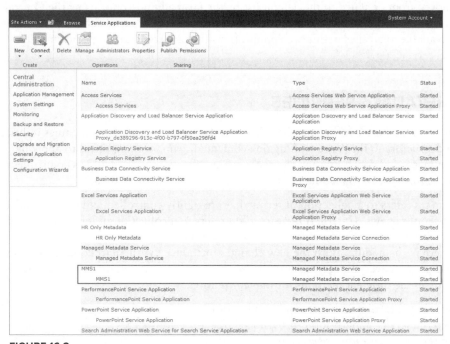

FIGURE 16-3

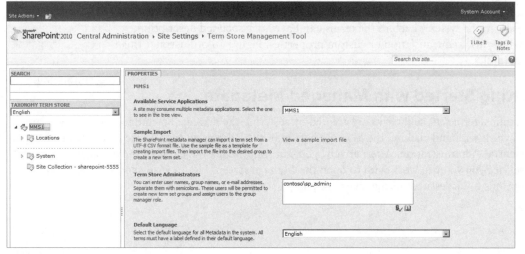

FIGURE 16-4

Connecting to a Web Application

Whenever a new web application is created, it can either be automatically associated with the default service applications or it can be configured using a custom set of service applications. Whenever you create a new Managed Metadata service application, one of the menu options will be adding it to the list of default service applications. After the service application has been created, it can only be removed from or added to the default list by the farm administrator using the Central Administration Farm Association page. If it is added to the default service applications when created, it will be available to all sites within web applications that are configured to consume the default services.

MANAGED METADATA SERVICES

The managed metadata services available in SharePoint 2010 provide a way for companies to bring organization and structure to the process of tagging content. *Tagging content* refers to applying metadata to documents and content within the organization. SharePoint 2010 allows companies to define and manage this process, including both structured and unstructured data.

Structured metadata refers to a collection of terms that are tightly controlled and only modified through a strict set of reviews. *Unstructured metadata* refers to a collection of terms that can be updated by users at will. These are two extreme ends of the spectrum, and most organizations operate somewhere in the middle. With the new changes introduced with SharePoint 2010, both ends of the spectrum and everything in the middle can be implemented and managed. The rest of this section discusses the different methods for implementation.

Metadata services in SharePoint 2010 are implemented through the use of a *term store*. When the service application is provisioned, the term store is created. Within the term store, *groups* are created that are used to house the term sets and terms. Groups are important because they are used primarily as a security boundary. *Term sets* are the groupings that are used to organize the terms. At the lowest level are the *terms*, which are the values selected by users in the system. Each of the terms can have an associated description, synonyms, and translation or custom properties. Figure 16-5 illustrates this hierarchy.

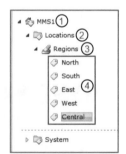

FIGURE 16-5

Getting Started with Managed Metadata

Groups, term sets, and terms are created by selecting the managed metadata service you want to work with and clicking the Manage button in the Ribbon on the Service Applications page in Central Administration. Alternatively, you can simply click the name of the managed metadata service you want to work with to open the Manage screen. Figure 16-6 shows the Ribbon menu options for accessing this management page.

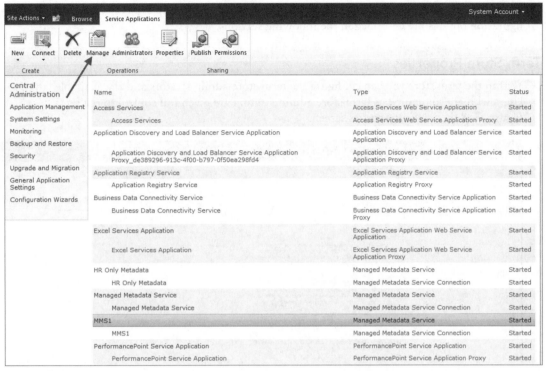

FIGURE 16-6

From within this management screen you can create and customize new content. Key actions include creating new groups, assigning group management permissions, and creating new terms and term sets. In most cases, the option to create the next level of content is provided on the parent level drop-down menu. For instance, the option for creating a new group is available on the Service Application dropdown, and the option to create a new term set is on the Group dropdown menu. An example of the Group dropdown menu is shown in Figure 16-7.

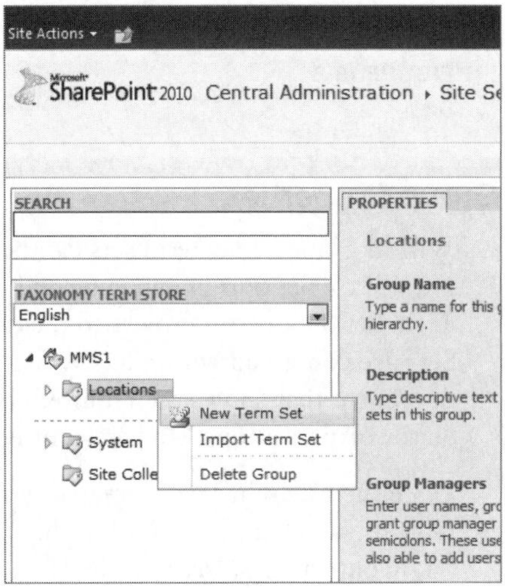

FIGURE 16-7

For each of the different levels of content, different menu options are available. The available configuration options are described in the following sections.

Term Store Properties

Within the term store you can configure the term store administrators and the available languages. Users who are configured as term store administrators are given full control to the term store. Figure 16-8 shows the Properties screen.

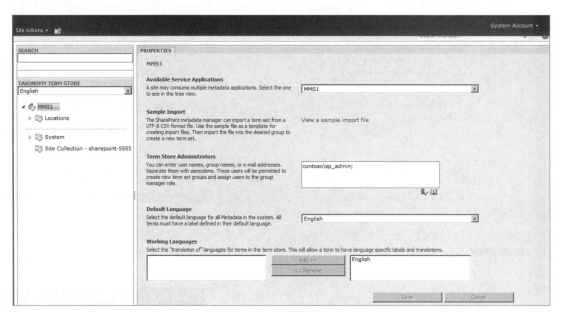

FIGURE 16-8

Group Properties

Within groups, new term sets can be imported or created. To create a new term set, simply select the New Term Set option and enter the required information. To import a term set, select the Import Term Set option and browse to the document that contains the term set to be imported. Import Term Sets are contained within a .csv file. Out of the box, Microsoft provides a sample term set import document that shows the required formatting. This sample import file can be accessed from the Service Applications Management page.

Once the group has been created, you can configure various properties for it. In addition to the Group Name and Description, there are two levels of configurable permissions: Group Managers and Contributors. Users in the Group Managers list may add items to the group as well as assign other users to the Contributor role. Users with the Contributor role will only be able to add terms and configure group hierarchies. Figure 16-9 shows the properties available for a group.

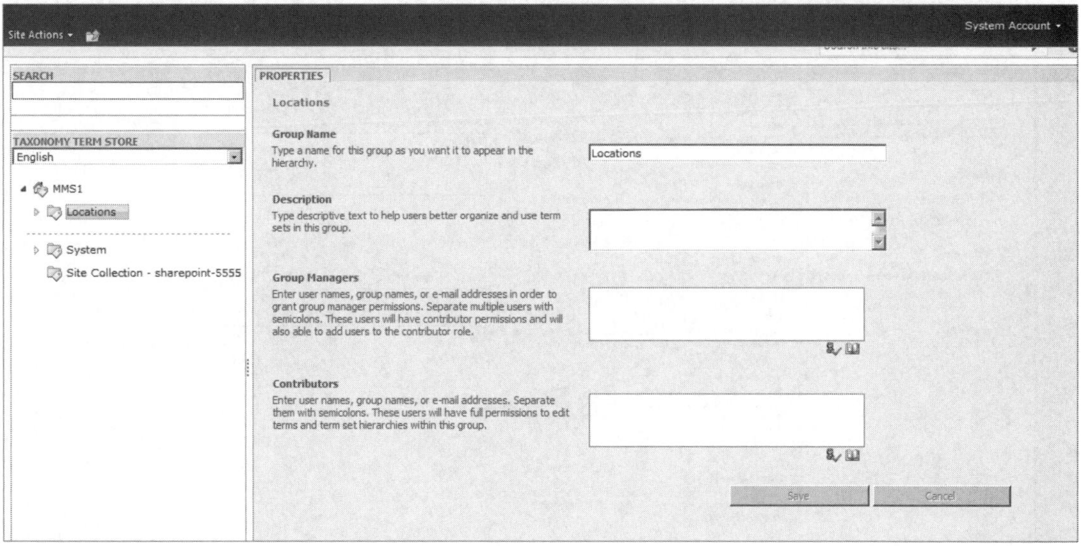

FIGURE 16-9

Term Set Properties

Within each term set you can configure several different properties in addition to the name and description properties. These properties can be divided into two areas: ownership and usability. From an ownership perspective, there are three different properties to be configured: Owner, Contact, and Stakeholders. The Owner property should be configured to the group or user who will have primary ownership and responsibility for the term set. The Contact property provides an e-mail address where users can submit feedback on the term set. This feedback will be valuable in determining any updates or modifications that can be made to improve the term set. The Stakeholders property enables you to keep track of various users and groups within the organization that should be notified whenever changes are made to the term set.

From a usability perspective, the following properties can be configured for the term set: Submission Policy, Available for Tagging, and Custom Sort Order. The submission policy is where the term set is configured to allow users to add items (open) or to restrict them from adding additional values (closed). If this term set is configured as an open term set, users will be able to add items to the term set whenever they are selecting values. The tagging property of the term set determines whether the items will be visible in the UI when users are selecting values. The custom sort order property allows the term set to be sorted using a custom order. A great example of this would be a term set that includes the days of the week. Logically, users would want to see the list sorted Sunday through Saturday and not in alphabetical order.

This is also the location where new terms are created. Selecting the dropdown menu from the Term Set in the tree view gives you several options for creating new terms and managing existing terms. From this menu you can create new terms, move entire term sets to new locations, create copies of term Sets, or delete entire term sets. Figure 16-10 shows the Term Set properties page; note that the options for custom sorting are located on a separate tab called Custom Sort.

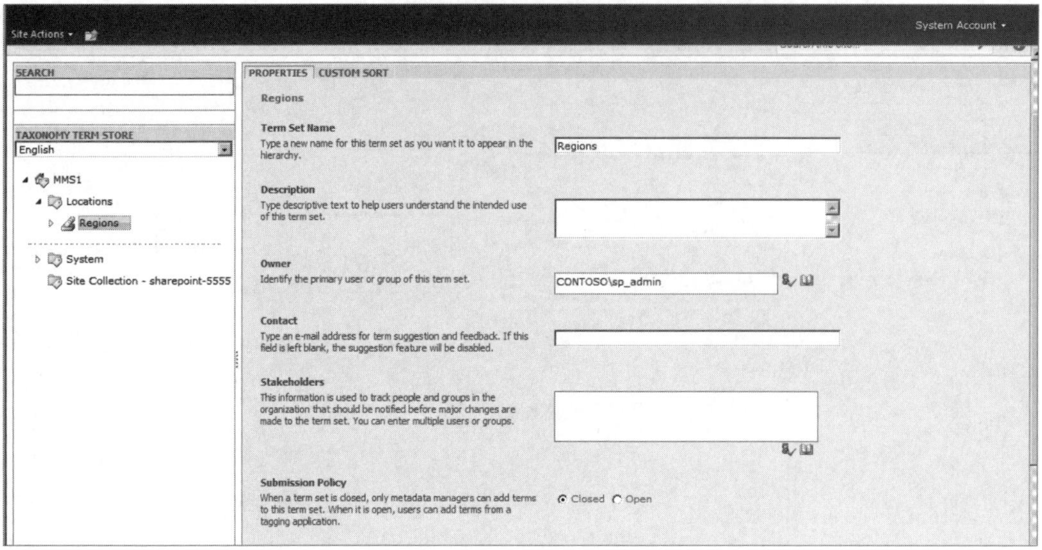

FIGURE 16-10

Term Properties

Each property within the term store can be configured with the following properties: Available for Tagging, Language, Description, Default Label (name) and Other Labels (synonyms). These properties can be configured per language. This means you can have separate synonyms for English and French, for example, if you have the French language pack installed on the server. Once a synonym has been created, whenever it is entered, the value is stored as the default label instead. This allows users to enter the same data in multiple formats and still store the same values.

An example of this is the term set for Regions, which contains a term for the Northeast region. There are many different ways to abbreviate this term set; one user may enter NE while another enters N.E. and yet another enters North East. By creating synonyms for each of the examples listed, all users will be storing the same value of Northeast, even though they entered an alternative value for the term. Figure 16-11 shows this configuration page.

Using Managed Metadata in Sites

Once the Term Stores have been configured within Central Administration, any site associated with the service application can create list columns based on entries in the Term Store. These columns can be created as site columns or list columns, and they can be associated with content types. Figure 16-12 shows the Create Column page where new managed metadata columns are configured. Figure 16-13 shows the list view of a library that is using managed metadata columns. Notice that the columns are displayed like any other list metadata column.

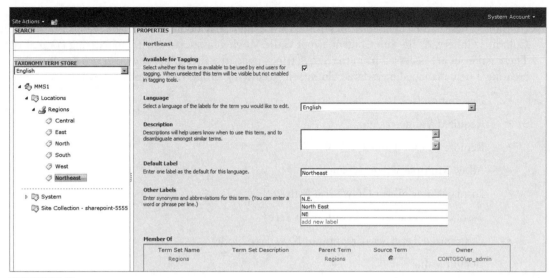

FIGURE 16-11

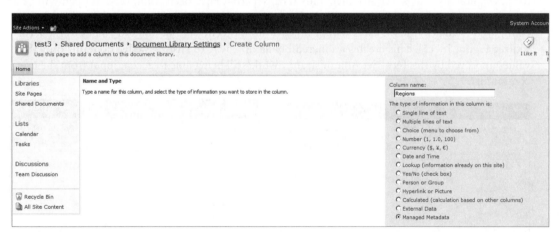

FIGURE 16-12

FIGURE 16-13

The process for creating new managed metadata columns is the same as creating traditional list columns. These can be created from within a list using the Ribbon or the List Settings page, the Site Columns Gallery, or the Site Content Types Gallery (when associated with an existing content type). These galleries are accessed from the Site Settings page in a site, under the Galleries heading. When creating a new managed metadata column, the following properties can be configured:

➤ Description (text)

➤ Required Value (yes/no)

➤ Require Unique Value (yes/no)

➤ Allow Multiple Values (yes/no)

➤ Display Value (Term Only/Term with Path)

➤ Associated Term Set (Selection from Tree)

➤ Customized Term Set (Creation of New Tree Node)

➤ Default Value

The specific settings configured in the Managed Metadata Services management screen will be applied to these column settings. For instance, only term sets that have been configured as open will be able to support fill-in values (see Figure 16-14). For term sets that have been marked closed but have a configured feedback e-mail, users will be able to submit feedback but not add values to the term set (see Figure 16-15). This creates an incredibly flexible way to ensure the list contains only those values approved by the Term Set Administrator, while still being able to accept input from the user community.

FIGURE 16-14

FIGURE 16-15

Column-Specific Term Sets

When creating a managed metadata site column, you can choose the option "Customize your term set" to create a *column-specific term set*. This term set will be created and stored in the service application that is configured as the default storage location; however, it will only be available for use in this specific location. This implies that if it is created at the list level, it can only be referenced in that specific column within the list; and if it is created at the site level, it can only be referenced within that site. If it is created as part of a content type that is published, it would be available wherever that content type is available, thereby facilitating enterprise manageability to that term set.

Key Usability Features

Managed Metadata columns provide several key usability features that will help define the end user experience. These rich features provide a clear and easy way to create, manage, and maintain global tagging structures. These features enable users to easily use, define, and communicate suggestions for existing structures. All the commands are located within the user interface, so users will not have to leave the entry screen to take advantage of these various features.

Type Ahead

When a user is entering the value for a field by directly typing the value into the text field, the field will identify what is being typed and provide selections based on the values being entered. For example, as a user types the value "Nor" into the text field, the field control will offer the selections of "North," "Northeast," and "Northwest." A user can then select from among these options, without having to type the complete value. Values for synonyms are also identified; for example, if the user enters "N," the field control would recognize the value as a synonym for the value "Northeast."

For fields that are part of open term sets, any previously typed values are displayed for the user. This valuable feature enables users to quickly zero in on previously created entries. Figure 16-16 demonstrates this feature.

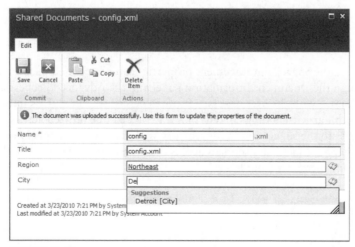

FIGURE 16-16

Browsing for Valid Options

Instead of manually typing the desired value, users can select the Browse icon located to the right of the field control. This option enables users to browse the tree structure of the values and select the desired value. If users don't see the desired value, they can suggest a new value or create a new value, if the term set allows. Users can drill down multiple levels within the tree view to select their desired value. Figure 16-17 illustrates the Browse feature.

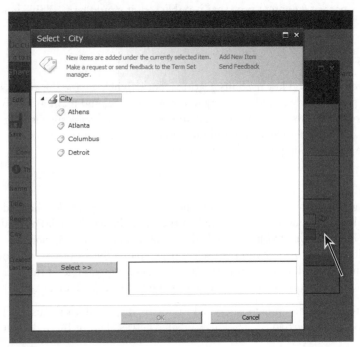

FIGURE 16-17

Office UI

From within the Office applications, the SharePoint document properties can be accessed in several ways. Two specific ways are through the Document Information Panel and the Advanced Properties screen. Each of these options integrates with the user interface features described above. This integration enables users to become familiar with adding content in a way that can be utilized across multiple applications. Having access to the suggestions and tree view within the Office application greatly increases the usability of managed metadata services across the organization. Figures 16-18 and 16-19 show examples of entering metadata from Excel.

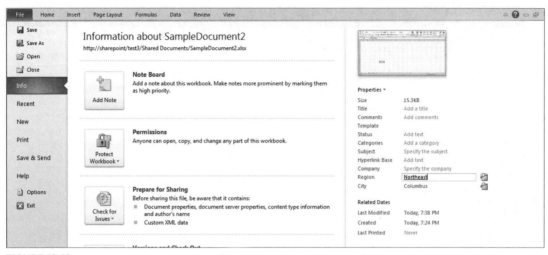

FIGURE 16-18

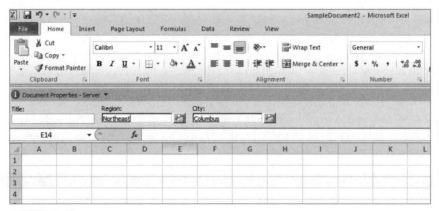

FIGURE 16-19

Metadata Navigation

Another new feature in SharePoint 2010 is the capability to create dynamic filters based on metadata. These new filters are referred to as *Metadata Navigation* and can be configured from the List Settings page. From the List Settings page you can configure Navigation Hierarchies and Navigation Filters. Hierarchies display in a tree view below the Quick Launch and enable you to drill down to filter through the various list metadata. Navigation Filters enable you to enter a specific value from the tree for filtering. Figure 16-20 shows a filter for the city of New Orleans.

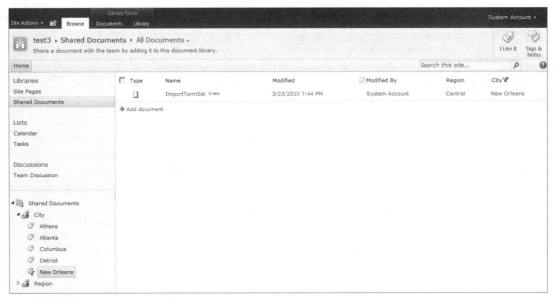

FIGURE 16-20

In addition to these navigation options, the filter can also be configured through the column drop-down menu. From this menu you can select which node of the tree to filter on and to include or exclude the descendants from the list. Note that if the column is configured to be part of the Key Filters, then filtering from the column drop-down is not enabled. Figure 16-21 shows the column filtering options. Metadata-driven, filter-based navigation is a logical and helpful addition to SharePoint 2010. Before this version of SharePoint, this type of navigation was only possible through localized customization of a SharePoint list.

FIGURE 16-21

CONTENT TYPES

Content types are a powerful feature within SharePoint that provide a single point of management of common document or list types. Content Types were introduced with SharePoint 2007 and could be used within any single site collection. If you needed to use content types across multiple site collections, the content types had to be deployed and managed at each of the site collections. This restriction made the use of global content types difficult in many organizations.

With the release of SharePoint 2010, many of these restrictions have been removed. Within managed metadata services, along with the Enterprise Term Stores, SharePoint administrators can configure a Content Type hub. This Content Type hub will be responsible for managing content types that can be published to all site collections that are consuming the services provided in the managed metadata service. Keep in mind that a single site collection can consume multiple managed metadata services.

The Content Type hub is configured once for each managed metadata service. Any site collection to which the Service Owner has access can be configured to be the site collection hub. Figure 16-22 shows the Managed Metadata Service configuration screen with the option for selecting the Content Type hub to be associated with the specific managed metadata service. Content Type hub configuration settings can be found in the Managed Metadata Service properties page.

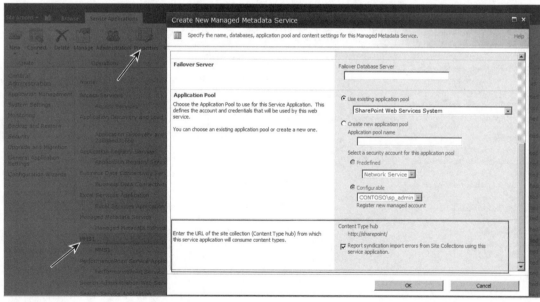

FIGURE 16-22

When selecting the Content Type hub, you also have an option to report any syndication errors. This is important because it provides detailed information about specific content that is not correctly deployed to all consuming site collections. When a site collection is configured as a Content Type hub, the Content Type Syndication Hub feature is automatically activated, enabling the necessary features to become available for the site collection to publish content types.

Additionally, several new options become available on the Site Settings page and the Content Type settings page. These new options control the ability to publish content types and review specific errors from the publishing process.

Content type publishing is controlled by two different timer jobs, the Content Type Hub and the Content Type Subscriber. The Content Type Hub timer job manages the maintenance logs and the unpublished content types. When this timer job is run, content types that have been identified to be published are made available to the Content Type Subscriber timer job. The Content Type Subscriber job is created for each of the web applications and is responsible for retrieving published content types and making them available in the local content type galleries for the subscribed site collections. The timer jobs are run on a default schedule, but you can update the schedule to match your organization's needs. Figure 16-23 shows the different timer jobs; notice that there is one global Content Type Hub timer job but a Content Type Subscriber job is created for each web application.

Title	Web Application	Schedule Type
Application Addresses Refresh Job		Minutes
Application Server Administration Service Timer Job		Minutes
Application Server Timer Job		Minutes
Audit Log Trimming	SharePoint - 80	Monthly
Audit Log Trimming	SharePoint - 8080	Monthly
Audit Log Trimming	SharePoint - 9090	Monthly
Audit Log Trimming	SharePoint - 9191	Monthly
Audit Log Trimming	SharePoint - portal.contoso.com80	Monthly
Bulk workflow task processing	SharePoint - 80	Daily
Bulk workflow task processing	SharePoint - 8080	Daily
Bulk workflow task processing	SharePoint - 9090	Daily
Bulk workflow task processing	SharePoint - 9191	Daily
Bulk workflow task processing	SharePoint - portal.contoso.com80	Daily
CEIP Data Collection		Daily
Cell Storage Data Cleanup Timer Job	SharePoint - 80	Weekly
Cell Storage Data Cleanup Timer Job	SharePoint - 8080	Weekly
Cell Storage Data Cleanup Timer Job	SharePoint - 9090	Weekly
Cell Storage Data Cleanup Timer Job	SharePoint - 9191	Weekly
Cell Storage Data Cleanup Timer Job	SharePoint - portal.contoso.com80	Weekly
Cell Storage User Data Deletion Job	SharePoint - 80	Disabled
Cell Storage User Data Deletion Job	SharePoint - 8080	Disabled
Cell Storage User Data Deletion Job	SharePoint - 9090	Disabled
Cell Storage User Data Deletion Job	SharePoint - 9191	Disabled
Cell Storage User Data Deletion Job	SharePoint - portal.contoso.com80	Disabled
Change Log	SharePoint - 80	Weekly
Change Log	SharePoint - 8080	Weekly
Change Log	SharePoint - 9090	Weekly
Change Log	SharePoint - 9191	Weekly
Change Log	SharePoint - portal.contoso.com80	Weekly
Content Organizer Processing	SharePoint - 80	Daily
Content Organizer Processing	SharePoint - 8080	Daily
Content Organizer Processing	SharePoint - 9090	Daily
Content Organizer Processing	SharePoint - 9191	Daily
Content Organizer Processing	SharePoint - portal.contoso.com80	Daily
Content Type Hub		Minutes
Content Type Subscriber	SharePoint - 80	Hourly
Content Type Subscriber	SharePoint - 8080	Hourly
Content Type Subscriber	SharePoint - 9090	Hourly
Content Type Subscriber	SharePoint - 9191	Hourly
Content Type Subscriber	SharePoint - portal.contoso.com80	Hourly
Crawl Log Cleanup for Search Application Search Service Application.		Daily

FIGURE 16-23

Creating and Publishing Content Types

Once the Content Type hub has been created, users who have access to the hub can create and manage the content types that will be published to the subscribing sites. The creation of the published content type follows the same creation process for nonpublished content types. The difference is that when a user is working within a site that has been created as a Content Type hub, additional configuration options are available in the Content Type management screen. The additional options are shown in Figure 16-24 and explained in detail in the following sections below.

FIGURE 16-24

Publishing, Unpublishing, and Republishing Content Types

Once a content type has been created in the Content Type Gallery on the hub site collection, it can be published to the subscribing site collections. The Content Type Publishing dialog, shown in Figure 16-25, allows you to Publish, Unpublish, or Republish a content type. Notice that it also displays the timestamp for the last successful publication.

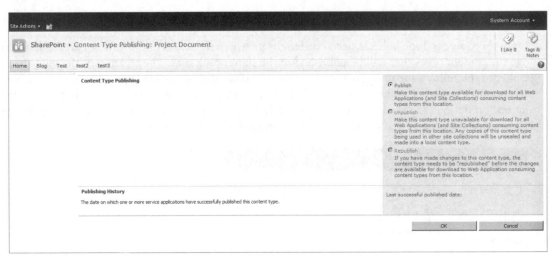

FIGURE 16-25

There are three specific publishing options, explained in Table 16-3.

TABLE 16-3: Content Type Publishing Options

PUBLISHING TYPE	DESCRIPTION
Publish	Make this content type available for download for all web applications (and site collections) consuming content types from this location.
Unpublish	Make this content type unavailable for download for all web applications (and site collections) consuming content types from this location. Any copies of this content type being used in other site collections will be unsealed and made into a local content type.
Republish	If you have made changes to this content type, the content type needs to be "republished" before the changes are available for download to web applications consuming content types from this location.

When a content type is initially published, it becomes available to the subscribing site collections. Within the subscribing site collection, the various published content types can be viewed using the Content Type Publishing option, available in the Site Collection Administration section on the Site Settings page. This configuration screen, shown in Figure 16-26, shows the different hubs that the site is subscribed to, the specific content types that have been published from those hubs, as well as a link to see the publishing error log.

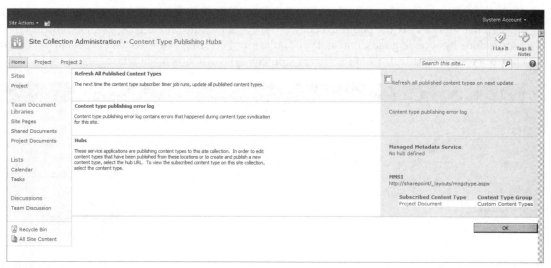

FIGURE 16-26

When site collection administrators click on a published content type, they will be directed to the settings page within their site collection. From this screen, site collection administrators can configure the advanced settings options for this content type, as shown in Figure 16-27.

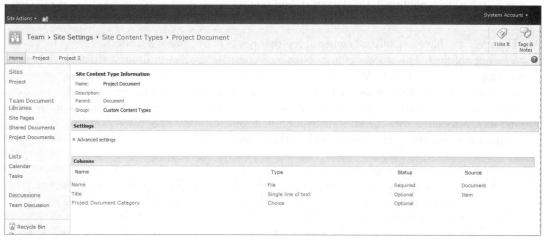

FIGURE 16-27

From here, the site collection administrator can configure a custom template for the content type, mark the content type as read only, and enforce an update to all content types that inherit from this content type.

Once a content type has been published to the subscribing sites, site collection administrators in the subscribing sites can use the published content type as a parent content type for new content types. This is done by accessing the Content Type Gallery and creating a new content type. All published content types are available from the Parent Content Type dropdown, shown in Figure 16-28.

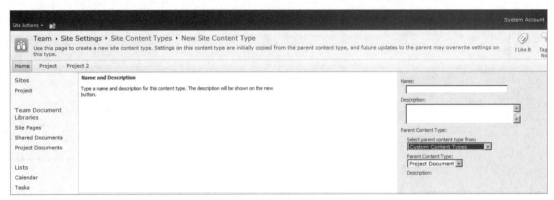

FIGURE 16-28

Whenever the content type is updated at the hub, it needs to be republished in order for the subscribing sites to receive the updates. The process for republishing is the same as publishing. Within the Content Type management screen, select the option to Manage Publishing Options. You will see that once the item has been published, the default option on the screen is set to republish. Clicking OK on this screen will cause the content type to be updated the next time the timer jobs run.

Whenever you have a published content type that needs to be removed from the hub, it first needs to be unpublished. The process of unpublishing a content type has a minimal effect on the sites subscribing to the content type. When a content type is unpublished from the hub, for any subscribing sites that have implemented the content type, a local content type will be created within the Content Type Gallery. The content type can then be updated within the gallery; however, any documents that were associated with the previously published content type will become read-only, and will not be updated if the associated content type in the gallery is updated.

 Not all items associated with a content type can be published through the Content Type hub. Two specific examples include associated workflows and lookup columns. Any time a content type with associated workflows is published, the workflows will only work on the subscribing sites if the workflow is currently available within that site.

Content Type Service Application Error Log

The Content Type Publishing hub includes a feature that allows for the reporting of syndication errors. This syndication error list is available within the Content Type hub site collection. The list is updated whenever the update timer jobs are run and provide detailed information about any specific errors that occurred during the synchronization. Figure 16-29 shows an example of this log.

FIGURE 16-29

Table 16-4 identifies the information presented within this log.

TABLE 16-4: Error Log Fields

FIELD	DESCRIPTION
Title	Error title.
Taxonomy Service Store ID	ID of the service.
Taxonomy Service Name	Name of the service.
Content Type Subscriber Site	Link to site with syndication errors.
Syndication Item	The content type that is unable to synchronize.
Syndication Failure Stage	The stage at which the syndication failed. Examples include pre-import checks or importing of workflows.
Syndication Failure Message	The specific details outlining what caused the syndication errors.
Syndication Failure Time	The timestamp of the error.

SUMMARY

The Managed Metadata service enables you to create, organize, and maintain a complete data-tagging solution for your organization. By providing the capability to create open term sets, SharePoint 2010 enables any organization to deploy both controlled and ad hoc content to users in a way that is familiar and easily accessible through products they already know and use. Content types enable you to create repeatable content structures that can be managed in a single location and deployed globally.

17

Social Computing and SharePoint 2010

WHAT'S IN THIS CHAPTER?

- ➤ Managing, using, and synchronizing user profiles

- ➤ Setting up and customizing My Sites

- ➤ Creating and using wikis and blogs

- ➤ Applying ratings

- ➤ Using the Outlook 2010 Social Connector plug-in

- ➤ Searching for people in SharePoint using People Search

Social computing is one of the fastest evolving trends on the Internet. This dynamic trend has touched the corporate environment and most, if not all, companies are thinking about using social computing in some capacity, but we are yet to see broad-scale adoption like we have seen on the public Internet. Social computing is generally about establishing communities, and building and maintaining relationships. It is usually recognized as involving blogs, wikis, social networks like Facebook, and micro-blogging like Twitter. Social computing (usually referred to as Web 2.0 on the Internet and Enterprise 2.0 in the corporate setting), is representative of a collection of different technologies. But in its most general sense, social computing is people interacting and sharing information, which is the exact goal of SharePoint and collaboration. SharePoint's social computing capability addresses the following areas:

- ➤ Capturing and sharing information

- ➤ Enabling people to find and engage experts

- ➤ Improving productivity

SharePoint 2010 social computing features include a new and better organized My Site, which provides dynamic news feeds so that people can stay up-to-date on colleague's activities. Central to the social computing capability is the User Profile Service, another service application in SharePoint 2010 new service architecture. Content tagging is a new introduction and all types of content can be tagged, categorized and viewed in the person's Tag Cloud Web Part, which is one of the built-in web parts. Tagged content can also be located more easily using search. Search and People Search have been improved and they provide excellent tools for finding information and experts. Blogs and wikis have been improved, and they now include the ability to host rich media such as audio and video. All of these topics are discussed in this chapter, which introduces you as an administrator to social computing and provides the information for installing and configuring the numerous options. The chapter begins with a discussion of the User Profile Service, which is at the heart of SharePoint's social computing capability.

THE USER PROFILE SERVICE APPLICATION

The User Profile Service Application is a managed application, and it is where the social computing setup begins in SharePoint 2010. This application stores information about all users, which can include profile properties from Active Directory, My Site configurations, and profile synchronization settings. This section describes the uses and configuration settings in the User Profile Service Application. Figure 17-1 displays the main screen of this managed application.

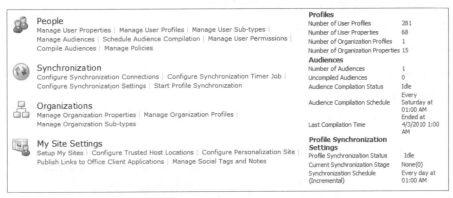

FIGURE 17-1

User Profiles and Properties

The People section of the User Profile Server Application contains information about all of the individuals in the organization, and the properties associated with their user profiles.

Manage User Properties

User properties are all of the fields associated with the database of users in the organization, referred to as a *directory service*. A long list of properties is included and already configured by default. These properties are also set up in visual groupings called *sections*, mostly for the purpose of organizing them. User properties can be set up in order to automatically pull or push data to the directory service, or configured to be editable by end users from within their SharePoint My Site. A user property is composed of the following:

➤ **Property Settings** — The property name is permanent and cannot contain any spaces, but the display name is what is shown to the end users. The type of property is a field type, such as a string, a date, or an integer. Fields of the type single or multi-value string also provide an option to configure a term set to be used for the property. (See Chapter 16 for more information on the concept of a *term set* and how to set one up.) Multi-value strings are properties that can contain more than one value, and properties can support multiple languages, using the Edit Languages button.

➤ **Sub-Type of a Profile** — Subtypes can be used to more granularly categorize the people, such as by a company's major divisions. Each profile property can be selectively added or removed from these subtypes.

➤ **Policy Settings** — Use this section to configure settings such as whether fields are required and who should be able to see them. The privacy setting determines just that — how private is the information in this property? For example, a property such as Home Phone will most likely be set up with a default privacy setting of Only Me or My Manager. If the organization's policy is that end users are allowed to modify the privacy setting, check the box next to User can override. When the default privacy setting is set to Everyone, the property may also be set as Replicable. This means that the property will be propagated down to each site's user information list.

 On any SharePoint site, click your user name drop-down button at the top-right corner of the site, and click My Settings. User properties that are set as Replicable will appear on this screen. Replicable properties also become available properties in the settings of the out-of-box Web Part called the Current User Filter.

➤ **Edit Settings** — Use this section to specify whether users should be allowed to edit the value of this property. For properties that are automatically populated from the directory service, it is a best practice to choose Do not allow users to edit values for this property, because the value will be overwritten during the next synchronization.

➤ **Display Settings** — If a property is set as visible to everyone in the policy settings, there will be an option to Show in the profile properties section of the user's profile page. This means that when a user's My Site profile is being viewed, this property will be displayed. When Show on the Edit Details page is enabled, it will be available as an editable property when a user clicks Edit my profile, which is a link located under the user photo on the My Site. If the Edit Settings section is set to *not* allow users to edit the property value, then selecting to Show on the Edit Details page will not have any effect. Enable the Track updates to the property in the User Profile change log option to display changes to this property as part of the newsfeed of activities in SharePoint 2010, which can be seen on the My Network page on any user's My Site. Figure 17-2 shows the Policy, Edit, and Display settings sections.

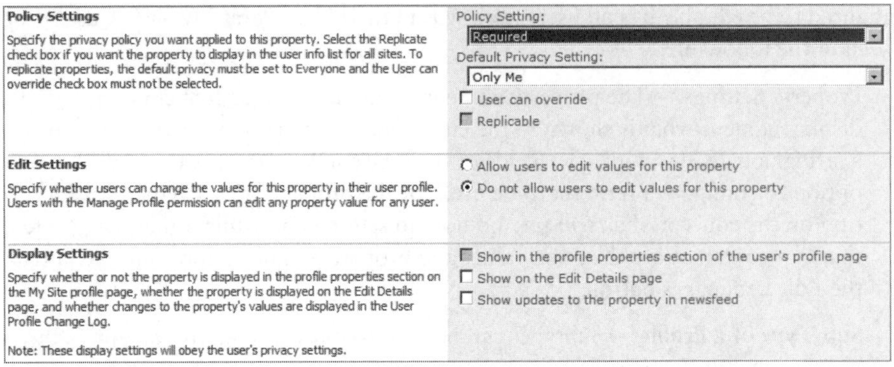

FIGURE 17-2

➤ **Search Settings** — The Alias setting is used only for the unique fields associated with each user, such as Account name, Name, User name, and Work e-mail. When a property is configured as indexed, this allows the data to be searched when searches for people are performed in SharePoint.

➤ **Mapped Data** — Each property in the list can be mapped to a specific attribute in another line-of-business directory service, such as Active Directory. First, pick a Source Data Connection. (The upcoming "Synchronization" section covers how to create these data connections.) Then, from within that source, pick an attribute, which is a field in the user database. Lastly, choose whether to either import this attribute into SharePoint, or export it from SharePoint.

ACTIVE DIRECTORY ATTRIBUTE NAMES

When mapping attributes from Active Directory to the profile properties in SharePoint, sometimes it is a little difficult to discern the correct attribute, simply because the names don't necessarily match up. For example, when creating a new profile property called Zip to map to the Zip Code attribute in Active Directory, it took a while to figure out that Zip is actually called postalCode.

You can use ADSI Edit to take a look at the real attribute names. From a server with the Active Directory domain services role installed, click Administrative Tools in the Start menu and choose ADSI Edit. Click Action, click Connect to, and type your domain name. Then, navigate through the Active Directory structure to where the user objects are. Right-click on a user's name and choose Properties. Scroll through the Attribute Editor tab to see the names of the attributes and the data in them.

Manage User Profiles

Once user profiles have been synchronized, they are available in the Manage User Profiles interface. Scroll through the list of users, or use the Find Profiles box to search for specific users by name. To modify a profile, click an account name and choose Edit. You can also use the New Profile button to create a new user profile. When the profiles are imported using a synchronization connection, it is not usually necessary to create new ones from here.

 When editing an individual user profile, note that icons next to profile properties give a quick indication as to which ones are required, and which properties were imported through a data connection.

Profile Services Policies

The Profile Services policies settings are used to determine how to share personalized information, along with who can view this information about users. Use these policies to configure privacy settings and access for My Site personalization features and user profile properties. Administrators can configure policies for each specific feature or user profile property, allowing them to align to the organization's existing privacy and sharing policies. Some of the types of policies that can be configured in this interface are as follows:

➤ SharePoint site and distribution list memberships

➤ Auto-population and recommendations of colleagues

➤ My Links on My Site

➤ Personalization site pinning

➤ User profile properties

Follow these steps to change the settings of a profile service policy in the User Profile Service Application:

1. In the People section, click Manage Policies.

2. Click the drop-down box on a policy and click Edit Policy.

3. The policy setting can be enabled or disabled. The default privacy setting configures who is allowed to see the information in this property. In addition there is an option that allows users to override the default policy setting.

4. Click OK after changes have been made.

Manage User Sub-types

From the User Profile Service Application you can easily access the Sub-types page by clicking the Manage User Sub-types link. As shown in Figure 17-3, you can create new user sub-types or remove existing ones from this page. Use sub-types for classification of user properties, which means that if desired, user properties can be associated with only specific sub-types. An example of the use of sub-types would be for a large company that has many user accounts for vendors with whom it does business. A user subtype called "Vendors" could be created, and a new property called "Vendor Company" could be created. This property could be set up to be associated only with the users that are categorized into the Vendors sub-type.

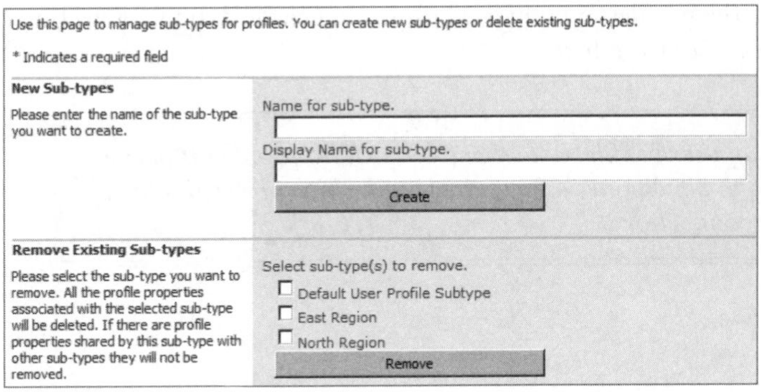

Use this page to manage sub-types for profiles. You can create new sub-types or delete existing sub-types.

* Indicates a required field

New Sub-types

Please enter the name of the sub-type you want to create.

Name for sub-type.

Display Name for sub-type.

Create

Remove Existing Sub-types

Please select the sub-type you want to remove. All the profile properties associated with the selected sub-type will be deleted. If there are profile properties shared by this sub-type with other sub-types they will not be removed.

Select sub-type(s) to remove.

☐ Default User Profile Subtype
☐ East Region
☐ North Region

Remove

FIGURE 17-3

Manage User Permissions

Within the User Profile Service Application, administrators can configure permissions to control whether or not users can create their own My Sites, and if they can use personal features or social features. Figure 17-4 shows the default permission setting, which allows all authenticated users to use all personalization features.

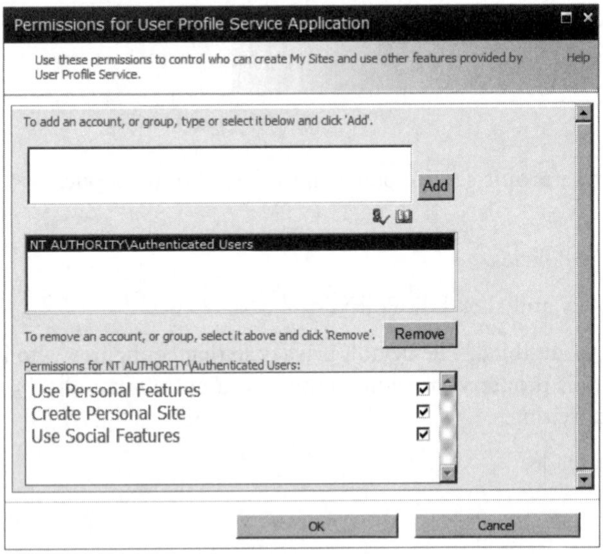

Permissions for User Profile Service Application   ☐ ✕

Use these permissions to control who can create My Sites and use other features provided by User Profile Service.   Help

To add an account, or group, type or select it below and click 'Add'.

Add

NT AUTHORITY\Authenticated Users

To remove an account, or group, select it above and click 'Remove'.   Remove

Permissions for NT AUTHORITY\Authenticated Users:

Use Personal Features   ☑
Create Personal Site   ☑
Use Social Features   ☑

OK   Cancel

FIGURE 17-4

The top portion of the permissions screen allows you to add groups, which then appear in the list in the middle section. Select a group from the middle section, and assign it permissions using the checkboxes at the bottom.

Synchronization

Within the User Profile Service Application, synchronization is set up between SharePoint and other directory services applications, such as Active Directory, an LDAP directory, or other line of business (LOB) applications. User profile data is stored in a database inside of SQL Server.

Synchronization Connections

Synchronization connections are set up in order to either pull profile property data from directory services into SharePoint or export it back out.

Active Directory

Follow these steps to create each synchronization connection from within the User Profile Service Application:

1. In the Synchronization section, click Configure Synchronization Connections.
2. Click Create New Connection.
3. Type a descriptive name as the Connection Name.
4. The type of connection can be one of the following: Active Directory, Active Directory Logon Data, Active Directory Resource, Business Data Connectivity, ITDS, Novell eDirectory, or Sun Java System Directory Server.
5. Once a Type has been selected, the rest of the settings on the screen vary according to connection type.

Table 17-1 describes the settings for the most common connection type, Active Directory.

TABLE 17-1: Create Active Directory Synchronization Connection

SETTING	DESCRIPTION
Connection Name	A descriptive name of the connection.
Type	Active Directory.
Connection Settings	Type the name of the Active Directory forest, and either choose auto-discovery of a domain controller or type a specific one.
Authentication Provider Type	Choose from Windows Authentication, Forms Authentication, or Trusted Claims Provider Authentication.
Account Name and Password	Account credentials for Active Directory access.
Port	The default port is 389.
Containers	Click the Populate Containers button to see a hierarchical view of Active Directory. From this view, a specific Organizational Unit (OU) or other containers may be selected.

Figure 17-5 displays the Add new synchronization connection screen:

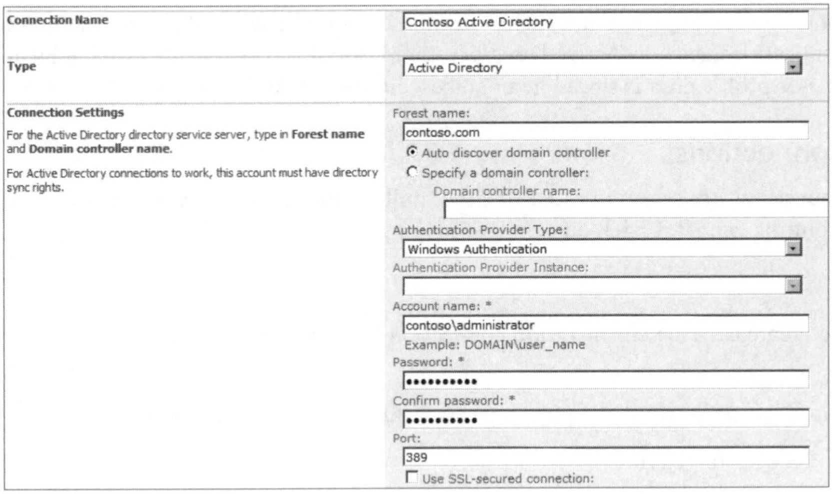

FIGURE 17-5

Business Data Connectivity

When external content types have been created in SharePoint 2010, they can be used as synchronization connections. Learn more about external content types in Chapter 24. When an external data source is selected as a Business Data Connectivity entity, there are additional options to connect the user profile store to the business data connectivity entity as either a one-to-one mapping or a one-to-many mapping. Once the BDC connection has been created, this is treated as secondary to the Active Directory connection, and does not overwrite existing imported data.

Connection Filters

Connection filters enable users to filter the data that is imported into SharePoint. By default, all user accounts are imported, including disabled accounts. One way to use the connection filter is to selectively import only active user accounts from Active Directory. Follow these steps to create a filter that excludes disabled accounts from the import:

1. In the User Profile Service Application, click Configure Synchronization Connections.

2. Hover over the name of any connection that has been created, click the drop-down box, and choose Edit Connection Filters.

3. Under Exclusion Filters for user, click the Attribute drop-down box, and choose the userAccountControl.

4. Choose the operator "equals."

5. In the Filter text box, type the number 0x10222. (After saving these settings, the next time you look, the number will be 66082)

6. Click the Add button, and then click OK. During the next import, those accounts will be excluded.

Synchronization Timer Job

Once synchronization connections have been set up, you will need to configure a schedule for when this synchronization is to take place. An import should be performed at a frequency that matches how often the data source content changes. In the User Profile Service Application, click Configure Synchronization Timer Job. Use this screen to set the timer job to run on a recurring schedule according to minutes, hours, days, weeks, or months. In addition, you can start the synchronization immediately by clicking the Run Now button.

Synchronization Settings

In the User Profile Service Application, click Configure Synchronization Settings. This page enables you to change more specific configuration settings regarding the data synchronization connections that have been created. Several options are available, such as whether to import only Users, or Users and Groups.

Organizations

The concept of organizations in the User Profile Service Application is similar to the user profiles, the difference being that user properties are related to individual people, and organization properties are related to entire organizations. Organization sub-types can be used to more granularly categorize multiple organizations, such as by a company's major divisions or subsidiaries.

On the main User Profile Service Application screen, there is an area called Organizations that contains links to Manage Organization Properties, Manage Organization Profiles, or Manage Organization Sub-types.

A multinational company with different subsidiary companies is one example of how this feature might be used. The company could use these Organizations in order to specify different information about the subsidiary. Some users can actually have multiple profiles, one for each of different subsidiaries that they may work with.

Audiences

SharePoint audiences, which are used to target content to specific sets of users, can be quite powerful when used to their full extent. Audiences are defined here in the User Profile Service Application, and can be used in many ways in sites and lists to display information relevant to specific users. Audiences are not a security setting, but are simply used to display pertinent information to certain people.

Before creating audiences, it is important to plan audience use. Audiences cannot be used to their full advantage unless the user data is accurate in the user profiles and properties. Whether this information comes from Active Directory or another line of business directory services such as PeopleSoft, correct and consistent profile data is imperative. Once this profile data is accurate and useful, you should understand how to use audiences before going through the process of defining them.

The following is a list of places in SharePoint 2010 where audiences are applicable:

➤ List items displayed in a Content Query Web Part

➤ Personalization Site links and Publish links to Office client applications

➤ Web Parts

➤ Web Part pages

➤ Navigation links

Setting Up an Audience

Follow these steps in order to set up audiences in the User Profile Service Application:

1. In the People section, click Manage Audiences.

2. Click the New Audience button. The screen shown in Figure 17-6 will appear.

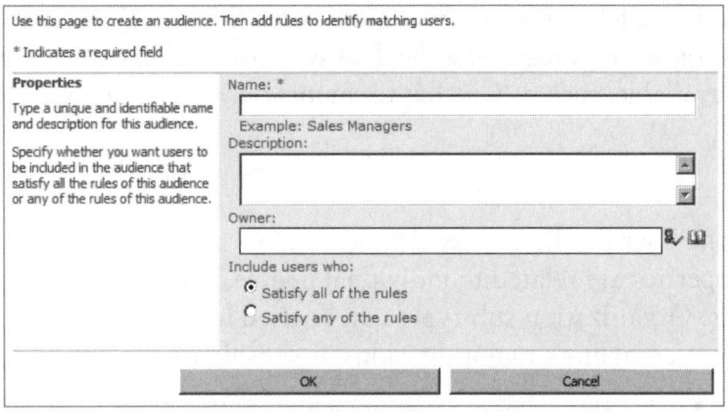

Use this page to create an audience. Then add rules to identify matching users.

* Indicates a required field

Properties

Type a unique and identifiable name and description for this audience.

Specify whether you want users to be included in the audience that satisfy all the rules of this audience or any of the rules of this audience.

Name: *

Example: Sales Managers

Description:

Owner:

Include users who:
- Satisfy all of the rules
- Satisfy any of the rules

OK   Cancel

FIGURE 17-6

3. Give the audience a Name and Description.

4. Define the audience owner.

5. Multiple rules can be defined, so specify whether all or any of the rules need to be satisfied in order for a user to be included in the audience. Click OK.

6. Using the screen shown in Figure 17-7, set up a rule that defines the audience.

7. Create a rule based on either the User or Property Operand. Click OK.

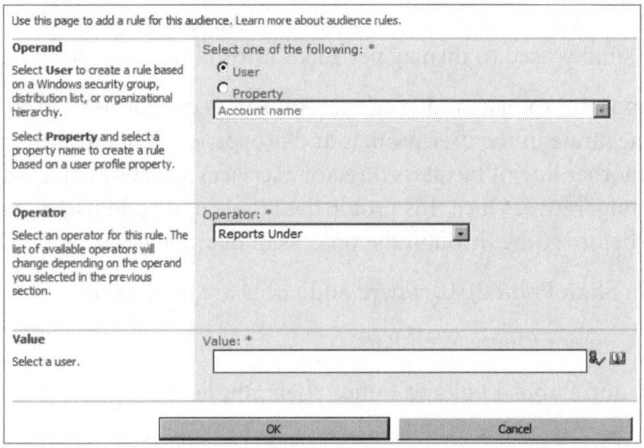

Use this page to add a rule for this audience. Learn more about audience rules.

Operand

Select **User** to create a rule based on a Windows security group, distribution list, or organizational hierarchy.

Select **Property** and select a property name to create a rule based on a user profile property.

Select one of the following: *
- User
- Property

Account name

Operator

Select an operator for this rule. The list of available operators will change depending on the operand you selected in the previous section.

Operator: *

Reports Under

Value

Select a user.

Value: *

OK   Cancel

FIGURE 17-7

Audience Targeting Rules and Logic

This section uses some examples to describe the rules for audience targeting and the logic behind them.

For the first example, suppose you want to make sure that new employees see Web Parts and content relevant to those new to the company, such as forms to fill out and orientation announcements to read. You could create an audience called "New Hires." The rule that defines it can be as follows:

➤   Property of Hire Date >= 1/1/2010

This rule could be changed once per year to include everyone hired in the past year as new hires.

The second example uses an audience called Marketing, with three possible ways to define this group of people:

➤   Define an audience according to a group of people who report to the same manager. This option is useful as long as the Manager property is accurate in the user profiles. The downside to this option is handling employee attrition. Because this rule is based on an individual person, when that person leaves the company, this audience must be redefined to include the new marketing manager's name. The rules for this example would be:

  ➤   **Operand** — User

  ➤   **Operator** — Reports under

  ➤   **Value** — Select the name of the manager of the marketing department.

➤   Define an audience based on group membership. Any security-based distribution list in Active Directory can be selected as the basis for an audience. In this example, we have already created a group called Marketing, which contains all of the members of the marketing department. The rules for this example would be:

  ➤   **Operand** — User

  ➤   **Operator** — Member of

  ➤   **Value** — The name of the group, in this case "Marketing"

➤   Define an audience based on information in user profile properties. In this example, the Department property contains the word "Marketing." The rules for this example would be:

  ➤   **Operand** — Property

  ➤   **Operator** — Contains

  ➤   **Value** — Marketing

Given the different rules that might define the marketing department in the company, think about how restrictive the audience definition should be. In Figure 17-7, under the Audience settings, you could include users who satisfy all of the rules if each person must report to the specific marketing manager *and* have membership in the Marketing group in Active Directory *and* have "Marketing" as part of their department name. Alternately, you could choose to include users who satisfy any of the rules, if at least *one* of these criteria needs to be met. The second option allows for a broader audience, of course.

Audience Compilation

The list of audience members can be compiled on a schedule. This compilation entails a scan of changes in the user profiles, and changing the audience member list accordingly. For example, if a user was not in the marketing department during the last compilation, then the new compilation will recognize the changes to the user's profile, and add them as a member of the audience automatically. All audiences are compiled on the same schedule. Follow these steps to set up an audience compilation schedule in the User Profile Service Application:

1. In the People section, click Schedule Audience Compilation.

2. Check the box to Enable Scheduling.

3. Configure settings for daily, weekly, or monthly compilation. Click OK.

At any point, a manual compilation of all audiences can be started by clicking Compile Audiences in the People section. Any individual audience can be manually compiled from that audience's properties screen by clicking Compile audience.

Targeting Content to Audiences

We create audiences in SharePoint, so that some content can be targeted to be seen by certain people. It is a good idea to first determine where audiences will need to be used, before going through the process of creating them.

> *Several bullet points on this page note that audiences do not need to be created at the Central Administration level in order to target content. In some cases, the audience settings allow for the selection of already existing SharePoint or Active Directory Groups.*

This section describes several targeting methods, along with instructions to carry them out.

> ➤ **List Items displayed in a Content Query Web Part** — In the settings for any list or library, click Audience targeting settings, and check the box to Enable audience targeting. There will be a new field in the list, called Target Audiences. Set target audiences on individual items in the list, from the Edit Properties page. The way that the audience targeting is made applicable is to display the list in a Content Query Web Part on a Web Part page on a site in the same site collection. In the Web Part's tool pane settings, note two checkboxes: In the Query section, there is an Audience Targeting area. Once the setting to Apply audience filtering is selected, you can optionally choose to include items that are not targeted. Pick from audiences, distribution lists, or SharePoint groups for targeting. This means that if an audience for a Content Query Web Part simply needs to be an Active Directory or SharePoint group, then it is not necessary to define this audience in the User Profile Service Application.

> ➤ **Personalization Site Links and Publish Links to Office Client Applications** — In the My Site Settings section of the User Profile Service Application, the Personalization Site Links and

the Publish Links to Office Client application options both allow for content to be audience targeted. Read more about these features in the "My Sites" section of this chapter.

➤ **Web Parts** — Any Web Part can be targeted to an audience. In the Web Part's properties tool pane, expand the Advanced section, which contains a Target Audiences field at the bottom. Pick from audiences, distribution lists, or SharePoint groups for targeting. This means that if an audience for a Web Part simply needs to be an Active Directory or SharePoint group, then it is not necessary to define this audience in the User Profile Service Application.

➤ **Web Part Pages** — In SharePoint publishing sites, there is a library called Pages. Click to Edit Properties of any individual page in the library, to see the field called Target Audiences. Pages that have been targeted to audiences will be displayed only to that audience, within the site's navigation. Pick from audiences, distribution lists, or SharePoint groups for targeting. This means that if an audience for a Web Part page simply needs to be an Active Directory or SharePoint group, then it is not necessary to define this audience in the User Profile Service Application.

➤ **Navigation Links** — Within the navigational structure of the site, individual links may be targeted to audiences. On a SharePoint Server 2010 site, click Site Actions ➪ Site Settings. In the Look and Feel section, click Navigation. Click a link in the navigation, and then click the Edit button. (Some items are not editable because they are part of the built-in site structure.) This screen is displayed in Figure 17-8. Type an audience name and click OK. Pick from audiences, distribution lists, or SharePoint groups for targeting. This means that if an audience for a link simply needs to be an Active Directory or SharePoint group, it is not necessary to define this audience in the User Profile Service Application.

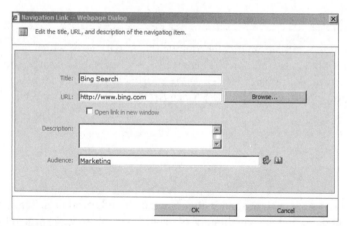

FIGURE 17-8

➤ **Trusted My Site Hosted Locations** — In larger SharePoint deployments with geographically distributed User Profile Service Applications, administrators manage a list of Trusted My Site host locations, which can be targeted to audiences. These different locations can exist as multiple web applications in a farm. This setting is found in the My Sites section of the application.

Remember that audiences are not a method of controlling security. Items that are not targeted to specific users are not inaccessible to those users. Navigation in SharePoint will automatically be security trimmed, which means that users who don't have access to a list, library, or site, will not see that link in navigation. When it comes to navigation, audience targeting is most useful with links that have been manually added, such as links to external websites, or links to other site collections.

TAGS AND NOTES

Interfaces for social interactivity and feedback on content are pervasive throughout SharePoint 2010. Users are encouraged to tag items everywhere in the environment, which makes their experience more interactive and collaborative. This section explains the tagging and notes interface, including steps for tagging and making notes.

First, take a look at the top-right corner of any site in SharePoint 2010 to see the I Like It and Tags & Notes buttons, shown in Figure 17-9.

These icons will become very familiar, as they appear pretty much everywhere in SharePoint 2010.

FIGURE 17-9

ACTIVITY FEED TIMER JOB

By default, SharePoint does not automatically compile the activity feed, which is the list of user activities like tags and notes. There is a server timer job that needs to be enabled first. In Central Administration, click Monitoring in the quick launch. In the list of timer jobs, click the User Profile Service Application ➪ Activity Feed Job, and click the Enable button.

Tagging

In SharePoint Server 2010 discussions, you hear a lot about metadata and social tags. Tags are basically keywords, or data about data. To tag something is to assign keywords to it, separated by semicolons, and these keywords can be associated with anything. End users are able to "tag," which not only adds a level of rich interactivity, but enables participation in the SharePoint community in the organization. The I Like It button, next to Tags & Notes, enables users to quickly identify content that they like. These tags can also be managed, and even structured, from within Central Administration and at other levels. Read Chapter 16 for a thorough understanding of this managed metadata. Here is a list of some objects that can be tagged in SharePoint 2010:

➤ Pages

➤ Libraries

➤ Lists

➤ List items

➤ Documents

➤ External websites

➤ My Sites

➤ Tag profiles

➤ Images

When tagging pages, libraries, lists, My Sites, and tag profiles, the experience is similar. Simply navigate to that location in SharePoint, and use the Tags & Notes button at the top-right corner of the page. Figure 17-10 shows an example of the Tags & Notes interface after some user activity.

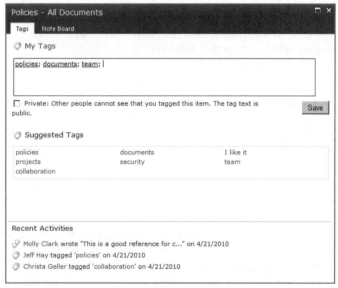

FIGURE 17-10

My Tags are tags that you have added, and the Suggested Tags section shows what others have added to the same object. As you start typing a new tag, SharePoint will automatically suggest similar tags that already exist as managed metadata.

In document libraries, the content tagging setting is not turned on by default. To enable it, in the library settings, click Enterprise Data and Keyword Settings. There are two check boxes on the Enterprise Metadata and Keywords Settings screen:

➤ **Add Enterprise Keywords** — Check this box in order to make use of any legacy keywords associated with the items in this list. In the Office applications, on the File Save As screen, there is a Tags field. The words entered here automatically populate a new Enterprise Keywords column in the document library. Once this check box is selected and OK is clicked, this option cannot be turned back off. The new column can then be added to any views in the library. When only this option is selected, tags added to the Enterprise Keywords column are not part of the Tags & Notes for the item.

➤ **Metadata Publishing** —When this option is selected, tags can be added to the item using the Tags & Notes button, and those tags are saved as social tags in the Managed Metadata.

When both of the above items are selected, the Enterprise Keywords for an item are the same as the Tags in the Tags & Notes screen. For example, when a document is created, tags can be added on the Save As screen in Word. These tags not only get passed to the Enterprise Keywords column in the library, but they show up when viewing the Tags & Notes screen for the item. Why participate in tagging? Tagging something helps to describe it, and enables it to be found again by browsing or searching. When you identify and classify items this way, it aids in information retrieval for not only the individual doing the tagging, but also for other people who visit SharePoint sites. The tags themselves each have their own page, or Tag Profile, and can be followed by other people in their My Site activity feeds.

Shown in Figure 17-11 is the out-of-the-box Web Part called the Tag Cloud Web Part, which can be found in the Social Collaboration category when adding the Web Part.

FIGURE 17-11

A tag cloud is a listing of recent tags related to the current page. Tags that have been used more often are displayed in a larger font, with the font size decreasing for tags that have been used less often. By default, this Web Part displays tags created by the current user only, but the Web Part's properties can be changed to show tags by everyone. The Web Part can also be configured to display a maximum number of tags, or to display a number in parentheses next to each tag (Show Count), indicating the exact number of times it has been used. By default, the date range of tags is one month, but it can be changed to one year or all dates. A tag cloud is also displayed on the Tags & Notes tab of each user profile.

The Note Board

The Note Board is new in SharePoint 2010, and it is pervasive throughout all sites in the environment. Notes in SharePoint 2010 are literally free-form notes that users add to SharePoint objects, as a running commentary. Like the tags described in the preceding section, these notes exist within the same interface. Notes are an integral part of an activity feed in the social network of SharePoint 2010. Figure 17-12 displays the Note Board portion of the Tags & Notes interface.

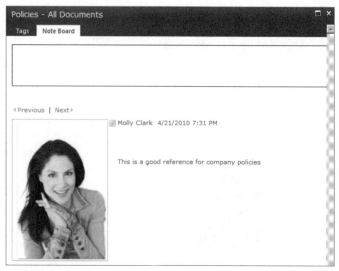

FIGURE 17-12

The Note Board is also an out-of-the-box Web Part that can be added to any page in SharePoint, and can be found in the Social Collaboration category of Web Parts. Web Part settings include the capability to configure the number of recent notes that are displayed, and whether or not to include the new note entry text box. Even if the option to enable new note entry is unchecked, users may still add new notes by using the Tags & Notes button at the top-right corner of the page.

Tag Profiles

For every tag that has been added to content in SharePoint 2010, there is a special page called a Tag Profile, as shown in Figure 17-13.

In this case, the tag profile is for the tag "policies." It includes a list of recent items that have been tagged with the word, a Get Connected section, and, of course, a Note Board.

The Get Connected section is another way in which personal interactivity with SharePoint is enhanced, and it contains the following links:

➤ **Follow this tag in My Newsfeed** — When this link is clicked, the tag is added to the current logged-in user's newsfeed, as a keyword that is "followed." This newsfeed can be accessed by clicking My Profile ➪ My Network. After this link has been clicked, the tag is automatically added to the user's profile, in a property called Interests. Profile editing is covered later in this chapter in the section "My Sites."

➤ **Add to "Ask Me About" in My Profile** — When this link is clicked, the tag is added to the current logged-in user's profile, in a property called Ask Me About.

➤ **View people who are following this tag** — Clicking this link will elicit a People search on the tag, for people with the word in their Ask Me About property or in the Interests property of their profile.

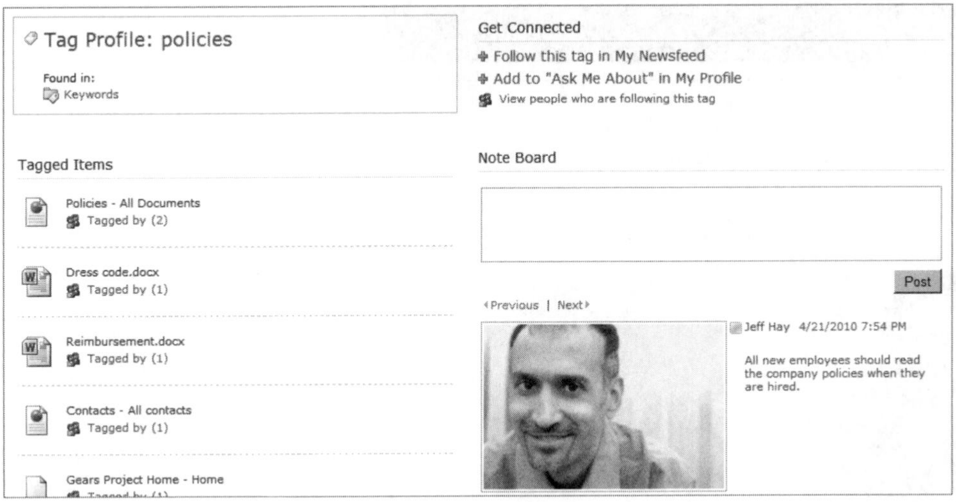

FIGURE 17-13

Also included for each tag profile is a link called See all results for this tag in Search. Clicking this link elicits a search on All Sites, for items that have been tagged with this keyword. The search syntax for a tag called "policies" is as follows: socialtag:"policies."

MY SITES

In SharePoint, My Sites are personal sites that not only display information about each user in the organization, but also are used as a personal landing page and storage site for individuals. My Sites can be used to both enter information about yourself, such as demographics, current projects, and areas of expertise, and to view an activity feed of information about colleagues' activities in SharePoint.

This section explains how to set up My Sites on the server, and then discusses their components and how they can be used.

Setting Up My Sites

Basically, each My Site is a site collection, and each user is the site collection owner of his or her My Site. Some planning should be done before jumping right into the setup. The following should be determined ahead of time:

> **Storage requirements** — Each My Site is a site collection in which each owner can create multiple libraries and lists, and subsequently upload many files to these libraries. Because of this, site sizes can easily get out of hand if storage and quotas are not considered at the time of creation. Consider setting up a relatively small site quota as a default, such as 50MB. Multiply this number by the number of users in the organization, for a potential total. Keep in mind that as more storage is needed, it can be handed out on a per-user basis, or the default quota can be changed. A lot of the size planning for My Sites is based on how many users will *actually* be using them and storing data in them, and only you know this about your own company.

➤ **URL planning** — What URL will be used for My Sites? It is a best practice to create a new web application for this purpose. Some commonly used URLs for the My Site web application are "my" or "mysite." For example, if your company were called Contoso, and the main SharePoint site were `http://intranet.contoso.com`, then the My Sites web application would be `http://my.contoso.com`.

Here are the steps to take to set up My Sites in SharePoint Server 2010:

1. Create a new web application by following the instructions in Chapter 4. Use the naming convention that was determined in the URL planning phase. Here's an example of what a few of the fields would contain if "my" was determined to be the DNS name of the web application:

My Sites New Web Application

FIELD	CONTENTS
IIS Web Site Name	My Sites
Port	80
Host Header	my.contoso.com
URL	http://my.contoso.com

2. After the web application has been created, a confirmation pop-up window will appear. Click this link on this window called Create Site Collection.

3. Fill out the following fields on the Create Site Collection screen:

Create My Sites Site Collection

FIELD	CONTENT
Title	My Sites Home
Web Site Address (URL)	Leave this as the default of "/", which is the root of the web application.
Template Selection	In the Enterprise tab, select My Site Host.
Site Collection Administrators	Designate primary and secondary site collection owners.
Quota Template	This is the quota discussed above in the storage requirements bullet point. There is a default quota template called Personal Site, with a storage limit of 100MB. Use this one, or go to Specify Quota Templates in Application Management to create a custom one. This can be changed at any time.

4. In Central Administration, click Manage web applications in the Application Management section. Click to select the My Sites web application.

5. In the Ribbon at the top of the screen, click Managed Paths. Add two managed paths as shown in Figure 17-14. Note that "personal" is a wildcard, whereas "my" is explicit.

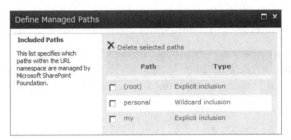

FIGURE 17-14

6. Now that the site collection has been created, the My Sites configuration is next. In Central Administration, click Manage Service Applications, in the Application Management section.

7. Click the User Profile Service Application and click Manage in the Ribbon. Alternately, click the hyperlink text on the name of the application to access it.

8. In the My Site Settings section, click Setup My Sites. Here are some settings to consider:

My Site Settings

FIELD	CONTENT
My Site Host Location	This is the URL to the My Site web application, with /my at the end. This will be the beginning of the URL to each user's public profile — for example: http://my.contoso.com/my. The profile page of a user with the login name of mollyc on the contoso domain will have a URL of http://my.contoso.com/my/Person .aspx?accountname=CONTOSO%5Cmollyc.
Personal Site Location	This is the beginning of the URL for each user's content area, which is different from the user's profile page URL. This is the personal site collection for each user, where they can store their data in lists and libraries. An example URL is http://my.contoso.com/personal.

FIELD	CONTENT
Site Naming Format	This is the suffix of the personal site location URL. For single-domain environments, the first option called "User Name" is a good choice. Inherently, because there are no duplicate usernames in a single domain, there will be no conflicts. In multiple-domain environments, pick one of the second two options. In a single-domain environment, a user with the login name of "mollyc" will have a personal site collection URL of `http://my.contoso.com/personal/mollyc`.
Read Permission Level	By default, all authenticated users are given Read permissions to new personal sites as they are created, which is a best practice for My Sites.

9. After all of these steps have been completed, try it out by clicking your name at the top-right corner of a SharePoint site. Click My Profile. This is your profile page. Click My Content at the top of the screen to generate your own personal site collection.

Trusted My Site Host Locations

In larger SharePoint deployments with geographically distributed farms and User Profile Service Applications, multiple My Site host locations can exist. In these scenarios, administrators manage a list of Trusted My Site host locations, and then target each location to the audiences of users who need to view those locations. Follow these steps to set up multiple My Site trusted locations in the User Profile Service Application:

1. In the My Site Settings section, click Configure Trusted Host Locations.
2. Click the New Link button.
3. The URL field should contain the link to the top level of the location in which the My Sites are located.
4. The Description field should contain the text that is displayed to the users, as a clickable link.
5. In the Target Audiences box, chose one or more audiences who will use that URL location as their My Site host.

Personalization Site Links

Personalization site links are links that are added to the top navigation within My Sites. Each link that is added can be targeted to a specific audience or to the default audience of All Site Users. This enables end users to quickly navigate from their My Site to other locations that are relevant to them.

The following example demonstrates how personalization site links can be used to target departmental home pages to users in each company department. The company, called Contoso, has five major departments, each with its own SharePoint departmental home page that is used for team collaboration. Five different audiences have been created, one for each department; and five personalization site links have been created, each one a link to the departmental home page, and targeted to users in the departmental audience. For example, when users in the marketing department navigate to their My Site, the appropriate link is displayed in the top navigation, as shown in Figure 17-15.

FIGURE 17-15

Follow these steps to set up personalization site links in the User Profile Service Application, per the preceding example:

1. In the My Site Settings section, click Configure Personalization Site.

2. Click the New Link button.

3. Fill in the URL to the departmental team site.

4. The Description will be the text that is displayed, such as "Marketing Site" in Figure 17-15.

5. The owner is a required field, and represents the person responsible for maintaining this link.

6. The Target Audience in this example is called "Marketing," composed of all users in an Active Directory, security-based e-mail distribution list called "Marketing."

7. Take a look at Figure 17-16, and click OK to save the new link. Follow the preceding steps for each company department.

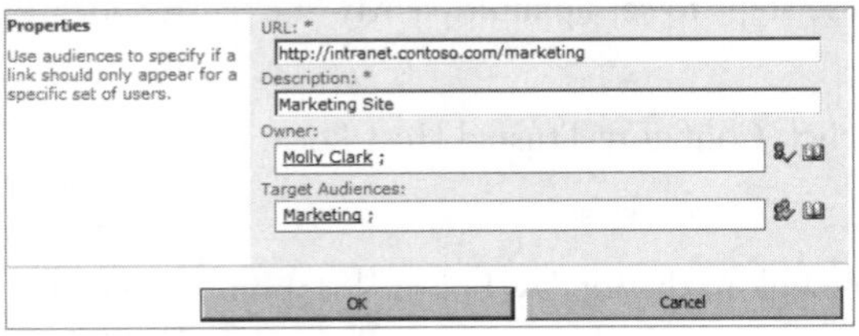

FIGURE 17-16

Publish Links to Office Client Applications

The configuration to publish links to Microsoft Office client applications is conceptually similar to the personalization site links. This setting enables SharePoint links to be pushed out, so that they are available to end users *within* the Office applications, such as Word and Excel. When users have such quick and easy access to open and save files to common SharePoint locations, their daily work processes can be even more efficient.

In the My Sites section, click Publish Links to Office Client Applications. The steps to create a new link are identical to the personalization site link steps in the previous section, except that there is an additional drop-down box to select what type of item is being published, such as a document library or a team site.

Where does the end user see the published links? In any Office 2010 application, click the File tab at the top left, choose the Share tab, and click Save to SharePoint. This section lists the published links on the right side, which the file can then be saved in as long as the user has Contribute rights to the library selected.

 Chapter 18 includes a section called "Managing Office 2010 and SharePoint through Group Policy" with information about using Active Directory Group Policy to control the SharePoint site links in Microsoft Office 2010 applications. This is simply another method of globally configuring the links that are published to Office clients.

Manage Social Tags and Notes

Within the My Site Settings section of the User Profile Service Application is a setting called Manage Social Tags and Notes. The concept of tags and notes was described earlier in this chapter.

As shown in Figure 17-17, SharePoint 2010 includes a management console for administrators that enables them to perform searches on existing tags and notes, as well as delete specific ones as needed.

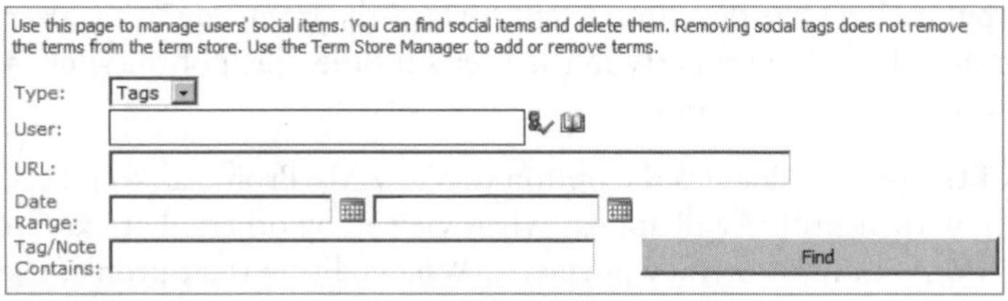

Use this page to manage users' social items. You can find social items and delete them. Removing social tags does not remove the terms from the term store. Use the Term Store Manager to add or remove terms.

Type:	Tags ▾
User:	
URL:	
Date Range:	
Tag/Note Contains:	Find

FIGURE 17-17

To perform a search for either tags or notes, the username or URL must be specified. You can narrow down the search results by specifying a date range or keyword or both. Click the Find button to see the results of the query. When the list of results is displayed, the only action that can be taken on an item is to delete it. Only the person who created a note is allowed to edit it.

My Sites User Experience

This section covers My Sites from the user's perspective. It explains the different parts of the user's My Site and profile, along with how they are used.

Once My Sites have been set up in the SharePoint environment, users have access to their own My Site profile, and can navigate through other users' profiles. At the top-right corner of any site, logged-in users can click their name to see a drop-down box. The My Profile option is selected in order to display the profile portion of My Site. Figure 17-18 displays the top portion of a user's profile, as seen by the user.

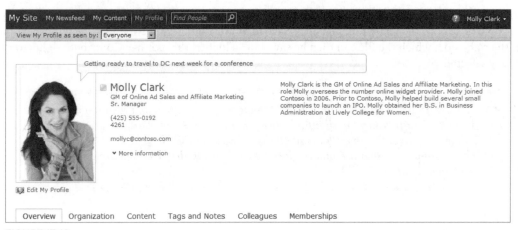

FIGURE 17-18

The user's status update appears in the dialog bubble by the user's image. To update your own status, simply type inside this bubble. This brief status update is known in social computing as *micro blogging*. Some important properties are displayed under the user's name, such as phone number and e-mail address. The fields that are displayed here are configured in the user property display settings in the User Profile Service Application. The descriptive text toward the right side of the user's name in Figure 17-18 comes from the About Me property in the user's profile. Each of the subheadings described next appear as tabs on the My Site profile.

A light-blue band across the top of the profile includes the option to View My Profile as seen by. This setting enables users to test how their profile will appear when viewed by others. For example, users may want to preview their information for privacy purposes. When editing their profile, users can specify that their home phone number should be visible only to their manager. To be absolutely certain that the home phone number is not shown publicly, users can view the profile as seen by everyone (for example) and ensure that the home phone field does not show.

Overview

The Overview tab displays some basic information about the person and their activity in SharePoint. Within each user's profile, by default there is an editable field called Ask Me About. This is a place for users to type in keywords regarding their areas of expertise. On this overview tab, the Ask me about section contains that person's expertise keywords as hyperlinks. When one of these links is clicked, text is automatically inserted into a new Note Board note. For example, if the user's profile has an Ask Me About link called "marketing," clicking this link will insert this text "Question on marketing:", which enables My Site visitors to type in their own text before posting the note.

The Note Board on My Site can be likened to the "wall" on the Facebook social networking site. This is a place for colleagues to post public comments to each other.

Another prominent part of the Overview tab is a list of recent activities, as shown in Figure 17-19.

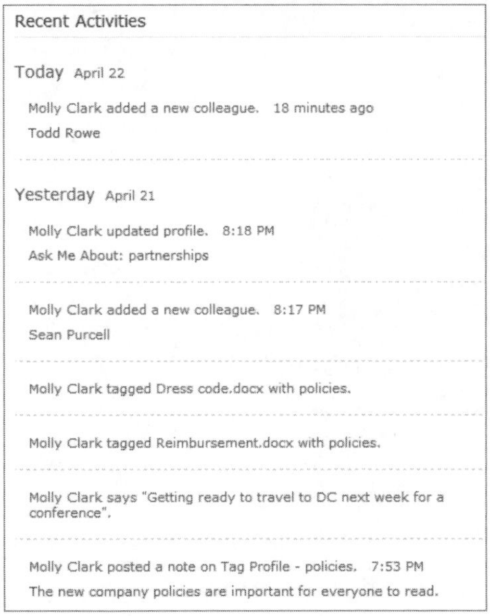

FIGURE 17-19

Recent Activities is a list of what the person has been doing in SharePoint, such as updating information about themselves, tagging items, and making notes on note boards.

When viewing user profiles other than your own, the In Common With You section displays a list of commonalities between the logged-in user and the user whose profile is being viewed. Above this section is a small organization chart with a link to view the Organization Browser, which is a link to the Organization tab.

Organization

The Organization tab contains the Organization Browser, an interactive Silverlight Web Part. (Microsoft's Silverlight software must be installed on client machines in order for them to enjoy not only this Web Part, but also several other enhanced interfaces within SharePoint 2010.) The entire structure of this interface is based upon the accuracy of the Manager field in the user profiles. Click any name to see the profile page for that person. The Organization Browser Web Part is shown in Figure 17-20.

Note that non-Silverlight clients can view a simple HTML view via a link at the bottom-left corner of the Organization tab.

Content

The Content tab is where each user stores his or her own content, such as documents and spreadsheets in libraries, and personal SharePoint lists and subsites. Click the Content tab on any user's My Site to see content that has been shared publicly, such as shared documents and blogs. Each of these personal sites is a site collection, and each user is the owner of his or her own site collection.

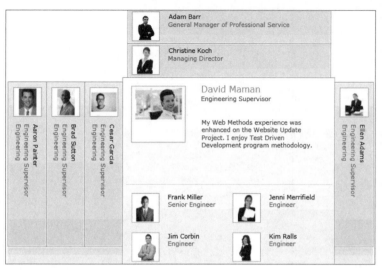

FIGURE 17-20

Tags and Notes

The Tags and Notes tab displays a running list of all tags and notes that the user creates in SharePoint. Figure 17-21 shows an example of the information in the Tags and Notes section. You can optionally refine the list on the right to show either tags or notes, and scroll between months. The tag cloud on the left shows the most frequent tags by this person. Users can go to their own Tags and Notes and either edit or delete them individually. When viewing your own Profile, there is also the option to filter the list to display only private or public items.

Colleagues

In SharePoint, all users keep their own list of favorite colleagues with whom they would like to keep current and share certain information. This tab enables users to manage and organize colleagues, such as by group. A person's colleagues can be added as follows:

- ➤ **Automatically** — Some colleagues will be automatically added, such as direct reports and people who report to the same manager. As mentioned earlier, this data is drawn from the Manager property under User Properties, and is therefore only as accurate as the data entered in Active Directory.

- ➤ **Suggestions** — Some colleagues will be suggested by SharePoint, based on commonly sent Exchange e-mails, Office Communication Server contacts, and websites for which multiple individuals are included in the Members group.

- ➤ **Manually** — When viewing a person's profile page, you can click the Add as a Colleague button, which is located below the person's profile picture, to add them to your own list of colleagues.

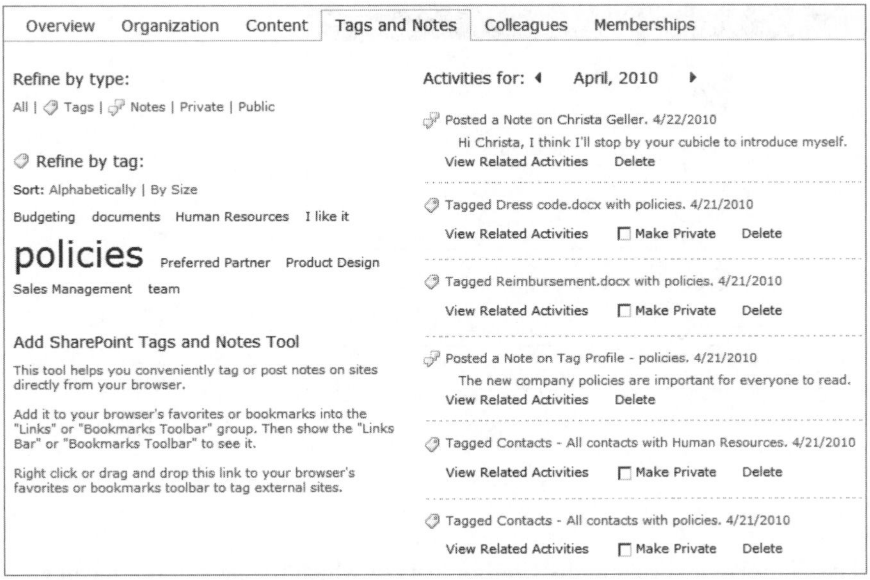

| Overview | Organization | Content | Tags and Notes | Colleagues | Memberships |

Refine by type:

All | Tags | Notes | Private | Public

Refine by tag:

Sort: Alphabetically | By Size

Budgeting   documents   Human Resources   I like it

policies   Preferred Partner   Product Design

Sales Management   team

Add SharePoint Tags and Notes Tool

This tool helps you conveniently tag or post notes on sites directly from your browser.

Add it to your browser's favorites or bookmarks into the "Links" or "Bookmarks Toolbar" group. Then show the "Links Bar" or "Bookmarks Toolbar" to see it.

Right click or drag and drop this link to your browser's favorites or bookmarks toolbar to tag external sites.

Activities for: ◄   April, 2010   ►

Posted a Note on Christa Geller. 4/22/2010
  Hi Christa, I think I'll stop by your cubicle to introduce myself.
View Related Activities   Delete

Tagged Dress code.docx with policies. 4/21/2010
View Related Activities   ☐ Make Private   Delete

Tagged Reimbursement.docx with policies. 4/21/2010
View Related Activities   ☐ Make Private   Delete

Posted a Note on Tag Profile - policies. 4/21/2010
  The new company policies are important for everyone to read.
View Related Activities   Delete

Tagged Contacts - All contacts with Human Resources. 4/21/2010
View Related Activities   ☐ Make Private   Delete

Tagged Contacts - All contacts with policies. 4/21/2010
View Related Activities   ☐ Make Private   Delete

FIGURE 17-21

There are a couple of different reasons to add people to your personal list of colleagues. First, the activity of colleagues will be displayed in your newsfeed, also known as the My Network page, which is covered later in this section. All of the colleagues' social interactivity within SharePoint is displayed on this continuous feed. Second, when people are added as colleagues, it is possible to granularly share profile information with them. The Add Colleagues screen, shown in Figure 17-22, contains the following options:

➤ **Add to My Team** — Enable this option in order to use the privacy settings. This allows for granular sharing of certain information with the given colleague.

➤ **Add to a Group** — Colleague groups provide a simple organization method for handling a long list of colleagues.

➤ **Show to** — Use this option to specify which people are allowed to see that this person is in your list of colleagues.

"Colleagues" is also an out-of-the-box Web Part that users can add to their own My Content sites.

In SharePoint 2010 My Sites, a drop-down box called Show To appears in several places. This is a privacy setting, which allows control over what personal information is displayed, and to whom it is displayed. Five different levels are possible, listed in order from the most private to the most public: Only Me, My Manager, My Team, My Colleagues, and Everyone.

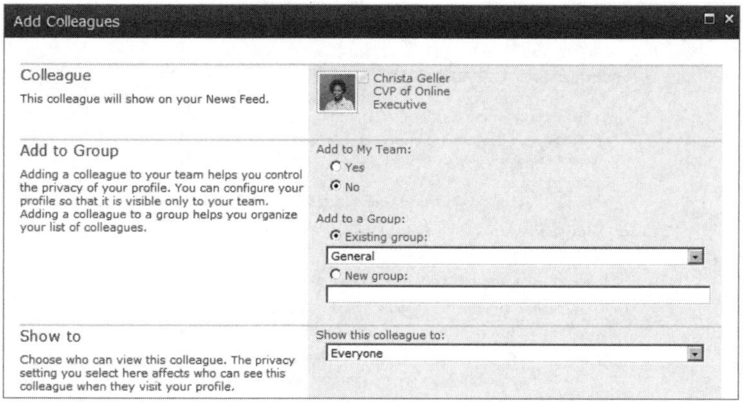

FIGURE 17-22

Memberships

This section displays SharePoint sites and distribution lists of which the person is a member. Each item in the list has a privacy setting that determines who is allowed to view that membership. Memberships is also a Web Part that users can add to their own My Content sites.

My Newsfeed

The next few sections regarding My Newsfeed, My Content, and My Profile refer to the top navigation items on My Sites. My network is the activity feed, and displays all of the activities of the current user's colleagues, along with activity related to tags in which the user is interested. Figure 17-23 shows an example of an activity feed.

An out-of-the-box Web Part called What's New can be used on My Site content pages to display the same information as this activity feed. The top of the My Network page displays the following three links:

➤ **My Colleagues** — Link directly to the Colleagues tab on the My Site.

➤ **My Interests** — Link directly to the current user's profile page, and the Interests property.

➤ **Newsfeed Settings** — Link directly to the current user's profile page, and the Activities I am following section.

My Content

With My Sites, each person has his or her own site collection for storing personal content, which can be accessed by clicking My Content at the top of the My Site. The first time a user clicks on My Content, the site collection is automatically created. Also, if the client computer has Microsoft Office installed, then the first time the content site is accessed the user will be prompted to allow Microsoft Office to remember the My Site location. After clicking Yes to this prompt, Microsoft Office applications will have the user's My Site as a SharePoint location in which to save documents. For example, in Microsoft Office, click the File menu at the top, select the Share tab on the left, and then click Save to SharePoint. My Site will be listed under My SharePoint Locations.

FIGURE 17-23

My Profile

This link simply takes the current user to his or her My Site profile page. On this page, there is an Edit My Profile link under the user's photo. Profile editing is covered shortly in the section "Edit My Profile."

My Links

SharePoint users can save their favorite links to their own list called My Links. Although it is not apparent as a tab in the interface, there are two ways to add links and to manage a list of personal links:

➤ **Document Libraries** — Follow these steps to add to My Links from within document libraries:

1. In any document library, click the Library tab in the Ribbon at the top of the page.

2. In the Connect & Export section of the Ribbon, click the Connect to Office button, shown in Figure 17-24.

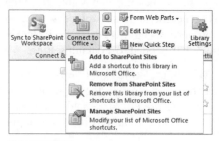

FIGURE 17-24

3. From this drop-down box, you can add or remove a link to this library, or manage your own personal list of links.

➤ **My Content Site** — Follow these steps to add to My Links from within the personal My Content site:

1. Click to edit the page and click to Add a Web Part.

2. In the Recommended Items category of Web Parts, add the My Links Web Part to the page. This Web Part contains the list of My Links, along with a button to Manage Links.

Edit My Profile

All SharePoint users have their own personal profile and can modify certain properties in it. The properties that can be edited are controlled from within the user profiles and properties in the User Profile Service Application, which was covered at the beginning of this chapter.

When viewing your own My Site profile, click the Edit My Profile button, located below your photo. Figure 17-25 displays an example of part of the edit screen of a user's profile.

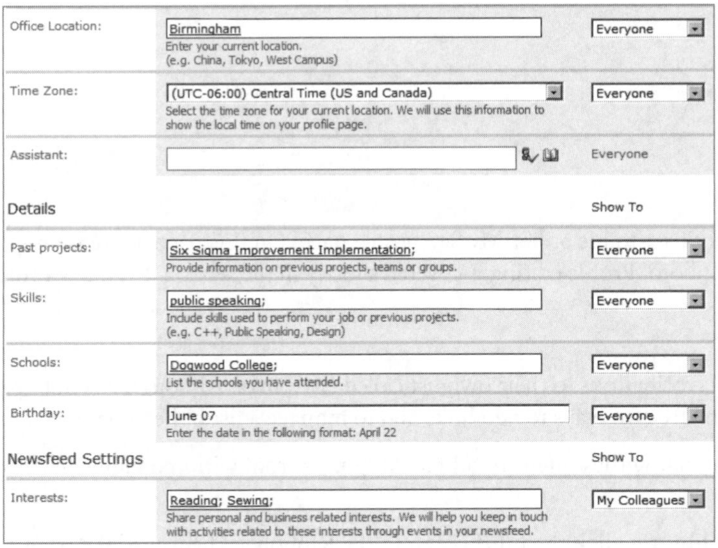

Office Location:	Birmingham Enter your current location. (e.g. China, Tokyo, West Campus)	Everyone
Time Zone:	(UTC-06:00) Central Time (US and Canada) Select the time zone for your current location. We will use this information to show the local time on your profile page.	Everyone
Assistant:		Everyone
Details		Show To
Past projects:	Six Sigma Improvement Implementation; Provide information on previous projects, teams or groups.	Everyone
Skills:	public speaking; Include skills used to perform your job or previous projects. (e.g. C++, Public Speaking, Design)	Everyone
Schools:	Dogwood College; List the schools you have attended.	Everyone
Birthday:	June 07 Enter the date in the following format: April 22	Everyone
Newsfeed Settings		Show To
Interests:	Reading; Sewing; Share personal and business related interests. We will help you keep in touch with activities related to these interests through events in your newsfeed.	My Colleagues

FIGURE 17-25

On the right side of each property is a Show To setting indicating who is able to see that particular piece of information. The Manage User Properties section earlier in this chapter describes how administrators can configure these settings globally. For some properties, end users can change the Show To setting using a drop-down box, whereas other settings are hard-coded to a default setting.

In some properties of the profile, such as Ask Me About, Skills, and Interests, tags are used. When tagging, you are not simply typing text in a text box. The keywords that are used in profiles become part of the farm's metadata term set. The tags that are used in these fields are interactively tied to many other social aspects of SharePoint 2010. Read more about term sets in Chapter 16.

Another important part of the edit screen of the user's profile is the Preferences section, shown in Figure 17-26.

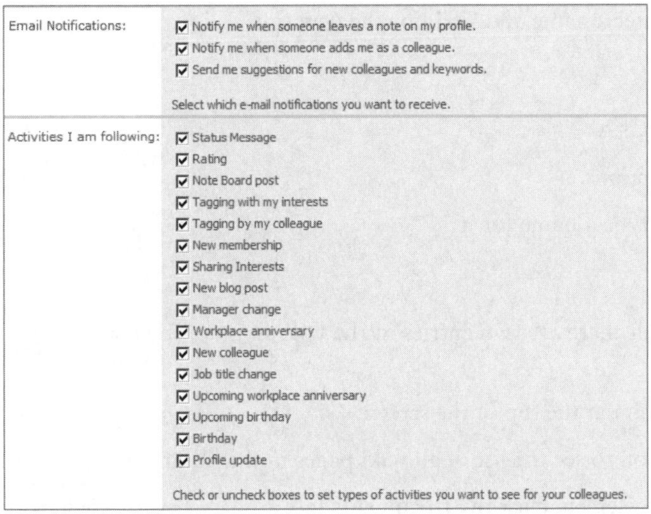

Email Notifications:	☑ Notify me when someone leaves a note on my profile.
	☑ Notify me when someone adds me as a colleague.
	☑ Send me suggestions for new colleagues and keywords.
	Select which e-mail notifications you want to receive.
Activities I am following:	☑ Status Message
	☑ Rating
	☑ Note Board post
	☑ Tagging with my interests
	☑ Tagging by my colleague
	☑ New membership
	☑ Sharing Interests
	☑ New blog post
	☑ Manager change
	☑ Workplace anniversary
	☑ New colleague
	☑ Job title change
	☑ Upcoming workplace anniversary
	☑ Upcoming birthday
	☑ Birthday
	☑ Profile update
	Check or uncheck boxes to set types of activities you want to see for your colleagues.

FIGURE 17-26

Set your own e-mail notification preferences here, along with activities to follow. To *follow an activity* means to see that type of activity listed in your My Network page.

WIKIS AND BLOGS

Wikis and blogs are considered part of social media on the web, and are both highly interactive types of web pages. Before delving into how to use them in SharePoint, we will quickly define each of these concepts.

A *wiki* is a web page that allows users to freely create and edit content through a web browser interface. This open editing concept is useful in the creation of collaborative websites, in obtaining community input, or for personal note taking. Wikis are exceptionally useful when it comes to maintaining knowledge management systems, such as a knowledge base for an information technology help desk.

A *blog* is a personal web log, and can be thought of as an individual's journal on a particular topic. Blog posts can be written about either personal or business-related topics, and are usually created for consumption by the general public. Each new entry made in the blog is referred to as a blog *post*, and readers of the blog are usually allowed to comment on each of these posts.

Wikis

In SharePoint, a wiki can be created using a site template, or a wiki can simply be created as a library within an already existing site. This section covers both methods, along with concepts of working within a wiki.

To create a Wiki site:

1. Click Site Actions ➪ New Site.

2. Click Enterprise Wiki, and enter a name and URL for the new site.

3. Click the Create button.

To create a Wiki library in an existing site:

1. Click Site Actions ➪ More Options.

2. Click Wiki Page Library and type a name for it.

3. Click the Create button.

When a new wiki is created, by default there are two entries in the wiki library. To create a new entry in the library:

1. Click the Page tab in the Ribbon at the top of the screen.

2. Click the View All Pages button to see the list of all wiki pages in the library.

3. In the Ribbon at the top of the screen, click the Documents tab.

4. Click the New Document button.

A wiki site has quite a few more features than a wiki library. The following wiki site benefits aren't included when simply creating a wiki library:

➤ Page ratings included on each wiki page

➤ Page categories (tagging) on each wiki page

➤ An Edit This Page button on each wiki page, for quick editing

➤ Three different wiki page templates

➤ The capability to insert multimedia into a wiki page

Blogs

Blogs are composed of a blog site, blog posts, and blog comments. When it comes to the social features that SharePoint 2010 offers, blogs play an integral part. In the corporate environment, blogs can be used to post current information on projects, highlight departmental achievements, or serve as a log of technical trials and tribulations. Each user's My Site content site contains a "Recent blog posts" Web Part by default. When people create blog posts in SharePoint, they become part of the bigger picture of social activity.

Unlike wikis, which can be created as sites or just libraries, blogs can only be created as sites. Besides being included as part of My Sites, blogs can also be created anywhere in SharePoint. For example, suppose your IT department wants to publish an "IT Blog" by the CIO, which is a subsite of the public IT departmental site.

Follow these steps to create a new blog site:

1. Click Site Actions ⇨ New Site.

2. Choose Blog, and type a name and URL for it. Click Create.

3. You are now the proud owner of a new blog site, as shown in Figure 17-27.

FIGURE 17-27

One of the first things to consider when creating a blog site is the blog categories. Notice that the Quick Launch bar on the left lists categories 1 through 3 by default. Obviously, there's a button to Add New Category, but you'll probably want to modify the existing ones first. Click All Site Content, and then go to the Categories list to edit each of the default categories.

In addition to creating your own set of categories, create an image and description for this new blog. The About this Blog Web Part is simply a Content Editor Web Part that can be modified.

Blog Tools

On the right side of the blog is a set of links called Blog Tools, which can be viewed only by users who have at least Contribute permissions on the blog posts. The following are options available in the Blog Tools:

➤ **Create a Post** — Create a new item in the list on the site called Posts. The most recent blog post is listed first, on the blog site.

➤ **Manage Posts** — Navigate to a list view of the Posts list on the site.

➤ **Manage Comments** — Navigate to a list view of all comments that have been made on blog posts. This is a list on the site called Comments.

➤ **Launch blog program to post** — Open Microsoft Word in order to create a blog post. Chapter 18 has detailed information on how to create blog posts in Word.

Allowing Comments

In a typical blog scenario, one or two people create blog posts in any given blog site, and then the general visitors to the site are able to make comments on those posts. By default, the Comments list is set up to inherit permissions from the site level, but in order to allow comments on a blog, some permissions need to be changed, as described in the following steps:

1. On the blog site, click Manage Comments on the right side of the page.

2. In the Ribbon at the top of the screen, click the List tab.

3. Click the List Permissions button.

4. Click the Stop Inheriting Permissions button.

5. According to your company's requirements, give the appropriate group of people Contribute permissions on this screen, to allow them to add blog comments. Click the Grant Permissions button to add new groups or individuals, or click the check boxes next to existing ones to change their permissions. A good example is where the site visitors group may have Read access, change that group's permission to Contribute.

Users can now add and edit comments on this blog site, but we don't want them to be able to edit other people's comments. This is a simple setting change in the Comments list, following these steps:

1. On the blog site, click Manage Comments on the right side of the page.

2. In the Ribbon at the top of the screen, click the List tab.

3. Click the List Settings button.

4. Click Advanced Settings.

5. Look at the Item-Level Permissions section. In the Create and Edit access option, select Create items and edit items that were created by the user. Click OK.

Another action that can be taken in order to have a bit of control over the comments that are posted is to turn on content approval. Follow these steps to turn on comment approval:

1. On the blog site, click Manage Comments on the right side of the page.

2. In the Ribbon at the top of the screen, click the List tab.

3. Click List Settings.

4. Click Versioning Settings.

5. In the Content Approval section, choose Yes. Click OK.

There's one more step. How will you know when new comments are added to the blog? The comments have to be approved, so someone needs to know when to approve them. Set up an alert for yourself on the Comments list, to be notified when new items are added.

To approve or reject an item, go to the Comments list and click the drop-down box on the item. Choose Approve/Reject, and then pick whether you approve or reject the item, and add optional comments.

RATINGS

In SharePoint 2010, you can rate content on a scale from zero (the lowest rating) to five (the highest). In addition to tags and notes, this is yet another way that people are encouraged to participate by giving feedback in SharePoint. This section covers the rating setup steps, along with ways that this rating information can be utilized.

Turning on Ratings

In a list or library's settings, click Rating Settings. Choose Yes to allow items in this list to be rated. Once this rating feature has been enabled, a new column called "Rating (0-5)" appears in the list. This field can be added to any views, and it is displayed on the View Properties and the Edit Properties form for each item in the list or library. Figure 17-28 shows an example of a document library view in which ratings have been enabled.

Type	Name	Modified	Rating (0-5)
			Average= 3.27
	Absenteeism	1/22/2010 10:14 PM	★★★★☆
	Accounting Projections	1/27/2010 2:57 PM	★★☆☆☆
	brochure	1/27/2010 3:01 PM	★★★☆☆
	Computer security	1/22/2010 10:14 PM	★★★★☆
	Corporate aircraft	1/22/2010 10:14 PM	★★☆☆☆
	Corporate Party Policy	2/5/2010 2:44 PM	★★★★★
	Dress code	1/28/2010 10:24 AM	★★★☆☆

FIGURE 17-28

Hover over any individual item's star rating to see text about your own rating of the item. Click to assign a rating is shown, along with My Rating, which reminds you, the logged-in user, of any rating that you have already assigned. As items are rated, they are listed in activity feeds.

The Ratings Timer Job

In order for current ratings to be displayed as the appropriate number of stars next to each rated item, there is a timer job on the server. The User Profile Service Application - Social Rating Synchronization Job runs hourly by default. This timer job aggregates all of the past hour's ratings, and calculates totals and averages for each rated item.

OUTLOOK 2010 SOCIAL CONNECTOR

A new Outlook plug-in called the Social Connector enables connections to social networks to be created within Outlook. These social connections become apparent when reading and writing e-mails, and in the Outlook contacts lists.

When you select an e-mail, the bottom of the screen displays icons of people, gray by default, each representing a person addressed in the e-mail. Clicking a small chevron button next to these icons expands what is called the People Pane.

To connect SharePoint 2010 to the Social Connector in Outlook 2010 on a client desktop, follow these steps:

1. In Outlook 2010, click the View tab.

2. Click the People Pane button.

3. Click Account Settings.

4. On the Social Network Accounts screen, click the checkbox next to My Site.

5. Type the URL to your personal My Site site collection, and your username and password.

6. Click the Connect button.

7. Click Finish.

8. A "Congratulations!" screen will let you know that you have successfully connected. Click Close.

Once SharePoint has been added to the list of social networks, the News Feed will appear in Outlook 2010, on the left side, in the list of folders. This is the continuous feed of all activities that are being followed on the user's My Site in SharePoint. Profile settings on My Site enable each user to choose what types of activities to follow. This is the same list of activities that are displayed on the My Network page on the My Site.

Now that SharePoint 2010 has been added as a social network, you can add individuals to your own network in order to add individuals from the SharePoint network to your own contacts list in Outlook. In an e-mail, each person's image has an Add button below it, as shown in Figure 17-29.

FIGURE 17-29

To add a person to your SharePoint 2010 social network in Outlook, click the green Add button and choose SharePoint. The person's photo will be displayed after they've been added to your network. Also, a SharePoint icon will appear next to the Add button. After people have been added, they will appear in the Contacts list in Outlook, as a folder underneath the default Contacts list. This list will be called "SharePoint___," with the name and URL of the SharePoint My Site at the end. Edit this contacts list to modify the people who have been added to your network. Tabs are listed next to each person's image, to quickly view content related to that person, such as activities in the social network, e-mail, attachments, meetings, and status updates.

Other social networks are also available in the Social Connector, such as Facebook, MySpace, and LinkedIn, which are separately installed Outlook plug-ins. Each social network that is added includes its own separate contacts list in Outlook.

PEOPLE SEARCH

When searching for people in SharePoint 2010, the interface has advanced filtering capabilities, and interactivity with the search results. This capability brings into play the concept of *knowledge mining*, centered around the SharePoint tagging covered earlier in this chapter. There is a give-and-take with knowledge mining, centered around the following concepts:

➤ Everyone in the SharePoint community participates in tagging. This practice benefits yourself and others in the organization, and the searching of content.

➤ Using the Ask Me About property, individuals indicate their areas of expertise.

➤ Using the Interest property, users can indicate their interests. As opposed to a topic of expertise, an interest reflects something that the person would like to learn more about.

In addition to responsibilities and interests, any profile properties that have been set by the administrator as "indexed" are also searchable. Configuring properties as indexed in the Search Settings was covered in the "User Profiles and Properties" section at the beginning of this chapter.

In knowledge mining, the idea is that when metadata associated with a person is accurate, they can be found easily. Consider the need to pull together a team of people when starting a new project. Knowledge mining enables you to search for people in the organization based on areas of expertise related to the skill sets needed for the project. This can save valuable time when searching for, discovering, and using people's proficiencies.

People Search Configuration

In Search Administration there is a scope called People, in addition to the default scope of All Sites. The definition of this scope is that a property called contentclass is equal to urn:content-class:SPSPeople. As long as the user profiles exist and a full crawl has been performed, people searches are possible whether or not My Sites are used in the environment. By default, this People scope is available in the search drop-down box in site collections. Take a look at Chapter 14 for more information about configuring search scopes.

Performing a People Search

When site users would like to search for people, using keywords, the People scope can be selected next to the search box at the top of the SharePoint site, as shown in Figure 17-30.

FIGURE 17-30

An advanced people search can also be performed. From the Search Center, click the People tab, and then the Search Options link, to see more options, as shown in Figure 17-31.

All Sites   People

🔍	Preferences
	Search Options

Find People by...   ✕

Last name

First name

Title

Person Keywords

FIGURE 17-31

The search options enable specific properties to be searched. There is also another way to perform a search on a specific property. The syntax for a search on anyone who has the word "marketing" selected as one of their interests, for example, would be **Interests:"marketing"**.

The People Search Results Page

When searches for people are performed, the results page is highly integrated with the knowledge mining concept discussed in the last section. Figure 17-32 displays the People results page.

The left side of the screen contains a Web Part called the People Refinement Panel. Use this panel to further filter the results that are displayed. Some examples of properties that can be used to filter are Focus, Job Title, School, Past projects, and Office Location. The Sort by drop-down box at the top right enables the results to be sorted on the page, and there are additional links to set up a search alert, view an RSS feed, or click to search from Windows, which enables the Search Connector to be added to Windows.

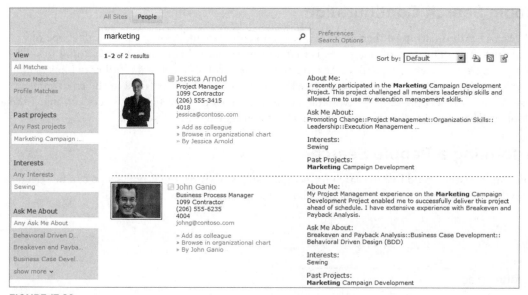

FIGURE 17-32

Several actions can be taken on each of the people profiles that are displayed in the results. As you can see in Figure 17-32, pertinent information about each user is displayed, with the search term in bold letters.

➤ Click any person's name to view their profile.

➤ The listed profiles of people who are not in the My Colleagues list of the currently logged-in user will contain a link to Add as colleague.

➤ The relationship of each person to the currently logged-in user will be listed under their photo, such as "My Colleague" or "My Colleague's Colleague."

➤ Click the Browse in organizational chart link for any person, to navigate to that person's profile within the Organization tab.

➤ Click "By person's name," which elicits a JavaScript control to view that person's recent content. By default, a tab is shown, About "keyword," where the keyword is the search term that was used. There is also a tab under "By person's name" called "More by person's name," where you can quickly view the most recent documents and pages that the person has worked on.

When the currently logged-in user's profile is displayed among the search results, something special happens. Detailed information is provided regarding searches that were performed that lead to that person, as displayed in Figure 17-33.

Notice the section called Help People Find Me. You can see the number of times that searches led to your profile, and a list of the exact keywords that were used when people found you in search results and clicked on your name. There are also quick links to navigate to your own profile to modify it or add more keywords to it.

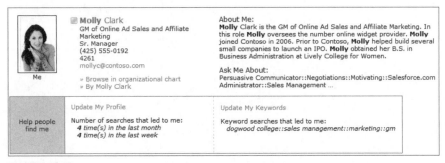

FIGURE 17-33

SUMMARY

In this chapter, you learned about social computing concepts and how those concepts are now used in SharePoint 2010. Now you have the tools to be able to set up your own SharePoint implementation to take advantage of all of these new features, like tagging, notes, My Sites, and even rating content.

18

Integrating the Office 2010 Clients with SharePoint 2010

WHAT'S IN THIS CHAPTER?

➤ Common SharePoint integration points that exist in all of the Office suite products

➤ Integration of each Office 2010 application with SharePoint

➤ Setting up Office 2010 integration from within Central Administration and Group Policy settings

Microsoft Office 2010 is now more tightly integrated with SharePoint than any previous version. Collaboration has become an intuitive part of the user experience, and it is a familiar ingredient of all the Office 2010 applications. With SharePoint 2010 and Office 2010 together, teams will be able to communicate effectively, stay in touch, share questions or concerns, and, of course, work on shared content.

Believe it or not, many workers still send e-mail attachments back and forth as their only form of collaboration. There are several reasons why this is not the most efficient way to accomplish the task at hand. There can be confusion about which version of the document is the most recent, who is working on it, and who made which changes to the file. In addition, each time a document arrives in a mailbox, it takes up more space on the Exchange server. Consider the cumulative effect of a single file being sent back and forth between a handful of people four or five times — and this happening many times a day between hundreds or thousands of users. This can significantly affect server storage, especially when you compare it to saving each file in a single place in SharePoint and using version control. This simple example alone makes a great case for utilizing SharePoint integration to its fullest.

In this chapter, you will learn about the SharePoint 2010 integration features that are part of several different Office 2010 applications.

OFFICE 2010 APPLICATION COMMONALITIES

All of the Microsoft Office applications have a common look and feel. The menus are similar, and so is the contextual Office Fluent UI or Ribbon that is part of the user interface, first introduced in Office 2007. Once users are familiar with one Office application, it becomes easy to switch between different applications and quickly find those common commands and buttons. With this in mind, it is logical that many SharePoint collaboration and integration features are also the same across the Office applications. There are also a multitude of points where Office and SharePoint talk to each other. If a user would like to take an action such as upload a document to SharePoint, for example, or even edit or tag an existing document, those tasks can be done from either within SharePoint or from the client application.

This section describes the many convenient ways to make the most of Office 2010 collaboration and integration. This integration is covered from two points of view. The first perspective is from working within the Office applications; the second perspective looks at Office integration options from within SharePoint in the browser.

Connecting to SharePoint from within Microsoft Office 2010 Applications

People work in Office applications all day long, so saving files to SharePoint should be a convenient process. In the name of efficiency, files can be accessed, worked on, and saved without ever having to open SharePoint in the browser. This section covers the concepts of live co-authoring, the Backstage view, and the Document Information Panel in Office.

Live Co-authoring

Gone are the days where you have to wait until another user checks a document library file back in before you can make your own changes! Now, with Office 2010, multiple users can work on the same file at the same time, and communicate with each other during the process. Whether using OneNote, Word, PowerPoint, or the Excel Web Application, the new live co-authoring feature promises to bring a higher level of efficiency to your daily work and collaboration.

What does the live co-authoring experience look like? The following example demonstrates Word 2010 co-authoring. As shown in Figure 18-1, when a document is being edited from a document library in SharePoint, the familiar Save button at the top-left corner of the application looks a little different. It also has a small "refresh" symbol as an overlay. This means that if the document is being co-authored, when you click the Save button it will be saved and also refreshed at the same time, to show any changes that other users have made to the document concurrently.

FIGURE 18-1

While working in the document, an icon at the bottom left indicates the number of users simultaneously editing the document, as shown in Figure 18-2. Two people are working on the example document.

Page: 1 of 1 | Words: 67 | 2

FIGURE 18-2

Clicking on the people icon with the number 2 on it will display a list of the users' names. Each name is clickable, and can be expanded to display more information about the person, with various ways to contact them. The paragraphs that other users are working on are locked for editing, as shown in Figure 18-3.

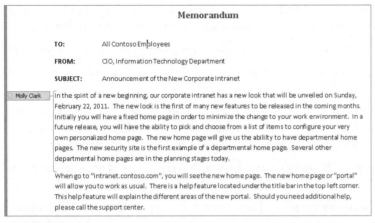

FIGURE 18-3

A vertical line appears down the left side of the locked paragraph, with the user's name and contact information next to it. When you click the Save button, if another user concurrently edited the document a notification pops up, letting you know that Word has refreshed your document with changes made by other authors.

Backstage View

Microsoft Office 2010 applications all have what's called the Backstage view. Think of this view as an amplified replacement for the old File menu at the top-left corner of previous versions of the applications. As shown in Figure 18-4, click the File tab to bring up the Backstage view.

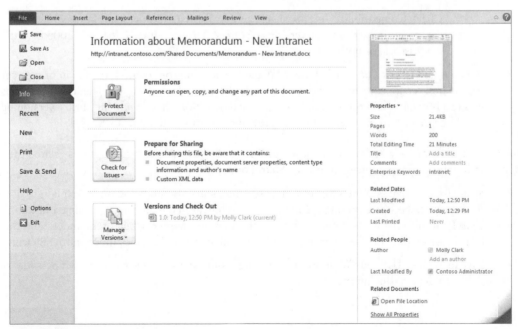

FIGURE 18-4

Notice that there are several tabs down the left side of the Backstage view. The Info tab contains vital information about the file, along with some buttons for interactivity with SharePoint.

➤ **Permissions** — Click the Protect Document button to carry out any of the following actions:

   ➤ **Mark the document as Final** — A document is marked as final indicates that editing is complete.

   ➤ **Encrypt with Password** — Require that a password is used in order to open this document. When collaborating on documents in SharePoint, this archaic option is a bit redundant, because SharePoint permissions can be used on documents instead.

   ➤ **Restrict Editing** — This option enables users to segregate parts of a file and define which users can edit each different part.

   ➤ **Restrict Permission by People** — This option makes use of Microsoft's Information Rights Management Service, which is a separate product that can be purchased.

   ➤ **Add a Digital Signature** — Insert a digital signature box into the document or spreadsheet when an official signature of approval needs to be obtained. This digital signature option is also available on the Insert tab, and it can be used in conjunction with the out-of-box workflow called "Collect Signatures - SharePoint 2010".

➤ **Prepare for Sharing** — Click the Check for Issues button to carry out any of the following actions:

   ➤ **Inspect Document** — Check the document for items such as comments, personal information, or hidden text.

   ➤ **Check Accessibility** — Inspect the document for any content that people with disabilities may find difficult to read.

   ➤ **Check Compatibility** — This checker looks for issues in the file that may exist due to compatibility with earlier versions of Office. Display either Office 97–2003 or Office 2007 issues, or both.

➤ **Versions and Check Out** — Click the Manage Versions button to check the file in or out, compare major versions, recover draft versions, or delete all draft versions. The list of previous versions is displayed in this section for easy reference. Note that document library versioning should be turned on in order to look at previous versions of the document.

The Backstage view's Save & Send tab, shown in Figure 18-5, contains several options related to document collaboration and integration with SharePoint.

➤ **Send Using E-mail** — When this option is selected, some useful dialog boxes explain to users the difference between sending the file as an attachment in e-mail versus sending a link to the SharePoint document. As stated at the beginning of the chapter, when users understand the benefits of keeping the files within SharePoint, collaboration becomes much more efficient.

➤ **Save to Web** — Use your Windows Live login account to save a file to your own personal or public folders on the Internet.

➤ **Save to SharePoint** — This option shows the current location, recent locations, and My SharePoint locations. In order to save to SharePoint, the current logged-in user must have at least Contribute permissions on the target library.

➤ **Publish as Blog Post** — This option enables the capability to publish to a SharePoint blog. It is covered in more detail later in this chapter.

➤ **Workflows** — This section shows SharePoint workflows that can be run on the current file.

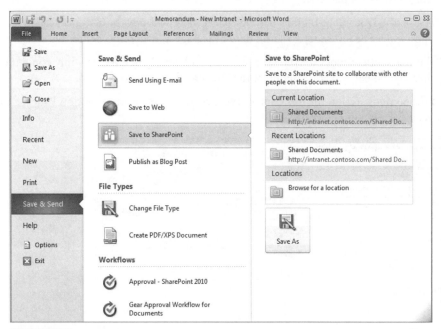

FIGURE 18-5

The Document Information Panel

In Microsoft Word, Excel, and PowerPoint, the document information panel is where you can view the metadata associated with a file, from within the application. *Metadata* refers to the properties associated with each file in a library. Columns in libraries are considered metadata, and contain information about each file, such as the create date and creator. You can add custom metadata to libraries simply by creating new columns. (See Chapter 16 for more about metadata.) Figure 18-6 shows an example of a default Document Information Panel.

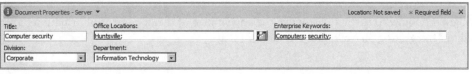

FIGURE 18-6

By default, the document information panel is not displayed when documents are opened, but this can be remedied with a quick setting change in the document library:

1. In the document library's Library tab, click Library Settings.

2. In the General Settings section, click Advanced Settings.

3. In the Content Types section, the Allow management of content types option should be changed to Yes. Click OK.

4. Back on the Document Library Settings page, there will now be a section called Content Types. It may be necessary to scroll down the page a little bit to get to this section.

5. All of the content types for the library are listed here. By default, the only content type is called Document. Click the name of the Document content type.

6. In the Settings section for this content type, click Document Information Panel settings. This screen is shown in Figure 18-7.

Document Information Panel Template

Specify the type of Document Information Panel template to show in Microsoft Office compatible applications.

Note: Creating a custom Document Information Panel template requires Microsoft InfoPath.

- ● Use the default template for Microsoft Office applications
- ○ Use existing custom template (URL, UNC, or URN)

  Edit this template
- ○ Upload an existing custom template (XSN) to use

  [Browse...]

  Create a new custom template

Show Always

Require that the Document Information Panel is displayed automatically for the user under specific conditions.

- ☑ Always show Document Information Panel on document open and initial save for this content type

FIGURE 18-7

7. The Show Always section enables you to force the document information panel to be displayed each time files of this content type are opened.

8. The Document Information Panel Template section enables customization of the panel itself, which is covered in the section "Integrating SharePoint 2010 with InfoPath."

> *You can configure a document information panel globally so that all documents of a certain content type in the site collection are affected. To do so, click Site Settings at the site collection level. In the Galleries section, click Site Content Types. Start at step 6 in the preceding set of instructions.*

For information on how to further customize the appearance of the document information panel, skip ahead to "Integrating SharePoint 2010 with InfoPath."

Connecting to Office 2010 from SharePoint 2010

Each library and list in SharePoint 2010 can be connected to the logged-in user's Office client software. From a library, there will be a Library Tools section of the contextual Ribbon, as shown in Figure 18-8.

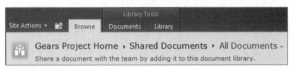

FIGURE 18-8

Click the Library tab inside the Library Tools section. This displays the Ribbon containing all of the options available at the library level. Figure 18-9 shows a document library, with the Library tab displayed.

FIGURE 18-9

In the Ribbon, the section labeled Connect & Export contains buttons related to Office integration. Depending on the current type of list or library, different options will appear in this area. Many of these concepts are expounded upon later in this chapter:

> ➤ **Sync to SharePoint Workspace** — Create a synchronized copy of the current library on your local computer using SharePoint Workspace 2010. SharePoint Workspace is an Office application that enables entire SharePoint sites or site lists and libraries to be synchronized to an offline copy.

> ➤ **Connect to Office** — Users can save their personal favorite SharePoint links to their own list. This list within SharePoint is similar to saving items as Favorites in the browser but even better. When items are saved in this list, these bookmarks are available no matter which computer a user logs into. These locations are also available on the Save & Send tab in the Backstage view.

> ➤ **Connect to Outlook** — In SharePoint, certain types of lists and libraries can be connected to Outlook. This means that the list itself is added as a type of folder in the Outlook client, and the list items are accessible and editable from within Outlook. Document libraries can be connected to Outlook, and the types of lists that can be connected are Contacts, Calendars,

Tasks, and Discussion Boards. External content types can even be connected to Outlook! Learn more about external content types in Chapter 16. Once a list or library has been connected, it will be displayed at the bottom of Outlook's folder view, under SharePoint Lists.

Right-click on any SharePoint list from Outlook and click Open in Web Browser to get back to the associated SharePoint site.

➤ **Export to Excel** — Take a look at the columns and data in the current view of the list. This option enables you to export the data to an Excel spreadsheet. The column order and filtering of the current view are carried over in Excel. This is a useful feature when you want to further analyze data, or when the need arises to send static list information to an individual outside of the organization.

➤ **Create Visio Diagram** — This option is available in a task list, and creates several visual representations of the task list in a new Visio diagram. Note the tabs across the bottom of Figure 18-10. Each tab displays a different visual representation of the list, such as Task Status, Workload Distribution, and Incomplete Tasks by Assigned To.

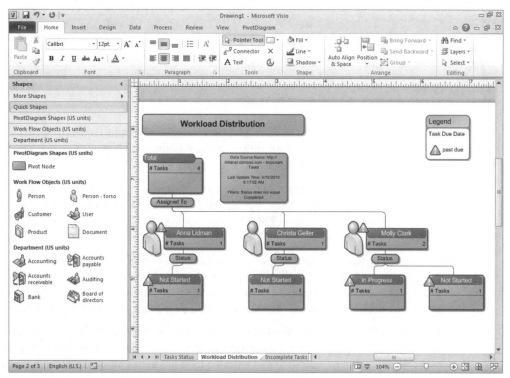

FIGURE 18-10

➤ **Open With Access** — This handy integration functionality enables you to connect a SharePoint list to Microsoft Access. When this is done, the live SharePoint list data is available as a table in an Access database.

➤ **Open Schedule** — From a SharePoint task list, click Open Schedule to export tasks in the current list to Microsoft Project.

Now that some of the more common integration features have been covered, the rest of this chapter details each of the Microsoft Office 2010 applications as they relate to SharePoint.

INTEGRATING SHAREPOINT 2010 WITH WORD 2010

Microsoft Word 2010 is used for document creation and editing, and has its own set of unique integration points with SharePoint. This section covers the following Word capabilities:

➤ Comparing document versions

➤ Document barcodes

➤ Quick Parts

➤ Blogging

Comparing Document Versions

From the Review tab in Word, you can compare various document versions to each other. Of course, multiple versions of a document will not be saved unless versioning is enabled in the library's settings. By default, versioning is not enabled. Follow these steps to enable versioning:

1. Click to select the target document library.

2. In the contextual Ribbon at the top of the screen, under the Library Tools tab, click the Library tab.

3. Click the Library Settings button.

4. In the General Settings section, click Versioning Settings.

5. Choose Create major versions so that each time the file is saved, it becomes a new version number. You can create major and minor (draft) versions if it is necessary to work on drafts and publish each file when it is ready for public consumption (major versions).

6. To access the file's versions from SharePoint, click the drop-down box on the file name and select Version History (see Figure 18-11).

FIGURE 18-11

The version history shows file version numbers, along with the dates and names of the users who modified them. These file versions can be opened, but sometimes it's hard to tell exactly what was changed in the document, especially if it's a large document or only very minor changes were made. In situations like this, Word can be used for more than just listing the versions. Documents can be visually compared side by side.

In Word, open a document from a SharePoint document library. On the Review tab in the Ribbon, click the Compare button. Figure 18-12 shows the options to compare specific versions to each other, or even to combine versions.

When versions are compared side by side, the differences are indicated in red, making it readily apparent exactly who made which changes during the collaboration process.

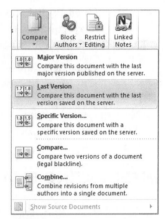

FIGURE 18-12

Document Barcodes

The Information Management Policy settings in SharePoint have several capabilities, but the main one related to Office integration is the capability to insert barcodes into documents when your document management solution requires that unique barcodes be associated with, and inserted into, each document. Barcodes policies can be set up at the site-collection level, or on an individual document library. Follow these steps to turn on the barcode functionality for a library:

1. In the document library's Library tab, click Library Settings.

2. In the General Settings section, click Advanced Settings.

3. In the Content Types section, Allow management of content types should be changed to Yes. Click OK.

4. Back on the Document Library Settings page, there will now be a section called Content Types. You may have to scroll down the page a little bit to get to this section.

5. Click Information Management Policy Settings.

6. On the Edit Policy screen, check the box next to Enable Barcodes, and optionally select to prompt users to insert a barcode before saving or printing.

Quick Parts

Quick Parts in Word are yet another point of integration with SharePoint 2010. Quick Parts are fields that you can insert into a Word document. Metadata (columns) from the document library can be inserted into the associated document. Insert a Quick Part into a document as follows:

1. Open a Word document from a SharePoint library, and ensure that it is in Edit mode.

2. Click on the Insert tab in the Ribbon at the top of the page.

3. In the Text section, click Quick Parts.

4. Choose Document Property and then, in the fly-out, choose the name of the field to insert.

Notice that the document library's column data for that document is displayed in a Content Control box in the document. When the metadata in the library is changed, the Word document will display the updated information the next time it is opened.

Blogging in Microsoft Word

Microsoft Word can be used to quickly create and post blog entries to SharePoint and other types of blog sites. This section covers the Word 2010 blog integration with SharePoint 2010. Here is a list of some blog terminology to be aware of:

➤ **Blog posts** — These can be thought of as journal entries that chronicle information on a general topic. Some blog posts are of a personal nature, and some are more educational or technical.

➤ **Blog site** — This is the web location where blog posts are posted. SharePoint provides a Blog template that enables you to easily and quickly get your own blog up and running.

➤ **Blog account** — The account is simply the URL and login information associated with the blog site.

Read more about blogging and social media in Chapter 17.

To quickly create a new blog site in SharePoint, click Site Actions ➪ New Site. Click the Blog template, specify a Title and URL for the new blog, and click the Create button. There's your new blog site! All that is needed now is the site's URL from the Address bar in the browser, to be used later in this section.

The New tab in Word's Backstage view has an option to create a new blog post, as shown in Figure 18-13.

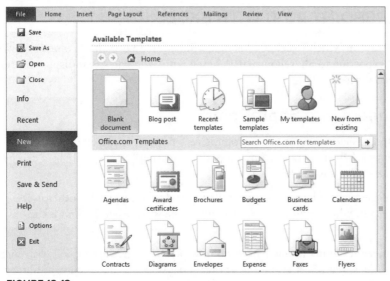

FIGURE 18-13

The first time a blog post is created in Word, the user is prompted to Register a blog account, with options to register now or later. Click Register Now, and follow these steps to set up Word for blogging:

1. On the New Blog Account screen, choose SharePoint Blog from the list of providers, and click Next.

2. On the New SharePoint Blog Account page, enter the URL of the blog site in SharePoint. An example is shown in Figure 18-14. Note that the "default.aspx" part has been left out. Click OK. The Picture Options button enables users to select where pictures in blog posts are stored. By default, they are uploaded to a picture library called Photos on the blog site.

FIGURE 18-14

3. An Account registration successful dialog will pop up. Click OK.

4. Once this new blog post has been written, simply click the Publish button in the Ribbon.

There is yet another way to create a new SharePoint blog post in Word. On the blog site in SharePoint, there is a set of links called Blog Tools on the right side of the page, which is only visible to content owners and editors. Click Launch Blog Program to Post, which will launch Microsoft Word, and the new blog post creation (blank) page.

If you have a regular Word document that wasn't originally created as a blog post, you can post it to a blog site. On the Save & Send tab of the Backstage view in Word, click Publish as Blog Post. Then, inside the newly formatted Word document, click the Publish button.

INTEGRATING SHAREPOINT 2010 WITH EXCEL

This section describes the ways in which Excel 2010 is tightly integrated with SharePoint 2010. We cover importing from and exporting to SharePoint 2010, along with Web Parts that display charts, and a little bit about Excel Services.

Importing Spreadsheets into SharePoint

The capability to import spreadsheet data into SharePoint is very powerful, and enables workers to become more efficient in their daily tasks. Any properly formatted Excel spreadsheet can be imported into SharePoint as a new, custom list.

If you can simply upload a spreadsheet into a document library and take turns with other users checking out and working on it, why would you want to import the spreadsheet? What is the difference?

The difference is quite significant. Think about a scenario in which managers are tasked with entering their daily sales figures in a spreadsheet every day. If that spreadsheet is in a document library, those managers can collaborate on it by taking turns checking it out, adding their sales numbers, and remembering to check it back in. When the spreadsheet is a custom list in SharePoint instead, users are simply creating new items in the same list. Besides the obvious efficiency increase, a benefit of working in a SharePoint list is the capability to use SharePoint alerts. Once the data has been collected, it can still be exported back out to spreadsheet format if needed.

A spreadsheet must be properly formatted in order for it to be imported. Each column heading becomes a new column in the SharePoint list, so make sure that row 1 (and only row 1) contains the column headings. The list data must begin at row 2, and there should be no blank rows among the data portion of the spreadsheet.

Because column headings will become SharePoint list column names, it's a good idea to keep these short and sweet. Keep in mind that if a more descriptive column heading is needed, there is a Description field associated with each SharePoint column that can be used for further clarification to the end users. Column A in the spreadsheet will become the Title column in the SharePoint list, so it is a good idea to use a Text field as this first column before importing.

A common reason for import failure is your IE settings. It most cases, the site you are trying to import needs to be in the Local intranet or Trusted sites zone.

The following steps can be taken to import a spreadsheet into SharePoint:

1. In SharePoint, click Site Actions, and choose More Options….

2. Select Import Spreadsheet in the list of templates in the middle of the screen. Click the Create button on the right.

3. In the Name box, type a name for the new list, and in the Import from Spreadsheet section, click the Browse button.

4. Navigate to the current location of the spreadsheet, click to select the spreadsheet name, and click Open.

5. Back on the New screen in SharePoint, click the Import button. The spreadsheet will be automatically opened in Excel, with a dialog box called Import to Windows SharePoint Services list. If there are no named ranges used in the spreadsheet, choose Range of Cells in the Range Type box.

6. The Select Range box allows for selection of the cells that need to be imported as a list in SharePoint. After a range has been selected, click the Import button.

7. The new SharePoint list is automatically created, and you will be taken to the default view of this list.

Another way to move data from Excel to SharePoint is from within Excel. Select the spreadsheet's data region, click the Format as Table button, and pick a style. From this new table, click the Design tab in the Ribbon. The Export button will provide the option to Export Table to SharePoint List.

Exporting to Excel

As mentioned earlier in the section "Connecting to Office 2010 From SharePoint 2010," there is an Export to Excel button in lists and libraries that you can use to export the current view to Excel. Another way to export the data to Excel is a hidden task pane that exists in the list's Datasheet view.

1. Click the Datasheet View button in the List tab of a SharePoint list (or the Library tab in a library). This view is displayed in Figure 18-15.

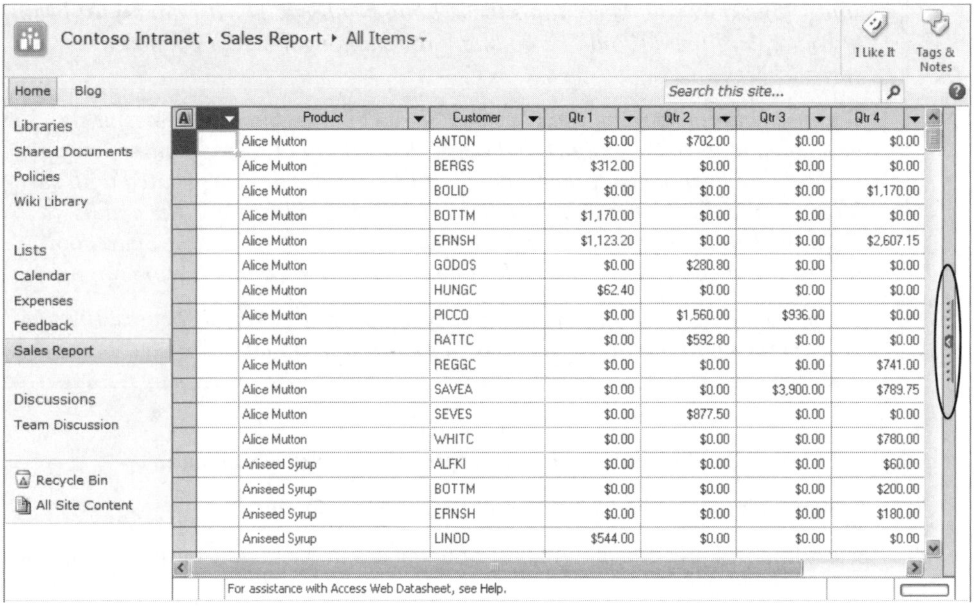

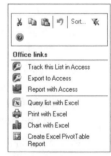

Contoso Intranet ▸ Sales Report ▸ All Items
I Like It
Tags & Notes
Home
Blog
Search this site...
Libraries
Shared Documents
Policies
Wiki Library
Lists
Calendar
Expenses
Feedback
Sales Report
Discussions
Team Discussion
Recycle Bin
All Site Content
Product | Customer | Qtr 1 | Qtr 2 | Qtr 3 | Qtr 4
Alice Mutton | ANTON | $0.00 | $702.00 | $0.00 | $0.00
Alice Mutton | BERGS | $312.00 | $0.00 | $0.00 | $0.00
Alice Mutton | BOLID | $0.00 | $0.00 | $0.00 | $1,170.00
Alice Mutton | BOTTM | $1,170.00 | $0.00 | $0.00 | $0.00
Alice Mutton | ERNSH | $1,123.20 | $0.00 | $0.00 | $2,607.15
Alice Mutton | GODOS | $0.00 | $280.80 | $0.00 | $0.00
Alice Mutton | HUNGC | $62.40 | $0.00 | $0.00 | $0.00
Alice Mutton | PICCO | $0.00 | $1,560.00 | $936.00 | $0.00
Alice Mutton | RATTC | $0.00 | $592.80 | $0.00 | $0.00
Alice Mutton | REGGC | $0.00 | $0.00 | $0.00 | $741.00
Alice Mutton | SAVEA | $0.00 | $0.00 | $3,900.00 | $789.75
Alice Mutton | SEVES | $0.00 | $877.50 | $0.00 | $0.00
Alice Mutton | WHITC | $0.00 | $0.00 | $0.00 | $780.00
Aniseed Syrup | ALFKI | $0.00 | $0.00 | $0.00 | $60.00
Aniseed Syrup | BOTTM | $0.00 | $0.00 | $0.00 | $200.00
Aniseed Syrup | ERNSH | $0.00 | $0.00 | $0.00 | $180.00
Aniseed Syrup | LINOD | $544.00 | $0.00 | $0.00 | $0.00
For assistance with Access Web Datasheet, see Help.

FIGURE 18-15

2. Click the task pane. This is a little hard to find at first. It is a long, vertical bar that goes down the right side of the datasheet view (highlighted in Figure 18-15). The contents of this task pane are displayed in Figure 18-16.

3. You can choose from several Excel options, including Query list with Excel, Print with Excel, Chart with Excel, or even Create Excel PivotTable Report. The Access options are discussed later in this chapter.

Sort...
Office links
Track this List in Access
Export to Access
Report with Access
Query list with Excel
Print with Excel
Chart with Excel
Create Excel PivotTable Report

FIGURE 18-16

When you are in the Datasheet view and the Datasheet View button is grayed out, it is most likely because this capability has been disabled on the list. In the list settings, an administrator can go to Advanced Settings and change Allow items in this list to be edited using the datasheet? to Yes.

Chart Web Part

The new Chart Web Part is a fantastic addition to the already long list of SharePoint's out-of-the-box Web Parts. Many SharePoint projects require a graphical display of data as a Web Part on a page. Figure 18-17 shows an example of the Chart Web Part.

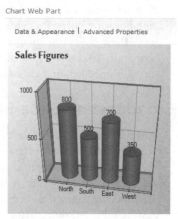

The data in this Web Part can come from a SharePoint list, an external content type (previously known as the BDC), Excel Services, or even another Web Part on the same page. The Data & Appearance button directs you to a screen with wizards to Customize Your Chart or Connect Chart to Data. The interface and configuration screens are very intuitive, and the chart itself is highly customizable, which makes this Web Part perfect for business users, thereby making the job of the SharePoint administrator and developer easier!

FIGURE 18-17

Publishing to Excel Services

The Save & Send tab in Excel's Backstage view has an option to Publish to Excel Services. Excel Services is a SharePoint technology that is used in facilitate sharing, securing, and ease of use when it comes to Excel spreadsheets as interactive entities in the enterprise. If a spreadsheet will be used in Excel Services, publishing the file to a library is the preferred method over simply saving the file. Click the Excel Services Options button in order to specify spreadsheet components to be published, such as individual sheets and charts. Excel Services are covered in more detail in Chapter 20.

Excel Web Access Web Part

The Excel Web Access Web Part can be used to display data from within a spreadsheet that has been published to Excel Services. You can display the entire spreadsheet or just specific portions of it such as ranges and charts. When typing interactivity is enabled in the Web Part properties and Office web applications are installed on the server, the spreadsheet is editable right in the Web Part. Charts in this Web Part are different from the Chart Web Part described earlier because the chart's configuration is done within Excel. The Chart Web Part is set up within the Web Part settings. For more information on the fun you can have with Excel Web Access check out Chapter 20.

INTEGRATING SHAREPOINT 2010 WITH POWERPOINT

PowerPoint is an application that is used to create powerful and portable presentations, and PowerPoint 2010 has more multimedia capabilities than ever. This section covers the ways in which SharePoint and PowerPoint are integrated. Live co-authoring, covered earlier in the chapter, is also available in PowerPoint presentations. This allows multiple users to work on the same file, and each user's currently edited slide is locked from editing by the other collaborators. Because PowerPoint presentations consist of slides, our first stop is a look at slide libraries.

Slide Libraries

First introduced in SharePoint 2007, slide libraries are used to provide a list of individual slides for collaboration purposes. Slide libraries not only enable you to view an inventory of slides, you can piece these slides together to create new presentations. In a slide library, each slide has a checkbox next to it. To create a new presentation based on slides in the library, simply check the boxes next to the slides needed, and click the Copy Slide to Presentation button.

Broadcasting Slide Shows

PowerPoint 2010 offers the capability to broadcast a PowerPoint presentation straight to the Web browser, which can be offered publicly on the Internet or locally on the intranet, via SharePoint Server. To broadcast a presentation means to make a live view available in a web browser. Individuals who are viewing the web page will see the slides as they are being clicked through. In other words, the presenter's current slide is displayed as they are discussing it. Here are the steps involved in broadcasting a PowerPoint 2010 presentation:

1. In PowerPoint, go to the Backstage view by clicking the File menu at the top left.

2. Click the Save & Send tab on the left side.

3. In the Save & Send section, click the Broadcast Slide Show button, as shown in Figure 18-18.

FIGURE 18-18

4. On the right, click the larger Broadcast Slide Show button.

5. By default, there is a public service called the PowerPoint Broadcast Service that only requires a Windows Live ID. Click Start Broadcast to use this service, or click Change Broadcast Service to use a custom one, such as a SharePoint site. The creation of a PowerPoint broadcast site in SharePoint is covered in the next section, "PowerPoint Service Application."

6. A URL link will automatically be generated and displayed on the screen. Hand this out to anyone who will need to view this live presentation, i.e., the intended audience.

7. Click the Start Slide Show button to begin the presentation, which entails a live view of the current slide.

Note that no audio is associated with this live broadcast. The intent is that a company conference line or direct phone call can be used, in order for the audience to hear the presenter's voice. When the presentation is over, click to end the broadcast.

PowerPoint Service Application

When Office 2010 Web Applications have been installed and deployed from Central Administration in SharePoint as covered in Chapter 19, listed among the service applications is the PowerPoint Service Application. This service enables you to set up your own internal PowerPoint broadcast URL. Follow these steps to create a SharePoint broadcast site:

1. In Central Administration, click Create Site Collections in the Application Management section.

2. Create a new top-level site collection, in the web application of your choosing. A good name and URL for this site would be "Broadcast."

3. In the Template Selection section, click the Enterprise tab and choose PowerPoint Broadcast Site.

4. Pick a site administrator and click OK.

5. On the Top-Level Site Successfully Created screen, click the link to the new site collection.

6. Click People and Groups on the left.

7. Configure the permissions on the site. Users who will be broadcasting slides are Broadcast Presenters, users who will view the slides are Broadcast Attendees, and obviously administrators of the permissions on this broadcast site are the Broadcast Administrators.

From this point on, when users are broadcasting PowerPoint presentations and are prompted to pick a broadcast service, they will use the URL of this new Broadcast site. The "Managing Office 2010 and SharePoint through Group Policy" section in this chapter shows how Group Policy can be used to block the default PowerPoint Broadcast Service. Your own custom internal broadcast URLs can be set in Group Policy also.

INTEGRATING SHAREPOINT 2010 WITH OUTLOOK

Outlook is Microsoft's e-mail management program, integrating e-mail with personal lists such as contacts, calendars, and tasks. With Outlook 2010, you can find and view information, customize your user interface, and connect to SharePoint and other social media networks. This section focuses specifically on the ways in which Outlook 2010 is used with SharePoint 2010.

In particular, you will learn how to manage SharePoint alerts from Outlook, the types of SharePoint lists and libraries that can be connected to Outlook, and how you can integrate Exchange calendars with SharePoint calendars in the browser.

Managing SharePoint Alerts

In SharePoint, alerts are e-mail notifications that are set up by end users, per document library and list. When alerts are set up, automatic e-mails arrive when items in a list are added or changed, and at the frequency that the user specifies. Users can manage all of their own alerts on various SharePoint sites from a single location in Microsoft Outlook.

In Outlook, on the Home tab of the Ribbon, click the Rules button in the Move section. Click Manage Rules & Alerts, and then choose the Manage Alerts tab. This screen displays a list of all your existing alerts, which can each be viewed and modified. To create a new alert, click the New Alert button.

SharePoint Lists and Libraries

Many types of SharePoint lists and libraries can be connected to Outlook for interactivity from within the Outlook client software. Using Outlook for e-mail is a standard part of life for many people, so the convenient accessibility of SharePoint data in Outlook is yet another way that Office and SharePoint integration drives efficiency. The following types of lists and libraries can be connected to Outlook:

- ➤ Calendars
- ➤ Tasks
- ➤ Project tasks
- ➤ Contacts
- ➤ Discussion boards
- ➤ Document libraries
- ➤ Individual document sets
- ➤ Picture libraries

In the Library or List tab in the Ribbon (depending on whether it's a library or a list), each of these types of lists has a Connect to Outlook button. Users can click this button to link their own Outlook client to SharePoint. When this is done, a new PST file is automatically created on the client hard drive, called `SharePoint Lists.pst`. Take a look at Outlook's Folder view, which usually has this file as the last PST at the bottom. Items in these SharePoint lists are synchronized, and editable from either SharePoint or Outlook 2010.

All lists and libraries that are connected to Outlook are actually full, offline copies of the libraries in their entirety. From a client support perspective, this could be a nightmare. Imagine end users flippantly clicking the Connect to Outlook button for document libraries with hundreds of files in them. Those hundreds of files are then copied to the PST on that client hard drive. A new setting in SharePoint 2010 enables site administrators to avoid this scenario: Offline Client Availability. Follow these steps to disable the offline availability of a library:

1. In the Library tab in the library's Ribbon, click the Library Settings button.

2. In the General Settings section, click Advanced Settings.

3. Scroll down to the section called Offline Client Availability. The default setting for the question Allow items from this document library to be downloaded to offline clients? is Yes. Change it to No and click OK.

When offline availability is turned off, the Connect to Outlook button in the library is grayed out and disabled. If clients have already created offline copies of the library, they will still exist as disconnected, and will not receive any further updates from the library.

There are a couple of options other than completely blocking users from downloading offline copies of the libraries to Outlook, but these options entail giving a bit of guidance to library owners and contributors:

➤ **Teach users the practice of setting up multiple document libraries on each site, as opposed to one large one** — A good way to carry this out would be when the site is provisioned. Create new sites with no default document libraries, and instruct the new site owner to create new, separate libraries for different topics.

➤ **Use document sets** — New to SharePoint 2010, document sets enable you to group similar documents together. Multiple document sets can be created in each document library. One of the great things about document sets is that the set itself can be connected to Outlook.

➤ **Sync to a SharePoint Workspace instead** — There is an option to download only headers, which would take up less space than the full files. SharePoint Workspaces are discussed later in this chapter.

Calendars and Meetings

As discussed previously in this chapter, SharePoint calendars can be connected to Outlook clients — but the integration doesn't stop there! Now, when SharePoint 2010 and Outlook 2010 are used in conjunction for meeting planning, the experience is quite seamless.

Using an overlay view, you can now add Outlook calendars to SharePoint calendars in the browser, enabling a quick visual comparison of the team's personal calendar with the appointments in a SharePoint calendar. On the left side of a SharePoint calendar in the browser, click Calendars in View. This allows for up to 10 additional calendars to be displayed in the view, which includes not only SharePoint calendars from multiple sites, but Exchange calendars also!

 Outlook 2010 also has a new feature called the Outlook Social Connector. This is covered in detail in Chapter 17.

INTEGRATING SHAREPOINT 2010 WITH INFOPATH

Since its inception in Microsoft Office 2003, InfoPath has been highly integrated with SharePoint. SharePoint 2010 offers a plethora of new integration points with InfoPath 2010.

A part of the Microsoft Office suite of applications, InfoPath is used for the creation and filling out of forms. This powerful program enables business users to easily create and customize their own forms. A lot of time and money can be saved by using InfoPath forms, as no programming knowledge is required, and the interface and form publishing process are simple and familiar.

InfoPath Forms Services was first introduced in Microsoft Office SharePoint Server 2007. It is a SharePoint technology that allows for centralized administration of forms in an organization, and also provides the ability for forms to be filled in using the browser instead of relying on client software.

If you have used InfoPath, then you know that in the past it was a single application in Office. In Office 2010, the product has been divided into Microsoft InfoPath Designer 2010 and Microsoft InfoPath Filler 2010. Because designing a form and filling out a form are two distinct tasks, typically performed by different types of users, it is logical to provide two different entry points to the program.

When forms are created, one of the first choices to make is whether the form will be *browser-based*, that is, it can be opened and filled out in the browser. If a form has not been set up as browser-based, it must rely on client software. The latter option requires that all client computers have InfoPath software installed as part of the Microsoft Office suite. Different types of controls and capabilities within InfoPath forms are compatible with different versions of the InfoPath client, so compatibility with clients is a consideration that is best tackled at the beginning of the form creation process.

When a new form is created for use in a SharePoint form library, you have three different options for publishing the form to SharePoint:

➤ **Form Library** — This method entails publishing the form to a single library on a SharePoint site. When you know that the form will not be needed in other sites or libraries, use this option. Browser-based forms are optional here. Note that at the SharePoint library level, there is a setting that the administrator can use to force the way the client machine opens forms.

➤ **Site Content Type** — The form is published to a SharePoint site as a content type. This type of form can then be used in multiple libraries and subsites, and the content type is managed from one location.

➤ **Administrator-approved form template** — These types of forms are to be uploaded to InfoPath Forms Services in Central Administration, and can be globally available in the organization. This option requires that the browser-based option is selected. This does not mean that the form can be *only* browser-based, but that it at least must be available in that format. The next section describes how to manage these administrator-approved forms.

To open documents in the browser, in the Form Library settings, click Advanced Settings. Figure 18-19 shows the options for Opening Documents in the Browser.

Default open behavior for browser-enabled documents:
- Open in the client application
- Open in the browser
- Use the server default (Open in the browser)

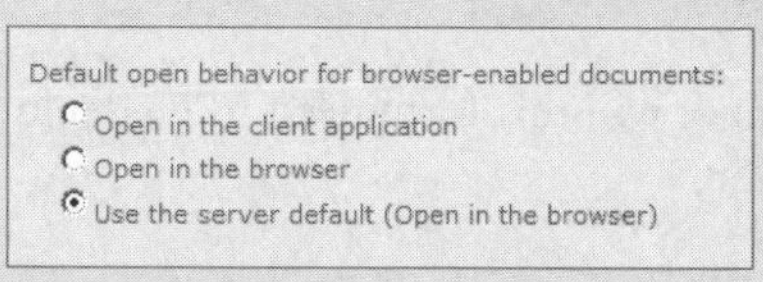

FIGURE 18-19

In the case of form libraries, InfoPath is the applicable client application.

The following sections describe the administrator-approved templates in relation to InfoPath Forms Services, which entails some Central Administration settings, and step-by-step instructions on how the form deployment process is carried out. A few other concepts covered are the new InfoPath Form Web Part, customizing the document information panel using InfoPath, and customizing SharePoint list forms.

InfoPath Forms Services in Central Administration

In Central Administration, click General Application Settings on the left side of the screen. Figure 18-20 shows the InfoPath Forms Services section.

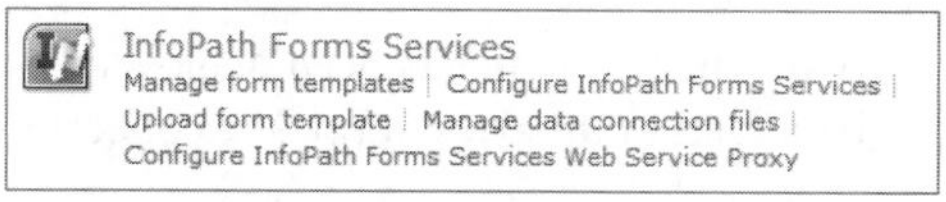

 InfoPath Forms Services
Manage form templates | Configure InfoPath Forms Services | Upload form template | Manage data connection files | Configure InfoPath Forms Services Web Service Proxy

The following list describes the options available for managing InfoPath Forms Services:

FIGURE 18-20

- ➤ **Manage form templates** — This is the master list of all templates that exist in InfoPath Forms Services. By default, there are already several in the list, which are associated with some out-of-the-box workflows in SharePoint 2010.

- ➤ **Configure InfoPath Forms Services** — This page contains general settings such as timeouts, authentication, and postback thresholds.

- ➤ **Upload form template** — Once an administrator-approved template has been created as described in the previous section, it can be uploaded to InfoPath Forms Services on this screen.

- ➤ **Manage data connection files** — Upload existing data connection files here so that they can be globally accessed from multiple InfoPath forms.

- ➤ **Configure InfoPath Forms Services Web Service Proxy** — Use this page to enable the web service proxy for forms.

Deploying Forms in InfoPath Forms Services

Deploying a form template to InfoPath Forms Services is typically done by a SharePoint administrator. This section covers the steps required to take a form from inception to "going live" on a SharePoint site.

What you will need:

➤ **The template file** — The person who has created the InfoPath form will send the form template to the administrator as an XSN file.

➤ **Site Collection URL** — To which site collection(s) will this form need to be deployed? The form creator should also supply this information.

Once the form template and site collection URL have been obtained, take the following steps:

1. On the General Application Settings page in Central Administration, click Upload Form Template.

2. Browse to the form template, which is the XSN file that the form creator supplied.

3. Optionally, click the Verify button, to verify that the form does not contain any errors.

4. Click the Upload button; and after the process has completed, a Form Template Status screen will indicate success.

5. On the Manage Form Templates screen, hover over the name of the template that was just uploaded. Click Activate to a Site Collection.

6. Pick a site collection from the drop-down box and click OK.

After the template has been deployed to the site collection, it is available as a content type that can be added to libraries in the site collection.

InfoPath Form Web Part

One of the new SharePoint 2010 out-of-the-box Web Parts is called the InfoPath Form Web Part. This Web Part allows for the insertion of any browser-based InfoPath form right onto a Web Part page. The following steps are taken as a form is inserted on the home page of a company's departmental site. The availability of the Web Part makes it a few clicks easier for the site visitors, as filling out this form is the most commonly performed task done on the site in this example:

1. At the top left, click Site Actions and choose Edit Page.

2. On the Ribbon at the top, click the Insert tab, and then click Web Part.

3. In the Forms category, select InfoPath Form Web Part, and click Add.

4. Click the link that says "Click here to open the tool pane," and the Web Part tool pane will appear on the right side of the screen. Figure 18-21 shows some tool pane settings.

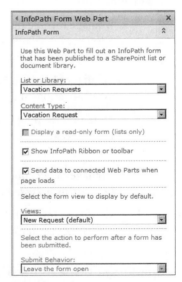

FIGURE 18-21

5. The first drop-down box, called List or Library, contains multiple options, depending on how many forms have been published to the current site. The names of these forms are listed, along with names of lists on the site that have custom InfoPath forms (customizing SharePoint list forms is covered later in this chapter). There is also an extra option called Deployed Forms. Pick the desired form name; or if the form was deployed via InfoPath Forms Services, pick Deployed Forms.

6. The rest of the Web Part options are pertinent to the way the form will be displayed, and the behavior when the Submit button is clicked.

7. Click OK at the bottom of the Web Part tool pane to save the changes.

The InfoPath form will be displayed directly on the SharePoint page, which can now be easily and quickly filled out by site users.

Customizing the Document Information Panel

An earlier section of this chapter, "Connecting to SharePoint from within Microsoft Office 2010 Applications," introduced the document information panel. To change the appearance of the document information panel, such as displaying it in a color other than the default blue, or inserting a company logo or other graphics, you can use InfoPath to perform this type of customization.

Inherently, a Document Information Panel is going to be associated with a content type in SharePoint. When a custom document information panel is created, the process involves InfoPath communicating with a specific document library in order to obtain information about the content types and metadata (columns) associated with the library. Therefore, before the form is created, obtain the URL of the target document library. Once you have the URL, use the following steps to customize the look and feel of the document information panel using InfoPath 2010:

1. On the Backstage view in InfoPath Designer 2010, click the New tab on the left. Figure 18-22 shows some of the Available Form Template options when creating new forms.

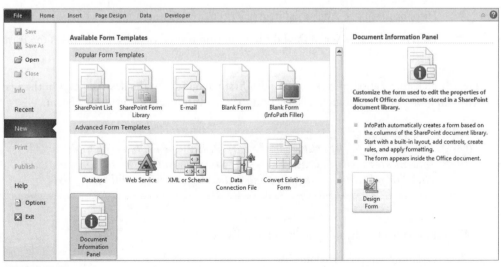

FIGURE 18-22

2. In the Advanced Form Templates section, choose Document Information Panel, and click Design This Form on the right.

3. On the first screen in the Data Source Wizard, enter the URL to the target document library, and click Next.

4. Choose the content type that the custom document information panel will be associated with and click Next.

5. Click Finish. At this point, a new form will be displayed in Design view in InfoPath, with all of the library fields already inserted. Customize this form by changing the background color, adding a company logo, or rearranging the form fields.

6. It is recommended that you save your own local copy of the form template as a backup, so click the Save button at the top of the screen.

7. Click the Quick Publish button, located in the Quick Access Toolbar at the top left of InfoPath, above the File menu. (Alternately, click the File menu, and on the Info tab, click the Quick Publish button). This publishes the custom document information panel back to the document library specified in step 3.

From this point on, files in that document library will display the new custom Document Information Panel instead of the default blue one.

Customizing SharePoint List Forms

By default, lists in SharePoint have a standard look and feel. In previous versions of SharePoint, form customization was not an easy or intuitive endeavor. With SharePoint 2010, you can use InfoPath to do advanced customizations of regular list forms.

Typical SharePoint lists have three associated forms:

➤ **NewForm.aspx** — This is used when a new item is created in a list.

➤ **DispForm.aspx** — After a list item has been created and it is opened to view, this form is used.

➤ **EditForm.aspx** — When the Edit Item button is used on a list item, this is the form that is filled out.

The form customization process starts with first navigating to the desired list. On the List tab in the Ribbon, look in the Customize List section for the button called Customize Form.

 If the icon does not exist, then the current list type is not compatible with InfoPath form customization. To verify this, go to the list settings screen and click Form Settings. A message will indicate non-compatibility.

Follow these steps to customize a SharePoint list form:

1. Open the target SharePoint list.

2. Click the Customize Form button in the List tab in the Ribbon.

3. The Microsoft InfoPath Designer 2010 application will start running.

4. A very basic version of the current list form will be displayed in InfoPath Designer, with a Fields pane displayed on the right side of the screen.

5. Customize the form by changing the background color, adding a form title, or rearranging the form fields. See Figure 18-23 for the Design view of this Sales Report form.

FIGURE 18-23

6. Once the form customizations are complete, click the Quick Publish button, located in the Quick Access Toolbar at the top left.

7. A notification will pop up, saying that the form was published successfully. Click OK and close InfoPath Designer.

Figure 18-24 shows the list form after it has been customized.

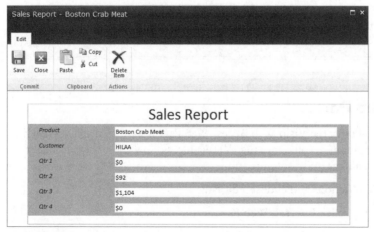

FIGURE 18-24

All three of the list default forms are automatically changed to be displayed with the new colors and title. This example shows an `EditForm.aspx` file of an existing list item. Think of the possibilities! No client software is required to work in SharePoint lists that have been customized in this manner, as the forms are browser-based by default.

INTEGRATING SHAREPOINT 2010 WITH MICROSOFT VISIO

The Microsoft Visio application enables the creation of advanced visuals such as charts, diagrams, flowcharts, and even floor plans and network diagrams. This section covers several ways that you can use Visio and SharePoint in conjunction. Chapter 25 explains how SharePoint workflows integrate with Visio Services.

The Visio Graphics Service is a service application in Central Administration. SharePoint users can create Visio diagrams on their client machines and publish them to the server, after which point the client software is no longer needed. After the diagram has been published to the Visio Graphics Service, the server can take care of refreshing that diagram and maintaining the data connections inside of it.

Visio Graphics Service Configuration

In Central Administration, click Manage Service Application, and see that the Visio Graphics Service is listed. Click the Visio Graphics Service link to get to the Visio Graphics Services Management page. There are two different pages here, where service customization options are located:

➤ **Global Settings** — This page contains settings such as the maximum diagram size, maximum and minimum cache sizes, and the maximum data refresh duration. Also, if external data connections are to be used in Visio graphics, there is a section here for an unattended service account's Application ID.

➤ **Trusted Data Providers** — This page contains a list of default data providers, with databases such as SQL and Oracle. You can add new, custom trusted data providers here.

 You can save Visio files as web drawings. You can view these files in the browser. They have a file extension of `.vdw`.

Visio Web Access Web Part

When added to a page in SharePoint, the Visio Web Access Web Part is used to display Visio files that have been saved to SharePoint as a Web Drawing (VDW) file. Follow these steps to insert a Visio Web Access Web Part on a page and configure it:

1. At the top left, click Site Actions and choose Edit Page.

2. On the Ribbon at the top, click Insert ➪ Web Part.

3. In the Business Data category, select Visio Web Access, and click the Add button.

4.   Click the link that says Click here to open the tool pane, and the Web Part tool pane will appear on the right side of the screen. Figure 18-25 shows some tool pane settings.

5.   Click the ellipses button next to the Diagram URL box, navigate to the document library in which the VDW file exists, select the target file, and click OK.

6.   Click OK at the bottom of the Web Part tool pane.

Figure 18-25 shows an example of a Visio diagram being displayed in a Visio Web Access Web Part. You can make further customizations in the Web Part tool pane. In addition to the settings displayed in Figure 18-26, there are sections to configure the Toolbar and User Interface, and the Diagram Interactivity.

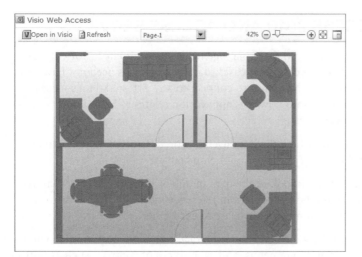

FIGURE 18-25

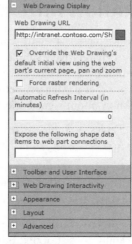

FIGURE 18-26

INTEGRATING SHAREPOINT 2010 WITH ONENOTE

OneNote is an Office application that is used to quickly take notes and organize them. Not only are there note typing and writing capabilities, you can insert many different types of objects into OneNote files, such as images, links, and even video or voice clips. Putting notes in OneNote gives you a visually clear and easily searchable solution.

The capability for OneNote to be shared and integrated with SharePoint and the other Office applications makes it a very useful and easily accessible tool. The live co-authoring feature discussed at the beginning of this chapter also applies to Office OneNote.

To create a new shared notebook for collaboration from a document library in SharePoint, follow these steps:

1.   Click the File tab to open the Backstage view.

2.   Click the New tab on the left side of the screen.

3. Choose Network, type a name for the new file, and choose the URL of the target document library.

4. Click the Create Notebook button.

5. Once the new file is created, OneNote offers you the option to send the link in an e-mail to someone.

From this point on, users who have at least Contribute permissions on that document library will be able to open the file and make their notes. The left side of the screen contains a vertical button with the name of the current file. Right-click on this button to view several options, such as the capability to Sync this notebook now.

INTEGRATION WITH ACCESS 2010 AND ACCESS SERVICES

Microsoft Access is a small-scale relational database management system. It has historically been used to create relatively simple solutions; and in most cases, database creators need not have any programming knowledge. Access provides the ability to connect to any external data sources, such as SQL or other databases. Before delving into how this application relates to SharePoint, you should know about some basic Access objects:

➤ **Tables** — Tables are the location where the data itself is stored. Everything that you do in Access is going to be based upon the information in your tables.

➤ **Queries** — Queries provide a way to look at the data in one or more tables. For example, using a query you can filter and refine information, reference information from various tables, and define the way that common fields relate to each other.

➤ **Forms** — Forms are the means by which end users interact with data in the tables. These generally consist of text boxes, drop-down menus, and other types of controls, such as buttons. Forms are the user interface when adding or modifying table data.

➤ **Reports** — Reports are used to display or print the Access data. Business users generally view reports in order to quickly assess numbers, using tables or graphs.

In scenarios where multiple users are attempting to access and modify the data within Access database tables, which can be difficult to accomplish, SharePoint integration provides a solution. If you think of lists and libraries in SharePoint as tables in a database, it is easy to understand the natural integration with Microsoft Access.

This section describes how to use SharePoint lists as tables in Access databases and the new concept of Access Services in SharePoint 2010.

SharePoint Data As a Table

The data in SharePoint can easily be connected to serve as live table data in an Access database, which can be queried and reported on. There are a couple of ways to accomplish this. In this section, you'll learn the methods that you can use to establish communications between SharePoint and Access.

Connecting to Access from SharePoint

From a SharePoint 2010 list, on the List tab in the Ribbon, click the Open with Access button in the Connect & Export section. Figure 18-27 shows the screen that appears.

If the desired database already exists, navigate to it or otherwise customize the name of the new database to be created. The option to link to the dynamic data is the default, but the data can optionally be exported from SharePoint as static.

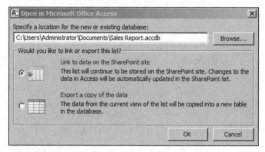

FIGURE 18-27

 SharePoint libraries do not have the Open with Access button that exists in lists, but they can be connected to Access. Refer to the "Exporting to Excel" section and Figure 18-16 earlier in this chapter, which demonstrates how to access the hidden task pane.

Connecting to SharePoint from Access 2010

When armed with the URL of the target SharePoint site, you can create a dynamic connection to SharePoint from within the Access 2010 software. This section describes the various ways to go about this.

Figure 18-28 displays the External Data tab in Access 2010. Both the Import & Link section and the Export section contain drop-down boxes called More, each of which contains an option for SharePoint List.

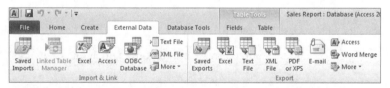

FIGURE 18-28

Data can be imported from SharePoint into Access, and it can even be exported from Access, to become a table in SharePoint.

Using the Create tab in Access 2010, you can also create several different types of SharePoint lists right from Access! The Database Tools tab contains a button called SharePoint, which you can use to move the tables to a SharePoint list and create linked tables in the database. In previous versions of Access, this was a manual operation, per table. The last step, which is new in Office 2010, is to upload the database file to a SharePoint document library, where it can be opened and interacted with.

A REAL-WORLD EXAMPLE

A project management department at a small company has an Access database on a file share, which they have always used to enter new projects. Some fairly complex Access reports are run on the project data. These reports are based on multiple tables and queries, are full of advanced calculations, and need to be shown to the company president every month.

The problem with this archaic solution is that it is not easy for multiple people to enter data at the same time. This is a good scenario in which the tables can be added to SharePoint as lists, and connected to Access. The Access database itself can then be uploaded to a document library, and the original copy on the file share can be deleted. Multiple users can access the Project Management SharePoint site and enter and edit project data, and those monthly reports can still be run from within the Access database in the document library.

Note that changes to the database design itself (not the data) will require that the database file be downloaded, changed, and then uploaded to the document library again. When multiple users change the database design simultaneously, one user's version of the file can be overwritten.

Access Services

There seems to be something missing when it comes to the way Access and SharePoint work together. How can legacy Access databases be fully translated into purely SharePoint applications? It shouldn't be necessary to have to keep queries and reports in Access, and only tables in SharePoint. SharePoint 2010's answer to this need is called Access Services.

Table 18-1 shows the additional functionality that Access Services brings to SharePoint.

TABLE 18-1   Additional Functionality with Access Services

FUNCTIONALITY	JUST SHAREPOINT	SHAREPOINT AND ACCESS SERVICES
Data in SharePoint lists	✔	✔
Centrally deployed interface	✔	✔
Collaborative design		✔
Web forms in the browser		✔
Web reports in the browser		✔
Server-side macros		✔

Existing Access databases can be published to Access Services, which will convert them to SharePoint web objects. The SharePoint user and permissions model is leveraged, and the databases then become more collaborative. For design and structure changes, the database is only locked per object, as opposed to per the whole database. One user can redesign a report while another user modifies a form or creates a new one. Once a database has been published in Access Services, the database objects are all run completely within the web browser, and no client software is needed, except for those users who will be redesigning the database.

Access Services Web Service Application

In Central Administration, Access Services is listed as one of the Service Applications by default, and is considered a middle-tier service that handles the query processor and the data access layer. Access Services also manages communication between the Access application and the SharePoint content database, which enables the use of large lists. In addition, SharePoint 2010 adds some advanced database concepts to SharePoint lists, which were fairly basic in the past. These new capabilities are relationships between lists, unique column constraints, and data-level validation.

 Access Services are configured like other service applications, which are discussed in Chapter 7.

You can configure numerous settings to optimize the performance of Access Services as an application. For example, there are several query settings, such as maximum columns per query, maximum sources (lists) per query, and maximum calculated columns per query. The setting called Maximum rows per query enables you to control how many rows can be viewed at once. For instance, if there are 2 million rows, a default of 50,000 rows per query is a good setting. Another setting called Maximum records per table enables you to set a limit on the table's size. For example, the IT department may want to reassess the use of a database when it reaches a certain size. At that point, it can be further determined whether the data may be better suited to a different type of database, such as SQL. There are several settings related to the maximum number of sessions, and even a maximum size for the log file. To access the settings described, go to Central Administration and click Access Services.

To get started publishing an existing Access 2010 database to Access Services, follow these steps:

1. In the database, click the File menu. The Backstage view will be displayed.

2. On the Save & Publish tab, click Publish to Access Services.

3. Click to Run the Compatibility checker. Some items may be flagged as incompatible with the web, such as certain types of characters in field names. When there are incompatibility issues, a new table called Web Compatibility Issues is automatically created. You will need to resolve any issues before the database can be published to the web.

4. The database will be published as a subsite, so fill in the URL of the top-level SharePoint site. As shown in Figure 18-29, enter a site name, and then click the Publish to Access Services button.

5. Once the Access database ACCDB file has been published to Access Services, it is not needed anymore and can be deleted or archived.

FIGURE 18-29

Note that during the web compatibility troubleshooting process, you can right-click on any object in Access, such as a table, and run the compatibility checker on just that object. This enables you to gradually work through the issues, especially when there is a long list of them.

One of the first things that is apparent on the New tab of the Backstage view in Access 2010 is an option to create a new "Blank Web Database." Once SharePoint 2010 with Access Services has been deployed in the organization, users can be trained to get in the habit of always choosing Blank Web Database when creating new databases. When creating these databases, the design interface is trimmed down to only allow for functionalities that are web friendly. This will ensure SharePoint compatibility going forward, with no web compatibility issues to work through when it's time to go live with the database.

After databases have been published to Access Services, they can be saved as templates to be used later, which is a similar concept to saving a SharePoint site as a template. Follow these steps to save the template and deploy it:

1. On the Settings page of the published database in SharePoint, click the Options drop-down and choose Open in Access.

2. Click the File menu, and on the Save & Publish tab on the left, click Save Database As.

3. For the format, choose Template (ACCDT).

4. The Create New Template from This Database screen will display (see Figure 18-30). Type a name for the template, and at the bottom optionally choose to include the data in the template.

5. The template file can then be uploaded to the Solution gallery on a SharePoint site, and activated.

6. From that point on, when users click to create a new subsite, there will be a new option with the same name as the template that was created. The nice thing about this method is that the person creating the new site based off the Access template need not have Microsoft Access installed on his or her client machine.

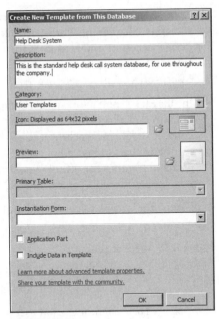

SHAREPOINT 2010 WORKSPACE

FIGURE 18-30

Previously known as Microsoft Office Groove 2007, SharePoint Workspace is an application that enables you to take a SharePoint site's data offline. With this tool, SharePoint sites, along with all of their content, become convenient and portable. SharePoint content can be set up for automatic synchronization that is able to be customized at a granular level. Although some list types are not compatible with offline synchronization, for the most part this is a wonderful tool for those of us who are frequently on-the-go.

Earlier in this chapter, it was mentioned that some list types and document libraries can be connected to Microsoft Outlook for use from within the Outlook client and offline. Compared to the offline capabilities of Outlook, SharePoint 2010 Workspace provides a much more granular synchronization interface, and the capability to select an entire SharePoint site for offline accessibility.

The Site Actions menu on a SharePoint 2010 site contains an option called Sync to SharePoint Workspace. Also, from within each document library in the browser, the Library tab in the Ribbon contains a link to Sync to SharePoint Workspace. The same goes for lists, and the button is on the List tab in the Ribbon.

The first time the SharePoint Workspace software is elicited, the user is prompted to create a new account or restore an existing account. This "account" will contain the user's connection settings for the different SharePoint sites to which they need to have offline access, and which libraries and lists are set up to synchronize to this offline copy. The user's e-mail account is used to initially configure the account, or an Account Configuration Code can be used in conjunction with an Account Configuration Server.

Groove Server 2010 is a different product that can be used to manage SharePoint Workspace accounts. SharePoint Workspace account management is beneficial because it expedites the setup of new accounts and facilitates the restoration of backed-up accounts. Detailed information about Groove Server 2010 is beyond the scope of this chapter, but you can find more information on Microsoft's TechNet site: `http://technet.microsoft.com`.

In this SharePoint Workspace example, an account will be created simply using the logged in user's domain e-mail account. Once an account is created, the user is first asked whether all of the site's content should be synchronized to their Workspace. At this point, it is a good idea to click the Configure button instead of the Yes button. The configuration screen enables users to select specific lists and libraries for offline synchronization. For each list or library that is clicked, a drop-down box enables selection of all content, headers only, or no content.

Follow these steps to connect SharePoint Workspace to a SharePoint site:

1. At the top left of the site, click Site Actions, and choose Sync to SharePoint Workspace for the first time.

2. On the Account Configuration Wizard's Welcome to SharePoint Workspace screen, choose Create a new account, and click Next.

3. The current logged in user's name and email address will automatically be filled in. Click Finish to accept these default settings.

4. At the security prompt called Sync to SharePoint Workspace, click OK.

 If the site has a large amount of content, click the Configure button instead, in order to selectively choose lists and libraries to be synchronized offline.

A dialog box will be displayed, showing the progress of the synchronization. When complete, the status of each list and library will be displayed as in Figure 18-31. Notice that the types of objects that are not supported are indicated in this list, such as calendars and data connection libraries.

5. Click Open Workspace to open this SharePoint site in SharePoint Workspace.

Each SharePoint site that is synchronized is shown as a different Workspace in a window on the screen called Launchbar. From this Launchbar, click to open any SharePoint

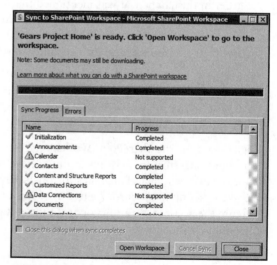

FIGURE 18-31

Workspace. Notice that navigating through the site's document libraries and folders is a faster experience than waiting for web pages to load in the browser. Many document library and list functionalities exist in this application, such as document upload, file check in or out, version history, and even filling out of forms.

SharePoint Workspace also contains a unique functionality that enables users to mark items as read or unread. When SharePoint Workspace is running in the toolbar of the client computer, a small notification message pops up to indicate that an item in a certain location is unread. Within a library in the Workspace, a special green, ring-shaped icon is displayed next to items that are unread. Figure 18-32 shows a document library called Shared Documents that exists in a site called Gears Project Home. This library has two unread items, as indicated by the ring-shaped icons.

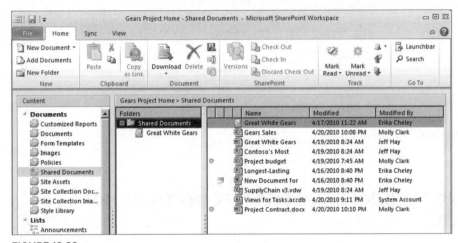

FIGURE 18-32

You can also configure many options within the SharePoint Workspace client via the Backstage view by clicking the File menu. In addition, from this screen you can set up desktop alerts and change account and connection settings.

PUBLISHING LINKS TO OFFICE CLIENT APPLICATIONS

In SharePoint, Personalization Site Links are special links that can be set up and pushed to client Office applications, such as links to commonly used document libraries or sites. The end user can view these links on the left side of the Save As and the Open dialog boxes in each Office Application. This allows the user quick access to commonly used SharePoint locations. Using Audiences, you can set up these links to be available to users in specific groups or specializations. For example, a Team Site for users who work in the company's Human Resources department could be created as a Personalization Site Link, targeted only to members of the Active Directory group called Human Resources. The following steps demonstrate how to create a Personalization Site Link.

1. In Central Administration, in the Application Management section, click Manage Service Applications.

2. Scroll down and click User Profile Service Application.

3. In the My Site Settings section, click Publish Links to Office Client Applications.

4. Click the New Link button. Figure 18-33 shows the Properties page for the new link, which will become available to all clients in their Office applications.

FIGURE 18-33

MANAGING OFFICE 2010 AND SHAREPOINT THROUGH GROUP POLICY

Active Directory and Group Policy administrators will be excited to know that they can now standardize a plethora of SharePoint and Office 2010 settings across a large organization. Basically, ADMX files are administrative templates that are used in Group Policy management. These files allow for client registry settings to be configured in a central location and deployed in Active Directory containers. To learn more about managing Group Policy, step by step, refer to `http://go.microsoft.com/fwlink/?LinkId=75124`.

Figure 18-34 shows the Group Policy Management Editor on a domain controller.

For the Office suite, more than three thousand settings can be modified via Group Policy. This section highlights some of the more useful user configuration settings that are pertinent to Office integration and SharePoint. Table 18-2 applies to the entire suite of applications; Tables 18-3, 8-4, and 18-5 are each pertinent to a specific Office application. The Policy column contains the name of the Group Policy Object, the GPO Path column shows the path to navigate to that setting, and the last column describes the purpose of the setting.

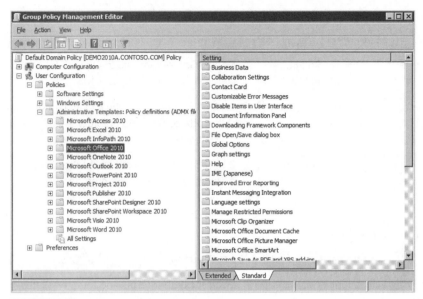

FIGURE 18-34

TABLE 18-2 Microsoft Office 2010 System

POLICY	GPO PATH	DESCRIPTION
Places Bar Locations	File ➪ Open/Save Dialog Box	Configure the list of items displayed in the Places Bar of the Common File dialog boxes.
User templates path	Shared Paths	Specify the location of user templates.
Disable Document Information Panel	Document Information Panel	Control whether users can view document information in the document information panel.
Maximum number of items to scan from today to determine the user's colleagues for recommendation	Server Settings ➪ SharePoint Server	Max number of items to scan in the Outlook mailbox to determine the user's colleagues. Larger = more accurate; Smaller = faster.
Control Blogging	Miscellaneous	Enable only SharePoint blogging, or disable blogging altogether.
Home Workflow Library	Miscellaneous	Allow administrators to make workflows from a specified list or library available within the workflow-enabled Office applications.

TABLE 18-3   Microsoft Outlook 2010

POLICY	GPO PATH	DESCRIPTION
Default SharePoint lists	Account Settings ⇨ SharePoint Lists	Deploy SharePoint lists to Outlook by providing a list of SharePoint list URLs.
SharePoint folder sync interval	Account Settings ⇨ SharePoint Lists	Define the interval in which Outlook automatically updates SharePoint folders. The default is 20 minutes.
Default servers and data for meeting workspaces	Meeting Workspace	Define up to five servers to be listed when meeting workspaces are created.

TABLE 18-4   Microsoft InfoPath 2010

POLICY	GPO PATH	DESCRIPTION
Control behavior for Microsoft SharePoint Foundation gradual upgrade	Security	Control whether forms and form templates follow URL redirections provided by Microsoft SharePoint Foundation during a gradual upgrade.
Turn off InfoPath Designer mode	Miscellaneous	Control whether InfoPath users can design new or existing form templates.

TABLE 18-5   Microsoft PowerPoint 2010

POLICY	GPO PATH	DESCRIPTION
Disable default service	Broadcast	Remove the default broadcast service from the Broadcast Slide Show dialog box.
Default file location	PowerPoint options ⇨ Save	Specify the default location for presentation files.

Although these are only a few of the thousands of settings you can deploy globally, they can be pretty powerful. Consider using some of these settings to encourage users to save Office documents to SharePoint, or to automatically see a shared list of the company's vendors in their Outlook application. You don't want users to have to "go find" SharePoint when it is time to upload a document for collaboration, or search for a company policy.

SUMMARY

Microsoft Office 2010 and its corresponding web companions, the Office Web Applications, are very tightly integrated with the SharePoint server functionality. SharePoint 2010 and the Office 2010 desktop applications all include the distinctive Ribbon interface. This provides a common user experience across the platform, which also helps to facilitate adoption. Each desktop application has a new set of key features that improve the user experience and provide integration between documents.

19

The Office Web Applications

Office Web Applications (OWA) are the web browser–based companions to the Office 2010 suite of desktop products for Word, Excel, PowerPoint, and OneNote. These applications enable users to access documents, and view, edit, and share content with other users across personal computers, mobile phones, and the Web using various web browsers. They are available on Windows Live at no cost to users as an ad-supported service, and for enterprise users, they can be hosted on SharePoint 2010. When enabled, these applications enhance the experience of the SharePoint user and greatly expand the possibility of collaboration.

Office Web Applications can be deployed to a SharePoint farm that has either SharePoint Foundation Services or the full SharePoint Server 2010 product installed. As the topic of this book is SharePoint Server 2010, we will be discussing the deployment of the OWA to the SharePoint Server 2010 product. This chapter begins with an overview of the OWA architecture, then walks you through the steps an administrator must take to get the OWA installed and configured. We also briefly discuss the OWA features to ensure that administrators are familiar with OWA's capabilities and its impact on the SharePoint environment.

OWA OVERVIEW

Before you dive into the installation and configuration process, we will briefly discuss web technologies that OWA utilizes, the components that make-up the OWA architecture and how they work.

Web Technology Utilized by OWA

The Office Web Applications provide the capability to view and edit your documents in the web browser. This is accomplished using three technology components that are fundamental to Web 2.0 and Rich Interactive Applications (RIA) — Asynchronous JavaScript (AJAX), Silverlight, and XML — plus good old HTML. These technologies are not unique, or specific to OWA, but OWA utilizes them to provide an enhanced user experience.

AJAX

For those readers who aren't familiar with Web 2.0 and RIA, AJAX is not a new programming language, but a new way to use the existing JavaScript and HTTP standards to create a better, faster, and more interactive web application. AJAX provides a dynamic mechanism for updating a web page without doing a complete page reload. This is accomplished using asynchronous data transfer (HTTP requests) between the browser and the web server, allowing web pages to request small bits of information from the server instead of whole pages. Overall, this reduces postbacks to the server, which makes the user interface more responsive.

Silverlight

Silverlight is a plug-in that installs into the browser. It provides new capabilities for the web browser, such as high-performance multimedia and animation. This functionality extends the web application capability far beyond the limitations of HTML and JavaScript. Silverlight works equally well on the Windows and Macintosh platforms and with Internet Explorer, Firefox, and Safari web browsers. Silverlight is not required for the OWA to function, but the user's experience will be much better with Silverlight installed. For example, the Word 2010 web application offers the following viewing experience benefits from Silverlight:

➤ Documents are loaded faster because, typically, fewer bytes need to be downloaded before displaying the document.

➤ Text fidelity is improved across zoom levels, including better text spacing and rendering.

The PowerPoint 2010 web application will provide smoother animations and better slide scaling with changes to the browser's window size. You can download and install the Silverlight plug-in from `http://www.microsoft.com/silverlight/get-started/install/default.aspx`. The administrator can deploy Silverlight across the enterprise using a number of different approaches, all of which are covered in the "Silverlight Enterprise Deployment Guide" located at `http://download.microsoft.com/download/7/8/d/78da8ec9-8801-42e5-89e5-3809386f1316/Silverlight%20Deployment%20Guide.doc`.

Browser Compatibility

The Office Web Applications will work with a diverse set of web browsers but three different browsers are officially supported:

➤ Internet Explorer 7 and 8 on Windows

➤ Firefox 3.5 on Windows, Macintosh, and Linux

➤ Safari 4 on Macintosh

Keep in mind that different browsers have different functionality, so the user experience will not necessarily be the same even within the supported list of browsers. For example, with Internet Explorer you can copy text using the Copy button on the ribbon, but Firefox doesn't support copying to the clipboard through mouse actions so the user will be required to use keyboard shortcuts. For an up-to-date listing of browser support, refer to the following link: `http://technet.microsoft.com/en-us/library/cc263526(office.14).aspx`.

Accessibility Features

The Office Web Applications have been designed to ensure that they are accessible to people with disabilities. Specifically, they have been designed to support people who are blind or have reduced vision, and people with limited mobility. Therefore, the focus has been on three objectives:

➤ Enable screen reader support.

➤ Ensure that all functionality is keyboard accessible.

➤ Ensure that the applications are high contrast and support different zoom modes.

Screen Reader Support

Screen reader support is based on XHTML compliance and Accessible Rich Internet Applications (ARIA) standards. ARIA, an initiative of the World Wide Web Consortium (W3C), defines a way to make web content and web application functionality more accessible to people with disabilities. Specifically, it helps with dynamic content and advanced user interface controls developed with AJAX, HTML, JavaScript, and related Web 2.0 technologies. ARIA markup has been included in the OWA so that browsers and screen readers that support the ARIA standard can provide an experience that is comparable to a fully accessible desktop application.

The Word, OneNote, and Excel web applications are XHTML Strict compliant and use cascading style sheets (CSS) for document layout. In addition, the PowerPoint and Word application viewers render documents as images, or use Silverlight if it is installed. Clearly, an image represents a challenge to a screen reader, so a text-based version of the document is also provided that contains both the text and the structure of the content contained in the image. Word documents can also be opened as a tagged PDF document, allowing the PDF viewer that is compatible with the user's screen reader to be used. A structured outline of the PowerPoint presentation is also provided that contains the text content of the presentation organized by slide. It includes list hierarchy and tabular data in simple HTML that a screen reader can interpret.

Keyboard Accessibility

The set of most frequently used Office desktop suite shortcuts (Ctrl+B, Ctrl+S, and Ctrl+C) all work as expected in the web applications. Also, the Ctrl+F6 shortcut enables the user to navigate between different regions or areas in the OWA view, such as between the ribbon, the navigation pane, and the content.

Architecture

The Office Web Application's architecture utilizes the SharePoint Web Front End (WFE) and a set of services which reside on the application server to generate the browser-based representation of the document.

➤ **Web Front End** — The WFE consists of the OWA web pages and the ASP.NET page handlers that are responsible for generating and returning the HTML that represents the document to the browser. These components may also rely on assistance from the service applications when generating the HTML representation of the document. The PowerPoint web application also provides the Broadcast Slide Show (BSS) functionality, which is a new feature in the desktop version of PowerPoint 2010. BSS enables presenters to broadcast a slide show from PowerPoint 2010 to remote viewers who watch in a web browser. We discuss BSS later in this chapter.

➤ **Service Applications** — The OWA installation adds the Word Viewing Service application, the Excel Calculation Service application, and the PowerPoint Service application to the list of available SharePoint service applications (see Chapter 7 for details on the service application architecture). These services are responsible for performing Excel calculations and generating the image representation for Word and PowerPoint. Additional SharePoint services are not required to edit in Word or OneNote files.

From an architecture and deployment point of view, these components can be installed either on a single physical server or on multiple servers where the different layers reside on different physical servers. With that basic understanding of the OWA, let's turn to deployment.

DEPLOYMENT

OWA deployment consists of a series of steps that must be completed after SharePoint Server 2010 has been installed. A few of the more pertinent steps in the server installation process are reviewed in this chapter. The steps required for OWA deployment can be categorized into several phases:

➤ Installation

➤ Service activation

➤ Feature activation

We start this section with a brief overview of each of these phases and then turn to the specific steps involved in the installation and configuration.

The install process you should follow for OWA will vary according to the status of your SharePoint 2010 Server install. Determine which of the following describes your status:

➤ You have not yet installed the SharePoint 2010 Server, or have already installed the SharePoint 2010 Server but have not yet run the Configuration Wizard.

➤ You have already installed the SharePoint 2010 Server and have run the Configuration Wizard.

For either type of install, you should start with the information in the following section and then proceed to the appropriate instructions for your situation.

 Chapter 4 covers the SharePoint 2010 Server installation; look there for more details if you still need to install the server.

Installing SharePoint 2010 Server and Preparing for OWA

The OWA can be installed on a single standalone server or on multiple servers in the farm. Let's start with some review of the SharePoint Server installation process covered in Chapter 4. Recall that during the initial steps of installing the server product, the user is prompted to choose between the Server Farm and Standalone type of installation, as shown in Figure 19-1.

FIGURE 19-1

You should choose the Server Farm option; the Standalone option should not be used unless you are creating a single-server development environment installation on Windows 7 or Windows Vista. See Chapter 4 for a thorough explanation of why to avoid the Standalone option. Also keep in mind that a single-server development environment is not a supported environment for running SharePoint in production; it is only for developers needing a desktop development environment.

The capability to install SharePoint server on the Windows desktop operating system is new for the 2010 server product. The Server Farm installation is used for installing either a single-server or multi-server SharePoint farm. Both types of installations require that the OWA setup application (WCSetup.exe) be installed on each SharePoint server that will be involved in hosting the OWA.

The next step in the SharePoint server installation requires you to choose between a Complete install and a Stand-alone, as shown in Figure 19-2.

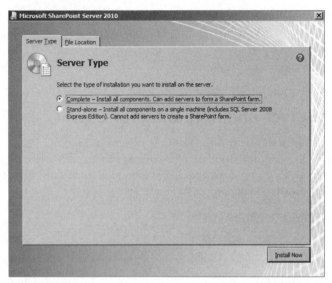

FIGURE 19-2

Choose the Complete install option because you will want to use a separate installation of SQL Server and not the SQL Server 2008 Express Edition.

Once setup is complete, you are prompted with the Run Configuration Wizard dialog, as shown in Figure 19-3.

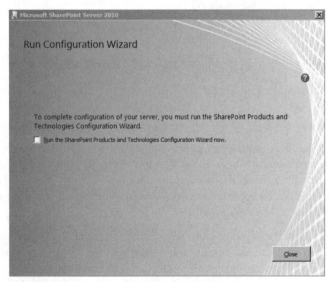

FIGURE 19-3

At this point in the typical installation, you would want to run the wizard to complete the installation of the farm. Because the Office Web Application software is not a part of the SharePoint Server 2010 install, it needs to be installed separately, so you should postpone the execution of the wizard until after the web applications are installed. If you are installing the server now, make sure the "Run the SharePoint Products and Technologies Configuration Wizard now" checkbox is not checked. Close this dialog and then proceed to install the OWA, as described in the "OWA Installation" section.

It is still possible to install the OWA software even after the configuration wizard has already been run, but that requires additional steps to complete the OWA configuration. This scenario is covered in the "OWA PowerShell Activation" section later in the chapter.

Service Activation

Recall that as part of the SharePoint Server 2010 installation in Chapter 4, the Post Setup Configuration Wizard application (PSConfig) or the SharePoint Farm Configuration Wizard may have been run to complete the installation. These two wizards alter the state of the SharePoint farm. Therefore, activating the OWA service applications for either the single-server or multi-server farm installation will depend on the state of the SharePoint farm when the OWA are installed.

For the single-server installation or farm installation, if PSConfig or the Farm Configuration Wizard have not been run, then running the corresponding wizard will automatically activate the required service instances, service applications, and service application proxies during an OWA installation. The setup application and PSConfig will install the SharePoint binary code, configure security permissions, configure the registry, create and configure the configuration and content database, and install the Central Administration web site.

Next, the Farm Configuration Wizard will configure the SharePoint farm, allow the administrator to select the specific services to use in the farm, and create the first site collection. All of this configuration can be done manually if you prefer, as described in the "Manual Activation" section.

If the wizards have already been run prior to installing the OWA, then the OWA service instances, service applications, and proxies must be created, started, and activated manually, or using PowerShell commands, as described in the "OWA PowerShell Activation" section later in this chapter.

Manual Activation

It is important for the administrator to know how to manually install any service and not have to rely on the wizard. This knowledge provides a much deeper understanding of what is involved, which will be helpful during troubleshooting. Manual activation requires that the OWA service instances be started and the service applications and proxies be created. Service instances are started using the Services on Server web page in SharePoint Central Administration, or by running a Windows PowerShell script. The Services on Server web page can be accessed using the Manager Services on Server link on the Central Administration home page. Service applications and their associated proxies can be created by using the Manage service applications page in SharePoint Central Administration, or by running a Windows PowerShell script (provided later in this chapter). Once created, the service applications will start running on each service instance automatically.

Feature Activation

Each site collection that will host the OWA functionality needs to be configured. This is accomplished by activating the OWA feature. The activation process can be done manually by browsing to each and every site collection's Site Collection Features page and activating the feature or by running a Windows PowerShell script. It is also possible to activate the feature for every site collection in the farm at once using a PowerShell script.

OWA INSTALLATION

The following installation instructions assume that SharePoint Server 2010 has not been installed yet, or that you have begun the installation but have not yet run the Configuration Wizard. If you have already run the Configuration Wizard, proceed to the "OWA PowerShell Activation" section at the end of the chapter.

Single-Server Farm Install

Install SharePoint Server 2010 according to the instructions in Chapter 4 and using the settings described earlier for the Server Farm and Complete Install options. In the dialog shown in Figure 19-3, leave the checkbox to automatically run PSConfig blank. This will postpone running PSConfig; the administrator may choose to run it later after the OWA are installed.

Installing the Office Web Applications

1. Make sure the user performing the installation is logged on with the built-in administrator account.

2. Extract the OWA files to a folder on your system by using the `/extract:c:\OWAfiles` switch, where `c:\OWAfiles` is the location to extract the files.

3. At the root of the `OWAfile` folder, run the OWA setup application `setup.exe`, which will display the Enter your Product Key dialog, shown in Figure 19-4.

4. After your key has been verified, click Continue to display the Microsoft Software License Terms dialog. Check the box to accept the terms and then click Continue.

5. On the Choose a file location dialog, shown in Figure 19-5, click Install Now to install to the default location. The Installation Progress dialog will be displayed during the installation.

6. The setup process should take only a few minutes. Once it is complete, the Run Configuration Wizard dialog (refer to Figure 19-3) will be displayed. Be sure that the "Run the SharePoint Products and Technologies Configuration Wizard now" checkbox is selected, and then click Close to start the configuration wizard.

 Step 6 assumes that the SharePoint Post-Setup Configuration Wizard has not been run after the original SharePoint server setup. If the wizard has already been run, then the OWA services need to be created and activated, either manually as described in Chapter 7 or using the PowerShell scripts provided at the end of this chapter.

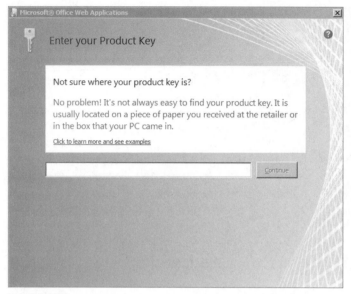

FIGURE 19-4

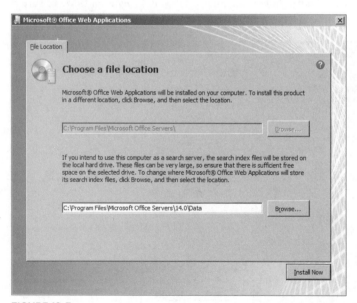

FIGURE 19-5

7. The configuration wizard's Welcome to SharePoint Products page, shown in Figure 19-6, is displayed. Click Next to continue.

8. The next dialog notifies you that some services might need to be restarted or reset during configuration. Click Yes to continue.

FIGURE 19-6

9. The Connect to a server farm dialog (see Figure 19-7) is shown next. Make sure the Create a new server farm option is selected, and then click Next.

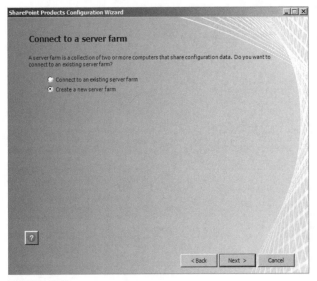

FIGURE 19-7

10. The Specify Configuration Database Settings dialog (see Figure 19-8) appears. Enter the appropriate value for the name of the database server, accept the default configuration database name or enter your own choice, enter the access account information for the administrator account, and click Next.

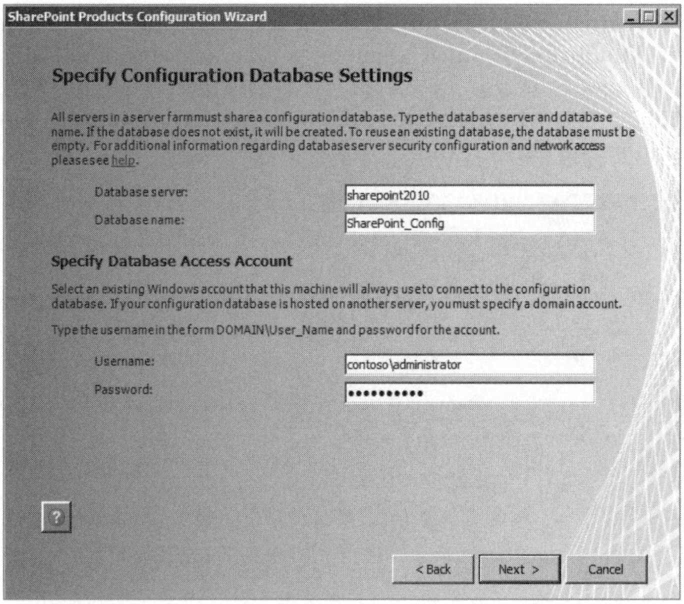

FIGURE 19-8

11. The Specify Farm Security Settings dialog shown in Figure 19-9 asks you to enter a passphrase. The purpose of the passphrase is to ensure that no other SharePoint servers can join the farm unless they have the proper credentials. Enter whatever you like here or enter something like the administrator account password. You can change this password later if you choose.

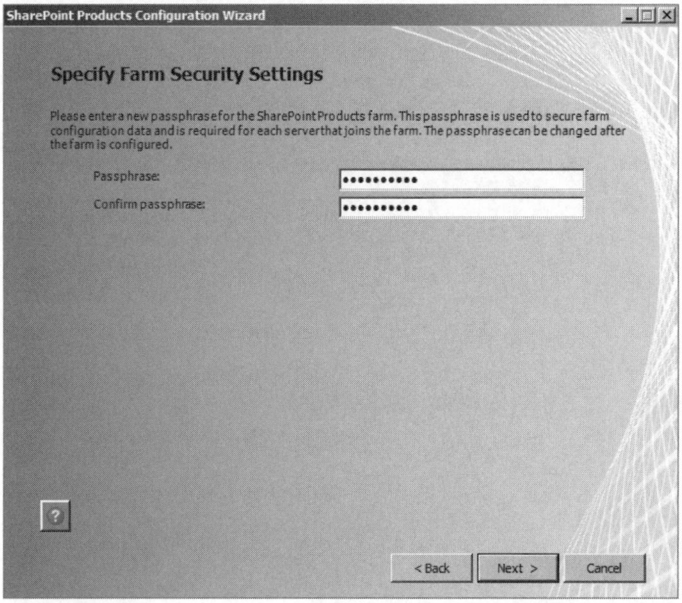

FIGURE 19-9

12. Figure 19-10 shows that the administrator can define a specific port for the Central Administration web application or utilize a randomly generated port number. The option to choose NTLM or Kerberos is also presented. It is usually best to choose Kerberos for SharePoint web sites but NTLM will suffice for the administration web site. Enter the appropriate information and click Next.

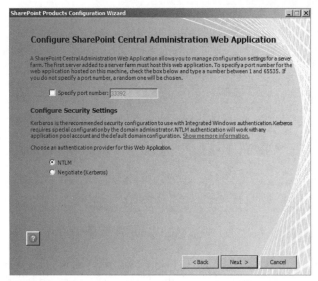

FIGURE 19-10

13. The next screen, shown in Figure 19-11, summarizes the information that you entered. Review the information and click either Next to begin the configuration process or Back to make any changes.

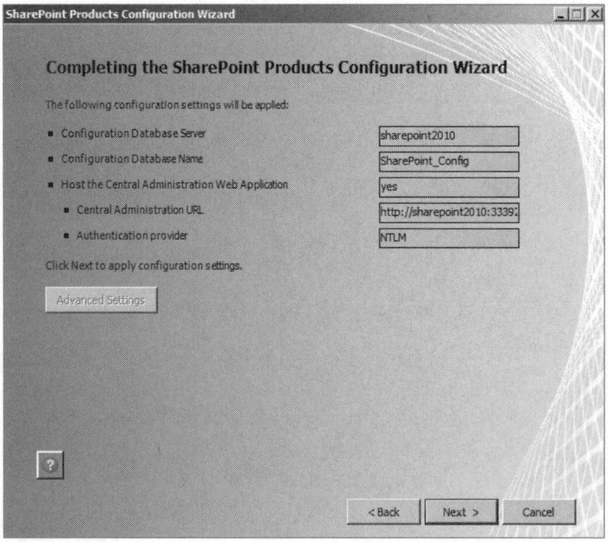

FIGURE 19-11

14. The Configuring SharePoint Products screen displays the progress for the configuration process. Once configuration is complete, you will receive confirmation stating that the configuration was successful. Click Finish on the Configuration Successful dialog to display the Central Administration dialog shown in Figure 19-12. This completes the configuration.

FIGURE 19-12

 Open SQL Server Management Studio and view the two different databases that have been created, SharePoint_Config and SharePoint_Admincontent, which represent the configuration database and the Central Administration web site databases, respectively.

Service Activation

From the Central Administration web site, click the "Manage servers in this farm" link located beneath the System Settings heading to see the Servers in Farm information shown in Figure 19-13. You can see that SharePoint Server 2010 and the Office Web Applications are installed. The next step is to create and configure the necessary services to support the web applications. You can do this task using the Farm Configuration Wizard, via manual configuration, or using PowerShell commands.

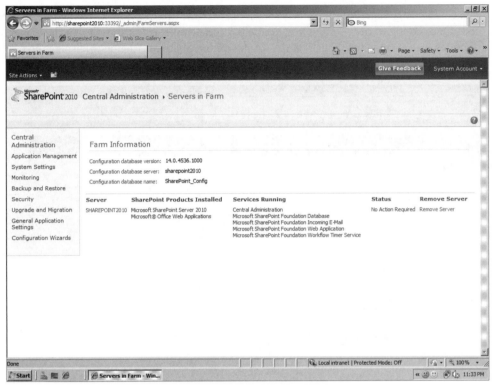

FIGURE 19-13

The following steps take you through the Farm Configuration Wizard. This procedure must be completed only if the wizard has not been previously run. If the wizard has already been run, the OWA can be activated using the PowerShell scripts at the end of the chapter.

 You can also configure the services manually. See the "Manual Activation" section earlier in this chapter.

1. On the SharePoint Central Administration home page, click the Configuration Wizards hyperlink in the lower right-hand corner of the page. On the Configuration Wizards page, shown in Figure 19-14, click Launch the Farm Configuration Wizard hyperlink.

2. The Farm Configuration Wizard welcome page is shown in Figure 19-15. Choose "Walk me through the settings using this wizard," and then click Next.

3. The purpose of running the wizard is to configure the desired services. On the Configure your SharePoint Farm page, in the Service Account section, make sure "Create new managed account" is selected and type a username and password for the service account. If you have not previously created an account specifically for services, then create the following account in Active Directory for use as your service account: contoso\sp_admin.

FIGURE 19-14

FIGURE 19-15

4. The contents of the Configure your SharePoint farm web page are shown in Figure 19-16 and Figure 19-17. In the Services section, select as many services as you would like, but specifically ensure that the PowerPoint service application and the Word Viewing Service checkboxes are selected. For this install, select all the checkboxes except the one for the Lotus Notes Connector and then click Next.

FIGURE 19-16

The next screen displayed indicates that processing is in progress. Service instances and their corresponding proxies are being created during this time.

5. At this point, the services have been created and the administrator now has the option to create a new top-level web site. On the Create Site Collection page, shown in Figure 19-18, add the necessary information and click OK when you are finished.

6. On the Configure your SharePoint Farm page, shown in Figure 19-19, review the list of services and click Finish.

This completes the OWA setup. Next you will proceed with testing the web applications to ensure they are working.

The installed service application instances can be viewed from the Manage Service Applications web page in Central Administration. Make sure that the PowerPoint service application and proxy instances are listed and the services are started. Also, make sure the Word Viewing Service and proxy instances have been created and started.

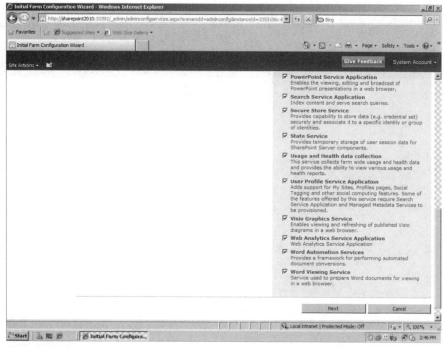

FIGURE 19-17

FIGURE 19-18

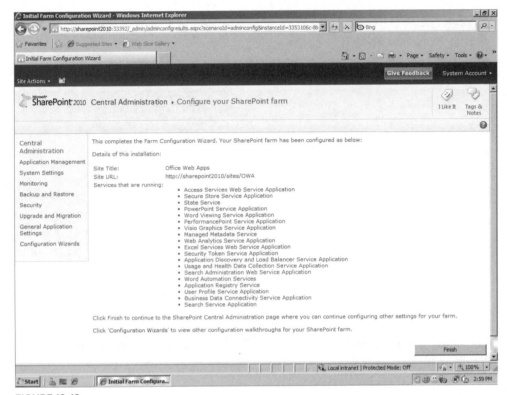

FIGURE 19-19

Feature Activation and OWA Testing

The last step in the installation and configuration is to activate the Office Web Apps feature at the site collection level and ensure that the apps are functioning properly.

1. Using the newly created site collection as the test case, navigate to the Features page for the site collection and confirm that the Office Web Apps feature has been activated, as shown in Figure 19-20.

FIGURE 19-20

2. The administrator should also confirm that the Shared Documents library that has been provisioned as part of the new web site in the site collection has been configured to open documents in the browser by default, as shown in Figure 19-21. Do this by navigating to the Advanced Settings page for the Shared Documents library.

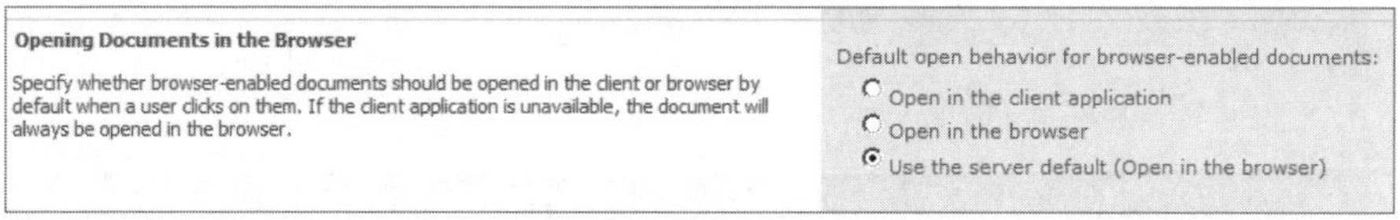

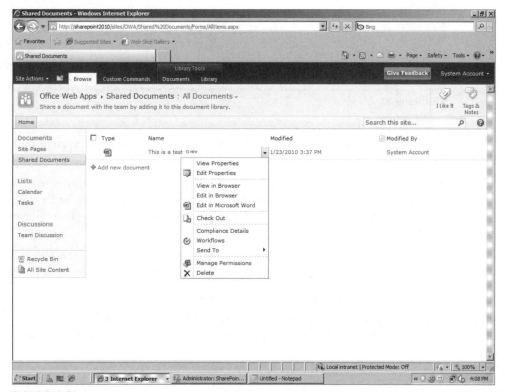

FIGURE 19-21

3. Add a document to the Shared Documents library so that the View in Browser functionally can be tested. You can do this by either creating a new document from scratch and then saving the document to the Shared Documents library or uploading a document to the library directly. Then select the View in Browser menu option from the drop-down menu, as shown in Figure 19-22. This will open the document in the web browser using the Office Web Application functionality.

FIGURE 19-22

4. If everything has been configured properly, the Word document will open in the browser (see Figure 19-23), indicating that the Word web application is functioning properly. The browser may also display the banner shown here above the document, indicating that the Word viewing experience can be improved by installing the Silverlight plug-in. To do so, click the link and complete the steps on the corresponding web pages.

FIGURE 19-23

You should test the Excel and PowerPoint web applications in the same way to confirm that they are configured properly.

If the OWA have been installed on a single server that is also functioning as an Active Directory domain controller, you will likely encounter the error shown in Figure 19-24. To fix the error and complete the configuration of the Word web application, you need to run the PowerShell commands using the following steps.

1. Open the SharePoint 2010 Management Shell from the Start menu in the Microsoft SharePoint 2010 Products heading. Type and execute the following two sets of commands:

> *See Chapter 10 for a refresher on running PowerShell commands.*

Available for download on Wrox.com

```
Get-SPServiceApplication

$e = Get-SPServiceApplication | where {$_.TypeName.Equals("Word
Viewing Service Application")}
$e.WordServerIsSandboxed = $false
$e.WordServerIsSandboxed
```

Code file Chapter19_code.txt

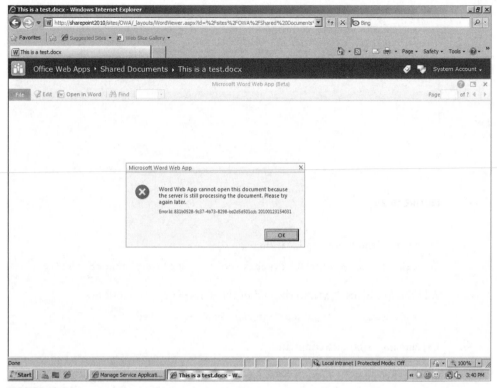

FIGURE 19-24

The first command, `Get-SPServiceApplication`, will provide a list of the installed service application instances. This command needs to be run first so that the correct names of the service application instances can be determined. Keep in mind that in different languages, service application names could be localized. These service application names are then utilized in the second set of PowerShell commands. In this case, the Word Viewing Service and PowerPoint service application are the services of interest.

2. Type and execute the following two PowerShell commands to activate the PowerPoint service application. Respond to the prompts with a "Y" for yes after each command is executed, as shown in Figure 19-25. (Each of these commands belongs on a single line; they are broken here to fit on the page.)

```
Get-SPPowerPointServiceApplication | Set-SPPowerPointServiceApplication -
EnableSandboxedViewing $false

Get-SPPowerPointServiceApplication | Set-SPPowerPointServiceApplication -
EnableSandboxedEditing $false
```

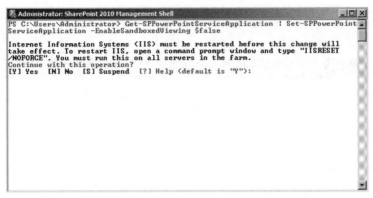

FIGURE 19-25

3.   Navigate to the following location:

    c:\windows\system32\inetsrv\config\applicationHost.config

Add the following XML to the end of the dynamicTypes section:

    <add mimeType="application/zip" enabled="false" />

4.   Execute an IISRESET command.

This completes the manual configuration necessary to activate the OWA on a server that is also functioning as a domain controller. Proceed with testing the Excel and PowerPoint web applications to ensure that they are functioning properly.

 Keep in mind that installing the OWA on a domain controller is not a supported configuration for a production environment. It is to be used as a development environment only.

PowerPoint Broadcast Slide Show

The Office 2010 Broadcast Slide Show (BSS) capability enables presenters to broadcast a PowerPoint 2010 slide show to remote users who can view the slide show using their web browser. The BSS service is hosted on a SharePoint server with the OWA installed and utilizes the PowerPoint service application. You create one or more broadcast services by creating sites that use the PowerPoint Broadcast site template, and set permissions for those individuals who can use the service through group membership on the site.

Installation and Configuration

The BSS requires that the PowerPoint service application be created and started. As demonstrated earlier, this is accomplished by running the Farm Configuration Wizard after the OWA have been installed. OWA installation adds the PowerPoint Broadcast site template to the server. A SharePoint site collection created from this template is required to utilize the BSS capability. Users who will utilize the BSS connect to the URL of this site collection to start a broadcast, and attendees also utilize this link to view the presentation in their browser. Multiple BSS sites may be created, each with its own URL.

As part of the OWA installation, a default BSS site collection is created within the default web application at `http://<default web application>/sites/broadcast`, which may be this URL: `http://<server name>/sites/broadcast`, where `<server name>` refers to the name of the server. In our specific installation, Figure 19-26 displays this default site collection's home page.

FIGURE 19-26

Specific SharePoint groups are automatically created to help manage user access permissions. You can view these groups by clicking the Groups hyperlink on the left-hand side of the site, as shown in Figure 19-27. The groups include the following: Broadcast Administrators, Broadcast Presenters, Broadcast Attendees, and Broadcast Content Access Users. The Windows group NT Authority/ Authenticated Users is automatically added to the Broadcast Presenters and Broadcast Attendees groups of this default site, granting all users access to create and view broadcasts. Also notice that the Administrator account is added to the Broadcast Administrators group.

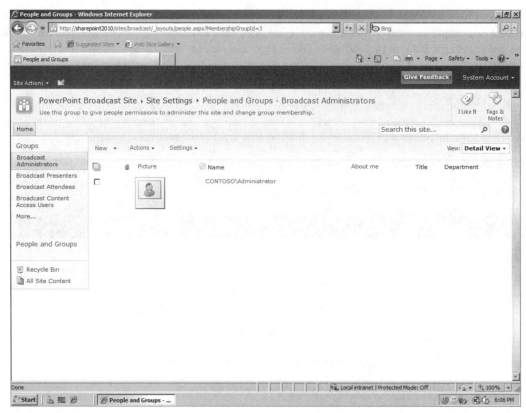

FIGURE 19-27

BSS sites can also be created manually by creating a new site collection using the PowerPoint Broadcast Site template as described in the following steps.

1. From the Central Administration web site home page, click the Create site collections hyperlink. This displays the Create Site Collection page shown in Figure 19-28.

2. Create a new site collection using the PowerPoint Broadcast Site template, which is located on the Enterprise tab of the Template Selection section, shown in Figure 19-29. Once the new site collection has been created, the administrator should confirm that no permissions are granted by default, and assign permissions manually.

3. The broadcast site administrator must assign users permissions to broadcast and attend slide show broadcasts as recommended below. Permission assignment is done from the People and Groups web page (refer to Figure 19-27).

    ➤ Users who need to broadcast should be added to the Broadcast Presenters group.

    ➤ Users who need to attend a broadcast should be added to the Broadcast Attendees group.

    ➤ Users who need to administer the site and change group membership should be added to the Broadcast Administrators group.

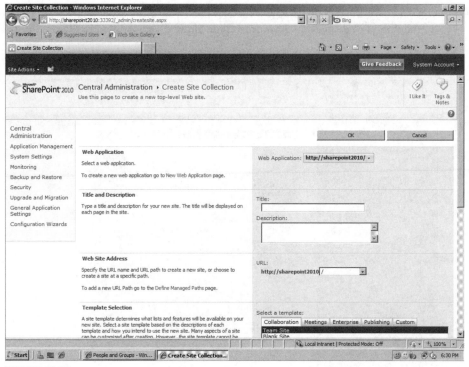

FIGURE 19-28

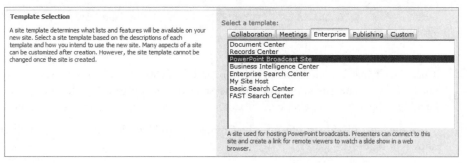

FIGURE 19-29

Once security is configured, the broadcast service needs to be made available to individual PowerPoint 2010 users. Presenters can connect to the site and start a broadcast from their desktop PowerPoint 2010 application, and viewers can see the presentation from their browsers. Group policy can also be used to advertise the service to users so they don't need to enter the broadcast site URL manually. Those interested in using group policy should download the PowerPoint 2010 Administrative template and follow the instructions in the article "Enforce settings by using Group Policy in the 2007 Office System," located at http://technet.microsoft.com/en-us/library/cc179081.aspx. Group policy can also be used to disable the broadcast capability.

4. Open a PowerPoint slide deck. On the Slide Show tab, click the Broadcast Slide Show button on the ribbon to display the Broadcast Slide Show dialog, shown in Figure 19-30.

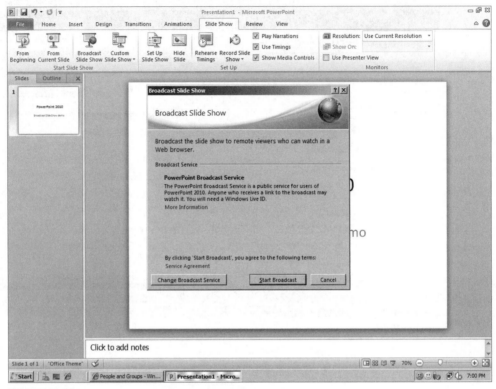

FIGURE 19-30

5. Click the Change Broadcast Service button, and then click the Add a new service... link. Type the URL of the new site in the Add Broadcast Service dialog and click the Add button. The result of adding the `http://sharepoint2010/sites/broadcast` site is shown in Figure 19-31.

6. Click the Start Broadcast button. The Connecting to SharePoint2010 dialog will appear as shown in Figure 19-32.

7. The final screen before starting the slide show provides the presenter with an option to copy the URL of the broadcast site or send an e-mail so that attendees can be informed. This screen is shown in Figure 19-33. To start the slide show, click the Start Slide Show button.

8. The slide show should begin, as shown in Figure 19-34. The presenter can press the Escape key to exit the presentation but won't be able to edit it until the broadcast is ended. This completes the configuration.

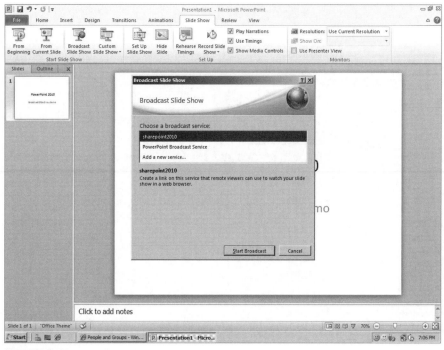

FIGURE 19-31

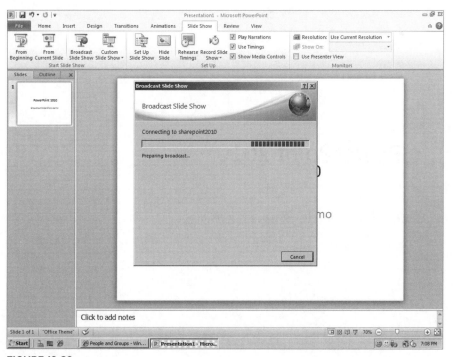

FIGURE 19-32

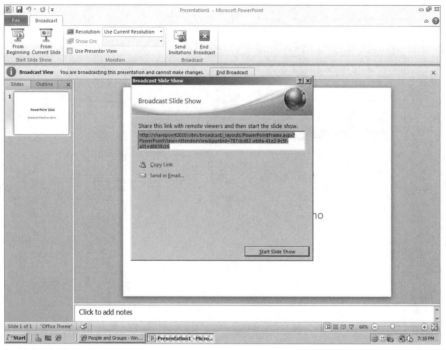

FIGURE 19-33

FIGURE 19-34

Multiple-Server Farm Install

The multiple-server install process is exactly the same as the single-server install except that the setup application must be executed on every server in the server farm that will host the Office Web Application functionality. The other difference is that the PowerShell commands for activating the services on a single server that is also a domain controller may not need to be executed because in a multiple-server install the domain controller is usually a separate physical server.

OWA POWERSHELL ACTIVATION

PowerShell commands can also be used to create and activate the OWA service applications. The PowerShell commands can be executed from any server in the farm that has the OWA installed. SharePoint administrators are likely to be only now becoming familiar with PowerShell, as SharePoint 2010 is the first SharePoint version to recommend use of the technology.

PowerShell Permissions

Historically, SharePoint administrators have used Central Administration and the command-line tool STSADM for administering the SharePoint farm. One of the challenges of using these tools was the specific permissions that were required.

The SharePoint administrator needed to be a Farm Administrator to access the Central Administration (CA) web site; this meant that the administrator had to be a member of the Farm Administrators Group. This membership gave the administrator access to use the CA web site to execute operations against the configuration database through the CA web application. These operations were executed in the security context of the application pool account for the web application, not the administrator. This situation differs with the STSADM command environment and PowerShell.

STSADM and PowerShell commands are run in the security context of the user executing the commands. The good news is that this enables commands to be run from any server in the farm because CA is not required. The challenge is that this requires the user to have the necessary permissions to complete the operation the commands are implementing. With STSADM, the user is required to be a local administrator, a SharePoint Farm Administrator, and have specific SQL Server permissions.

In general, PowerShell simplifies this because the administrator or user who is executing the PowerShell commands against the SharePoint 2010 farm only requires PowerShell and SQL Server permissions. Obviously, because each PowerShell command utilizes the SharePoint object model, additional permissions may be necessary for specific PowerShell commands, such as installing SharePoint 2010, Windows file system manipulation, and registry changes. Therefore, in general, administrators need to have the following two permissions to execute PowerShell commands:

➤   The user must be a member of the Windows group WSS_ADMIN_WGP on the server being used to execute the commands.

➤   The user must be a member of the SQL Server role called SharePoint_Shell_Access on the configuration database.

At this point in the installation, the administrator should confirm that the WSS_ADMIN_WGP group exists and that the Administrator account has been added to the group. The SharePoint_Shell_Access role exists on the configuration database but does not show any members, but keep in mind that the Administrator account is the owner of the role.

A PowerShell command called SPShellAdmin has been added to the list of preconfigured SharePoint commands to simplify the management of these roles. SPShellAdmin will add and remove Shell Administrators. Let's take a look at this command.

1. From the Start menu, type **PowerShell**, right-click the Windows PowerShell ISE option from the list, and click Run as administrator. The PowerShell Integrated Scripting Environment (ISE) is displayed, as shown in Figure 19-35. This environment provides a better approach to using and investigating PowerShell commands.

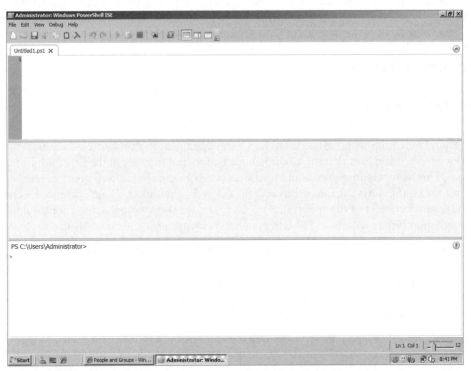

FIGURE 19-35

Unfortunately, the SharePoint 2010 PowerShell commands are not automatically loaded and registered into the environment like they are when you click the SharePoint 2010 Management Shell shortcut, so the SharePoint commands must be added manually.

2. At the PS C:\Users\Administrator prompt inside the ISE window, type the following command to register the SharePoint commands:

```
Add-PSSnapin Microsoft.SharePoint.Powershell
```

3. Type **Get-Help SPShellAdmin** at the shell prompt in the window as before. Three separate commandlets are listed, along with their synopses (summaries of their parameter requirements):

```
Get-SPShellAdmin
Add-SPShellAdmin
Remove-SPShellAdmin
```

These three commands have a database parameter that allows the administrator to designate a specific database, because by default the SharePoint_Shell_Access role allows access only to the configuration database. Each additional database access required must be given individually. Try adding a user to the SharePoint_Shell_Access role using the SPShellAdmin commandlet. Keep in mind that the syntax for the Add-SPShellAdmin commandlet is as follows:

```
Add-SPShellAdmin [-UserName] <String> [-database <SPDatabasePipeBind>]
```

4. Before you can execute the Add-SPShellAdmin commandlet, you need the SPDatabasePindBind value for the SharePoint_config database. This is obtained by executing the following command:

```
Get-SPDatabase
```

The Name, Id, and Type property information should be displayed in the ISE. The value of the Id is the SPDatabasePipeBind value that you will need to include in the Add-SPShellAdmin commandlet.

5. Type and execute the following command. Copy the Id value for the SharePoint_config database into the command. Make sure the sp_admin account exists or utilize another account. The command should add the sp_admin account to the SharePoint_Shell_Access role in the SharePoint_config database. The results are shown in Figure 19-36.

```
add-spshelladmin -username "contoso\sp_admin"
-database 67256615-0d6f-467f-b17a-9de983c71563
```

After this brief tutorial, you should be ready to use PowerShell to manually create and activate the OWA service applications, as discussed in the next section.

Service Creation and Activation

Manual activation of the Office Web Applications is only required if the Farm Configuration Wizard has already been executed, as this process creates and registers the service and proxy instances. Before executing the PowerShell commands, it is advised that you check the state of your SharePoint farm services and service applications in the Manage services on server and Manage service applications pages in SharePoint Central Administration. If the OWA services are not running, or the service applications do not exist, you will need to perform the following steps.

1. Verify that the user executing the PowerShell commands meets the following minimum requirements:

➤ Is a member of the SharePoint_Shell_Access role on the configuration database

➤ Is a member of the WSS_ADMIN_WPG local group on the computer where SharePoint 2010 is installed

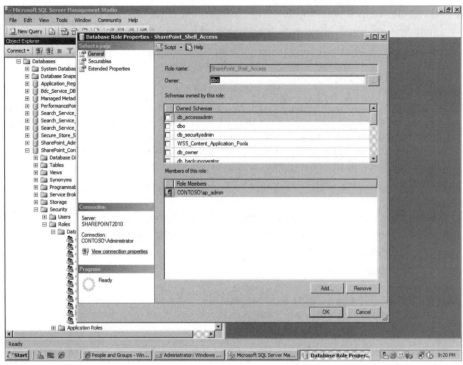

FIGURE 19-36

2. Open the PowerShell ISE with administrator privileges. You can also open the shell environment by using the SharePoint 2010 Management Shell if you prefer.

3. In the PowerShell console, at the command prompt, type and execute the following command as described in the previous section so that the SharePoint commandlet library is available:

```
Add-PSSnapin Microsoft.SharePoint.Powershell
```

4. The environment needs to be configured to execute PowerShell scripts in an unrestricted manner. Execute the following command to set policy. When prompted with the Execution Policy Change dialog, click Yes.

```
set-executionpolicy unrestricted
```

5. Next, the service instances must be started for each server that is executing the OWA service applications. Execute the following script. Replace the sharepoint2010 and server2 names with your specific server names, adding additional servers as appropriate:

```
$machinesToActivate = @("sharepoint2010", "server2")
$serviceInstanceNames = @("Word Viewing Service", "PowerPoint Service",
"Excel Calculation Services")
```

Available for
download on
Wrox.com

```
foreach ($machine in $machinesToActivate) {
foreach ($serviceInstance in $serviceInstanceNames){
    $serviceID = $(Get-SPServiceInstance | where
        {$_.TypeName -match $serviceInstance} | where
        {$_.Server -match "SPServer Name="+$machine}).ID
    Start-SPServiceInstance -Identity $serviceID
  }
}
```

6. The next step is to create the service applications and proxies after the service instances have been started. The applications and proxies connect the WFE to the service applications. Execute the following script to create the applications and proxies:

```
$appPool = Get-SPIisWebServiceApplicationPool -Name "SharePoint Web Services
Default"
New-SPWordViewingServiceApplication -Name "WdView" -AppPool $appPool |
New-SPWordViewingServiceApplicationProxy -Name "WdProxy"
New-SPPowerPointServiceApplication -Name "PPT" -AppPool $appPool |
New-SPPowerPointServiceApplicationProxy -Name "PPTProxy"
New-SPExcelServiceApplication -Name "Excel" -SPIisWebApplicationPool
$appPool |
```

7. The OWA feature can be manually activated on specific site collections in the farm or activated across all site collections using the following script:

```
$webAppsFeatureId = $(Get-SPFeature -limit all | where {$_.displayname
-eq "OfficeWebApps"}).Id
Get-SPSite -limit ALL |foreach{
Enable-SPFeature $webAppsFeatureId -url $_.URL }
```

8. Once the OWA feature is activated, documents will be opened using the corresponding web application, not the desktop application. This can be reconfigured so that documents are opened in the desktop application but not the web application. The following two sets of scripts reconfigure the default behavior for all site collections and all document libraries in the finance site, respectively. This completes the manual OWA activation. You can proceed with testing the install as previously discussed in the "Feature Activation and OWA Testing" section.

```
$webAppsFeatureId = $(Get-SPFeature -limit all | where {$_.displayname
            -eq "OpenInClient"}).Id
Get-SPSite -limit ALL |foreach{
            Enable-SPFeature $webAppsFeatureId -url $_.URL }


Get-SPWeb -site http://www.demo.com/sites/finance |% {}{$_.Lists}{$_.Update()
}|% {$_.DefaultItemOpen = $false}
```

SUMMARY

The Office Web Applications enhance the productivity of SharePoint users and information workers by providing the capability to access, create, and edit Word, Excel, PowerPoint, and OneNote documents using a web browser. These applications are deployed to SharePoint Server 2010 and can be installed in single-server or multiple-server SharePoint farms.

The installation requires three phases. First, the OWA are installed using a setup application. Second, the service applications that support this functionality must be created and activated. Finally, the OWA feature must be activated for each site collection in the farm that will utilize the functionality. SharePoint administrators can rely on the configuration wizards to assist in the configuration of the second and third phases, or use PowerShell commands for these phases.

20

PerformancePoint Services and Business Intelligence

WHAT'S IN THIS CHAPTER?

➤ Installing and configuring PerformancePoint Services

➤ Dashboard Designer

➤ Importing PerformancePoint Server 2007 content to PerformancePoint Services 2010

PerformancePoint Services (PPS) is one of the built-in services in SharePoint Server 2010. PPS is a performance management application that individuals use to monitor and analyze business data to help improve effectiveness and efficiency. Microsoft's Business Intelligence (BI) solution is based on using PPS in SharePoint 2010, SQL Server, and the Office Platform. PPS is available to any company that installs SharePoint Server 2010 using an Enterprise key, and has purchased Enterprise Client Access Licenses (CALs) for its employees.

Microsoft introduced PerformancePoint capability in a stand-alone product called PerformancePoint Server 2007 (PPS2007), and this capability integrated with SharePoint Server 2007 through the use of Web Parts. With the introduction of SharePoint Server 2010, PPS is now an integrated part of SharePoint 2010's architecture and exists as one of the available services. PPS retains many of the same features and functionality as its predecessor while including additional benefits, enhancements, and new functionality. PPS provides the capability to create and utilize BI objects referred to as dashboards, scorecards, and key performance indicators (KPIs). PPS also provides the capability to upgrade PPS2007 content using a wizard-driven process.

Using PPS begins with creating objects using a rich client tool called Dashboard Designer. Dashboard Designer provides a What-You-See-Is-What-You-Get authoring experience.

Designer objects are stored in SharePoint lists and libraries so that they can be utilized by other SharePoint 2010 features. Once these objects have been created, they are published or deployed to SharePoint 2010 websites so that their information can be viewed by individuals across the enterprise.

To do justice to the PerformancePoint capability in SharePoint Server 2010, we would need to write a whole book just to introduce the numerous features. The good news is that you will find books dedicated to PPS if you are interested, as well as books that are dedicated to specific elements of PPS. Yes, it is both deep and wide. Our purpose in this chapter is to provide the administrator with the information necessary to install and configure PPS, while briefly introducing the BI capability and features. We start with a very brief introduction of key PPS features and terminology.

PPS FEATURES AND TERMINOLOGY

This section introduces the PerformancePoint Services capabilities, and provides a table summarizing the relevant terminology that is used in Microsoft BI and in this chapter.

➤ PerformancePoint is one of the services in SharePoint Server 2010. The administrator will utilize the new service application architecture to install and configure PPS.

➤ PPS is used to create, display, and interact with first-class objects (FCOs). FCOs are dashboards that contain scorecards, reports, KPIs, filters, and data sources. FCOs bring data together from multiple data sources. Table 20-1 provides descriptions of the FCOs.

➤ FCOs are stored as content types and secured within SharePoint Server 2010 lists and libraries, providing a single repository for the information. Specifically, data sources are stored in document libraries, and all other FCOs are stored in lists. Dashboards that are stored in the list as FCOs represent dashboard pages, while dashboards that have been deployed are stored in a different document library. Under the covers, an FCO is defined by XML data in the content type.

➤ Because PPS is now built into SharePoint Server 2010, it can take advantage of the other SharePoint Server 2010 features, such as the security framework, scalability, collaboration, backup and restore, search, and disaster recovery capabilities.

➤ PPS Web Parts can link to other PPS Web Parts or other SharePoint 2010 Web Parts on the same page.

➤ PPS includes a new type of report called the *Decomposition Tree*. The Decomposition Tree simplifies the display of a multi-dimensional data set so that the data can be more readily interpreted. Because easy visualization and interpretation is at the heart of the BI process, this is going to be a very popular view.

Before we introduce Dashboard Designer and demonstrate how BI objects are created and published, we need to describe how to install and configure PPS. This is a key aspect for the administrator, so it represents the bulk of the chapter.

TABLE 20-1: First-Class Object Terminology

OBJECT	DESCRIPTION
Dashboard	A visual display of information that helps promote collaboration and improve decision making. This display includes scorecards, KPIs, reports, and filters. A dashboard is created using Dashboard Designer and published to SharePoint Server 2010.
Scorecard	One or more elements of a dashboard that represent a compilation of KPIs. They are used to track status, and they help measure KPIs.
Key Performance Indicator (KPI)	Measures the performance or success against some metric defined by the organization. This usually involves comparing a target value to an actually achieved value. For example, you could compare target sales by geography to actual sales by geography.
Filter	Controls the view of a dashboard so that only select items are available.
Indicator	A visual element of a KPI that quickly displays the status without drilling into the data. The iconic example is the red, yellow, and green colors of the traffic light.
Data Source	Provides the information for PPS to connect to a back-end system that contains information. PPS can connect to Analysis Services, Excel Services, Excel Workbooks, SharePoint Lists, and SQL Server Table and Views.
Reports	Allows data to be visualized and summarized using charts. PPS includes several types of reports: Analytic Chart, Analytic Grid, Strategy Map, KPI Details, SQL Server Reporting Services reports, and Excel Services.

PPS INSTALLATION AND CONFIGURATION

The installation and configuration of SharePoint 2010 was presented in depth in Chapter 4, so only the pertinent details for installing and configuring PerformancePoint Services are discussed in this chapter. You should review Chapter 4 to ensure you have a good understanding of the SharePoint 2010 installation and the wizards that are available to assist in the configuration, but some of the relevant details are repeated here for simplicity.

After SharePoint 2010 is installed, the administrator must configure the SharePoint farm. There are two wizards: the SharePoint Products and Technologies Configuration Wizard, which is used to create a new SharePoint farm or add your server to an existing farm, and the Farm Configuration Wizard (or Central Administration Wizard), which is used to help you provision service applications. Our interest is in the second wizard. Both of these wizards were run as part of the installation instructions in Chapter 4; but you should know that the Farm Configuration Wizard can be launched from the Central Administration home page using the Configuration Wizards link and the Launch the Farm Configuration Wizard link on the Configuration Wizards web page. This should display the web page shown in Figure 20-1.

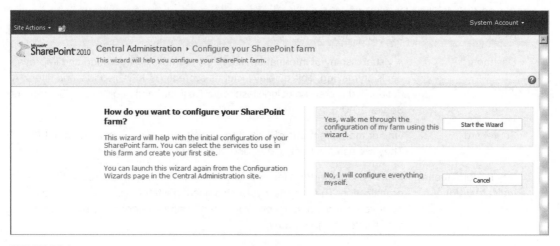

FIGURE 20-1

At this point, you have two options. The first option activates the wizard discussed in Chapter 4, whereas the second option returns you to the Central Administration default page. If you don't use the wizard, you will have to manually create the default web application, the default site collection, and activate any service applications that are necessary to support the PerformancePoint capability. Because the wizard has likely already been run, it is possible that the necessary services are already available and PerformancePoint is ready to be used. However, SharePoint administrators should know how to enable and configure the PerformancePoint capability regardless of the state of the server farm, so we will discuss the manual configuration approach here in order to ensure that you have a thorough understanding of the details.

PerformancePoint Service Application and Proxy

The first step in configuring PPS is to ensure that the PPS service application and proxy have been created, along with the corresponding applications for the Secure Store Service. The following steps take you through this process.

1. Ensure that the PerformancePoint Service and the Secure Store Service have been started. These services need to be running on the application servers to support PerformancePoint capability.

Browse to the Services on Server web page in Central Administration (see Figure 20-2). You should see a list of the different services and their status.

Scroll down the page until you can see the two services and verify that they are both in the Started state. If not, click the Start link directly to the right of the Stopped value in the Status column and start the service.

The PerformancePoint service application calls instances of these services to process requests. As you can see, these service instances can be started on a per-instance basis. Therefore, administrators only need to start the services that will be used, which is one of the key advantages of the SharePoint 2010 service architecture. Contrast this to SharePoint

2007, where the shared service provider included a fixed set of services that were all running all of the time, regardless of which was actually needed.

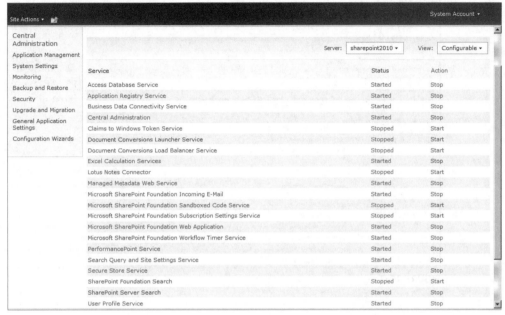

FIGURE 20-2

2. The next step is to ensure that a PerformancePoint service application has been created and is running.

Creating the service application creates the service application proxy that facilitates web service calls between the WFE and the application server using the Windows Communication Framework. This is accomplished by confirming that the PerformancePoint Service Application is running. To do so, browse to the Manage Service Applications web page. If the service application does not exist, click the New button in the Ribbon and choose PerformancePoint Service Application from the list of options, shown in Figure 20-3.

The set of service applications can also be obtained using the PowerShell cmdlet `Get-SPServiceApplication.`

A unique name and an application pool are required for configuring a new service application, as shown in Figure 20-4. The name is the display name of the service, and differs from the service application's identity, which is a GUID that is automatically assigned when the application is created. The identity is used to distinguish the service application from any other service application, as two different applications cannot have the same GUID. The identity can be viewed using PowerShell, with the `Get-SPServiceApplication` cmdlet.

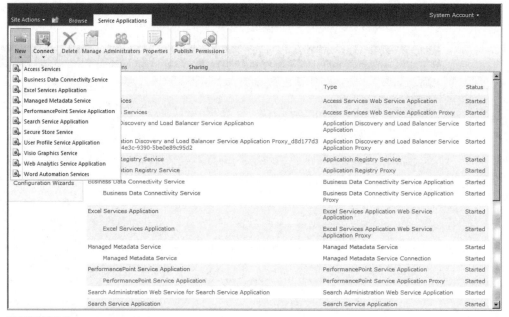

FIGURE 20-3

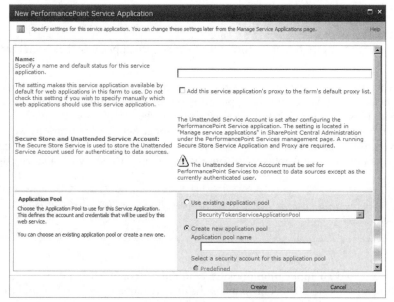

FIGURE 20-4

As part of creating a new service application, you have the option to specify whether this service application instance should be available by default for use by web applications in the farm. Checking this option adds the instance to the farm's list of default service applications. However, even though a service application proxy exists within the default group, it does not automatically make it the default application proxy within the default group.

Let's see what it means to enable this option. A default application proxy is used by all service applications in a given web application to communicate with that service application's web service. For a proxy to be the default of the default group, it must be designated as such on the Service Application Associations page. The Service Application Associations web page displays the relationships between the web applications in the farm, the Application Proxy Group, and the Application Proxies, as shown in Figure 20-5.

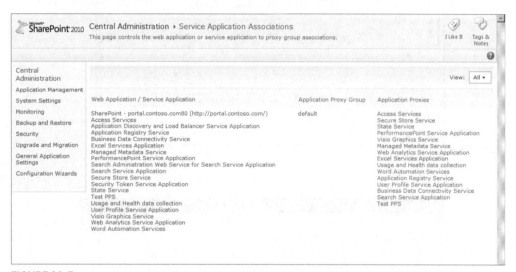

FIGURE 20-5

Only one proxy group can be associated with a web application. Within that proxy group, you can enable as many proxies as necessary. If you disable proxies, the associated service applications won't be available for use within the web applications associated with that proxy group. As shown in Figure 20-5, two different PerformancePoint service applications exist: the PerformancePoint Service Application created by the wizard during the install and the Test PPS service application that the author created manually for illustration. By clicking on the default proxy group link, you will see (as shown in Figure 20-6) that Test PPS is not the default of the default group. You can change the default association by clicking the [set as default] link.

Now that you better understand what enabling this option means, you can complete creating the service application by defining an application pool. You can use an existing application pool or a new application pool. A new application pool requires the use of the Configurable option because the Predefined option is not available for creating PerformancePoint dashboards, and the recommendation is to use a domain account. After the Name and Application Pool sections are complete, finish the process by clicking the Create button. After the service application and proxy have been created, the

New PerformancePoint Service Application dialog is displayed, as shown in Figure 20-7. You should review this dialog, especially the additional steps required to complete the configuration.

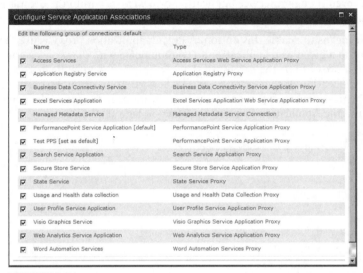

FIGURE 20-6

FIGURE 20-7

3. PerformancePoint Services service applications utilize a SQL Server database for storing information. This database is created when the service application is created and can be viewed by opening SQL Server Management Studio. As shown in Figure 20-8, the two PerformancePoint service applications that have been created are displayed here: PerformancePoint Service Application and Test PPS. As you can see, there are several different databases, each associated with different service applications. These databases are created automatically and usually append a GUID to the end of the database name to help ensure a unique database name. By default, all new PerformancePoint service application databases are installed on the same server as the configuration database. The data displayed in PerformancePoint dashboards can be stored in any SQL Server instance, assuming that the proper security context has been set up for the users who view and create those dashboards.

FIGURE 20-8

4. Browse to the PerformancePoint Service Application web page by clicking the service application link on the Manage Service Applications web page. As shown in Figure 20-9, there are four different categories of options that further specify the PerformancePoint configuration. We will return to these later in this chapter.

FIGURE 20-9

Secure Store Service Application and Proxy

The Secure Store Service is a new capability in SharePoint 2010 that replaces the single sign-on (SSO) capability present in SharePoint 2007. SharePoint 2010 stores the credentials for accessing the external data in the database associated with the service application.

PerformancePoint Services requires the use of the Secure Store Service to connect to external data sources on behalf of users or groups using the unattended service account. The unattended account utilizes a domain account whose password is stored in the secure store. The secure store is configured by providing a passphrase, and the passphrase is used to generate a key that is used to encrypt and decrypt the credentials stored in the Secure Store Service database.

The following list details a few key aspects of the Secure Store Service.

➤ The service provides the capability to store and retrieve access credentials to external systems. These credentials consist of a user identity and password that are mapped to an application ID. The Secure Store Service supports both individual mappings and group mappings.

➤ Application IDs are used to map individual users or groups of users to credential sets. Individual users are mapped to a unique set of credentials, while individuals in a group will all receive the mapping designated for the specific domain group.

➤ SharePoint 2010 or custom applications access the external data using the application ID on behalf of the user or group.

➤ Security governs each application ID, so each ID can have permissions applied that specify which users or groups can access the credentials stored for the application ID.

➤ The Secure Store Service runs on the application server, and it is a claims-aware authorization service. (For a review of claims-based authentication, read Chapter 9.)

In our example, the wizard created a Secure Store Application instance, and the Chapter 4 installation instructions configured the instance by supplying the passphrase. If the store had not been set up, you would have seen a warning on the PerformancePoint Service Application Settings page indicating that a secure store hasn't been configured. Therefore, we will proceed assuming a store doesn't exist, and the first step is to ensure that a Secure Store Application instance and proxy have been created.

1. Create a new Secure Store Service application and proxy called Test Secure Store using the same process used previously to create a new PerformancePoint Service application—clicking the New button in the Ribbon on the Manage Service Applications web page. The resulting Secure Store Service Application: Test Secure Store page is shown in Figure 20-10. As indicated in the figure, you must first generate a new key before you can use the store.

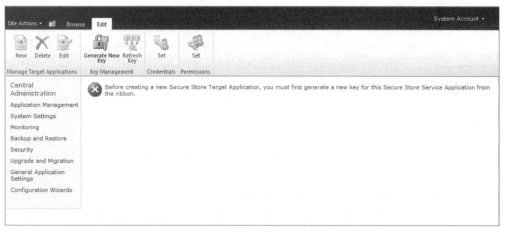

FIGURE 20-10

2. Click the Generate New Key button located in the Key Management Group to reveal the Generate New Key dialog shown in Figure 20-11.

FIGURE 20-11

3. Type a passphrase string inside the Pass Phrase box and retype the same string in the Confirm Pass Phrase box. Keep in mind that the passphrase string is not stored, so ensure that it is written down and stored in a safe place. Administrators will need the passphrase string to refresh the key, which is necessary whenever a new application server is added to the farm or during a restore of a previously backed up Secure Store Service database. The string must be at least eight characters and must have at least three of the following four elements:

➤   Uppercase characters

➤   Lowercase characters

➤   Numerals

➤   Any of the following special characters: "! " # $ % & ' ( ) * + , - . / : ; < = > ? @ [\ ] ^ _ ` { | } ~

4.   Click the OK button to complete the process.

5.   Now you need to configure the unattended service account. From the Manage Service Applications web page, click the PerformancePoint Service Application, and then click the Manage button. Click the PerformancePoint Service Application Settings link, and enter a username and password in the respective boxes in the Secure Store and Unattended Service Account section. This information is used for authenticating and querying data sources.

6.   Click the OK button when finished, leaving all other sections and their values at their defaults. If everything worked correctly, when you return to the settings page you will see the Secure Store Service name and the user representing the unattended service account, as shown in Figure 20-12.

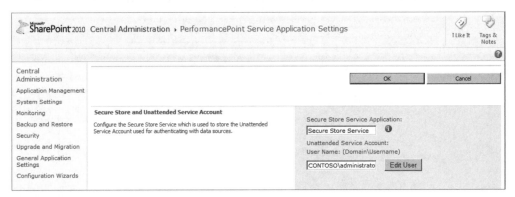

FIGURE 20-12

7.   Browse to the Secure Store Service settings page. You should see that the PerformancePoint Service Application has been added as a target application of the secure store, and an application ID has been generated, as shown in Figure 20-13. PerformancePoint will always try to use the Secure Store Service in the default proxy group, even if you have multiple Secure Store Service instances.

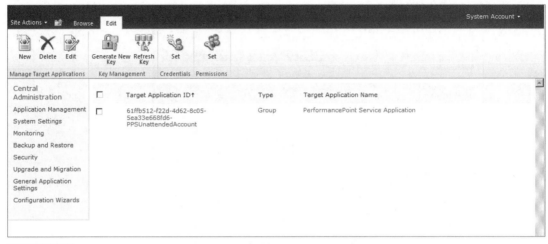

FIGURE 20-13

You can now install PerformancePoint Services using the wizard as described in Chapter 4, and manually using the process described in this chapter. Each approach has its advantages, but a good administrator needs to know both. The wizard enables administrators to create new service applications for each service in the farm and assign a single application pool account to run all of the service applications, and those service applications will use the default proxy group to connect to the application server.

The wizard should not be used when you need to install and run different service applications on different application servers. Also, you still have to configure the secure store and define an unattended service account even if the wizard was used.

The final step in the installation and configuration is validating that everything was done correctly. We will create a new website and install the new Dashboard Designer so you can see that all is working as planned.

Installing the Business Intelligence Center Website

The Business Intelligence Center Web site is created using a new BI template. Dashboard Designer is installed once the new BI site has been created. These steps are discussed below.

1. Create a new web application if you have not already done so. Use the instructions in Chapter 4 if you need assistance. As you proceed through the configuration, you have two options: Classic Mode Authentication (NTLM) or Claims-Based Authentication, as shown in Figure 20-14. Claims-based authentication is discussed in detail in Chapter 9. You should be aware of this new capability, but in this example we will use Classic Mode, which uses Windows authentication to validate users.

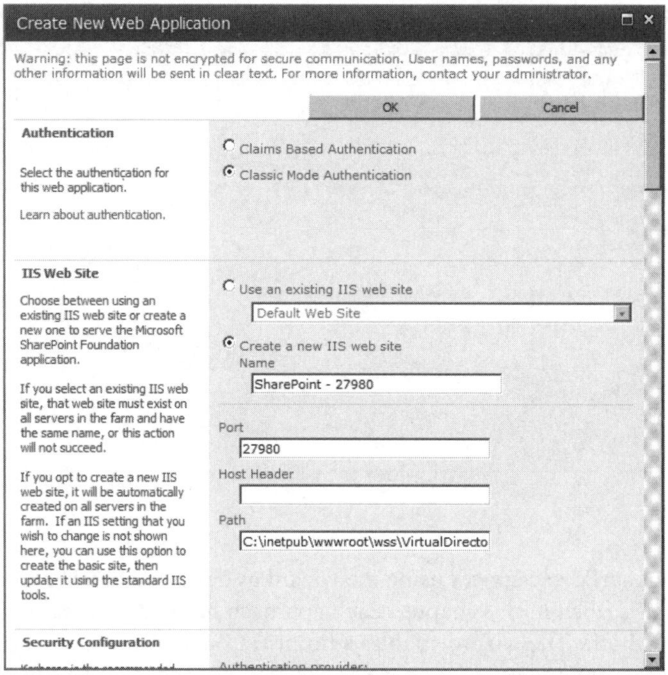

FIGURE 20-14

2. Create a new site collection (refer to Chapter 4 for instructions if needed). Use the Business Intelligence Center template on the Enterprise tab to provision the site collection, as this is the standard template for PerformancePoint objects. This template contains all of the necessary SharePoint content types used to create BI dashboards. You can certainly add PerformancePoint content types to standard Web Part pages, lists, and libraries in order to create deployment targets, but it's much easier to use the Business Intelligence Center template.

 If the Business Intelligence Center template isn't visible, then you probably installed SharePoint 2010 server using a Standard license key. PerformancePoint Services requires an Enterprise license key.

3. Browse to the business intelligence site collection created in step 2 and you should see the Business Intelligence Center, shown in Figure 20-15. Mouse over each of the descriptions on the right—Monitor Key Performance, Build and Share Reports, and Create Dashboards—to review the different capabilities that are available.

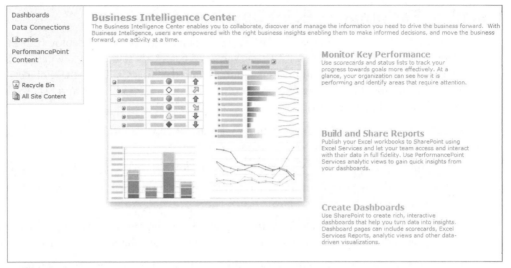

FIGURE 20-15

4. You should also be aware of the features that have been activated by provisioning the site using the Business Intelligence Center template. Figure 20-16 shows a portion of the site collection Features web page. Note that the Publishing and PerformancePoint features are enabled.

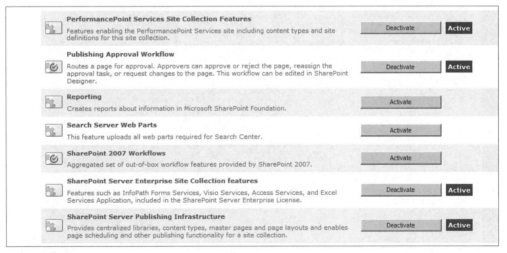

FIGURE 20-16

The final steps in validating the installation is to install and use the PerformancePoint Dashboard Designer to create a data source, a scorecard, and a dashboard. The next section describes how to install the Dashboard Designer 2010 application. Actual creation of PerformancePoint objects is done in the section "Creating an Analytic Chart Report and Dashboard."

Installing PerformancePoint Dashboard Designer

PerformancePoint Dashboard Designer 2010 is the tool used to create and deploy your business intelligence objects to the SharePoint 2010 server. Specifically, these include key performance indicators (KPIs), scorecards, reports, filters, data sources, and dashboards. Once these objects have been created, they are stored in one or more SharePoint 2010 document libraries and lists so that they can be reused in different dashboards.

Dashboard Designer is a desktop application that must be deployed to an author's desktop before it is available for use. It requires several prerequisites on the author's desktop:

➤ Dashboard Designer is a .NET Framework ClickOnce application that requires the .NET Framework 3.5 SP1 or later. If this is not installed on the client machine, Dashboard Designer will not install.

➤ Visio 2007 or 2010 Professional for creating or editing strategy map reports. Strategy maps are reports that enable you to connect KPI data to Visio shapes in order to visualize data.

➤ Report Viewer 2008 for creating or editing SQL Server Reporting Services reports.

It's time to install the designer tool. Follow these steps:

1. From the home page of the Business Intelligence Center, hover over the Create Dashboards heading to reveal the view shown in Figure 20-17. Click the Start using PerformancePoint Services link contained in the Add Insight to Information With Dashboards section.

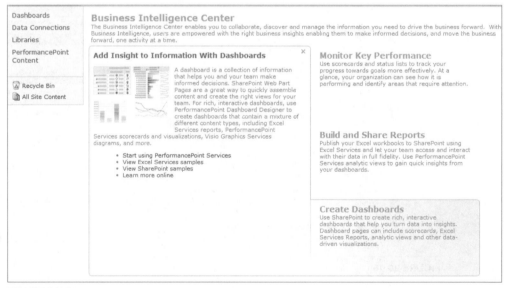

FIGURE 20-17

2. This should reveal the web page shown in Figure 20-18. From this page, click the Run Dashboard Designer button to initiate the ClickOnce deployment process. Dashboard Designer 2010 is automatically deployed to the client desktop using ClickOnce technology. After a few checks, the designer is downloaded and installed to the client's desktop and opened to the design pane. Installation is quick, without any need for installation media or files. The application is hosted on the SharePoint 2010 server, so software patches are applied automatically the next time the designer is launched, assuming any software updates have been applied to the SharePoint 2010 server. This is all handled by the ClickOnce technology.

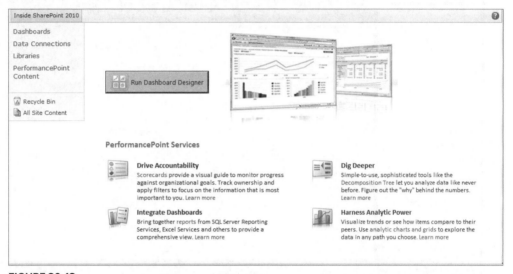

FIGURE 20-18

After Dashboard Designer has been downloaded and installed on the client desktop, it can be launched from the desktop using the PerformancePoint Dashboard Designer shortcut in the SharePoint folder on the Start menu. It can also be launched from the SharePoint list that contains the PerformancePoint Designer objects. At the time of this writing, Dashboard Designer does not operate in offline mode, so the author must be connected to the SharePoint 2010 server to edit and create designer objects.

INTRODUCTION TO DASHBOARD DESIGNER

The visual elements of Dashboard Designer are displayed in Figure 20-19. Across the top of the designer display is a ribbon with three tabs: Home, Edit, and Create. There is a Workspace Browser pane on the left-hand side of the designer, and a centrally located pane that contains two tabs. A SharePoint tab displays a view of the items that have been deployed to the SharePoint server, and a Workspace tab (shown in Figure 20-19) displays a view of the items in the local workspace. A third pane, Details, is not shown, but will appear at different points in the process of creating objects, as you will see in the following example.

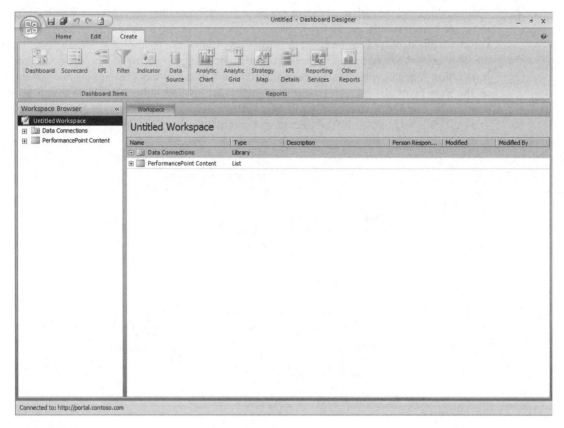

FIGURE 20-19

As new objects are created using the designer, these objects are stored inside the Business Intelligence Center. Specifically, the objects are stored inside the provisioned lists and libraries that were previously shown in Figure 20-15. These lists are called Dashboards, Data Connections, and PerformancePoint Content. Each has a special purpose, as summarized in Table 20-2.

TABLE 20-2: Business Intelligence Center Lists

LIST	DESCRIPTION
Dashboards	This library contains dashboard objects that have been deployed (published) to the server.
Data Connections	This library contains data sources that are available for use by PerformancePoint objects. These sources contain server connection and security information.
PerformancePoint Content	This list contains scorecards, reports, filters, and unpublished dashboards.

There are two key benefits to saving objects to these lists: the objects are centrally managed and they are reusable across multiple dashboards. Dashboard authors with the proper permissions can reuse any of the objects by adding them to their own dashboards. SharePoint requires that authors have Contribute permission in order to save items to SharePoint server, and they must have Design permission to deploy dashboards. All objects are stored in a SharePoint database. At this point, you are ready to create your first designer objects.

Creating an Analytic Chart Report and Dashboard

Analytic reports are dynamic, visual representations of data that can be displayed as interactive line charts, bar charts, pie charts, and tables (also called grids). PerformancePoint analytic reports remain connected to the data, which means their content is always up to date. This walk-through requires SQL Server Analysis Services to be installed and available to the SharePoint Server, and the Adventure Works Data Warehouse cube database should also be installed. SharePoint administrators can check with their SQL Server database administrator if uncertain about the availability. These Adventure Works databases for SQL Server 2008 and the instructions for installing can be obtained from the CodePlex web site using the following link: `http://msftdbprodsamples.codeplex.com/Wikipage`.

Analytic reports pull information from Analysis Services cubes. These cubes consist of concepts called *dimensions*, *members*, and *named sets*, which are summarized in Table 20-3.

TABLE 20-3: Cube Concepts

CONCEPT	DESCRIPTION
Measure	A cube member that associates a numeric value with one or more dimension members. For example, measures might include Sales Amounts and Gross Profit.
Dimension	A structured, hierarchical approach to organizing data. For example a Customers dimension could represent a hierarchy such as Sales Region, State, and City.
Named Sets	A collection of one or more dimensions that are defined in the database.

These concepts will be important as you define and configure the types of information that will be displayed in the chart report. Let's begin the process of creating the chart report:

1. Open Dashboard Designer. Click the Home tab and then click the Refresh button.

2. You will need to first create a connection to your data source, which will be SQL Server 2008 Analysis Services. Click Data Connections inside the Workspace Browser and then click the Data Source button in the Ribbon. The Select a Data Source Template dialog will appear, as shown in Figure 20-20. Briefly browse the different types of templates. Note that five different data source types are available: Analysis Services, Excel Services, Import From Excel Workbook, SharePoint List, and SQL Server Table.

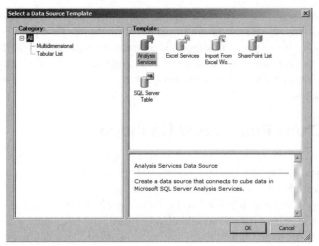

FIGURE 20-20

3. Select the Analysis Services template and click OK. You need to add several values on the Connection Settings view, which is located in the middle of the designer. Add the name of your server to the Server box. Once you add your server name and click in the Database box, it will be populated with the appropriate database options. Select a database. Enter the values shown in Figure 20-21 or choose your own values. Once complete, click the Test Data Source button to verify you have connectivity. You should see the Test Connection modal dialog, confirming you have successfully connected to the data source.

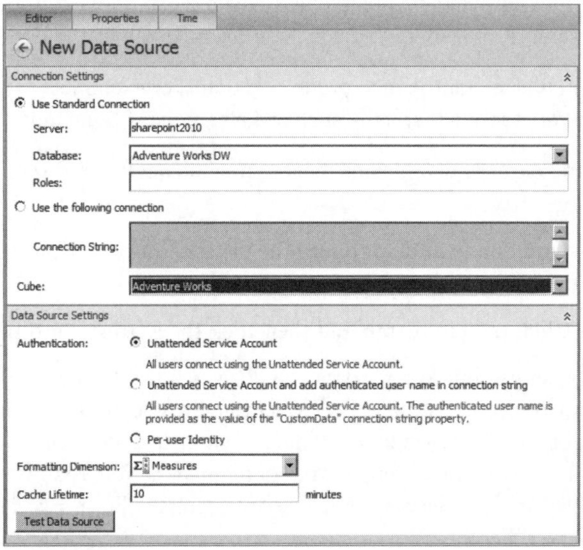

FIGURE 20-21

4. Choose an appropriate name, like ADW Cube Source, and assign it to the connection you just created in the Workspace Browser. Once assigned, right-click on the name and choose the Save option. Verify that a new entry called ADW Cube Source (or whatever you named your connection) has been added to the Data Connections library in the Business Intelligence Center, as shown in Figure 20-22. You should also confirm that the Dashboard Designer can be launched using the Edit in Dashboard Designer option on the object item menu. This enables you to open the designer directly from one of the object libraries.

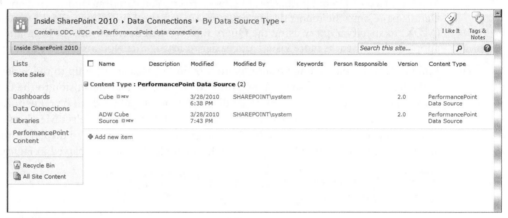

FIGURE 20-22

5. To create the chart report, select PerformancePoint Content in the Workspace Browser. Click the Create tab, followed by clicking Analytic Chart in the Reports group. This should open the Create an Analytic Chart Report wizard, shown in Figure 20-23.

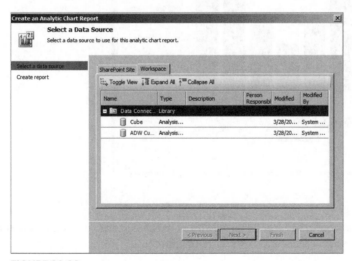

FIGURE 20-23

Notice that you can choose data connections that exist either on the SharePoint Server or in the designer workspace. For this example, select the ADW Cube Source connection created previously, and then click the Finish button. Once the wizard has completed, an entry called New Report is added to the Workspace Browser, and the analytic report opens for editing in the center pane of the workspace. Rename this entry **Chart Report**. You should also notice that a Details pane is displayed on the right-hand side of the workspace.

At this point, you need to define the information that will be displayed in the chart report. You have two different approaches to choose from: You can drag-and-drop items from the Details pane onto the report design pane or you can use Multidimensional Expressions (MDX) to specify a query using the Query tab. We will demonstrate the drag-and-drop approach because it is more visual and easier to learn when you are first beginning.

6. From the Details pane, drag Order Quantity from the Measures group to the Series panel at the bottom of the workspace. Next, drag the Date.Calendar dimension to the Bottom Axis panel. You should see a new chart displayed, but it still needs to be refined. Right-click the Date.Calendar entry in the Bottom Axis panel and choose the Select Members option. Choose calendar years 2002 and 2003 and their respective quarters to display in the report, and then click OK. Your chart report should resemble the chart displayed in Figure 20-24.

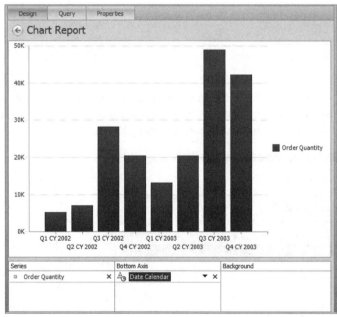

FIGURE 20-24

7. Save the report and confirm that it has been stored in the PerformancePoint Content library in the Business Intelligence Center, as shown in Figure 20-25.

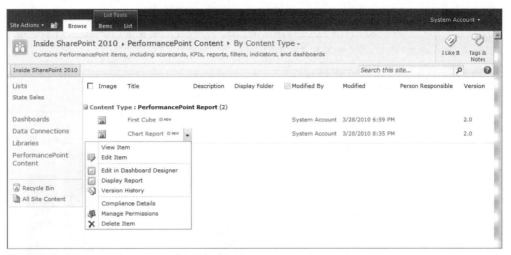

FIGURE 20-25

8. Figure 20-25 also displays the object menu for the chart. Click the Display Report option and a new browser window will open displaying the chart. There is a wealth of information in this report. First, notice that you can toggle between different chart types using the icons located at the top of the report. Second, you can drill into additional information by right-clicking on any of the bars in the chart and choosing from any of the different options, as shown in Figure 20-26. Close the browser window when you have finished exploring the different options.

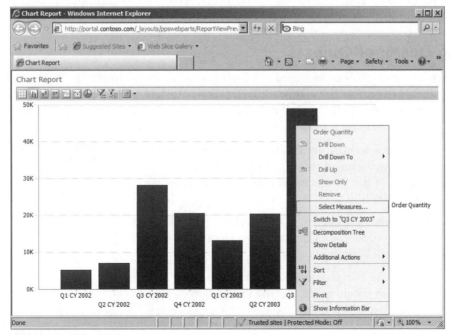

FIGURE 20-26

9. This chart report can now be added to a dashboard, and then Designer can be used to publish the dashboard to the Dashboards library. This exercise is left to readers to do on their own. The result is displayed in Figure 20-27.

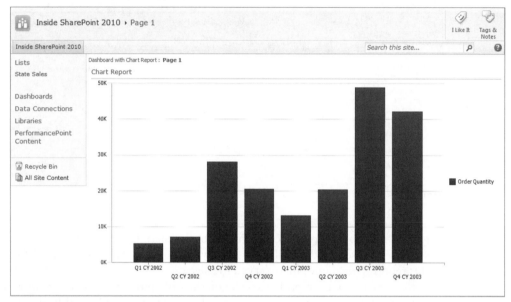

FIGURE 20-27

This completes the process for verifying the PerformancePoint installation and configuration, as well as the brief introduction of the Dashboard Designer's capabilities.

Reusing Designer Objects

PerformancePoint objects can be reused by different authors. For example, the Workspace Browser can copy and paste items in the same or different display folders, provided the items remain within the same site collection. To illustrate this capability, you will make a copy of an object, make some changes to it, and then save it to a different website in the same site collection:

1. Create a new website in the same site collection as the Business Intelligence Center, and use the Business Intelligence Center template. For this example, name the site BI Center II.

2. Open Dashboard Designer. In the Workspace Browser, click PerformancePoint Content. In the Home tab of the Ribbon, click Refresh.

3. Click the Add Lists button in the Workspace group in the Ribbon. This should reveal the Add Lists dialog shown in Figure 20-28. You should see an entry for BI Center II,

FIGURE 20-28

and Data Connections and PerformancePoint Content. Click BI Center II and then click OK. This should add a second PerformancePoint Content entry to the Workspace Browser. The first entry is for the original website; the second is for the website you just created in step 1.

4. You now need to make a copy of the objects that you would like to modify and reuse. Expand the folder that contains the dashboard item you want to reuse. Select the object and then right-click the object and choose Copy. For this example, select the Chart Report.

5. Select the new PerformancePoint Content entry and paste the object there as shown in the Workspace Browser in Figure 20-29.

6. Rename the Chart Report to Chart Report v2. Save the copy of the chart to SharePoint, and confirm that the report has been saved to the PerformancePoint Content library in the BI Center II website. You can now make any necessary changes to this report without affecting the original report or any dashboards that use the original report.

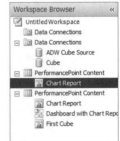

FIGURE 20-29

The previous discussion focused on reusing PerformancePoint objects by different authors in the same site or across different sites in the same site collection. This is a very practical use case that occurs frequently within an organization. Another scenario that is also very common and critical to an organization is the *object promotion* process, which takes PerformancePoint objects created in one SharePoint farm and then copies them to another farm. This example includes creating objects in an authoring or development environment, moving them to a test environment, and then finally moving them into a production environment. You'll learn how to do that next.

Promoting PerformancePoint Objects across Environments

Dashboard Designer should be used to create PerformancePoint objects in a development environment so that the authoring process does not negatively impact the production environment. Obviously, once the objects have been developed, there needs to be a promotion process to move them into a test environment and subsequently into a production environment. Dashboard Designer content includes metadata with information about objects such as dashboards, KPIs, filters, scorecards, data sources, and reports. As you plan your promotion process, there are several things to keep in mind:

➤ Moving content across servers requires that the destination SharePoint Server's version, service packs, hotfixes, and so on are the same as those of the source SharePoint Server.

➤ Dashboard Designer objects need to have unique names to ensure that objects on the destination server are not overwritten. Obviously, this requires some planning as you set up each of the different source and destination environments. You can simplify this by implementing an object naming convention that includes information such as server, site, library, etc.

➤ Make sure there are no missing dependencies when you import objects and when you are creating the workspace file. As you've seen, the objects have dependencies on data connections, just as dashboards have dependencies on the objects contained in the dashboard.

➤ All data sources must have unique names—even when the data sources reside in different display folders.

➤ When promoting objects to production, make sure that your data sources point to the production server.

The process used in this example imports the workspace containing the objects to be promoted into the designer and then deploys them to the proper server. Let's see how the promotion process works using Dashboard Designer:

1. Open Dashboard Designer in the SharePoint site to which you want to promote the content. Ensure that you are connected to the site by checking the lower-left corner of the designer for connection information.

2. Click Import Items on the Home tab to open the Import Items dialog.

3. Navigate to the workspace file (`<name>.ddwx`) in the Import Items window. Select the file and then click Open. This will display the Import Items to SharePoint dialog, shown in Figure 20-30.

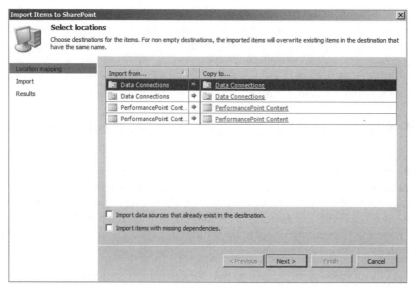

FIGURE 20-30

4. As you can see, Figure 20-30 displays the first step to import content using a wizard. There are three steps in the process: location mapping, importing, and the results. The purpose of this dialog is to choose the destination for the items to be imported. Administrators are warned that imported items will overwrite existing items in the destination that have the same name.

The window contains a list of folder names beneath two column headings labeled Import from and Copy to. If items have the same name, as shown in the figure, you can distinguish source and destination by placing the cursor over the item; a tooltip will display the necessary information. Note that items beneath the Copy to column are hyperlinked so that the specific location at the destination can be selected. For each location under Copy to, click the destination folder. The Add List dialog opens, enabling you to select a destination for the dashboard content or object. You must select a destination list or library in order for the Next button to be enabled.

5. Once the destination information is selected, you have two other options to consider, although neither option is enabled by default or required for the import:

➤ Import data sources that already exist in the destination—This option will overwrite data sources that already exist in the destination if the workspace file being imported contains a data source with the same name and display folder. If this option is not selected, data sources with the same name and display folder will be skipped.

➤ Import items with missing dependencies—This option will import items that have missing dependencies. These objects must be repaired manually at the destination. For example, if a scorecard is missing a related KPI, the import process will import the scorecard but a warning dialog appears in the wizard if the condition is detected in the workspace file.

6. Once selected, click Next. On completion, the dialog shown in Figure 20-31 is displayed. This dialog indicates the status of the import, the number of new items created, the number of items updated, the number of items skipped, and the number of items that failed to be imported. There is also an option to view a log with a more detailed summary.

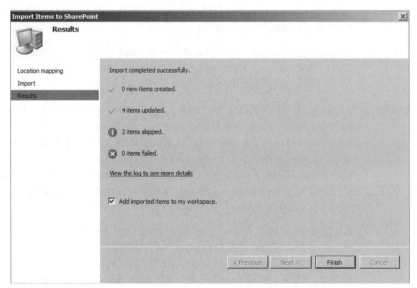

FIGURE 20-31

7. You'll also notice in Figure 20-31 an option to add the imported items to your workspace, which is enabled by default. Click Finish to complete the promotion process.

IMPORTING PERFORMANCEPOINT SERVER 2007 CONTENT TO PERFORMANCEPOINT SERVICES 2010

The following discussion applies to companies that have dashboard content stored inside PerformancePoint Server 2007 that they would like to import into PerformancePoint Services 2010. Content import must be performed by a SharePoint 2010 farm administrator.

Planning

SharePoint 2010 provides a wizard-driven process for importing dashboard content from PerformancePoint Server 2007 (PPS2007) into PerformancePoint Services (PPS2010) in SharePoint Server 2010. The import wizard walks the administrator through the process of importing dashboards, scorecards, data sources, KPIs, and so on. After the data import process is complete, the administrator or object author must deploy each individual dashboard to their new SharePoint Server 2010 locations. Before performing the import, you must be aware of several key factors that may affect the integrity of the import. These are summarized in Table 20-4.

TABLE 20-4: Factors for Consideration When Planning the Import Process

TOPIC	DESCRIPTION
Report types	PerformancePoint Services does not support all the report types that were available in PerformancePoint Server 2007. The following report types are not supported and will not be imported: Trend Analysis Charts, Pivot Tables, Pivot Charts, and Spreadsheets.
Local administrators	PPS2007 makes the local server administrator a PPS2007 administrator. In SharePoint Server 2010, that individual is not automatically made an administrator, but can be assigned manually if necessary.
Dashboard creation and deployment	These apply to PPS2010. The farm administrator requires at least Contribute permissions on content lists and data source libraries to create and edit dashboard items. Site collection administrators need at least Contribute permissions on data source libraries only. The site administrator or site member needs at least Contribute permissions on content lists and data source libraries. Anyone deploying objects from Dashboard Designer to SharePoint Server 2010 must have at least Designer permissions.
User access and content security	PPS2010 uses the SharePoint Server 2010 user access and content security model, which is very different from that of PPS2007. PPS2007 has its own server and database for storing metadata and content, and security is applied globally at the server level and on each individual object. In PPS2010, metadata and content is stored in lists and libraries.

Dashboard Designer Tasks and Necessary Permissions

Those familiar with PPS2007 and Dashboard Designer need to become familiar with the specific credentials necessary to perform the same authoring tasks in PPS2010. Table 20-5 summarizes the relationship between PPS2010 user permissions and authoring capability. The Dashboard Designer task capabilities are cumulative as you progress down the column.

TABLE 20-5: Relationship between Designer Task and User Permission

DASHBOARD DESIGNER TASK	PPS2010 PERMISSION
View PPS2010 dashboards	Read
Create PPS2010 dashboard items and save them to a list or library	Contribute
Publish PPS2010 dashboards	Design
Manage user permissions for dashboard objects	Full Control or Site Collection Administrator

Preparation before Running the Wizard

The import process will take PPS2007 dashboards and scorecards and store them in a single SharePoint 2010 list, and imported data sources will be placed in a single document library. To the extent possible, keep an inventory of the objects that should be redeployed and the locations that will store the newly imported objects once redeployed. To ensure that the process is as effective and efficient as possible, gather the necessary information and review the following steps before attempting the import:

➤ Establish how PPS2010 data source security needs to be configured. PPS2010 stores the security information inside the data source itself, whereas PPS2007 stores the security setting for its data sources in the `web.config` file at `C:\Program Files\Microsoft Office PerformancePoint Server\3.0\Monitoring\PPSMonitoring_1\WebService`. Administrators should review which of the three different PPS2007 security methods were used by examining the appSettings node of the `web.config` file.

➤ Know your username and password for logging onto the PPS2007 server because the wizard will prompt you for those credentials.

➤ Know the names of the content databases that contain the PPS2007 data.

➤ Create the website and list that will store the imported dashboard items. You will need to provide the name of the site collection, website, and list during the process.

➤ Create the document library that will store the imported data sources. This library needs to be configured to support the Data Source content type. As you've seen, this library is automatically provisioned by creating a new site using the Business Intelligence Center template.

Once the import process in initiated, its progress is displayed with a status bar, and a running summary of all objects that have been imported is provided. When complete, the final import results list each imported item by category (Data Sources, KPIs, Scorecards, and so on), with information about any issues or errors that were encountered. The results also specify whether data source names were changed in the event of duplicates. Now you are ready to run the wizard.

Using the Import Wizard

Keep in mind that the farm administrator running the import wizard must be a SharePoint administrator on the PerformancePoint 2010 target website so that the user context running the wizard is able to create SharePoint security groups. PerformancePoint 2007 secured dashboard elements using custom security groups managed in SQL Server. PerformancePoint 2010, however, uses standard SharePoint groups. To maintain the same level of security, the wizard will create new SharePoint security groups based on those in PerformancePoint 2007.

1. Navigate to the PerformancePoint Services settings page inside the SharePoint Central Administration website. This page is shown in Figure 20-32.

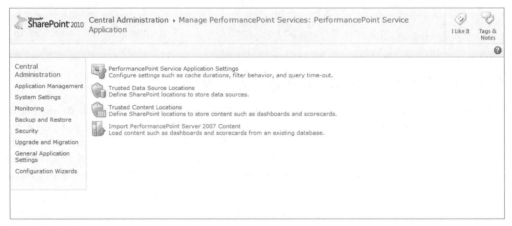

FIGURE 20-32

2. Click Import PerformancePoint Server 2007 Content to launch the import wizard. The first page explains what will be imported. You should typically review this content, but in this case there shouldn't be any surprises because this information was covered in the previous section. Once the information is reviewed, click Next.

3. The next page, titled "How was security configured on the original server?" is shown in Figure 20-33. This is where you will need to know the data source security information discussed in the previous section. Select the appropriate type of security and click Next. Keep in mind that if you choose Per-user identity (which, by the way, is the most common method for PerformancePoint 2007), then your SharePoint 2010 farm must have Kerberos Delegation configured between all instances of the PPS service application and the data sources.

4. Type the SQL Server name/instance of the PerformancePoint Server 2007 content server. Then select the method of authentication and enter the appropriate username and password. Click Next.

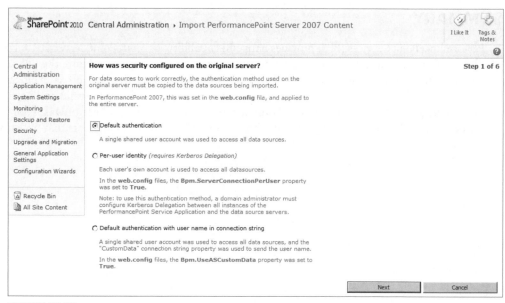

FIGURE 20-33

5. On the Connect to the PerformancePoint 2007 content database page, select the PerformancePoint Server 2007 database that you want to import. The default database is titled PPSMonitoring. Click Next.

6. On the next page, select the site collection, site, and list where your dashboard items are to be imported. Click Next.

7. Select a site and a document library where your data sources will be stored. Click Next. Keep in mind that data sources must be imported into the same site collection as your dashboard items.

8. The last step is to review the settings you have chosen. Click Back to make any necessary changes. If the settings are correct and you are ready to proceed, click Import. Once the import process begins, it cannot be stopped. Once complete, a summary page will appear that shows the results of the import process. It includes the status of the items that successfully imported; and, if there were any errors, what didn't import successfully. Click the View List or View Library links to view the actual data that was imported.

9. Click Done to close the wizard.

Administrators and site owners will need to review the security of the imported objects because it is set at the individual item level. Additionally, two new security roles will be created in the SharePoint 2010 environment to match what existed in PPS2007. These roles are called PerformancePoint Editors and PerformancePoint Readers. Users who were in these roles in PPS2007 will be placed in the corresponding roles in PPS2010. You will likely want to modify this to match the security plan that has already been established for the organization.

SUMMARY

PerformancePoint Services (PPS) provides native BI capability for SharePoint Server 2010. Providing PPS capability to the enterprise requires administrators to install and configure the PPS service application and proxy, along with the Secure Store Service application and proxy. You can install these applications using a wizard or manually, although you should understand and be able to use both approaches. You also need to be familiar with the installation and use of Dashboard Designer for creating and deploying FCOs, along with the SharePoint libraries and lists that will store the FCOs.

21

New Content Management Capabilities in SharePoint 2010

WHAT'S IN THIS CHAPTER?

➤ Using metadata for Enterprise Content Management

➤ Creating and configuring document sets

➤ Using the Document ID service for persistent links

➤ Automatic routing with the Content Organizer

This chapter covers the new document management capabilities in SharePoint 2010. Specifically, these new capabilities include the following:

➤ **Managed metadata** — This is the capability to centrally define taxonomies that can be leveraged within and across the SharePoint farm to categorize, navigate, and locate content quickly. This topic was covered in-depth in Chapter 16; this chapter focuses on how to establish the right metadata for the organization.

➤ **Document sets** — Documents can now be grouped together and treated as one asset. Document sets share the same metadata, and you can version the entire document set as a whole or version each document individually.

➤ **Document IDs** — Documents can be assigned a unique ID, which can be used to locate the document regardless of its physical location within the farm. This ID remains the same even when the document is moved manually or moved by an automated process. If a copy is made, the copy is assigned a new ID.

➤ **Content Organizer and automatic routing** — This very powerful feature provides the capability to automatically route content to a desired location based on its metadata and content type. When users submit content, it is routed to the proper library and/or folder based on a set of rules established by the site owner or administrator.

As in previous chapters, the focus here is to provide administrators with the necessary knowledge to understand, configure, and utilize the details of each of these new capabilities.

MANAGED METADATA

MOSS 2007 introduced the concept of content types to the SharePoint platform. A *content type* describes specific details about content, such as the properties or metadata that will be associated with the content. For example, a Word document could have been associated with the Change Request content type and therefore, by definition, have a predefined set of metadata called date, originator, approver, and so on. The metadata would remain with the document and surface as the names of the columns in the document library for this specific type of content. This provided a mechanism for associating metadata with content and for storing different types of content in a single document library. Because this was the first introduction of this capability to SharePoint, it did not have all the functionality necessary for enterprise adoption. Specifically, this capability was lacking as follows:

➤ It didn't enable a standardized set of corporate approved content types and metadata to be deployed easily.

➤ It didn't provide the capability to utilize hierarchies of metadata.

➤ It lacked an easy mechanism for navigating and filtering content based on content type or metadata.

➤ It didn't provide an easy way to manage content types and metadata across the farm.

➤ It was difficult for end users to enter data.

➤ It did not provide an easy extensibility mechanism.

➤ It lacked the ability to use the terms as enterprise search filters.

Managing and utilizing metadata is essential to establishing enterprise taxonomy and the tagging of content. SharePoint 2010 addresses each of these gaps by introducing the Metadata Service and Enterprise Content Types.

SharePoint 2010 Metadata Service and Enterprise Content Types

The Metadata Service and Enterprise Content Types are central to providing the Enterprise Content Management (ECM) capability across the enterprise. ECM refers to capabilities and features that are utilized across numerous web sites or across all web sites in the company, as opposed to just a few sites. The creation and configuration of the Metadata Service and its use was covered extensively in Chapter 16. Enterprise Content Types (ECTs), which solve the problem of having to keep content types synchronized across site collections, refer to the same content type being used across site collections. Content type publishing, also covered in Chapter 16, provides the capability to reuse content types across the enterprise. Keep in mind that in the past you had to create a content type in one site collection and then duplicate the content type in another site collection (or use the feature framework to deploy). Then, you were responsible for updating all the instances when changes were made. The power of ECTs is that they enable you to define one site collection as the hub and then the Metadata Service periodically updates all other site collections with any changes.

You are encouraged to review Chapter 16 for a refresher because of its tremendous application to ECM.

Because several metadata-related words are used throughout this chapter, they are summarized in Table 21-1 for reference.

TABLE 21-1 SharePoint 2010 Vocabulary

NAME	DEFINITION
Term	A word or phrase that is associated with content. A term can be a managed term or a managed keyword. Terms are also referred to as *facets*.
Term set	A collection of related terms that can be hierarchical. Terms and term sets are referred to as *taxonomy*.
Managed term	A term that is controlled and can only be created by those with appropriate permission
Keywords	Words defined by users to "tag" content. This is referred to by some as creating a *folksonomy*.
Managed keywords	Keywords kept in a non-hierarchical list

 A managed keyword can also be a managed term, which enables SharePoint 2010 to blend both taxonomy and folksonomy.

Establishing the "Right" Metadata

Now that you have the capability to utilize enterprise metadata, you must define the specific vocabulary you wish to use across the corporation. Even though many organizations appreciate the value of metadata, there is no general consensus about how it should be created, stored, and applied across the enterprise. Therefore, there is no one-size-fits-all approach to establishing and managing relevant metadata, but we can provide a few suggestions based on experience with numerous companies and their successful or not so successful use of metadata. The definition of metadata terms is not a technical exercise; you should have representation from several key business areas throughout your enterprise. SharePoint 2010 merely facilitates the technical implementation of a business definition of terms.

The benefits of establishing the right metadata can be summarized as follows:

➤ Uniformity and consistency of metadata and taxonomy across the organization improves the information's value and makes the system more useful.

➤ Defining the business value for metadata use establishes the need for adoption.

➤ Documenting and understanding metadata use identifies gaps so that information can be located and utilized much more efficiently.

➤ Establishing metadata taxonomy provides an agreed upon approach to how content should be communicated and discussed.

Clearly, there is value in planning your metadata deployment, just as you would plan any other deployment. The intent here is to educate administrators about a few key concepts, as these are the people who will be involved in implementing and managing any enterprise system. They will definitely not have to design the system themselves, but rather work with a multi-functional team. The following steps should get them started:

➤ **Perform a metadata audit** — The first step is to define what you already have and are using, if anything. Along with the audit, you should document not only the terms being used, but also how they are being used, where they are being used, and the purpose of each. This includes defining which terms and content types should be standardized across the enterprise. Because metadata will be added, deleted, and changed, it is important to know where the metadata is being used and the applications that rely on it so that the effects of any change will be understood. You should also define who, if anyone, owns the metadata and how often it changes.

➤ **Define how metadata is used** — Once you establish an inventory of the metadata, the next step is to understand how metadata is being assigned. This includes how the people in the organization, the business processes, and the information systems assign metadata. Typically, numerous business processes are involved, and it is important not to get bogged down trying to specify everything; focus on the key processes. Your assessment should include who or what is applying metadata to the content, how it is being applied, and where in the process it occurs.

➤ **Define where the metadata is stored** — It's likely that every system and application associated with content creation and possibly storage is storing some type of metadata. Metadata can be associated with the content or found within the content itself. As you can see, multiple systems, varying formats, and different storage mechanisms can result in a very complex metadata picture. It is essential that you understand where your existing metadata is located, but don't get bogged down in the complexity and attempt to unify these systems to a single location. Your purpose here is to identify where it is, how it is applied, and its potential uses.

At this point, you should have a much better idea of where you are with regard to metadata use and you can begin to plan your way forward. Just as any SharePoint implementation is more apt to succeed with an executive sponsor, your implementation of managed metadata will have a greater chance of succeeding if you have an owner from the business overseeing and owning the definition of metadata terms. The more relevant the data is, the more value your users will find in using it. Remember, SharePoint 2010 merely facilitates the implementation of a business definition. As you proceed, here are a few questions that you will need to answer:

➤ What are the business needs that drive the use of the metadata system?

➤ Who are the key decision makers that need to agree to the metadata system?

➤ What industry standards can and should be used to simplify metadata creation and management?

➤ Who should take responsibility and ownership for the enterprise metadata system?

➤ How will the system be maintained and updated?

Table 21-2 provides key online references for establishing and implementing your enterprise metadata system.

TABLE 21-2 Metadata System Key References

TOPIC	REFERENCE
Planning Managed Metadata	http://technet.microsoft.com/en-us/library/ee530389(office.14).aspx
Managed Metadata Roles	http://technet.microsoft.com/en-us/library/ee424398(office.14).aspx
Planning Terms and Term Sets	http://technet.microsoft.com/en-us/library/ee519604(office.14).aspx
Planning to Import Managed Metadata	http://technet.microsoft.com/en-us/library/ee424393(office.14).aspx
Planning to Share Terminology and Content Types	http://technet.microsoft.com/en-us/library/ee519603(office.14).aspx

DOCUMENT SETS

SharePoint 2010 provides the capability to group documents together in sets that can be treated as one logical unit. A *document set* is a content type. Specifically, it's a folder content type, which means that other items can attach to the document set, as you'll see in the "Configuring Document Sets" section of this chapter. Just like other content types, the documents in the set can share metadata, workflows, and policies.

New to SharePoint 2010 is the *welcome page*. The welcome page of a document set is a customizable page that enables users to discover the content in the set, view and synchronize metadata between items in the set, and manage the set. Key functionality includes the following:

➤ Document sets utilize SharePoint 2010 content types, and they are enabled at the site collection level by feature activation. Similar to how content types were used in SharePoint 2007, they can be can be used as is, they can be customized and used as a standard template for enterprise-wide use, and they can be customized after they are added to a document library.

➤ Document sets can share the same metadata.

➤ Document sets can be versioned. This mechanism is independent of individual document versioning, and it does not replace versioning of individual documents in the set. Both versioning features can both be used simultaneously.

➤ Workflows can be associated with the group.

➤ Permissions can be defined for the group.

➤ New pages are provisioned for the document set. The welcome page is essentially a landing page that displays the contents of the set and its properties. This Web Part page can be used directly or it can be customized as needed.

Clearly, this type of capability has immediate use for things like sales proposals or Request for Proposal (RFP) documents, which are composites of multiple documents. Both of these examples typically require the creation of multiple documents, and document sets automate this process. The customizable landing page, or welcome page, provides users with guidance on how to use the document set and what is contained in the set. The capability to update metadata for all content within the set at one time is a huge advantage.

Configuring and Creating Document Sets

Before attempting to configure a document set, ensure that the Document Sets feature has been activated. Navigate to the Site Settings page for your site collection as shown in Figure 21-1 and click the link for Site Collection features beneath the Site Collection Administration heading.

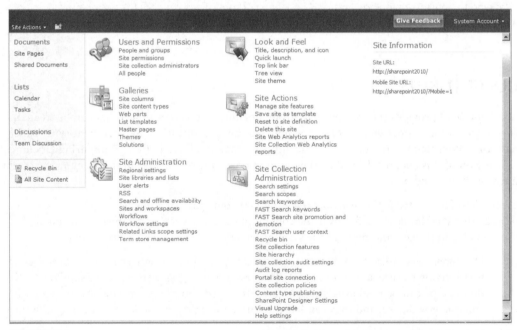

FIGURE 21-1

Scroll down the list of features until you see the Document Sets feature and activate the feature if it is not already activated, as shown in Figure 21-2. Once the feature has been activated, use the following steps to configure the specific document library to allow document sets:

1. Navigate to the specific library of interest and select the Library tab that is part of Library Tools on the Ribbon. Click the Library Settings button on the far right of the ribbon to reveal the Document Library Settings page, as shown in Figure 21-3.

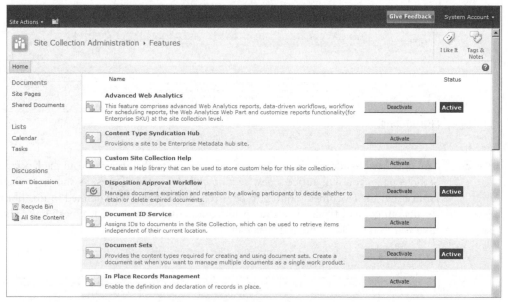

FIGURE 21-2

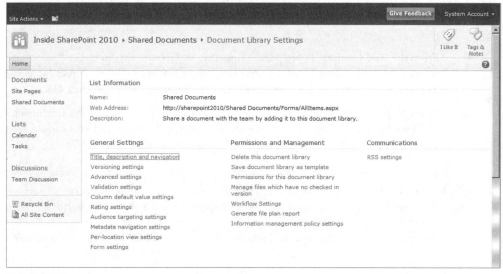

FIGURE 21-3

2. Under the General Setting category on the Document Library Settings page, click the Advanced settings link. Ensure that "Allow management of content types?" is set to Yes, as shown in Figure 21-4, and click OK.

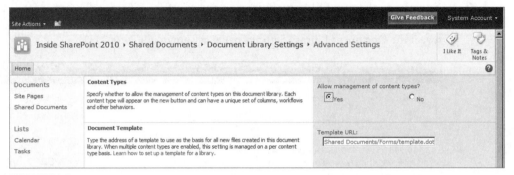

FIGURE 21-4

3. You now need to add the Document Set content type to the library. From the Document Library Settings page, you will notice a new section called Content Types, as shown in Figure 21-5. Notice that the Document content type is the only content type defined in this library. This is the default content type. Click the "Add from existing site content types" link. This should take you to the Add Content Types page.

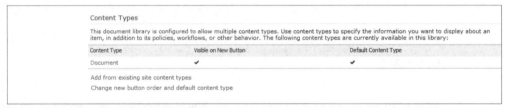

FIGURE 21-5

4. From the Add Content Types page, select the All Groups option in the "Select site content types from:" drop-down box. Choose Document Set from the list of Available Site Content Types: and click the Add > button as shown in Figure 21-6. Then click OK.

5. This completes the configuration and now it's time to create a new document set. Click the New Document button from inside the configured library and you should see that the Document Set content type has been added to the list (see Figure 21-7).

 You can change the order of the two different content types from the Library Settings page if necessary. This could be important if a large number of content types have been configured.

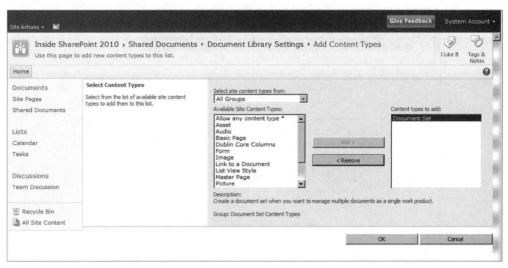

FIGURE 21-6

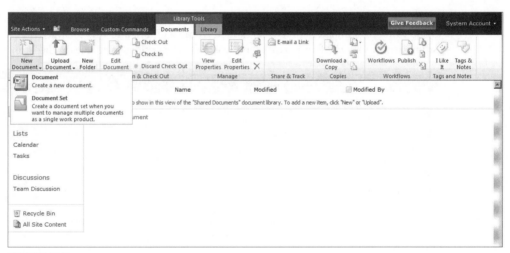

FIGURE 21-7

6. Click the Document Set option from the New Document menu. Enter a name and a description for the document set and then click the OK button as shown in Figure 21-8.

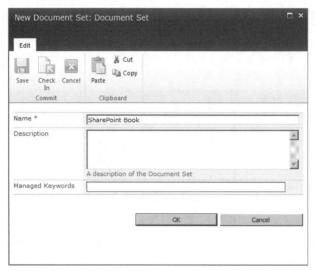

FIGURE 21-8

This will produce the document set's welcome page, shown in Figure 21-9. Notice that a new group called Document Set has been added to the Ribbon, and this includes the Manage tab. Administrators should familiarize themselves with the options available on the Manage tab.

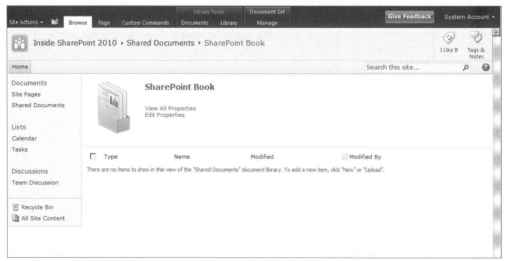

FIGURE 21-9

7. To upload multiple documents, select Upload Document from the Ribbon, and then select Upload Multiple Documents. The new Upload Document dialog is displayed, as shown in Figure 21-10. Documents and folders can be dragged directly onto the window or you can browse for the documents. Upload several documents to the document set. An example is shown in Figure 21-11. Notice that several options are available from the Manage tab. If the Capture Version and Version History buttons are disabled, you need to enable versioning for this document library.

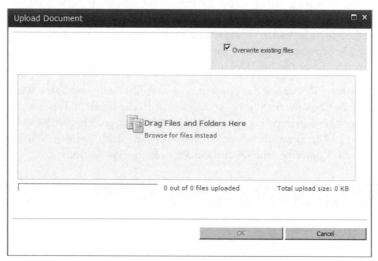

FIGURE 21-10

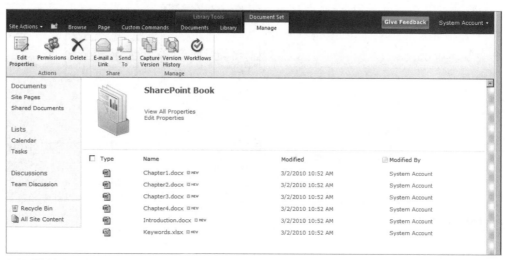

FIGURE 21-11

Returning to the default library view, note that the document set is classified as a single object. Take some time to review the options available from the drop-down menu for the document set.

Customizing the Document Set

Document sets can be customized. There is a settings page that provides additional configuration options so let's take a brief look. In general, a specific document set that is associated with a document library can be customized using the process described here. In addition, an enterprise document set could also be created. If so, it is best to create a custom Document Set content type that inherits from the base Document Set content type, and then perform the customization on the inherited content type. This keeps the out-of-the-box Document Set content type unmodified.

You can view the settings for a Document Set content type that has been associated with a library by clicking the Document Set link on the library settings page in the Content Types section, and then clicking the Document Set Settings link on the Document Set page. This will reveal the settings page shown in Figure 21-12. The figure shows only some of the available options; scroll down to review all of them. Table 21-3 describes the Document Set content type options.

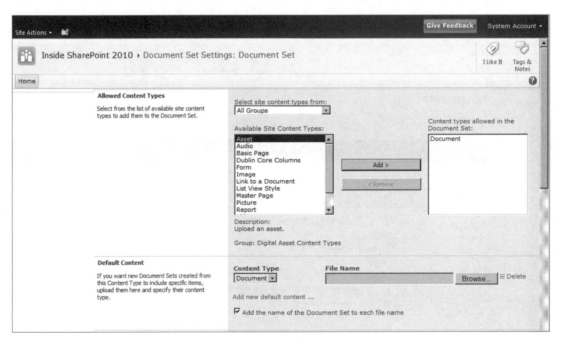

FIGURE 21-12

Because the Document Set is a content type, you can in fact add additional content types to your document set. You can also predefine content that you would like included in the document set and it will be automatically added when new sets are created. Metadata columns can be shared across items in the set. If you add a new column to the document set itself, that column becomes available for sharing with the documents contained in the document set. The columns that are displayed on the document set home page can also be defined. Lastly, you can even edit the home page's layout, design, and contents.

TABLE 21-3   Document Set Content Type Settings

OPTION	DESCRIPTION
Allowed Content Types	Other existing content types can be added and removed from the Document Set content type.
Default Content	This allows the newly created document set to include specific items, content, documents, etc. Content can be selected by browsing directly to the files.
Shared Columns	A shared column is a column that is available for all documents in the set. Each of the columns in the content type can be shared, which means the column values will be automatically synchronized to all documents in the set.
Welcome Page Columns	This option defines which columns are displayed on the welcome page for the document set.
Welcome Page View	The specific view that is used to display the document set's contents can be chosen with this option.
Welcome Page	This option enables the welcome page to be customized either directly in the browser or using SharePoint Designer 2010.

DOCUMENT ID SERVICE AND IDS

The Document ID service is a new capability at the site collection level that adds a unique identifier to all documents throughout the site collection. This ID is used to locate and retrieve documents regardless of their current or future location.

In SharePoint 2007, links break if you rename or move a file. Therefore, one of the desired features that users of SharePoint 2007 asked for is *persistent links*. This is the capability to link directly to a unique object ID. Using this system, each document or individual piece of content, or content object, would have its own unique ID that doesn't change regardless of where it is stored or moved in the repository. Persistent linking enables the management of compound documents, as discussed earlier in the section on document sets, and the capability to link directly to an older version of a document. In SharePoint 2010, document IDs provides absolute reference to objects regardless of file renames or content moves.

Document ID capability is activated and managed at the site collection level. This capability includes an ID value and the ID service. IDs can be used to retrieve items independent of their current location. The ID service supports this process by generating and assigning the IDs. Once the ID is assigned, a static URL can be used to locate the document based on its ID. Static URLs work correctly at the site collection level because the web browser manages the redirect before it invokes the specific Office client application. The ID service generates IDs for all documents in the site collection, but it does not generate IDs for other types of list items. IDs are generated every time a new document is created. The ID is retained during move operations and a new ID is created when a document is copied.

Configuring the Document ID Service

The Document ID capability is enabled and configured at the site collection level. This provides more granular control for implementing this functionality. The following instructions walk you through this configuration.

1. Activate the Document ID Service feature for the specific site collection of interest, as shown in Figure 21-13. Figure 21-13 shows the status of several different features. The Document ID Service feature is the fifth feature from the top, right beneath the Disposition Approval Workflow feature. Administrators can also activate this feature using the following PowerShell cmdlet (the -Url parameter needs to be changed to match the URL of your site collection):

```
Enable-SPFeature -Identity DocID -Url http://sharepoint2010
```

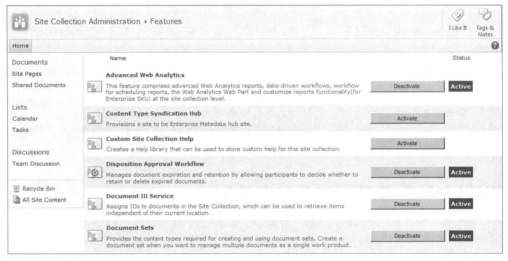

FIGURE 21-13

2. Once activated, a new link called Document ID Settings will appear in the Site Collection Administration group of the Site Settings page. Click this link to display the Document ID Settings page, shown in Figure 21-14.

The Assign Document IDs section section contains three different configuration options:

➤ The Assign Document IDs checkbox is enabled by default, which ensures that IDs are automatically assigned to all documents in the site collection.

➤ A randomly generated ID for each document will begin with the characters displayed in the textbox immediately below the checkbox. By default, this ID prefix is a set of numbers and letters that varies by site collection, which ensures uniqueness across the entire farm. Administrators can enter their own set of characters, but then they need to ensure that these represent a unique value.

➤ There is an option to reset all IDs in the site collection using the defined character string.

The second section, Document ID Lookup Search Scope, allows a specific search scope to be used to look up documents using their IDs. Searching for a specific document based on its ID is a key advantage of the ID.

One last thing to note is the text (shown in bright red on screen) which indicates that the ID feature is scheduled to be completed by an automated process. This indicates that there must be a timer job responsible for completing feature activation. Once this page has been configured, click the OK button.

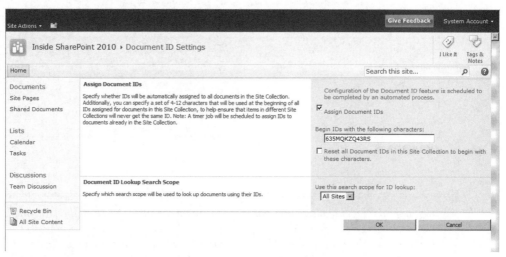

FIGURE 21-14

3. Ensure that the IDs are being assigned by uploading a document to a library in the site collection, as shown in Figure 21-15. Also open the default view of the document library to ensure that the Document ID field is available, as shown in Figure 21-16. In this case, the Document ID column is in position 12, but you can change the position by altering the Position from Left attribute.

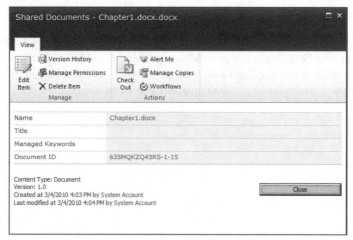

FIGURE 21-15

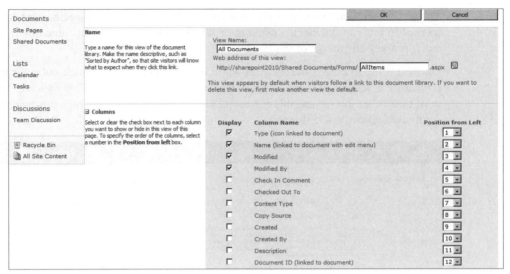

FIGURE 21-16

 If you used a Document Center template to create the site collection, the Document ID feature is enabled by default. If you manually activated the Document ID feature, then the feature is enabled by a daily timer job. You can manually run the timer job; it is called the Document ID enable/disable job. You can also run the Document ID assignment job to assign IDs to all of the documents in your site collection. New documents will be assigned a document ID immediately.

4. To ensure that the ID column is available and IDs have been assigned, you can manually execute the timer jobs that complete these processes. By default, these jobs execute once per day. From the Central Administration website, click the Check job status link in the Monitoring group. Then click the Scheduled Jobs link on the left-hand side of the page to reveal the Scheduled Jobs page. Scroll down the page until you locate the Document ID enable/disable job and the Document ID assignment job links, as shown in Figure 21-17. Click either one of the links to reveal the Edit Timer Job page, shown in Figure 21-18. For both jobs, you can configure when the timer job is executed and you can manually execute the job by clicking the Run Now button. Once completed, all documents should be assigned an ID, and the ID column should be available.

Document ID enable/disable job	sharepoint2010	SharePoint - 80
User Profile Service Application - User Profile Change Cleanup Job	sharepoint2010	
Document ID assignment job	sharepoint2010	SharePoint - 80

FIGURE 21-17

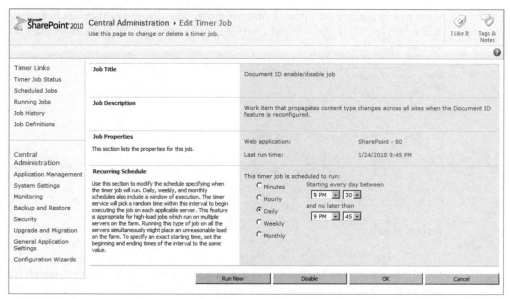

FIGURE 21-18

5. View the properties of any of the documents in the library and copy the shortcut for the Document ID value in the properties dialog. The URL should resemble the following:

```
http://sharepoint2010/_layouts/DocIdRedir.aspx?ID=635MQKZQ43RS-1-15
```

The general URL has the following format, with the specific ID of the document at the end of the string:

```
http://<sitecollectionurl>/<web>/_layouts/DocIdRedir.aspx?ID=635MQKZQ43RS-1-15
```

The preceding URL indicates that there is a new web page in the layouts directory called `DocIdRedir.aspx`; this is the document redirector page. This page accepts the ID as a parameter value in the query string. As is evident from the URL, there is no specific reference to the document's actual location. You can use this link to provide others with a consistent link to your documents. Even if the document is moved to another folder in the same document library or to a different document library in the same site collection, the ID will still enable the document to be located.

6. Now that you've seen how the ID approach works, let's deactivate the ID feature and see what is affected. Deactivating the Document ID Service feature removes the Document ID settings link from the Site Collection Settings page. The ID column is still visible in the document library. If you click the hyperlink in the ID column or click the hyperlink in the document properties window, you will receive the error shown in Figure 21-19. Deactivating the feature has disabled the redirector functionality and turned off the ID service, and IDs are no longer being assigned. Any document that has been assigned an ID will retain its ID. If and when the service is restarted, any document with an ID can once again be located.

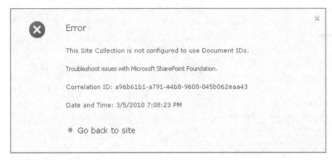

FIGURE 21-19

7. Recall from Chapter 14 that you can define managed search columns, which then enable you to search directly on the values in these columns. Therefore, you can configure the search service to look up documents based on their IDs by adding the ID column as a managed search column. Refer to Chapter 14 to review how to create the managed column. You can also use the `New-SPEnterpriseSearchMetadataManagedProperty` PowerShell cmdlet to perform this function.

8. The last configuration option we will discuss is the Document ID Lookup Box Web Part, which is displayed in Figure 21-20. This Web Part enables you to enter an ID. It then constructs a static URL, looks up the item, and then opens the appropriate viewer or application.

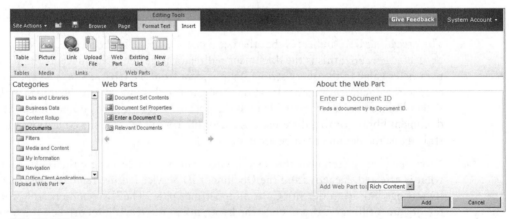

FIGURE 21-20

CONTENT ORGANIZER

Information routing, or content routing, is a very powerful capability. Those of you who are familiar with and use Outlook are very familiar with content routing. Outlook's rule capability enables the automatic routing of different types of e-mail messages to different folders. This is extremely efficient for organizing and managing your Outlook Inbox. In SharePoint 2007, the Records Center site template has a routing engine that routes records to the proper location within the Records Center site collection. The Content Organizer feature in SharePoint 2010 is a new routing feature that extends, enhances, and makes more broadly available the routing engine used in the Records Center site template from SharePoint 2007.

The Content Organizer automatically routes documents that users upload to libraries and folders based on rules that are defined by site administrators. Document routing is based on content types and the metadata within those content types. The following list summarizes the Content Organizer features:

➤ The Content Organizer feature must first be activated to provide this capability. This feature is installed and visible at the site level by default, not the site collection level, but it is not activated. Once the feature has been activated, site administrators can configure both the organizer settings and the organizer rules. Organizer settings determine whether to route documents and rules determine where the documents are routed.

➤ Feature activation also creates a special document library called the Drop Off Library (DOL). This library acts as location where users can upload content, where content that needs to be routed is temporarily stored, and where content that needs to be routed but does not contain all the necessary metadata can be stored. For example, when users upload multiple documents at the same time, the documents are stored in the DOL until metadata is defined and the documents are checked-in.

➤ The organizer only routes documents that are based on the Document content type or are derived from the Document content type. Therefore, it cannot be used to automatically organize and manage lists.

➤ Documents can be automatically routed to different libraries, and folders within those libraries. This is accomplished without user intervention.

➤ It can be used to control the number of documents in a specific folder, and create a new folder when the document limit has been met. This is yet another way that SharePoint 2010 works to ensure that large lists (in this case, libraries) are appropriately managed as were discussed in Chapter 3.

➤ The user who uploads a new document is notified that the document has been routed and given the URL to the document's location so that it can be found in the future.

Configuring the Content Organizer

Configuring the Content Organizer involves choosing options for both the organizer settings and the creation of rules. Because each of these has several different options, the configuration discussion is divided into two sections, one for settings and one for rules.

Organizer Settings

The first step in configuring the content organizer is to configure the settings.

1. You first need to activate the Content Organizer feature at the site level. The Manage site features link is located in the Site Actions section on the Site Settings page. Click the Activate button on the Site Features page to activate the organizer feature, as shown in Figure 21-21.

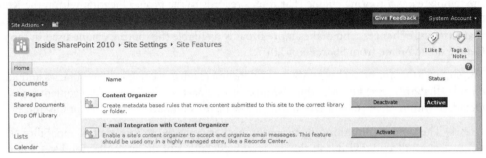

FIGURE 21-21

Feature activation adds two new menu items, or links, to the Site Administration section of your Site Settings page: Content Organizer Settings and Content Organizer Rules, as shown at the bottom of the list in Figure 21-22. The settings determine whether to route documents that are added to the site collection based on rules. Any changes made here affect routing for the entire site. Rules are used to route individual documents based on metadata attributes, which are configured by the site administrator.

FIGURE 21-22

Also added is the new Drop Off Library document library, described earlier. The link to the DOL should be added to the Documents sections on the left-hand navigation pane of the site. It is just a standard SharePoint document library with a timer job that processes outstanding items. This library is used for several different purposes. Essentially, this library is a temporary location for documents that will eventually be moved to the correct library or folder. Once their metadata have been filled out, files uploaded to this library are automatically moved according to rules created by the site owner or administrator. Users can upload their documents to this library when they are unsure where they go, and this library can be used as a staging area for documents that do not have all the required metadata. The document's properties need to be edited and all required metadata filled out in order to have the routing rules applied.

If none of the rules apply, then the document remains in the DOL and the user who uploaded the document receives a message indicating that. In addition, the site owner is notified that a new rule may be created. Items that remain in the DOL generate e-mails to those individuals defined as rule managers in the Content Organizer settings page. Those e-mails are only sent, however, if the Content Organizer Settings page is properly configured — for example, the options to send e-mails when submissions do not match a rule, and/or send e-mails when content has been left in the DOL for three days have been enabled.

Because the DOL is a standard SharePoint document library, it has all the features available to a library. Therefore, the following features can be used with automatic document routing: SharePoint workflow and content approval, check in and check out, alerts, and permissions.

2. The next step is to configure the organizer's settings. Several different options are available for configuring the organizer. This will be accomplished over the next several steps. Navigate to the Settings page and review the different options. This page is partially shown in Figure 21-23, and the options are summarized in Table 21-4 (which appears at the end of this section).

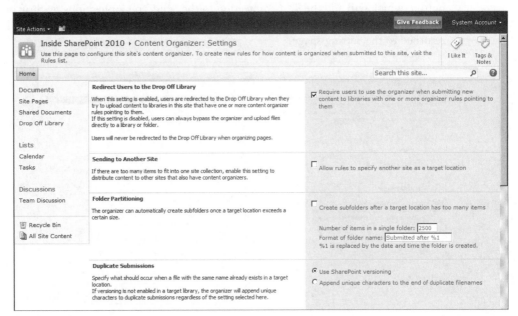

FIGURE 21-23

The Settings page contains configuration options that will affect document routing for the entire site. The Redirect Users to the Drop Off Library option is enabled by default. Leave this option enabled so that all users will be required to use the organizer for this site.

3. Enable the Allow rules to specify another site as a target location option. Doing so enables you to see what configuration needs to be done to support this option. You will see the benefit of this option when you configure the organizer's rules in the next section. Navigate to the Central Administration home page, click the General Application Settings link, and then click the Configure send to connections link, which will reveal the page shown in Figure 21-24 (only the bottom half of the page is shown in the figure). Note that Send To connections are created and configured on a per-Web-application basis. We will focus on creating a new connection, so review the Connection Settings section. Enter the title Test into the Display name textbox. For the Send To URL value, you need to configure another site for organizer use, as shown previously. Once you have done this, the URL you will need is shown at the bottom of the Settings page in the Submission Points section. Copy this value to the Send To URL textbox and click the option Click here to test to ensure you have copied a URL that is an accessible location. Note the format of this URL, and that the reference is calling a Web service:

```
http://sharepoint2010/_vti_bin/OfficialFile.asmx
```

The general format of this URL is shown below. You will not be allowed to add a URL to a site in which the organizer feature has not been activated:

```
http://server/site/_vti_bin/OfficialFile.asmx
```

Select the Move option for the Send To action. Once complete, click the Add Connection button, which will add the Test connection to the Send To Connections textbox on the same page. Select Test and click the OK button at the bottom of the page. You will then be returned to the Settings page.

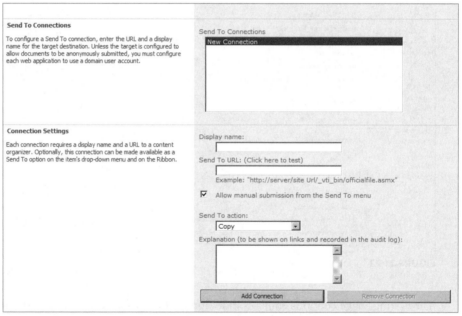

FIGURE 21-24

4. From the Settings page, enable Folder Partitioning by selecting the checkbox. Set the number of items in a single folder to a value of 1. This option enables administrators to manage libraries with a large number of items. For SharePoint 2007, it was recommended to limit the number of items in a single container or view to fewer than 2,000. This was managed through the use of folders, but it had to be implemented manually. The Content Organizer in SharePoint 2010 can automate this process. In SharePoint 2010, the recommendation is to limit a container or view to fewer than 5,000 items. Farm administrators can use the organizer and list throttling to help manage this on a per-Web-application basis.

5. For the Duplicate Submissions section, leave the Use SharePoint versioning option enabled.

6. Enable the option for Preserving Context. This option is especially important when using Records Center websites so that you retain all of the historical information about an item. When retained, you can click Compliance Details from the View Properties page of an item to review this information.

7. Keep the remaining options with their default configuration settings, and click the OK button at the bottom of the page to save the options configured for the organizer. This completes the configuration.

Table 21-4 reviews the Content Organizer settings.

TABLE 21-4   Content Organizer Settings

OPTION	DESCRIPTION
Redirect Users to the Drop Off Library	This option requires users to use the Content Organizer. If this option is enabled, then all document uploads are automatically placed in the DOL regardless of which library the user initially chose in the site for their upload. If this option is not checked, documents can still be routed but users have to upload their documents directly to the DOL. Once uploaded, they will be routed according to the organizer's rules.
Sending to Another Site	This option allows rules to be created that will route documents in the current site to another site that also has the Content Organizer feature enabled. Rules utilize a Send To connection, which is configured in Central Administration, so the site owner may need to work with a farm administrator to complete this process.
Folder Partitioning	This option enables the Content Organizer to automatically create subfolders once the target location exceeds a pre-defined size. Site owners can provide two additional parameters: the maximum number of items per container before a new one is created, and the format of the folder name that will be automatically created.
Duplicate Submissions	This option controls what the Content Organizer does when a submitted item has the same name as a document already in the destination library. Administrators can either use SharePoint versioning or append unique characters to the end of duplicate filenames.

continues

TABLE 21-4 *(continued)*

OPTION	DESCRIPTION
Preserving Context	This option ensures that the original audit logs and properties of the document are retained after the item is routed.
Rule Managers	Users who will create, edit, and manage rules need to be added here. These users also need the Manage Web Site permission in order to modify rules. You can also configure whether to e-mail the rule managers either when content has been added to the DOL and not moved out of it, or when an item was moved there during upload but an applicable routing rule was not found to apply to it. In that case, after it sits in the DOL for three days, an e-mail will be sent to all rule managers informing them that items are still in the DOL.
Submission Points	The URL provided is used for configuring Send To connections so that other sites can send documents or e-mail to this site.

Organizer Rules

The final step in configuring the content organizer is to define the rules used by the organizer to route the content.

1. Click the Content Organizer Rules link on the Site Settings page to display the Content Organizer Rules: Group by Content Type page. This page is a standard SharePoint list that uses the custom Rule content type. Notice that the Group by Content Type heading is actually a drop-down list containing several options for displaying the items in the list, as shown in Figure 21-25. The items in this drop-down menu represent different views of the list. The Group by Content Type view is the default view because content types are the primary criteria upon which rules are based. There is an All Items view, and a Group by Target Library view, plus several other items for modifying, configuring, and creating a new view.

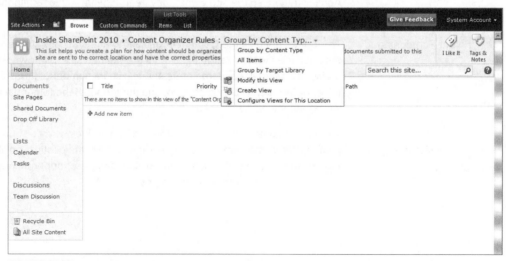

FIGURE 21-25

Each rule contains all of the criteria used to determine where new items should be routed. Rules provide a wide array of configuration options to ensure that you can develop a routing plan for almost any situation. A summary of the options available for creating rules are shown in Table 21-5 at the end of this section.

2. Now it's time to create a new rule. Click the Add new item link or the New Item button in the Ribbon to reveal the Content Organizer Rules: New Rule dialog, shown in Figure 21-26. Only a portion of the New Rule web page is shown in the figure.

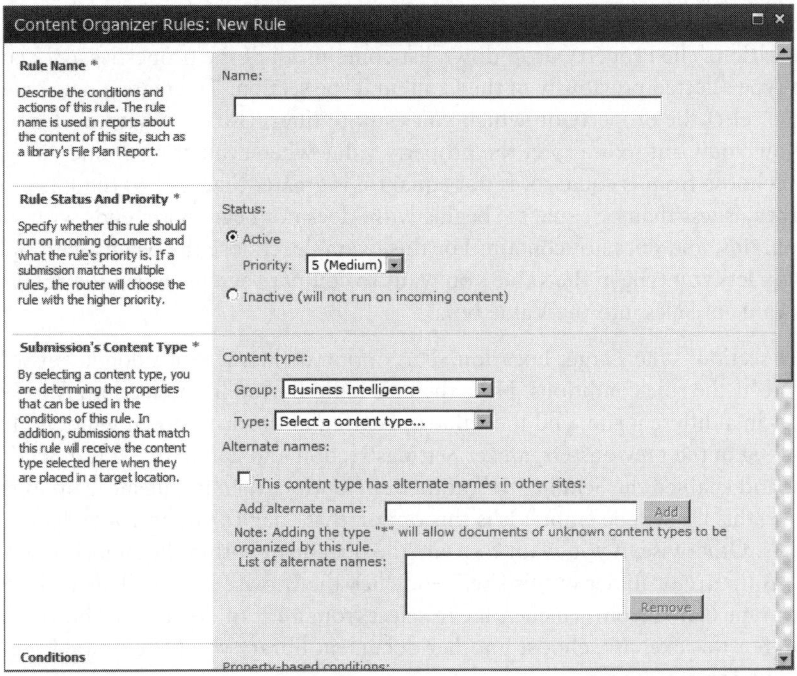

FIGURE 21-26

3. Assign a name to the rule, such as "My First Rule" or similar. In general, you should adopt a naming convention that describes the function of the rule so that its function can be distinguished from other rules, since multiple rules will usually be present. Leave the status and priority at their default values of Active and 5.

4. You need to make a few choices in the Submission's Content Type section, where you make selections in two drop-down lists. First, for the group content type, choose Document Content Types or any other group you prefer. The Group drop-down list contains the content type group names that are being used in the site collection and the current site. Once you pick a group name, the values in the Type drop-down list are filtered to show only those content types that are part of the selected group. Routing in the Content Organizer feature works only for Document content types or content types that inherit from the Document content type. If a group doesn't contain any content types that inherit from Document, then it won't be included in the Group drop-down list. As you might expect then, if a content type is not Document or inherit from Document, it will not show up in the Type drop-down list. Choose the Document content type for the Type value. You can also use content type *aliases*, as used in Record Center sites in SharePoint 2007. Aliases are alternative names for content types that may exist in other sites. These can be also be configured in this section.

5. The two remaining sections on the New Rule page are Conditions and Target Location. These sections are not shown in Figure 21-26 so you will have to browse to the New Rule web page and scroll to the bottom of the page to view these sections. You can specify up to six different conditions in the Conditions section. This is a very powerful option that governs whether a submitted document matches the rule and will be routed according to the rule's target location. The Property drop-down list contains all of the properties associated with the content type selected previously in the Content Type section. To create a new property-based filter, you select the property on which you want to filter. Use the Operator drop-down list to define how you want to interpret the property value when evaluating an incoming document. You can choose from is equal to, is not equal to, is greater than, is less than, is greater than or equal to, is less than or equal to, begins with, does not begin with, ends with, does not end with, contains, and does not contain. For this example, choose the begins with operator. The Value box lets you type in the value you want to compare against when the rule is processed. Enter a value of Sales into the Value box.

6. The final section is the Target Location. This option defines where a document will be routed once it meets the rule conditions. Note the first radio button in the section, Another content organizer in a different site, and the value appearing in the drop-down window. If you followed along in the previous Organizer Settings section and configured a test Send To connection, and enabled the Sending to Another Site option, then it will show up in this list; otherwise, this list will be empty. It is this option that enables you to route documents to other sites. Otherwise, if you want to route the document within the site, choose the radio button "A library or folder in this site:" and click the Browse button. This will open a built-in picker-type dialog from which you can select from a list of document libraries in the current site. For this exercise, choose another document library you have created previously, such as Enterprise Content.

After you've made your selection it is plugged into the Edit box in a URL format that is relative to the specific site collection. For example, if you are in the top-level site and you are routing to a library called Enterprise Content, the value in the Edit box would be `/Enterprise Content`. You can also choose to have folders created automatically for items based on one of the properties of the content type. To do so, enable the "Automatically create a folder for each unique value of a property:" checkbox. It also has a drop-down list of properties associated with the content type. However, unlike the drop-down list used in the property-based filters above, this drop-down contains only properties required by your content type. This prevents adding folders that have no values for a property. You can also specify a format for the folder name. By default, it is "%1 — %2", where %1 is replaced with the name of the property, and %2 is replaced with the value of the property. There is no need to make any other additions to the rule for our testing purposes, so this completes the rule configuration. At this point, click OK, and the new rule is added as shown in

Figure 21-27. Whenever a new rule is created, the Content Organizer checks whether that specific content type has been added to the DOL. If it hasn't, then the content type is added to the library so that when the edit form is displayed after an item has been uploaded, users can select any one of the content types used in the routing rules.

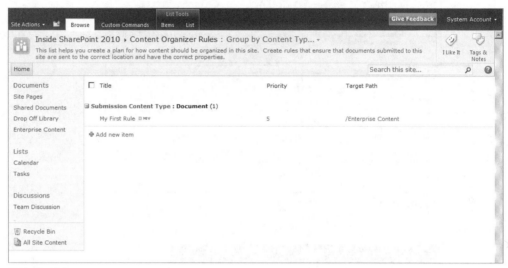

FIGURE 21-27

7. Add a second rule called "My Second Rule" or similar and configure the Group and Type content types to be Document Set Content Types and Document Set, respectively. Configure the condition to use the Name property, the *ends with* operator, and a value of "IT." Route all documents to a different library called Enterprise Document Sets. If your target library does not have the content type specifically chosen in the rule, you will receive the message shown in Figure 21-28 and the new rule will not be saved. Therefore, you need to add this content type to the Enterprise Document Sets library and then re-create the rule. Once you have successfully created the rule, confirm that the Document Set content type has been automatically added to the DOL Content Type list.

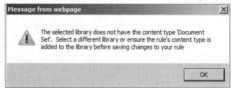

FIGURE 21-28

8. To test the functionality, upload a Word document called Sales Brochure to the Enterprise Content library. You will see the dialog shown in Figure 21-29. Choose the Document content type and click the Submit button. The dialog shown in Figure 21-30 will appear. This dialog informs the submitter that the uploaded document has been saved to its final location and provides a URL for the location. Confirm that it was successfully routed to the Enterprise Content library.

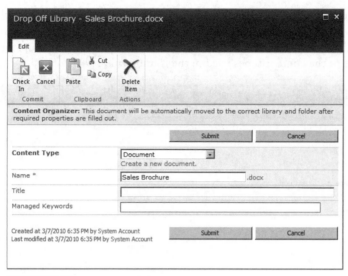

FIGURE 21-29

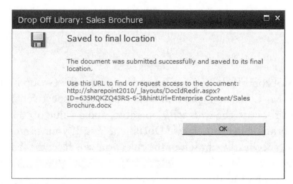

FIGURE 21-30

9. Upload a Word document titled Sales Business Rules to the Enterprise Document Sets library, and configure Document as the content type. Confirm that the document was routed to the Enterprise Content library; but notice that the confirmation dialog indicates that a folder was created, as shown by the link in Figure 21-31. You can confirm this by navigating to the Enterprise Content library, as shown in Figure 21-32. The folder appears exactly as you configured it in the Organizer Settings earlier.

10. You can confirm that an uploaded document of content type Document Set was routed to the Enterprise Document Sets library. This completes the configuration and testing of the Content Organizer routing capability.

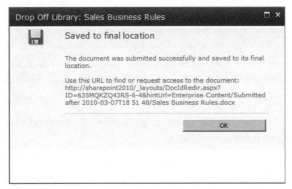

FIGURE 21-31

FIGURE 21-32

Table 21-5 summarizes the options for creating new rules.

TABLE 21-5 New Rule Configuration Options

OPTION	DESCRIPTION
Rule Name	The name of the rule. When creating the name, keep in mind that the rule name is used in reports, so make the name as descriptive as possible.
Rule Status and Priority	The status of a rule is either active or inactive. If active, you can choose a priority for the rule, from 1 (highest priority) to 9 (lowest priority); an active status with a priority of 5 is the default. If more than one rule matches the criteria for a document, the rule with the highest priority is applied.
Submission's Content Type	The site owner or administrator must choose a content type, which will determine which properties (metadata) can be used in the rule's conditions. Uploaded documents that match this rule will be assigned this content type when they are routed to the target location.

continues

TABLE 21-5 *(continued)*

OPTION	DESCRIPTION
Conditions	This defines the conditions for matching the rule. An uploaded document's properties must match all of the specified property conditions. A maximum of six conditions can be specified.
Target Location	This specifies the location where submitted content will be redirected once the conditions of the rule have been satisfied.

SUMMARY

This chapter introduced several new content management features of SharePoint 2010, including managed metadata, document sets, document IDs and the Content Organizer. The focus has been on understanding each of these tools, the different options available for each tool, and how to configure them. These features have broad-scale application to a large number of uses for SharePoint websites, so administrators should take the time to understand them thoroughly.

22

Working with SharePoint Designer 2010

WHAT'S IN THIS CHAPTER?

➤ Introduction to SharePoint Designer

➤ The new user experience

➤ Controlling the use of SharePoint Designer

➤ Uses of SharePoint Designer

Organizations purchase SharePoint to help them do more with less. SharePoint is a tool to help companies work smarter as opposed to harder. Although SharePoint is very powerful and has a long list of features and capabilities out of the box, it is fair to assume that most companies are going to want to customize the product in some way. This is where SharePoint Designer (SPD) fits into the picture; it is the preferred tool for customizing SharePoint.

Before we get too far into this chapter, we need to address the elephant in the room. Whether you are a developer or an administrator, you've probably already formed an opinion about SharePoint Designer or have heard co-workers and friends saying negative things. This book is family friendly and many of the comments about SPD shouldn't be repeated — let's just say that most folks seem to think that the tool does more harm than good.

The bad reputation started back with Microsoft FrontPage, a product that made creating websites easy, almost too easy in many cases. Bad websites created using FrontPage began to pop up all over the place. FrontPage's reputation was so toxic that there are tales of web developers not being hired because they listed FrontPage on their resumes.

However, aside from making bad websites, FrontPage was also the tool of choice for customizing SharePoint 2003. It wasn't until organizations started upgrading to SharePoint 2007 that everyone realized the full extent of the problems that were caused by FrontPage. Entire migration efforts were made significantly more difficult because of how FrontPage customized SharePoint sites.

When SharePoint 2007 was released, FrontPage was split into two products: Microsoft Office SharePoint Designer 2007 and Expression Web Designer. The name FrontPage was conspicuously dropped from both products. SPD 2007 was a vast improvement over FrontPage. The tool was designed to be the primary way to customize SharePoint 2007, and it enabled users to not only change the user interface but also to build powerful applications without writing any code. This meant that any business user was able to use SPD 2007 to create functionality, such as a custom workflow, that previously required a developer and significant effort to accomplish.

Despite the name change and all of the new functionality in SPD 2007, the negative perceptions persisted. Many users described their "love-hate" relationship with the product. The common feeling was that although SPD 2007 was one of the most powerful software tools they had ever used to create valuable business solutions with SharePoint, it was also very quirky. For example, SPD 2007 enabled users to back up a site as long as the site was not larger than 24MB. In other cases, users would get frustrated with SPD 2007 because it would rewrite the code for their web page without asking. Additionally, SharePoint administrators were frustrated by SPD 2007 because of the lack of control they had over the tool being used in their environment.

Yes, FrontPage and SPD 2007 both had some issues; but all of these things are behind us now. When SharePoint Designer 2010 was created, it was done so with many of these complaints and pain points in mind. Therefore, for those of you who have written off SPD and called it nasty names, it's time to give the tool another chance. The whole product has been revamped to place more of an emphasis on integrating with SharePoint and less on being a tool for editing web pages that also kind of has something to do with SharePoint.

This chapter provides a high-level overview of the features and capabilities of SharePoint Designer 2010. You'll take a look through the various menus and see some examples of how to perform several common tasks, including the following:

➤   Managing your sites

➤   Working with data sources

➤   Views and forms

➤   Workflows

➤   Branding

Sit back, relax, and take a deep breath as we venture off on a tour of SharePoint Designer 2010.

WHO SHOULD USE SHAREPOINT DESIGNER?

SPD is a very powerful tool, and despite many of the improvements for SPD 2010 that simplify its use, in the wrong hands it can cause problems. Whether you are a SharePoint administrator, developer, or end user, make sure that when you first start using SPD you are doing so from a place where you can do no harm.

With that public service message out of the way, who *should* use SPD? The tool is intended to be used by site owners and power users to create and add functionality to SharePoint, without needing to know how to write code. The same reasons that make SPD an ideal tool for end users also make it an ideal tool for developers and administrators.

INTRODUCTION TO SHAREPOINT DESIGNER 2010

The name "SharePoint Designer" suggests that it is a tool for website designers, but customizing your site's look and feel is just one of many tasks that SPD is capable of doing. Perhaps a better name would be something like "SharePoint Management Studio" because SPD 2010 acts as a central location to manage your SharePoint sites.

There have been a number of improvements to SPD 2010, starting with a new UI. Like everything else in SharePoint 2010, SPD has been updated with a new user interface that introduces the fluent UI, otherwise known as "The Ribbon." By now this isn't a new concept. Aside from the Ribbon, the menus themselves have been updated to make it easier to do many common tasks. Those familiar with SPD 2007 would often use the tool to make changes to web pages or create a custom workflow. With SPD 2010, most of the functionality from the previous version is still there (and improved), but it is now possible to manage your SharePoint sites directly from the tool. In this section we'll discuss the basics you'll need to begin using SharePoint Designer 2010.

Requirements for Using SPD 2010

On April 2, 2009, Microsoft announced that SharePoint Designer 2007 would be available as a free download. Many assumed that this was an April Fool's Day joke that came a day too late, but it was no joke. Microsoft made this move because several organizations decided not to purchase the tool based on its original cost. When SPD 2010 was announced, many wondered if the tool would still be offered as a free product. The good news is that SPD 2010 will indeed be available as a free download, at `www.microsoft.com/spd`. Following are the necessary requirements:

➤ **Supported operating systems** — Windows 7; Windows Server 2003; Windows Server 2003 Service Pack 1; Windows Server 2003 Service Pack 2; Windows Server 2008 R2; Windows Server 2008 Service Pack 2; Windows Vista Service Pack 1

➤ **Computer and processor** — 500 MHz processor or higher

➤ **Memory** — 256 megabytes (MB) of RAM or higher

➤ **Hard disk** — 2.5GB minimum

SharePoint Designer 2010 works only with SharePoint 2010. If you try to open your MOSS sites with SPD 2010, it won't work. Although this might be frustrating for some users, it was a decision made by the SharePoint Designer product team in order to make it possible to implement all of the changes for the new version of the project.

In environments where SharePoint 2007 and SharePoint 2010 are both installed, it might be necessary to have SPD 2007 and SPD 2010 installed side by side on the same machine. If this applies to you, make sure you install the same version of SPD 2010 that you did with SPD 2007. Because SPD 2007 only came in x86, if you wanted to install SPD 2010 on the same machine it would be necessary to install SPD 2010 x86.

OVERVIEW OF THE NEW UX

It should be pretty obvious by looking at SharePoint Designer 2010 that there have been some significant improvements to the user interface. Aside from the Ribbon, the entire user experience for SPD 2010 now reflects the stronger focus on SharePoint itself. Users can now easily see all the components that make up their sites, and the various relationships between the components. In general, users can now control most of the common pieces of their SharePoint site directly from SPD 2010 without having to wade through several disconnected settings screens.

Before we proceed, it would probably be helpful to actually open SharePoint Designer so that it is easier to follow along: Click Start ➪ All Programs ➪ SharePoint, and then click Microsoft SharePoint Designer 2010.

The first screen that opens is referred to as the Sites place. This screen is divided into four self-explanatory areas: Open SharePoint Site, New SharePoint Site, Recent Sites, and Site Templates.

In the Site Templates section, by default you'll only see three options for templates: Blank Site, Blog, and Team Site (see Figure 22-1). Clicking on one of these templates will open up a dialog that enables you to create a new site once you specify a URL. If you want to create a new site based on a different template that isn't specified, you can click the More Templates button and type in the URL of a site that has more options. For example, typing in the URL for a site created using the Enterprise Wiki template would allow you to choose from additional templates such as Enterprise Wiki, Publishing Site, and so on.

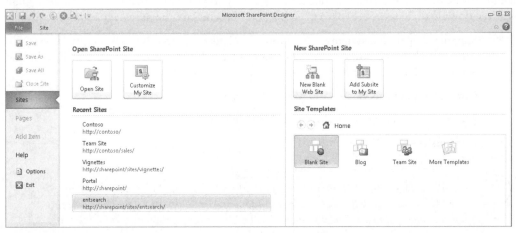

FIGURE 22-1

If this is the first time you've opened SharePoint Designer, the Recent Sites area will be blank and you'll need to click the Open Site button. Once the Open Site dialog opens, you can type in the address of your site in the format of `http://contoso` or `http://contoso/subsite` and then click Open.

Your site will open to what is referred to as the *settings page*, shown in Figure 22-3, which displays high-level information such as the title, description, URL, SharePoint version number, permissions, subsites, etc. The settings page for the site is the starting point from which all changes to your site can be made. Previously, when SPD 2007 opened, users were presented with a multi-paned interface that contained a blank HTML page and other areas that allowed you to edit the parts of your page (see Figure 22-4). SPD 2010 has an updated user interface that puts more of a focus on SharePoint itself. All aspects of your SharePoint site should be easily accessed from this page.

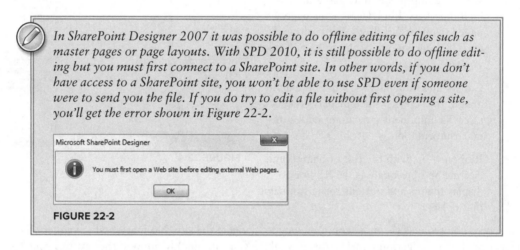

In SharePoint Designer 2007 it was possible to do offline editing of files such as master pages or page layouts. With SPD 2010, it is still possible to do offline editing but you must first connect to a SharePoint site. In other words, if you don't have access to a SharePoint site, you won't be able to use SPD even if someone were to send you the file. If you do try to edit a file without first opening a site, you'll get the error shown in Figure 22-2.

FIGURE 22-2

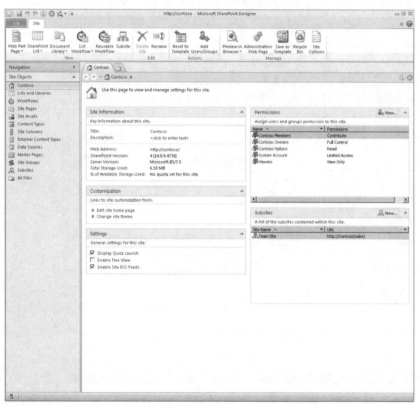

FIGURE 22-3

The user interface, shown in Figure 22-5, is divided into three main areas:

➤ **Navigation** — This pane shows the various components that make up a site, including lists, libraries, master pages, page layouts, workflows, content types, etc. Clicking on one of the links will take you to a Gallery page.

➤ **Gallery and Summary** — This is the main area of the screen, which displays the lists of each component type along with summary information.

➤ **Ribbon** — As with the rest of SharePoint, electing an object causes the Ribbon to display menus and options for customizing that object.

FIGURE 22-4

The navigation panel is the most common way to navigate the site. No matter which gallery has been clicked, the navigation panel is always visible. You can quickly jump to the settings page by clicking the Site link (listed first in the navigation) or jump to any of the other areas of the site.

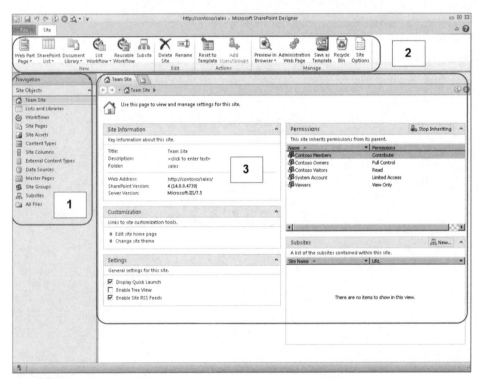

FIGURE 22-5

The gallery pages provide a high level view of each of the various areas of the site. Whether you are trying to determine how many lists there are or what workflows are available, the galleries provide a quick way to get whatever information you need about the site. Additionally, clicking on a gallery will cause the Ribbon to change context and show buttons related to what's selected. For example, if you are on the site settings page, then the Ribbon displays common actions you might perform at the site level; but if you click the Lists and Libraries gallery, the Ribbon changes to show options specifically related to lists and libraries. In most cases, the options available in SPD are the exact same options that are available from the SharePoint user interface. The advantage of SPD is that it provides a single place to quickly navigate through the different areas of the site.

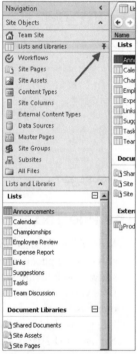

Another thing to note is that a gallery can be opened as a "mini-gallery" below the navigation pane. To do this, hover your mouse over the link for a gallery in the navigation and you'll see a pin icon (see Figure 22-6). Clicking the pin icon displays the mini-gallery. This mini-gallery will continue to show even when you select a different gallery. However, it is only possible to pin one gallery at a time.

Once you click the link in the navigation, the contents of the gallery will be displayed. In most of the galleries, clicking the name of an item once will open its settings page, but double-clicking on the item will open its editor. For example, if you click the Lists and Libraries gallery and then click the title for the Announcements list, the settings page will open; but if you were to instead double-click on the list, the editor will open for the list, showing the various columns along with new options available from the Ribbon.

Opening the editor for an object can be tricky, though. The easiest way is to ensure that you double-click away from the name of the object you are clicking on. For the Announcements list, it might be easier to click on the item near the Type column, rather than the Name column.

FIGURE 22-6

Bread Crumbs, Tabs, and Navigation

The way that you navigate throughout SPD 2010 has also changed significantly. As mentioned previously, the site settings page is now the common area that can be used to access all other areas of the site; but as you navigate from the site settings page, there are now additional ways that make it easier to get around. Users who are familiar with Windows 7 will find the navigation aspects of SPD 2010 to be very familiar.

There are forward and back buttons that function the same as if you were navigating around in your favorite web browser. If you click on an area of the site and want to go back to the place you just were, simply click the back button to return to the page. Additionally, if you've got forward and back buttons on your mouse they can also be used in the same way that they work with Web pages in a browser.

There is also a bread crumb navigation that shows where you are in relation to the site. For example, if you were to click on Lists and Libraries and then the Announcements list, the bread crumb would have a link for each level if you wanted to jump up in the site hierarchy (see Figure 22-7). The bread crumb links themselves can be expanded, enabling you to quickly jump to other areas of the site.

As you click on different files, they will open as different tabs in your site. This works very similarly to how tabs work in a web browser. Each tab maintains a history, so it is easy to quickly jump back to something you were working with earlier (see Figure 22-8).

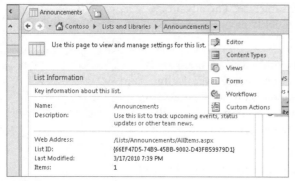

FIGURE 22-7

FIGURE 22-8

The File Tab

Most of us are used to the concept of a File menu that can be accessed in the upper-left corner of all software applications. SPD 2010 is no different; a quick glance in the upper-left corner of the screen shows the File tab, which is highlighted in orange so it is tough to miss. Clicking the File link will take you to a page that looks very similar to the one you first see when you start SPD 2010. This menu is the place for doing things above and beyond working on the site you might be editing. The File tab is the location from which you can open other sites, add pages, import files, or view and change SPD 2010's settings. If you need the Help menus or want to find the version number for SPD 2010, that would also be accessed from this menu. To exit out of this screen, click the tab to the immediate right of the File tab to go back to where you were.

Checking and Changing the Current User

You may have noticed a small icon in the bottom left corner of your SPD 2010 window that looks like a person (see Figure 22-9). If you hover your mouse over this icon, it will highlight the name of the user currently logged in to SPD 2010. Clicking this icon enables you to log in with a different user account. This is useful for testing permissions scenarios or support issues to determine what access a specific user might have.

FIGURE 22-9

RESTRICTING ACCESS TO SHAREPOINT DESIGNER

Early in the chapter we mentioned the negative feelings that many users have had about previous versions of SPD. These feelings weren't just isolated to individuals; many organizations also decided not to use SPD. Despite the fact that SPD 2007 was a very powerful tool, one of its major shortcomings was that it was very difficult to control access. If you had enough access to a site, then you could use SPD. This problem was magnified when the tool was made available as a free download. Organizations wrote lengthy governance documents that outlined how SPD was to be used in their environment, but unfortunately those words didn't actually stop brave users from downloading the tool and doing things they shouldn't be doing.

SharePoint administrators everywhere can breathe a sigh of relief, because SharePoint 2010 now provides much tighter control over how SPD can be used in an organization with the following settings:

➤ **Enable SharePoint Designer** — Determines whether SharePoint Designer can be used at all.

➤ **Enable Detaching Pages from the Site Definition** — Allows edited pages to be customized, which detaches them from the site definition.

➤ **Enable Customizing Master Pages and Layout Pages** — Removes the Master Page link from the navigation pane and prevents users from updating master pages and layout pages.

➤ **Enable Managing of the Web Site URL Structure** — Removes the All Files link from the navigation pane.

These new options enable organizations to control SPD 2010 at the level appropriate to their requirements. SharePoint 2010 allows access to SPD to be controlled at two different levels:

➤ **Central Administration** — Accessed from the General Application Settings menu, this enables farm administrators to control SPD at the web application level. Disabling the options here prevents site collection administrators from enabling the functionality.

➤ **Site Collection** — Accessed from the Site Collection Administration section in Site Settings, this enables site collection administrators to control SPD access for Designers and Site Owners.

The following example walks you through the process of updating the SPD settings from Central Administration:

1. Open Central Administration from your SharePoint server by clicking Start ➪ All Programs ➪ Microsoft SharePoint 2010 Products ➪ Microsoft SharePoint 2010 Central Administration.

2. Click General Application Settings in the left navigation.

3. From the SharePoint Designer section, click Configure SharePoint Designer settings (see Figure 22-10).

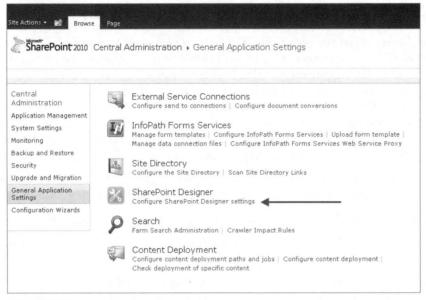

FIGURE 22-10

4. From the settings page, select the appropriate web application from the drop-down at the top right. By default, all the options should be selected. Leave the first box checked, which enables the use of SPD, but remove the checks from the other boxes, as shown in Figure 22-11. Click OK.

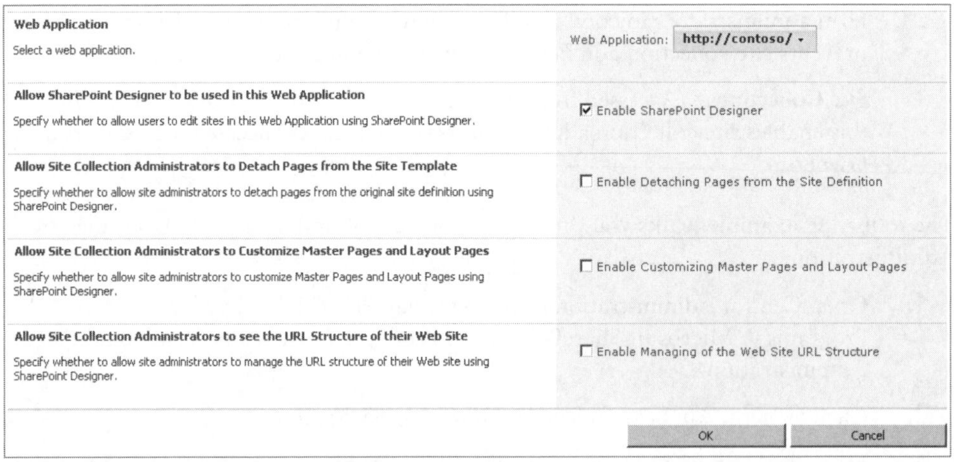

Web Application

Select a web application.

Web Application: **http://contoso/ ▾**

Allow SharePoint Designer to be used in this Web Application

Specify whether to allow users to edit sites in this Web Application using SharePoint Designer.

☑ Enable SharePoint Designer

Allow Site Collection Administrators to Detach Pages from the Site Template

Specify whether to allow site administrators to detach pages from the original site definition using SharePoint Designer.

☐ Enable Detaching Pages from the Site Definition

Allow Site Collection Administrators to Customize Master Pages and Layout Pages

Specify whether to allow site administrators to customize Master Pages and Layout Pages using SharePoint Designer.

☐ Enable Customizing Master Pages and Layout Pages

Allow Site Collection Administrators to see the URL Structure of their Web Site

Specify whether to allow site administrators to manage the URL structure of their Web site using SharePoint Designer.

☐ Enable Managing of the Web Site URL Structure

OK Cancel

FIGURE 22-11

5. To test the changes, navigate to the URL of the site collection in your web browser to be used for testing, and log in as a site collection administrator. In this example, we use http://contoso. In order for this example to work, the ID that is used must be a site collection administrator.

If you were to test with an account that has more permissions, such as a farm administrator account, you might not notice any changes. Since administrator accounts have more rights to the site collection, these changes won't impact their ability to use SharePoint Designer.

6. From the Site Actions button, choose Edit in SharePoint Designer (see Figure 22-12).

7. SharePoint Designer should open. Note that the Master Page, Page Layouts (only shows in sites with Publishing enabled), and All Sites links should be missing from the left-hand navigation pane (see Figure 22-13). If the links are still there, verify that you are logged in as a site collection administrator, not a farm administrator. You can check by clicking the icon in the bottom-left corner of the SPD window, which displays the name of the logged-in user.

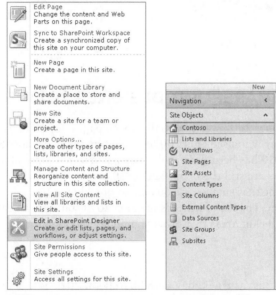

FIGURE 22-12   **FIGURE 22-13**

Also, if you were to click Site Pages and try to edit the home.aspx, you'll notice that Advanced mode is grayed out (see Figure 22-14). The page can only be edited in Normal mode, which means that only content in Web Part zones can be edited.

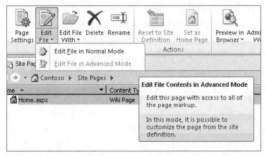

FIGURE 22-14

8. For the next step, we are going to test what happens when you completely disable SPD access. Close the instance of SPD that you were using for the last example. It's OK to leave your web browser open.

9. Repeat steps 1–3 and remove the check from the Enable SharePoint Designer box. Press OK.

10. Repeat step 5. Now when you try to open SPD, you should see the prompt shown in Figure 22-15.

FIGURE 22-15

WHAT CAN YOU DO WITH SHAREPOINT DESIGNER 2010?

Back in the dark ages, SharePoint Designer 2007 was essentially a web page editor with the ability to do various SharePoint tasks. For many who used SPD 2007, it didn't do many of those SharePoint tasks very well. SharePoint Designer 2010 has been drastically redesigned to put more of a focus on SharePoint. The page editing capabilities are still there, but SPD 2010 can be thought of as more of a SharePoint site management tool — one that enables site owners to quickly manage and update all areas of their site from a central location. The list of features for SPD 2010 could fill an entire book, so this section focuses on the most significant areas that provide unique functionality.

Data Sources

The old adage that "Content is king" is just as true today with SharePoint 2010 as it ever was. SharePoint Designer 2010 can be used to create and manage data sources whether the data is coming directly from SharePoint or from external sources. *Data sources* is the term used by SPD 2010 to refer to these sources of content.

Lists and Libraries

The most basic types of data in SharePoint are lists and document libraries; and in terms of SPD 2010, the concepts don't change at all. However, creating and managing lists and libraries is much easier with SPD 2010 than in the past. Clicking the Lists and Libraries link in the navigation in your site with SPD 2010 will open up the Lists and Libraries gallery. The gallery shows all of the lists and libraries associated with this site. The gallery interface makes it easy to create new lists and libraries based on a template, create your own with custom columns, or update existing ones by adding columns or modifying the settings.

Data Source Connections

Clicking the Data sources link in the navigation will open the gallery, which at first glance looks exactly like the Lists and Libraries gallery. Although lists and libraries are data sources, the important difference in this gallery can be seen if you look at the Ribbon — you'll notice several new options. In many cases, the data that you want to interact with in your SharePoint site is actually coming from a source outside of SharePoint. The following types of data source connections are supported:

➤ External database

➤ SOAP Web Service

➤ REST Web Service or RSS Feed

➤ XML File Connection

Clicking the corresponding button in the Ribbon of SPD will open a wizard that enables you to quickly connect to each of the different data sources. Once you've connected to the data sources, SharePoint Designer 2010 can be used to combine the information from multiple sources into a single view. Many would refer to this as creating a *mashup*, but in SharePoint terminology this is referred to as a *composite application*. An example would be if you wanted to combine product information stored in a SQL Server database with customer information stored in another system, which is exporting to an XML file. All of the data is coming from different places and combined into a single view by using SharePoint Designer 2010.

External Data Integration

One of the most powerful features of SharePoint 2007 was the capability to connect to line-of-business (LOB) systems through the use of the business data catalog, more commonly referred to as the BDC. In theory, it sounded like a great idea that would solve many common business problems that organizations face. However, the BDC wasn't widely adopted because a number of obstacles made implementation difficult.

Connecting to the LOB systems required the creation of an XML file called an *application definition*, which was very difficult to create by hand. Most companies either decided it was too tough to create the file or relied on a third-party product to generate the file. However, even when a company was able to get the BDC connected, out of the box it only sent information in one direction. Although data from external sources could be read from the BDC in SharePoint, it wasn't possible to easily write changes made from SharePoint back to the LOB systems. At the end of the day, most companies felt that although the BDC sounded like a good idea, it was too much work to implement and there were too many limitations to work through.

SharePoint 2010 greatly enhances the capability to connect to LOB systems — using a feature that has been renamed *Business Connectivity Services (BCS)*. SPD 2010 can now be used to create the connections into LOB systems such as SQL Server databases, PeopleSoft, SAP, and more. Once the connections are made, the information can be surfaced as an external content type (ECT) in an external list. This enables business users to interact with external data in SharePoint just like any other type of list. For example, if you were to connect to your customer database in SQL Server and add it as an external list, you could update the content in SQL Server directly by making changes to the data in SharePoint. The BCS now enables changes from SharePoint to be written back to LOB systems.

As a practical application for the BCS, once you've connected to LOB systems the data returned in the external list behaves just like any other data in SharePoint. This means that not only can you make updates to it, but it can also be indexed and searched, or used as metadata in lists and libraries. For example, it would be possible to connect to an external products database and then add a Products field to a document library. When a document is added to this library, a user could select a product name as metadata, and other fields could then be selected to be added from the database as metadata. If the product name were selected as metadata, then the price, color, and weight would be automatically added.

Using SharePoint Designer 2010 to Create an External List

The goal of this example is to walk you through the steps for creating an external list with SharePoint Designer 2010. Business Connectivity Service (BCS) is covered in more detail in Chapter 24. For this example, we'll be using the AdventureWorks sample database. If you do not yet have it installed, you can download it from `http://msftdbprodsamples.codeplex.com/`. Be sure to download the correct version based on the version of SQL Server you have installed. The examples in this chapter are shown using the SQL Server 2008 R2 databases.

After downloading and installing the database, follow these steps:

1. Open SharePoint Designer 2010 and open your SharePoint site.

2. From the navigation pane, click the link for the External Content Types gallery.

3. Click the External Content Type button in the Ribbon (see Figure 22-16).

4. Enter a Name and Display Name. Clicking the words "New external content type" will allow you to edit the name. For this example, enter **Products** as the value for both fields.

5. Click the link that says "Click here to discover external data sources and define operations" (see Figure 22-17), which will open a new page that will enable you to configure the connection to your external data source.

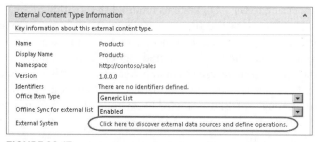

FIGURE 22-16   **FIGURE 22-17**

6. From the new screen, click the Add Connection button located in the upper left hand corner of the center panel. This will open up a series of windows that will walk you through the process of configuring the connection to the external data source. With previous versions of SharePoint, this process needed to be done either by hand, which was extremely complex, or through the use of third-party products.

7. From the first pop-up, select the External Data Source Type as SQL Server and click OK.

8. Next, specify the Database Server and Database Name for the database to which you want to connect (see Figure 22-18) from the second pop-up. Click OK.

9. When the Data Source Explorer is loaded, expand the Tables section, select the Product table, right-click on it, and click Create All Operations (see Figure 22-19). You might receive a warning when you expand the tables saying that some columns have unsupported data types. If you do receive the warning, press OK to move past it and continue with the demo. It will not impact the rest of the steps.

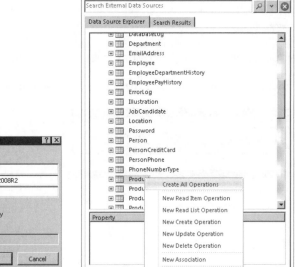

FIGURE 22-18   **FIGURE 22-19**

10. The All operations window will open, which enables you to specify more details about how the external content type works. For this example, leave all of the default settings and click Finish.

11. You'll notice that there's now a green check mark displayed under the External Content Type Operations section, indicating that everything is working as expected. However, before you can use the external content type, it is necessary to save it. To do so, press the Save icon in the upper-left corner of the screen (see Figure 22-20), which will save it to the Business Data Connectivity Metadata store.

12. Click the Create Profile Page button in the Ribbon (see Figure 22-21) to create a profile page that will be used to display the information from external data when it is shown in SharePoint.

> *You might receive an error when you try to create the profile page stating that you must first set up a host site. If this is the case, you will need to log in to Central Administration to make the change. Click on Manage service applications from under the Application Management section. Next, click on the link for the Business Data Connectivity Service. Then you'll need to create the host page by clicking the Configure button in the Ribbon. In the dialog that opens, accept the default settings and then click on the OK button. You should now be able to create the Profile Page from within SPD.*

13. Once SharePoint has connected to the data source, you'll make an external list so that you can interact with the data in SharePoint. To do this, click Lists and Libraries in the Site Objects panel in SPD.

14. From the Ribbon, click the External List button (see Figure 22-22).

FIGURE 22-20

FIGURE 22-21

FIGURE 22-22

15. From the External Content Types Picker, choose Products and click OK (see Figure 22-23).

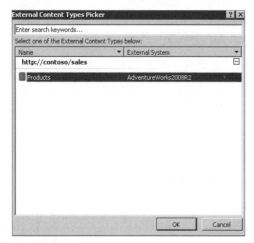

FIGURE 22-23

16. Enter Products as the name for the new external list and click OK.

17. If you browse to your SharePoint site and click on the list, the content from the SQL Server table should be returned. If everything looks good, skip to step 20. If this is the first time you've configured a BCS connection, you'll probably get an error stating "Access denied by Business Data Connectivity" (see Figure 22-24). To resolve this, open Central Administration and go to Application Management and then click Manage service applications. Click the Business Data Connectivity Service. Place a check in the box next to the new connection you made, and click the Set Object Permissions button in the Ribbon.

18. The Set Object Permissions dialog, shown in Figure 22-25, will open. In the top box, specify the accounts to grant permissions to and then click the Add button.

19. Once the account has been added, select the permissions the account should have. For this example, you've just added the account that will be browsing the external list. This account was granted all permissions and the option to Propagate permissions to all methods was checked. Click OK.

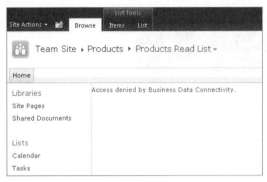

FIGURE 22-24

The content in the external list should now be displayed without the error. In a production environment, it would be necessary to specify the users and/or groups who have permission to read from and write to this data source.

 If you are still having issues, it might be necessary to check the permissions to the AdventureWorks database in SQL Server.

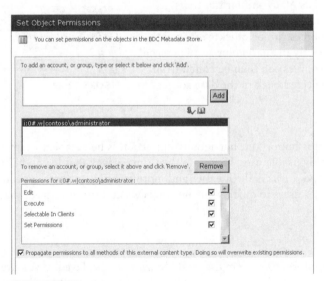

FIGURE 22-25

20. The external list should display the information from the SQL table. As you can see, it looks very similar to a SharePoint list, and in fact it can be edited just like one. Select the first item called Adjustable Race with a product number of AR-5381. The Ribbon will change to display new options. Click the Edit Item button.

21. Update the ProductNumber field and click the Save button (see Figure 22-26).

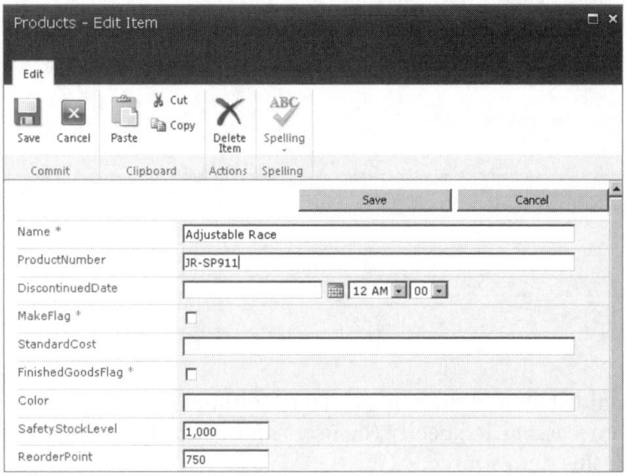

FIGURE 22-26

22. Now, not only has the field been updated in the external list, but if you were to look in SQL Server you'd find that the field has also been updated there (see Figure 22-27).

As shown in this example, BCS has many similarities to its predecessor, the BDC, but it offers significant improvements. Connections to external data sources can be quickly made with SPD 2010 and then surfaced directly in SharePoint as an external list; and content from the data sources can then be edited from the external list, and changes reflected back in the data source.

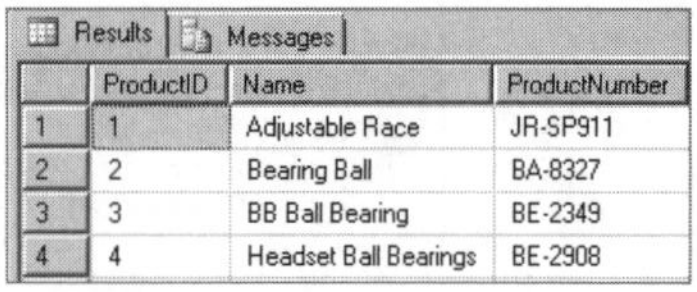

FIGURE 22-27

Views and Forms

The content stored in SharePoint is important, but equally important is being able to capture and display the information in a highly usable way. *Views* are the primary way that list and library content is displayed back to users; and *forms* make it easier and more intuitive for users to enter content into SharePoint. SPD 2010 enables users to quickly customize views and forms to meet the needs of their organization.

Views

Views are the primary way that information from lists and libraries are displayed. If you are familiar with the concept in SharePoint 2007, you'll find very little has changed in SharePoint Designer 2010, which enables you to customize the out-of-the-box views or create new ones for the lists and libraries in your site. To access the views for a list, click the Lists and Libraries link in the navigation pane and then click once to open the settings page for a list. The list of views is displayed at the right side of the center column of the summary panel. Clicking the name of a current view or pressing the New button will enable you to edit the view as an XSLT List View.

XSLT List View Web Part

With SharePoint Designer 2007, once content was added to the site, the information could be displayed on the site using views and List View Web Parts. Customization was limited to a few out-of-the-box options. To get more flexibility, many users opted for the Data View Web Part, which was created with SPD and could be styled using XSLT to provide many more custom display options. The downside to the Data View Web Part was that once it deployed, it wasn't easy to update. Basically, users had to edit the page in SPD to make changes to the Web Part. When it came to showing information on the page, users were forced to choose between the flexibility to make changes in the browser and custom design. SharePoint 2010 addresses this issue by combining the best of both options into the XSLT List View Web Part. All lists and libraries are now shown on pages as the XSLT List View Web Part, which can be both styled using SPD and edited in the browser.

Editing Views and Forms with SharePoint Designer

In this example, you are going to walk through the various options available in SPD 2010 for views and forms. You'll create a list with a few fields, customize the list form in InfoPath, edit the view to add conditional filtering, and then create a custom view.

1. Open SharePoint Designer and connect to a site.

2. From the navigation pane at the left, click Lists and Libraries to open the gallery.

3. To create a new list, click the Custom List button in the Ribbon.

4. Name the list **Championships** and click OK.

5. The new list should be added to the gallery. Click the name of the list to open its summary page.

6. From the summary page, in the Customization section which is located in the middle of the center panel, click the Edit list columns link, which will open the editor for this list.

7. There should already be a column on the list called Title. Click on the name of column and change the name to **Team Name**.

8. Click the Add New Column button in the Ribbon (see Figure 22-28) and select to add a Number column. Name the column **Number of Championships**.

9. To add the final column, click the Add New Column button in the Ribbon once again and select to add a Choice column. The Column Editor dialog window will open which allows you to customize the choices for the drop-down. For the choices, enter the following values on separate lines (see Figure 22-29):

> ➤ NFL

> ➤ MLB

> ➤ NHL

> ➤ NBA

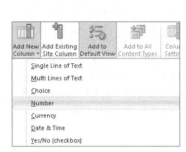

FIGURE 22-28   **FIGURE 22-29**

10.   While still in the editor for the Choice column, delete the value from the Default Value field, leaving the field empty, and click OK. You'll be returned to the screen showing the list of columns on the list. Be sure to name the new column **League**.

11.   The list is created and the fields are updated, but you'll need to save the list for the changes to be applied. Click the Save icon in the upper-left corner of the browser.

Now that the list has been created, you can view it from the web browser by going to the site. If the site is a Team Site, the link for the list should show in the left navigation. Clicking on the list name should display the list with all of the custom fields. There's nothing too fancy here; if you click to add a new item to the list, you'll see the standard form with the various fields displayed. Because this is a special list, you can customize this form using SharePoint Designer and InfoPath.

12.   From SharePoint Designer, navigate to the new Championships list summary page by clicking on the Lists and Libraries link in the navigation at the left if it isn't already open.

13.   In the Ribbon, click the button called Design Forms in InfoPath. As shown in Figure 22-30, another small window will open below the button; click Item and the form will open in InfoPath.

FIGURE 22-30

14.   After the form opens in InfoPath, give the form a title and highlight and remove the Attachments row, as you won't be using that. When you've completed your changes, click the Quick Publish button in the upper-left corner (see Figure 22-31). You should get a message that says your form was published successfully.

15.   Now when you try to create a new item you'll see the fancy new form.

FIGURE 22-31

The list is all set to go with a custom form and ready for content to be entered. Once the content has been entered, you can use views to help visualize and filter the data:

16. Click Lists and Libraries and then click the Championships list to get to the list settings page. Click the All Items view to edit it (see Figure 22-32). For this example, you'll be editing the All Items view, but in a production environment the best practice would be to create a new view, rather than modify this one.

17. The XSLT List View Web Part will open. In order to make this a little easier to work with, you can add sample data. From the Ribbon, click the Design tab under the List View Tools section and place a check in the Sample Data box, as shown in Figure 22-33. If you don't see the Design tab, you might first have to click on the XSLT List View Web Part.

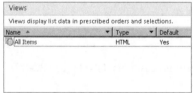

FIGURE 22-32

FIGURE 22-33

18. Because you've removed the attachments field from the entry form, you can remove the paper clip icon from the left column. First, click the icon in the header of the table and press the Delete key. Next, select the icon in the second row and press the Delete key again. This should remove all of the remaining icons.

19. To the left of the Team Name column in the XSLT List View is a column for attachments. The heading for the column is a paper clip icon and there are paper clip icons in each cell below it. Click on the paper clip icon in the heading row for table to select it and press Delete. This will remove only the one icon from the heading row. To remove the icons for each of the data rows, click on the paper clip icon in the next row and press Delete (see Figure 22-34).

20. After deleting the paper clip icons for each of the data rows, the left-most cell should still be selected. It is important that the whole cell be selected — if the whole cell is selected it will be gray; if it isn't selected it will show only the border but the center will be white. If the cell isn't selected, click on the small td tab above the cell (see Figure 22-35).

Right-click on the cell and select Conditional Formatting to add conditional formatting to this cell, then click the Conditional Formatting button in the Ribbon and choose Format Column.

FIGURE 22-34

FIGURE 22-35

20. In the Condition Criteria window, shown in Figure 22-36, specify the field name as Number of Championships Equals 0 (zero). Click the Set Style button.

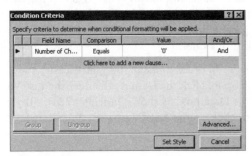

FIGURE 22-36

21. In the Modify Style window, choose the Background category (see Figure 22-37). Change the background color to red (#FF0000) and click OK.

22. Save the changes to the view by clicking the Save button in the upper-left corner.

23. If you were to add a new item to the Championships list with 0 wins, the background of the cell at the left for the item would be highlighted red, shown as shading in Figure 22-38. (This would be similar to how you could create a simple KPI for any list or library, no matter which version of SharePoint you had.)

The final step is to create a custom view that shows only the values you are interested in.

24. From the Championships list settings page, click the New button, shown in Figure 22-39, to create a new view called **NFL** and click OK.

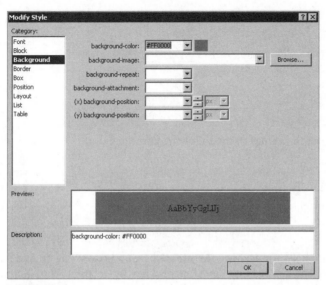

FIGURE 22-37

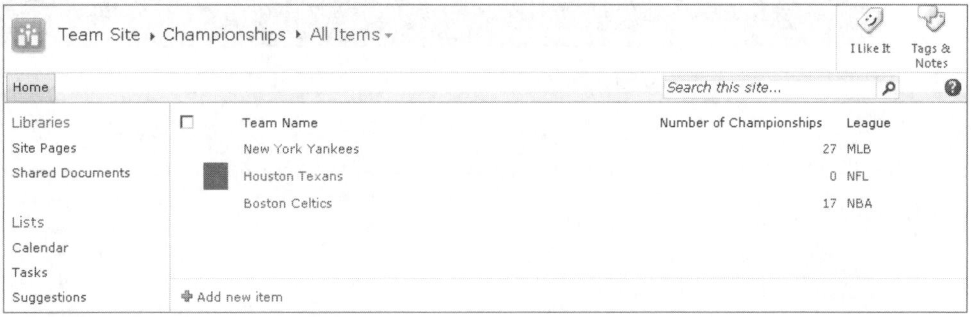

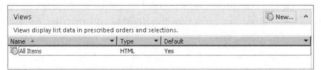

FIGURE 22-38

FIGURE 22-39

25. The new view will be created and appear in the list of views. Click the new view to edit it.

26. Press the Filter button in the Ribbon (see Figure 22-40). If you don't immediately see it, select the Options tab under List View Tools.

FIGURE 22-40

27. For the Filter Criteria, set the values to the following criteria:

➤ Field Name: League

➤ Comparison: Equals

➤ Value: NFL

28. Click OK.

29. The new has been created. To test it, open the site in the web browser again and navigate to the list. When the list opens it will show the All Items view by default. To switch to the new view, with your mouse hover over the All Items link in the bread crumb, you'll be able to switch to the NFL view, which will now show only the NFL teams (see Figure 22-41).

FIGURE 22-41

This example walked though many of the common tasks related to views and forms in an organization. SharePoint Designer 2010 makes it easy to customize the display of information with the XSLT List Web Part and integration with InfoPath forms.

Workflows

One of SharePoint's biggest selling points is the capability to use workflows to manage business processes. SharePoint Designer is the preferred tool for creating custom, rules-based declarative workflows that don't require any code. For more specific information on workflows in SharePoint 2010, see Chapter 25, which is dedicated entirely to this subject.

SharePoint Designer 2010 can create three types of workflows:

➤ **List workflow** — These workflows are directly associated with a list. This was the only type of workflow supported by SPD 2007.

➤ **Reusable workflow** — These workflows can be associated with many lists or libraries or content types, and can be reused throughout your SharePoint sites as needed.

➤ **Site workflow** — These workflows are not associated with a specific list or content type.

Another new workflow capability in SharePoint 2010 enables you to import the out-of-the-box workflow templates into SPD 2010 and modify them as necessary. However, note that modifying a workflow template from the top-level site in your site collection means that you are modifying the template used by all sites in the site collection. If you choose to use one of the out-of-the-box templates as the basis for your workflows, it is best to make the changes to workflows from a subsite. This is actually a copy of the workflow, so making changes here will not cause changes to all workflows based on that template in the site collection.

Workflow Designer

The Workflow Designer has been significantly changed to enable visualization of the entire workflow from a single screen. To open the Workflow Designer, click the Workflows link in the navigation pane and then select the option to create a new workflow from the Ribbon (any of the workflow types will work).

As mentioned previously, SPD 2010 workflows are declarative in nature. Declarative workflows are rules-based workflows, which use conditions and actions to define a process. This is very similar in concept to how rules are defined in Outlook; when an e-mail arrives it is evaluated against the first rule and then subsequent rules until a condition is found that applies to the e-mail. When your workflow requires more complexity than what is provided by the out-of-the-box workflows, declarative workflows are a valuable alternative. Because they don't require any code, they can be quickly created and deployed. Developers can even use SPD to help prototype workflows, which can then be imported into Visual Studio 2010 for further customization.

The Workflow Designer provides a visual representation of the declarative workflow, separated into the various steps, conditions, and actions. With the designer open, clicking on the Step button in the Ribbon adds a new step to which *conditions* and *actions* can be added:

➤ **Conditions** — These are the rules that are used to drive the workflow. If a condition is true, then whatever is contained within the conditional block will be processed. If a condition isn't true, then the workflow will move along to the next condition, assuming there is another one. Clicking the Condition button in the Ribbon will display the complete list of available conditions.

➤ **Actions** — These are the statements that perform a specific activity, such as sending an e-mail or modifying a field. Clicking the Actions button in the Ribbon will display the complete list of actions available for use in workflows.

Once the conditions and actions are added to the workflow, you can click the specific steps of the workflow to more specifically define what should happen in that step. For example, if you were to add an action that sends an e-mail, you'd need to click on the action itself to define the e-mail's recipient, subject, and body. You can also use variables in these workflow steps so that depending on who started the workflow and other information that's been captured, the resulting actions can vary. An example of this would be that the subject of an e-mail can be written based on the value of a field in the list that a workflow is attached to. Similarly, because another new feature in SPD 2010 makes it easy to look up a given user's manager, you could create an approval workflow that is automatically sent to an employee's manager.

Creating a Site Workflow That Writes to a Custom List

Creating standardized forms that have basic workflows is a common scenario in many companies. This example uses a site workflow to capture employee reviews submitted by employees, which their managers will then need to review and approve. To do this, you'll create a custom list, customize the fields on the form that are used to start the workflow, look up the manager of the person submitting the workflow, write it all to a list, and then assign a task to the manager.

1. Open your site in SharePoint Designer and click Lists and Libraries in the navigation pane on the left.

2. Click the Custom List button in the Ribbon to create a new list called **Employee Review** with the following fields:

    ➤ Rename Title to Employee

    ➤ Manager: Single line of text

    ➤ Rating: Single line of text

    ➤ Comments: Multiple lines of text

3. After all of the fields have been added click the save button to save the changes to the list.

4. Click the Workflows link in the navigation pane on the left.

5. Next from the Ribbon, click the Site Workflow button to create a new workflow (see Figure 22-42).

6. Name the workflow **Employee Reviews** and click OK. The Workflow Designer for the new workflow will automatically open.

7. With the Workflow Designer open, you should see a blinking horizontal orange line, which is used to indicate where the next action or condition will be inserted. But before you add any steps to your workflow, from the Ribbon, click the Initiation Form Parameters button (see Figure 22-43). This allows you to define parameters that are used to collect data when the workflow is started. In this case you want the user to fill out the form and then use the information that was entered throughout the workflow.

FIGURE 22-42

FIGURE 22-43

8. From the Association and Initiation Form Parameters dialog, click the Add button (see Figure 22-44).

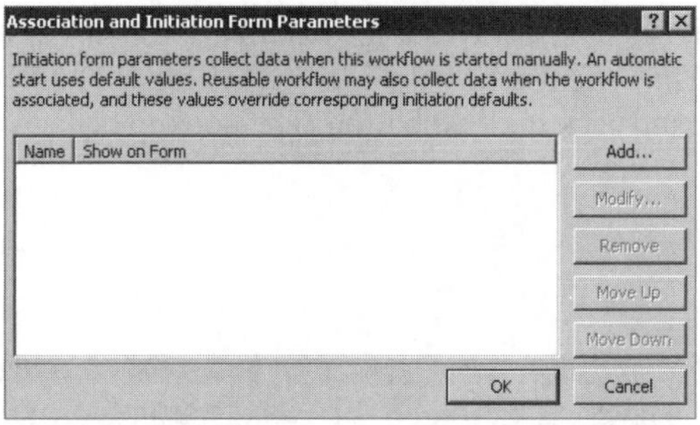

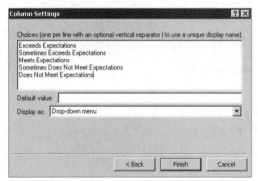

FIGURE 22-44

9. Name the field **Rating**, choose Choice as the Information type (i.e., a menu to choose from), and click Next. On the Column Settings screen, enter the values shown in Figure 22-45 and click Finish.

FIGURE 22-45

10. Press the Add button to add another field. Name this field **Comments**, set it as Multiple lines of text, and click Next and then Finish. Click the OK button from the Association and Initiation screen.

> *Workflows make use of two concepts that are sometimes confused: variables and parameters. Variables are defined during the workflow process and can be referenced throughout the workflow. In this example, the name of the initiator's manager is a variable that is later written to a field in a list. Parameters are user-entered information that's captured during the workflow. In steps 9 and 10, parameters are defined that will be filled out by the user before the workflow process begins.*

11. The Workflow Designer should open and there should be a horizontal, orange blinking cursor in a box titled Step 1. From the Ribbon, click the Action button and then click Lookup Manager of a User (see Figure 22-46). Optionally, instead of clicking the Actions button, you can start typing and SPD will try to figure out what you want it to do.

12. A description of the action will be added to step 1. Click the link that says "this user" to specify whose manager will be looked up. The Select Users dialog, shown in Figure 22-47, will open. Select Workflow Lookup for a User and click the Add button. The Lookup dialog will display.

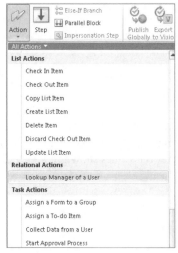

FIGURE 22-46

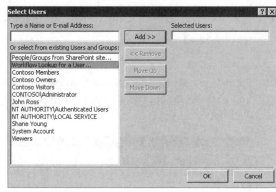

FIGURE 22-47

13. In the Lookup dialog, set the following options:

➤ Data source: Workflow Context

➤ Field from source: Initiator

➤ Return field as: Login Name

Click OK when you are done.

The capability to look up a user's manager in an SPD workflow is a new feature for this version. In this last step, the action looks at the Workflow Context to get the name of the Initiator, which has been set to return the Login Name of the user, which in turn is used to look up the name of the user's manager.

The manager lookup is performed against the user profile. In order for this capability to work properly, user profile synchronization needs to be configured and a manager needs to be specified for the user. See Chapter 25 for details on this feature.

14. Click just below the action that was just completed but still within the Step 1 box. The orange cursor should show where the next action will be added. Click the Action button again in the Ribbon and select Create List Item (see Figure 22-48).

15. In the new action, click the "this list" link. Select Employee Review. Click the Employee field and then click the Modify button to specify the values for this field. In step 9 and 10 you defined the values to be entered by the user. Because the name of the employee doing the review is the same as the person starting the workflow, you can get that automatically.

16. Click the function button (see Figure 22-49) and set the following values in the Lookup dialog:

➤ Data source: Workflow Context

➤ Field from source: Initiator

➤ Return field as: Display Name

Click OK and then click OK again.

FIGURE 22-48

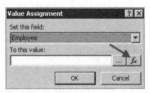

FIGURE 22-49

17. Repeat the same steps described in step 15 for the Rating field, but select the following values for the lookup:

➤ Data source: Workflow Variables and Parameters

➤ Field from source: Parameter: Rating

➤ Return field as: As String

Click OK and then OK again. You'll be returned to the Create New List Item dialog.

18. From the Create New List Item dialog window, click Add and choose the Manager field. Press the function button as described previously. Set the following values for the lookup:

➤ Data source: Workflow Variables and Parameters

➤ Field from source: Variable: Manager

➤ Return field as: Display Name

Press OK and then OK again. You'll be returned again to the Create New List Item dialog window.

19. Click Add and choose the Comments field. Click the function button and set the following values for the lookup:

➤ Data source: Workflow Variables and Parameters

➤ Field from source: Parameter: Comments

➤ Return field as: As String

Press OK and then OK again. Verify that all of the fields have been created and then from the Create New List Item dialog shown in Figure 22-50, click OK. You should find yourself back at the Workflow Designer.

20. With the Workflow Designer open, click the Action button in the Ribbon and select Assign a to-do item.

21. Click the link for "a to-do item" and the Custom Task Wizard will open. Click Next. On the second page of the wizard, enter **Employee Review** in the Name field and click Finish.

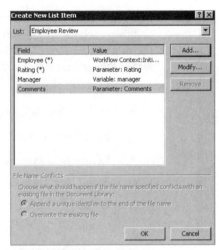

FIGURE 22-50

22. Next, from the Workflow Designer click the "these users" link in the create to-do item action that you've been editing. From the Select Users dialog, click Workflow Lookup for a User, and then click Add. The Lookup for Person or Group dialog window will open.

Set the following values for the lookup in the top section of the window:

➤ Data source: User Profiles

➤ Field from source: Manager

➤ Return field as: Login Name

23. For the fields at the bottom of the Lookup for Person or Group dialog window, for the Field value choose Account Name from the drop-down. Next press the function button to the right of the Value field. In the dialog that opens, set the fields as follows:

➤ Data source: Workflow Context

➤ Field from source: Initiator

➤ Return field as: Login Name

Similar to step 13, the name of the manager is being returned, but in this case it is for the purpose of assigning a task to the manager, which is why the Login Name is used as the return field.

24. Press OK on all the dialogs to accept the changes.

25. The workflow is now complete and should look similar to Figure 22-51. From the Ribbon, click the Save button (see Figure 22-52). Before the workflow can be used, it must first be published. To do so, click the Publish button in the Ribbon.

FIGURE 22-51

FIGURE 22-52

26. To try the site workflow, go back to your site and click Site Actions ⇨ View All Site Content. At the top of the page, click the Site Workflows link.

27. Click the Employee Reviews link (see Figure 22-53), which will open the page where you can fill out the form to start the workflow. Fill out the form and press Start. To make this form easier to access, you can copy the form's URL and create a link directly to the form.

FIGURE 22-53

28. If you go back to the Employee Review list, you'll see that a new item has been created, the manager has been successfully looked up, and the information entered into the form has been added (see Figure 22-54). A task should have also been created for the manager, which you can see by clicking Site Actions ⇨ View All Site Content then clicking on the Site Workflows link.

FIGURE 22-54

This example showed how you can create a workflow that captures information into a form, looks up the manager of the person who started the workflow, writes the information to a list, and then assigns a task to the manager. Although this was a very basic workflow example, these concepts can be expanded and repeated to create much more robust and complex workflows that don't require any custom code.

Branding

As mentioned at the beginning of this chapter, most people associate SharePoint Designer with designing websites. When the product was introduced with SPD 2007, it was obvious by looking at the interface that the tool was intended for editing HTML pages. Although the focus on SPD 2010 seems to be more on managing SharePoint sites, SPD 2010 is still the primary tool for customizing the look and feel of your SharePoint site to reflect your corporate brand. The common term used for this task is *branding*.

Branding is covered in more detail in Chapter 23, but in terms of SharePoint, it refers to the objects that work together to create the look and feel for the site. This includes the master pages, page layouts, CSS, HTML, fonts, and so on. The following three elements are particularly relevant to SharePoint:

➤ **Master page** — Registers all of the SharePoint controls on the page and then arranges them via HTML, CSS, and content placeholders. It is a primary factor in influencing the look and feel of a site or page. Every page that is rendered in SharePoint requires a master page.

➤ **Page layout** — Basically a template for content. Using field controls, users enter content that is then rendered as a web page based on the design of the page layout itself. It can be thought of as a more heavily styled version of entering content into a list. Page layouts are available only with sites where Publishing has been enabled.

➤ **Cascading style sheets (CSS)** — Used heavily throughout SharePoint to determine the overall look and feel. Branding a SharePoint site usually requires creating custom CSS.

Regardless of your skill level with branding, SPD is often the first place to begin when trying to change the look and feel of your SharePoint site.

Hiding the All Site Content and the Recycle Bin in Your Master Page

Editing master pages is covered in more detail in Chapter 23, but SharePoint Designer offers some new functionality that makes the branding process even easier. The following example walks through the process of performing one of the more common branding requests: hiding the All Site Content and Recycle Bin links from the left navigation. This example makes changes to a Team Site, so if your site uses a different template the steps may vary slightly.

1. Open your site in SPD and click the Master Pages link in the navigation pane.

2. Click v4.master to bring up the settings page for the file. For this example, you'll be making changes directly to this master page, but in a production environment it is recommended that you first copy any system files before making any changes.

3. Click the link to Edit file from from under the Customization section of the summary page. If you are using a publishing site you might be prompted to check out the file before proceeding.

4. Click the Skewer Click link in the Ribbon (see Figure 22-55). Skewer Click is a new functionality in SPD 2010 that enables you to see the various CSS that is responsible for rendering an element.

5. With Skewer Click selected, hover over the area near where the Recycle Bin and All Site Content links are located. Move your mouse around the area and you should see the name PlaceHolderQuickLaunchBottom faintly appear above the link for the Recycle bin. Click on it to select it, which will open another window displaying a list of styles and then select the style called ul.s4-specialNav... (see Figure 22-56).

FIGURE 22-55

FIGURE 22-56

6. To edit the style you first need to add a new panel. From the Ribbon, click the Style tab and select the CSS Properties button (see Figure 22-57).

7. When the new panel opens, you'll see the top section is called Applied Rules. The style you need (.s4-specialNavLinkList) should be already selected. It may be tough to read the entire name of the style so it might be easier to make the right panel a little wider. Right-click on the style and select New Style Copy (see Figure 22-58).

FIGURE 22-57

FIGURE 22-58

8. At the top of the New Style dialog, shown in Figure 22-59, set the new style to be defined in the Current page. Be sure to check the box Apply new style to document selection, and then select Layout category and set the visibility to hidden. Click OK.

9. Save the changes made to the master page. When you view the site now, the links for All Site Content and the Recycle Bin will be hidden. You might get a warning after you save the file that says "Saving your changes will customize this page so that it is no longer based on the site definition." Click Yes to continue. When you browse back to your site, the All Site Content and Recycle bin links are now hidden (see Figure 22-60).

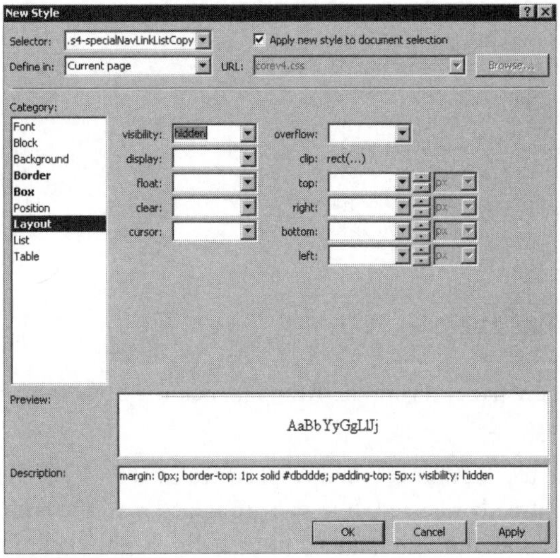

FIGURE 22-59

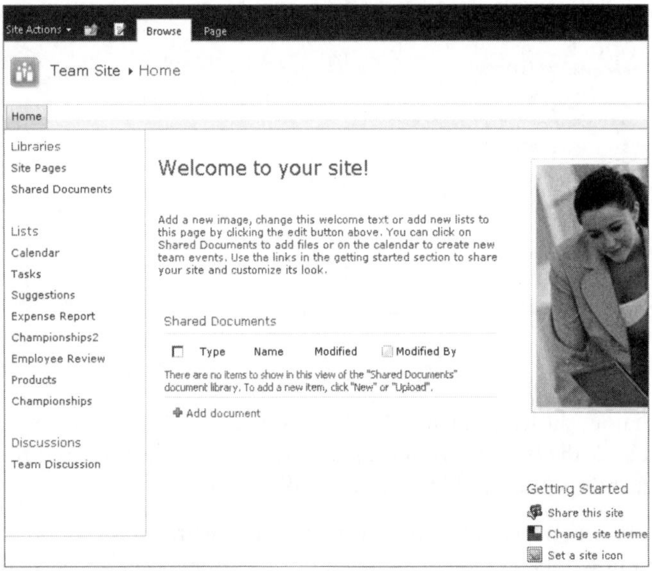

FIGURE 22-60

In this example you used the New Style Copy feature, which is new to SharePoint Designer 2010. This feature makes it quick and easy to safely update CSS for your site. Selecting New Style Copy makes a copy of the style you want to edit and then defines it where you specify — in this case, it made the changes inline at the top of the master page. If you look at the Design view of the master page, you'll see the following code has been added:

```
        <style type="text/css">
    .s4-specialNavLinkListCopy
```

```
{
        margin: 0px;
/* [ReplaceColor(themeColor:"Light2-Lightest")] */      border-top: 1px solid
#dbddde;
        padding-top: 5px;
        visibility: hidden;
}
</style>
```

Notice that the style was copied and appended with "Copy." Simply selecting New Style Copy creates this reference, but it is necessary to check the Apply new style to document selection option, which changes the reference of the style you want to change to the copied style. Without checking the box, you'd need to make manual changes in order to get the style to apply your changes properly.

Instead of applying the styles inline, you can also choose to apply the changes to a separate CSS file. The result is the same, but instead of the code being inline, the custom CSS file would be automatically referenced. If you are making several changes to CSS, it is recommended that you use the option to reference a separate CSS file in order to keep the master page code cleaner.

SUMMARY

This chapter discussed the many capabilities of SharePoint Designer 2010. Users who are familiar with the previous version should appreciate the improvements made to this latest version, which include the following highlights:

➤   The user interface for SharePoint Designer 2010 has been redesigned to put more focus on the various SharePoint objects and less focus on being a page editor.

➤   SPD 2010 has been divided into three areas: Navigation, Ribbon, and Gallery and Summary.

➤   Access to SPD can be controlled by farm administrators from Central Administration or by site collection administrators from the site settings page.

➤   To prevent users from getting into trouble, you can restrict SPD by customizing specific pages or more broadly by removing the permission to use SPD altogether.

➤   Connections to LOB systems such as external databases can now be made directly from SPD using the BCS. Information from these external systems can be surfaced in SharePoint as an external list, where users can interact with it just as if it were a regular SharePoint list. Changes made to the external list are reflected in the LOB system.

➤   SPD 2010 enables users to quickly customize views using the XSLT List View Web Part.

➤   List forms can be customized in InfoPath directly from SPD.

➤   Declarative workflows can be created with SPD, which enables users to create no-code solutions to streamline business processes.

➤   There are three types of SPD workflows: List, Reusable, and Site.

➤   SPD is the primary tool for customizing the look and feel of your SharePoint site.

23

Branding SharePoint 2010

WHAT'S IN THIS CHAPTER?

➤ Understanding branding in SharePoint

➤ Themes

➤ Master pages

➤ Page layouts

➤ Cascading style sheets

➤ Controlling access to branding in SharePoint

When you think of administering SharePoint, branding and user interface design is usually not the first thing that comes to mind. While most farm administrators are not very interested in tweaking colors and fonts, you need to understand how the process works behind the scenes. This is especially important with SharePoint because unlike many traditional web development projects, SharePoint projects require a high level of interaction between IT professionals, administrators, designers, and developers. As designers and developers create user interfaces, administrators need to ensure that those design assets live and play well with everything else that is part of a SharePoint farm.

WHAT IS BRANDING?

Branding is the act of creating a specific image or identity that people will recognize in relation to a company. When you think of Coca-Cola, you probably first think of their distinctive red and white logo; and when you think of United Parcel Service (UPS), the first image that comes to mind is either their brown trucks or uniforms. When you see these colors, you are immediately reminded of the products or services for which each of these companies is known. One reason is probably because of all the advertising that bombards you on a daily basis; but it's also because both of these companies have a strong branding strategy, one that permeates all of their products and advertising, including their websites.

For websites, branding usually refers to the colors, font, and images that are seen on the page, as well as the HTML, CSS, and images that together make that page render properly. Branding for SharePoint websites includes all of this, but it also refers to technologies such as master pages, page layouts, and Web Parts.

This concept has been traditionally known as *design*, or more specifically *user interface design*. The term "branding" is used frequently with SharePoint projects because the word "design" often means different things to people in other technology roles. In enterprise software projects, "design" often refers specifically to the act of planning and architecting a software application. To alleviate this confusion, the term "branding" has become quite popular in recent years to refer to the act of creating an effective user interface design.

UNDERSTANDING YOUR REQUIREMENTS

Because SharePoint is a big product that can be used to solve a lot of IT problems, it's a good idea to spend some time up front thinking about your specific project requirements. This process typically involves asking a lot of questions in order to break down the large goal of having a successful SharePoint site into smaller requirements that can be measured and achieved. The act of branding a SharePoint site is no different; there are a few specific high-level decisions that need to be made before starting, such as which edition of SharePoint will be required to achieve the project goals or what the intended audience expects to see or not see on the page. The following sections will discuss a few high level considerations that should be made based on your project's requirements.

SHAREPOINT VERSIONS AND PUBLISHING

As discussed in Chapter 3, SharePoint 2010 is available in several different versions. SharePoint Foundation 2010 is the new version of the free Windows SharePoint Services version 3 (WSSv3), and SharePoint Server 2010 is the new version of Microsoft Office SharePoint Server 2007 (MOSS). While it's tempting to say that any project can be achieved using just SharePoint Foundation 2010, the Server version of SharePoint includes the Publishing feature, which is particularly useful for branding projects. Here are a few reasons why publishing is useful for branding, including areas where publishing is superior to standard non-publishing SharePoint features:

➤   Publishing enables designers to create templates for page content that are known as *page layouts*. Non-publishing wiki sites have a different form of page template with several pre-wired page content arrangements, known as *text layouts*. Unlike page layouts, text layouts are not editable by content authors or designers.

➤   Publishing contains navigation providers that are more flexible, and can be managed more easily from the SharePoint web user interface.

➤ Publishing enables site administrators to change a master page for their site and all subsites easily from the SharePoint web user interface.

➤ Publishing enables more flexibility with themes, including the capability to apply the theme to all subsites at the same time.

For these reasons, it is often a good idea to plan for SharePoint Server 2010 publishing when high levels of branding customization are required.

 For SharePoint websites with a significant amount of branding customization, it's a good idea to create the top-level site collection as a publishing site. This is often true even if the intent is to have many Team subsites. Having publishing enabled at the top level of a site collection enables easy manipulation of master pages and themes throughout all the subsites.

Creating a Publishing Site Collection

This example assumes that you have already created a web application that can be used for the new site collection. If you have not created a web application, or would like to create a new one, see Chapter 4.

1. Open Central Administration on the SharePoint server.

2. Under Application Management, click Create site collections.

3. Note the Web Application selector in the upper-right corner of the screen. Be sure to select the correct web application; this is where the new site collection will be created (see Figure 23-1).

4. Provide the Title, Description, and Web Site Address (the URL of the site collection).

5. For Template Selection, click the Publishing tab and then select Publishing Portal. Figure 23-2 shows the Publishing tab. Note that Enterprise Wiki is also a viable option because it too has the Publishing Feature enabled.

6. Enter the name of a Primary Site Collection Administrator and a Secondary one if desired, and select a Quota Template, which limits the amount of resources allowed on the site collection.

7. Click OK. After a few seconds the new site collection will be created and you are presented with a link to open it in a new browser window.

Figure 23-3 shows the newly created Publishing Portal site collection.

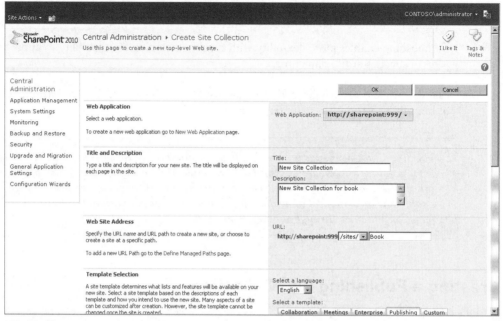

FIGURE 23-1

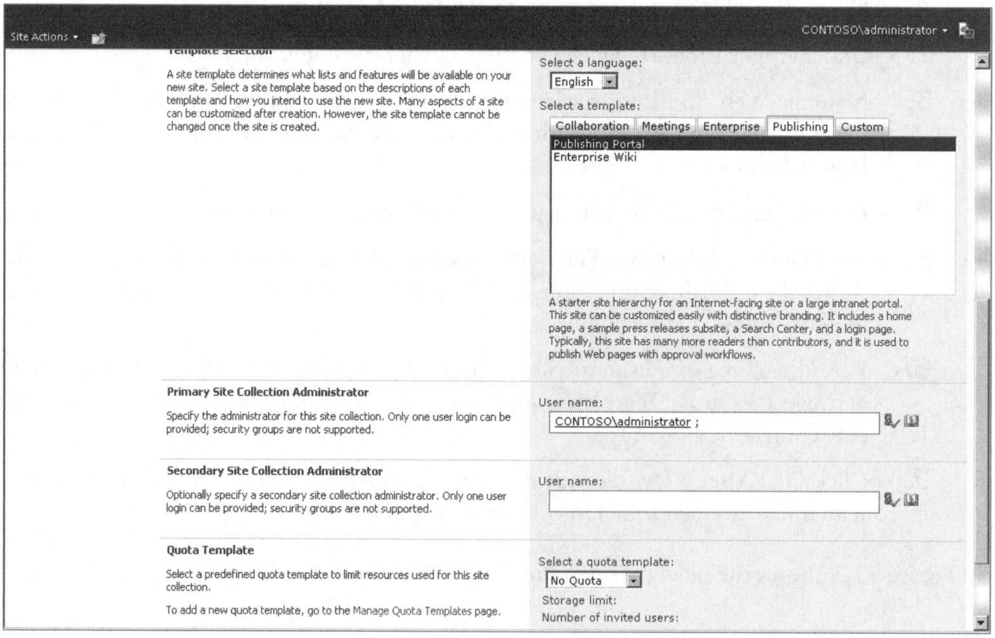

FIGURE 23-2

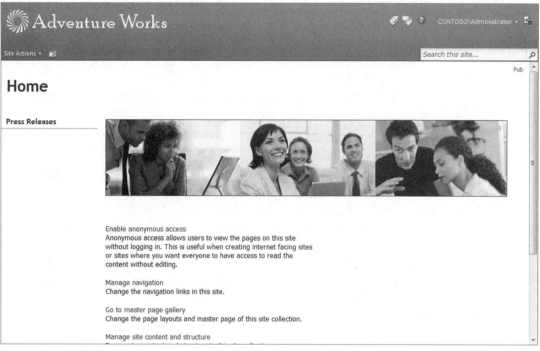

FIGURE 23-3

Activating Publishing on a Team Site Collection

If you would prefer not to start with one of the publishing templates such as Publishing Portal or Enterprise Wiki, you can still take full advantage of the Publishing Feature in SharePoint Server 2010 by activating it on other types of site collections. The following steps will walk you through the process of activating publishing on a Team Site collection:

1. Click Site Actions ⇨ Site Settings, and under Site Collection Administration click Site collection features.

2. Scroll down to SharePoint Server Publishing Infrastructure and click the Activate button (see Figure 23-4). This enables the infrastructure for the Publishing feature but it does not activate publishing for the site itself.

3. Click Site Actions ⇨ Site Settings. Under Site Actions, click Manage site features.

4. Scroll down to SharePoint Server Publishing and click the Activate button, as shown in Figure 23-5. This enables publishing on the site and creates the Pages library that will contain new web pages.

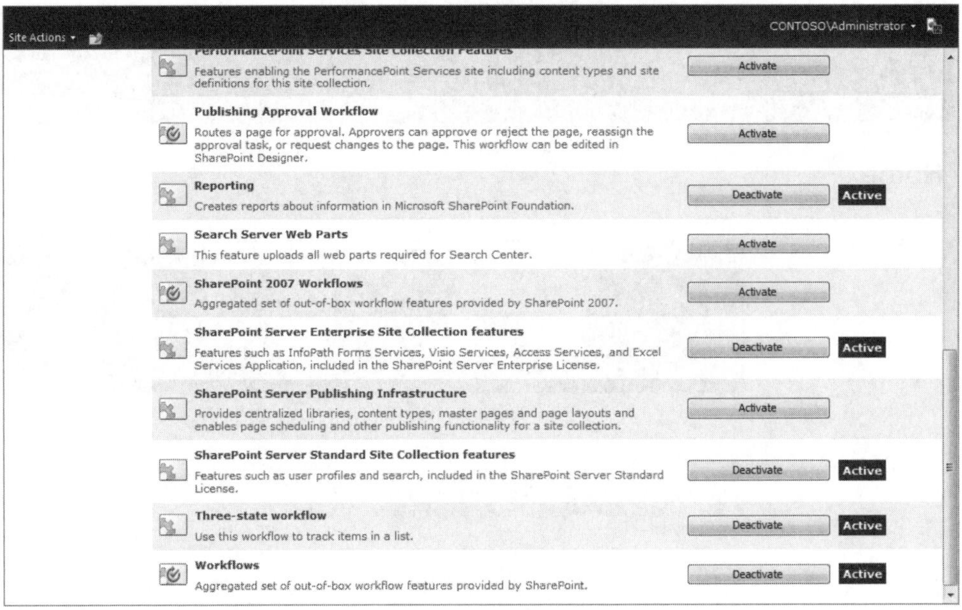

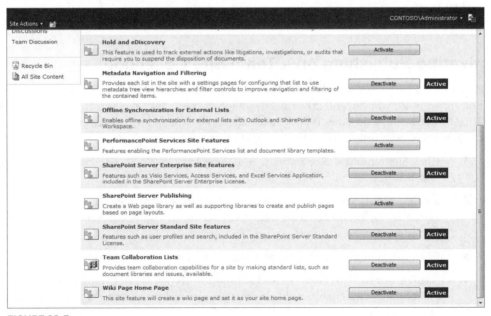

FIGURE 23-4

FIGURE 23-5

With these two features activated, publishing is enabled. New pages can be created in the Pages library with page layouts attached, and the master page selection menu becomes available from the Site Settings menu. The home page of the site collection will still be based on the Team Site template, though. Because the site collection will be using publishing from now on, you may want the home page to be based on a publishing page as well. The following steps walk you through changing the home page.

Changing the Welcome Page on a Site Collection

The following steps will create a new publishing home page and enable it as the welcome page:

1. Navigate to the Pages directory, which will be located at `http://YOURSERVER/Pages/`. You can also get there by clicking Site Actions ➪ View All Site Content and clicking Pages.

2. Click Site Actions ➪ New page, give the page a name like "Home Page," and click Create (see Figure 23-6).

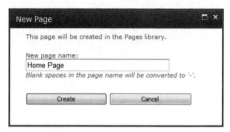

FIGURE 23-6

3. Enter some page content like "Welcome Home." If you want, you can switch the page layout by clicking the Page tab in the Ribbon and selecting Page Layout.

4. When you like the way the page looks, click Save & Close from the Ribbon (see Figure 23-7).

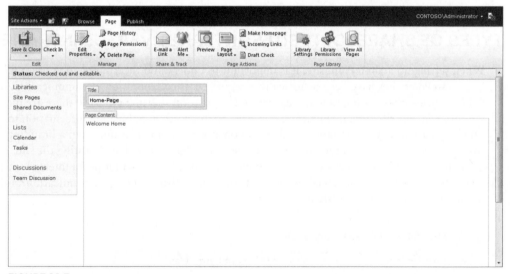

FIGURE 23-7

5. To make this page the starting page, click Site Actions ➪ Site Settings, and under Look and Feel, click Welcome Page.

6. Browse and select your new home page, which should be in the Pages library. The relative URL should be `/Pages/Home-Page.aspx`. Figure 23-8 shows the Site Welcome Page window.

FIGURE 23-8

7. Click OK. Now when you browse to the root of your site, it should open your new publishing home page.

TYPES OF SHAREPOINT SITES: INTERNET VERSUS INTRANET

When setting up a SharePoint site, it is important to understand the kind of content it will be hosting. SharePoint sites have been historically categorized as collaboration, communication, or both. *Collaboration sites* are focused on facilitating information sharing; typically there are many content authors and contributors. *Communication sites* are focused on publishing information to users and typically have few content authors and many consumers of information. From a branding perspective, however, it's important to also consider the general audience that is visiting the site. Is the site going to be a public Internet site where communication is key, or will it be an internal intranet site where the focus is typically collaboration but sometimes also includes communication? Table 23-1 highlights some of the key differences between the two.

TABLE 23-1   Internet versus Intranet Sites

INTERNET SITES	INTRANET SITES
Public facing	Internal facing.
Marketing driven	Information and collaboration driven.
Mostly anonymous users	Typically all users authenticate.
Few authors, many viewers	Many authors, collaborators, and viewers.
Tightly controlled content	Freely created content.
Many different types of browsers	Browsers can be controlled by administrators.

Because Internet sites are public facing, they often feature heavily customized branding. Two great examples of branded Internet sites that were built with SharePoint are SharePoint911.com (see Figure 23-9) and Kroger.com (see Figure 23-10).

 You can find many excellent examples of public-facing SharePoint sites at `http://www.wssdemo.com/Pages/websites.aspx.`

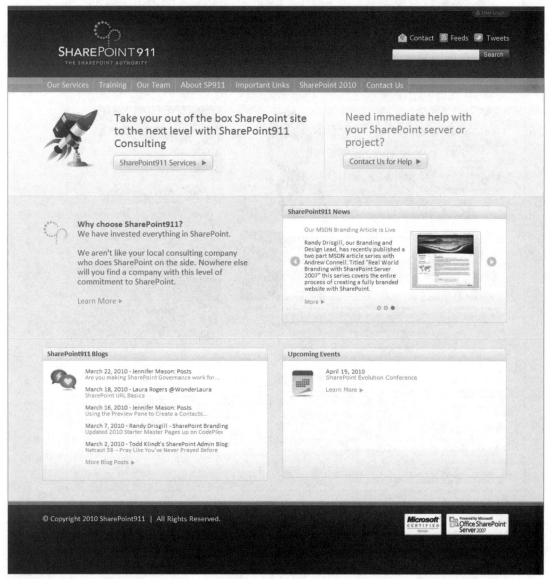

FIGURE 23-9

FIGURE 23-10

Intranet sites typically feature less branding than Internet sites; often the focus is on getting work done rather than marketing something. The out-of-the-box default SharePoint 2010 Team Site layout is often a good starting point for SharePoint intranet site designs. Figure 23-11 shows the default layout for Team Sites.

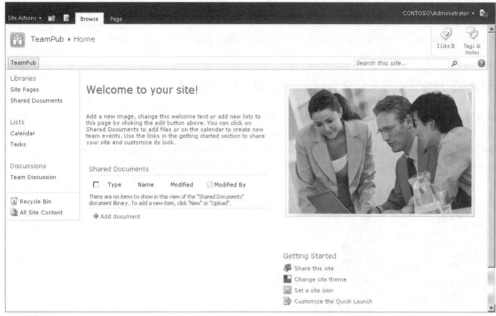

FIGURE 23-11

This doesn't mean that all corporate intranets need to be identical. Often, companies want to have their branding apply to their intranet sites even if it's just a hint of their corporate style. Figure 23-12 shows a sample branded SharePoint 2010 intranet site.

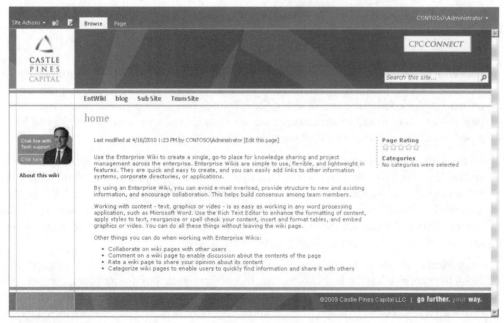

FIGURE 23-12

Because Internet sites and intranet sites focus on such different goals, administrators need to consider these differences when configuring SharePoint. For example, intranet sites often need more site collection owners and more intricate security groups than public Internet sites.

BRANDING BASICS FOR SHAREPOINT 2010

Depending on your skill level with traditional web development, ASP.NET, and SharePoint, it can be intimidating to consider all of the options for creating a branded SharePoint site. In fact, there are three major approaches to creating branding in SharePoint 2010, ranging from very simple (low effort) to complex (high effort). Figure 23-13 shows the three approaches.

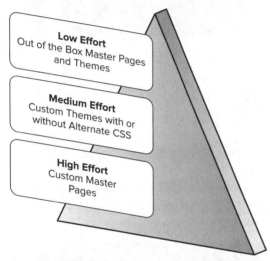

FIGURE 23-13

➤ **Low effort** — This approach uses the out-of-the-box SharePoint master pages and themes to create a simple branded SharePoint site. Without doing anything custom, you can create many color combinations and styles. SharePoint Server 2010 provides two master pages — v4.master and nightandday.master — to choose from, both of which can be styled using any of the 20 out-of-the-box SharePoint 2010 themes.

➤ **Medium effort** — This approach combines the out-of-the-box master pages with custom themes and/or Alternate CSS, which is covered later in the section "Applying CSS to SharePoint." You will see in the next section that themes are much easier to create in SharePoint 2010 than they were in SharePoint 2007. Themes can be used with the out-of-the-box master pages to add corporate colors and fonts, but the medium effort approach can be taken even further by adding custom background images through the use of Alternate CSS.

➤ **High effort** — To create Internet and intranet sites that have a high level of customization, the high-effort approach is the best choice. It includes creating custom master pages, custom CSS, and even potentially some custom page layouts. This approach is good if you have prior experience with traditional web design or some knowledge of how master pages work in ASP.NET.

To understand how branding works in SharePoint 2010, it's important to talk about the major technologies that are involved. These include themes, master pages, page layouts, and cascading style sheets (CSS), so we turn to those topics now.

Themes

In many ways, SharePoint themes are the first and easiest option for creating light branding for a SharePoint site. They enable site owners and designers to apply a set of 12 colors and 2 fonts throughout any of the out-of-the-box branding and even custom branding. If you are used to how themes worked in SharePoint 2007, you may be in for a shock with SharePoint 2010, as Microsoft has completely revamped the way themes are created and how they work in SharePoint.

In SharePoint 2007, creating a theme involved creating a lot of CSS and images, placing them on the file system in the 12 folder, editing both an .INF file and an XML file, and then, for icing on the cake, you also had to run IISRESET and select and apply the theme on every site. This process was difficult for both those creating the themes and those who had to administer and maintain them. Behind the scenes, when a page was loaded, both the SharePoint core CSS file and the theme CSS file would be loaded by the browser, with the theme's CSS usually showing on the page because it was loaded last.

That entire process has changed for SharePoint 2010; now themes can be created in the Microsoft Office client software (either Word 2007/2010 or PowerPoint 2007/2010). This creates a .THMX file, which describes the 12 theme colors and 2 fonts available in the new SharePoint themes. These .THMX files can be uploaded into SharePoint and applied to any site. Unlike in SharePoint 2007, the new themes do not apply CSS after the core CSS; instead, SharePoint actually looks for a special type of CSS comment and injects the new CSS into the core CSS so that only one file has to be loaded by the web browser. If you were to look at coreV4.css, you would see many comments like the following throughout:

```
/* [ReplaceColor(themeColor:"Accent1")] */
color: red;
```

When a theme is applied, SharePoint will look for these comments and apply the Accent 1 color to whatever CSS rule is directly below it.

Unlike SharePoint 2007 themes, the new themes in SharePoint 2010 do not have the capability to define custom background images. If you have a SharePoint 2007 theme that uses a lot of custom background images, probably the best way to move forward to SharePoint 2010 is to either convert that theme into a custom master page or perhaps use the Alternate CSS feature in SharePoint Server 2010.

Although you cannot define a custom background image in SharePoint 2010 themes, a feature unique to SharePoint 2010 enables you to tint or color existing images with the theme comments. To put it another way, any background images that are being defined in the SharePoint core CSS or custom CSS, whether they are applied with a master page or Alternate CSS, can be colored on the fly by themes. Here is a sample of what the CSS comment would look like:

```
/* [RecolorImage(themeColor:"Accent2",method:"Tinting")]*/
background:transparent url("Header.png") no-repeat scroll top left;
```

When SharePoint sees this comment it will create a version of the `Header.png` image that is tinted in the same color as Accent 2.

From an administrative standpoint, note that when applying themes to custom branding, the custom CSS and image files should be located in one of several `Themable` directories:

➤ On the server file system in 14 folder:

`14\TEMPLATE\LAYOUTS\1033\STYLES\Themable`

➤ In the site collection's Style Library directly under the root:

`/Style Library/Themable/`

➤ In the site collection's Style Library directly under any language code folder:

`/Style Library/en-us/Themable/`

By placing your CSS files in these locations or any subdirectories created below them, SharePoint will look for any valid CSS comments and apply the colors and fonts. Anywhere else will be ignored and the theme colors will not be applied.

Using Microsoft Office Themes in SharePoint 2010

Here are the steps for creating and using a Microsoft Office theme in SharePoint 2010 using PowerPoint 2010:

1. Open PowerPoint (2010) and either create a new PowerPoint file or use an existing PowerPoint presentation.

2. On the Ribbon, switch to the Design tab and click Colors, and then select Create New Theme Colors (see Figure 23-14).

Notice that there are two dark and two light Text/Background colors, six Accent colors, and two Hyperlink colors. One thing to consider here is that the Accent 1 through 6 colors correspond well to the bullet indention levels in PowerPoint, but they are more subjective in SharePoint. Some experimentation is typically needed before getting the right combination. One good strategy is to pick colors that are similar or complementary. Figure 23-15 shows the menu for creating new theme colors (this figure loses some impact in a black-and-white book).

3. After selecting a color scheme, click Save.

4. Back on the Ribbon, click Fonts ➪ Create New Theme Fonts (see Figure 23-16).

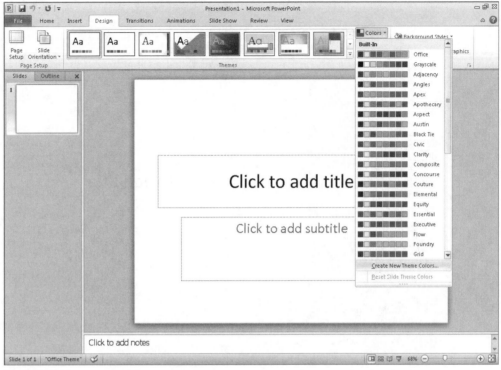

FIGURE 23-14

FIGURE 23-15

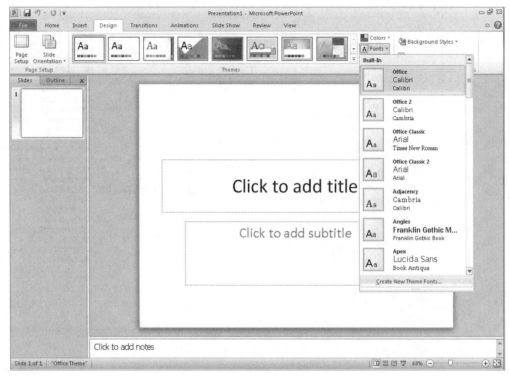

FIGURE 23-16

Notice that there are options to set both the Heading and Body font and that the selection includes many of the fonts installed on the client computer. Because these fonts will be used in SharePoint and loaded from an Internet browser, be sure to pick fonts that are common across multiple operating systems. Figure 23-17 shows the dialog for creating new theme fonts.

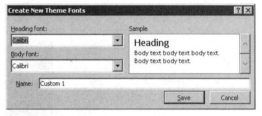

FIGURE 23-17

5. After selecting the two fonts, click Save.

6. Up until now, your selections were being saved in the local PowerPoint file. To export the theme for use in SharePoint, click the small "more" button (the downward-pointing arrow) on the right side of the Themes section of the Design tab in the Ribbon (see Figure 23-18).

FIGURE 23-18

7. At the bottom of the All Themes dialog, shown in Figure 23-19, click Save Current Theme, select a location, name it `demo.thmx`, and click Save. This saves the .THMX file so that it can be used in SharePoint.

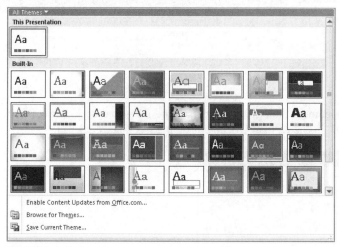

FIGURE 23-19

8. Open a SharePoint 2010 site in a browser, login, and click Site Actions ➪ Site Settings ➪ Galleries ➪ Themes. This will load the document library view of the available themes, as shown in Figure 23-20.

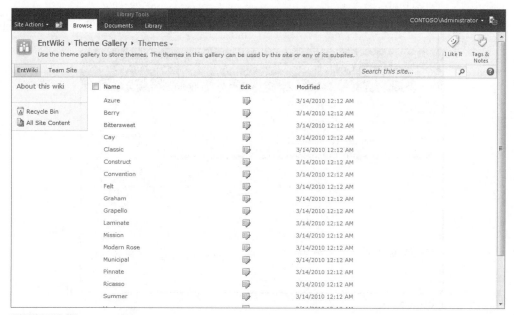

FIGURE 23-20

9. To add the new theme, from the Ribbon select Documents ⇨ Upload Document (see Figure 23-21).

FIGURE 23-21

10. From the Upload Document dialog, click Browse, find the saved demo.thmx file, and click Open. Then click OK in the Upload Document dialog (see Figure 23-22).

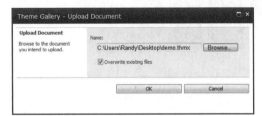

FIGURE 23-22

11. When the save dialog opens, you can change the filename here or just save the selection by clicking Save (see Figure 23-23). Now the new theme is ready to be selected for use in SharePoint.

12. To select the theme, click Site Actions ⇨ Site Settings ⇨ Look and Feel ⇨ Site Theme.

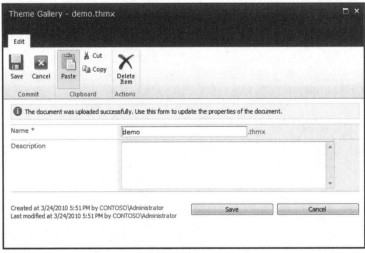

FIGURE 23-23

13. From the Select a Theme dialog, select your new theme from the list. If you have SharePoint Server, you can preview the theme by clicking Preview or you can apply it to the site immediately by clicking the Apply button. Figure 23-24 shows the Select a Theme options.

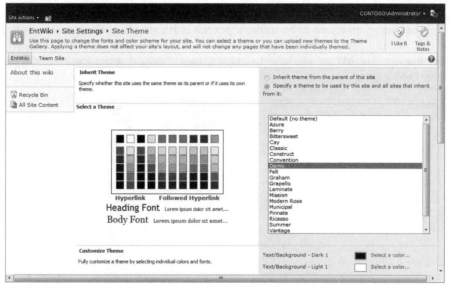

FIGURE 23-24

Figure 23-25 shows the SharePoint site with the theme applied. Of course, because this book is in black and white, you'll have to try it yourself if you want to see the results.

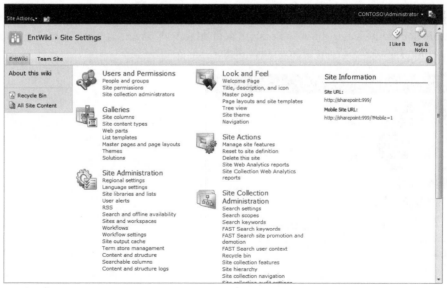

FIGURE 23-25

Adjusting a Theme with SharePoint Server 2010

SharePoint Server 2010 has unique functionality that enables site owners and designers to adjust the theme color and fonts directly in the web user interface. SharePoint Foundation users are limited to editing SharePoint themes using the Office client software.

To change the theme attributes in SharePoint Server 2010, simply click Site Actions ⇨ Site Settings ⇨ Look and Feel ⇨ Site Theme. From there, the Customize Theme section will display all of the same options that are available from the Office client software. Figure 23-26 shows the Customize Theme options.

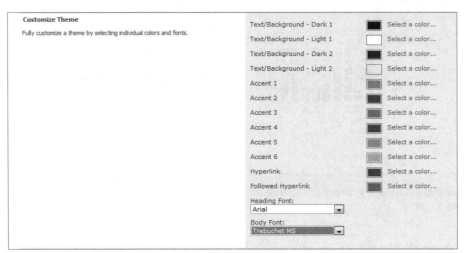

FIGURE 23-26

The color picker is a very useful addition to this dialog. Site owners and designers do not have to rely on previous knowledge of how colors are defined in web pages. To see a color in action, click Select a color. Figure 23-27 shows the color picker.

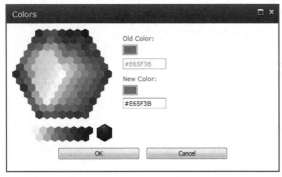

FIGURE 23-27

Along with the colors, two font options can be changed from the Customize Theme dialog. Note that all of the fonts installed on the server are available for selection. This can be particularly troublesome because site owners can select inappropriate fonts such as Wingdings.

One last design option that is available in SharePoint Server 2010 publishing sites is the capability to apply the theme to the current site and reset all of the subsites below it to the same theme. There was no equivalent option in SharePoint 2007 themes, and it can be quite useful for projects with many subsites. Once all of the changes are made, clicking Apply will refresh the site with the new colors and fonts that were selected.

The great thing about how themes work in SharePoint 2010 is that they are self service. From an administrative standpoint, your users should be able to create their own color-schemed sites without needing to ask you to mess with XML files or put files in the SharePoint root folder.

Master Pages

If you think back to the olden days of web development, every page on a website contained all of the HTML and design elements that made up what was seen. If a change had to be made to the general look and feel, every single page had to be edited individually. This led to websites that were difficult to maintain, and often resulted in pages being skipped or errors being introduced. ASP.NET 2.0 fixed this problem by providing a separate *master page* that controls the many aspects of the layout of each page from one central location. Because SharePoint is built on top of ASP.NET, master pages in SharePoint work very similarly to those in traditional ASP.NET sites.

Master pages can be thought of as the glue that holds together, and arranges and styles, all of the SharePoint functionality that is seen when a page is loaded in the browser. Pretty much every page in SharePoint requires an associated master page. When a page is loaded in the browser, SharePoint sees the reference to a master page and combines the page content with the master page to create one seamless page that is displayed to the user. Figure 23-28 shows the relationship between master pages and page content.

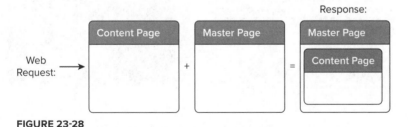

FIGURE 23-28

Unlike themes, custom master pages enable you to change almost all aspects of how SharePoint looks. From a branding point of view, master pages can be thought of as the outer design or "chrome" of a website. Master pages in SharePoint consist of HTML for layout, CSS for styles, SharePoint controls, and content placeholders. Content placeholders can be thought of as a type of container that loads matching pieces of content from the referring page.

Out of the box, SharePoint 2010 includes a few master pages that can be used for branding without any extra effort:

➤ **Default.master** — Only used when a SharePoint 2007 site is being upgraded to 2010. It is virtually identical to the default master page in SharePoint 2007. Note that this master page can only be used when SharePoint 2010 is in SharePoint 2007 mode via Visual Upgrade.

➤ **Minimal.master** — Only used on pages that have their own navigation or need extra space, such as dedicated application pages or the search center. Unlike the concept of minimal master pages in SharePoint 2007, this master page is not intended for use as the starting point for branding, as it is missing several common SharePoint controls.

➤ **V4.master** — The default master page used for much of SharePoint 2010 (refer to Figure 23-11). In many ways, it is similar to the default master page in SharePoint 2007, but the look and feel has been refreshed with new design and cleaner markup.

➤ **NightandDay.master** — This master page, shown in Figure 23-29, is accessible only in a SharePoint Server 2010 site that has the Publishing Feature enabled. It is similar to the Blueband master page in SharePoint 2007, but with an updated look and feel. It is intended for use as a simple Internet or intranet publishing site.

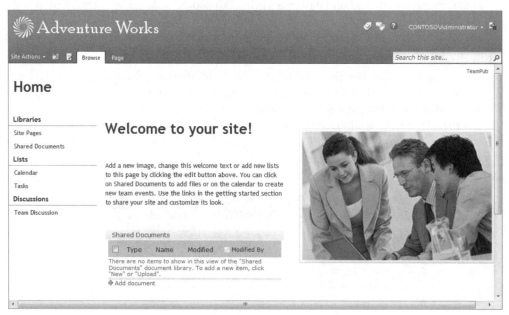

FIGURE 23-29

You can see a list of all available master pages in a SharePoint site by loading the Master Page Gallery. Open your SharePoint site and click Site Actions ➪ Site Settings ➪ Galleries ➪ Master pages and page layouts. Figure 23-30 shows the Master Page Gallery.

This page shows both master pages and page layouts, which are discussed in the next section. Anything with an extension of .master is typically a master page.

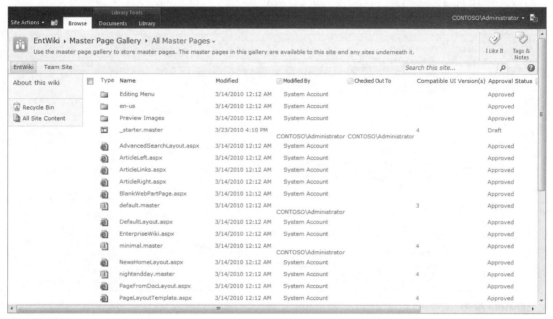

FIGURE 23-30

Applying Master Pages to Application Pages

One major limitation to custom master pages in SharePoint 2007 has been alleviated in SharePoint 2010. In SharePoint 2007, master pages did not apply any formatting or styling to application pages, which included the Site Settings and several other key locations, all of which can be identified with "_layouts" in the URL. These pages did not receive the custom master page because they were hard-wired to always use something known as Application.master, which was shared across all sites on the farm. As a result, heavily branded sites often had a few rogue pages sticking out like sore thumbs, showing the default yellow and blue look and feel. In SharePoint 2010, custom master pages can apply to almost all pages on a SharePoint site, including the Application pages. Note that there are some cases where a custom master page wouldn't apply by default, for example the error pages use a specific simple master page to ensure that they remain consistent no matter what has happened.

To apply a master page to the Application pages, be sure to set the System master page to the custom master page. In SharePoint Server you can find this setting at Site Actions ➪ Site Settings ➪ Look and Feel ➪ Master page.

Figure 23-31 shows the Master Page Setting menu.

FIGURE 23-31

Making Application Pages Behave Like They Did in SharePoint 2007

If you decide that you don't want this new master page feature on your SharePoint site, you can turn it off from Central Administration:

1. Open Central Administration on the SharePoint server.

2. Under Application Management, click Manage web applications.

3. Select the desired web application from the list and then, from the Ribbon, click General Settings (see Figure 23-32).

4. In the dialog that appears, scroll down to Master Page Setting for Application _Layouts Pages and select No (see Figure 23-33).

5. Scroll to the bottom of the dialog and click OK.

Now custom master pages for this entire web application will not apply to the Application pages, and SharePoint 2010 will behave just like SharePoint 2007 did in this regard.

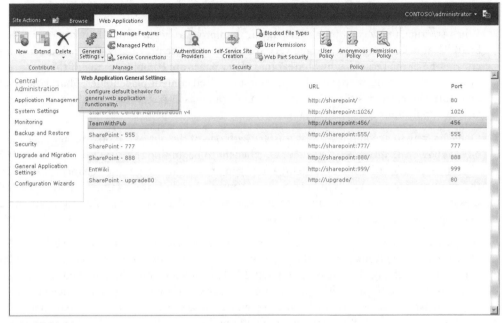

FIGURE 23-32

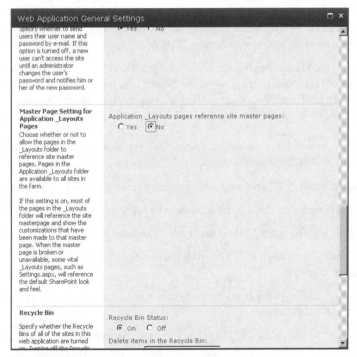

FIGURE 23-33

Creating Custom Master Pages

When starting a new custom master page, it's tempting to begin with a blank master page, but SharePoint master pages have some very specific needs. The previously mentioned content placeholders are one of the reasons why SharePoint master pages are complex; many of them are required in order for SharePoint to operate. If you omit a required content placeholder, SharePoint will display an error. Therefore, it's often best to start a custom master page with some sort of skeleton to which you can apply your custom branding.

One easy way to accomplish this is to start with one of the out of the box master pages such as `v4.master` or `nightandday.master`. One benefit to beginning this way is that Microsoft has already done a lot of testing on them, and if you are only making minor changes, this decreases the amount of testing you will need to do. Chapter 22 includes an example that uses SharePoint Designer 2010 to edit an existing master page. You could also use SharePoint Designer to copy an existing master page and create a new one.

Another popular way to start a custom branded master page is by utilizing something known as a *starter master page*. Starter master pages were known as *minimal master pages* in SharePoint 2007. The name has changed because SharePoint 2010 already has something named `minimal.master`, which is intended for use with applications that have their own navigation or need extra space. Starter master pages are usually well commented and contain all of the required content placeholders, but they have little to no styling or layout applied to them.

At the time of writing, there are two popular choices for starter master pages in SharePoint 2010:

➤ **Microsoft's Starter Master Page** (`http://code.msdn.microsoft.com/ odcSP14StarterMaster`) — This starter master page was built for SharePoint Foundation 2010 but it will also work in SharePoint Server 2010.

➤ **Randy Drisgill's Starter Master Pages** (`http://startermasterpages.codeplex.com`) — These consist of two starter master pages, one for SharePoint Foundation 2010 and the other for SharePoint Server 2010 publishing sites. They are less minimal than Microsoft's starter master page and have most of the common SharePoint functional controls displayed.

The following example demonstrates how to create a new custom master page based on a starter master page in a SharePoint Server 2010 publishing site:

1. Open SharePoint Designer 2010 and load a SharePoint Server 2010 site.

2. From the Site Objects menu on the left, click Master Pages.

3. Click Blank Master Page from the Ribbon and name it `demo.master`.

4. Click `demo.master` and then click Edit File from the Ribbon. When you are asked if you want to check it out, click Yes.

5. Download the starter master pages from `http://startermasterpages.codeplex.com` and unzip the files to the local computer.

6. Copy the contents of `_starter.master` to the clipboard. Switch to SharePoint Designer 2010 and make sure you are in Code View, and then paste over the contents of `demo.master`, replacing the basic master page content that was included in `demo.master`.

7. Save the master page by pressing Control+S.

8. Right-click on `demo.master` in SharePoint Designer, select Check In, and then select Publish a major version. SharePoint will warn that "This document requires content approval. Do you want to view or modify its approval status?" Click Yes. A browser window will open to the Approval status page.

9. Click the arrow that appears next to demo and select Approve/Reject; and from the next screen click Approved and OK. This will allow other users to see the changes.

10. Click Site Actions ⇨ Site Settings ⇨ Look and Feel ⇨ Master page.

11. Select `demo.master` for both the Site Master Page and the System Master Page. Make sure Alternate CSS URL is set to Use Microsoft SharePoint Foundation default styles. Click OK.

This will apply the new master page throughout the site, even to the Site Settings pages. Figure 23-34 shows the SharePoint site with the starter master page applied. Notice that it contains very little styling or formatting.

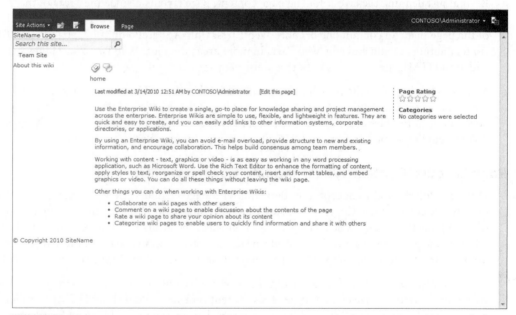

FIGURE 23-34

Upgrading SharePoint 2007 Master Pages

One common question when upgrading an existing SharePoint 2007 environment to SharePoint 2010 is, can existing branding be updated to work in SharePoint 2010? The answer is definitely yes, but there are a couple of options for using SharePoint 2007 master pages with SharePoint 2010. SharePoint 2007 master pages can be used as is if SharePoint 2010 is set to use SharePoint 2007 visuals using visual upgrade mode. For more information on visual upgrade mode, see Chapter 5.

Because visual upgrade is meant to be a temporary solution when upgrading an old SharePoint server, it is not intended for SharePoint 2007 master pages to be used long term in this way. To fully update an existing SharePoint 2007 master page to work with SharePoint 2010, several steps need to occur. These steps include adding the SharePoint Ribbon control and removing redundant and old 2007 controls. For more information on this process, check out the MSDN article "Upgrading an Existing Master Page to the SharePoint Foundation Master Page" (`http://msdn.microsoft.com/en-us/library/ee539981(office.14).aspx`).

Page Layouts

SharePoint Server installations that have the Publishing Feature enabled include another type of branding that is not available with SharePoint Foundation or Team Sites: *page layouts*. Page layouts are essentially templates for arranging and creating page content. They enable content authors to create pages that are based on defined templates. For instance, the same page content could be set up like a news article or as a landing page just by switching the underlying page layout.

Beyond just defining the layout for the page content, page layouts also define areas of the page that can be edited, known as *field controls*, as well as Web Part zones. *Web Part zones* are special areas of the page that can contain one or more Web Parts. Unlike SharePoint 2007, SharePoint 2010 allows content authors to add and edit Web Parts in more areas than just Web Part zones; they can also be added to HTML content fields in both publishing pages and wiki pages.

You can see a list of all the page layouts available in SharePoint from the same gallery as the master pages. Select Site Actions ➪ Site Settings. Under Galleries, click Master pages and page layouts. Several out-of-the-box page layouts are available when creating new pages in SharePoint Server 2010, including Article layouts and Welcome layouts, among others.

Page Layouts, Content Types, and Site Columns . . . Oh, My!

One particularly tricky concept to understand with page layouts is that they are always based on exactly one content type. Content types are themselves made up of site columns, which can be thought of as containers for data. When a page layout is created, the available editable field controls that can be added to the page layout are defined by which site columns are available in the underlying content type. To put it another way, editable field controls have their data stored in the site columns that define them.

For example, the Article Left page layout that is available out of the box in SharePoint Server is based on the Article Page content type. This content type has a Publishing HTML site column named Page Content. The Article Page content type has an editable field control for Page Content; and any page created from Article Page, when edited, can have Page Content information entered and saved. When creating custom page layouts, you can use either existing content types, which are named Article Page and Welcome Page, or you can create your own custom content types.

Using a Page Layout to Create a Page

You can see page layouts in action by creating a new page in a SharePoint Server publishing site:

1. Click Site Actions ➪ New Page.

2. Enter a page name and click Create.

3.   Click the Page tab in the Ribbon and then click Page Layout (see Figure 23-35).

FIGURE 23-35

4.   Choose one of the available page layouts, as shown in Figure 23-36.

As soon as the page layout is selected, the page changes immediately to reflect the new layout.

FIGURE 23-36

Creating a Custom Page Layout

While using the existing page layouts is certainly nice, sometimes you may need to create your own custom page layout. The following steps describe how to create your own custom page layout with SharePoint Designer 2010:

1.   Open your SharePoint Server site in SharePoint Designer.

2.   From the Site Objects menu on the left side, click Page Layouts.

3.   From the Ribbon, click New Page Layout.

4.   From the New dialog, leave Content Type Group set to Page Layout Content Types. For Content Type Name, select Article Page, and then enter a URL Name of DemoLayout.aspx and a Title of "Demo Page Layout," and click OK. SharePoint Designer will create a basic page layout and open it.

5.   Select the Toolbox pane on the right (if it's not showing, you can click View from the Ribbon and then click Task Panes ⇨ Toolbox), and scroll down to the bottom and expand SharePoint Controls.

6.   Expand Page Fields and Content Fields. Content Fields shows all of the site columns that were added to the actual content type from which the page layout was created, and Page Fields shows all of the site columns that were inherited from the parent content type.

7.   From the Toolbox Pane, under SharePoint Controls ⇨ Content Fields, drag Page Content into the PlaceHolderMain. If you are in Code view, you should see something like the following:

```
<asp:ContentContentPlaceholderID="PlaceHolderMain" runat="server">
<PublishingWebControls:RichHtmlFieldFieldName="f55c4d88-1f2e-4ad9-aaa8-
819af4ee7ee8" runat="server" id="RichHtmlField1">
</PublishingWebControls:RichHtmlField>
</asp:Content>
```

This adds the Page Content field control to the page layout, enabling users to add content to the page layout.

8. Save the page layout by clicking Control+S.

9. Now the page layout needs to be checked in and approved. To do this, click the Page Layouts item in the Site Objects menu, find `DemoLayout.aspx`, and click on its icon.

10. From the Ribbon, click Check In, select Publish a major version, and click OK.

11. When SharePoint asks whether you want to view or modify the approval status, click Yes. This opens a view of the Master Page Gallery sorted by Approval Status.

12. Click the arrow to the right of DemoLayout and select Approve/Reject. Then, from the Approve/Reject dialog, click Approved and OK.

13. Now the page layout is available for use. Click Site Actions ⇨ New Page. Give the page a name and click Create.

14. SharePoint creates a new page based on the default page layout. You can switch the page layout to the new one. From the Ribbon click Page ⇨ Page Layout and select Demo Page Layout.

15. Because this example created a very simple page layout, only the title and the page content are editable. Edit the content and click Save & Close.

If you make further changes to the page layout, all pages based on the page layout will be automatically updated.

Creating Custom Site Columns and Content Types for Page Layouts

The previous example demonstrated how to create a page layout based on an existing content type. In this example, you will create a custom site column and add it to a custom content type and then use that content type to create a page layout:

1. Open your SharePoint Server site in SharePoint Designer.

2. From the Site Objects menu on the left side, click Site Columns.

3. From the Ribbon, click New Column ⇨ Multi Lines of Text.

4. Name the Site Column "Secondary Content" and select Custom Columns from Existing group. Click OK.

5. Click Column Settings from the Ribbon, and check the box next to Enhanced Rich Text. Click OK.

6. Click the disk icon on the top left of SharePoint Designer to save the site column.

7. From the Site Objects menu on the left side, click Content Types.

8. From the Ribbon, click Content Type New.

9. For the Name, enter "Demo Content Type," set Select parent content type to Publishing Content Types. Set Select parent content type to Page (all page layouts need to inherit the Page content type), and set Existing group to Page Layout Content Types, and click OK.

10. From the Ribbon, click Edit Columns ⇨ Add Existing Site Column.

11. Scroll down to Custom Columns and select Secondary Content and click OK.

12. Click the disk icon on the top left of SharePoint Designer to save the content type.

Now that the content type is saved, you can follow the preceding steps to create a page layout based on it. Just be sure to select the Demo content type when creating the new page layout.

Controlling the Available Page Layouts

As a site administrator, sometimes you may wish to control or change the available page layouts that content authors can use when creating pages. This can be easily managed by clicking Site Actions ➪ Site Settings ➪ Look and Feel ➪ Page layouts and site templates. From this menu you can allow users to select any page layout or you can create a list of page layouts from which users must select. This menu also enables you to select the default page layout that will be used when pages are first created. Figure 23-37 shows the Page layouts and site templates menu.

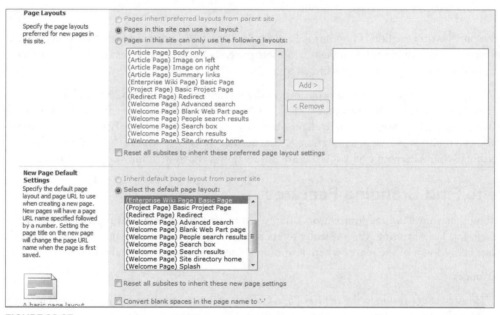

FIGURE 23-37

Cascading Style Sheets

Cascading style sheets (CSS) are a type of markup language that is focused on defining the look and feel of data, most often HTML content. CSS is a very important concept for creating a branded SharePoint site. Many of the aspects of the way SharePoint displays information are ultimately controlled by the CSS that is loaded. Master pages almost always have CSS that is loaded, Web Parts often have CSS that styles them, and even themes inject colors and fonts into CSS. Before undertaking any decent amount of SharePoint branding, one should be well versed in how CSS works in traditional web design. For more information about CSS, check out *Professional CSS: Cascading Style Sheets for Web Design*, 2nd Edition, by Christopher Schmitt et al. (Wrox, 2008).

CSS in SharePoint 2010 is loaded differently from how it was loaded in SharePoint 2007. SharePoint 2007 loaded almost all of its CSS via the `core.css` file. SharePoint 2010 contains a similar file named `corev4.css` that loads a large amount of CSS, but several other CSS files are loaded onto the page dynamically based on what controls are being used at any given time.

Applying CSS to SharePoint

When custom CSS is being used to create a branded SharePoint site, you have several options for applying the CSS. The most popular way to load custom CSS is to reference it from a custom master page. The command for adding CSS to a master page is as follows:

```
<SharePoint:CssRegistration name="/Style Library/sitename/style.css"
  After="corev4.css" runat="server"/>
```

One reason why this method is popular is because for heavily branded sites, custom CSS is often tied directly to custom HTML in a custom master page. By applying CSS inside the master page, the CSS and the master page are always linked together.

SharePoint Server publishing sites have one other easy method for adding CSS to a SharePoint site, known as *Alternate CSS*. This method enables the CSS styles to be easily selected and applied to a site and all of its subsites without having to change the master page at all. In SharePoint Server publishing sites, you can find this setting at Site Actions ➪ Site Settings ➪ Look and Feel ➪ Master page. Scroll to the bottom to find Alternate CSS URL. Figure 23-38 shows the System master page setting.

Where to Find Branding Features

One thing that SharePoint administrators often want to understand better is where everything lives in SharePoint. For branding, this typically refers to master pages, themes, page layouts, and CSS. Here is a breakdown of the places where branding frequently is found in SharePoint:

Master pages

➤ Master pages reside in the Master Page Gallery of a site collection's content database. From SharePoint Designer, this can be found at `_catalogs/masterpage`.

➤ The master pages in the Master Page Gallery are often provisioned there automatically when the site collection was created. These provisioned files are based on master pages that have been loaded in the SharePoint root folder, either out of the box or via SharePoint solution packages.

Themes

➤ Custom themes are uploaded to the site collection's content database and live in the Themes Gallery. From SharePoint Designer, this can be found at `_catalogs/theme`.

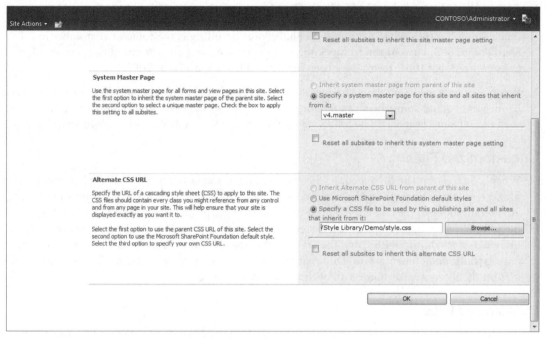

FIGURE 23-38

Page Layouts

➤ These reside in the Master Page Gallery of a site collection's content database. From SharePoint Designer, this can be found at _catalogs/masterpage.

➤ The page layouts in the Master Page Gallery are often provisioned there automatically when the site collection was created. These provisioned files are based on page layouts that have been loaded in the SharePoint root folder, either out of the box or via SharePoint solution packages.

CSS

CSS can live in many locations in SharePoint. Here are some of the more common:

➤ Most custom CSS lives in the site collection's content database under the Style Library folder.

➤ Much of the out-of-the-box CSS is loaded from the SharePoint root folder from subdirectories under 14\TEMPLATE\LAYOUTS.

Customization and Solution Packages

One common pitfall when dealing with SharePoint branding is the topic of customization. In SharePoint 2003, customization was known as *unghosting* and uncustomized pages were referred to as *ghosted*, but those terms have been deprecated since SharePoint 2007.

Because branding in SharePoint frequently involves changing out-of-the-box files, customization can happen easily (and sometimes happens unexpectedly when someone who is inexperienced is working with SharePoint Designer). The following sections describe how these files work in SharePoint.

Uncustomized Files

When a SharePoint site is created, its files are actually instances of files from the SharePoint server's file system that are provisioned into the content database. When a browser visits one of these pages, SharePoint looks in the content database and sees that the page is based on a file that resides in the file system, retrieving it from the file system and presenting it to the user. These types of files are known as *uncustomized* files, and they represent many out-of-the-box files such as master pages, page layouts, and content pages. Different SharePoint sites on the same farm can point to the same files on the file system as long as all of them are uncustomized.

Customized Files

Any time one of these uncustomized files is changed via the SharePoint web user interface or through SharePoint Designer, the changed version is stored in the content database and the file becomes *customized*. When a browser visits a customized page, SharePoint looks in the content database, sees that the file is customized, and simply displays the contents of the file as it was stored in the content database. On the face of things, this doesn't seem too bad, but from an administrative perspective there can be maintenance issues with customized files.

For example, if a master page is installed via a SharePoint solution package (WSP) and activated on a site collection as a feature, and then later that master page is customized in the site collection with SharePoint Designer, subsequent changes to the original solution file will not affect that customized master page. This can get even more confusing when several site collections are all based off of the same solution package and then one of the sites is customized. The sites' branding can become out of sync; and depending on how long the customizations go undetected, synchronizing them could be challenging.

Using SharePoint Solution Packages to Apply Branding

If customization can cause problems, how is SharePoint Designer effectively used to create branding without customizing everything? The answer to this is simple: SharePoint Designer can be used to create branding on a development server or a local virtual machine that is set up to closely mimic the production environment. When the branding files are completed, they can be packaged for proper deployment to the production server.

This involves loading all of the master pages, page layouts, custom CSS, and images, and any other branding assets, into a Visual Studio project and creating a SharePoint solution package (WSP). Branding that is installed on a SharePoint server via a WSP will create files that are uncustomized. You can learn more about creating solution packages in Chapter 13, "Adding Functionality with Features and Solution Packages."

Controlling Access to Branding in SharePoint

As an administrator, you may need to control user access to branding on a particular server. The easiest way to control access to branding in SharePoint is to add or remove users from the Designers group. Among other permissions, by default, users in this role have the following branding-related permissions automatically applied to them:

➤ **Approve Items** — Approve a minor version of a list item or document.

➤ **Add and Customize Pages** — Add, change, or delete HTML pages or Web Part pages, and edit the website using a Microsoft SharePoint Foundation–compatible editor.

➤ **Apply Themes and Borders** — Apply a theme or borders to the entire website.

➤ **Browse Directories** — Enumerate files and folders in a website using SharePoint Designer and WebDAV interfaces.

➤ **Use Self-Service Site Creation** — Create a website using Self-Service Site Creation.

➤ **Use Remote Interfaces** — Use SOAP, WebDAV, the Client Object Model, or SharePoint Designer interfaces to access the website.

Adding Users to the Designer Group

To add users to the Designers group follow these steps:

1. Open your SharePoint site and click Site Actions ➪ Site Settings ➪ Users and Permissions ➪ People and groups.

2. In the Groups menu on the left-hand side of the screen, click Designers.

3. To add a new user, click New ➪ Add Users (see Figure 23-39).

FIGURE 23-39

4. From the Grant Permissions dialog, type in a username or browse for one and click Enter. If the username is valid it will be underlined (see Figure 23-40).

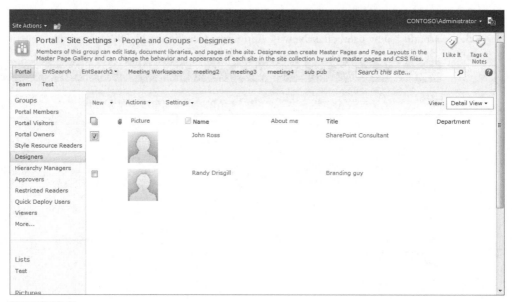

FIGURE 23-40

5. Click OK to add the user to the group.

Removing Users from the Designer Group

Removing a user from the Designer group is equally simple:

1. Open your SharePoint site and click Site Actions ➪ Site Settings ➪ Users and Permissions ➪ People and groups.

2. In the Groups menu on the left-hand side of the screen, click Designers. Place a checkmark next to the user you want to remove, as shown in Figure 23-41.

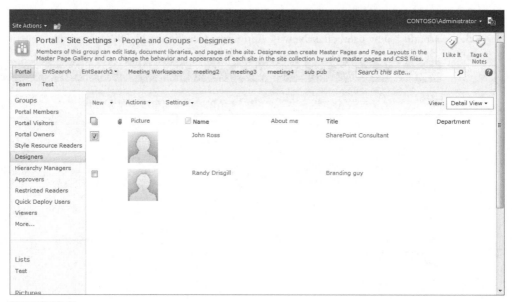

FIGURE 23-41

3. Click Actions ➪ Remove Users from Group (see Figure 23-42).

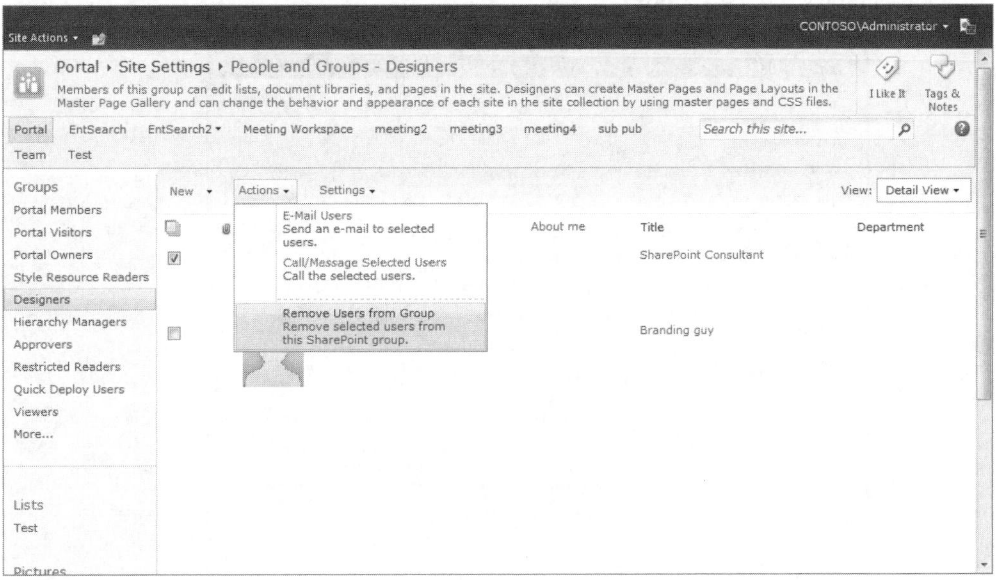

FIGURE 23-42

4. When you are asked if you are sure you want remove the user or users from the group, click OK.

Adding Design Permissions to Individual Users

While adding users to groups is the recommended method for controlling access to branding in SharePoint, there may be special cases for which you want individual users to have access to the Design permission level. The following steps will set up an individual user's permission levels:

1. Open your SharePoint site and click Site Actions ➪ Site Settings ➪ Users and Permissions ➪ Site permissions.

2. From the Ribbon, click Grant Permissions (see Figure 23-43).

FIGURE 23-43

3. In the Grant Permissions dialog, enter or browse for a username and click Enter.

4. Under Grant Permissions, click the radio button next to Grant users permission directly, as shown in Figure 23-44.

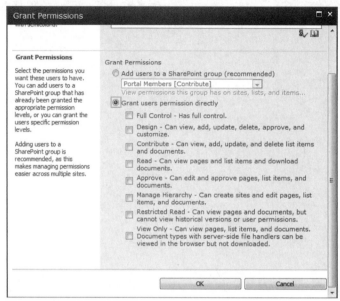

FIGURE 23-44

5. Select the Design permission level (or any others that are needed) and click OK.

Editing Permissions in the Design Permission Level

Another option for controlling access to branding in SharePoint is to edit the individual permissions that are available for the Design level. The permissions that are related to branding were listed at the beginning of this section. Follow these steps to add or remove permissions from the Design permission level:

1. Open your SharePoint site and click Site Actions ➪ Site Settings ➪ Users and Permissions ➪ Site permissions.

2. From the Ribbon, click Permission Levels.

3. From the Permission Level screen, click Design.

4. Scroll down to Permission and select the permissions that you want applied to the group. Figure 23-45 shows some of the Permissions list.

5. When you are finished, click Submit.

Because SharePoint Designer is frequently used to create branding, you might want to refer to the previous chapter to learn how you can restrict access to SharePoint Designer.

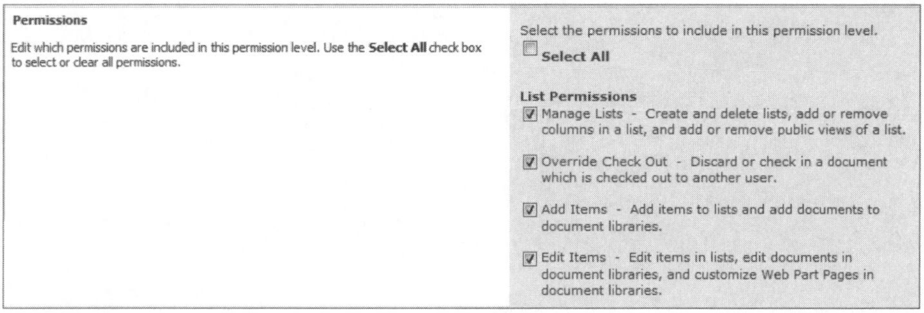

Permissions	Select the permissions to include in this permission level.
Edit which permissions are included in this permission level. Use the **Select All** check box to select or clear all permissions.	☐ **Select All** **List Permissions** ☑ Manage Lists - Create and delete lists, add or remove columns in a list, and add or remove public views of a list. ☑ Override Check Out - Discard or check in a document which is checked out to another user. ☑ Add Items - Add items to lists and add documents to document libraries. ☑ Edit Items - Edit items in lists, edit documents in document libraries, and customize Web Part Pages in document libraries.

FIGURE 23-45

SUMMARY

In this chapter you looked at how branding works in SharePoint 2010 and how it affects SharePoint administrators. You also learned about how customization and solution packages work, and the various security roles that are involved in SharePoint branding. Now that you have completed the chapter, you should have a good understanding of what branding is and how it is applied to SharePoint. Of course, a single chapter can't cover every aspect of SharePoint branding. For more information on creating great-looking SharePoint 2010 sites, check out *Professional SharePoint 2010 Branding and User Interface Design* by Randy Drisgill et al. (Wrox 2010).

24

Business Connectivity Services in SharePoint 2010

WHAT'S IN THIS CHAPTER?

- ➤ An overview of BCS architecture
- ➤ Creating a BCS solution
- ➤ Service applications and BCS
- ➤ Design considerations for BCS solutions
- ➤ Upgrading the Business Data Catalog to BCS

Business Connectivity Services (BCS) represent a comprehensive set of capabilities that integrate and connect SharePointServer 2010 applications with data that resides in external systems. BCS, which is based on a set of services and features included in SharePoint Foundation 2010, provides out-of-the-box support that simplifies the development of solutions that use external data and services. BCS is a major enhancement to its predecessor in SharePoint 2007, the Business Data Catalog (BDC). Using BCS, you can design and build solutions that extend SharePoint collaboration capabilities to include external business data and the processes that are associated with that data.

BCS uses a new concept in SharePoint 2010 called *external content types* (ECTs), which should not be confused with the enterprise content types mentioned in other chapters. ECTs are a content type that is based on external data. Just as with any content type, they are associated with lists. In this case, the list is called an *external list*, and it provides the viewing and storage mechanism for the external data.

BCS solutions can be created using SharePoint Designer 2010 or Visual Studio 2010. Which tool is best depends on both the skill set of the creator and the features and complexity requirements of the solution. For example, you can create a BCS solution that uses Outlook 2010 to manage customer information that resides in a CRM system. This solution would use an external content type created with SharePoint Designer 2010, and an external list created using the web browser. The data in the external list can be taken offline into Outlook as a set of contacts. Updates to the contact list can be made in Outlook and synchronized with the external data source. Many types of BCS solutions can be created without writing any .NET code, which fosters the development of such solutions and encourages those without professional development skills to get involved. BCS also includes a runtime environment in which solutions that include external data are managed and executed.

This chapter provides a BCS introduction and overview in order to familiarize you with its capabilities. Because these capabilities are both wide and deep, expect to see entire books dedicated to BCS coming along soon.

CAPABILITY OVERVIEW

BCS is an enhancement to the functionality that was provided in the SharePoint 2007 Business Data Catalog. The BDC was a first-generation technology for connecting SharePoint to external data. Before looking at the specific capabilities of the SharePoint 2010 BCS, let's review some of the gaps in the BDC:

➤ The BDC did not provide the capability to truly integrate external data into SharePoint 2007. BDC data could be displayed using four out-of-the-box Web Parts and by adding a column to a list with the Business Data data type. This provided a copy of the specific data.

➤ The BDC data was essentially read-only, unless you wanted to write the custom .NET code necessary to perform the write-back capability. External data was displayed using a number of different out-of-the-box Web Parts, but there was no direct provision for updating the back-end data system.

➤ There was no support for integrating external data with Office desktop client applications like Outlook, Word, or Excel. The BDC provided integration with SharePoint Server 2007. To provide client integration, you would need to create a web service that would access the BDC Object Model and then the client would interact with the web service to surface the data. This approach would work, but it required a lot of custom .NET development, and there was no capability to manipulate the data once in the client, such as a client object model, which also had to be developed.

➤ BDC content could not be taken offline or used in a disconnected fashion.

➤ The BDC did not support streaming BLOB content. This caused problems when the BDC was used to index content that was contained in SQL Server and stored as BLOBs.

The BCS represents a second-generation technology for connecting to external systems, and specifically addresses all of the aforementioned gaps:

➤ BCS uses content types and external lists to integrate external data in SharePoint 2010. SharePoint 2010 features and services that utilize list data can utilize the external list data as well.

➤ BCS provides complete CRUD (create, read, update, and delete) operation capability on data returned from external systems.

➤ BCS provides direct integration of external data with client applications like Outlook 2010, Word 2010, and SharePoint Workspace 2010. This integration does not require any custom programming.

➤ External list data can be taken offline in Outlook 2010 and SharePoint Workspace 2010. The external data source can be updated with changes made in the offline environment, and in general the two environments can remain synchronized.

➤ BCS provides the capability to index and search content stored in BLOBs. Specifically, this requires defining a method in the XML access model, defining a content source with the ECT, and having the necessary IFilters installed for the specific file types of interest.

➤ BCS provides a more extensive set of authentication mechanisms for connecting to the external systems and retrieving data. This also includes greater control over access to the external data once it has been retrieved.

BCS capability is provided by SharePoint Foundation 2010, whose predecessor is Windows SharePoint Services version 3, and by SharePoint Server 2010. Table 24-1 summarizes which BCS functionality is available in SharePoint Foundation and SharePoint Server 2010. SharePoint Server 2010 functionality also includes that provided by SharePoint Foundation. Details about each of the features are discussed later in the chapter.

 Just as you saw in SharePoint 2007, there are two different types of client access licenses (CALs) for SharePoint Server 2010: Standard and Enterprise. These different licenses entitle the user to different types of BCS features. Table 24-1 and this chapter in general do not discuss the licensing requirements for utilizing these features. Administrators should consult a licensing specialist for details.

TABLE 24-1: BCS Functionality for SharePoint Foundation and Server 2010

PLATFORM	FUNCTIONALITY
SharePoint Foundation 2010	**Business Data Connectivity Service** — Manages and provides the storage and retrieval capability.
	External lists and External data columns — Enables the display of external data.
	BDC connectors — The actual binary logic that communicates with the data store.
	Custom connectors can be created and made available using the **Connector Framework**.

continues

TABLE 24-1 *(continued)*

PLATFORM	FUNCTIONALITY
SharePoint Server 2010	**Search Capability** — To index and access external data.
	Secure Store Service — Stores access credentials to the external data.
	External Data Web Parts — Display external data.
	User Profiles — For managing and displaying external data.
	Workflow Capability — For using external data.
	Rich Client Integration — Integrates external data with Office 2010 client applications like Outlook and Word.

ARCHITECTURE

The BCS architecture consists of service applications that manage and provide the connectivity to external systems; client and server runtime applications, which deliver the capability to the server and Office desktop clients; external content types, which provide the XML description that governs how to access the store and what to retrieve; and the built-in connectors, which contain the actual programming logic that communicates with the data store. Each of these architectural components is discussed in the following sections.

Service Applications

BCS utilizes two service applications, just as you've seen other SharePoint 2010 functionality use the service application architecture. These services are called the Business Data Connectivity Service (BDCS) and the Secure Store Service (SSS).

Business Data Connectivity Service

The BDCS provides a means for storing, accessing, and utilizing external data. Specifically, this includes external content types (ECTs) and related objects. This service provides connectivity capability to several different types of external systems, and there is out-of-the-box support for the following data sources:

- ➤ Databases
- ➤ Web services
- ➤ .NET Framework assemblies
- ➤ Custom connectors

This new service can be compared to the Business Data Catalog in SharePoint Server 2007, but there are some big differences. One of the differences is that this service is provided by a new service architecture, which is available in SharePoint Foundation 2010. Previously, in order to use the Business Data Catalog, you had to have SharePoint Server 2007 installed; this functionality was not available in Windows SharePoint Services version 3. From a licensing perspective, your users had to have the Enterprise client access license.

In SharePoint 2010, BCS functionality is provided by SharePoint Foundation and SharePoint Server 2010. The specific functionality provided by each was discussed earlier in the "Capability Overview" section. Note that this service also provides support for custom connectors, which the BDC did not. These connectors are discussed later in the section "Connectors and the Connector Framework."

BDCS is implemented as a service application in SharePoint Foundation 2010. Like other SharePoint 2010 services discussed in previous chapters, there is an associated service application and proxy called Business Data Connectivity. You can view this service application and proxy from the Manage Service Application web page in Central Administration. Multiple instances of the BDCS can exist in the same farm, each with a unique set of administrators if necessary, and an instance of the BDCS can be shared across farms. The BDCS uses ECTs to define the connectivity and information to be retrieved.

ECTs define quite a bit of information. They are discussed in their own section a bit later, but the following is a brief summary of their contents:

➤ A named set of fields in the external data. This could include things like Customer, Products, and so on.

➤ The specific CRUD operations that will be used for interacting with the external data system.

➤ Connectivity information that BCS solutions will use to connect the external content type to the external system.

External content types are stored in a dedicated BDCS database, which by default is called Bdc_Service_DB and can be viewed using SQL Server Management Studio.

Secure Store Service

As you saw in Chapter 20 with PerformancePoint Services, the SSS securely stores credentials for external systems and then associates those credential sets with identities of individuals or groups. The SSS replaces the Single Sign-on capability that was available in SharePoint Server 2007. This service enables the BCS solution to authenticate users and groups on external data sources. It also enables the same user or group to have different user accounts and credentials for the different external systems compared to their enterprise log-in credentials.

For example, suppose John Doe logs into SharePoint Server 2010 using his enterprise username and password, and he uses a different set of credentials for logging into the corporate financial system. Using SSS, Mr. Doe's financial system access credentials can be stored with his user profile. The benefit of this is that when Mr. Doe uses a BCS solution from within SharePoint Server 2010 to access data from the financial system, SharePoint server obtains his credentials from the SSS and provides a single sign-on mechanism. Thus, this eliminates the need for Mr. Doe to manually log into the financial application. You can also configure the SSS so that multiple users can access an external system by using a single set of credentials.

Another potential issue that the SSS can solve when accessing external systems is the *double hop* problem. This occurs because a SharePoint web page or Web Part tries to access resources that are located on a server other than the web server. You can use SSS to map the user's account with his credentials for the external store. In the terminology of the SSS, external data stores are referred to as *target applications*. A target application needs to be configured in the SSS in order for the BCS solution to connect to and utilize the data.

SSS credential sets are stored in a dedicated, secure database, which by default is called Secure_Store_Service_DB. The BDCS data and the SSS data are also cached on client computers that are using the BCS solution. For more information, see Chapter 20 and the discussion on PerformancePoint Services and SSS.

For more information about the double hop problem, see `http://support` `.microsoft.com/default.aspx?scid=kb;en-us;329986.`

Connectors and the Connector Framework

BDCS provides connectivity to the external data. It does this by utilizing ECTs and built-in connectors. The ECTs provide the metadata description of the connectivity information, and the connector provides the actual binary logic to communicate with the data store. External data that resides in a database such as SQL Server, Oracle, etc. is accessed by using the appropriate ADO.NET database provider. Data that doesn't reside in a database but is accessible via web services is accessed using the Windows Communication Foundation connector for web services. There is also a .NET Framework Assembly connector for accessing .NET assemblies. All of these connectors are available out-of-the-box and don't require any custom programming.

For those data stores that don't comply with either an ADO.NET provider or a web service, or access via the .NET assembly connector, a custom connector can be built. The custom connector would plug into the connector framework, and then it could be utilized by the BDCS to provide access to the data source. The process for creating a custom connector is beyond the scope of this chapter and this book, but interested readers should begin by understanding the differences between the custom connector and the .NET assembly connector. Learn more about this at `http://msdn.microsoft.com/en-us/` `library/ee554911(v=office.14).aspx.`

BDC Client and Server Runtime

Different runtimes provide the necessary capability to access and utilize external data. One runtime exists on the SharePoint server, and the other exists on the client computer. Together, they deliver the server functionality to the desktop client. These different runtimes are discussed in the following sections.

Server Runtime

The Business Data Connectivity Server runtime understands how to reach into the back-end store and connect to data based on the external content types defined within the content type store. The server runtime exists on the SharePoint 2010 web front-end servers, and it utilizes two shared services: the BDCS and the SSS, discussed previously. It uses information from these services to access external systems and execute operations on the external systems for access by web browsers. The server runtime provides the connectivity to external sources such as SQL Server and other relational databases, web services, and custom data connectors. SharePoint websites display external data in the web browser using Business Data Web Parts and SharePoint external lists.

The runtime also contains a data cache called the *metadata cache*, which provides caching of the runtime BDCS data. This data can be encrypted for additional security if necessary. The runtime also provides the mechanism for clients to synchronize with the BDCS data and SSS data.

Client Runtimes

Two different runtimes provide BCS functionality on the client: the Business Data Connectivity Client Runtime (client runtime), and the Office Integration Client Runtime (integration runtime). These runtimes are installed along with the installation of SharePoint Workspace 2010, Word 2010, and Outlook 2010 desktop client applications. The integration runtime integrates with the client runtime to surface external data and functionality to the desktop client. The client runtime is a connector between the server runtime and the integration runtime.

The client runtime provides integration with the server runtime. This connectivity between the client and the server occurs via the client-side cache, which contains the BDCS data and SSS data to connect to and execute operations on external systems for access by supported desktop clients. The client-side cache is periodically refreshed to ensure that data is synchronized with the BDCS and SSS data. This cache provides the capability to take solutions offline and then update the server when reconnected. From a technology point of view, the client-side cache leverages the SQL Server Compact database as its durable store. This should provide a strong sense of reliability to developers because it leverages proven and widely adopted technologies.

The SSS is also accessible from client applications through the Client Secure Store Service, which enables end users to configure their client mappings in the credential database. The client runtime also supports connecting to SQL Server and other relational databases, web services, and custom data connectors.

External Content Types

External content types (ECTs) are a critical component of the BCS architecture and functionality. Recall that content types were introduced in SharePoint 2007. Content types provide a mechanism for standardizing and reusing metadata information for a specific type of content, as well as associating such functions as workflows and policies with the content. We will not review content types in this chapter, but for those who may need a refresher of the types of capabilities available to content types, you can browse to the Site Content Types web page from the Site Settings page of your SharePoint website, and select a content type such as Document. On the Document content type web page, you can review all the different aspects of content types.

What is important to us in this chapter are ECTs, which are an extension of the content type concept to external data. Specifically, they contain connectivity information for accessing external data, specifications for the type of data to be accessed, and actions that you want to apply to external data. An ECT is defined using XML markup. This is very similar to how an entity was defined with the Business Data Catalog in SharePoint 2007, so you may hear and read the terms *ECT* and *entity* used interchangeably, but the ECT has additional functionality, as you will see. In general, you can consider an ECT a data source. Using the ECT as a data source, you can view the external data on the server using an external list, an external data column, and external data Web Parts. These different approaches to viewing ECT data in SharePoint 2010 are described in Table 24-2.

TABLE 24-2: Viewing External Content Type Data in SharePoint 2010

APPROACH	DESCRIPTION
External List	An external list is a new type of SharePoint list that displays data using the ECT as the data source. This provides direct integration of the external data in SharePoint so it can be manipulated using CRUD operations just like any other SharePoint list data, and the list and external data can be kept synchronized. External lists can be taken offline using Outlook 2010 and SharePoint Workspace 2010. Unlike standard SharePoint lists, external list data is not stored in the content database, but remains in the external data store. Also, external lists do not have all the standard features of regular lists, such as versioning, check-in, check-out, workflows, and content type association.
External Data Column	The Business Data list column type introduced in SharePoint 2007 has been renamed the External Data Column in SharePoint 2010. This adds a single column of information from the ECT to standard SharePoint lists. Unlike the external list, External Data Columns provide all the other features of standard SharePoint 2010 lists.
External Data Web Parts	Just as SharePoint 2007 provided Web Parts that displayed data from the BDC, SharePoint 2010 provides five Web Parts that do not require any custom programming to use and display BCS data on SharePoint 2010 web pages: External Data List, External Data Item, External Data Item Builder, External Data Related List, and External Data Connectivity Filter Web Part. These Web Parts are read-only and do not provide write-back capability to the external data.

Security

BCS provides extensive authentication and authorization capability for accessing external systems and consuming data. BCS security will govern access to external data in a wide variety of scenarios, which can be categorized by the tool or application desiring access to the data:

➤ Web browser

➤ Office client

➤ Custom application

A comprehensive discussion of BCS security is beyond the scope of this one chapter, as it would involve the overall security architecture, both client and server, which authentication modes are available for external content types, the type and options for configuring permissions on objects, and the specific steps to configuring authentication and authorization. Interested administrators are encouraged to review the information referenced in Table 24-3. An understanding of this information is not required to get starting using BCS, and readers can complete the hands-on exercise in the section "Creating a BCS Solution" without this knowledge.

TABLE 24-3: BCS Security Topics and References

TOPIC	REFERENCE
Planning SharePoint 2010 Authentication	http://technet.microsoft.com/en-us/library/ cc262350(office.14).aspx
BCS Security Overview	http://technet.microsoft.com/en-us/library/ ee661743(office.14).aspx.
BCS Authentication	http://msdn.microsoft.com/en-us/library/ ms566523(office.14).aspx
BCS Authorization	http://msdn.microsoft.com/en-us/library/ ms497953(office.14).aspx
BCS Permissions	http://blogs.msdn.com/bcs/archive/2009/11/24/ permissions-in-business-connectivity-services.aspx

CREATING A BCS SOLUTION

In this section, you'll create an example solution that illustrates the concepts of external content types and external lists. BCS solutions are created using SharePoint Designer 2010 and Visual Studio 2010. These solutions can be packaged as a Visual Studio Tools for Office (VSTO) package that is easily distributed to SharePoint Workspace, Word, and Outlook 2010 client desktops by leveraging the ClickOnce capabilities in the.NET Framework. BCS also exposes APIs to extend solution packaging to target additional clients. A BCS solution can be created using SharePoint Designer 2010, an external data source, and SharePoint Server 2010. The following exercise creates a BCS solution that requires the following:

➤ The Business Data Connectivity Service application and proxy must be created and started. This can be checked by browsing to the Manage Service Applications web page in Central Administration. A service application instance can be created using the wizard as part of the installation, as shown in Chapter 4. A new service application instance can also be created manually or by using PowerShell. The manual approach was demonstrated in Chapter 20 and discussed in Chapter 7, so readers are encouraged to review this information if necessary.

➤ SQL Server 2008 must be installed on the same physical server as SharePoint Server 2010, including an instance of the Northwind database. The Northwind database can be downloaded and installed from http://msdn.microsoft.com/en-us/library/ms143221.aspx. If SQL Server is installed on a server other than the SharePoint server, then you need to create a target application in the SSS. This is also discussed in Chapter 20 as part of configuring PerformancePoint Services.

➤ SharePoint Designer 2010 must be installed on either the same SharePoint server or another computer that has access to the SharePoint server.

Creating an External Content Type

An external content type can be created using SharePoint Designer (SPD) 2010. In the following example, using SPD, you will create an ECT named Products that is based on the Products table in the Northwind SQL Server sample database:

1. Browse to a SharePoint site you have created previously or create a new website for use with this exercise. This example uses a website called Inside SharePoint 2010.

2. Start SharePoint Designer 2010 and click the Open Site button (see Figure 24-1). When the Open Site dialog appears, enter the URL of your website and click Open. SPD should display a dialog while the website is loading. Once the site is loaded, review the different types of information displayed. If you are familiar with SharePoint Designer 2007, then you will notice a big difference with SPD 2010. The most obvious is the Ribbon navigation at the top and the new navigation pane on the left-hand side, which displays all of the SharePoint objects that you can create and edit in SPD. See Chapter 22 for full details of SPD.

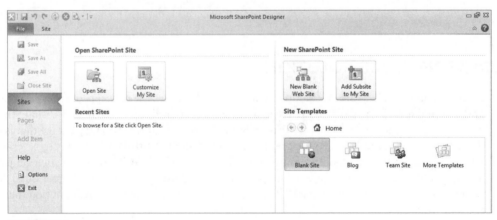

FIGURE 24-1

3. Begin the process of creating an ECT by clicking External Content Types in the navigation pane. An empty tab called External Content Types should be added to the display, as shown in Figure 24-2. Note that the Ribbon has changed, as it is also contextual, as you have seen throughout SharePoint Server 2010.

4. Open the content type designer by clicking the External Content Type button on the Ribbon.

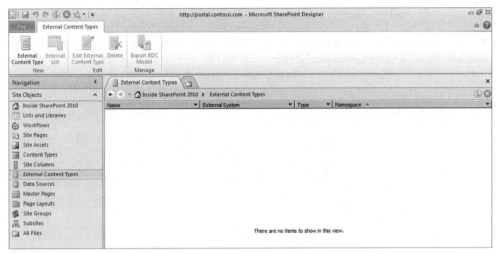

FIGURE 24-2

5. For your new content type, specify the Name, Display Name, and the Office Item Type, as shown in Figure 24-3. The Office Item Type determines the Outlook behavior that you can associate with this content type. You won't be using Outlook for this example, so select Generic List. The Offline Sync for external list field option enables the content type to be taken offline in Outlook or SharePoint Workspace.

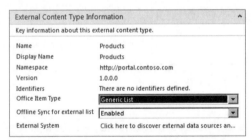

FIGURE 24-3

6. The next step is to specify the data source for the content type. Click the Click here to discover external data sources and define operations link, which will display the Operation Designer page shown in Figure 24-4.

7. Click the Add Connection button and choose SQL Server for the Data Source Type in the External Data Source Type Selection dialog. Notice that the other two options are .NET Type and WCF Service. Click the OK button when finished.

8. The next step is to configure the SQL Server Connection dialog. Enter the name of your database server in the Database Server box and Northwind for the Database Name in the SQL Server Connection dialog. Note that Connect with User's Identity is the default authentication mode for connecting to the database. Referred to as *pass-through authentication*, this is the simplest type of authentication to configure, and all you need for this exercise. Click OK when finished. This should establish a connection to the Northwind database, and an object called Northwind should be added to the Data Source Explorer window as shown in Figure 24-5. Expand the Northwind object to display the Tables, Views, and Routines object hierarchy. Expand the Tables object and select the Products table.

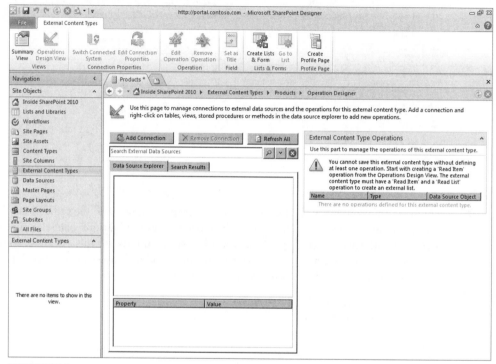

FIGURE 24-4

 In the SQL Server Connection dialog, other than Connect with User's Identity, two other options are available: Connect with Impersonated Windows Identity, and Connect with Impersonated Custom Identity. If you choose either of these options, the grayed-out Secure Store Application ID box is enabled and you have to enter a value. If your SQL Server instance were on a different server than the SharePoint server, then you would need to configure a secure store target application and use the secure store to access the database, and you would need to create a target application for the Northwind database in the SSS before you create the external content type in SPD. Once you have configured the target application, you would use the target application ID value in the ID box inside the connection dialog.

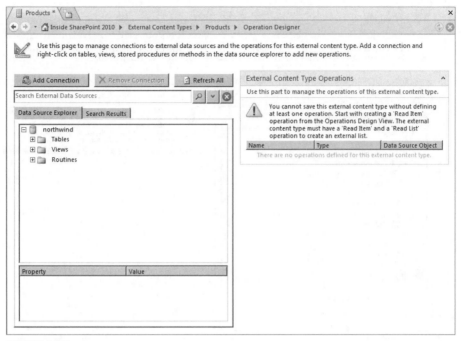

FIGURE 24-5

9. Next you define the types of CRUD operations that can be performed on this content type. You should see a window to the right of the Data Source Explorer labeled External Content Type Operations. This window should be empty, because no operations have been defined yet.

10. Right-click the Products table in the Data Source Explorer and notice the different types of operations that can be created. Select the Create All Operations option, as shown in Figure 24-6. The Create All Operations command is only available for creating commands on SQL Server tables and views. Once you select the menu option, this should display the All Operations wizard. The Create, Read Item, Update, Delete, and Read List operations will be automatically created. You also have the option to manually create each operation, as you probably noticed when you viewed each of the options on the shortcut menu. Creating a subset of operations is valuable if you don't want to allow users to perform all of the CRUD operations or if the database does not support certain operations.

11. Click the Next button to configure the parameters. The Parameters Configuration dialog, shown in Figure 24-7, is displayed. By default, all the columns in the Products table are selected. For this example, keep the default selections. Enable this option for all of the fields except the Discontinued field. This is accomplished by selecting each field and enabling the option. This will make the field available in the External Content Type Picker. Click Next when you are finished. The Filter Parameters Configuration dialog should be displayed.

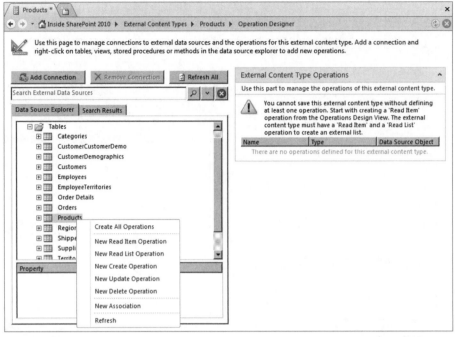

FIGURE 24-6

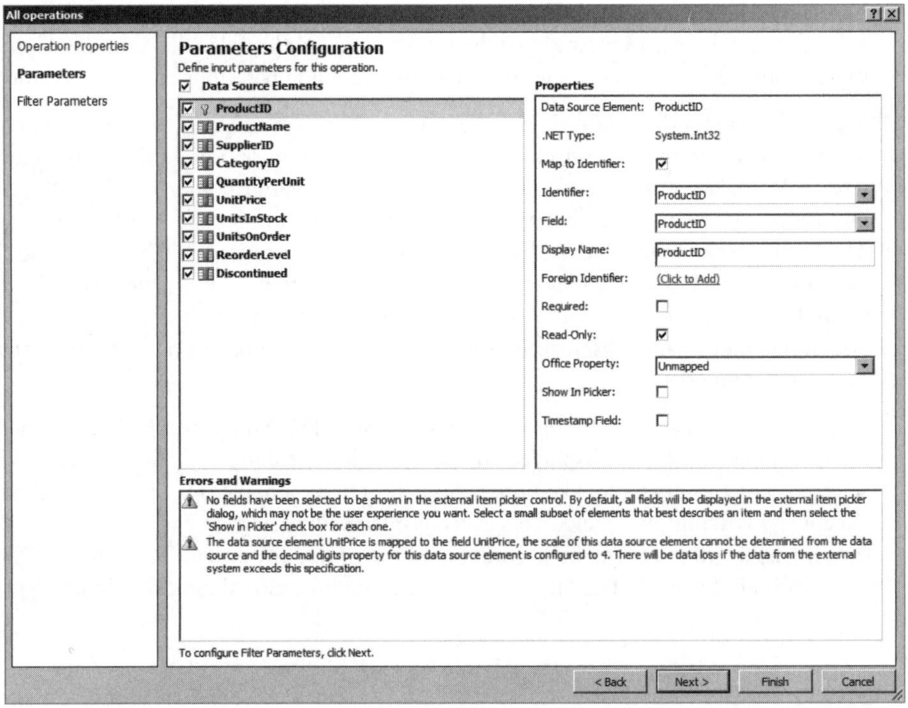

FIGURE 24-7

12. The Filter Parameters Configuration dialog enables you to define filters that will limit the number of items — in this case, table rows — that are returned by the operation from the external data source. You should always specify a limit filter during a Read operation. To add a limit filter, click Add Filter Parameter. In the Properties pane, click (Click to Add). Add the value SQL Limit Filter for the name of the new filter in the Filter Configuration dialog. Select the Limit option for the Filter Type field, and then click OK.

13. Specify a value of 500 in the Default Value field. This will limit the number of rows returned by an operation to 500. Click the Finish button. You will be returned to the Operation Designer page and you should see that the External Content Type Operations window is now populated with the operations you just created, as shown in Figure 24-8.

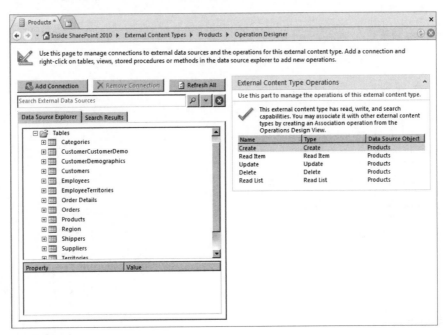

FIGURE 24-8

14. Click the Save button using the floppy disk icon above the Ribbon or the Save option from the File tab. This will store the Products external content type definition in the BDC metadata store on the SharePoint Server.

15. Browse to the Business Data Connectivity Service web page in Central Administration. You will notice that a Products external content type has been created, as shown in Figure 24-9. You can click on the Products hyperlink to view the ECT information.

16. To view the XML model definition that was automatically created for you when SPD created the ECT, select the drop-down menu at the top of the page and choose the BDC models option. If you don't see the drop-down menu, make sure you are using the Edit tab on the Ribbon. On the BDC models page, you should see a single entry named SharePointDesigner-northwind-Administrator, or something similar. Click the menu associated with this entry and select the Export BDC Model option. This page is shown in Figure 24-10.

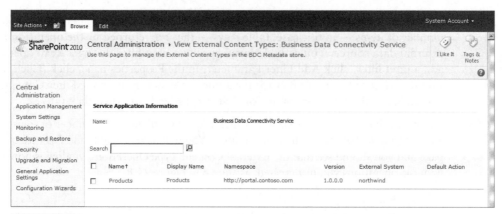

FIGURE 24-9

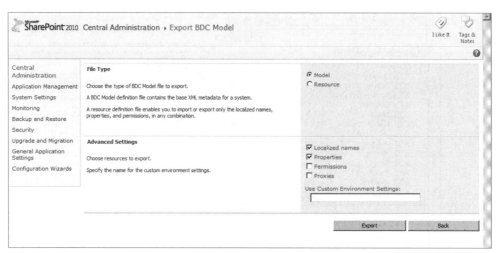

FIGURE 24-10

17. Click the Export button and save the BDC model definition file to a location of your choice so you can view the definition. Once the file is saved, open the file using the Notepad application; you should see something similar to Figure 24-11. If you have ever created a Business Data Catalog application definition file in SharePoint 2007, you know that this is not very easy, and SPD has done all the work for you.

Creating an External List

SPD can be used to create an external list but the following walk-through utilizes the web browser to illustrate this process:

1. Browse to the SharePoint website you used to create the Products external content type.

2. Click the View All Site Content option from the Site Actions menu.

3. Click the Create button at the top of the All Site Content page.

4. On the Create web page, filter the display options by clicking the List option in the Filter By category on the left-hand side of the page. Select the External List option, and click the Create button to display the New page, shown in Figure 24-12. If the External List option is not shown, you may need to activate the Team Collaboration Lists feature for the website. (As a reminder, to activate this feature, click the Manage site features link in the Site Actions section of the Site Settings page of the site, and activate the Team Collaboration Lists feature.)

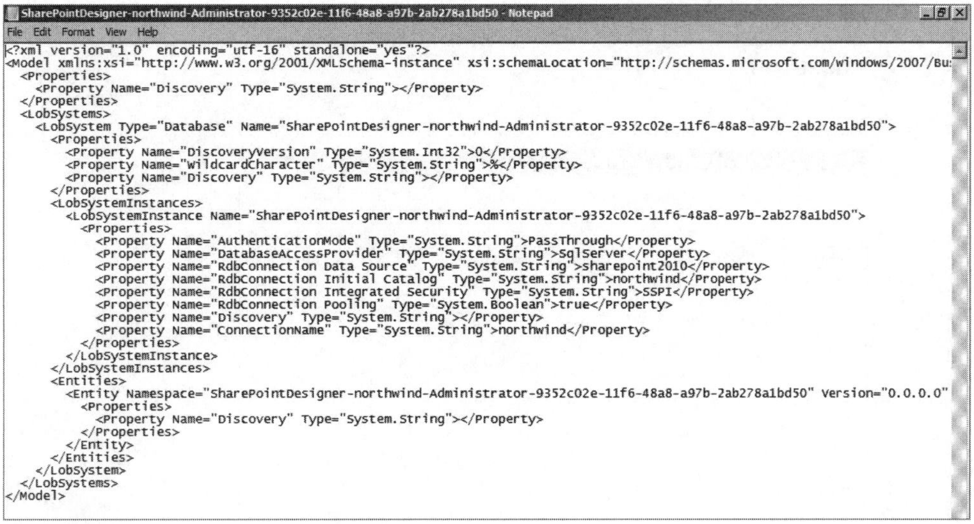


```
<?xml version="1.0" encoding="utf-16" standalone="yes"?>
<Model xmlns:xsi="http://www.w3.org/2001/XMLSchema-instance" xsi:schemaLocation="http://schemas.microsoft.com/windows/2007/Bu
  <Properties>
    <Property Name="Discovery" Type="System.String"></Property>
  </Properties>
  <LobSystems>
    <LobSystem Type="Database" Name="SharePointDesigner-northwind-Administrator-9352c02e-11f6-48a8-a97b-2ab278a1bd50">
      <Properties>
        <Property Name="DiscoveryVersion" Type="System.Int32">0</Property>
        <Property Name="WildcardCharacter" Type="System.String">%</Property>
        <Property Name="Discovery" Type="System.String"></Property>
      </Properties>
      <LobSystemInstances>
        <LobSystemInstance Name="SharePointDesigner-northwind-Administrator-9352c02e-11f6-48a8-a97b-2ab278a1bd50">
          <Properties>
            <Property Name="AuthenticationMode" Type="System.String">PassThrough</Property>
            <Property Name="DatabaseAccessProvider" Type="System.String">SqlServer</Property>
            <Property Name="RdbConnection Data Source" Type="System.String">sharepoint2010</Property>
            <Property Name="RdbConnection Initial Catalog" Type="System.String">northwind</Property>
            <Property Name="RdbConnection Integrated Security" Type="System.String">SSPI</Property>
            <Property Name="RdbConnection Pooling" Type="System.Boolean">true</Property>
            <Property Name="Discovery" Type="System.String"></Property>
            <Property Name="ConnectionName" Type="System.String">northwind</Property>
          </Properties>
        </LobSystemInstance>
      </LobSystemInstances>
      <Entities>
        <Entity Namespace="SharePointDesigner-northwind-Administrator-9352c02e-11f6-48a8-a97b-2ab278a1bd50" Version="0.0.0.0"
          <Properties>
            <Property Name="Discovery" Type="System.String"></Property>
          </Properties>
        </Entity>
      </Entities>
    </LobSystem>
  </LobSystems>
</Model>
```

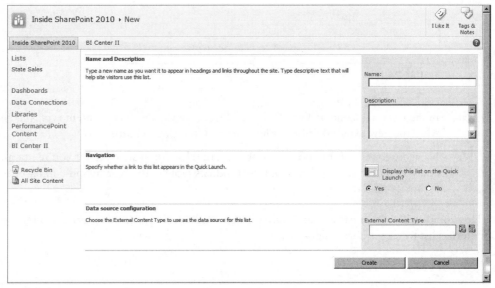

FIGURE 24-11

FIGURE 24-12

5. Enter a name and a description for the external list on the New page. Leave the Navigation section with the default value. In the Data source configuration section, click the external content type picker icon, which is the icon without the checkmark to the far right of the text box in Figure 24-13. Clicking the icon will reveal the External Content Type Picker dialog shown in Figure 24-14.

Data source configuration

Choose the External Content Type to use as the data source for this list.

External Content Type

FIGURE 24-13

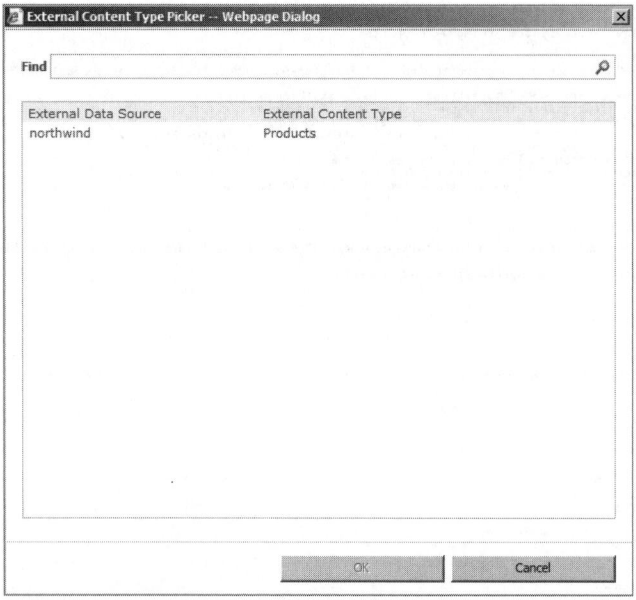

External Content Type Picker -- Webpage Dialog

Find

External Data Source	External Content Type
northwind	Products

OK   Cancel

FIGURE 24-14

6. In the External Content Type Picker dialog, select the Products content type and click OK. After the new external list is configured, click the Create button.

7. Navigate to the site and browse to the external list you just created if you're not already there and you should see the data from the Products table in the Northwind database, as shown in Figure 24-15.

This completes the exercise demonstrating how a BCS solution uses an external content type and an external list to view external data.

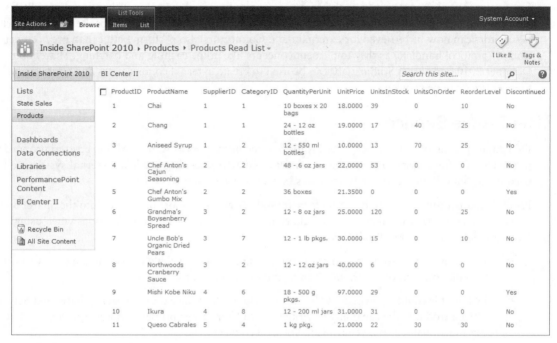

FIGURE 24-15

SERVICE APPLICATIONS THAT USE BCS

BCS solutions are a powerful mechanism for utilizing external data, but BCS capability extends beyond the discussion in this chapter. SharePoint Server 2010 uses BCS as the foundation for SharePoint 2010 Search crawl functionality and social computing by augmenting User Profile Service functionality. SharePoint Search is discussed in Chapter 14, and the User Profile Service is discussed in Chapter 17, so the information below is specific to how BCS affects these two services and their capability.

Search Service

SharePoint 2010 Search uses the BCS connector framework discussed earlier to crawl content. This is a change and improvement over the protocol handlers that were used in previous versions of SharePoint. Protocol handlers are very difficult to create and generally need to be written in C++, which negatively impacted handlers that were available for the wide variety of external systems that are in use today.

Connectors also support richer crawl options than protocol handlers in previous versions of SharePoint. For example, they support the full-crawl mode that was implemented in previous versions and they support timestamp-based incremental crawls. However, they now also support change-log crawls, which can remove items that have been deleted since the last crawl.

Connectors can also now crawl attachments and content in e-mail messages. When crawling a BCS entity, additional related entities can be crawled by virtue of the entity relationships. Item-level security descriptors can now be retrieved for external data. Connectors also perform better than previous versions of protocol handlers, as they implement concepts like inline caching and batching. SharePoint Designer 2010 and Visual Studio 2010 can be used to create external content types and entities, and these entities can be crawled.

User Profile Service

BCS augments the out-of-the-box User Profile Service properties as well as adding custom properties to the User Profile Service. This enables user data and attributes that reside in external systems to be used inside SharePoint Server 2010 for tasks like audience targeting.

Profile import connections can be set up for external systems to import properties into the SharePoint Server 2010 user profile database. You should be aware of the following considerations when using BCS to supplement the User Profile Service:

➤ BCS cannot be used as the primary connection for a User Profile import. It can only work in conjunction with other primary profile import connections.

➤ BCS profile connections cannot be used to write back to the external system. SharePoint Server 2010 introduced the capability to write back to User Profile property source connections, but this functionality is not yet available for BCS connections.

➤ A common property is required between the primary user profile import connection and the BCS import connection. The property is used to identify and associate the properties with the appropriate user profile when performing a user profile import from BCS.

DESIGN CONSIDERATIONS FOR BCS SOLUTIONS

As part of implementing BCS solutions, you need to be aware of several design considerations that will affect the efficiency and effectiveness of these solutions:

➤ Assign appropriate permission to users who are managing the BCS service application.

➤ Define and govern the number of people who can create external content types.

➤ Define and implement appropriate throttling limits for external lists. These limits are likely different from throttling limits defined for normal lists on the Central Administration website.

➤ Create limit filters on external content types to retrieve a limited amount of data from external stores.

➤ Use SSS as the preferred mechanism to authenticate against external systems.

➤ Implement write-back capability via external content types only when absolutely necessary and with caution.

➤ Use Feature and deployment packages for installing external content types.

➤ External lists based on an external content type do not have all the functionality of standard SharePoint lists. The following limitations may affect your design:

  ➤ Workflows cannot be configured directly on external lists.

  ➤ Item-level permissions cannot be configured from the list properties page.

  ➤ Versioning and item history are not available.

  ➤ Ratings, RSS feeds, and Datasheet view are not available.

UPGRADING THE BUSINESS DATA CATALOG TO BCS

There are several differences between the functionality of the Business Data Catalog in SharePoint Server 2007 and the BCS in SharePoint Server 2010. Table 24-4 summarizes what you need to consider both as you upgrade and after the upgrade is complete. Refer to Chapter 5 for details on the different approaches to upgrading SharePoint Server 2007 to SharePoint Server 2010. These should only be considered guidelines; these recommendations will likely be revised as the product is used more extensively.

TABLE 24-4: Factors to Consider When Upgrading BDC Applications to BCS Solutions

BUSINESS DATA CATALOG	POINTS TO CONSIDER
Upgrading external system metadata in the application definition file	Use the database upgrade approach, as it automatically upgrades the metadata to the new schema used in BCS. This also migrates all permissions in the definition files.
	Once the database attach upgrade approach has been completed, SharePoint Server 2007 application definition files cannot be imported. It is possible to manually re-create the definitions using SPD, but a better approach is to use an in-place upgrade. Use your original SharePoint Server 2007 data and perform an in-place upgrade to SharePoint Server 2010. Then export the models from the upgrade and import them into the SharePoint Server 2010 farm that was originally created using the database attach method.
Single Sign-on Service	The SSO service in SharePoint Server 2007 Business Data Catalog has been replaced by the Secure Store Service. This may require creating target applications, so the SSS will need to be tested to ensure it is working properly.
Profile Pages	Profile pages in SharePoint 2007 need to be re-created in SharePoint 2010 if the database attach upgrade process was used.
Application Security	If the upgraded application is going to use claims-based identity, you need to ensure that the permissions defined in the metadata model will work as expected after an import.

SUMMARY

Business Connectivity Services (BCS) are a set of capabilities that SharePoint Server 2010 and Office 2010 clients use to provide access to external data. This chapter was designed as a general introduction to BCS and its capabilities, not a comprehensive guide to its use, so administrators are encouraged to delve deeper into the topic. Creating and implementing BCS solutions requires a number of different tools, so you will need to be aware of their use and the potential impact they may have on the overall SharePoint environment. One such tool is SharePoint Designer 2010. In the example, SPD was used to create an external content type. You also saw that BCS is utilized in combination with two other service applications. Even though we are very early in the experience cycle for SharePoint 2010 usage, the chapter gave several recommendations to consider when planning to use BCS.

25

Building Workflows in SharePoint 2010

WHAT'S IN THIS CHAPTER?

➤ Why workflow is important

➤ Core workflow topics

➤ Configuration options for workflow

➤ Using workflow tools such as SharePoint Designer and Visual Studio 2010

It's no secret that user collaboration using SharePoint 2010 improves overall efficiency and productivity within organizations. To successfully accomplish this, clearly defined and reliable business processes must be in place to govern how collaboration within an organization will occur. These processes can be managed several ways, but the most effective way is to leverage the workflow capabilities of SharePoint 2010.

Workflow is an automated business process. Rather than have users manually track and manage a process, you can create a workflow that predefines the necessary steps and actions needed to complete the task at hand. By automating this process, human error is eliminated, responses can be tracked, actions are consistent, and user responsibility is kept at a minimum. Workflows provide an easy way to improve the overall effectiveness of your solution while minimizing the costs of managing business processes.

In this chapter you will learn about workflow in SharePoint 2010 and the vital role it plays in an effective enterprise solution. You will also learn how to create workflows and use them in real-life scenarios.

WHY USE WORKFLOW?

Organizations work hard not only to fill their staff with highly qualified employees, but also to train them how to perform their daily tasks. In the ever-evolving scheme of things, whereby business processes change, document templates are updated, and new tasks are assigned, even the most attentive, responsible, and well-trained employee has moments of fallibility. Human-based processes are never 100% effective. Workflows provide a dependable solution to this fallibility, one that enables users to focus on actually doing their day-to-day work, rather than on *how* the work needs to be done. Workflows execute with a level of consistency that is unmatched by user-managed processes, and their flexibility enables them to be configured and reconfigured to meet the needs of your organization.

In addition to being more effective than manual processes, workflows can be very easy to set up. The options in the browser provide users with the necessary tools to create workflow associations; and with a little training, users can also be taught how to create their own workflow solutions. The only options that will be out of the reach of typical SharePoint users are custom solutions built in Visual Studio.

WINDOWS WORKFLOW FOUNDATION

The workflow technology used in SharePoint 2010 is based on the latest version of Windows Workflow Foundation (WF), WF4. First introduced in 2005, Workflow Foundation is a framework created by Microsoft to provide a consistent development experience with other technologies based on the .NET Framework. This framework fully supports Visual Basic, .NET, and #C programming languages. For building custom activities, an extensible model and designer is also provided. For the release of SharePoint 2010, a new set of features will be available for developers to create custom workflow solutions. The following are just a few of the improvements available with the latest version:

➤ A new workflow designer allows for working with much larger and more complex workflows without sacrificing performance.

➤ The data flow model has been greatly improved, providing simplified definition of the flow of data both into and out of workflows, as well as data storage.

➤ The introduction of Flowchart, a new activity that enables developers to map out the workflow process from a more logical perspective.

➤ A new programming model allows for simpler workflow authoring.

➤ Windows Communication Foundation (WCF) integration now enables new messaging activities and improved communication.

If you are not a developer, the technology specifics behind workflows in SharePoint 2010 may be of little value and/or concern to you. You are probably more concerned with why workflows are used and when to deploy them in your environment. However, it is still valuable to understand the underlying technology and to be aware that the various tools you will use to create and participate in workflows utilize this same technology.

WORKFLOW BASICS

Before getting into the nitty-gritty details of SharePoint 2010 workflow, it is important to have a good grasp of the basics. Like anything else, you need to make sure you can walk before you run.

Terminology

First and foremost, you need to be familiar with the proper terminology:

➤ **Workflow template** —A workflow template is a reusable workflow solution that has been deployed and installed in your SharePoint environment as a feature. Like all features, it must first be activated before it can be used. By default, the out-of-the-box templates are activated, but if you create a custom workflow template, make sure to check whether the feature is activated before you attempt to create a workflow based on that template. Use the following steps to check the feature settings in your site collection (you must be a site collection administrator):

1. From the top-level site in your site collection, click Site Actions ⇨ Site Settings.

2. Under the Site Collection Administration section, click Site Collection Features.

3. Ensure that the workflow features have a status of Active, as shown in Figure 25-1.

FIGURE 25-1

➤ **Workflow association** —A workflow association is a specific connection between a workflow and a target list, library, content type, or site. For example, when you add an out-of-the-box workflow to a document library, you are taking the existing workflow template and creating a workflow association between the workflow and the document library.

➤ **Workflow instance** —A workflow instance is the individual workflow process running on a specific item or site, based on a specific workflow association. When you are using an approval workflow in a list and the workflow is set to start on item creation, when an item is created, a new workflow instance starts running on the item.

➤ **Reusable workflow** —As the name suggests, a reusable workflow is any workflow that can be reused in your SharePoint environment. However, this can be a bit confusing. In the past, workflows were reusable only if they were created as workflow templates. This meant that a workflow had to be an out-of-the-box template or a custom solution created in Visual Studio. However, Microsoft Office SharePoint Designer 2010 is now capable of creating "reusable workflows." These workflows will not be as reusable as workflow templates, but nonetheless they are reusable. These types of workflows are covered later in the section "SharePoint Designer 2010."

Although several workflow instances can be running on an item, only one workflow instance of a given workflow association can run on an item at one time. Depending on how you start a workflow, there could be situations in which a workflow will run on creation and restart when the item is edited. In this case, starting the new workflow instance terminates the old workflow instance.

Workflow Association Types

In addition to having various methods of starting a workflow, workflows can be associated at different levels within SharePoint:

➤ **Lists/Libraries** — By creating the association at this level, the workflow will run only on items created within the specified list or library. If you were to save this list or library as a template, any out-of-the-box workflow templates used would be associated with the template, making them part of anything created from the template.

➤ **Content types** — By associating the workflow with a content type, the workflow will run on all items created with this content type. This allows for a reusable workflow solution if you were to use the specified content type in multiple lists or libraries. The management features in Central Administration enable you to reuse a content type with a workflow across sites, site collections, and web applications.

➤ **Sites** — Some workflows aren't associated with list and/or library items and are triggered by a different mechanism. Workflows of this nature can be associated at the site level. The ability to associate workflows with sites means workflow authors are no longer required to use list and library items. Possible scenarios for this would be for the workflow to run when the home page of the site was edited or a new Web Part was added to the page. Only workflows created with SharePoint Designer 2010 and Visual Studio 2010 can be associated at the site level.

Using the Ribbon

Now that you have the basic vocabulary down, it's time to locate the workflow options using the SharePoint 2010 user interface. Throughout this book, a common theme for SharePoint 2010 and other Microsoft applications is the Ribbon. It is here that you will find workflow options for sites, lists, libraries, items, and documents.

We will first look at the Site Workflows option, which you can find on the All Site Content page of the current site (see Figure 25-2). By clicking the link for Site Workflows, your browser will take you to the "Workflows: [your site]" page, where you can start a new site workflow or view information about existing workflows.

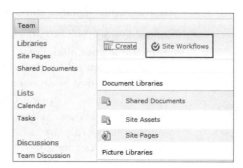

FIGURE 25-2

The more commonly used workflow links are located in the Lists and Libraries ribbon. When you navigate to a list or library, you will see a new tab of options related specifically to that list or library, List Tools or Library Tools. If it is a list, you will see two options. These vary according to the type of list, but for a custom list you will see Items and List. If it is a library, you will also see two options, but these options will be related to the library and will vary by library type. For a document library, these options are Documents and Library.

In a document library, when you click on the Documents tab under Library Tools, the Ribbon will contain a set of available options that you can perform on a document. Toward the right, there is a section titled Workflows (see Figure 25-3). This section has several options:

> **Workflows** —This is the link you will primarily be concerned with. By clicking the Workflows link, called out in Figure 25-3, you will be taken to the "Workflows: [document name]" page. From here you can manually start a new workflow or view information related to workflows that are currently running on the item. Workflows that you can start on the item are displayed at the top of the page. These options vary according to the type of library or list that you are in. For a document library, you should see options for several out-of-the-box workflows. For lists, these same workflows may not be available. If you have created a specific workflow association that is set to start manually, you should also see the option to start that workflow.

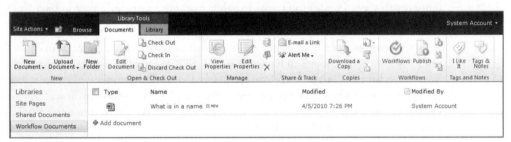

FIGURE 25-3

> **Publish** — If versioning is enabled, this link will publish a major/minor version of the document.

> **Unpublish** — If versioning is enabled, this link will unpublish the current version of the selected document.

> **Approve/Reject** — If Content Approval is enabled, this option will be available to users with Approval permissions to reject or approve documents.

> **Cancel Approval** —This option will cancel the approval of the selected document.

If no documents have been selected, many of these options will be grayed out. When you select a document, these options become available, although for some documents these options may not be available until you create a specific workflow association or you enable specific features such as Versioning and Content Approval.

The other option you will see under Library Tools is Library. Clicking this tab displays all of the options you have for configuring the document library itself. On the far right is the option for Workflow Settings. Clicking this drop-down menu will display several options, as shown in Figure 25-4.

FIGURE 25-4

➤ **Workflow Settings** — Selecting this option will take you to the "Workflow Settings: [library]" page. Here you can see all workflow associations that exist on the library. If you have several workflows running on multiple content types, a drop-down menu enables you to select a content type to view. In addition to the existing workflow associations, you have links to Add a workflow, Remove a workflow, and View workflow reports.

➤ **Add a Workflow** —Although this option is also available through the Workflow Settings link, it is important enough to have it here as well. Clicking this link takes you to the "Add a Workflow: [library]" page. Here you can select a workflow template to create a workflow association with your library. Depending upon the template you choose, you will be prompted for various configuration options, but each template should require you to enter a unique name, task list, history list, and start options.

➤ **Create a Workflow in SharePoint Designer** —When you click on this link, SharePoint Designer 2010 will open and pop up a new window for creating a new workflow. This option is covered later in the section "SharePoint Designer 2010."

➤ **Create a Reusable Workflow in SharePoint Designer** —When you click on this link, SharePoint Designer 2010 will open and pop up a new window for creating a new reusable workflow. This option is also be covered later in the section "SharePoint Designer 2010."

Workflow Initialization

The first, and sometimes the most crucial, step in workflow creation is deciding what action will trigger a workflow to start, also called *initialization*. This one starting point will play a major role in the structure of the workflow. Following are the ways to initialize workflows in SharePoint 2010:

➤ **Start manually** —This option enables users to manually start a workflow on an item of their choosing. The only requirement is that the user must have Participate permissions on the item where the workflow will run. However, if the creator of a workflow association selects the option to start the workflow manually, he or she may also choose to configure the workflow so that only users with the Manage Lists permission can start the workflow. Manually starting the workflow is not the ideal option, as it puts additional responsibility on the user.

➤ **Start on item creation** —This option will start the workflow as soon as a user creates or uploads a new item to the list or library. This start method is more commonly used because it requires less user responsibility and the workflow is guaranteed to run for every content type in the list or library.

➤ **Start when an item is changed** —This option will start the workflow when an item is edited. If a workflow instance is already running on an item, then it will be terminated and the workflow will restart. You can have only one workflow instance running on an item at a given time.

➤ **You can select multiple or all options** — Make sure you understand the implications of having multiple start methods. The obvious concern is interference with the business process: Triggering a workflow to start when another workflow is running will cancel the previous instance. It is also possible to use this feature to create an infinite loop, which is never a good thing.

Now that you've learned some of the basic components of workflows in SharePoint 2010, the next few sections cover the different tools that you use to create and participate in workflow solutions. As with most things in SharePoint, there are several options for creating similar workflow solutions. These sections will clarify the benefits of using one option over another.

CONFIGURING WORKFLOWS USING THE BROWSER

Because the workflow information for Windows SharePoint Foundation 2010 and Windows SharePoint Server 2010 is very similar, this section groups both of these versions together. Any variations between the features and functionalities of the two versions are noted.

Out-of-the-Box Templates

To get you started, SharePoint 2010 ships with templates you can use to begin creating workflows. With simplicity, ease of use, and quick deployment in mind, these templates provide users with a great out-of-the-box solution set that can be used to create a variety of workflows:

➤ **Three-State** —This workflow is used to track items in a list. It does this by using a predefined choice column. The column has three choice values that correspond to the three "states" of the workflow: Initial State (Active), Middle State (Resolved), and Final State (Closed). In the configuration page for this workflow, you specify this column and then set the task details for each choice value. When an item is running an instance of this workflow, as the item's specified choice column is updated, the task details for that choice column value, or state, is triggered, and then moves on to the next state. An example of this workflow would be on a Help Desk item that had three states defining its status: Open, Pending, and Closed. Different users would be assigned tasks based on the status of the item.

➤ **Approval** —This template routes a document for approval. Users that have been assigned as approvers can approve or reject the document, reassign the approval task, or request changes to the document. During the configuration process, you can specify the approvers and define stages of the workflow. If the workflow is started manually, the user who starts the workflow can specify which users the workflow notifies for document approval. Each stage can have a different set of approvers; and you can also define whether you want the stage approval to run serially or in parallel. Serial approval causes the workflow for that stage to request approval for each specified user, one at a time. The workflow will move on to the next stage, or complete the workflow, when the last user has completed his or her task. Parallel approval creates tasks for every user specified at the same time, and waits for all of them to complete their tasks before moving on. An example of this workflow would be a defined two-stage approval process for a Time Off request submitted as a Microsoft Word document. The first stage might be manager approval, and the second stage could be the Human Resources department confirming that the employee has available time off.

➤ **Disposition Approval** —This template supports both records and document management. Working in conjunction with a preconfigured Expiration Policy section of an Information Management Policy, this workflow will assign a task to a specified user who reviews the item and then approves or rejects the item's deletion. This workflow is invaluable in situations where records and document management are paramount. A common example would be an organization that has a mandatory three-year retention requirement for storing documents related to a project. The organization could use the Disposition workflow to work with an expiration policy so that the project manager would be assigned the task of deleting the project documents after the necessary time had elapsed.

➤ **Collect Signatures** —This template will automatically request assigned users to add their signatures to a document. These requests are similar to the Approval workflow, but you aren't able to configure the notification message, duration information, and other configurations. The Collect Signatures workflow request is very basic. The assigned users can be specified when the workflow association is created and/or when a user manually starts the workflow. Even though the usage information of users can be tracked within most applications, some organizations still require an actual signature on documents. For those situations, this workflow is ideal.

➤ **Publishing Approval** — Similar to the Approval template, this template is specifically for the approval of publishing page items.

➤ **Collect Feedback** —This template forwards the document to assigned users who will provide feedback. These requests can be configured the same way Approval workflows can be configured. Once the workflow is completed, all the feedback is compiled and forwarded to the user who initiated the workflow.

The only workflow that ships with SharePoint Foundation 2010 is the Three-State workflow. All other templates are only available with the installation of SharePoint Server 2010 (both Standard and Enterprise versions have the full set of templates).

Microsoft Office 2010 Integration

One of the major assets of leveraging workflows in SharePoint 2010 is the complete integration with Office 2010 applications, including Outlook. Although users cannot create workflows from Office applications, they can participate in workflows through the various applications. From the File button, users can manually start workflows. In Outlook, when users are e-mailed Tasks or Workflow e-mails, they can click on usable links both in the body of the e-mail as well as the Outlook application itself to update tasks and workflow items. This smooth integration enables users to work on daily tasks in Office without ever having to switch back and forth from their browser.

 Unfortunately, the workflow options that exist in the Microsoft Office 2010 applications are only available when you are running SharePoint Server 2010. The workflow integration features are not available with SharePoint Foundation 2010. This applies not only to the out-of-the-box workflow templates, but to custom workflow solutions as well.

Creating a SharePoint 2010 Workflow for a Real World Scenario

This section introduces an example scenario for using a workflow and then walks you through the steps to create it.

Expense Report Approval Scenario

An organization has a group of users who need to submit expense reports and have them approved by both their manager and then a member of Accounts Payable. Currently, the users e-mail their requests or manually take their requests to their manager, who then e-mails or manually takes the requests to the Accounting department. During the two years they have used this system, countless reports have been lost, rejection reasoning is still unclear, and requests are rarely processed in a timely fashion. This was all fine and dandy back in the days of "sneaker net" but it is 2010 and computers can do this type of stuff far better than you or your intern.

After multiple complaints, the manager decides to create a workflow to manage the process. To his surprise, a simple template is available that would resolve all the issues they have been experiencing. From this template he configures the workflow to start when the users submit the form, assigning himself as the first approver; creating another stage for the second approver (Accounting department); and then setting a due date of five days from the date of submission for each request. Now, rather than guess where to find the requests, he can approve or reject requests from Outlook, or he can access his SharePoint site and look at a Tasks list that has been set up so that users can view items assigned to them. This list contains his tasks to approve expense reports. In the event that he or Accounts Payable rejects a request, they can provide feedback to the requester so that the request can be resubmitted. Since the approval workflow has been used, no requests have been lost, users are getting the necessary feedback, due dates are being tracked, and everyone's sneakers are still in great shape.

Creating the Workflow

The preceding scenario is a good example of a real-world situation for which an out-of-the-box solution is a perfect match for a desired business process. Because you already know how to create lists and libraries and configure their views, this step-by-step process describes how to create this workflow:

1. Although a Forms Library may be better suited for web forms, this example will use a simple Document Library. Click Site actions and New Document Library.

2. Enter a name and description for the new library and make any Navigation, Version, and/ or Template configurations. For this example, the name of this library will be Workflow Documents.

3. This example uses the out-of-the-box Approval template which requires the use of a Tasks list. You will need to create a Tasks list (many site templates will create this list for you), and configure it to send an e-mail when a task is assigned. Click on Site Actions and select More Options...

4. On the left, select Filter By: List.

5. Click on the icon for Tasks, and enter Workflow Tasks for the name. Click Create.

6. To enable e-mail notifications click the List tab from List Tools.

7. From the right side of the Ribbon click List Settings.

8. Under General Settings, click Advanced Settings.

9. In the E-Mail Notification section, select Yes for "Send e-mail when ownership is assigned?" as shown in Figure 25-5.

FIGURE 25-5

10. Scroll down the page and click OK.

11. Navigate back to the Workflow Documents library. In the Ribbon, click the Library Tools tab and then the Library tab (see Figure 25-6).

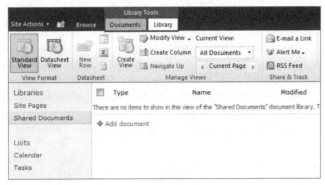

FIGURE 25-6

12. On the right side of the Ribbon, click the Workflow Settings drop-down menu and select Add a Workflow (see Figure 25-7).

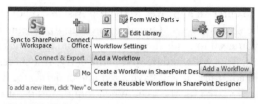

FIGURE 25-7

13. On the Add a Workflow page shown in Figure 25-8, in the Workflow section, select Approval – SharePoint 2010. Enter a name, Expense Report Approval.

14. From the same page, select a Tasks List and History List. This example will use the Workflows Tasks list we created earlier and the Workflow History list.

15. For Start Options, select "Start this workflow when a new item is created." Also, deselect the existing option "Allow this workflow to be manually started by an authenticated user with Edit Item Permissions."

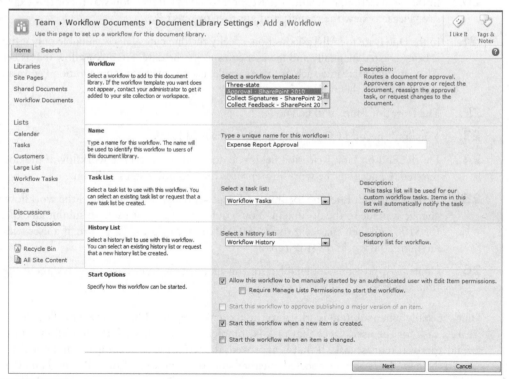

FIGURE 25-8

16. Click Next. You will be forwarded to the Change a Workflow ⇨ Expense Reports Approval page. All of the sections described in steps 17 through 26 are shown in Figure 25-9.

17. In the Approvers section, you need to enter an approver to the top Assign To box; the example shows Manager Smith. Leave the Order box as "One at a time (serial)." If this is your first time using a "people picker," you need to enter the user's name and then click the little person icon with the blue checkmark. This will validate that name entry. If it successfully validates the name, it will be underlined. If not, it will have a red line underneath. If this is the case, click the little book icon and do a search for the user. When found, add the user to the Assign To box.

18. Click Add a new stage. Add your next approver (accounts department) in the second Assign To box. Leave the Order box as "One at a time (serial)."

19. For the Expand Groups section, this value depends on whether or not you entered a group for the value in the Assign To box. If you didn't enter a group, then this section doesn't matter. If you did, then you have the option to either assign a task to every user who is a member of that group or assign one task to the group and then let someone claim that task and complete it. For this example, you can leave the box checked so that anyone in the Accounts department can give approval.

20. In the next section, configure the Request to say whatever you want. For this example, it will say "Please review the request and approve or reject."

21. In the Due Date for All Tasks section, specify the due date. This is valuable only if the workflow is being created manually and the user can specify the date. For a workflow that is being started when an item is created such as this example, use the next section, Duration Per Task. For this example, enter the number 5.

22. The Duration Units will be Day(s).

23. You don't need to CC anyone, so leave this field blank.

24. For the End on First Rejection field, you do want to cancel the workflow if the document is rejected. Cancelling the workflow ensures that no other steps will run.

25. In the next field, End on Document Change, you also want to cancel the workflow if a change is made to the document. You wouldn't want your users to submit an expense report for $100 and then change it to $1,000,000 after approval. Therefore, if a user tries to change anything, the workflow is rejected.

26. Content Approval is not enabled for this list, so you don't have to worry about the last section. Click Save.

That's it. Now when an item is added to the Expense Reports library, the workflow will start and create a task for the user. Once that task is completed and approved, the workflow will trigger the second approval request task. If that is approved, the workflow will complete and notify the user who created the item. If the item is rejected at either step, then the workflow will cancel and the approver can enter comments for the user, who can review them and then resubmit the form. If the user tries to edit the form while the workflow is running, the workflow will cancel.

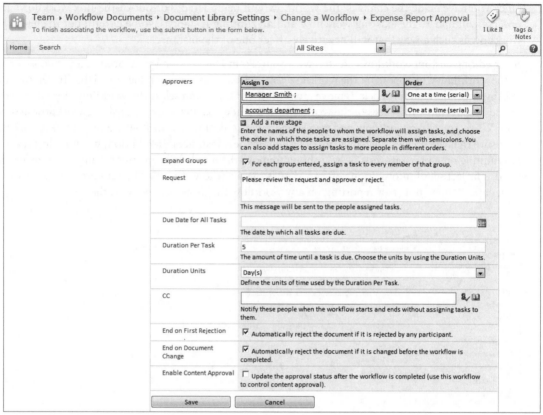

FIGURE 25-9

Editing/Deleting Workflows

As you have seen, using the out-of-the-box workflow templates to create workflows in SharePoint is a simple process. Continuing along the same lines, this section describes how to manage existing workflows and the process to edit and delete workflows.

As mentioned earlier, you can access the Site Workflows page from the All Site Content page. On this page you can view the existing workflows; and by clicking on any one of them, you can pull up the workflow information related to that instance. If that workflow is currently running, you will see the option to terminate the workflow. This will stop the workflow instance. To delete or edit a site workflow, you must do so through the client application used to create it. With regard to SharePoint 2010, this will be either SharePoint Designer 2010 or Visual Studio 2010.

To manage workflows running on a list or library, you need to navigate to that list's or library's work-flow settings page (refer back to Figure 25-7). From here you can view the current workflows run-ning on this list. If you want to make a change to a workflow on this list, you must know the type of workflow it is. If it is an out-of-the-box template, you can click on it and make your changes directly through the browser. If it is a custom workflow you must edit the workflow in its native application.

Once you have made the changes, the workflow will be updated. For out-of-the-box workflows this process will update the existing workflow and all running instances, so be careful not to change the workflow is such a way that will negatively affect one of the instances.

After editing custom workflows created with SharePoint Designer or Visual Studio, a previous version of the workflow will appear on the workflow settings page, as shown in Figure 25-10. To remove an existing workflow, simply click Remove a workflow, and you can select the workflows for which you would like to Allow instances of the workflow, Deny new instances, or Remove the workflow association. When you edit a workflow and two or more versions of that workflow are present, it is important to ensure that the previous versions are not allowing new instances. In addition, when no instances are running on a previous version, you should remove them to help keep your settings from being cluttered. The last set of information you can view is the workflow reports. This can provide activity duration, cancellation, and error reporting on any workflow that is associated with the given list.

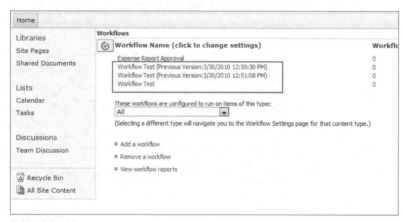

FIGURE 25-10

At the item level, your workflow management options are even simpler. Referencing Figure 25-3, navigate to the workflow settings page for an item. The page will be similar to the site workflows page. On this page you can view the same information. Click on a specific workflow to view information specific to that workflow instance. You can't edit the workflow instance or association, but you can terminate the workflow that is running on an item. You can also see the workflow history for an item. This can provide information regarding different steps of a workflow and when they were completed. It can also be used to help troubleshoot or debug any issues with an existing workflow.

WORKFLOW TOOLS IN SHAREPOINT DESIGNER 2010

Although we covered SharePoint Designer 2010 in Chapter 22, it is necessary to reiterate the important pieces specifically related to workflow. After all, when out-of-the-box workflow templates fail to meet your needs, SharePoint Designer 2010 can be used to create more complex workflow solutions. One distinct difference from the out-of the-box templates is that SharePoint Designer is capable of creating a variety of solution types. With the out-of-the-box templates, your options are fairly limited: Each template is a configurable solution, but the workflow itself cannot be edited via the browser. With SharePoint Designer 2010, you can create and/or utilize the following:

➤ Declarative workflows

➤ Direct workflow associations

➤ Reusable workflows

➤ Prototype workflows

➤ Edited versions of standard templates

➤ WSP files

➤ High-privilege workflows

➤ Office InfoPath 2010 forms

➤ Association columns

➤ Site workflows

The following sections describe each of these features.

Declarative Workflows

A declarative workflow is a code-free, rules-based workflow, using conditions and actions to define a business process. The structure is analogous to the way users define rules for their Outlook mail client. Shipping with an extensive set of conditions and actions, SharePoint Designer 2010 is capable of creating a wide range of workflow solutions. And for most cases these capabilities will far exceed your needs. If you find yourself wanting more you still have options. You can add to the out-of-the-box set of workflow tools by creating additional conditions and/or actions you may need, but this requires custom development using Visual Studio. You can also look into third-party solutions that have already laid the groundwork for you by creating extra conditions and actions that might meet your needs. That is the beauty of SharePoint being a platform, more is always an option.

Direct Workflow Associations

The workflows you have read about so far have all been templates. Obviously, the standard templates ship with SharePoint 2010, but additional template solutions must be created as Features, packaged as Windows Solution Packages (*.wsp) files, installed on the SharePoint server, deployed using STSADM or PowerShell commands, and activated at the appropriate level. In addition, several steps in that process require highly elevated permissions on the servers and with SharePoint. This is less than ideal for a scenario where you want "power users" designing their own workflows.

With SharePoint Designer 2010, you can bypass this whole process and create direct workflow associations to lists, libraries, content types, and sites. In SharePoint Designer 2010, you can select a target for the workflow and then write the workflow directly to it. This capability makes these solutions fast to deploy, and they require fewer permissions than would be needed to install solution packages to the SharePoint server. The downside to these solutions is that they are not considered to be the best option for creating reusable solutions. In other words, if the workflow is something you will likely create and use only once, then SharePoint Designer is the way to go. Conversely, if you want to reuse the solution several times, it is recommended that you take a close look at the requirements and ensure that the workflow is a good fit.

You can create a direct workflow association from the browser in SharePoint, as shown earlier in Figure 25-4, or from the client application. To create the solution from SharePoint Designer 2010, follow these steps:

1. Open SharePoint Designer 2010.

2. Once the application loads, you must first open the site you want to work with. To do so, click Open Site or, if you have recently opened this site in SharePoint Designer 2010, it might still be in the Recent Sites list (see Figure 25-11).

3. From the main site page, you can create a direct workflow association by clicking the Site tab ⇨ List Workflow in the Ribbon (see Figure 25-12). Another option is to click the link for Workflows in the Site Objects navigation section and then click the List Workflow link (see Figure 25-13).

4. After selecting List Workflow, select the list you want to target.

5. Once you have selected the list, enter a name and description for your workflow. For this example, the name will be **Workflow 1**.

FIGURE 25-11

FIGURE 25-12

FIGURE 25-13

6.   When your workflow opens, you will have a wide variety of configuration options to choose from the client Ribbon. For this example you will configure the workflow to e-mail a user after an item has been added.

7.   In the Ribbon, click on the Action drop-down menu and select Send An Email. This action will be added to steps area.

8.   Click on "these users". You will be prompted to specify a user to send the e-mail to, enter a value for the Subject line, and enter a value for the body of the e-mail. After you have made your configurations, click OK.

9.   Now that the workflow step is set up, click on Check for Errors. This will check the workflow for any possible errors that will prevent the workflow from working correctly. Any problems will be highlighted in red. If there aren't any errors, you will get the following message: The workflow contains no errors.

10.   Click Publish. Your workflow is now associated with the specified list.

Reusable Workflows

The capability to create reusable workflows is new to SharePoint Designer 2010. Previously, by creating quick workflow associations with specific lists and libraries, it was nearly impossible to reuse declarative workflow solutions. The only option was to replicate the solution. Fortunately, Microsoft felt your pain and has added the capability to simply create reusable workflows by attaching them to content types. In addition to creating workflow associations with lists and libraries, you can now create workflow associations with content types. By doing so, any list or library that uses the content type will include items that will be running workflow instances.

To reuse the workflow solution, simply enable the management of content types in your list and/or library and add the designated content type. Note that this is not as "reusable" as a workflow template would be. Depending upon the workflow requirements, a workflow template may still be the best approach when creating a reusable solution, but for a nondeveloper, this is a convenient work-around and an answer to many SharePoint 2007 user requests.

Creating a reusable workflow in SharePoint Designer is very similar to creating a list workflow. The main difference is that when you enter the name and description, you must also select a base content type to limit the workflow to (see Figure 25-14). This enables you to reuse the workflow by adding the designated base content type to a list or library.

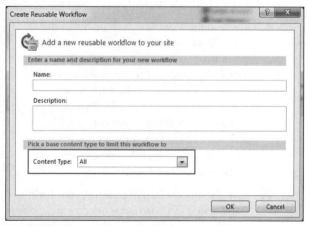

FIGURE 25-14

Prototype Workflows

Testing is an important part of any solution building — especially when you think that the current tool may be the cheaper, quicker way to go. However, in the event that it doesn't work out, it would be nice to have the capability to transfer the current solution in its incomplete state to another application that you know could finish the solution. With SharePoint Designer 2010, you can do exactly that. With its new graphical workflow designer, you can test your solution; and if it fails to meet the business requirements, you can export it to Visual Studio 2010 for completion. Few applications can offer that level of flexibility.

Edited Versions of Standard Workflow Templates

A common request that has hounded nondeveloper workflow creators for the past few years is the capability to easily edit the out-of-the-box workflow templates that ship with SharePoint. Organizations often find that the out-of-the-box templates only get them 80% of the way to their business processes. Unfortunately, that leads to one of two options: settling for less or paying to have a custom solution created from scratch. In most cases, a company with a tight budget ends up settling for less than what they want.

This dilemma has not fallen on deaf ears. With SharePoint Designer 2010, you can now edit and redeploy the out-of-the-box templates. The options to do this lie within the Ribbon on the application; one simple click pulls in the template of your choosing. Once you make the changes you want, save them back to the template and you are good to go. The following steps can get you started:

1. Open the SharePoint Designer 2010 application.

2. Open your site.

3. Click the Workflows link on the Site Objects navigation on the left. For this example, we will edit the Approval – SharePoint 2010 workflow template.

4. When the Workflows tab opens in the middle of the page, click the out-of-the-box template you want to edit. You can click the icon next to the workflow link, which will highlight the workflow so that you can click the Edit Workflow link in the Ribbon (see Figure 25-15), or you can click directly on the workflow link, causing it to open a new designer tab (see Figure 25-16).

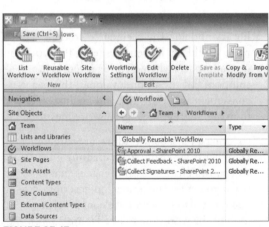

FIGURE 25-15

5. By clicking on Edit Workflow, the workflow designer will open. You will see the conditions and actions the current workflow design is using. Make the desired changes and then save the workflow. Saving the workflow will save your changes for the next time the out-of-the-box Approval – SharePoint 2010 template is used.

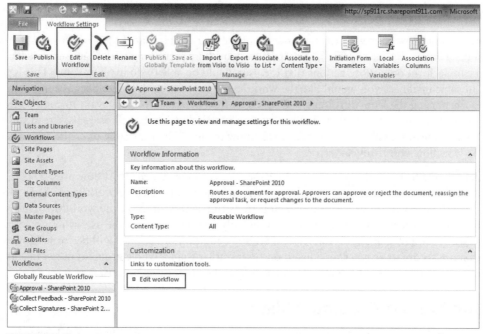

FIGURE 25-16

 A word of caution! One thing to keep in mind when editing out-of-the-box-templates is location. To edit the workflow in SharePoint Designer, you must first open it from a site in SharePoint Designer. If you open the top-level site of a site collection and make changes to the out-of-the-box workflow template, it will save the changes to the entire site collection and all of its child sites. If you open a web (aka a subsite) of a site collection and make changes, a new version of the workflow will be saved to that site and you will not overwrite the standard template for the entire site collection. In some scenarios, an organization might want to do each of these types of updates, so make sure that you know what change you want to make, and then that will determine where the change needs to take place.

WSP Files

Unlike the previous ways of creating workflows, in SharePoint Designer 2010 you now have the option of saving a reusable workflow as a template. By doing so, the template is saved as a .wsp file and can be transferred to another SharePoint server or to Visual Studio 2010 for editing. This provides yet another way in which SharePoint 2010 technology enables users to effectively collaborate on solutions — in this case, workflows — even if the users have different skill sets and are working in different applications. For more information on WSPs check out lucky Chapter 13.

High-Privilege Workflows

The standard workflow runs with the permissions of the user who initiated the workflow, so if a user submits a document for approval, that approval workflow is running with that user's credentials and can perform only those actions that the user would be able to do in SharePoint. This is limiting, as in some instances you would like the workflow to perform with higher permissions — for example, when using the Copy List Item or Create List Item actions. You may want to copy or create a list item to an archive list or library that has custom permissions so that all users have read-only access. This will be impossible for a standard workflow to run. When the copy or create action step is run, the workflow will throw an error.

Fortunately, a new feature allows you to change the user account that the workflow uses. This is known as an *impersonation step*, and it allows users to create high-privilege workflows. After this step is added to your workflow, any subsequent actions run as the author of the workflow. This is a great advancement for workflow creators, and the only restriction is that the user who is creating the workflow must have the appropriate access for any condition or action it will perform. However, it is much more secure to give permissions to one user, rather than a whole group of users. In some situations, a designated user account can be created specifically for this purpose.

Office InfoPath 2010 Compatibility

With SharePoint Server 2010, you can now create SharePoint Designer workflows that leverage Office InfoPath 2010 forms. These forms are much easier to create and edit than the previous ASPX forms used in 2007. You can also use the additional conditional formatting and easy branding that is included with the InfoPath client.

 For users to be able to have this type of integration with InfoPath browser-enabled forms, you must be using SharePoint Server 2010 Enterprise, which has the licensing for Forms Services. This integration is also possible with SharePoint Foundation 2010 and SharePoint Server 2010 Standard, but users will either have to have the InfoPath client installed on their machines or the environment will need to be licensed to support clientless forms.

Associated Columns

Another innovative feature available with SharePoint Designer 2010 is the capability to create associated columns. These columns are placeholders for information needed for the workflow to run, and will be added to the list or library schema when the specified workflow is associated. These can be columns that require user input, or they can simply be a choice column that contains status information used throughout the process of the workflow that defines the subsequent steps. However you choose to use them, they provide yet another advantageous feature that enables users to create successful workflow solutions.

Site Workflows

Although workflows can now be associated with sites, the out-of-the-box templates do not provide a workflow option that can be run at the site level. That may beg the question, why is this needed? In the past, workflows were designed for workflow instances to run on items. However, in the grand scheme of things, in some workflow scenarios list and/or library items aren't an integral part of a workflow process. Yet to create a workflow, an item had to be created to trigger the process. This led to workflow authors arbitrarily creating useless lists and libraries, simply out of the need to have a workflow run.

The ability to associate workflows at the site level enables workflow authors to write solutions that aren't dependent upon a list or library item. This is beneficial from both a user and management perspective, as unnecessary lists and libraries won't be created in their SharePoint sites. Unfortunately, this advantage is also this option's major drawback. Because these types of workflows are not dependent on items, they must be manually started from the SharePoint API or through the SharePoint UI. Any time a business process relies on human input, it will be prone to errors.

WORKFLOW VISUALIZATION USING VISIO PREMIUM 2010

In the previous SharePoint release, there was a noticeable gap between business analysts and information technology workers when it came to workflow. The flow, or path, of a workflow wasn't always clear. On the business side, users could create nice diagrams and outline what they wanted, but from their perspective, things still got lost in the mix. On the other side, you had IT members trying to decipher a request, without each party having a common tool to visualize or create the end solution.

Enter Visio 2010 and the new SharePoint workflow visualization feature in SharePoint 2010. Whether it's creating a flow chart in Visio 2010 and then exporting the Workflow Visio Interchange (*.vwi) file to SharePoint Designer 2010, or creating a workflow in SharePoint Designer 2010 and importing the .vwi file into Visio 2010, the solution provides the ultimate workflow collaborative tool. Although it is incapable of applying the conditions and actions that make up the bulk of a workflow, this new feature bridges the gap between the two sets of users and gets everyone on the same page.

In addition to playing a role in creating workflows and/or visualizing them, you can also view the status of workflows that are currently running in SharePoint 2010 environments. All that is required is to configure the workflow with the "Show workflow visualization on Status page" setting. Being able to view the individual steps of a custom workflow as they execute makes debugging and troubleshooting issues much easier. It's true that you could always log workflow history entries for every step in the workflow, but this new feature eliminates that tedious extra work.

 To fully utilize the visualization functionality, you must have Visio Premium 2010, SharePoint Designer 2010, and SharePoint Server 2010 Enterprise.

USING VISUAL STUDIO 2010 TO CREATE WORKFLOWS

The last option to create workflows for SharePoint 2010 is using Visual Studio 2010. This is by far the most flexible option and it can be used to create almost any type of workflow an organization could need. The major downside to this option is cost and time. Creating a workflow in Visual Studio requires a seasoned developer. Out-of-house developer resources can be expensive, and if you have developers in-house, they are typically in high demand, so availability may be nonexistent. Therefore, time is a factor not only from an availability standpoint, but depending upon the solution, chances are good that the solution itself will take some time to create.

In addition, best practices recommend that workflow solutions created with Visual Studio 2010 be packaged as .wsp files and installed and deployed to your SharePoint environment as Features. This is an added portion of time that must be accounted for when planning this type of solution. Even taking into account these disadvantages, Visual Studio 2010 is still the ideal method for creating complex reusable workflow solutions.

SELECTING A WORKFLOW METHOD

Finding the right method for creating a workflow solution can be relatively simple. The first step is clearly defining the workflow. This means creating a flow chart with the exact functionalities, conditions, and actions that are needed. Identify the plan, and then find the method. If the out-of-the-box workflows don't provide the functionality you need, then you have to go with SharePoint Designer (possibly in conjunction with Visio Premium 2010 and SharePoint Server 2010 Enterprise) or Visual Studio 2010. From there, look at the need for reusability. If you need a truly reusable template, Visual Studio may be the way to go. If you think you can use the reusable workflow in SharePoint Designer, that option would be best from a time and cost perspective.

We've said that both SharePoint Designer 2010 and Visual Studio 2010 can be used to create custom reusable workflows, but keep in mind that the SharePoint Designer 2010 reusable workflows are limited. To create a reusable workflow in SharePoint Designer 2010, the workflow is associated with a content type. This content type can then be reused in any list or library you want. The reusability of the workflow requires that the specified content type be added to a list or library for the workflow to be available.

Visual Studio 2010 reusable workflows are reusable in the sense that they are deployed as solutions, activated as features, and can be used wherever it is needed. This allows users to select a Visual Studio 2010 workflow template and associate it with any list, library, content type, or site of their choice. This makes the Visual Studio 2010 solutions a complete and unrestricted "reusable" option.

It sounds simple, right? In fact, *finding* the right method may be relatively easy, but actually *choosing* the method can be much more difficult. Unfortunately, everything comes into play: cross-department communication problems, office politics, money, time, and so on. This can make the process difficult to finalize. Moreover, the workflow requirements always seem to be in that little gray area where you are unsure whether the out-of-the-box options will suffice, whether SharePoint Designer will work, or whether you have the time and money to create something custom with Visual Studio. Ultimately, the best advice is to find what will work for your organization. Sometimes this means settling for less and going with the out-of-the-box templates, and sometimes this means going all out and creating a workflow to end all workflows. Either way, each scenario is unique, so be prepared and know what you have to work with.

SUMMARY

A successful SharePoint 2010 collaborative solution effectively incorporates workflow into its strategic layout. By utilizing the capability to automate various business processes, your organization can reap the benefits of consistency and efficiency without the negative costs related to process management.

Creating, editing, managing, and deleting workflows, workflow associations, and workflow instances can be done from several applications and user interfaces. As you learned in this chapter, each has its own advantages and disadvantages. SharePoint 2010, Office 2010, Visio 2010, SharePoint Designer 2010, and Visual Studio 2010 all contain several new and improved tool sets that can be leveraged to create workflow solutions. From the creation of flowcharts and defining processes through the building of the workflow solutions, users have the tools needed to implement successful solutions.

Index

INDEX

S